BIRT: A Field Guide to Reporting

Second Edition

SERIES EDITORS Erich Gamma ▪ Lee Nackman ▪ John Wieg

Eclipse is a universal tool platform, an open extensible integrated development (ronment (IDE) for anything and nothing in particular. Eclipse represents one of most exciting initiatives hatched from the world of application development long time, and it has the considerable support of the leading companies and or izations in the technology sector. Eclipse is gaining widespread acceptance in the commercial and academic arenas.

The Eclipse Series from Addison-Wesley is the definitive series of books dedic to the Eclipse platform. Books in the series promise to bring you the key tech information you need to analyze Eclipse, high-quality insight into this pow technology, and the practical advice you need to build tools to support this ev tionary Open Source platform. Leading experts Erich Gamma, Lee Nackman, John Wiegand are the series editors.

Titles in the Eclipse Series

For more information on books in this series visit www.awprofessional.com/series/ecli

BIRT: A Field Guide to Reporting

Second Edition

Diana Peh • Nola Hague • Jane Tatchell

✦ Addison-Wesley

Upper Saddle River, NJ • Boston • Indianapolis • San Francisco
New York • Toronto • Montreal • London • Munich • Paris • Madrid
Capetown • Sydney • Tokyo • Singapore • Mexico City

The publisher offers excellent discounts on this book when ordered in quantity for bulk purchases or special sales, which may include electronic versions and/or custom covers and content particular to your business, training goals, marketing focus, and branding interests. For more information, please contact:

U.S. Corporate and Government Sales
(800) 382-3419
corpsales@pearsontechgroup.com

For sales outside the United States please contact:

International Sales
international@pearsoned.com

Visit us on the Web: informit.com/aw

Pearson Education, Inc.
Rights and Contracts Department
501 Boylston Street, Suite 900
Boston, MA 02116
Fax: (617) 671-3447

ISBN-13: 978-0-321-58027-6
ISBN-10:   0-321-58027-3

Text printed in the United States at OPM in Laflin, Pennsylvania.
First printing, June 2008

Contents

Part V   Enhancing Reports. 557

Chapter 21   Designing a Multipage Report 559

Application development tools and technology have come a long way since the late 1970s, when I took my first job out of college in Hewlett-Packard Company's IT (Information Technology) department. Of course, IT was not the term we used to refer to the discipline back then; our preferred acronym was EDP (Electronic Data Processing).

And maybe that difference between simply "processing" data and delivering "information" was reflected in our development tools. We worked on TTY terminals connected to 16-bit mini-computers over 2400 baud lines. We used simple line editors to make changes to our COBOL programs, and we kept our application data in non-relational hierarchical databases. Debugging was COBOL WRITE statements, and source code control was keeping full copies of every version on tape or in separate directories.

Reports for our applications were typically afterthoughts, and they were done by hand in the same technology we used to develop the base application, i.e., COBOL. We designed them—when we did design—by laying them out in pencil on the report design pads that IBM had developed for RPG and COBOL programmers. Because we created them without much forethought, and because junior programmers like me often got the assignment of coding them, our users often found them inadequate, and the cost of making changes to accommodate their true requirements was high.

But while today's application developer may scratch his or her head in wonder at the primitive tools and technologies we employed in building our base applications in the late 1970s, he or she may not find my description of our approach to report development so very unfamiliar.

JSP = COBOL and Banded Report Writers = Report Design Pads

The majority of Java developers still hand-code reports for their applications using JavaServer Page (JSP) technology. This is analogous to our approach of hand-coding them in COBOL and has all the same downsides: high development cost, low user satisfaction, and inflexible, high-cost maintenance.

A minority of Java developers do use tools to develop reports; however, almost all of these tools—be they commercial or open source—are what's known as "banded report writers," and they support a design metaphor that has essentially evolved from the old IBM report pads. Each section in the report writer—header, detail, footer—corresponds to a section in the report with the detail sections repeating as needed to accommodate rows from the data source.

Because they were created before the advent of the internet, banded report writers are not intuitive to web application developers, who are most comfortable with the web page-oriented design metaphor that one finds in modern graphical web development tools. In addition, web concepts—such as tables, graphical object containment and inheritance, cascading style sheets (CSS), and scripting in web-oriented languages like Java and JavaScript—are not supported.

Enter BIRT

The Eclipse Foundation's Business Intelligence and Reporting Tools (BIRT) project takes report development into the age of the internet. Based on industry-leading Eclipse IDE and Rich Client Platform (RCP) technology, BIRT was built from the ground up for web applications.

As Senior Vice President of Engineering for Actuate Corporation, I'm proud of the leading role my company has played in the project. We've leveraged our 14+ years of experience in the reporting and business intelligence space and put to work a significant number of full-time developers (or "committers," in Eclipse Foundation parlance) on the development of the platform. In fact, Ohloh, the open source rating website, calculates that it would cost over $21M to hire a team to write the project from scratch. But more important than the investment is the result: BIRT is an extensible, full-featured reporting platform that is ready for use in and integration with production applications.

An impressive list of commercial adopters justifies this claim. BIRT is used extensively in IBM's Rational and Tivoli product lines, in Borland's Silk and Together product lines, in BEA's AquaLogic product line, in the Zend Platform to enable reporting in PHP, by Compuware and by SPSS. Likewise, enterprise IT developers and system integrators have embraced BIRT and are using it in important business applications.

All of these constituencies—ISVs, IT, and SI developers—contribute to the Eclipse Foundation BIRT community, which is a vibrant one. The BIRT newsgroup is especially active and BIRT is one of the most searched-for terms on the Eclipse website. Feedback from the community has helped to drive project priorities, give direction on feature implementation, uncover defects, and once in a while, deliver some "attaboys" to the project team. Here are just a few comments posted by developers in the Eclipse BIRT newsgroup:

> "I had installed BIRT the other day just to check it out and barely went through the introductory tutorial. Today I was able to drag and drop my way to replacing a broken report (600 lines of somebody else's perl) and all I can really say is it was almost too easy."

"I've gotten through what I think is a complex development and I'm impressed with exactly how much BIRT can do."

"BIRT is an inspiring piece of work that I chose over Crystal Reports."

"I find BIRT much easier to use and customize than JasperReports/iReport."

"I think BIRT is one of the best reporting tools today."

"Lots of credit to the BIRT crosstab team. The crosstab feature looks great."

"I will recommend BIRT and its community for other people."

"We love BIRT."

I hope that you will leverage the information in this book to become a successful member of the BIRT community as well. And, in the off chance that you are standing in a bookstore aisle, having picked up this book with no idea what BIRT is all about, may I suggest that you rush home—after buying the book, of course—and download the software from the Eclipse BIRT website:

```
http://www.eclipse.org/birt
```

Take it from me—it's the best way to prevent yourself from being lumped into the same category as 1970s COBOL programmers!

Mark Coggins
Senior Vice President of Engineering, Actuate Corporation

About this book

BIRT is a powerful reporting platform that provides end-to-end reporting solutions, from creating and deploying reports to integrating report capabilities into other enterprise applications. Two companion books, *BIRT: A Field Guide to Reporting* and *Integrating and Extending BIRT*, cover the breadth and depth of BIRT's functionality.

Using BIRT Report Designer's rich set of tools, report developers can create many reports, simple and sophisticated, without programming. This book teaches report developers how to create reports using the graphical tools of BIRT Report Designer. Report developers who want to go beyond the graphical tools to customize the report-generation process or incorporate complex business logic in their reports should read the second book, *Integrating and Extending BIRT*.

This second edition, newly revised for BIRT 2.2.1, adds updated examples and covers all the new and improved product features, including cross tabs and OLAP cubes, new chart types, web services as a new data source, new report output formats, the capability for reports to reference Cascading Style Sheets, and the localization of report parameter and data values.

Who should read this book

This book is intended for people who have a basic need for reporting. You need not be an expert at creating reports nor do you need years of programming experience. Familiarity with the following subjects, however, is useful:

- HTML, for formatting report content
- SQL, for writing basic queries to extract data from a database for a report
- JavaScript, for writing basic expressions to manipulate data in the report

This book provides many examples of formatting with HTML, and writing SQL queries and JavaScript expressions, but it is not designed to teach you HTML, SQL, or JavaScript.

Contents of this book

This book is divided into several parts. The following sections describe the contents of each of the parts.

Part I, Installing BIRT

Part I introduces the currently available BIRT reporting packages, the prerequisites for installation, and the steps to install and update the packages. Part I includes the following chapters:

- *Chapter 1, Prerequisites for BIRT.* BIRT provides a number of separate packages for BIRT Report Designer as downloadable archive (.zip) files on the Eclipse web site. Two of the packages are stand-alone modules and another requires an existing Eclipse environment. This chapter describes the prerequisites for each of the available report designer packages.

- *Chapter 2, Installing a BIRT Report Designer.* BIRT provides two report designers as separate packages, which are downloadable archive (.zip) files on the Eclipse web site. This chapter describes the steps required to install and update each of the available report designers. The chapter also shows how to troubleshoot installation problems and install a language pack that provides localization support.

Part II, Getting Started

Part II provides an overview of the report creation process and introduces the report design environment. Part II includes the following chapters:

- *Chapter 3, Learning the Basics.* This chapter presents fundamental concepts of reporting and provides a tutorial. Report developers learn that the report design process begins with a paper and pencil sketch of the proposed report layout and continues through specifying data, laying out the report, formatting, previewing, and testing. In addition, this chapter orients the reader to the software. To accomplish that objective, the chapter provides a tutorial that walks the reader through a creation of a complete report.

- *Chapter 4, Planning Your Report.* This chapter explains the planning process in greater detail. Planning is essential to creating effective and efficient reports. A thorough understanding of user requirements and objectives makes the development process smoother and achieves better results. This chapter discusses the types of requirements and other information that a report developer should consider when determining how to set up, format, and distribute a report.

Part III, Accessing and Binding Data

Part III discusses the tasks necessary to connect to an external data source, extract, and prepare data for use in a report. Part III includes the following chapters:

- *Chapter 5, Connecting to a Data Source.* Report data comes from many different information systems. An important step in developing a report is ensuring you can connect to a system that provides data. This chapter explains how to access data in JDBC databases, text files, XML documents, and web services.

- *Chapter 6, Retrieving Data.* Data sources typically contain more data than is needed in an effective report. This chapter explains how to define data sets to retrieve only the data required for a report. Specifically, this chapter describes retrieving data from JDBC databases, text files, XML sources, and web services.

- *Chapter 7, Binding Data.* The data sets you create retrieve the data you want to use in a report. Before you can use or display this data in a report, you must first create the necessary data bindings. A data binding defines an expression that specifies what data to display. This chapter explains how to create and manage data bindings.

Part IV, Designing Reports

Part IV describes the tasks that a report developer completes to design reports using BIRT Report Designer. Part IV includes the following chapters:

- *Chapter 8, Laying Out a Report.* A report developer places and arranges report data on a page to determine how report users view the information. This chapter provides an overview of the layout model and describes the report elements that BIRT Report Designer provides for organizing and displaying data. This chapter also describes techniques for creating report sections and placing report elements.

- *Chapter 9, Displaying Text.* Much of the information in any report is textual. Textual information can be static text or values derived from data set fields. Text can be as short as a single word, or span paragraphs or pages. This chapter describes the different types of textual elements that BIRT Report Designer provides, and how to use each type of element.

- *Chapter 10, Formatting Report Content.* Formatting different types of data within a report improves the clarity and visual appeal of the report. This chapter describes many formatting techniques, including how to change the display of dates, numbers, or currency values, format report elements based on conditions, and adjust the spacing between report elements.

- *Chapter 11, Sorting and Grouping Data.* Almost all reports require that a report developer structure the data that comes into the report. Grouping and sorting are two ways of structuring data to ensure that the critical relationships among various pieces of information in a report are apparent to the report user. For example, a report developer can use grouping and sorting with sales data to organize the data by region, then by office, and finally by sales representatives. This chapter also includes a tutorial.

- *Chapter 12, Aggregating Data.* One of the key features of any report is the ability to display summary, or aggregate, information. For example, a sales report can show the overall sales total, sales subtotals by product type, region, or sales representative, average sales amount, or the highest or lowest sales amounts. This chapter describes the common types of aggregate calculations, and explains how to write aggregate expressions and where to place them in a report.

- *Chapter 13, Writing Expressions.* To obtain the necessary data for a report, it is often necessary to use expressions to manipulate the raw data that comes from a data source. This chapter explains how to write JavaScript expressions and provides many examples of manipulating data, including how to convert numbers to strings, combine values from multiple data set fields, search and replace string values, get parts of a string, and calculate the time between two dates.

- *Chapter 14, Filtering Data.* Often the data from a data set includes information that is not relevant in a particular report. To exclude this extraneous information from the report, a report developer filters the data to use only the data that pertains to the report. This chapter discusses how to use BIRT Report Designer to filter data and how to enable filtering in the external data set.

- *Chapter 15, Enabling the User to Filter Data.* A report developer can use parameters to enable report users to determine which part of the data they see in the report. For example, in a report of nationwide sales figures, filtering can be used to display the data for a user-specified region. This chapter shows how to set up a report that enables a user to specify parameter values to determine what data appears in a report. This chapter also shows how to design report parameters to improve their usability and presentation.

- *Chapter 16, Building a Report That Contains Subreports.* This chapter provides examples of building and organizing subreports in a report. This chapter also includes a tutorial that provides an example of a master-detail report. This tutorial illustrates and reviews many of the topics from earlier chapters. A reader can complete the tutorial and practice applying the basic principles to build a more complex report that includes both side-by-side subreports and data set parameters.

- *Chapter 17, Using a Chart.* The graphical presentation of summary data is another way of improving the effectiveness of a report. A chart can serve as a report in itself or provide a synopsis of more complex data that appears in a report. Charts often provide an additional view of the data, highlighting or extending the information that appears in a report. This chapter introduces the types of charts that a developer can create and discusses the steps that are required to add a chart to a report. The chapter includes a tutorial that introduces a reader to the chart features.

- *Chapter 18, Displaying Data in Charts.* Setting up chart data differs somewhat from selecting typical report data and requires some specific knowledge about how to process data to produce effective charts. To modify which data appears and the arrangement of the data in the chart, you must use series, grouping, and axis settings. This chapter discusses how to link data to a chart, use the chart builder to filter data, plot the data by defining x-and y-axes, and sort and group data. You also learn how to create a combination chart and a meter chart.

- *Chapter 19, Laying Out and Formatting a Chart.* Like chart data, the steps to lay out and format a chart are distinct from the layout and formatting options for a typical report. This chapter explains how to work with the visual elements of a chart to produce the desired appearance. The tasks include positioning elements in the chart area, adding and formatting titles and labels, and changing the style of the series elements available in each chart type.

- *Chapter 20, Presenting Data in a Cross Tab.* A cross tab is ideal for presenting summary data in a compact row-and-column matrix that looks similar to a spreadsheet. This chapter explains how to prepare data for a cross tab and how to build a cross tab. The chapter also includes a tutorial that provides an example of building and formatting a cross tab.

Part V, Enhancing Reports

Part V discusses features you can add to a report to improve usability and increase productivity when working with suites of reports. Part V includes the following chapters:

- *Chapter 21, Designing a Multipage Report.* Most reports display on multiple pages. Often, report developers want to specify where page breaks occur and they want to display information, such as page numbers and report titles, on every page. This chapter explains how to control pagination in a report and how to design a page layout.

- *Chapter 22, Adding Interactive Viewing Features.* To make a report more useful, you can add interactive features, such as hyperlinks or bookmarks. This chapter describes how to create and use bookmarks and tables of contents. It also describes how to add interactive features, such as highlighting and Tooltips, to charts.

- *Chapter 23, Building a Shared Report Development Framework.* To support a consistent appearance for a suite of reports, BIRT provides two ways to share the report development among designers. A report library contains standard report elements, such as data sources, a company logo, or a set of styles. A report template combines report elements from libraries or the BIRT palettes to provide a predefined layout and master page. Report designers who use these tools increase their productivity.

- *Chapter 24, Localizing Text.* To support international data or produce reports that can be viewed in multiple locales or languages requires planning and an understanding of the issues that are associated with working with resource files. This chapter provides an overview of the localization process and procedures for localizing text in a report.

Glossary contains a glossary of terms that are useful to understanding all parts of the book.

Typographical conventions

Table P-1 describes the typographical conventions that are used in this book.

Table P-1 Typographical conventions

Item	Convention	Example
Code examples	Monospace font	`StringName = "M. Barajas";`
File names	Initial capital letter, except where file names are case-sensitive	SimpleReport.rptdesign
Key combination	A + sign between keys means to press both keys at the same time	Ctrl+Shift
Menu items	Capitalized, no bold	File
Submenu items	Separated from the main menu item with a small arrow	File➞New
User input	Monospace font	2008

Acknowledgments

John Arthorne and Chris Laffra observed, "It takes a village to write a book on Eclipse." In the case of the BIRT books, it continues to take a virtual village in four countries to create these two books. Our contributors, reviewers, Addison-Wesley editorial, marketing, and production staff, printers, and proofreaders are collaborating by every electronic means currently available to produce the major revisions to these two books. In addition, we want to acknowledge the worldwide community of Java programmers who have completed over three million downloads of the multiple versions of the software. Their enthusiastic reception to the software creates an opportunity for us to write about it.

We want to thank Greg Doench, our acquisitions editor, who asked us to write a book about BIRT and has been supportive and enthusiastic about our success. Of course, we want to acknowledge the staff at Addison-Wesley who worked on the first edition and this revision. In particular, we would like to acknowledge John Fuller, Michelle Housley, Mary Kate Murray, Julie Nahil, Stephane Nakib, Sandra Schroeder, Beth Wickenhiser, and Lara Wysong. We also want to thank Mike Milinkovich at the Eclipse Foundation and Mark Coggins at Actuate Corporation for continuing to provide the forewords for the books.

We particularly want to acknowledge the many, many managers, designers, and programmers too numerous to name who have worked diligently to produce, milestone by milestone, the significant upgrades to BIRT, giving us a reason for these two books. You know who you are and know how much we value your efforts. The following engineers have been of particular assistance to the authors: Linda Chan, Yasuo Doshiro, Wenbin He, Petter Ivmark, Rima Kanguri, Nina Li, Wenfeng Li, Yu Li, Jianqiang Luo, Zhiqiang Qian, Kai Shen, Aniruddha Shevade, Pierre Tessier, Krishna Venkatraman, Mingxia Wu, Gary Xue, Jun Zhai, and Lin Zhu. We want to recognize the important contribution of David Michonneau in the area of charting. In addition, we want to acknowledge the support and significant contribution that was provided by Paul Rogers. Dan Melcher's and Daniel O'Connell's insights into the techniques for building reusable components expand upon the ideas in the Libraries chapter and can be applied to building internationalized reports. Working examples are to be found at http://reusablereporting.blogspot.com/

Creating this book would not have been possible without the constant support of the members of the extended Developer Communications team at Actuate Corporation. Many of them and their families sacrificed long personal hours to take on additional tasks so that members of the team of authors could create this material. In particular, we wish to express our appreciation to four writers who contributed original material for these books. Mary Adler wrote the initial version of "Adding Interactive Viewing Features" and Alethea Hannemann wrote the initial version of the three charting chapters. Terry Ryan pulled together the terminology in the glossary that accompanies each of the books. In addition, Terry assisted Diana Peh by replacing screenshots throughout much of the book. Kris Hahn assisted Nola Hague by replacing screenshots and reworking content under her direction. Forest White assisted with testing information and developing online help. In addition, Frances Buran, Bruce Gardner, Mike Hovermale, Melia Kenny, Cheryl Koyano, Madalina Lungulescu, Liesbeth Matthieu, Audrey Meinertzhagen, James Monaghan, Jon Nadelberg, Lois Olson, and Jeff Wachhorst all contributed to the success of the books.

Actuate's active student intern program under the Executive Sponsorship of Dan Gaudreau, Chief Financial Officer, made it possible for Hamid Foroozandeh, Arvind Kanna, Arash Khaziri, Maziar Jamalian, Gene Sher, C. J. Walter-Hague, and Samantha Weizel to support the projects in Developer Communications while actively engaged in pursuing undergraduate and graduate degrees in accounting, business and information science, economics, physics, and technical writing at five different universities in California, New York, and Ontario, Canada.

Installing BIRT

Prerequisites for BIRT

There are two designer applications that you can use to create BIRT reports:

- BIRT Report Designer

  Requires multiple Eclipse platform components and a Java Development Kit (JDK). This designer version provides all the functionality of BIRT RCP Report Designer, plus support for writing Java code. BIRT Report Designer is useful for a report designer who wants to modify the underlying Java or JavaScript code that BIRT uses to create a report.

- BIRT RCP Report Designer

  A stand-alone module for report developers who do not have programming experience. This designer is based on the Eclipse Rich Client Platform (RCP). BIRT RCP Report Designer is a stand-alone package, which requires only a Java JDK as an additional resource.

This chapter describes the requirements for installing these BIRT Report Designers and related components.

Downloading Eclipse BIRT components

You can download BIRT 2.2.1 from the following location:

```
http://download.eclipse.org/birt/downloads/build.php?
    build=R-R1-2_2_1-200710010630
```

The download page contains a mix of packages. Some packages contain stand-alone modules while others require an existing Eclipse environment. Some packages provide extra functionality for BIRT report and application developers.

The BIRT 2.2.1 download site contains the following packages:

- Report Designer Full Install (All-in-One) for Windows

  Contains all the components necessary to run BIRT except the required Java 1.5 JDK. This all-in-one installation is the easiest way to install BIRT.

  In addition to the complete BIRT Reporting Framework, this package includes the following Eclipse components:

  - Software Development Kit (SDK)
  - Graphical Editing Framework (GEF)
  - Modeling Framework (EMF)
  - Web Tools Platform (WTP)
  - Axis plug-in

- Report Designer Full Install (All-in-One) for Linux

  Contains the same components as BIRT Report Designer Full Eclipse Install for Windows.

- Report Designer

  Contains only the BIRT Report Designer plug-ins for installing in an existing Eclipse Integrated Development Environment (IDE).

- RCP Report Designer

  Contains a simplified report designer that uses Eclipse Rich Client Platform (RCP) technology without the additional perspectives available in the standard Eclipse IDE.

- BIRT Data Tools Platform (DTP) Integration

  Contains the minimal set of Eclipse Data Tools Platform (DTP) plug-ins that BIRT requires when installing the Report Designer framework package.

- BIRT SDK

  Contains the source code for the BIRT plug-ins and examples.

- Report Engine

  Contains the report engine that you can install in a J2EE application server to run BIRT reports in a viewer.

- Chart Engine

  Contains the chart engine plug-ins for the Eclipse environment, run-time JAR files for Java applications, a WAR file for Web deployment, and SDK plug-ins, including source code, examples, documentation, and a web tools extension. The chart engine is a stand-alone library that supports adding a chart to a Java application that runs independent of a BIRT report.

- BIRT Web Tools Integration

Contains the plug-ins required to use the BIRT Web Project Wizard in a Web Tools Project, including the source code.

- BIRT Source Code

  Contains the BIRT source code for a specific build. All source code is in a plug-in format ready to import into a workspace to build BIRT. These plug-ins are the required libraries for a standard BIRT installation. Additional libraries may be necessary. For example, this package does not include the Data Tools Platform (DTP) source code.

- BIRT Samples

  Contains sample reports and charts, plus application examples that use the Chart, Report Engine, and Design Engine APIs.

- BIRT Demo Database

  Contains the package for defining and loading the demonstration database into Apache Derby and MySQL, including SQL and data files. The demonstration database package is a convenient way to install the Classic Models database schema and data in the Apache Derby and MySQL systems. The package does not include any BIRT software. The Report Designer and the RCP Report Designer packages include the demonstration database for Apache Derby.

  The demonstration database supports the following Apache and MySQL versions:

  - Apache Derby version 5.1 or higher
  - MySQL Connector/J version 3.1 or MySQL client version 4.x

BIRT Report Designer software requirements

Because BIRT is a Java-based platform, installing a required component typically involves only unpacking an archive. Unpacking the all-in-one archive places the components in the required locations in the installation path.

Most BIRT components are packed in archives that have an eclipse directory at the top level. As a result, you follow the same unpacking procedure for most modules.

If you install BIRT components from separate packages, examine the archive structure carefully before you unpack an archive to confirm that you are unpacking to the correct directory. A common installation mistake for a new BIRT user is to unpack the archives in the wrong directory.

BIRT Report Designer requires the software shown in Table 1-1. Table 1-1 lists the software versions required for developing report designs using BIRT

Report Designer 2.2.1. You cannot use other versions of these listed components.

Table 1-1   Supported configuration for BIRT 2.2.1

Component	Required version
Eclipse Platform	3.3.1
Data Tools Platform (DTP)	1.5.1
Eclipse Modeling Framework (EMF)	2.3.1
Graphical Editing Framework (GEF)	3.3.1
Web Tools Platform (WTP)	2.0.1
Java Development Kit (JDK)	1.5

The following section provides additional information about these software components:

- Eclipse Platform

  The Eclipse SDK is an archive file that you extract to your hard drive. The installation of Eclipse is complete once you extract this archive. The result is the creation of a directory named Eclipse.

  You must specify where to place the eclipse directory on your hard drive. You can extract the Eclipse archive to any location that you prefer. A typical location for Eclipse is the root directory of the C drive. If you specify this directory, the result of installing Eclipse is the following directory:

  ```
  c:/eclipse
  ```

- DTP

  The Data Tools Platform (DTP) is a collection of Eclipse plug-ins that BIRT uses to access data sources and retrieve data from those data sources. If you do not need the full functionality of DTP, you can use the BIRT DTP Integration package instead of the full DTP platform.

- EMF

  The Eclipse Modeling Framework (EMF) is a collection of Eclipse plug-ins that BIRT charts use. The required EMF download includes the Service Data Objects (SDO) component, which is a graph-structured data object that supports applying changes to a graph back to the data source.

- GEF

  Graphical Editing Framework (GEF) is an Eclipse plug-in that the BIRT Report Designer user interface requires. This framework provides a rich, consistent, graphical editing environment for an application running on the Eclipse Platform.

- WTP

  Eclipse Web Tools Platform (WTP) is a set of Eclipse plug-ins that support deploying the BIRT report viewer to an application server. The package includes source and graphical editors, tools, wizards, and APIs that support deploying, running, and testing.

- Java Development Kit (JDK)

  Eclipse recommends using the Java J2SE JDK 1.5 release with BIRT 2.2.1. JDK 1.5 is also known as JDK 5.0.

  The Java J2SE JDK 1.5 download is currently available at the following URL:

  ```
  http://java.sun.com/javase/downloads/index_jdk5.jsp
  ```

About types of BIRT builds

The Eclipse BIRT download site makes several types of builds available for BIRT. The following list describes these builds:

- Release build

  A production build that passes the complete test suite for all components and features. Use the release build to develop applications.

- Milestone build

  A development build that provides access to newly completed features. The build is stable, but it is not production quality. Use this type of build to preview new features and develop future reporting applications that depend on those features.

- Stable build

  A development build that is stable, but passes a reduced test suite. New features are in an intermediate stage of development. Use a stable build to preview new features.

- Nightly build

  The Eclipse BIRT development team builds BIRT every night. As an open source project, these builds are available to anyone. These builds are unlikely to be useful to a report developer.

  If a certain feature that you require does not work, you can provide feedback to the development team by filing a bug report. Later, you can download a new build to confirm that the fix solves the problem that you reported.

Installing a BIRT Report Designer

Installing BIRT Report Designer adds a report design perspective to the Eclipse Integrated Development Environment (IDE). You install BIRT Report Designer by downloading an archive file from the Eclipse web site and extracting it in your existing Eclipse environment. The following examples describe how to install BIRT Release 2.2.1.

Installing BIRT Report Designer Full Eclipse Install

If you are new to Eclipse and BIRT, you can download and install BIRT Report Designer Full Eclipse Install (All-in-One) package to start developing and designing BIRT reports immediately. This package includes the Eclipse Integrated Development Environment (IDE), BIRT Report Designer, and all other required Eclipse components. You must also download and install Java JDK 1.5.

Complete the following procedure to download this installation package on a Windows or Linux system.

How to install BIRT Report Designer Full Eclipse Install

1 Using your browser, navigate to the main BIRT web page at:

    http://www.eclipse.org/birt

2 From BIRT Project, choose Download.

3 From BIRT Report Downloads—More Downloads, choose Recent Builds Page.

This page shows all the downloadable BIRT projects.

4 From BIRT Downloads—Latest Releases, choose 2_2_1.

BIRT Downloads for build 2.2.1 appears.

5 On BIRT Downloads for build 2.2.1, perform one of the following tasks:

- ☀ If you are using Windows, choose the following archive file in Report Designer Full Eclipse Install:

  `birt-report-designer-all-in-one-2_2_1.zip`

- ☀ If you are using Linux, choose the following archive file in Report Designer Full Eclipse Install for Linux:

  `birt-report-designer-all-in-one-linux-gtk-2_2_1.tar.gz`

Eclipse downloads appears. This page shows all the sites that provide this archive file.

6 Choose the download site that is closest to your location.

The BIRT Report Designer all-in-one archive file downloads to your system.

7 Extract the archive file to a hard drive location that you specify.

The extraction creates a directory named eclipse at the location that you specify.

To test the BIRT Report Designer installation, start Eclipse, then start BIRT Report Designer as described in the following procedure. BIRT Report Designer is a perspective within Eclipse.

How to test the BIRT Report Designer installation

1 Start Eclipse.

2 From the Eclipse window menu, choose Open Perspective➤Report Design. If Report Design does not appear in the Open Perspective window, choose Other. A list of perspectives appears. Choose Report Design.

Eclipse displays the BIRT Report Designer perspective.

Installing BIRT RCP Report Designer

BIRT RCP Report Designer is a stand-alone report design application that enables report developers to produce reports in both web and PDF formats. This application uses the Eclipse Rich Client Platform (RCP) to provide a report design environment that is less complex than the full Eclipse platform. If you need the project-based environment that the full Eclipse platform provides, install BIRT Report Designer instead. BIRT RCP Report Designer runs only on Windows.

You install BIRT RCP Report Designer by downloading and extracting an archive file. The following examples use Release 2.2.1.

Complete the following procedure to download and install BIRT RCP Report Designer on a Windows system.

How to install BIRT RCP Report Designer

1 Using your browser, navigate to the main BIRT web page at:

   `http://www.eclipse.org/birt`

2 From BIRT Project, choose Download.

3 From BIRT Report Downloads—More Downloads, choose Recent Builds Page.

   This page shows all the downloadable BIRT projects.

4 From BIRT Downloads—Latest Releases, choose 2_2_1.

   BIRT Downloads for build 2.2.1 appears.

5 In RCP Report Designer, choose the following archive file:

   `birt-rcp-report-designer-2_2_1.zip`

   Eclipse downloads appears. This page shows all the sites that provide this download file.

6 Choose the download site that is closest to your location.

   The BIRT RCP Report Designer archive downloads to your system.

7 Extract the archive file to a hard drive location that you specify.

   The extraction creates a directory named birt-rcp-report-designer-2_2_1 at the location that you specify.

To test the installation, start BIRT RCP Report Designer as described in the following procedure.

How to test the BIRT RCP Report Designer installation

1 Navigate to the birt-rcp-report-designer-2_2_1 directory.

2 To run BIRT RCP Report Designer, double-click BIRT.exe. BIRT RCP Report Designer appears.

Troubleshooting installation problems

Installing a BIRT report designer is a straightforward task. If you extract the archive file to the appropriate location and the required supporting files are also available in the expected location, your BIRT report designer will work. One of the first steps in troubleshooting an installation problem is confirming that all files are in the correct location.

Verify that the /eclipse/plugins directory contains JAR files whose names begin with org.eclipse.birt, org.eclipse.emf, and org.eclipse.gef. The following sections describe troubleshooting steps that resolve two common installation errors.

Avoiding cache conflicts after you install a BIRT report designer

Eclipse caches information about plug-ins for faster start-up. After you install or upgrade BIRT Report Designer or BIRT RCP Report Designer, using a cached copy of certain pages can lead to errors or missing functionality. The symptoms of this problem include the following conditions:

- The Report Design perspective does not appear in Eclipse.

- You receive a message that an error occurred when you open a report or use the Report Design perspective.

- JDBC drivers that you installed do not appear in the driver manager.

The solution is to remove the cached information. The recommended practice is to start either Eclipse or BIRT RCP Report Designer from the command line with the -clean option.

To start Eclipse, use the following command:

```
eclipse.exe -clean
```

To start BIRT RCP Report Designer, use the following command:

```
BIRT.exe -clean
```

Specifying a Java Virtual Machine when starting BIRT report designer

You can specify which Java Virtual Machine (JVM) to use when you start a BIRT report designer. This specification is important, particularly for users on Linux, when path and permission problems prevent the report designer from locating an appropriate JVM to use. A quick way to overcome such problems is by specifying explicitly which JVM to use when you start the BIRT report designer.

On Windows and Linux systems, you can either start a BIRT report designer from the command line or create a command file or shell script that calls the appropriate executable file with the JVM path. The example in this section uses BIRT Report Designer on a Windows system.

How to specify which JVM to use when you start a BIRT report designer

On the command line, type a command similar to:

```
eclipse.exe -vm $JAVA_HOME/jdk1.5/bin/java.exe
```

Installing a language pack

All BIRT user interface components and messages are internationalized through the use of properties files. BIRT uses English as the default language, but supports other languages by installing a language pack that contains the required properties files. There are four language packs for BIRT packages.

Each language pack contains support for a specific set of languages. The names of the language packs are identical for each product, although the archive file names differ. The following list describes these language packs and the languages that they support:

- NLpack1

  Supports German, Spanish, French, Italian, Japanese, Korean, Brazilian Portuguese, traditional Chinese, and simplified Chinese.

- NLpack2

  Supports Czech, Hungarian, Polish, and Russian.

- NLpack2a

  Supports Danish, Dutch, Finnish, Greek, Norwegian, Portuguese, Swedish, and Turkish.

- NLpackBidi

  Supports Arabic and Hebrew. Hebrew is available only for the Eclipse, GEF, and EMF run times.

The following instructions explain how to download and install a language pack for BIRT 2.2.1 on Windows.

How to download and install a language pack

To download and install a language pack, perform the following steps:

1 Using your browser, navigate to the main BIRT web page at:

   `http://www.eclipse.org/birt`

2 From BIRT Project, choose Download.

3 From BIRT Report Downloads—More Downloads, choose Recent Builds Page.

   This page shows all the downloadable BIRT projects.

4 From BIRT Downloads—Latest Releases, choose 2_2_1.

   BIRT Downloads for build 2.2.1 appears.

5 In the Build Documentation section, choose Language Packs.

6 Download the language pack for the product and language that you need.

7 Extract the language pack archive file into the directory above the Eclipse directory.

For example, if C:/eclipse is your Eclipse directory, extract the language pack into C:/.

8 Start Eclipse and choose Window➤Preferences➤Report Design➤Preview.

9 Select the language of choice from the drop-down list in Choose your locale.

10 Restart Eclipse.

If Windows is not running under the locale you need for BIRT, start Eclipse using the -nl <locale> command line option, where <locale> is a standard Java locale code, such as es_ES for Spanish as spoken in Spain. Sun Microsystems provides a list of locale codes at the following URL:

```
http://java.sun.com/j2se/1.5.0/docs/guide/intl/locale.doc.html
```

Eclipse remembers the locale you specify on the command line. On subsequent launches of Eclipse, the locale is set to the most recent locale setting. To revert to a previous locale, launch Eclipse using the -nl command line option for the locale to which you want to revert.

Updating a BIRT Report Designer installation

Because BIRT Report Designer is a Java-based application, updating an installation typically requires replacing the relevant files. Eclipse supports the update process for BIRT Report Designer by providing the Update Manager. BIRT RCP Report Designer is a stand-alone product, so you must replace the existing version with a newer version.

This section describes the steps required to update the following BIRT packages:

- Report Designer
- RCP Report Designer

You can use the Eclipse Update Manager to find and install newer major releases of BIRT Report Designer.

How to update a BIRT Report Designer installation using the Update Manager

1 In Eclipse, choose Help➤Software Updates➤Find and Install. Feature Updates appears.

2 Select Search for updates of currently installed features, and choose Finish. The Update Manager displays a list of update sites. Choose one to continue. Search Results appears and displays any updates that are available.

3 Select a feature to update, then choose Next.

4 On Feature License, select I accept the terms in the license agreement. To continue installing the update, choose Next.

5 On Installation, choose Finish to download and install the selected updates.

To install a milestone release or other pre-release version, use the manual update instructions.

How to update BIRT Report Designer manually

1 Back up the workspace directory if it is in the eclipse directory structure.

2 To remove the BIRT files, use one of the following techniques:

- To prepare for a new all-in-one installation, remove the entire eclipse directory.

- To prepare for only a BIRT Report Designer installation, remove only the BIRT components.

  1 Navigate to the eclipse\features directory.

  2 Delete all JAR files and subdirectories with birt in their names.

  3 Navigate to the eclipse\plugins directory.

  4 Delete all JAR files and subdirectories with birt in their names.

3 Download and install BIRT Report Designer as described earlier in this book.

4 Restore the workspace directory, if necessary.

5 Restart BIRT Report Designer with the -clean option:

```
eclipse.exe -clean
```

Updating BIRT RCP Report Designer installation

Unlike BIRT Report Designer, BIRT RCP Report Designer is a stand-alone application. To update this application, you delete the entire application and reinstall a newer version. If you created your report designs and resources in the birt-rcp-report-designer-<version> directory structure, you must back up your workspace directory and any resources that you want to keep before you delete BIRT RCP Report Designer. After you install a newer version of the application, you can copy your files back to the application directory structure.

As a best practice, do not keep your workspace in the birt-rcp-report-designer-<version> directory structure. Keeping your workspace in a different location enables you to update your installation more easily in the future.

How to update BIRT RCP Report Designer

1 Back up the workspace directory and any other directories that contain report designs, libraries, and other resources, if they are in the birt-rcp-report-designer-<version> directory structure.

2 Delete the birt-rcp-report-designer-<version> directory.

3 Download and install BIRT RCP Report Designer as described earlier in this book.

4 Restore the directories that you backed up in step 1, if necessary.

5 Restart BIRT RCP Report Designer with the -clean option:

```
BIRT.exe -clean
```

Getting Started

Learning the Basics

This chapter provides an overview of the report design process and environment. The chapter also includes step-by-step procedures for building your first report.

About BIRT reports

A BIRT report is a structured document that displays data from an external information system, such as a database or application. Data in the report is organized and formatted so that it is meaningful and useful to the person who reads the report. A BIRT report is not a document that you type, like an essay or research paper, although you could use BIRT Report Designer to create such documents.

Using BIRT Report Designer, you can create operational reports, such as a bill of materials, a purchase order, or an invoice. You can also create reports that provide real-time information about business performance, such as the number of calls handled by your customer service organization, the number of problems handled, categorized by levels of complexity, and the number of repeat calls made by the same customer. You can use BIRT to create client-facing reports, such as account statements and transaction details. Any time that you need to gather, analyze, summarize, and present data from an information system, a report is the solution.

Overview of the report design process

Designing a report involves the following tasks. You do not have to perform all the tasks in the order in which they are presented here, but if you are new to BIRT Report Designer or learning how to design reports, you can use the following task list as a starting point:

- Plan the report.
- Start a new report design.
- Specify the data to use.
- Lay out the report.
- Format the report.
- Design a master page.
- Preview and test the report.

For those who do not have report development expertise, it is important to understand that the process of creating a report is iterative rather than linear. You typically perform each task multiple times and in different orders. You might specify the data to use, lay out data, preview the report, then modify the data set, change the layout, preview the report again, and so on, until you are satisfied with the report's contents and appearance.

Planning the report

Before you create a report, you should identify the information that you want the report to provide and decide how to present that information. It is important to think through these details, then draw a mock-up on paper, which you use to get feedback from your report users. Most people cannot visualize what a report could be without a paper and pencil sketch. Planning saves time in the long run because you do not waste time creating a polished report that contains the wrong information or layout. More frequently, you discover in this review process that the customer wants much more and can now articulate those requirements more successfully.

Starting a new report design

If you are using BIRT Report Designer, start Eclipse, and create a new project, if you have not already done so. Eclipse requires that all files are organized in a project. No project is required if you are using BIRT Rich Client Platform (RCP) Report Designer. After you create the project, create a new report using one of the following techniques:

- Start with a report template.
- Start with a blank report.

Specifying the data to use

A report can access data from a wide variety of sources, including databases, text files, XML documents, and web services. To set up the report to access data, complete the following tasks in this order:

- In BIRT Report Designer, choose the type of data source.

- Specify how to connect to the data source.
- Create a data set that identifies the data to extract from the data source.

Laying out the report

There are many ways to present information in a report. Different users have different expectations about how to visualize the data, and different types of layouts work better for different types of data. A report can display information in a tabular list, a cross tab, a series of paragraphs, a pie chart, a bar chart, a hierarchical list, or a series of subreports. These different layouts can be combined and customized. Laying out a report entails placing data on the page and organizing it in a way that helps the report user to grasp and analyze the information.

Formatting the report content

After you lay out data in a report, you format the report to give it a professional and polished appearance. Typical formatting tasks include highlighting certain data, applying styles to data, adjusting the spacing between rows of data, and conditionally hiding sections. You can also apply conditional formatting to data. One basic example is to display numbers in different colors depending on their values. Highlighting data makes the report more accessible to users. Key information stands out in the report, and users can absorb the information in layers.

Designing a master page

When you create a new report, BIRT Report Designer uses a default master page. The master page specifies default values for page size, orientation, and margins. It also defines a default page header and footer, where you can display page numbers or the date. You can modify the master page to design a custom page layout.

Previewing and testing the report

You should preview and test the report as you design it. The most important item to test is your data set. Verify that the data that is retrieved from the data source is what you expect before you start laying out the report. As you lay out and format the report, check the report output throughout the design process. If you add code, test and debug it as you go.

About the report design environment

BIRT Report Designer provides a flexible environment that meets the needs of both beginning report developers and experienced report developers who want the power of programming. It provides the following features:

- Report templates that include instructions to help new report developers get started quickly

- Customizable views that enable report developers to tailor the environment to their style of working

- User-friendly tools for designing, debugging, and previewing reports

- Sample reports that demonstrate how to use various product features

This section introduces the report design environment. If you are using BIRT Report Designer for the first time, reviewing the topics in this section can help you learn how to use BIRT Report Designer more effectively.

Procedures in this book apply to both BIRT Report Designer and BIRT RCP Report Designer unless the instructions explicitly state which platform to use. Both platforms provide the same reporting functionality. BIRT Report Designer appears within the Eclipse Workbench and therefore requires the installation of Eclipse. BIRT RCP Report Designer does not require all the Eclipse-specific tools because it is designed for report developers who want only the reporting functionality.

Starting BIRT Report Designer

The steps you take to start BIRT Report Designer depend on whether you are using BIRT Report Designer or BIRT RCP Report Designer. To start the designer, follow the instructions that are appropriate to the designer that you use.

How to start BIRT Report Designer

1 Start Eclipse by navigating to the Eclipse directory and performing one of the following tasks:

- If you are using a Microsoft Windows system, run eclipse.exe.

- If you are using a UNIX or Linux system, run eclipse.

2 On Workspace Launcher, shown in Figure 3-1, specify a workspace in which to store your report projects.

- To create a workspace in the default location, choose OK.

- To specify a different location, choose Browse to select a different folder, then choose OK.

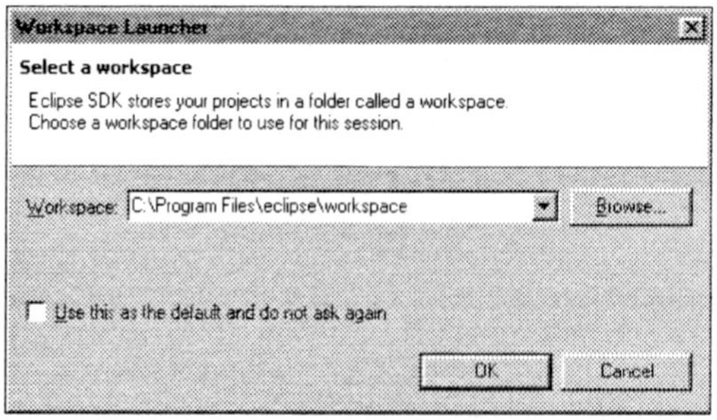

Figure 3-1   Workspace Launcher

3 From the main menu of Eclipse Workbench, choose Window➤Open Perspective➤Report Design to start BIRT Report Designer. The application window displays the Report Design perspective, as shown in Figure 3-2.

Figure 3-2   BIRT Report Designer

The Report Design perspective shows all the tools, which Eclipse calls views, for creating and managing reports. A perspective is an Eclipse mechanism for organizing the initial set and layout of views in the application window.

If you are new to the Eclipse environment, read the Eclipse online documentation at http://www.eclipse.org/documentation for information about perspectives, views, and other Eclipse user interface topics.

How to start BIRT RCP Report Designer

Start the Report Designer by navigating to the BIRT RCP Report Designer directory then running BIRT.exe.

BIRT RCP Report Designer appears, as shown in Figure 3-3. As the figure shows, this application is similar to BIRT Report Designer. BIRT RCP Report Designer, however, does not show the Navigator view and does not include menu items that provide access to Eclipse-specific tools.

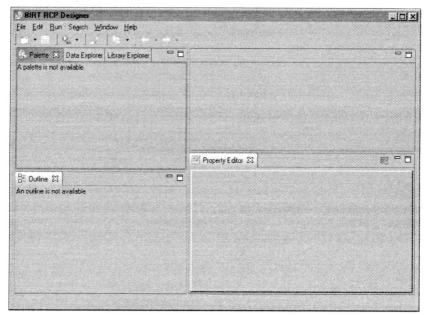

Figure 3-3   BIRT RCP Report Designer

Report design views

The BIRT Report Designer views provide tools that you use to build and customize a BIRT report design, preview the report, and debug the report. Figure 3-4 shows the views that open by default in the Report Design perspective.

Each view is a window you can close, resize, minimize, or maximize. You can also move each view to a different location, either inside or outside the application window. Change or rearrange the set of views to fit the way you work or the available screen space.

If you are using BIRT Report Designer, you can save each application window configuration as a named perspective. Then, as you work with different reports, you can choose a perspective from the list of saved perspectives. This technique is useful if the reports that you create require different sets of views or a different application window layout. For example, if some reports require access to the Library Explorer, but some do not, you can set up and save two perspectives, one with Library Explorer open, another with it closed. Similarly, if you create some reports in landscape orientation and some in portrait, you can save different perspectives with the report editor set to different sizes. Read the Eclipse online documentation for more information about working with perspectives.

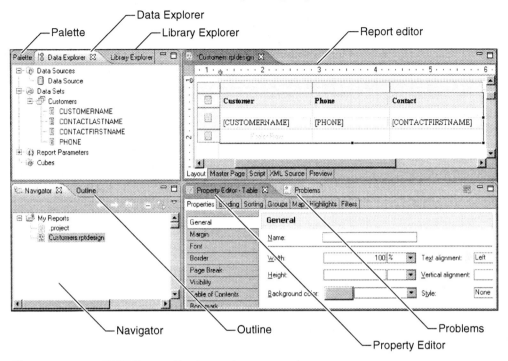

Figure 3-4 BIRT Report Designer views

Report editor

This window is where you design and preview your report. You can open multiple reports in the report editor. The report editor has five pages, which you access by choosing the tabs at the bottom of the report editor. The pages are

- Layout editor, where you create and edit your report design. Figure 3-4 shows the layout editor.

- Master Page, which shows items that appear on every page in a paginated report, such as a report in PDF format.

- Script editor, where you add JavaScript code to your report. You can create many reports without programming. Typically, you write code only if you want to change the way in which BIRT generates a report.

- XML Source, which shows the XML content that BIRT Report Designer generates when you create a report.

- Previewer, which runs your report and displays the output.

Palette

The palette shows all the elements that you can use in a report to organize and display data. To lay out a report, you can drag elements from the palette and drop them in the report page in the layout editor.

Data Explorer

Data Explorer shows the data sources, data sets, and report parameters that your report uses. You use Data Explorer to create, edit, or delete these items. You can also use Data Explorer to add data set fields to your report.

Library Explorer

Library Explorer shows the libraries that the report uses. A library is a shared resource that contains report elements that can be used by more than one report. Use Library Explorer to insert report elements from a library in a report.

Property Editor

Property Editor displays the properties of the report element currently selected in the layout editor. It organizes properties by functional categories. Use it to apply style or format settings to the contents of your report.

Navigator

Navigator shows all your projects and the reports within each project. Use it to manage your report files. Each project is a directory in the file system. Using Navigator, you can open files, delete files, rename files, or move files from one project to another. If you add files to a project directory through the file system, for example, through Windows Explorer, you need to refresh the project in Navigator to update the list of reports.

BIRT RCP Report Designer does not organize report files in projects. Therefore, it does not include a Navigator view.

Outline

Outline shows the structure of your report as a tree view. It shows the hierarchy of elements in a format that is similar to the outline view of a Microsoft Word or PowerPoint document. You expand or collapse parts of the report by choosing the plus (+) or minus (–) signs. Outline also shows all the resources that are used by or defined in a report, including data sources, data sets, libraries, and styles. You can select items in Outline to edit, delete, rename, or copy them.

Problems

Problems displays messages about errors in the report designs in the current project. It describes the error, says which report file contains the error, provides the location of the file, and indicates the line numbers in which the error occurs.

Report design files

BIRT Report Designer uses a simple document model. When you create and save a report design, BIRT Report Designer creates just one file with the .rptdesign file-name extension. This file contains all the information that is necessary for generating a report.

Unlike many report design tools that generate files in proprietary formats, BIRT design files are written in XML. XML is a widely used markup language specification that was designed especially for web documents. Because BIRT uses XML to define the structure and contents of a report design, developers can leverage their knowledge of XML to get a deeper understanding of how BIRT constructs a report design. BIRT's suite of report-specific XML elements and properties is called Report Object Model (ROM).

You open a report design (.rptdesign) file with the report editor, which, by default, displays the report design in the layout editor. The layout editor provides a graphical view of the report design. If you wish, you can view the report design in the XML editor. This editor displays the XML that BIRT Report Designer generates when you create a report.

View the report design in the XML editor to see its XML code or to locate, by line number, an error that was reported in the Problems view. To understand the XML code, you can consult the ROM specification at http://www.eclipse.org/birt/phoenix/ref/.

How to open a report design

- If using BIRT Report Designer, use one of the following methods:

    - In Navigator, double-click the .rptdesign file.

    - Choose File→Open File, then select the .rptdesign file from the file system.

    If someone sends you a .rptdesign file, first save the file in a project folder, then, in Navigator, right-click the project, and choose Refresh. This action updates the project folder to include the file, which you then open using one of these two methods.

- If using BIRT RCP Report Designer, choose File→Open File, then select the .rptdesign file from the file system.

Eclipse saves your environment settings when you exit. If you keep a file open when you exit Eclipse, this file opens automatically when you next start Eclipse.

How to view a report design in the XML editor

1 Open the report design file, using one of the procedures that is described in the previous section.

The layout editor displays the graphical view of the report, as shown in Figure 3-5.

Figure 3-5   Report design in the layout editor

2 Choose the XML Source tab at the bottom of the report editor.

The XML editor displays the XML that defines the report design, as shown in Figure 3-6.

Figure 3-6   XML code for a report design

Report output formats

You can save and view a report in the following formats:

- HTML

- Microsoft Excel document (.xls)

- Microsoft PowerPoint document (.ppt)

- Microsoft Word document (.doc)

- PDF
- Postscript

In addition, users who receive reports can export the data to any of these common office software formats, then edit and redistribute the reports to other users.

Previewing a report

As you work on the design of a report, you typically want to see the report as it would appear to the report user. Using BIRT, you can easily preview a report in any of the supported output formats. You can also view the report in the BIRT report viewer. The report viewer, shown in Figure 3-7, is an interactive viewer that provides report users with the capability to jump to specific pages or to specific sections of a report, to run a report to get the latest data, to print a report, and to export a report to any of the supported output formats.

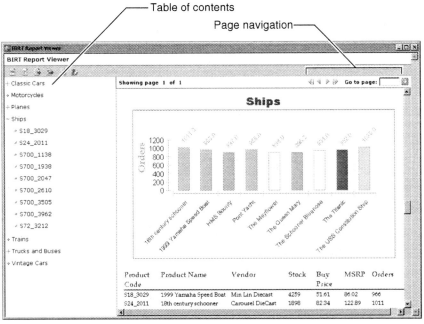

Figure 3-7 BIRT Report Viewer

The following list describes the ways to preview a report:

- To preview a report in BIRT Report Designer, choose the Preview tab at the bottom of the layout editor. The previewer displays the report in HTML format.

- To preview a report in the interactive report viewer, choose File➤View Report➤View Report in Web Viewer.

- To preview a report as a Microsoft Word document, choose File➤View Report➤View Report as DOC.

- To preview a report as a Microsoft PowerPoint document, choose File➤View Report➤View Report as PPT.

- To preview a report as a Microsoft Excel document, choose File➤View Report➤View Report as XLS.

- To preview a report in HTML format in a separate window, choose File➤View Report➤View Report as HTML.

- To preview a report in PDF format, choose File➤View Report➤View Report as PDF.

- To save a report as a PostScript file, choose File➤View Report➤View Report as POSTSCRIPT.

Viewing sample reports

BIRT Report Designer includes many sample reports that you can open to review how various product features are implemented. These sample reports access data from a sample database, Classic Models, that ships with BIRT Report Designer, so you can run the reports and view them with actual data. The sample reports are grouped by feature and common report types, and they are accessible through two views called Chart Examples and Report Examples.

How to access the sample reports

1 Choose Window➤Show View➤Other.

2 On Show View, expand Report and Chart Design. The Chart Examples and Report Examples views appear in the list, as shown in Figure 3-8.

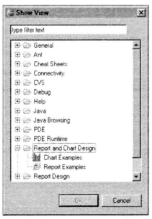

Figure 3-8   Show View displaying the items under Report and Chart Design

3 Select the view you want to open. To open both views, select both Chart Examples and Report Examples (press the Shift key as you click each item), then choose OK.

The Chart Examples and Report Examples views appear next to the Property Editor and Problems views. Figure 3-9 shows the Report Examples view and the categories of sample reports on the left side.

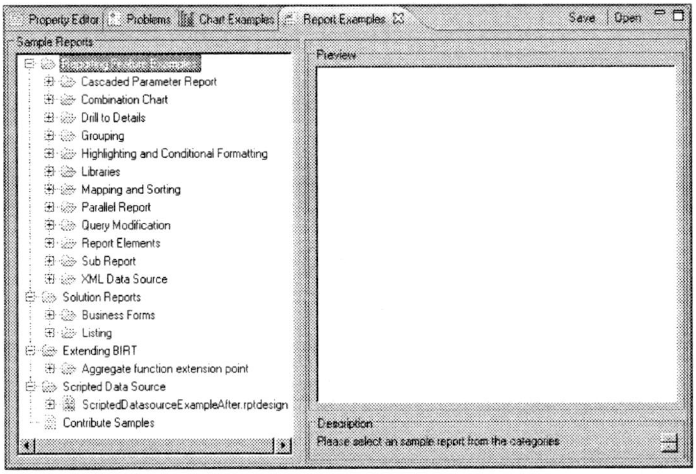

Figure 3-9   Report Examples view displaying the report categories

4 Expand the categories to view the list of report designs. To view a particular report, select the report design (.rptdesign).

As Figure 3-10 shows, the right side of the Report Examples view displays an image of the selected report's output, and provides a description of the report.

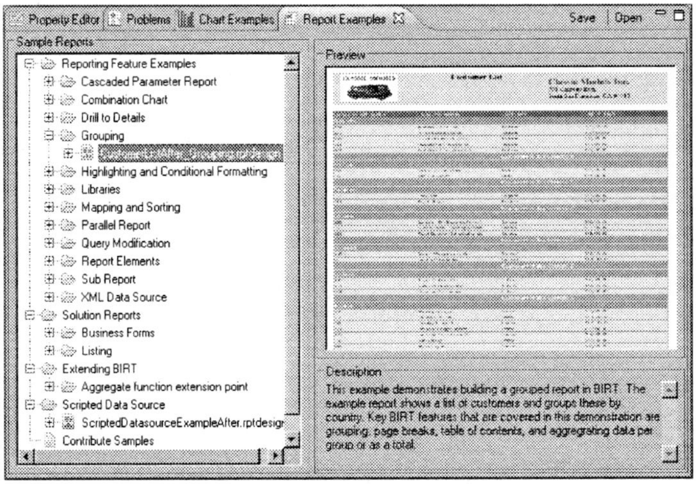

Figure 3-10   Report Examples view displaying an image and description of a selected report

5 Open a sample report in the report editor by doing one of the following:

- If you have already created a report project, choose Save on the title bar next to the Report Examples tab to save the report design in a project folder of your choice. Then, in Navigator, open the report from that folder.

- If you have not created any report projects, choose Open to create a report project and place the selected report design in the project folder. BIRT creates the project folder, which appears in Navigator. Open the report in that folder.

Tutorial 1: Building a simple listing report

This section provides step-by-step instructions for building a report that lists customer names, phone numbers, and contact names. The report uses data from the sample database that is supplied with BIRT Report Designer, Classic Models. Figure 3-11 shows a portion of the finished report.

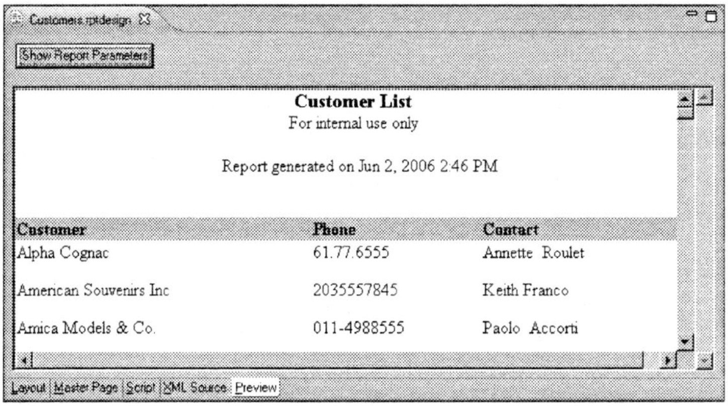

Figure 3-11   Report listing customer names, phone numbers, and contacts

In this tutorial, you perform the following tasks:

- Create a new project. If you are using BIRT RCP Report Designer, you do not complete this step.

- Create a new report.

- Build a data source.

- Build a data set.

- Lay out the report to display each row of the data set.

- Sort the data.

- Format the report to enhance its appearance.

- Create a report title.

Task 1: Create a new project

Eclipse organizes files by projects. You can create one project to organize all your reports or create multiple projects to organize your reports by categories. For each project that you create, Eclipse creates a directory in your file system.

If you are using BIRT RCP Report Designer, this task does not apply to you.

1   Choose File→New→Project. New Project, which appears in Figure 3-12, displays the types of projects that you can create.

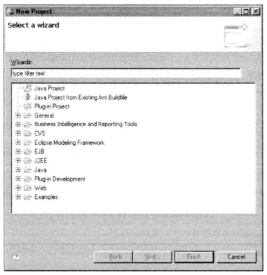

Figure 3-12   New Project

2   Expand Business Intelligence and Reporting Tools, select Report Project, then choose Next.

3   On New Report Project, in Project name, type the following text, as shown in Figure 3-13:

      My Reports

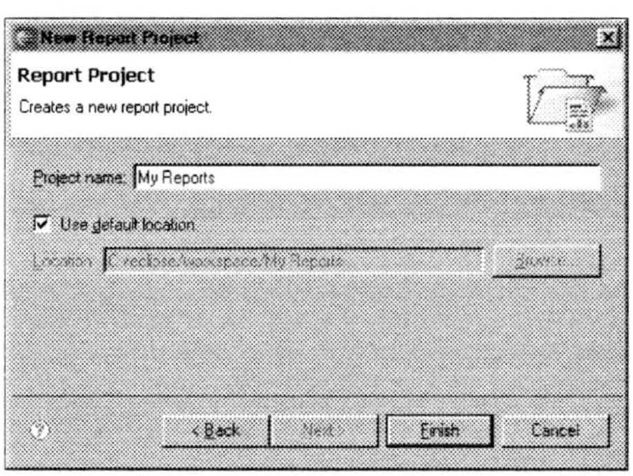

Figure 3-13   New Report Project

4 To add the project, choose Finish. You can now see the project in the Navigator view, as shown in Figure 3-14.

Figure 3-14   A project in the Navigator view

Task 2: Create a new report

You can create a report in the following ways:

- Start with a blank report design.

- Use a predefined report template.

  For each template, BIRT Report Designer provides a cheat sheet, which contains step-by-step instructions, to help you create the report.

For this tutorial, you start with a blank report design.

1 Choose File➤New➤Report. New Report appears. Figure 3-15 shows the window that appears in BIRT Report Designer. New Report is slightly different in BIRT RCP Report Designer.

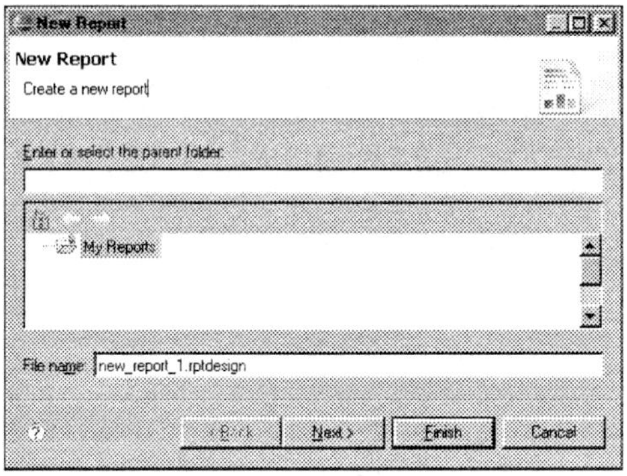

Figure 3-15   New Report in BIRT Report Designer

2 In BIRT Report Designer, in the tree view of the available folders, select the project that you created. This step applies only to BIRT Report Designer users.

3 Type the following text as the file name:

```
Customers.rptdesign
```

4 Choose Next. New Report provides options for starting with a blank report and several report templates, as shown in Figure 3-16.

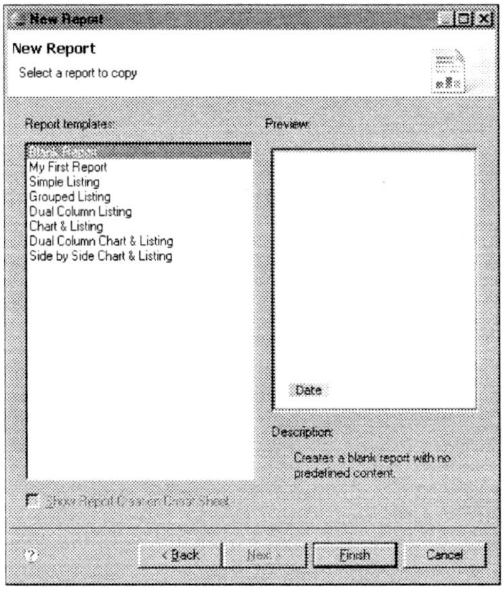

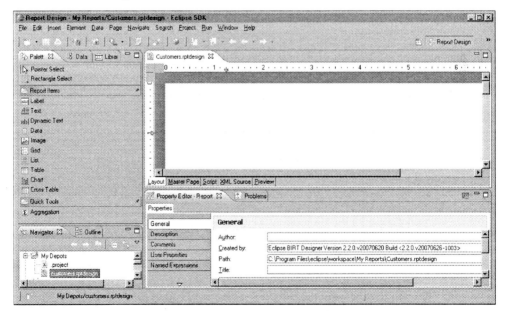

Figure 3-16   Report templates in New Report

5 Select Blank Report, then choose Finish. Your new report appears in the main window. This window displays the layout editor, as shown in Figure 3-17. The layout editor shows an empty report page.

The remainder of this tutorial provides the detailed steps for creating the customer report.

Figure 3-17   Blank report design

Task 3: Build a data source

Before you begin designing your report in the layout editor, you build a BIRT data source to connect your report to a database or other types of data sources. When you build a data source, you specify the driver class, data source name, and other connection information that is specific to the type of data source. For this tutorial, you use the sample database, Classic Models, that is already configured for use with BIRT Report Designer. You do not need to specify the connection information for this sample database.

1 Choose Data Explorer. If you use the default report design perspective, Data Explorer is to the left of the layout editor, next to Palette, as shown in Figure 3-18. If Data Explorer is not open, choose Window→Show View→Data Explorer.

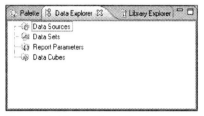

Figure 3-18   Data Explorer

2 Right-click Data Sources, then choose New Data Source from the context menu. New Data Source displays the types of data sources you can create, as shown in Figure 3-19.

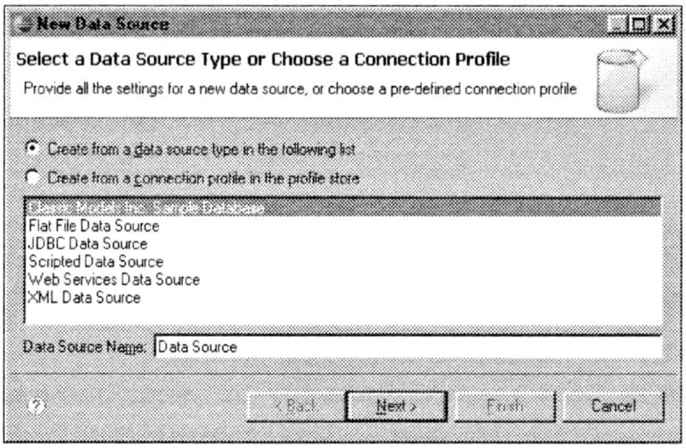

Figure 3-19   New Data Source

3 Select Classic Models Inc. Sample Database from the list of data source types. Use the default data source name, then choose Next. Connection information about the new data source appears.

4 Choose Finish. BIRT Report Designer creates a new data source that connects to the sample database. It appears within Data Sources in Data Explorer, shown in Figure 3-20.

Figure 3-20   Data Sources in Data Explorer

Task 4:   Build a data set

Now, you are ready to build your data set. A data set identifies the data to retrieve from the data source. If your report connects to a JDBC data source, you use a SQL SELECT statement to identify the data to retrieve.

1 In Data Explorer, right-click Data Sets, and choose New Data Set from the context menu.

2 On New Data Set, in Data Set Name, type the following text, as shown in Figure 3-21:

   Customers

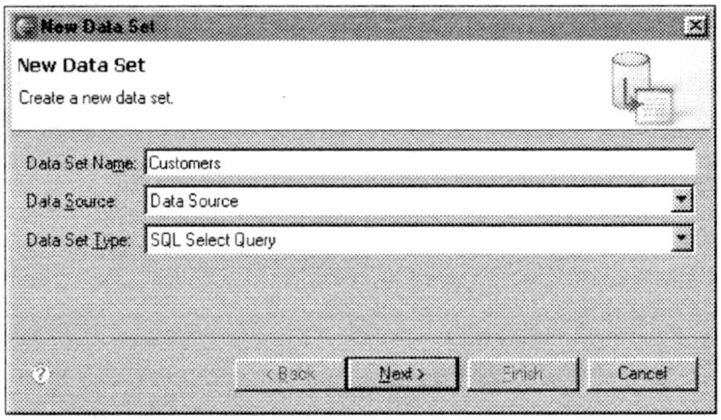

Figure 3-21   New Data Set

3 Use the default values for the other fields.

   ▪ Data Source shows the name of the data source that you created earlier.

   ▪ Data Set Type indicates that the data set uses a SQL SELECT query.

4 Choose Next.

   Query displays the information to help you create a SQL query. Available Items lists all the tables in the Classic Models database. You can click the plus (+) sign next to a table to display the columns in the table. The text area on the right side of this dialog shows the required following keywords of a SQL SELECT statement:

   select
   from

5 In the text area, type the following SQL SELECT statement to specify the data to retrieve:

```
select customerName,
contactLastName,
contactFirstName,
phone
from Customers
```

Although the data set editor shows table and column names in uppercase letters, you can type these names in the case you prefer because SQL is not case-sensitive. If you do not want to type the query, you can drag columns and tables from Available Items to the text area.

The SELECT statement that you created, which is shown in Figure 3-22, gets values from the CUSTOMERNAME, CONTACTLASTNAME, CONTACTFIRSTNAME, and PHONE columns in the CUSTOMERS table.

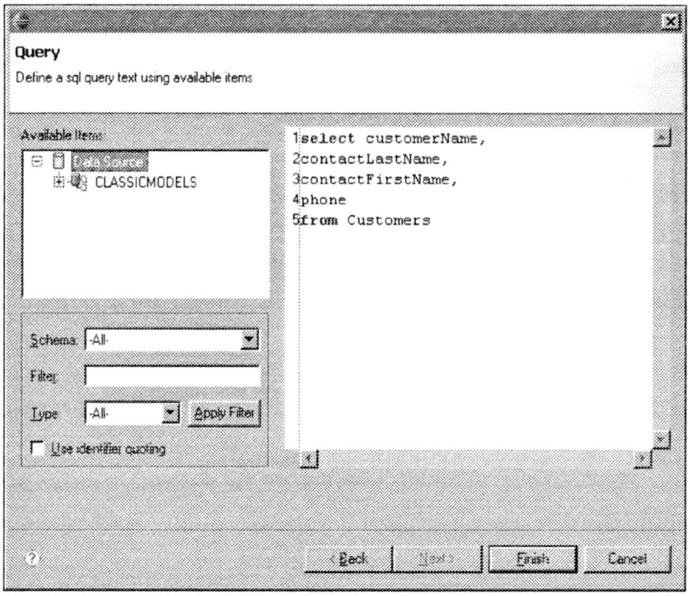

Figure 3-22   SQL SELECT statement in Edit Data Set

6 Choose Finish to save the data set. If you typed the query correctly, Edit Data Set appears. If you made a mistake, an error message appears before Edit Data Set opens. Edit Data Set displays the columns you specified in the query, and provides options for editing the data set, including correcting typing errors in the query.

7 Choose Preview Results to make sure the query is valid and that it returns the correct data. If you typed the SELECT statement correctly, you should see the results that are shown in Figure 3-23. These are the data rows that the query returns.

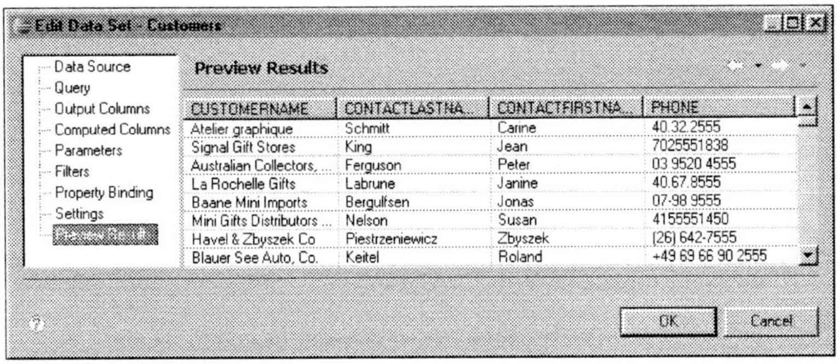

Figure 3-23 Data rows returned by a SQL SELECT statement

8 Choose OK.

Task 5: Lay out the report

In this procedure, you insert elements in the report page to display the data from the data set that you created previously. You start by inserting a table element, then you insert data elements in the table. It is important to understand the functionality that the table provides. The table:

- Iterates through all the data rows that a data set returns

- Enables you to lay out data easily in a row and column format

1 Choose Palette. The palette displays all the elements that you can place in a report.

2 Drag a table element from the palette, and drop it in the report in the layout editor. Insert Table prompts you to specify the number of columns and detail rows to create for the table. The dialog also prompts you to select a data set to bind with the table.

3 On Insert Table, specify the following values, as shown in Figure 3-24:

- In Number of columns, type 3.

- In Number of details, type 1.

- In Data Set, select Customers from the drop-down list.

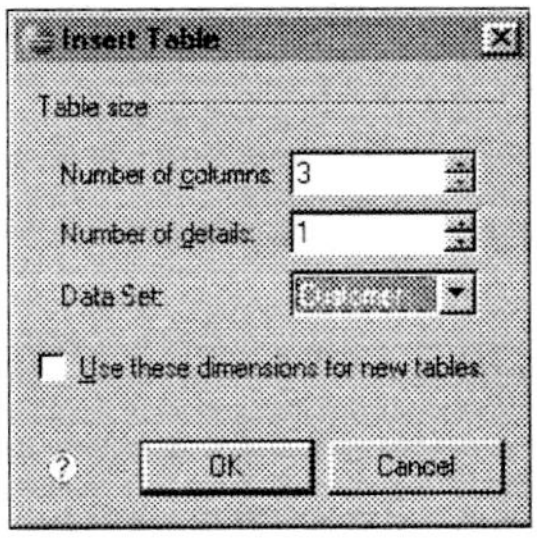

Figure 3-24 Table properties in Insert Table

Choose OK. A table with three columns and one detail row appears in the layout editor. Now, you are ready to insert data in the table.

4 Choose Data Explorer.

5 In Data Explorer, expand Data Sets, then expand Customers. The columns that you specified in the query appear below Customers.

6 Drag CUSTOMERNAME from Data Explorer, and drop it in the first cell in the table's detail row, as shown in Figure 3-25. The detail row displays the main data in the report. In the finished report, the detail row repeats to display all the data rows from the data set.

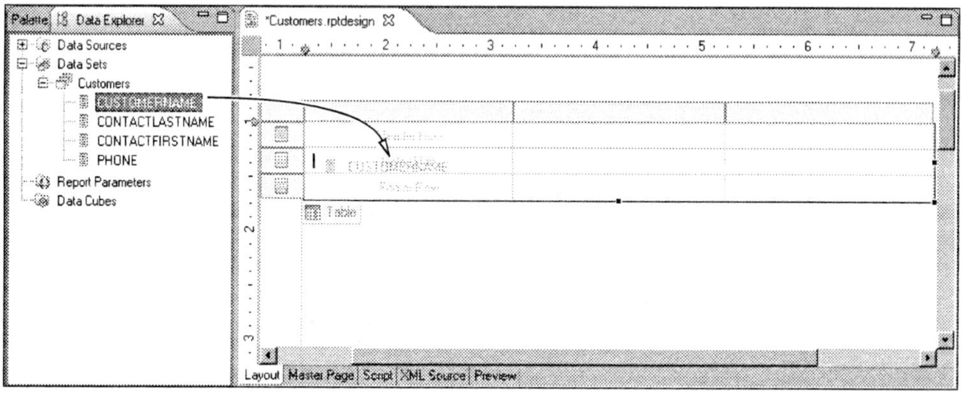

Figure 3-25   Dragging a column from Data Explorer and dropping it in a table cell

In the layout editor, the table cell in which you dropped the CUSTOMERNAME field contains a data element that displays [CUSTOMERNAME]. Above this data element is a label element that the layout editor automatically added to the header row. This label displays the field name as static text. It serves as the column heading. Figure 3-26 shows the data and label elements.

A label displays the field name as a heading

A data element displays the field data

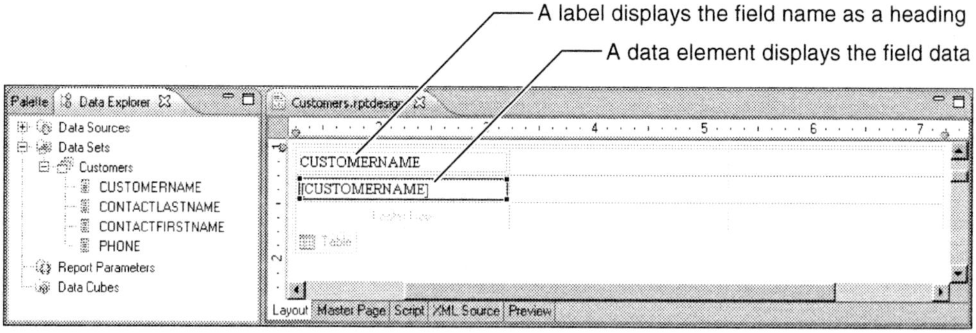

Figure 3-26   Data and label elements in a table

7 Drag PHONE from Data Explorer, and drop it in the second cell in the detail row.

8 Drag CONTACTFIRSTNAME, and drop it in the third cell in the detail row.

9 Drag CONTACTLASTNAME, and drop it in the third cell in the detail row, below CONTACTFIRSTNAME. The report page should look like the one shown in Figure 3-27.

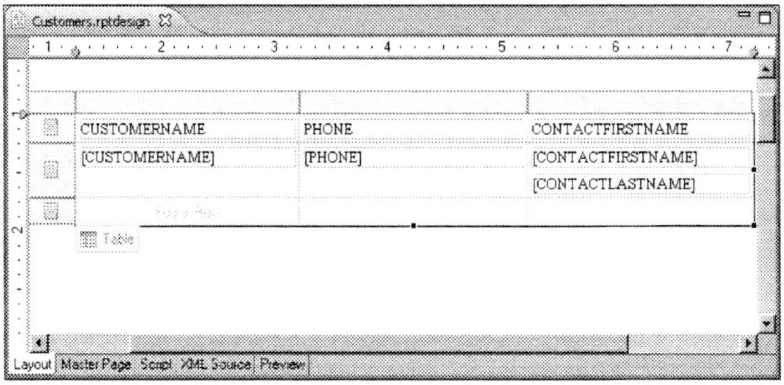

Figure 3-27 Customer and contact information added to a table

10 Choose Preview, the tab at the bottom of the layout editor. BIRT Report Designer generates and displays the report in HTML format, as shown in Figure 3-28. Scroll down to see the entire report. You can also preview a report in PDF. You do so by choosing File➤View Report➤View Report as PDF from the main menu bar.

As Figure 3-28 shows, the data is correct, but it appears in random order. It makes more sense to sort the data alphabetically by customer name. The report's appearance also needs improvement.

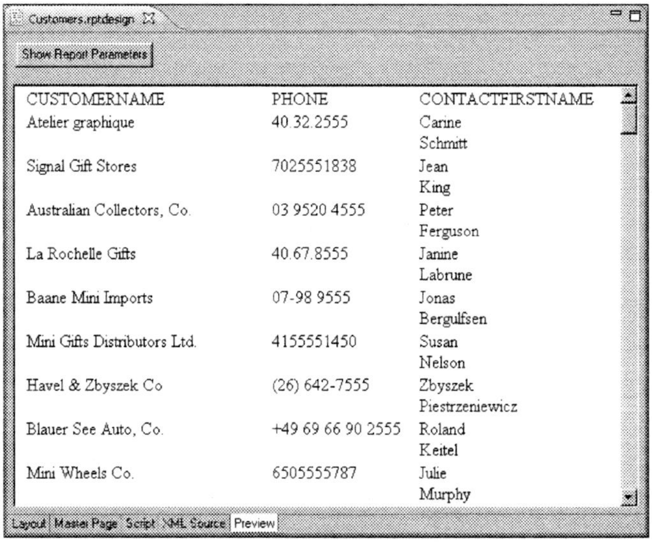

Figure 3-28 Preview of report data

Task 6: Sort the data

When you first create and preview a report, the report displays the data rows in the order in which the query returns them. The order can vary, depending on many factors, such as how data was supplied in the data source. In most cases, you will want to change the order in which data appears in the report.

1 Choose Layout to return to the layout editor.

2 Open Property Editor, if necessary. If you use the default report design perspective, Property Editor appears below the layout editor. If it is not open, choose Window➤Show View➤Property Editor.

3 In the layout editor, select the table by selecting the Table tab in the lower left corner. This tab appears when you hover the mouse pointer over this area. Property Editor displays the properties for the table, as shown in Figure 3-29.

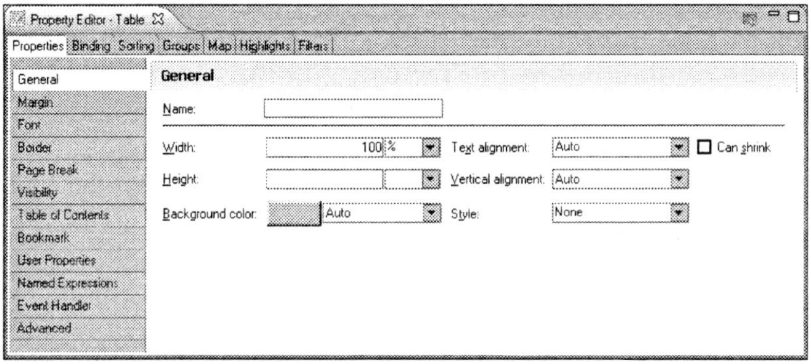

Figure 3-29   Property Editor

4 Choose the Sorting tab.

5 Choose Add to specify a sort key.

6 On New Sort Key, specify the following values:

■ In Key, select CUSTOMERNAME from the drop-down list.

■ In Direction, use the default value, Ascending.

Figure 3-30 shows the sort definition.

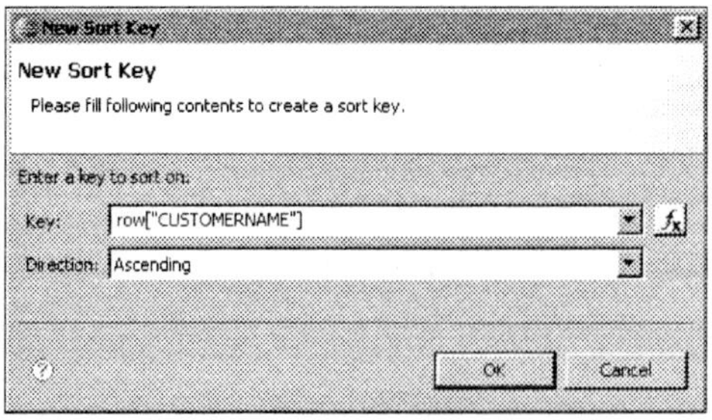

Figure 3-30   Sort definition in New Sort Key

Choose OK. The Sort page displays the sort key that you defined for the table.

7 Preview the report. The sorted data appears in ascending order by customer name, as shown in Figure 3-31.

Figure 3-31   Data sorted by customer name

Notice that names with uppercase letters appear at the top of the list. BIRT sorts string data by UCS2 code point values. In ASCII-based character sets, uppercase letters have lower code point values than lowercase letters. Therefore, uppercase letters appear before lowercase letters.

8 Sort the customer names case-insensitively so that ANG Resellers appears after American Souvenirs Inc., rather than before.

1 On the Sort page, shown in Figure 3-32, select the sort key, then choose Edit.

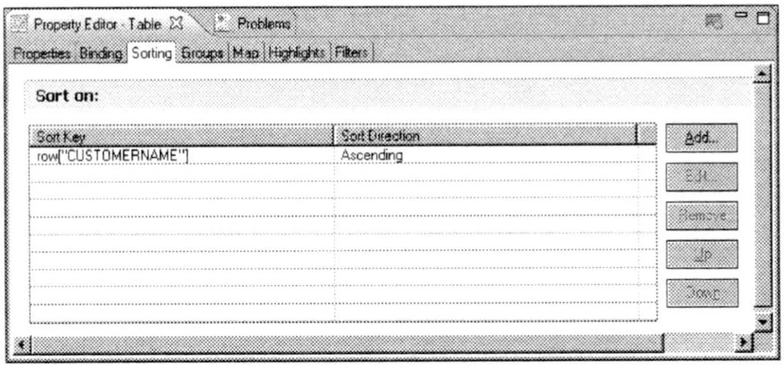

Figure 3-32   Sort key displayed on the Sort page

2 On Edit Sort Key, change the Sort Key expression to the following expression, then choose OK:

```
row["CUSTOMERNAME"].toUpperCase()
```

This expression uses the JavaScript toUpperCase( ) function to convert all the customer name values to uppercase before sorting. JavaScript function names are case-sensitive, so you must type toUpperCase( )

exactly as shown. References to column names are also case-sensitive. In this expression, row["CUSTOMERNAME"] is the correct name to use. If you type row["customername"], for example, BIRT Report Designer displays an error when you run the report. You can verify the capitalization of a column name by looking at the name that is displayed in Data Explorer.

9 Preview the report. The customer names appear in a different order. Names with uppercase letters do not appear at the top of the list.

Task 7: Format the report

Now that you verified that the report displays the correct data in the correct order, you can turn your attention to improving the report's appearance. You perform the following tasks in this section:

- Edit the text of the column headings.

- Format the column headings to differentiate them from the data rows.

- Display the contact first and last names on the same line.

- Increase the space between rows.

Edit the column headings

1 Choose Layout to return to the layout editor.

2 Double-click the first column heading, CUSTOMERNAME. The column heading is in the first row—the header row—of the table.

3 To replace all the highlighted text, start typing, then press Enter when you finish. To edit the text, click once to deselect the text, then position the cursor where you want to add or delete characters.

Replace CUSTOMERNAME with the following text:

    Customer

4 Repeat steps 2 and 3 to change the second and third column headings to the following text:

    Phone
    Contact

The report design should look like the one shown in Figure 3-33.

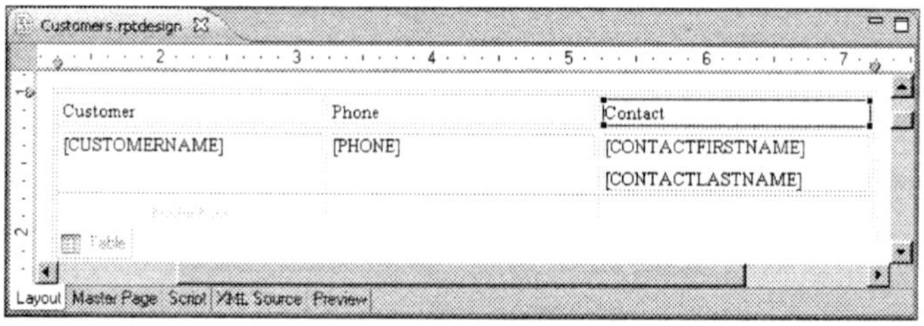

Figure 3-33   Revised column headings in a report design

Format the column headings

To format a report element, you set its properties. You can accomplish this task in one of the following two ways:

- Set an element's properties through Property Editor.

- Define a style that contains the desired properties, and apply the style to an element. Use this method to define format properties once and apply them to more than one element.

In this procedure, you use the first method to set the column headings to bold, and the second method to add color to the header row.

1 To set the column headings to bold using Property Editor:

   1 Select all the column headings. To select multiple elements, press the Shift key as you click each element. Property Editor displays the properties for the selected elements, as shown in Figure 3-34.

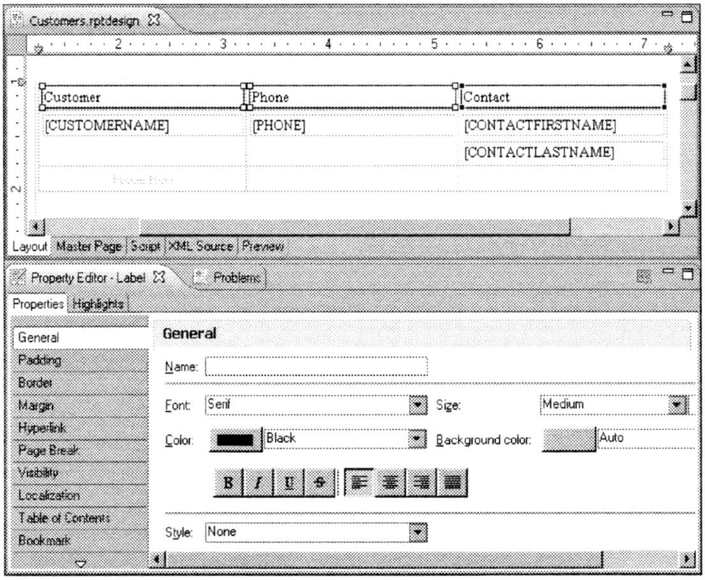

Figure 3-34   Properties for selected elements in Property Editor

   2 Choose B to format the column headings as bold text.

   3 To deselect the column headings, click the white space outside the table.

2 To add a background color to the header row, using a style:

   1 From the main menu bar, choose Element➤New Style.

   New Style appears, as shown in Figure 3-35. The left side displays the property categories. The right side displays the properties for the category that you select.

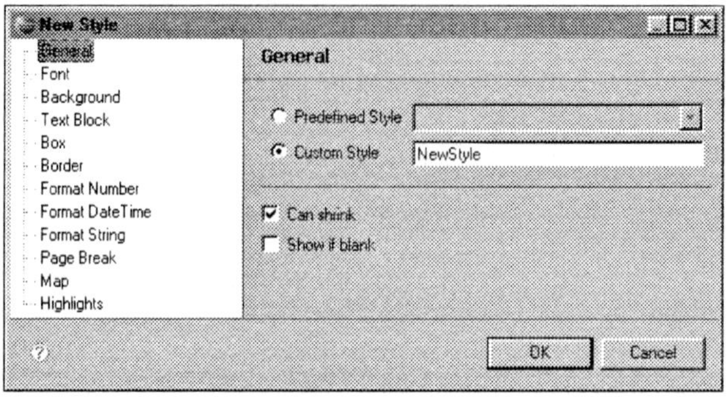

Figure 3-35   New Style

2   For Custom Style, specify the following name for the style:

    table_header_row

3   Choose Background from the list of property categories. New Style displays the background properties that you can set.

4   Specify a color for the Background Color property, using one of the following methods:

    ❑   Select the button next to the property, then select a color from the color palette that appears.

    ❑   Select a color from the drop-down list.

    Choose OK.

5   In the layout editor, select the table by selecting the Table tab in the lower left corner. This tab appears when you hover the mouse pointer over the lower left corner of the table. Clicking the table causes guide cells to appear at the top and left side of the table, as shown in Figure 3-36.

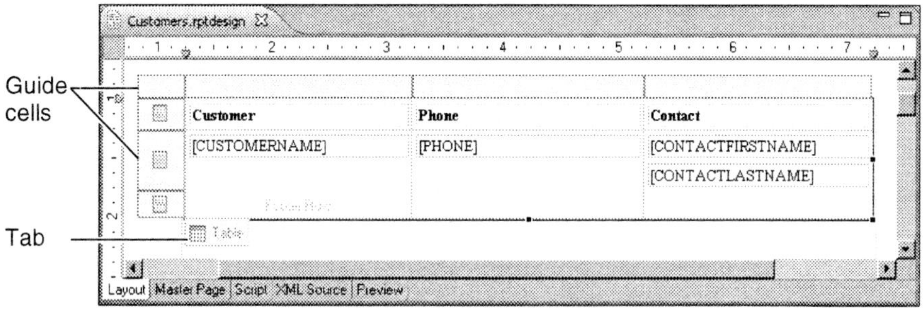

Figure 3-36   Guide cells at top and left of a table

6   Select the guide cell next to the header row. Property Editor displays the properties for the selected row.

7   Choose Properties then General to display the general properties for the row.

8 Apply the style that you just created by selecting table_header_row from the drop-down list next to Style. BIRT Report Designer applies the style to the header row and it appears in color.

3 Preview the report. The report should look like the one shown in Figure 3-37.

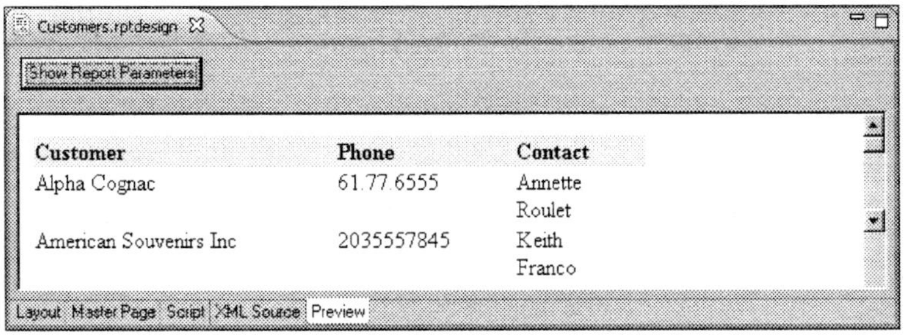

Figure 3-37 Report preview showing header row style

So far, the main improvement is that the headings are clearly visible and defined.

Display first and last names on the same line

When you place multiple elements in a single cell, BIRT Report Designer creates block-level elements. If you are familiar with HTML, you know that each block element starts on a new line. To display multiple elements on the same line, you need to set them as inline elements. Alternatively, you can concatenate the first and last name values to display in a single data element, as described in this procedure.

1 Choose Layout to return to the layout editor.

2 Delete the data element that displays [CONTACTLASTNAME].

3 Double-click the data element that displays [CONTACTFIRSTNAME].

Edit Data Binding, shown in Figure 3-38, shows information about the data associated with the current data element. In Expression, dataSetRow["CONTACTFIRSTNAME"] indicates that the data element displays data from the CONTACTFIRSTNAME field in the data set.

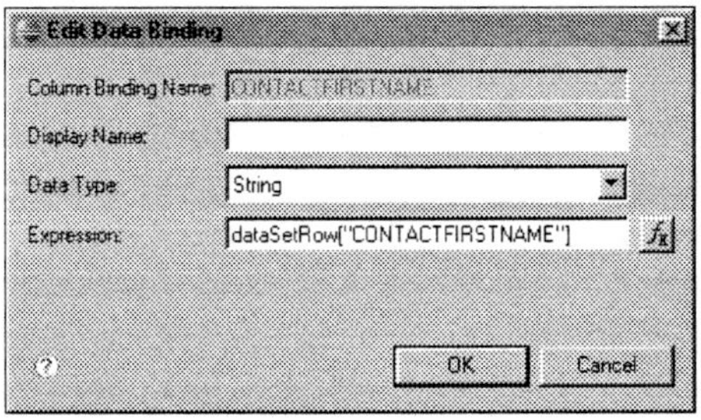

Figure 3-38 Edit Data Binding

4 Click the expression builder button next to
dataSetRow["CONTACTFIRSTNAME"].

The expression builder displays the expression in the text area at the top
of the window.

5 To concatenate the first and last names, edit the expression as follows:

```
dataSetRow["CONTACTFIRSTNAME"]+" "+
    dataSetRow["CONTACTLASTNAME"]
```

Figure 3-39 shows this expression in the expression builder. The empty
quotation marks (" ") add a space between the first name and last name.
You can type the expression in the text area, as shown in Figure 3-39, or
double-click an item in the lower right of the window to insert it in the
expression. Figure 3-40 shows a column name that you can double-click to
insert into the expression.

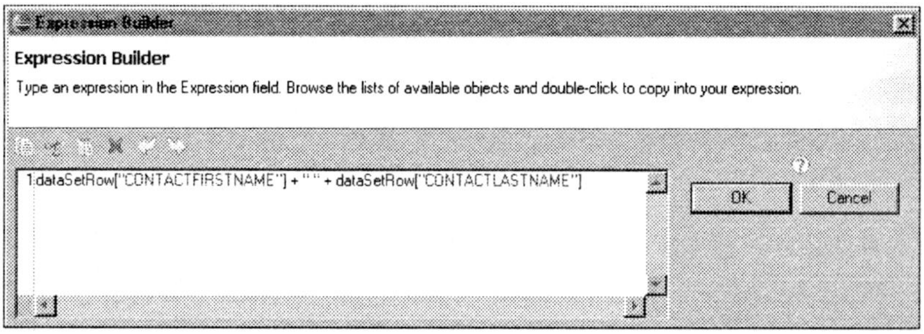

Figure 3-39   Concatenated data in the expression builder

Double-click to insert column
name into expression

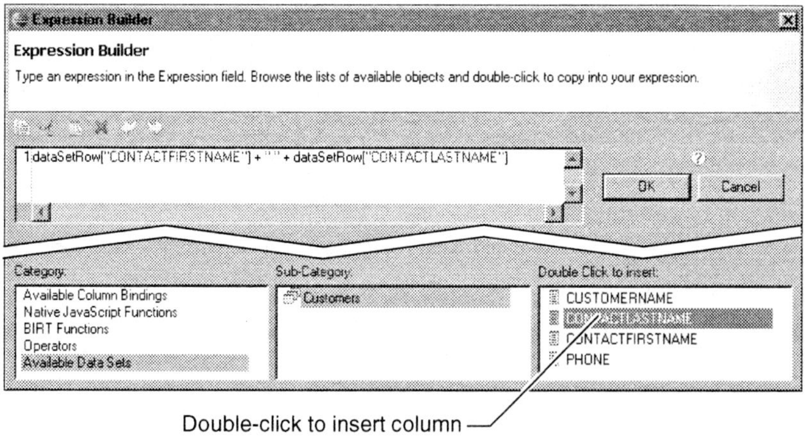

Figure 3-40   Concatenated data in the expression builder created by
choosing a data set field

6 Choose OK to close the expression builder.

The edited expression appears in Edit Data Binding. Choose OK to save the changes to the data element.

7 Preview the report. The report should look like the one shown in Figure 3-41.

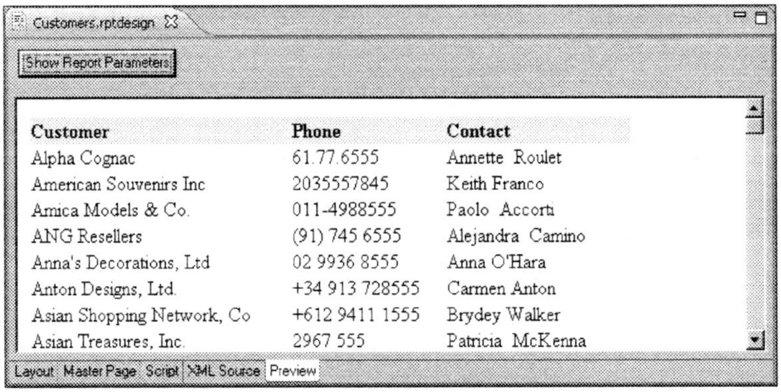

Figure 3-41 Report preview showing concatenated contact names

Increase the space between rows

The default layout adds a minimum space between table rows. Typically, you will want to adjust the spacing between rows.

1 Choose Layout to return to the layout editor.

2 Select the table's detail row, the middle row, as shown in Figure 3-42.

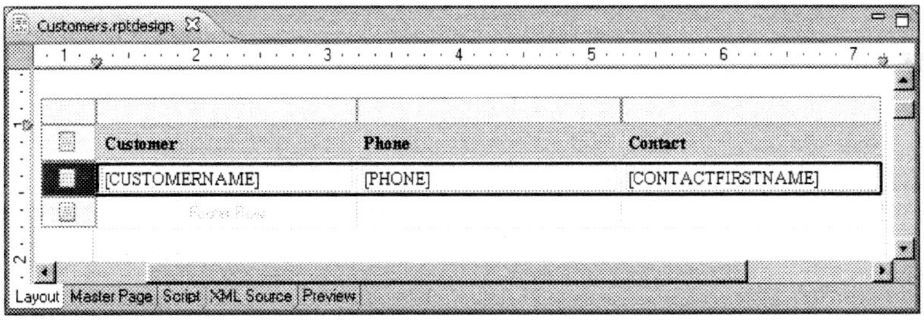

Figure 3-42 Selected table row in the layout editor

Property Editor displays the properties for the row. The title that appears in Property Editor shows the type of element that you select, so you should see Property Editor—Row.

3 In the General properties, set Height to 24 points. The height of the row increases, as shown in Figure 3-43.

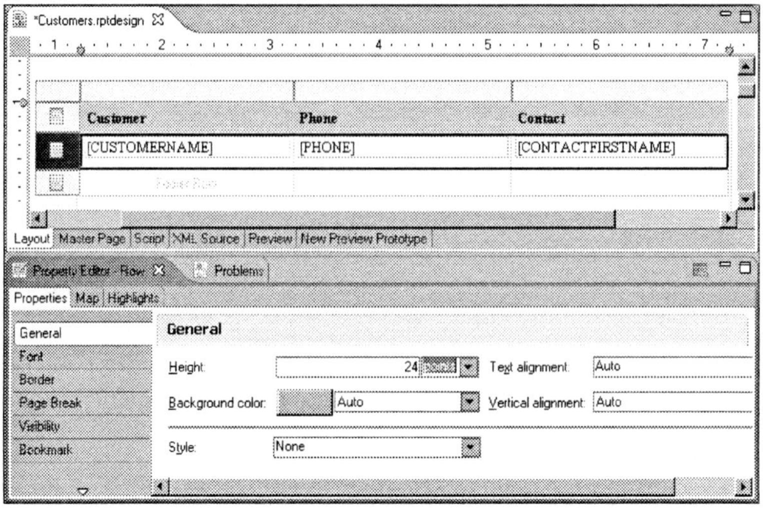

Figure 3-43   Row height set to 24 points

4 Preview the report. The report should look like the one shown in Figure 3-44. There is more space between the rows of data.

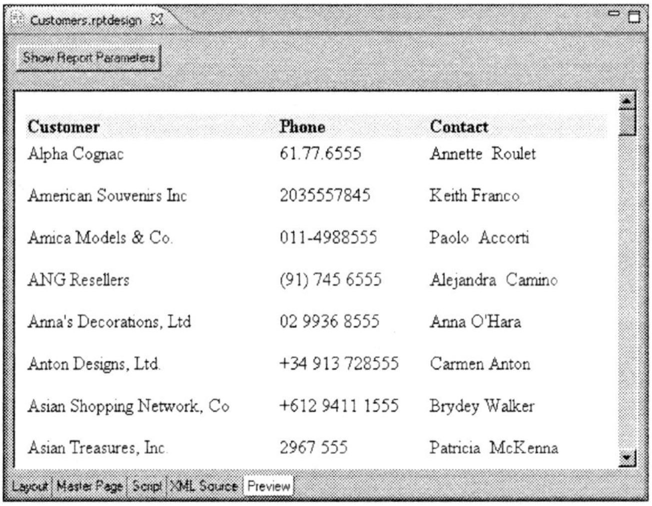

Figure 3-44   Report preview showing row spacing

Task 8: Create a report title

All your report needs now is a title. To display a title, you can use either a label element, a text element, or a data element. The following list describes each type of element:

- The label element is suitable for short, static text, such as column headings.

- The data element is suitable for displaying dynamic values from a data set field or a computed field.

- The text element is suitable for multi-line text that contains different formatting or dynamic values.

In this procedure, you use a text element and HTML tags to format the text. Note that you are not required to use HTML to create formatted text. If, however, you are well-versed in HTML or web design, you might prefer using HTML to create a block of formatted text.

1 Choose Layout to return to the layout editor.

2 Choose Palette.

3 Drag the text element from the palette, and drop it above the table.

4 On Edit Text Item, select HTML from the drop-down list that displays Auto.

When you select HTML, you can embed HTML tags or CSS properties in the text. You can type the tags or you can insert the commonly used HTML tags that the text editor provides.

5 Specify the following text in the text area, shown in Figure 3-45:

```
<CENTER><B><span style="font-size: larger">
Customer List
</B></span><BR>
<FONT size="small">For internal use only</FONT><BR><BR>
Report generated on <VALUE-OF>new Date()</VALUE-OF>
</CENTER><BR><BR>
```

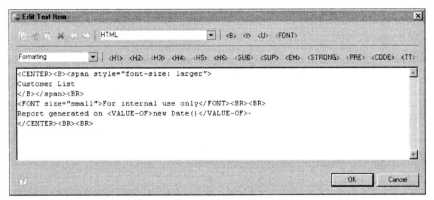

Figure 3-45 Text with HTML tags

6 Choose OK, then preview the report. The report should look like the one shown in Figure 3-46.

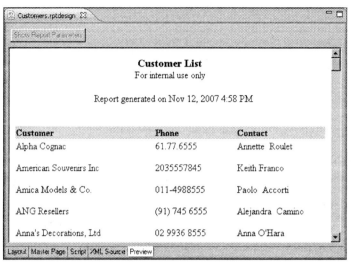

Figure 3-46   Report preview showing formatted report title

As you can see, using the text element with embedded HTML enables you to

- Use different formatting for each line in a multi-line text block.
- Insert dynamic values, such as the current date.

Alternatively, you can use

- Two label elements to display the first and second lines of static text
- A data element to display the third line that contains the dynamic value

Next steps

You just built your first report and worked with some of the basic tools and features of BIRT Report Designer. There are many more tasks that you can accomplish to build more sophisticated reports. Some of these tasks, described in other chapters of this book, include

- Connecting to your own data source
- Creating charts
- Creating cross tabs
- Creating report parameters for user input
- Building reports that contain subreports
- Formatting report elements based on conditions
- Hiding report elements or sections based on conditions
- Adding hyperlinks to link your report to web locations or to link one report section to another

Planning Your Report

The tutorial in the previous chapter demonstrates how easy it is to build reports using BIRT, so you may be puzzled when you next see a chapter recommending that you plan your report development. This chapter receives its prominent position because as you need to address more complex reporting requirements, you will find it is much more efficient to work from a plan.

You should always plan a report on paper before you begin to create the report with BIRT Report Designer. Planning helps clarify the report requirements and saves time in the long run because you do not waste time creating and fine-tuning a report that does not meet your users' needs.

Before you start creating a report, you should have the following documents prepared:

- A specification that describes the requirements for the report project

- A prototype, or mock-up, of the report

Ideally, your documents should be reviewed and approved by your report users to determine if the proposed layout meets requirements they may not be able to predict without seeing a mock-up on paper.

In organizations with large IT departments that have strong formal processes in place, report developers typically receive requests for new reports that are accompanied by a specification and perhaps a mock-up of the report. Sometimes, report developers discuss report requirements with the person who requested the report, and they develop the specification and mock-up together. Either way, both documents are essential planning tools before a report developer even starts BIRT Report Designer.

If you are responsible for writing the specification, you need to identify the information that the report should provide and determine how best to present the information. This chapter provides guidelines for defining the specification and designing a mock-up of the report. If you receive a specification from somewhere else, use the guidelines to ensure that the specification covers all the information that you need.

Identifying the content of the report

This step is the most important one in the planning process. To get started, answer the following questions:

- What is the purpose of the report?

  A purpose statement helps you determine the information that you need. It also gives the report a starting point.

  The following example is a sample purpose statement:

  > The purpose of this report is to show monthly sales by region, then by sales representatives, and to flag the representatives whose sales figures fall below a certain amount.

  Make the purpose statement as specific as possible. A vague requirement, such as a monthly sales report, does not help define the precise data requirements.

- Who is going to read the report?

  A report can be viewed by different types of users. For example, sales representatives, sales managers, and the vice president of sales can all use a sales report. Each type of user is interested in different types of information and different levels of detail. Knowing the users of your report helps you plan the report data accordingly. Reviewing the list of data to be included can ensure that the data needed by each of the users is, in fact, included in the design. Having a representative from each of the groups of users available to review your proposed layout assists in ensuring that you are meeting each set of requirements.

- What information should appear in the report, and where is it coming from?

  Much of the information in a typical report is taken directly from data fields in a database, application, or text file. First, you need to know the source or sources of data for the report. Second, you need to understand how the data is structured. If, for example, the data source is a database, you need to know what tables are in it, the relationships among tables, the columns in each table, the data types, and so on. If necessary, ask your database administrator for this information.

- Does any of the data need to be calculated?

  Some report data comes directly from data fields, such as sales representative names or addresses. Some information must be calculated, such as the percentage by which sales figures exceed or fall below a certain amount.

- How will the data be calculated?

  Some data can be calculated by performing a mathematical operation on data field values, such as multiplying Item.Quantity by Item.Price to get extended prices. Some data may need to be calculated by using a JavaScript function or a user-defined function.

- Do you want to enable the report user to specify what data to display?

  You can create a report that always displays a specific set of data from the data source. You can also create a report that lets users specify what information they want to see. For example, rather than displaying sales data for all regions, you can prompt the user to specify a region for which the sales data appears in the report.

Determining how the report will be viewed

When designing a report, you need to consider and test the environment in which the report will be viewed because the environment affects how a report appears and prints.

You should always design for the final delivery environment. This approach includes choosing the right fonts and colors, selecting the appropriate page size, fine-tuning the size of report fields and the amount of space between them, and so on.

Consider the following questions:

- Which is more important, viewing online or printing the report?

  Recognize that there are differences between online and printed reports; decide which is more important, and design for that output. For example, printed reports can vary in appearance depending upon the printer producing the output. If a report will primarily be viewed online, you can add interactive viewing features, such as hyperlinks or a dynamic table of contents.

- Will the report be viewed in HTML, a PDF file, or one of the other supported file formats?

  The appearance of the report differs depending on the file format. Pagination, for example, is a key difference between HTML and page-based file formats, such as PDF and Microsoft Word document (.doc). A report in PDF format, for example, appears on multiple pages of a fixed size. An HTML report, on the other hand, can appear on multiple pages or in one scrollable page, depending on what you specify.

- If distributing an HTML report, what browsers are you supporting?

  Different browsers can display results differently because they interpret HTML or CSS tags differently. If there are particular browsers that you must support, test the report in those browsers.

Considering international reporting requirements

BIRT Report Designer supports creating reports that contain international data for use in multiple locales. A locale defines a set of conventions for providing, displaying, and sorting data. Numbers, dates, and currencies appear differently in different locales. The following examples show dates in long date format when the locale is English (United States) and when the locale is German (Germany):

```
Wednesday, July 7, 2008
Mittwoch, 7. Juli 2008
```

BIRT reports automatically display date, number, and currency data according to the locale to which the report user's machine is configured. You do not have to do anything special to display these types of data in multiple locales.

When designing a report for international users, consider the following questions:

- Will the report be viewed in one locale? If yes, which locale?

  If your report will be used in a specific locale, design and test the report in that locale.

- Will the report be viewed by users in multiple countries?

  If your report will be viewed by users in multiple countries, you should consider internationalizing the report so that it appears correctly in multiple locales. For example, rather than specifying text directly in a report design, you can create text strings in an external source and provide translations of those strings. Using this technique, called localization, the report displays text in the language that is specified by the locale of the user's machine.

  Testing report output in multiple locales is an important early stage in the report design process. Develop a small sample and send that to recipients who can test the output in that locale and, in particular, can test printed output for possible glitches in fonts and layout. Even decisions such as how names are to be displayed can be challenging if the report is to be viewed by users with differing language competencies.

Deciding the layout and format of the report

After you identify the report's purpose and content, you should have a good idea about organizing and presenting the information. Consider these questions:

- What is the overall layout for the report data? Can all the data appear in a single section, or does the data need to be presented in multiple sections?

A simple listing of customer names and phone numbers, for example, can be presented in a two-column table. A financial statement, on the other hand, can be a multi-sectioned report that includes a form letter, a summary of accounts and balances, and transaction details for each account.

- Do you need to organize information into groups? If yes, how?

  For example, a monthly sales report can display sales figures by region, by sales representative, or by both. To display both, you can group the information by region first, then list the sales representatives for each region.

- How do you want to sort information?

  A report can present information in the order in which it is stored in the data source, in ascending order, or in descending order. The sort order affects the readability and usability of a report.

- Do you need to summarize the data? If yes, how?

  Reports that present numerical data, such as expense reports, financial statements, and earnings reports, always contain summary sections for totals, averages, or percentages. Decide if this summary information should appear in a table, a chart, a cross tab, or a combination of these display options.

- Do you want to highlight information based on certain conditions?

  It is common to use formatting to emphasize certain information. For example, if a report displays a long list of customers in alphabetical order, you can display the names of the top ten customers in blue.

- Do you need to display information in page headers and footers?

  Printed reports typically display information in the page header to help users navigate multi-page reports. For example, you can display the region name in the header, so users know that sales representatives on page n are part of region x. In the page footer, you can show the page number and the report's generation date. On the other hand, online reports that present data in one continuous page do not require page headers and footers.

- Are there corporate standards that you need to follow?

  If your company produces reports for external use, such as financial statements for clients, it is likely that a report that you create needs to use corporate styles. Corporate styles typically dictate the logos, security statements, fonts, and colors that you can use.

- Are there online style sheets that you can use?

  Most organizations maintain a corporate web site and frequently use CSS to format the look and feel of web pages. You can reuse CSS styles in your reports, which enables you to create reports with the corporate look without having to recreate the styles.

- Are there report templates you can use?

  Unless your organization is just starting up, chances are report templates are available. If there are no formal templates, look at existing reports to see if you can reuse and adapt their layouts. If you are in start-up mode, examine the sample reports, and consider establishing standards for organizational reporting in common areas, such as budget variance, expenses, and vacation reporting.

Drawing a mock-up

After you make the decisions that are described in the previous sections, you are ready to create a mock-up of the report. Use any tool with which you are comfortable, such as a word processor, graphics program, or pen and paper.

A mock-up should show approximately what the finished report will look like, including the report title, page header and footer information, and all the fields in the body of the report. Using a mock-up to get feedback and approval from your primary users can save you time. With this approval, you do not waste time creating a polished report that contains the wrong information or layout.

A mock-up is especially useful when you are first learning BIRT Report Designer. With a blueprint in hand, you can focus on learning and using the tool, rather than trying to design and learn at the same time.

Considering reuse of report components

Rarely do you create just one report. Often, you create reports for different departments in your company or to meet your clients' varying reporting needs. You can approach report creation one report at a time, or you can plan and design a suite of reports. Consider these questions to evaluate which approach is more suitable:

- How many reports are you creating?
- Do the reports require common elements and styles, such as connections to the same data source, page headers and footers that display the same information, report titles in a particular font and color, or tables with a certain format?
- Do you work in a group with other report developers? If yes:
  - How similar are the report projects?
  - Do you need to collaborate on the designs?

If you create more than a couple of reports, and they contain many common elements, or if you work with other report developers on similar reports, you can streamline the report creation process by creating a collaborative and shared report development environment. Using BIRT Report Designer, you can:

- Create and store common report elements in a library, which all reports can use.

- Create report templates that define a basic report structure on which new reports can be based.

With careful planning, you can create rich sets of libraries and templates that provide you and other report developers with a head start when you create a new report.

Managing report design resources

A report design typically uses external resources, such as image files, report libraries, Java files, and message files used for localization. If you work on a suite of reports that use multiple external files, you need a way to organize the files so that you can easily package and deploy them to an application server or migrate your reports to different machines.

BIRT Report Designer provides a resource folder as a way to organize all these external files for ease of deployment later. The default location of this resource folder is specified in the Preferences page, which you access by choosing Windows➤Preferences from the main menu, then choosing the Report Design Resource item. On this page, you can specify a different path for the resource folder option.

When you publish a library or create a message file in BIRT Report Designer, these files are automatically saved in the resource folder. To manage files that are created by other applications, such as image files, copy the files into the resource folder before you create the report. Then, when you insert the images in the report, select the image in the resource folder.

Deciding how the report will be deployed

Planning the report design is one phase of the planning process. You also need a plan for deploying or distributing the report. Consider these questions:

- How will the report be distributed to users?
  - Will the report be deployed from an application?
  - Will the report be sent through e-mail?

- If the report will be deployed from an application, address these questions:
  - How will the report integrate with the application?

- Will users need a secure login to access the report?

- Will users view a generated report, or will users generate the report to view it with real-time data?

Depending on your deployment strategy, there are a host of other questions to answer and programming tasks to perform. Deployment and integration are topics that are beyond the scope of this book and are covered in *Integrating and Extending BIRT* (Addison-Wesley, 2008).

Part

III

Accessing and Binding Data

Connecting to a Data Source

Enterprise report data is frequently stored in a variety of systems and formats. BIRT Report Designer provides wizards to set up access to the following types of data sources:

- JDBC data sources

- Text files

- XML documents

- Web services

A report, however, is not limited to using data from these data sources. Developers can write JavaScript or Java scripts to get data from Java objects, such as Enterprise JavaBeans. Developers can also use BIRT's Open Data Access (ODA) framework to write custom data drivers to access data from any source, including data stored in proprietary systems.

This chapter discusses how to use the wizards in BIRT Report Designer to set up access to a data source without programming. Information about writing scripts and developing custom data drivers is covered in *Integrating and Extending BIRT*.

About BIRT data sources

To access data for a BIRT report, you use a BIRT data source. A BIRT data source is an object that contains the information to connect to the database, text file, XML file, or web service. When you create a report, you use Data Explorer, as shown in Figure 5-1, to create and manage BIRT data sources.

Newly created data source

Figure 5-1   Data source in the data explorer

You can create as many data sources as necessary for a report. The data sources can be of different types. For example, a report can use data from a database and data from a flat file repository.

By default, BIRT Report Designer provides unique names with the prefix Data Source for each data source that you create in a report. If you create three data sources, the default names are Data Source, Data Source1, and Data Source2. It is good practice to provide descriptive names, such as SalesDB or BooksXml, so that you can identify easily the type or name of the data source.

Accessing data using JDBC

A report can access data from any database or other data source that uses a JDBC driver. Most relational databases, such as Oracle, SQL Server, or MySQL, use JDBC drivers. Make sure you have the appropriate JDBC driver for the database that you want to access.

Many databases also use a connection pool—a cache of database connection objects—to minimize the overhead of establishing a connection to the database. A connection pool optimizes database performance through the reuse of connections, which reduces the need to repeatedly open and close connections each time a report is run. If the database you want to connect to uses connection pooling, you can specify the path to the service.

Creating a JDBC data source

When you create a JDBC data source in BIRT, you select the driver class and provide a URL to connect to the data source. If necessary, you provide a user name, a password, and a path to a connection pooling service. Make sure you have all this information before you create the data source.

How to specify the connection information for a database or other JDBC data source

1 In Data Explorer, right-click Data Sources, then choose New Data Source.

2 On New Data Source, supply the following information:

   1 Select JDBC Data Source from the list of data source types.

2   In Data Source Name, type a name for the data source. The name must be unique in the current report. Figure 5-2 shows a default data source name.

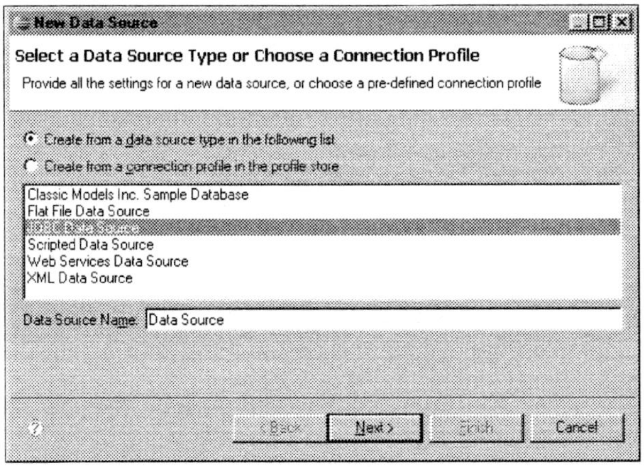

Figure 5-2   Creating a JDBC data source

3   Choose Next.

New JDBC Data Source Profile shows connection properties, as shown in Figure 5-3.

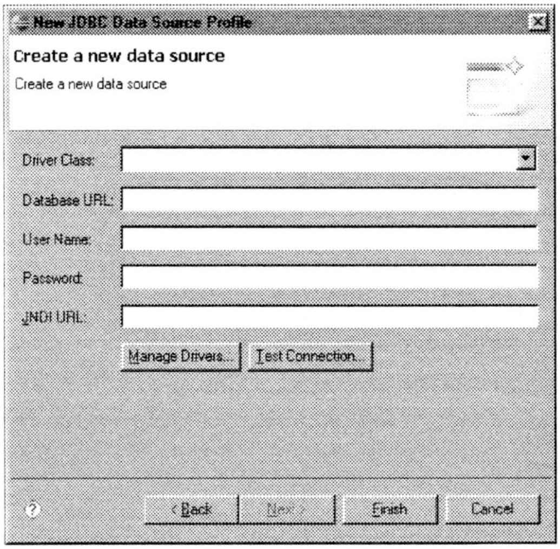

Figure 5-3   Defining JDBC connection information

3 Specify the connection information for the JDBC data source:

1   In Driver Class, choose a driver class from the drop-down list. If you do not see the driver class that you want to use, add a driver as described later in this chapter.

2 In Database URL, type the database URL, using the syntax that the driver requires. Typically, BIRT Report Designer displays the necessary syntax in Database URL. For a Sun JDBC/ODBC bridge, for example, the syntax is

```
jdbc:odbc:<data source name>
```

where <data source name> is the name of your data source. For example, the following URL identifies the sales database:

```
jdbc:odbc:sales
```

3 In User Name, type the user name to use when connecting to the JDBC data source. This field can be left blank if your data source does not require a user name.

4 In Password, type the password to use when connecting to the JDBC data source. This field can be left blank if your data source does not require a password.

5 In JNDI URL, type the full path to the connection pooling service, if applicable. The following path is an example:

```
java:comp/env/jdbc/MyDataSource
```

In the example, MyDataSource is the name of the JNDI database service.

4 To ensure that the connection information is correct, choose Test Connection. If Test Connection returns an error, repeat the preceding steps to correct the error. Then, test the connection again.

5 Choose Finish. The new JDBC data source appears under Data Sources in Data Explorer.

Managing JDBC drivers

BIRT supports JDBC 3.0 drivers. You can get these drivers from a data source vendor or third-party web site. BIRT Report Designer includes the Apache Derby JDBC driver and the Sun JDBC-ODBC bridge driver as part of a default installation. Use the bridge driver for prototype-development purposes only. We do not recommend using the bridge driver with ODBC data sources that do not have a JDBC driver because it is not a production quality driver. Instead, we recommend using a native JDBC driver whenever possible.

To indicate which drivers are available for use, the JDBC driver manager displays symbols next to the file names in the driver list. An x indicates that a driver is no longer available in the JDBC directory. An asterisk (*) indicates that a file does not exist in the specified location. A plus sign (+) indicates that a file has been restored. For example, in Figure 5-4, the driver manager indicates that the first driver is unavailable.

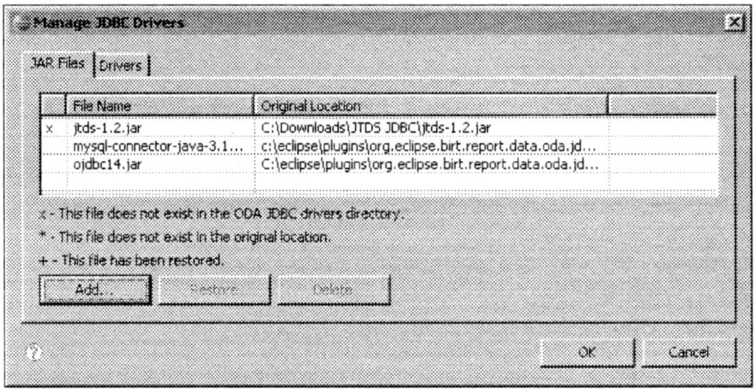

Figure 5-4   Managing JDBC drivers

Adding a JDBC driver

To install other JDBC drivers, use the JDBC driver manager. This tool supports the installation of JAR files that contain JDBC drivers. The JAR file you select is copied to the following directory:

```
eclipse\plugins
    \org.eclipse.birt.report.data.oda.jdbc_<version>\drivers
```

How to add a JDBC driver

This procedure assumes you are creating a new JDBC data source, and you need to install a new driver because the driver that your database requires is not available in the list of drivers.

1   On New JDBC Data Source Profile, shown in Figure 5-5, choose Manage Drivers.

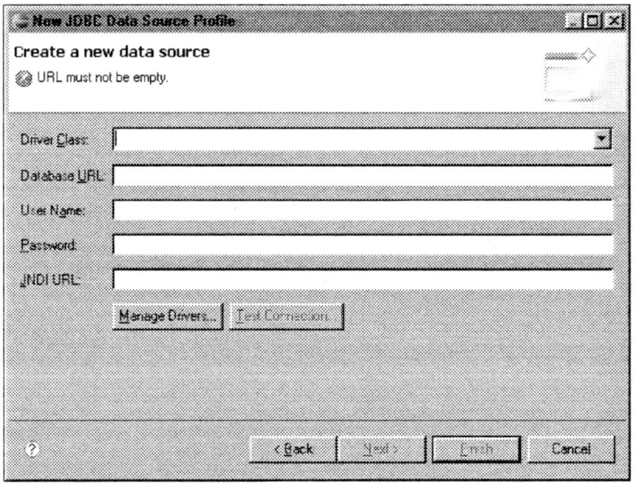

Figure 5-5   New JDBC Data Source Profile

2 On Manage JDBC Drivers, shown in Figure 5-6, choose Add to install the JAR file that contains the driver.

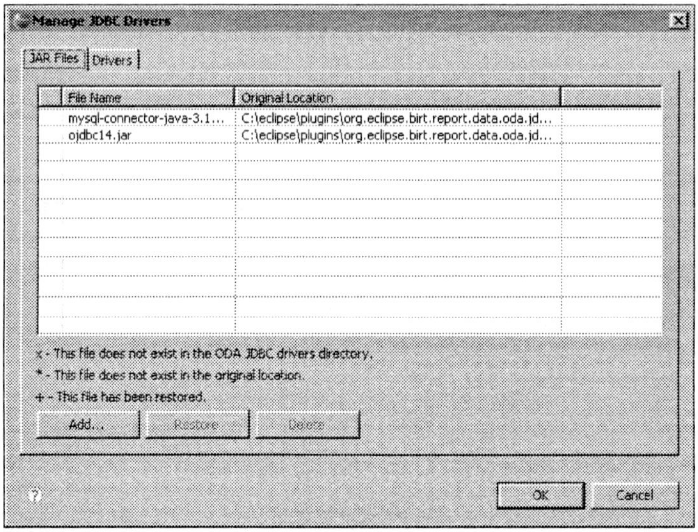

Figure 5-6　　　Managing JDBC drivers

3 Navigate to the directory that contains the JAR file. Select the JAR file and choose Open.

Manage JDBC Drivers shows the new JAR file. BIRT Report Designer copies the JAR file to the Eclipse JDBC directory.

4 Choose Drivers to see the list of installed drivers, as shown in Figure 5-7.

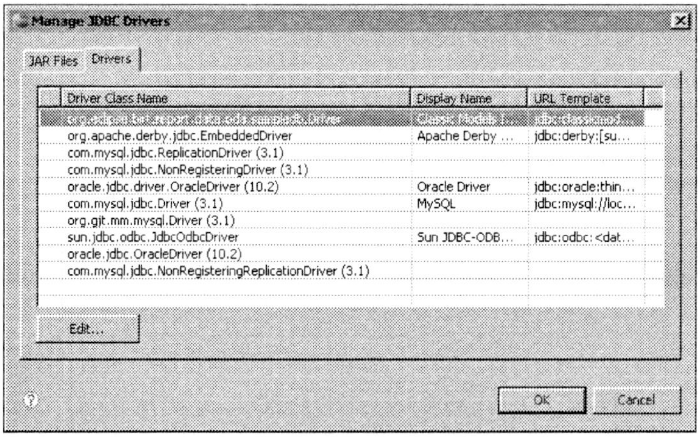

Figure 5-7　　　Viewing JDBC driver classes

5 Specify the properties for a driver, using the following steps:

1 Select the new driver, then choose Edit. Edit JDBC Driver appears, as shown in Figure 5-8.

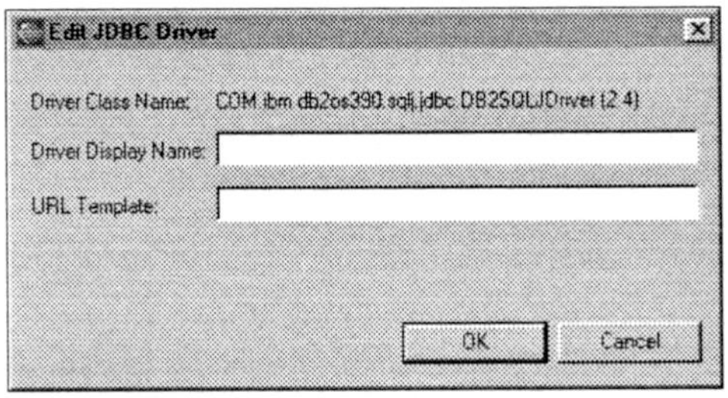

Figure 5-8   Editing a JDBC driver URL template

2 Specify settings for the JDBC driver.

    1 In Driver Display Name, type a name that appears in the Display Name column in Manage JDBC Drivers.

    2 In URL Template, type the syntax suggestion that appears for this driver in Database URL on New JDBC Data Source Profile.

    Choose OK. The driver manager displays the new display name and URL template syntax suggestion.

6 Choose OK.

Deleting a JDBC driver

To delete a JDBC driver, use the JDBC driver manager. If the JAR file contains more than one driver, the driver manager deletes all drivers that are in the JAR file. If you unintentionally delete a driver, you can use the restore feature to restore the driver.

How to delete all JDBC drivers that are in a JAR file

1 Right-click an existing JDBC data source, then choose Edit from the context menu. Edit Data Source appears.

2 Choose Manage Drivers to open the driver manager.

3 Select the JAR file that contains the driver, then choose Delete.

    BIRT Report Designer removes the JAR file and any drivers that it contains. BIRT Report Designer does not delete the JAR file from the file system.

Restoring a JDBC driver

You can use the JDBC driver manager to restore a driver that was accidentally deleted. When you restore the driver, the JDBC driver manager copies the driver file from a specified location to the JDBC driver folder in your Eclipse installation.

How to restore a JDBC driver

1 In Data Explorer, right-click a JDBC data source, then choose Edit from the context menu. Edit Data Source appears.

2 In Edit Data Source, choose Manage Drivers to open the driver manager.

3 Select the driver to restore, then choose Restore. BIRT Report Designer restores the driver from the original location to the Eclipse JDBC driver directory and replaces the asterisk (*) next to the file name with a plus sign (+), as shown in Figure 5-9.

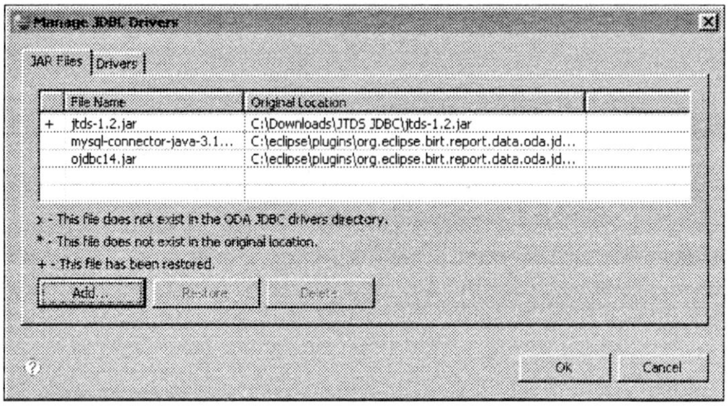

Figure 5-9   JDBC driver restored

Accessing data in a text file

A BIRT report can access data from a text file that conforms to a defined and consistent structure, as described in the next section. These files are typically generated by business systems and applications that create logs. These files can also be spreadsheets saved as CSV (comma separated values) files. Before you use text file data in a report, make sure the file uses a valid structure, and if necessary, edit the text accordingly.

Text file structure

A text file that you use for report data must follow these rules:

■ Optionally, the first line of the text file can contain the names of the columns, separated by commas. If the first line does not contain column names, BIRT assigns default names with the prefix Column, for example, Column_1, Column_2, and so on.

■ Optionally, the second line of the file can specify the data types of the columns. See Table 5-1 for a list of supported data types. If you use the second line to specify data types, list the data types in the same order as the columns, and separate the data types with commas.

- The remaining lines in the file must contain values for the columns. The values can be separated by commas, semicolons, tabs, or pipes.

- Each line must contain the same number of fields.

- The file cannot include empty lines between records.

- Each record must occupy a separate line, delimited by a line break, such as CRLF or LF. The last record in the file can either include or omit an ending line break.

- Data in a field can be surrounded by more than one set of quotation marks. Quotation marks are required only if the data contains one or more commas within a field.

- A field can enclose single quotation marks and commas with double quotation marks, such as:

    ```
    "He said, 'Yes, I do.'"
    ```

- If a field without content has zero or more spaces, the field is treated as NULL and evaluated as NULL in comparison operations.

- The file name and extension can be any name that is valid for your operating system. Although TXT and CSV are typical, you do not have to use either as the file extension.

The following example shows a valid sample text file. The text file has two lines of metadata and three lines of data:

```
FamilyName,GivenName,AccountID,AccountType,Created
STRING,STRING,INT,STRING,TIME
"Smith","Mark",254378,"Monthly",01/31/2003 09:59:59 AM
"Johnson","Carol",255879,"Monthly",09/30/2004 03:59:59 PM
"Pitt","Joseph",255932,,10/01/2005 10:32:04 AM
```

Text file data types

Table 5-1 lists and provides information about the abbreviations that you use for the data types.

Table 5-1   Supported data types in flat files

Abbreviation	Data type	Examples
BIGDECIMAL	java.sql.Types.NUMERIC	
DATE	java.sql.Types.DATE	YYYY-MM-DD or MM/DD/YYYY Examples: 2003-01-31 01/31/2003
DOUBLE	java.sql.Types.DOUBLE	

(continues)

Table 5-1   Supported data types in flat files *(continued)*

Abbreviation	Data type	Examples
INT	java.sql.Types.INTEGER	
STRING	java.sql.Types.VARCHAR	
TIME	java.sql.Types.TIME	hh:mm:ss and all DATE format strings such as "YYYY-MM-DD" Examples: 2003-12-31 12:59:59 A 01/31/2003 12:59:59 pm
TIMESTAMP	java.sql.Types.TIMESTAMP	YYYY-MM-DD hh:mm:ss.nnnnnn

Creating a flat file data source

When you create a flat file data source in BIRT, you specify its property values, such as the file location and the character set that the file uses. You should also know how the file is structured—whether the file uses commas, semicolons, tabs, or pipes to separate values, and whether the file specifies column names or data types.

How to specify the connection information for accessing a text file

1 In Data Explorer, right-click Data Sources, then choose New Data Source.

2 On New Data Source, supply the following information:

    1 Select Flat File Data Source from the list of data source types.

    2 In Data Source Name, type a name for the data source.

    3 Choose Next. New Flat File Data Source Profile appears, as shown in Figure 5-10.

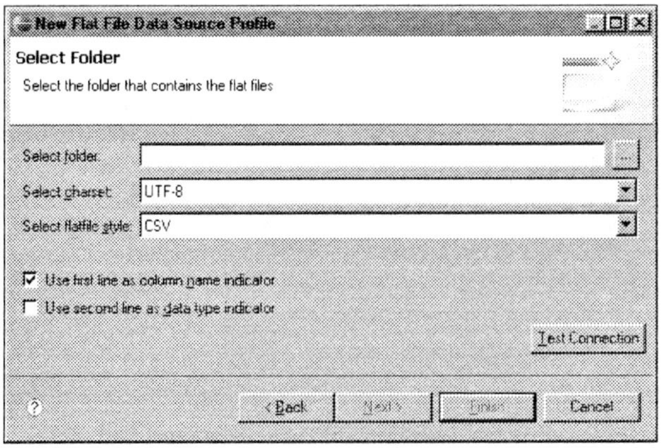

Figure 5-10   Selecting flat file directory and character set

3 Specify the following connection information for the text file:

1 In Select folder, type the location of the folder, or choose the ellipsis (...) button to navigate to and select the folder.

2 In Select charset, select the character set that the text files in this folder use.

3 In Select flatfile style, select either CSV, SSV, PSV, or TSV for a file that uses comma-separated values, semicolon-separated values, pipe-separated values, or tab-separated values, respectively.

4 If the first line of the text file specifies the column names, select Use first lines as column name indicator.

5 If the second line of the text file specifies the column data types, select Use second line as data type indicator.

4 Choose Finish. The new flat file data source appears under Data Sources in Data Explorer.

Accessing data in an XML file

An open specification recommended by the World Wide Web Consortium, XML has become a common mechanism for sharing structured data across different information systems. The XML document that a report accesses must be well-formed. To be well-formed, it must conform to the XML 1.0, third edition specification. You can find more information about this specification at the following URL:

```
http://www.w3.org/TR/REC-xml/
```

When you create an XML data source in BIRT, you specify the location of the XML file. Optionally, you can also specify the location of an XML schema. An XML schema contains a set of rules to which an XML file conforms, and you can use the schema to validate the XML file.

How to specify the connection information for accessing an XML file

1 In Data Explorer, right-click Data Sources, then choose New Data Source.

2 On New Data Source, supply the following information:

1 Select XML Data Source from the list of data source types.

2 In Data Source Name, type a name for the data source.

3 Choose Next.

New XML Data Source Profile appears, as shown in Figure 5-11.

3 Specify the following connection information:

1 In the first field, type the location of the XML file, or choose Browse to navigate to and select the file.

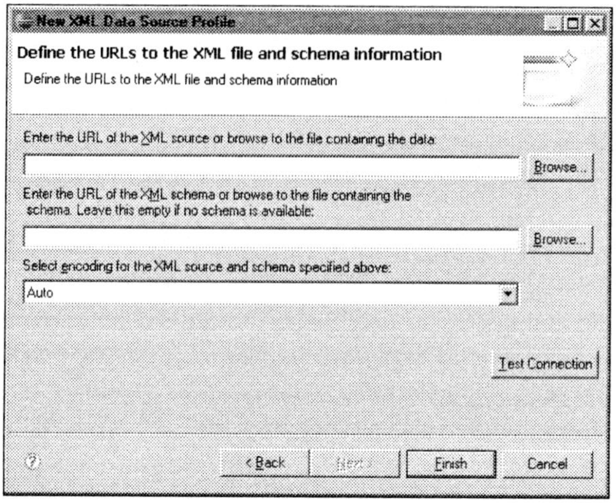

Figure 5-11 Defining XML source and schema information

2 In the second field, type the location of the schema file, if one is available, or choose Browse to navigate to and select the file. A schema is not required.

3 Select the type of encoding for the XML file and schema. Use the default value, Auto, to specify that the data source detect the encoding type specified in the XML file or schema.

4 Choose Finish. The new XML data source appears under Data Sources in Data Explorer.

Accessing a web service

Web services make software functionality available over the internet, using open and standard protocols, in the following manner:

- A web service defines a structured format for requests for its service and for the response the service generates.

- An application—a BIRT report, for example—makes a request for the web service over the internet.

- The web service performs an action and sends the results to the application.

The action can be calculating a monthly mortgage payment, retrieving stock quotes, converting currencies, getting the weather forecast for a particular city, or finding books by a particular author. If your report needs to present data that can only by generated by a program, you can save time and effort by looking for a web service that does the programming work and returns the data you need.

Web services use the following standard protocols:

- WSDL (Web Services Description Language) to describe the available services or operations provided by a web service
- SOAP (Simple Object Access Protocol) to transfer data
- XML to structure the data

Because web services are written and maintained by other developers, you should examine the web service definition to ensure that the web service does what you need. You should also verify that the WSDL document is well-formed. Remember, too, that you have no control over web services created by others, and if a web service your report accesses is modified significantly or removed, the functionality no longer works in your report.

When you create a web service data source in BIRT, you typically need to specify only the location of the WSDL file. A well-formed WSDL file defines the available services, and typically, the information to connect to the SOAP server identified by a SOAP endpoint URL.

Alternatively, you can connect to the web service through a custom driver class. You would create and use a custom driver, if, for example, the web service does not provide a WSDL document.

How to specify the connection information for accessing a web service

This procedure shows how to connect to a public web service that returns the weather forecast for a specified U.S. zip code. You can get information about this web service at the following location:

```
http://www.webservicex.net/WS/WSDetails.aspx?CATID=12&WSID=68
```

1 In Data Explorer, right-click Data Sources, then choose New Data Source.

2 On New Data Source, supply the following information:

 1 Select Web Services Data Source from the list of data source types.

 2 In Data Source Name, type a name for the data source. For this example, type

```
Weather_ws
```

 3 Choose Next.

3 On New Web ServicesData Source Profile, in WSDL URL or Location, type the following URL, as shown in Figure 5-12:

```
http://www.webservicex.net/WeatherForecast.asmx?WSDL
```

For well-defined web services, you need only specify the URL to the WSDL document.

4 Choose Test Connection to verify the connection to the web service.

5 Choose Finish. The new web service data source, Weather_ws, appears under Data Sources in Data Explorer.

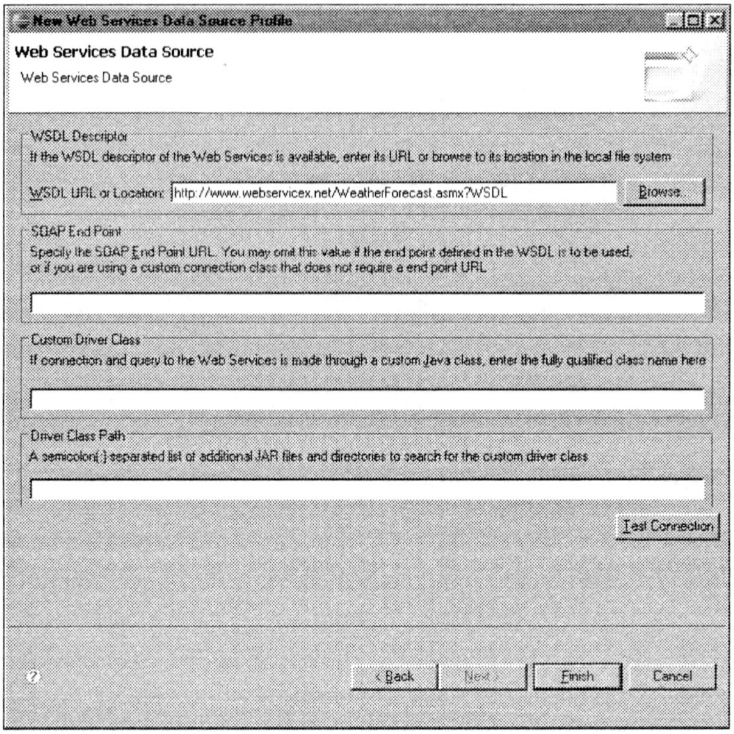

Figure 5-12   URL to WSDL specified

Creating reusable data sources

As discussed previously, each BIRT data source you create contains the connections properties required to connect to a database, flat file, XML document, or web service. Often, multiple reports require access to the same source. You might, for example, create a suite of reports that use data from the same corporate sales database. Rather than typing the same connection information repeatedly for each report, you can:

- Enter the connection information once in a file called a connection profile, then link the connection profile to any BIRT data source that requires that connection information.

- Create one BIRT data source, then store it in a library, which all reports can access.

The basic principles behind both techniques are simple: you define connection properties once, store the information in a shared location, and reuse the information in as many reports as needed. Another advantage that both techniques offer is the ability to update connection properties in one location and have the changes propagate to all reports.

This section describes how to create and use a connection profile. For information about sharing data sources in a library, see Chapter 23, "Building a Shared Report Development Framework."

Creating a connection profile

You use Data Source Explorer (not to be confused with Data Explorer) to create a connection profile. You can create a connection profile for any data source type, and you can create as many profiles as you need. If, for example, your reports frequently access data from a particular database and a particular web service, you can create one connection profile for the database, and one for the web service.

BIRT saves all the connection profiles in a single file named ServerProfiles.dat. This file is saved in the .metadata folder in your current workspace. The path is

```
...\workspace\.metadata\plugins\
     org.eclipse.datatools.connectivity\ServerProfiles.dat
```

If you want to share the connection profiles you create with other report developers, you can place ServerProfiles.dat in a central location. You can also rename the file in the event that there are other ServerProfiles.dat files in the central location.

How to create a connection profile

1 Choose Window→Show View→Other.

2 On Show View, expand Connectivity, select Data Source Explorer, as shown in Figure 5-13, then choose OK.

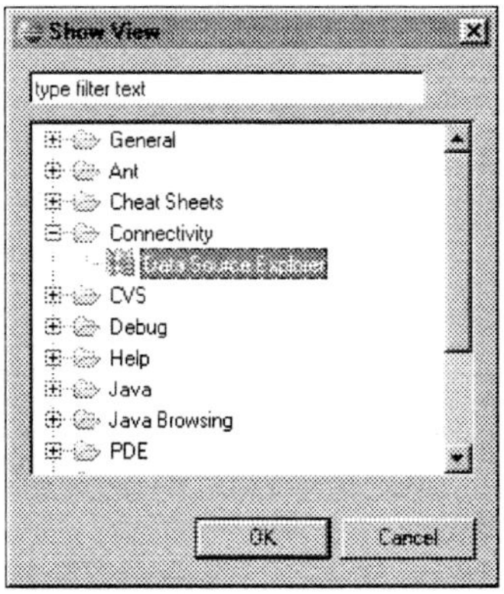

Figure 5-13   Select Data Source Explorer

3 In Data Source Explorer, expand ODA Data Sources. Data Source Explorer lists the data source types and connection profiles, if any were defined previously. Figure 5-14 shows the list of data source types in Data Source Explorer.

Figure 5-14   Data Source Explorer

The Legacy BIRT 2.1.x XML Data Source type is for backwards
compatibility with existing reports created with BIRT 2.1.x.

4 Right click the data source type for which you want to create a connection
   profile, then choose New.

5 On New <data source type> Data Source Profile, type a name and
   description for the connection profile. Figure 5-15 shows an example of
   information specified for a JDBC connection profile.

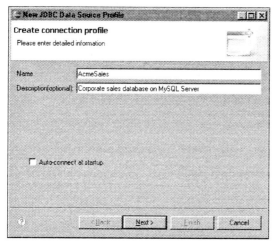

Figure 5-15   Name and description specified for a JDBC connection
                   profile

Choose Next.

6 On New <data source type> Data Source Profile, specify the connection
   values to connect to the data source. Figure 5-16 shows an example of
   connection properties to connect to a JDBC data source.

7 Choose Test Connection to verify the connection.

8 Choose Finish. The new connection profile appears in Data Source
   Explorer, as shown in Figure 5-17. It displays the name you specified
   when you created the connection profile.

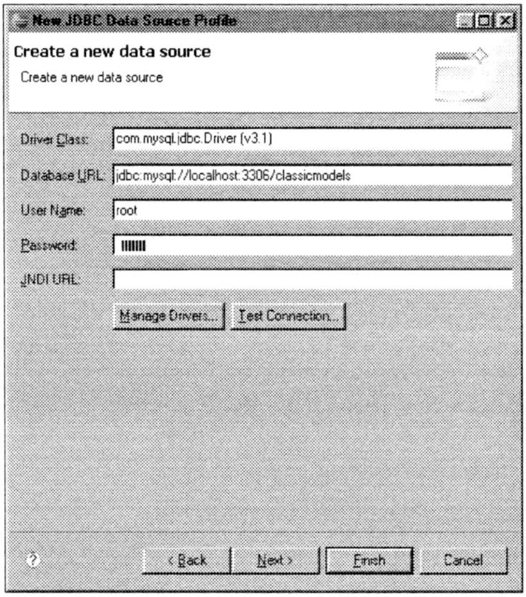

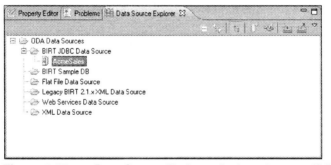

Figure 5-16   Connection properties for a JDBC data source

Figure 5-17   Data Source Explorer displays the new JDBC connection
                    profile

Using a connection profile

When you create a new data source, you have the option of creating it using
information stored in a connection profile. Using a connection profile saves
time and reduces the potential for connection errors because all you need to
do is supply the location of the profile. You do not need to know or remember
all the required connection information, and, presumably, the connection
profile has been tested. If you want to use a connection profile created by
another report developer, make sure you get the location of the profile.

How to create a data source that uses a connection profile

1   In Data Explorer, right-click Data Sources, then choose New Data Source.

2 On New Data Source, select Create from a connection profile in the profile store, as shown in Figure 5-18.

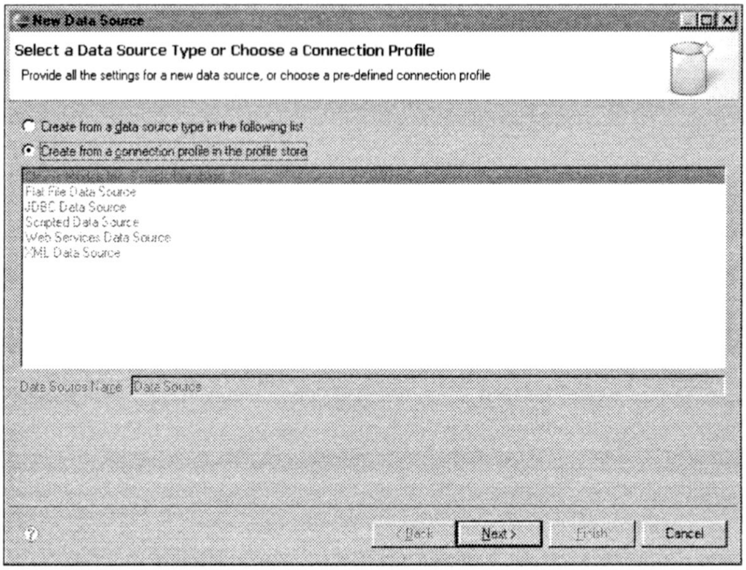

Figure 5-18   Creating a data source that uses a connection profile

3 On Connection Profile, in Connection Profile Store, specify the location of the file that contains the connection profiles. You can choose Browse to find and select the file. As described in the previous section, the default file name is ServerProfiles.dat, and BIRT saves this file, by default, in the .metadata folder in the workspace in use when the connection profile was created. The default path is

```
...\workspace\.metadata\plugins\
     org.eclipse.datatools.connectivity\ServerProfiles.dat
```

After you specify the location of the .dat file, Connection Profile displays all the available profiles. Figure 5-19 shows an example of two connection profiles, SystemLogs and AcmeSales.

4 Select the connection profile to use.

By default, Use the default data source name is selected. If you selected the SystemLogs profile, the new data source you are creating is also named SystemLogs by default.

5 Optionally, specify a different name for the data source.

6 Choose Next. New <data source type> Data Source Profile displays in read-only text the connection information derived from the connection profile.

7 Choose Finish. The new data source appears under Data Sources in Data Explorer.

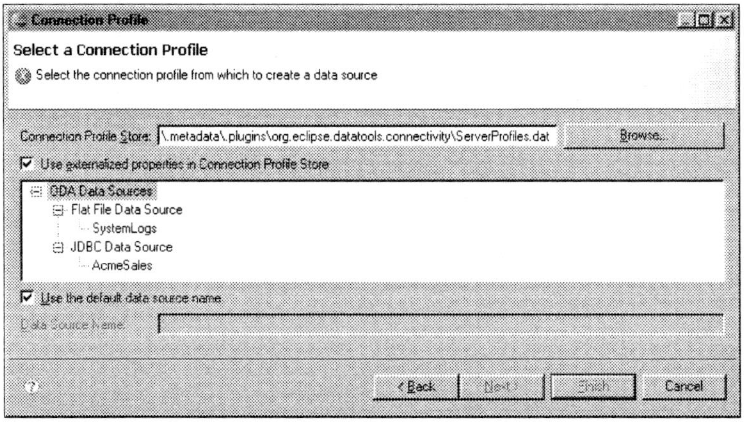

Figure 5-19   Connection Profile displays two predefined profiles

Setting connection properties when a report runs

When you first design and test a report, you create a BIRT data source that uses hard-coded information. All the procedures for creating data sources, described previously, used hard-coded information. For example, the procedure for creating a JDBC data source included providing a user name and password that the report uses to access a database. When the report is run, the database uses whatever roles and privileges are assigned to the hard-coded report user.

Production reports, however, cannot always use the hard-coded information specified at report design time. A typical example is allowing a report user to provide his credentials when he runs the report. Based on the specified credentials, the database authentication system determines the appropriate data to use to generate the report.

To support the setting of connection properties at report run time, the data source editor provides a feature called property binding. As its name suggests, this feature supports binding each connection property to a JavaScript expression that evaluates to a value that the report uses at run time. Because each data source type requires different connection information, the Property Binding page displays a different set of connection properties for each data source type. The Property Binding page is available only when you edit an existing data source. It is not available when you create a new data source.

Figure 5-20 shows the Property Binding page for a JDBC data source. Figure 5-21 shows the Property Binding page for a flat file data source. Notice that, for both data sources, all the connection properties that you set at design time can also be set dynamically at run time. As the figures also show, if the data source uses a connection profile, you can dynamically assign a connection profile and its location at run time.

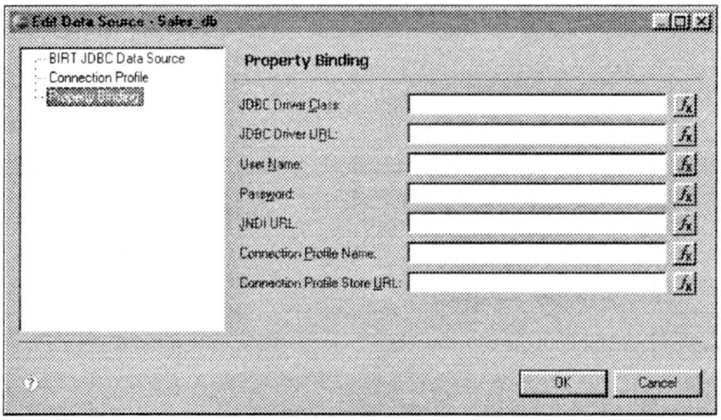

Figure 5-20   Property Binding page showing JDBC connection properties that
can be set at run time

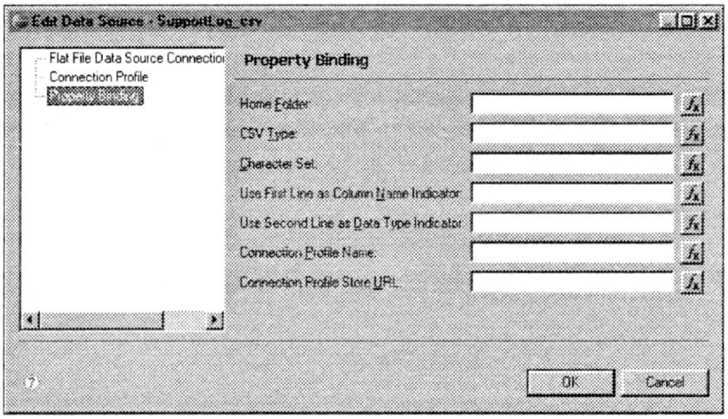

Figure 5-21   Property Binding page showing flat file connection properties
that can be set at run time

The following sections show two examples of setting connection properties at
run time.

Setting the folder path for text files at run time

To access a text file, one of the properties that you must specify is the path to
the folder that contains the text file. There are cases when the path to the
folder can be determined only at run time. Consider the following scenario: A
log file named log.csv is generated daily. Each daily log is stored in an auto-
generated folder whose name is the current date. Examples of the full path to
these folders are as follows:

```
C:\Logs\2008-03-01
C:\Logs\2008-03-02
C:\Logs\2008-03-03
```

You design a report that displays data from log.csv. When the report is run,
the report uses the log.csv data for the current day. For example, if the report
runs on March 1, 2008, the flat file data source uses the log.csv file in the

2008-03-01 folder. If the report runs on March 2, 2008, the data source uses the log.csv file in the 2008-03-02 folder. The following procedure shows how to write a JavaScript expression that returns the full folder path value based on the current date.

How to set the folder path for text files at run time

This procedure assumes that you have already created a flat file data source.

1 In Data Explorer, right-click the flat file data source, then choose Edit.

2 In Edit Data Source, choose Property Binding. The Property Binding page displays the flat file connection properties that you can set at run time.

3 Choose the expression builder button to the right of Home Folder.

4 In the expression builder, type the following expression:

```
function DF(n) {
return (n > 9 ? n : '0' + n);
}

var d = new Date();
shortDate = (d.getFullYear() + '-' + DF(d.getMonth() + 1) +
    '-' + DF(d.getDate()));

HomeFolder = "C:/Logs/"+shortDate;
```

The JavaScript functions, getFullYear( ), getMonth( ), and getDate( ), get the parts of the full date and time returned by new Date( ). The user-defined DF function formats the month and day parts of the date. The shortDate variable contains the date in 2008-01-01 format. The HomeFolder variable contains the full folder path, which is constructed by concatenating the static path with the shortDate variable.

5 Choose OK to save the expression.

Edit Data Source shows the JavaScript expression bound to the Home Folder property, as shown in Figure 5-22.

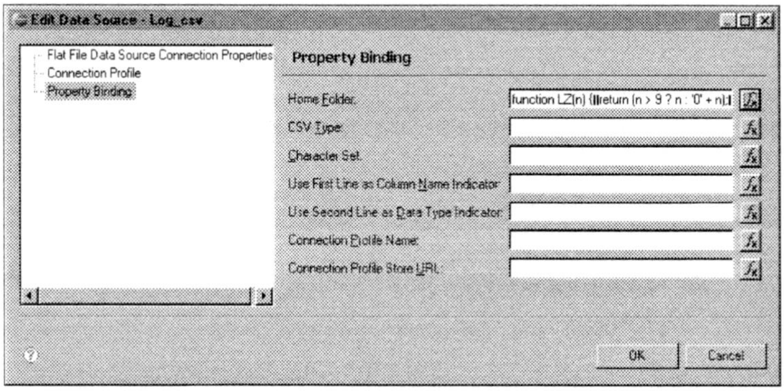

Figure 5-22   JavaScript expression bound to the Home Folder property

6 Choose OK to save your changes to the data source.

Setting the database user name and password at run time

When a report accesses data in a database, a typical action is to prompt the report user to type his user name and password at run time. You accomplish this action by using report parameters. Report parameters provide a mechanism for getting values at run time and passing the values to the report. For more information about report parameters, see Chapter 15, "Enabling the User to Filter Data."

The following procedure shows how to create report parameters and bind the parameters to the user name and password properties in a JDBC data source.

How to enable a user to provide a database user name and password when a report runs

This procedure assumes that you have already created a JDBC data source.

1 Create a report parameter to get the user name, using the following steps:

    1 In Data Explorer, right-click Report Parameters, then choose New Parameter.

    2 On New Parameter, supply the following information:

        ❑ In Name, type a name for the report parameter. For example:

            `username_param`

        ❑ In Prompt text, specify a word or sentence to prompt the report user to provide a user name value. For example:

            `User name`

        ❑ In Data type, select String.

    Figure 5-23 shows the completed report parameter definition.

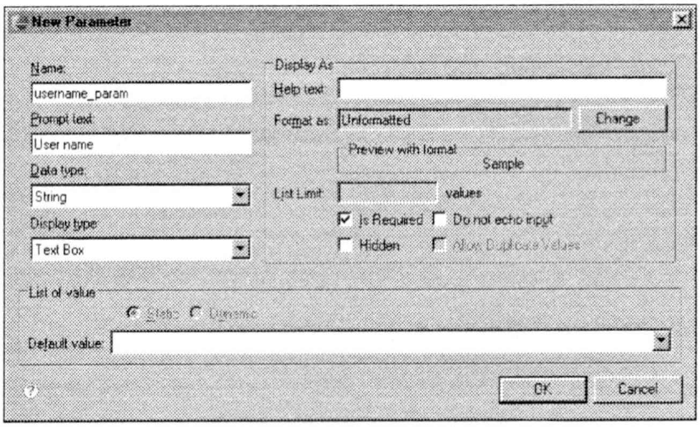

Figure 5-23   Report parameter to get the user name

3 Choose OK. The username_param parameter appears under Report Parameters in Data Explorer.

2 Use the previous steps to create a report parameter to get the password. Use the following values to define the report parameter:

- In Name, type

  ```
  password_param
  ```

- In Prompt text, type

  ```
  Password
  ```

- In Data type, select String.

3 Choose OK. The password_param parameter appears under Report Parameters in Data Explorer.

4 Bind the user name property to the username_param report parameter.

1 In Data explorer, right-click the JDBC data source, then choose Edit.

2 In Edit Data Source, choose Property Binding. The Property Binding page displays the JDBC connection properties.

3 Choose the expression builder button on the right of User Name.

4 In the expression builder, perform the following tasks:

1 Under Category, choose Report parameters. All appears under Sub-Category.

2 Choose All. Under Double Click to insert, BIRT Report Designer displays the report parameters that you created.

3 Double-click the username_param report parameter. The expression params["username_param"] appears in the text area, as shown in Figure 5-24.

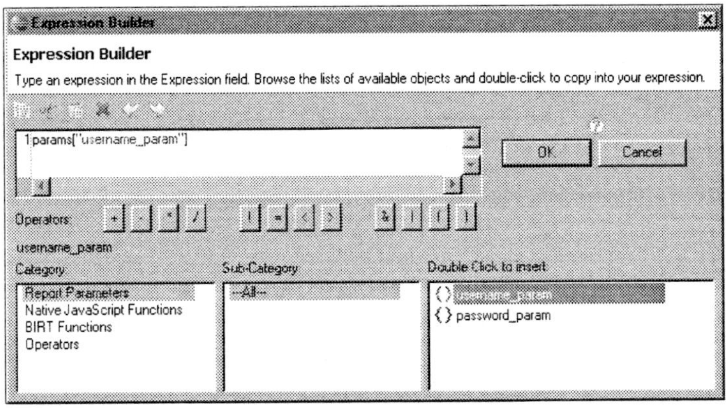

Figure 5-24   Choosing the username_param in the expression builder

4 Choose OK. The expression builder closes. The report parameter expression appears in the User Name field, as shown in Figure 5-25.

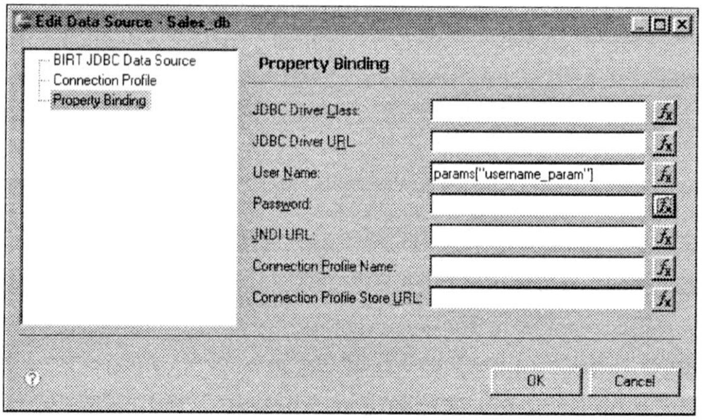

Figure 5-25 User Name property bound to the username_param report parameter

5 Using the previous steps, bind the password property to the password_param report parameter.

5 In Edit Data Source, choose OK.

6 Preview the report to confirm that the user is prompted for a user name and password. Figure 5-26 shows Enter Parameters, the dialog that prompts the user to enter a user name and password.

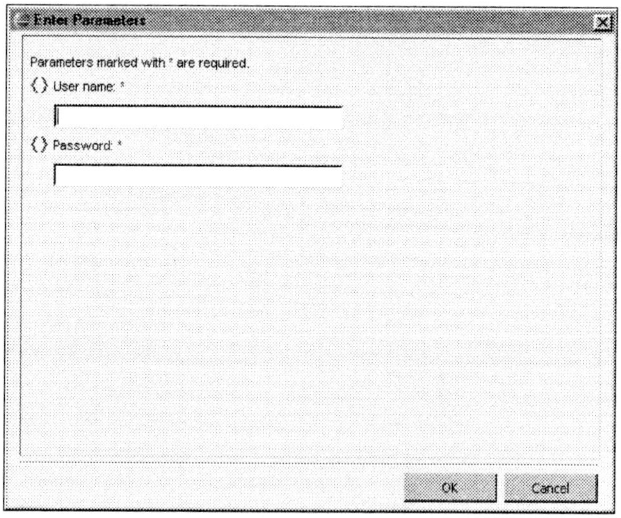

Figure 5-26 Enter Parameters prompts the user for a user name and password

The values that the user specifies are used to connect to the JDBC database.

Troubleshooting data source problems

BIRT Report Designer displays information about data source connection problems in several different places. Error reports can appear in the previewer, the problems view, the error log view, and as pop-up messages. Generally, BIRT Report Designer displays JDBC connection-related problems in pop-up error messages. If the connection information is syntactically correct, but the data source is not available, you see a pop-up message and entries in the error log view.

If a problem is an improperly defined data source, errors appear in the Problems view. You cannot manually delete items from the Problems view. They display until you resolve the problem or delete the object that is creating the problem.

If you have problems connecting to a data source from BIRT Report Designer, try connecting using a data source manufacturer or third-party tool to confirm that the connection string works as expected. This troubleshooting exercise can help you determine whether to focus your troubleshooting on a driver or on the parameters that you have provided.

If you make changes to your connection parameters and BIRT Report Designer behaves as though it is still using the original values for the parameters, restart Eclipse using the -clean option. What has happened is that Eclipse is using cached information that contains the previous values. To clear the cache, the only option is to exit Eclipse and restart using the -clean option.

Retrieving Data

Data sources, especially databases, generally contain more data than is needed for a report. After you create a BIRT data source to connect to a database, text file, XML file, or web service, you specify what data to retrieve from that source. This chapter discusses how to create different types of data sets to retrieve data from the different types of data sources.

About data sets

A data set is an object that defines all the data that is available to a report. To create a data set, you must have an existing BIRT data source. As with data sources, BIRT Report Designer provides wizards to create data sets. The first and the only required step in creating a data set is to select the data to retrieve from a data source. After this first step, you can optionally process the raw data as needed for the report. You can, for example, change the names of columns, create computed columns, and define filters to provide a subset of the data to the report.

You can create as many data sets as is necessary for a report. Typically, you create at least one data set for each data source. If, for example, you created a JDBC data source and an XML data source in a report, you would create a JDBC data set and an XML data set. You can also create multiple data sets that use a single data source. If, for example, a report displays sales data from the same database in a chart and in a table, you can create one data set to return data for the chart, and another data set to return data for the table. In this scenario, creating different data sets can improve performance because each data set gets only the specific data required by each report element. Alternatively, to use identical data, both items can share the same data set.

BIRT Report Designer, by default, provides a unique name for each data set you create in a report. The names have the prefix Data Set. If you create two data sets, the default names are Data Set and Data Set1. It is good practice to provide descriptive names, such as CorporateSalesDB or SupportLogXML, that enable you to identify easily the type of data that the data set provides.

Selecting data

BIRT uses data based on a relational model. A relational model organizes data in a two-dimensional table consisting of rows and columns, and a data set must return data in this format, as illustrated in Figure 6-1.

PRODUCTCODE	PRODUCTNAME	BUYPRICE	MSRP
S10_1678	1969 Harley Davidson Ultimate Chopper	48.81	95.7
S10_1949	1952 Alpine Renault 1300	98.58	214.3
S10_2016	1996 Moto Guzzi 1100i	68.99	118.94
S10_4698	2003 Harley-Davidson Eagle Drag Bike	91.02	193.66
S10_4757	1972 Alfa Romeo GTA	85.68	136
S10_4962	1962 LanciaA Delta 16V	103.42	147.74
S12_1099	1968 Ford Mustang	95.34	194.57
S12_1108	2001 Ferrari Enzo	95.59	207.8
S12_1666	1958 Setra Bus	77.9	136.67
S12_2823	2002 Suzuki XREO	66.27	150.62
S12_3148	1969 Corvair Monza	89.14	151.08
S12_3380	1968 Dodge Charger	75.16	117.44
S12_3891	1969 Ford Falcon	83.05	173.02
S12_3990	1970 Plymouth Hemi Cuda	31.92	79.8
S12_4473	1957 Chevy Pickup	55.7	118.5
S12_4675	1969 Dodge Charger	58.73	115.16
S18_1097	1940 Ford Pickup Truck	58.33	116.67

Figure 6-1   A data set returns data in a table consisting of rows and columns

A JDBC data source organizes data in exactly this way. Other types of data sources, such as XML and web services, do not. When you create a data set for these data sources, you map the data so that the data is organized in the structure that BIRT requires.

This section explains how to retrieve data from JDBC, flat file, XML, and web service data sources.

Using a SQL query to retrieve data from a JDBC data source

Typically, a JDBC data set retrieves data using a SQL query. SQL is a standard query language for requesting data from a database. Because there are many books about SQL, this section does no more than to discuss how to write a basic SQL query and how to combine data from multiple tables. In many cases, a basic knowledge of SQL is sufficient to get the data a report requires.

Writing a basic SQL query

A SQL query consists of one or more statements. The first statement of a SQL query is the SELECT statement that specifies which columns you want to retrieve from the database. The SELECT statement contains two required clauses: SELECT and FROM. The SELECT clause lists the columns that you want to retrieve. The FROM clause specifies the table from which you want to get the selected columns of data.

The following is an example of a SQL statement that selects the firstname and lastname columns from a table called customers:

```
SELECT customers.firstname, customers.lastname
    FROM customers
```

A SQL SELECT query can also include other clauses that limit what data a query returns. You use the WHERE clause to specify criteria that results must meet and use ORDER BY to sort results. The following is an example of the same SQL statement, with the addition of the WHERE and ORDER BY clauses:

```
SELECT customers.firstname, customers.lastname
    FROM customers
    WHERE customers.country = 'Japan'
    ORDER BY customers.lastname, customers.firstname
```

Combining data from multiple tables

Typically, you have to select data from two or more tables to get complete data for your report. This operation is called a join. You join tables in a database through a common column called a key.

For example, suppose you want to get the orders for every customer. The database, however, stores customer information in a Customers table, and order information in an Orders table, as shown in Figure 6-2. Both tables contain a column called CustomerID. You can join the customers and the orders table using the CustomerID column.

Customers

CustomerID	CustomerName
01	Mark Smith
02	Maria Hernandez
03	Soo-Kim Young
04	Patrick Mason

Orders

OrderID	Amount	CustomerID
110	251.49	02
115	145.75	03
120	176.55	01

Figure 6-2   Database stores customer and order information in two tables

To get order information for every customer, you can use the following SELECT statement:

```
SELECT Customers.CustomerName, Orders.Amount
    FROM Customers, Orders
    WHERE Customers.CustomerID = Orders.CustomerID
```

The WHERE clause in this example specifies that the query returns rows where the CustomerID in both tables match. Figure 6-3 shows the results that the SELECT statement returns.

Alternatively, you can use the JOIN keyword to select data from the two tables. The rest of this section describes the different types of joins you can use, and the results that each join returns. The following SELECT statement uses INNER JOIN and returns the same results shown in Figure 6-3:

```
SELECT Customers.CustomerName, Orders.Amount
FROM Customers
INNER JOIN Orders
ON Customers.CustomerID = Orders.CustomerID
```

Result

CustomerName	Amount
Mark Smith	176.55
Maria Hernandez	251.49
Soo-Kim Young	145.75

Figure 6-3   Results returned by SELECT statement

The INNER JOIN clause returns all rows from both tables where there is a match. If there are rows in the Customers table that do not match rows in the Orders table, those rows are not listed. In the example, Patrick Mason is not listed in the result set because this customer does not have a matching order.

To obtain all the customer names, whether or not a customer has an order, use the LEFT JOIN clause, as shown in the following example:

```
SELECT Customers.CustomerName, Orders.Amount
FROM Customers
LEFT JOIN Orders
ON Customers.CustomerID = Orders.CustomerID
```

LEFT JOIN returns all rows from the first (left) table, even if there are no matches in the second (right) table. Figure 6-4 shows the results of the SELECT statement that uses the LEFT JOIN clause. Here, Patrick Mason is listed in the result set even though he does not have an order, because the record is in the first table.

Conversely, if you want to get all rows from the second table (the Orders table in our example), even if there are no matches in the first table (the Customers table), use the RIGHT JOIN clause, as shown in the following example:

```
SELECT Customers.CustomerName, Orders.Amount
FROM Customers
RIGHT JOIN Orders
ON Customers.CustomerID = Orders.CustomerID
```

In our example, all the rows in the second table match rows in the first table, so the result is the same as in Figure 6-3. If, however, the Orders table had contained rows that did not have matches in the Customers table, those rows would also have been returned.

To get all customer names and orders from both tables, even if there are no matching values, you can use the FULL OUTER JOIN clause, as shown in the following example:

```
SELECT Customers.CustomerName, Orders.Amount
FROM Customers
FULL OUTER JOIN Orders
ON Customers.CustomerID = Orders.CustomerID
```

Result

CustomerName	Amount
Mark Smith	176.55
Maria Hernandez	251.49
Soo-Kim Young	145.75
Patrick Mason	

Figure 6-4   Results of a left join

In our example, the result is the same as in Figure 6-4. All the customer names and all the order amounts are returned. Note, however, that not all databases support FULL OUTER JOIN. In most cases, you can get the same results using the UNION operator.

Note that in all the examples, the SELECT statements specify the columns being joined: Customers.CustomerID and Orders.CustomerID. You must specify the columns to join. If you do not, the result is what is commonly referred to as a cartesian join. In a cartesian join, all rows in the first table are joined with all rows in the second table. If the first table has 1000 rows and the second table has 10,000 rows, the cartesian join returns 10,000,000 rows, a result you rarely want.

The inner, left, and right joins are the most common types of joins. For more information about these joins and others that your database supports, see the database manufacturer's documentation.

How to create a SQL query to retrieve data from a JDBC data source

This procedure assumes you have already created the JDBC data source that this data set uses.

1 In Data Explorer, right-click Data Sets, then choose New Data Set.

2 On New Data Set, specify the following information:

   1 In Data Set Name, type a name for the data set.

   2 In Data Source, select the JDBC data source to use.

   3 In Data Set Type, select SQL Select Query.

   4 Choose Next.

   Query displays the information to help you create a SQL query. Available Items lists the items in the data source.

3 To see the tables in a database, expand the data source, as shown in Figure 6-5.

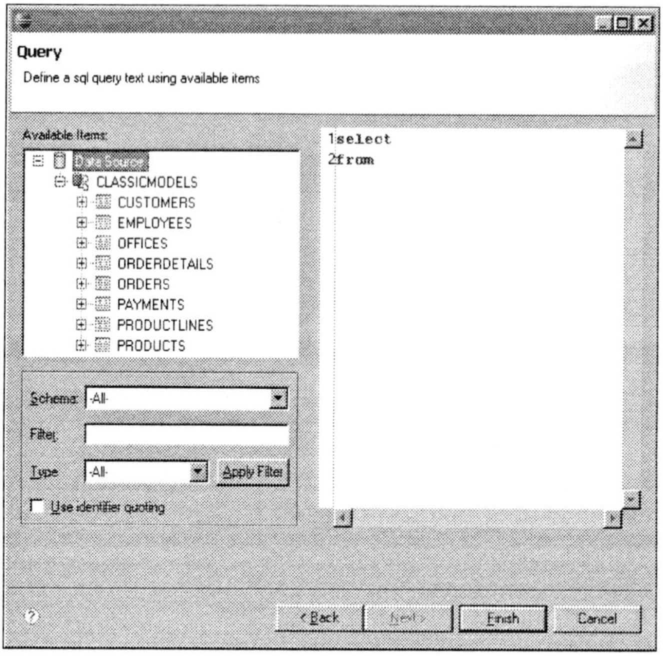

Figure 6-5   Viewing a schema

You can use the filter options to specify specific schemas or objects to
display.

- If you want to see only views in the JDBC data source, in Type, select
  View, and choose Apply Filter. If you want to see all tables, views, and
  stored procedures, select All, and choose Apply Filter.

- If the data source has a large number of objects, you can limit the
  number of object names that are retrieved by typing one or more letters
  in the Filter field and choosing Apply Filter. Available Items displays
  the objects that have names that begin with the same letter or letters
  that you typed. You also can use SQL filter characters for the database
  that you are using. For example, on some databases, an underscore (_)
  matches any single character, and the percent sign (%) matches any
  sequence of characters.

- If the database supports schemas, a Schema drop-down list is
  available. Select a schema to display only objects from that schema.

4 To display the columns in a table or view, click the plus sign (+) beside a
table or view name.

5 In the text area, type a SQL statement that indicates what data to retrieve
from the JDBC data source. You can also drag tables, views, and columns
from Available Items to the text area to insert their names in the SQL
statement at the insertion point, as shown in Figure 6-6.

For some databases, if a table or column name contains spaces or SQL reserved words, you must enclose the name in quotation marks (" "). If you drag and drop tables and columns, and those items need to be enclosed in double quotation marks, select the Use identifier quoting option. When this option is selected, the data set editor inserts the quotation marks around a table or column name when you drop it in the text area.

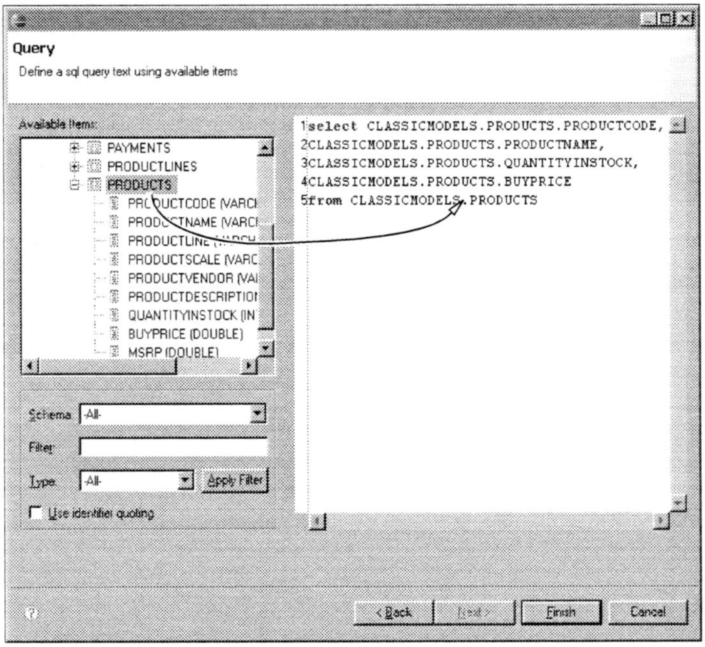

Figure 6-6   Adding a table to a SQL query

6 Choose Finish. Edit Data Set displays the columns specified in the query, and provides options for editing the data set.

Using a stored procedure to retrieve data from a JDBC data source

BIRT Report Designer also supports using a stored procedure to retrieve database data. Support for stored procedures, however, is limited in important ways. BIRT uses only one result set that is returned by a stored procedure. If your stored procedure returns multiple result sets, only the first result set that it returns is accessible to the report.

BIRT relies on the capabilities of the underlying JDBC driver in its support for stored procedures. For more robust support, a JDBC driver must fully implement the JDBC interfaces that are related to stored procedures, including those that provide its metadata. The jTDS project on SourceForge.net, for example, provides a pure Java (type 4) JDBC 3.0 driver for Microsoft SQL Server that does support stored procedures.

Unlike SQL queries, stored procedures can have output parameters, so BIRT Report Designer supports previewing output parameters that a stored procedure generates to confirm that the procedure is working as expected.

How to use a stored procedure to retrieve data from a JDBC data source

This procedure assumes you have already created the JDBC data source that this data set uses.

1 In Data Explorer, right-click Data Sets, then choose New Data Set.

2 On New Data Set, specify the following information:

    1 In Data Set Name, type a name for the data set.

    2 In Data Source, select the JDBC data source to use.

    3 In Data Set Type, select SQL Stored Procedure Query.

    Choose Next.

    Query displays a template for executing a stored procedure, as shown in Figure 6-7.

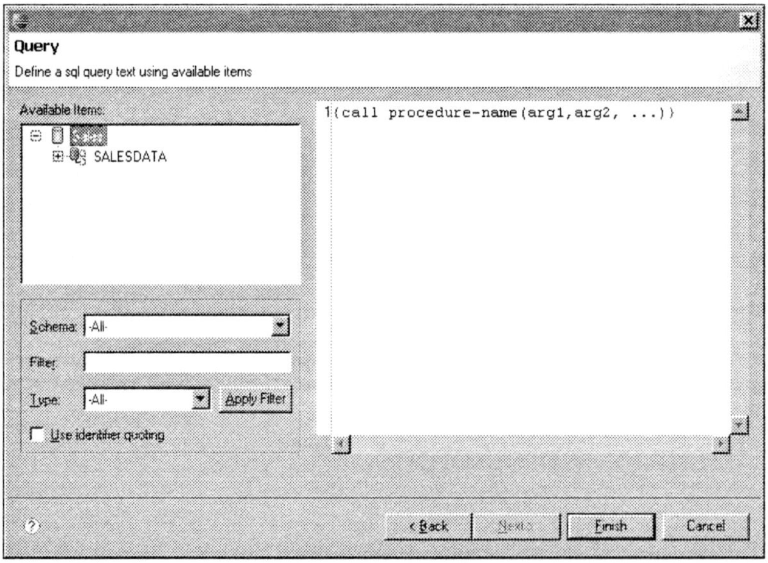

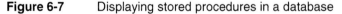

Figure 6-7   Displaying stored procedures in a database

3 In Available Items, navigate to the stored procedure. Select the stored procedure, and drag it to the text area. The stored procedure name appears at the insertion point. In the text area, type the required information to execute the stored procedure. For example, you should include any arguments that are passed to the stored procedure.

To type the stored procedure, enclose the call statement in left and right braces, for example:

```
{call getTable('ClassicModels.Customers')}
{call getClientOrders('103')}
```

If you type the stored procedure without the braces, BIRT treats the statement as a regular RDBMS call, so execution depends on the RDBMS of your data source.

4 Choose Finish to save the data set. Edit Data Set displays the columns returned by the stored procedure, and provides options for editing the data set.

Specifying what data to retrieve from a text file

The previous chapter described the structure of data in a text file and provided an example. If you review the example, you see that the structure of column names followed by rows of values resembles values stored in the table structure required by BIRT reports. This resemblance in data structure makes it easy to select the data to retrieve from a text file. The data set wizard displays the column names from the text file, and you select the columns that contain the data you want.

How to create a data set to retrieve data from a text file

This procedure assumes you have already created the flat file data source that this data set uses.

1 In Data Explorer, right-click Data Sets, then choose New Data Set.

2 On New Data Set, specify the following information:

   1 In Data Set Name, type a name for the data set.

   2 In Data Source, select the flat file data source to use.

   3 Choose Next.

3 On Select Columns, in File filter, select the file-name extension of the text file.

4 In Select file, select a text file from the drop-down list. The left pane displays the columns that are available in the selected file.

5 Select the columns to retrieve, and move them to the right pane. You can select columns in a few ways:

- Select a column, then choose Select.

- Press Shift while you click to select multiple columns, then choose Select.

- Choose Select All to include all columns. Figure 6-8 illustrates a text file in which all columns are selected.

6 Choose Finish to save the data set. Edit Data Set displays the columns you selected, and provides options for editing the data set.

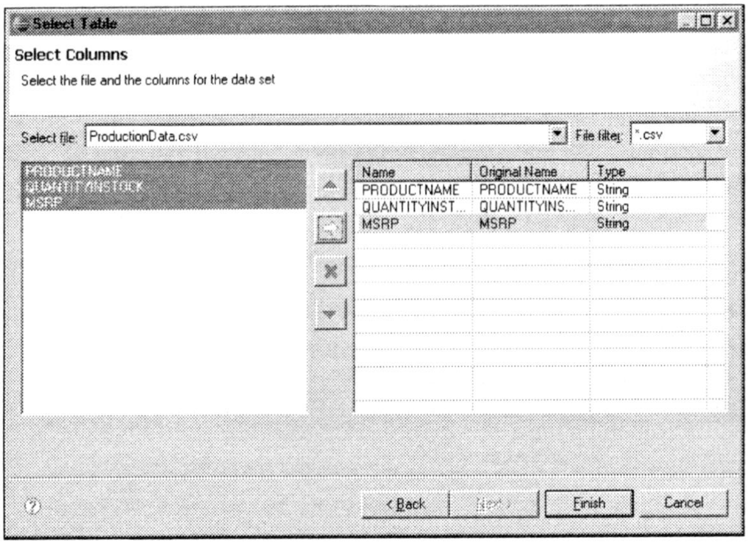

Figure 6-8   Selecting columns from a text file

Specifying what data to retrieve from an XML data source

As discussed earlier, BIRT reports must use data that is structured as a table that consists of rows and columns. XML documents use elements and attributes to present data. The data set wizard enables you to map a top-level XML element as a table, and other elements or attributes as columns. The wizard uses XPath expressions to define the paths to elements and attributes. XPath is a query language for accessing parts of an XML document.

When you select an element or attribute to map to a table or a column, the wizard generates the corresponding XPath expression. If you are familiar with XPath syntax and you want to do more than the basic mapping, you can edit the generated XPath expressions.

This section describes the most common ways to write an XPath expression to use an element or attribute as a table or column in an XML data set. This section is not a substitute for formal XPath user documentation. Examples in this section refer to sample XML data that appear at the end of the section.

The most important syntax rules to consider when you write XPath expressions to define tables and columns are as follows:

- Any path that starts with a forward slash (/) is an absolute path.
- The XPath expression that defines the table mapping must be an absolute path, for example:

    /library/book

- A path is considered relative to the table level that is defined when the XML data set was created, unless it begins with a forward slash.

- You can only use XPath expressions that locate elements along parent-child axes. For example, the following path is not valid:

  book/library

  The following path is valid:

  /library/book

- For attribute paths, you can use a single forward slash or left and right brackets. For example, the following paths are equivalent:

  title/@lang
  title[@lang]

- To define an element's attribute as a column, use either of the following syntax forms:

  author/@name
  author[@name]

- To define a table-level attribute as a column, use either of the following syntax forms:

  /@category
  [@category]

- To filter data rows, you can use either of the following predicate expression syntaxes:

  - Single-position predicates in the abbreviated form. The following example selects the first author listed:

    author[1]

  - Single-equality conditions based on an attribute value. For example, you can select an element by using the value of an attribute of the element. In the following example, only books that are in English are selected:

    title[@lang='eng']

- XPath functions are not supported.

The examples in the instructions in this section use the following XML data:

```
<?xml version="1.0"?>
<library>
    <book category="COOKING">
        <title lang="es">The Spanish Cook Book</title>
        <author name="Miguel Ortiz" country="es"/>
        <year>2005</year>
    </book>
    <book category="CHILDREN">
        <title lang="en">Everyone is Super Special</title>
        <author name="Sally Bush" country="us"/>
        <year>2005</year>
```

```
    </book>
    <audio format="CD" category="MUSIC">
        <title lang="en">We All Sing Perty</title>
        <artist name="Mary Rogers" country="us"/>
        <year>2005</year>
    </audio>
    <audio format="CD" category="MUSIC">
        <title lang="en">The Bluest Blues</title>
        <artist name="Barry Sadley" country="us"/>
        <year>2005</year>
    </audio>
</library>
```

How to create a data set to retrieve data from an XML file

This procedure assumes you have already created the XML data source that this data set uses.

1 In Data Explorer, right-click Data Sets, then choose New Data Set.

2 On New Data Set, specify the following information:

   1 In Data Set Name, type a name for the data set.

   2 In Data Source, select the XML data source to use.

   3 Choose Next.

3 On XML Data Set, specify the XML source in one of the following ways:

   ▪ In the text box, type the path to the XML file, or choose Browse to navigate to and select an XML file.

   ▪ To use the file specified in the XML data source, select Use the XML file defined in data source.

   Choose Next.

4 Define the table mapping, using the following steps:

   1 In XML Structure, navigate to the element in the XML data that represents the table level of your data, and select the element. Choose the right arrow.

      The Select or edit the XPath expression dialog displays the XPath expression that corresponds to the element you selected, as shown in Figure 6-9.

   2 Select the generated XPath expression or type another expression. For example, you can specify a filter expression to retrieve only data that meets a certain condition, as shown in the following example:

      `/library/book/author[@country="uk"]`

      Choose OK, then choose Next.

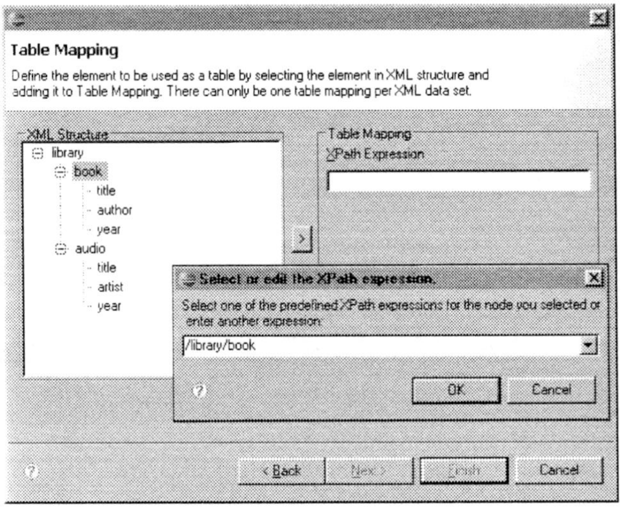

Figure 6-9   Creating an XML data set

5 Define the column mapping, using the following steps:

1 In XML structure, navigate to and select the element or attribute in the
XML data that represents a column, then choose the right arrow.
Column Mapping displays the default column mapping properties for
the element or attribute you selected. Figure 6-10 shows an example of
the default column mapping for an attribute named category.

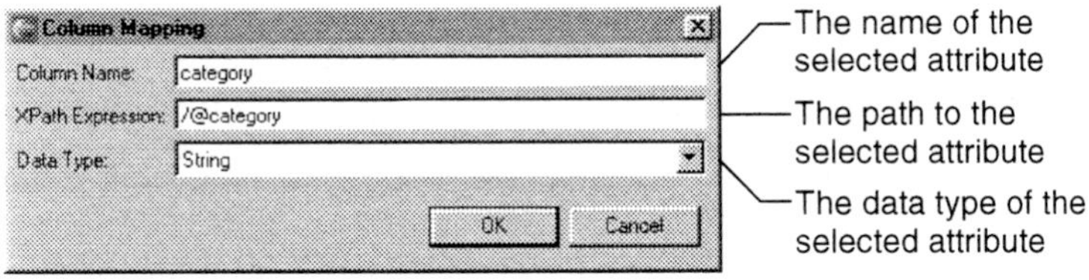

Figure 6-10   Column mapping properties

2 On Column Mapping, you can edit the column mapping properties.
Choose OK. The column appears and can be edited.

❏ To directly edit a path, select the XPath field, and edit the path.

❏ To remove a column, select the column, and choose the red x to
delete the mapping.

❏ In Table Preview, choose the Preview button to see a sample of
your data. See Figure 6-11 for an example.

6 Repeat the preceding steps for every column that you want to add to the
data set. Figure 6-11 shows an example of column mappings defined in a
data set.

7 Choose Finish to save the XML data set. Edit Data Set displays the
columns you mapped, and provides options for editing the data set.

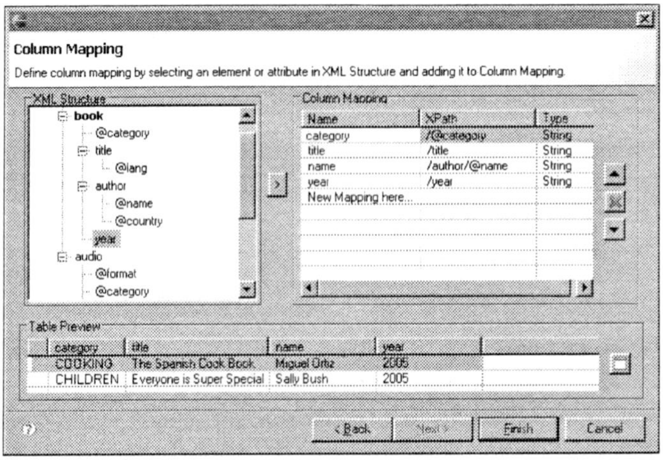

Figure 6-11   Mapping columns for an XML data set

Specifying what data to retrieve from a web service

Because a web service provides application functionality from a remote server, the creation of a web service data set is more complex than the other data set types. While the wizard guides you through the steps to supply the necessary information, it helps to understand generally how the data set communicates with a web service. The data set performs the following tasks:

- It sends a SOAP request to the web service. The request specifies the action you want the web service to perform and the parameter values to use when performing the action. For example, the request can be to run a mortgage calculator, and the parameter values to send are the loan years, interest rate, loan amount, annual tax, and annual insurance.

- The data set specifies the format of the SOAP response to use when the web service sends data back to the report.

- Finally, the data set specifies the data that the web service should return. In the case of a mortgage calculator, you can, for example, choose to get just the total monthly mortgage payment, or get additional data, such as monthly principal and interest, monthly tax, and monthly insurance.

The data set wizard constructs the SOAP request and response based on the web service operation and schema you select. For well-defined web services, you can use the generated SOAP request and response without any modifications, so while knowledge of SOAP can be helpful, it is typically not required. The wizard also displays, in XML format, all the data that the operation can return, so all you do is select the data that you want to use in the report, then map the data to a table and columns.

How to create a data set to retrieve data from a web service

This procedure shows how to retrieve data from a public web service that returns the weather forecast for a specified U.S. zip code. This procedure uses the web service data source, Weather_ws, whose creation procedure is provided in the previous chapter.

1 In Data Explorer, right-click Data Sets, then choose New Data Set.

2 On New Data Set, specify the following information:

    1 In Data Set Name, type a name for the data set.

    2 In Data Source, select the web data source to use, then choose Next.

New Web Services Data Set displays the URL to the WSDL document, which describes the services or operations provided by the web service. You specified the WSDL URL when you created the data source.

3 Expand the WSDL URL. Expand WeatherForecastSoap, then select GetWeatherByZipCode, as shown in Figure 6-12.

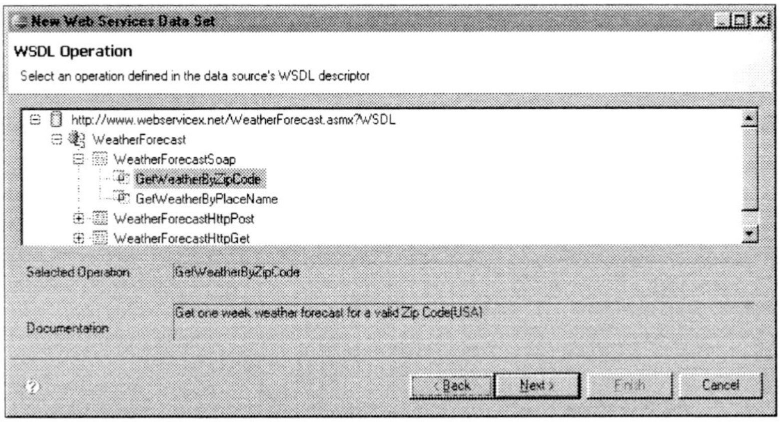

Figure 6-12   Select the GetWeatherByZipCode operation under WeatherForecastSoap

Choose Next.

New Web Services Data Set displays the parameter used by the GetWeatherByZipCode operation, as shown in Figure 6-13. The parameter, selected by default, is used to get the zip code whose weather forecast to return.

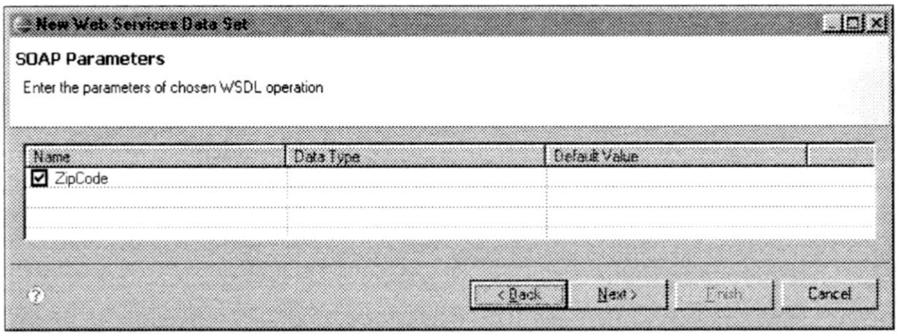

Figure 6-13   Parameters and specified default values

4 In Default Value, type a zip code, such as 94044. Choose Next.

BIRT generates a SOAP request template based on the WSDL document and your parameter selection, as shown in Figure 6-14. The body section of the SOAP request tells the web service to run the GetWeatherByZipCode operation and to use 94044 as the zip code parameter value.

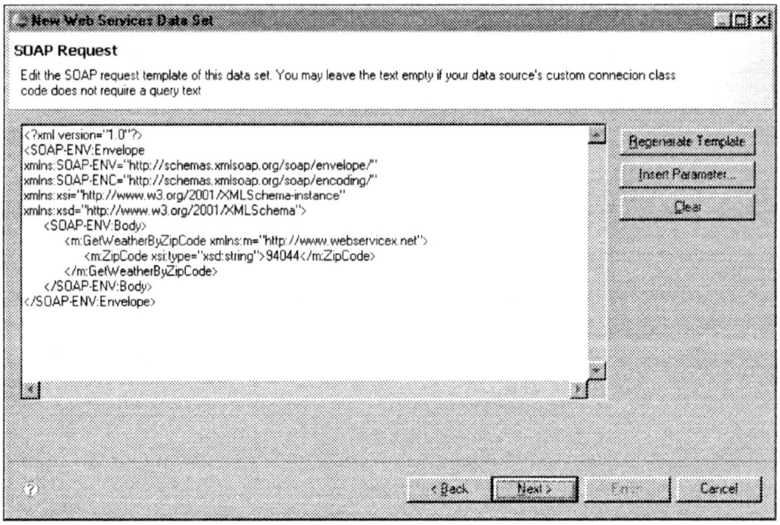

Figure 6-14   SOAP request template

Choose Next. New Web Service Data Set displays the options for constructing a SOAP response, as shown in Figure 6-15.

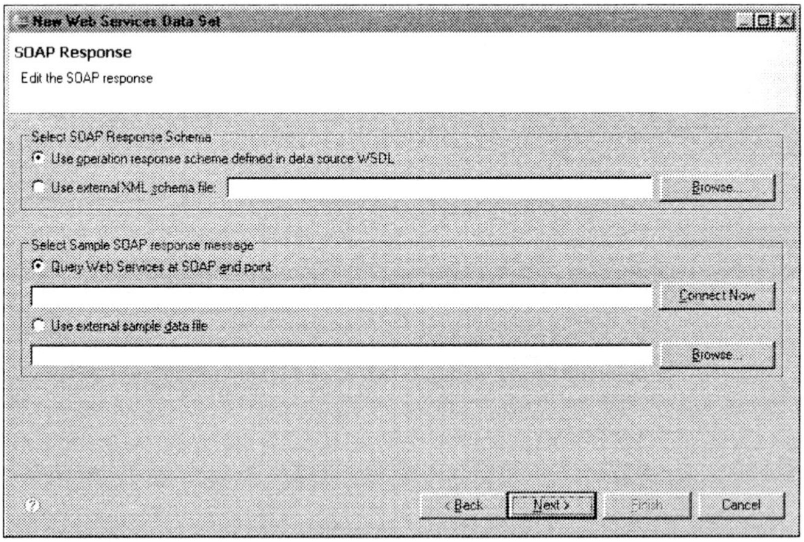

Figure 6-15   Options for constructing a SOAP response

5   Use the default options, which is the typical case for most well-defined web services.

Choose Next. New Web Services Data Set displays an XML structure from which you select an element to map as a table.

6   In XML Structure, expand all the items, then select GetWeatherByZipCodeResult, as shown in Figure 6-16. GetWeatherByZipCodeResult defines the data returned by the weather forecast service.

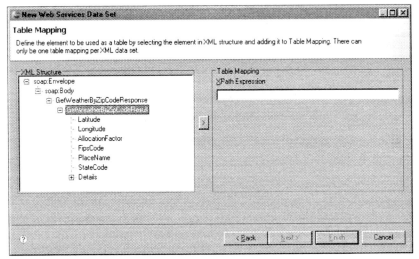

Figure 6-16   Select an element to map as a table

Click the > button, then choose OK to accept the generated XPath expression. Choose Next.

7   On Column Mapping, select the elements to map to columns.

1   In XML Structure, expand the Details element under GetWeatherByZipCodeResult. The GetWeatherByZipCodeResult operation returns a lot of information. For this example, assume that we want to retrieve only the following data: Day, MaxTemperatureF, and MinTemperatureF.

2   Select the Day element. Click the > button to create the XPath expression that maps the selected element as a column, then choose OK.

3   Select MaxTemperatureF and map it to a column.

4   Select MinTemperatureF and map it to a column.

Figure 6-17 shows the completed column mappings.

8   Choose Finish.

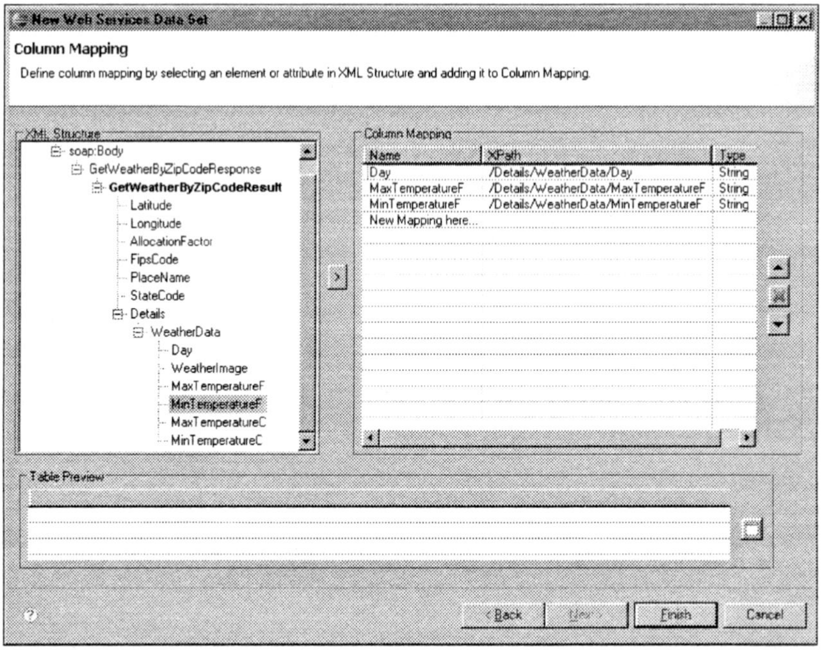

Figure 6-17   Column mappings

9 On Edit Data Set, choose Preview Results. The data set returns the date, and the maximum and minimum temperatures for zip code 94044, as shown in Figure 6-18.

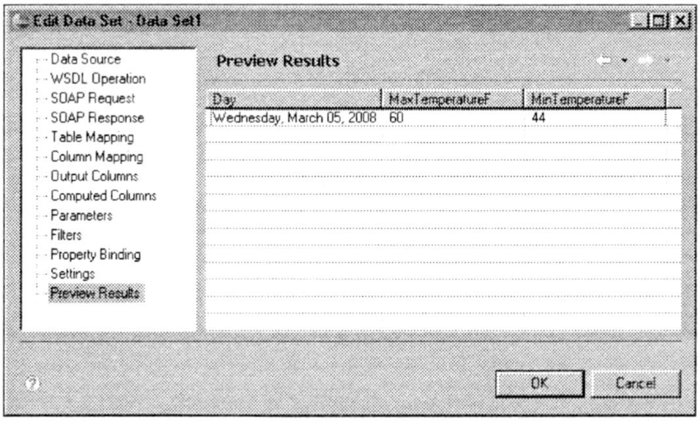

Figure 6-18   Results returned by the web service data set

When you use this data in a report, each time you run the report, the data set gets the weather forecast for the current day and for zip code 94044. While this data may be all you want to display in your report, the typical case when using a web service is to enable the report user to supply parameter values at run time. In our weather forecast example, we can make the report more interesting by prompting the user to specify the zip code for which to get weather information. For many web services, such as a mortgage calculator or a currency converter, incorporating web service data in the report makes sense only if users can specify parameter values to get the data they want.

The solution is to create report parameters to prompt the user for values. The user-specified values are then passed to the data set, which, in turn, passes it to the web service through the SOAP request. The procedure for implementing this solution is described next.

How to enable a user to provide values to a web service when a report runs

This procedure continues with the weather forecast example.

1 Create a report parameter to get the zip code at run time, using the following steps:

    1 In Data Explorer, right-click Report Parameters, then choose New Parameter.

    2 On New Parameter, supply the following information:

        ❑ In Name, type a name for the report parameter. For example:

            `zipcode_param`

        ❑ In Prompt text, specify a word or sentence to prompt the report user to provide a zip code. For example:

            `Weather forecast for this zip code`

        ❑ In Data type, select String.

        ❑ Use the default values for the other attributes.

Figure 6-19 shows the completed report parameter definition.

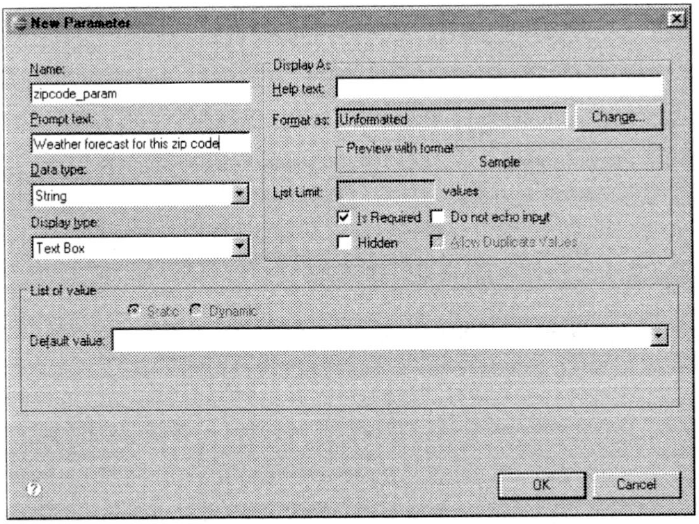

Figure 6-19   Report parameter to get the zip code

3 Choose OK. The zipcode_param parameter appears under Report Parameters in Data Explorer.

2 Create a data set parameter and link it to the report parameter.

1 In Data Explorer, right-click the web service data set, then choose Edit.

2 On Edit Data Set, select SOAP Request, as shown in Figure 6-20.

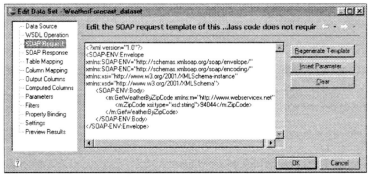

Figure 6-20 SOAP request

3 Choose Regenerate Template.

BIRT generates a new request template. Notice the change in the body section. The previously hard-coded 94044 zip code is replaced by the following parameter notation:

```
&?ZipCode?&
```

This parameter notation means that a value can be inserted in the SOAP request at run time.

4 Choose Insert Parameter, then choose OK when SOAP Request displays the ZipCode parameter. This action creates a corresponding ZipCode parameter in the data set.

5 Choose Parameters. Edit Data Set displays the default ZipCode parameter definition, as shown in Figure 6-21.

Figure 6-21 Default ZipCode parameter definition

6 Select the ZipCode parameter, then choose Edit.

7 On Edit Parameter, in Linked To Report Parameter, select zipcode_param, as shown in Figure 6-22, then choose OK.

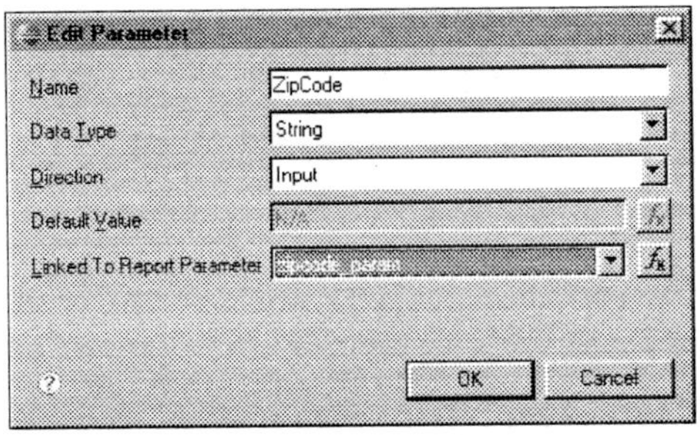

Figure 6-22   Link the data set parameter to the report parameter

3 Choose OK to save your changes to the data set.

4 Test the web service functionality in a report.

1 Drag the web service data set from the Data Explorer and drop it in the layout editor. BIRT creates a table and data elements to display the weather data, as shown in Figure 6-23.

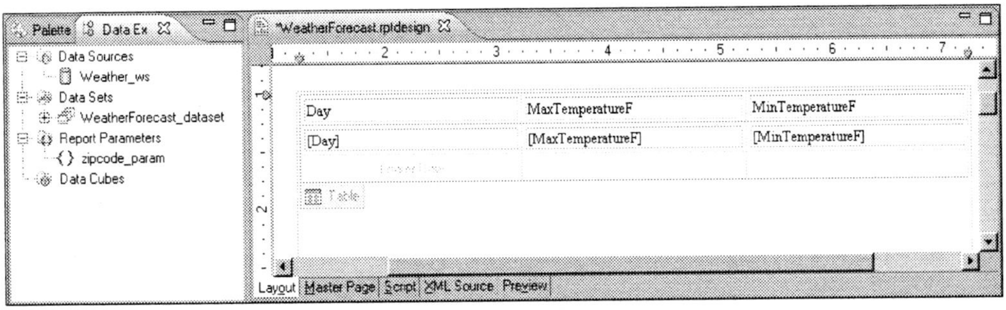

Figure 6-23   Report design to display the weather forecast data

2 Choose Preview. Enter Parameters displays the report parameter to get the zip code value, as shown in Figure 6-24.

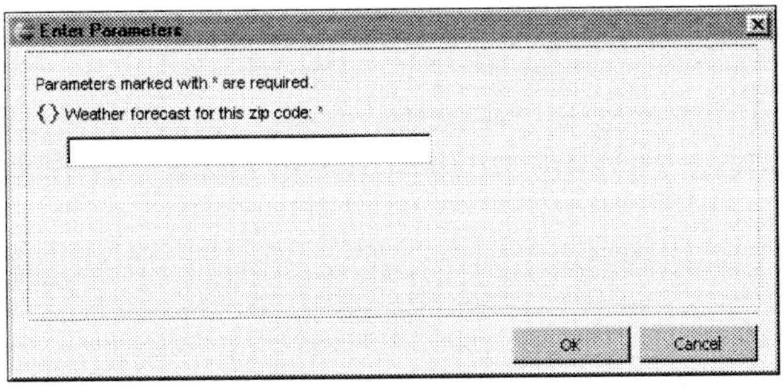

Figure 6-24   Enter Parameters displays the report parameter

3 Type a zip code, then choose OK.

The report displays weather data for that zip code. Figure 6-25 shows an example.

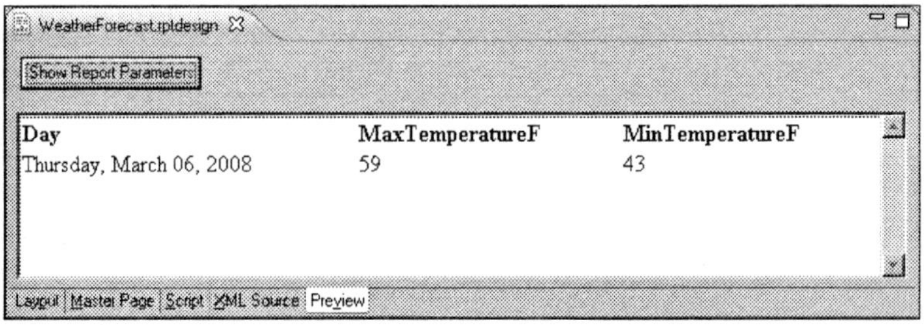

Figure 6-25   Report displays weather data for the specified zip code

Viewing and changing output columns

In Output Columns, you optionally can add an alias or display name for each column. BIRT Report Designer uses the display name in Data Explorer and for the column headings in a table. For example, you can give a column that is named $$CN01 a display name of Customer Name to make the column easier to identify in Data Explorer and more user-friendly in the column heading of a table.

Use an alias if you want to use a shorter or more recognizable name when you refer to the column in code. For example, you can give a column named $$CN01 an alias of custName so that you can write row["custName"] instead of row["$$CN01"]. If you do not specify a display name for the column, BIRT Report Designer displays the alias in Data Explorer and for the column headings in a table.

How to view and change output columns

1 To verify the list of columns selected for retrieval, choose Output Columns from the left pane of Edit Data Set. Output Columns displays the names of the columns, as shown in Figure 6-26.

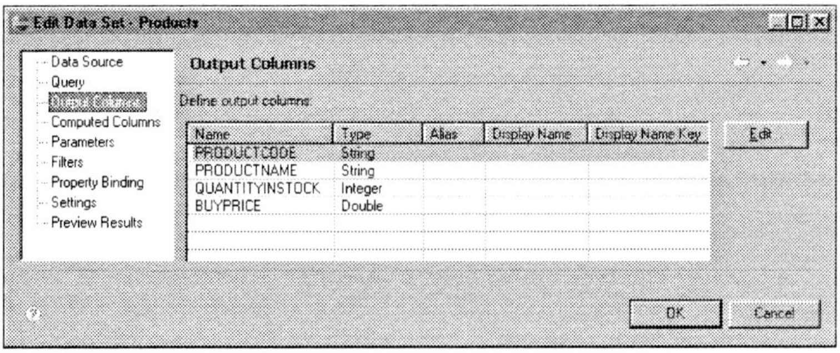

Figure 6-26   Viewing the output columns for a data set

2 To edit the properties of an output column, select the column name, then choose Edit. Edit Output Column displays the properties you can set.

For example, to display a name as the default column heading in the report, type the name in Display Name.

3 Choose OK to save your edits.

Adding a computed field to a data set

A data set can contain computed data as well as data that is returned from a data source. Computed data displays the result of an expression, typically involving one or more columns from a data source. For example, if each row that is returned from the data source contains a price and a quantity, you can create a computed field that calculates the total amount paid, using the following expression:

```
row["pricequote"] * row["quantity"]
```

You also can concatenate values from multiple fields, using the + operator, or calculate values using JavaScript functions. The expression builder provides a list of operators and functions that you can use to build expressions.

You can also define a computed field in the report layout. Defining computed fields in the data set is, however, the preferred approach. Defining the computed field in the data set separates business logic from the presentation of the data. Defining the computed field in the data set also enables you to verify the results of the calculation in the Preview Results page of Edit Data Set. You can determine whether the expression for the computed field is correct before you work on the report layout and how to display the computed field. Figure 6-27 shows an example computed field, Total_cost.

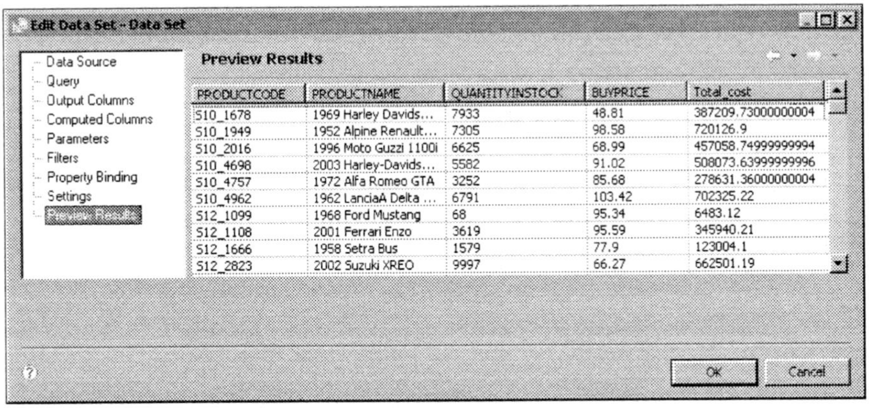

Figure 6-27   An example computed field, Total_cost

How to add a computed field to a data set

1 In Edit Data Set, choose Computed Columns.

2 Choose New to create a new computed field.

3 On New Computed Column:

    1 In Column Name, type a name for the computed field.

    2 In Data Type, select a data type for the computed field.

    3 In Expression, specify the expression to calculate the desired value. You can either type the expression or use the expression builder to construct the expression. To use the expression builder, complete the following steps:

        1 Choose the expression builder button to open the expression builder. In Category, select Available Data sets, then select your data set.

        In the top pane, type an expression. You can also double-click an item to add it to the expression at the insertion point. Figure 6-28 shows how to create an expression for a computed column.

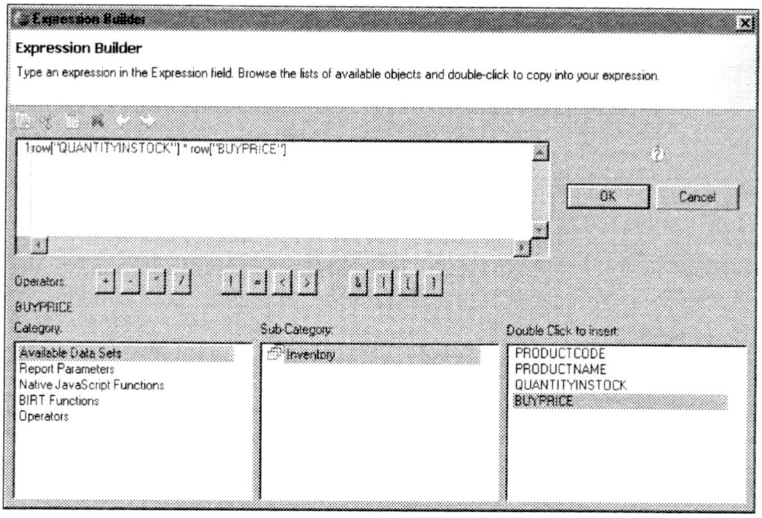

Figure 6-28   Creating an expression for a computed column

        2 Choose OK to save the expression. The expression appears in the Expression field in New Computed Column.

    4 Choose OK to save the computed field. Computed Columns displays the computed field and the expression you defined.

4 To see all the columns that are specified in the data set, choose Output Columns. The computed field you created appears on this page.

5 Choose Preview Results to confirm that the computed field returns the correct data.

6 Choose OK to save your changes to the data set.

Joining data sets

The capability to join data sets is a useful and easy way to combine data from two data sources. You can, for example, combine data from two XML files, or combine data from a text file with data from a database table. Before you can join data sets, you must, of course, create the individual data sets. For example, to combine data from an XML file with data from a text file, you must first create the XML data set and the text file data set.

Joining data sets is similar to joining tables in a database, described earlier in "Combining data from multiple tables," but with the following two limitations:

- You can join only two data sets. Within a database, you can join more than two tables.

- You can create only four types of joins: inner, left outer, right outer, and full outer.

Like the database joins, you must specify a column on which to join the two data sets. The four types of joins you can use to join data sets yield the same results as the similarly-named database joins. The following list summarizes the function of each join type:

- Inner join returns all rows from both data sets if there is a match.

- Left outer join returns all rows from the first data set, even if there are no matches in the second data set.

- Right outer join returns all rows from the second data set, even if there are no matches in the first data set.

- Full outer join returns all rows from both data sets, even if there are no matches in either data set.

Joining two data sets creates a BIRT object called a joint data set. Just as you can with a regular data set, you can add computed columns and filters to a joint data set, and preview the results it returns. Once you understand well the concepts of joining data sets, you can be creative about combining data from more than two sources, assuming the data from the various sources relate in some way.

Although each joint data set can join only two data sets, you can use a joint data set as one or both of those data sets. For example, you can create joint data set A and joint data set B, then join both of them. Doing so, in effect, combines data from four data sets. Figure 6-29 illustrates this concept.

As Figure 6-29 also shows, each data set can return data from different types of sources. You could also use joint data sets to join multiple tables in a single database. For performance reasons, however, this technique is not recommended. Where possible, you should always join multiple tables through the SQL SELECT statement, as described earlier in this chapter.

You should create joint data sets only to:

■ Combine data from disparate data sources.

■ Combine data from non-relational data sources, such as XML or text files.

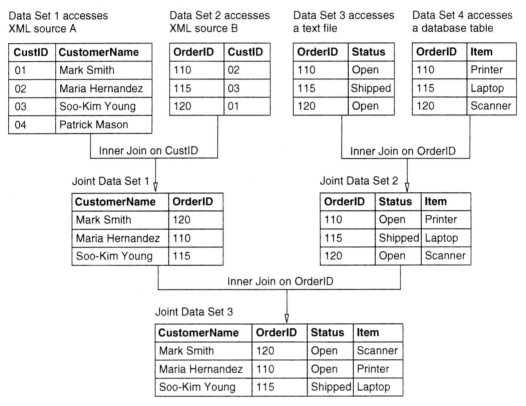

Figure 6-29   Combining data from four data sets

How to join data sets

You use New Data Set to join two existing data sets into a joint data set.

1   In Data Explorer, right-click Data Sets, and choose New Joint Data Set.

2   Select the first data set for the joint data set from the drop-down list at the left of New Data Set. The columns of the first data set appear in the panel below your selection.

3   Select the second data set for the joint data set from the drop-down list at the right of New Data Set. The columns of the second data set appear.

4   Select the columns to join. Select one column from the first data set, and one column from the second data set.

Typically, you select the columns that are common to both data sets. BIRT Report Designer does not prevent you from selecting two unrelated columns as long as both columns have the same data type. Doing so, however, typically does not provide the results you want. Figure 6-30 shows an example of a joint data set definition.

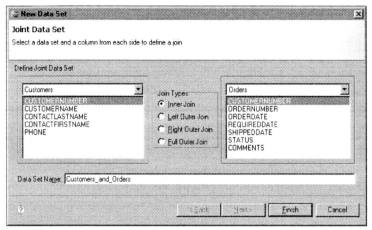

Figure 6-30   Joint data set definition

5 Select a join type, then choose Finish.

6 On Edit Data Set, choose Preview Results to see the rows returned by the joint data set.

Verifying the data returned by a data set

When you finish creating a data set, you should use Preview Results to verify that the data set returns the expected data. Figure 6-31 shows an example of a result set returned by a JDBC data set. Preview Results shows up to 500 data rows that are returned by the query or data definition in the data set. If you expect to preview data frequently, or if you are working with large or complex data sets, you can configure the data set cache, so you can work more efficiently.

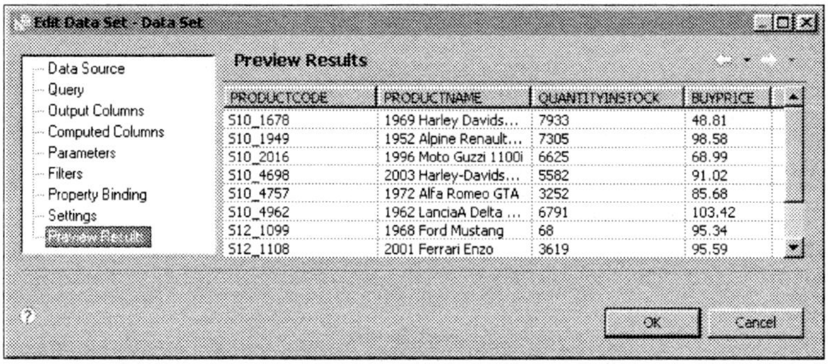

Figure 6-31   Previewing the results of a data set

How to change the number of rows that appear in Preview Results

1   Choose Window→Preferences.

2   On Preferences, click the plus sign (+) beside Report Design to expand the item.

3   Choose Data Set Editor.

4   On Preferences—Data Set Editor, in Maximum number of rows to display, type the number of rows to display, then choose OK.

Specifying the data to retrieve at run time

In all the procedures for retrieving the different types of data, described previously, the data you select is hard-coded at design time. Some reports, however, require the ability to display a different set of data based on run time criteria, such as user login or the data source that a report user selects.

If you recall from the previous chapter, the data source editor provides a feature called property binding to support the setting of connection properties at run time. Similarly, the data set editor provides the property binding feature to support the selection of data at run time.

Figure 6-32 shows the Property Binding page for a JDBC data set. The Query Text property is where you specify an expression that determines at run time what data to select. The Query Text property is also available to the flat file and web services data set.

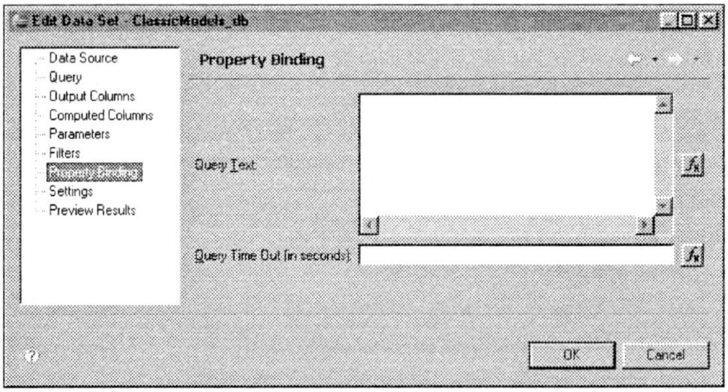

Figure 6-32   Property Binding page for a JDBC data set

About the Query Text property

When you select data, either by writing a SQL query, selecting a text file and columns, selecting XML elements, or specifying a SOAP request, BIRT stores that information in a property named queryText. If you choose the XML Source tab on the report editor, you see the XML source that BIRT generates when you create a report.

Figure 6-33 shows the part of the XML source that defines the value of the queryText property. In the example shown, the report uses data from the sample database, ClassicModels. The queryText property contains the SQL SELECT statement that specifies the data to retrieve.

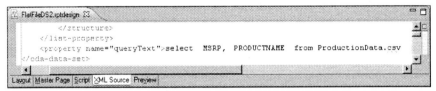

```
JDBC_ds.rptdesign ⊠
           <property name="queryText">select CLASSICMODELS.CUSTOMERS.CUSTOMERNAME,
CLASSICMODELS.CUSTOMERS.CUSTOMERNUMBER,
CLASSICMODELS.CUSTOMERS.CREDITLIMIT
from CLASSICMODELS.CUSTOMERS</property>
Layout Master Page Script XML Source Preview
```

Figure 6-33   Report's XML source showing the queryText property for a
                   JDBC data set

Figure 6-34 shows an example of a report's XML source, where the report uses data from a text file named ProductionData.csv. Although the flat file data set does not use a SQL query to select data, the queryText property contains a statement similar to a SQL query.

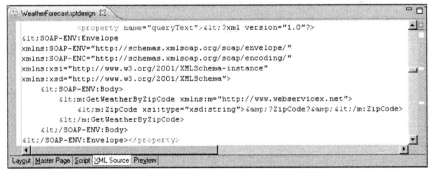

```
FlatFileDS2.rptdesign ⊠
         </structure>
      </list-property>
      <property name="queryText">select  MSRP,  PRODUCTNAME  from ProductionData.csv
</oda-data-set>
Layout Master Page Script XML Source Preview
```

Figure 6-34   Report's XML source showing the queryText property for a flat
                   file data set

Figure 6-35 shows the queryText property for a report that uses a web service data set. This property contains the SOAP request template.

```
WeatherForecast.rptdesign ⊠
           <property name="queryText">&lt;?xml version="1.0"?>
&lt;SOAP-ENV:Envelope
xmlns:SOAP-ENV="http://schemas.xmlsoap.org/soap/envelope/"
xmlns:SOAP-ENC="http://schemas.xmlsoap.org/soap/encoding/"
xmlns:xsi="http://www.w3.org/2001/XMLSchema-instance"
xmlns:xsd="http://www.w3.org/2001/XMLSchema">
    &lt;SOAP-ENV:Body>
        &lt;m:GetWeatherByZipCode xmlns:m="http://www.webservicex.net">
            &lt;m:ZipCode xsi:type="xsd:string">&amp;?ZipCode?&amp; &lt;/m:ZipCode>
        &lt;/m:GetWeatherByZipCode>
    &lt;/SOAP-ENV:Body>
&lt;/SOAP-ENV:Envelope></property>
Layout Master Page Script XML Source Preview
```

Figure 6-35   Report's XML source showing the queryText property for a web
                   service data set

Specifying a value for the Query Text property

The Query Text property on the Property Binding page of the data set editor is the same as the queryText property in the report source file. The value you specify on the Property Binding page updates the queryText property in the source file, and must use the same format you see in the report source file. In

addition, you must enclose the value you type in double quotation marks
(" ").

The following example shows the correct syntax for specifying a Query Text value for a JDBC data set:

```
"select CUSTOMERNAME, CUSTOMERNUMBER from CUSTOMERS where
    COUNTRY = 'Australia'"
```

The following example shows the correct syntax for specifying a Query Text value for a flat file data set:

```
"select Date, Open, High from StockHistory.csv"
```

The previous examples showed the syntax for a Query Text value, but both examples specified static data. Typically, when you specify a value for the Query Text property, you use variables or JavaScript expressions that evaluate to a specific value at run time.

The following example shows how to select a text file at run time. The JavaScript expression params["pTextFileName"] refers to a report parameter whose value evaluates to a file name specified at run time.

```
"select PRODUCTNAME, QUANTITYINSTOCK, MSRP from " +
    params["pTextFileName"]
```

The following example shows how to select from a database the customer rows for a particular country. The country value is specified by the user at run time through the report parameter p_Country.

```
"select CUSTOMERNAME, CUSTOMERNUMBER, COUNTRY from CUSTOMERS
    where COUNTRY =   " + "'" + params["p_Country"] + "'"
```

Binding Data

The data set or data sets you create return the data that you want to use in a report. Before you can use or display this data in a report, you must first create the necessary data bindings. As the first tutorial demonstrated, to display the data in a report, you simply drag data set fields from Data Explorer to a table in the layout editor. Each time you insert a data set field, BIRT creates a data binding automatically.

This data binding, called a column binding, defines an expression that specifies what data to display. The column binding also defines a name that report elements use to access data. To view the column bindings that BIRT creates automatically for each data set field that you place in a table, select the table, then, in Property Editor, choose the Binding tab. Figure 7-1 shows an example of column bindings created for each data set field in a table.

Understanding column bindings

For each piece of data to display or use in a report, there must be a column binding. For this discussion, note that data refers to dynamic data, and not static text that you type for a label. Dynamic data is data from a data set, or data that is calculated from a function or a formula. The data is dynamic because the values are not fixed at design time.

The default column binding, which BIRT Report Designer creates for a data set field, uses the data set field name as the name of the column binding. In Figure 7-1, the expression defined for the first column binding is dataSetRow["CUSTOMERNAME"]. This expression indicates that the column binding accesses data from the data set field, CUSTOMERNAME. In the layout editor, the column-binding name appears within square brackets ([]) in the report, as shown in Figure 7-1.

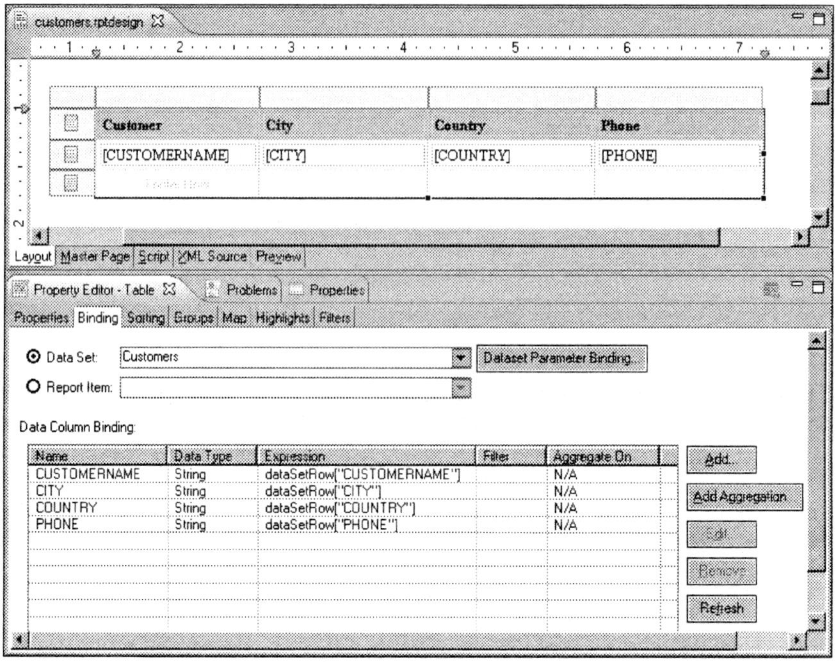

Figure 7-1　　Table's Binding page showing four column bindings

Column bindings form an intermediate layer between data set data and report elements—such as chart, data, dynamic text, and image elements—that display data. Figure 7-2 illustrates this concept. Report elements can access data only through column bindings.

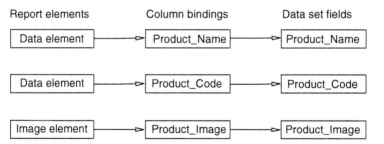

Figure 7-2　　Report elements access data set data through column bindings

The preceding examples show column bindings that access data set data. Column bindings can also access data derived from functions or user-defined formulas. For example, you can use a data element to display the current date derived from the JavaScript Date object. You would create a column binding that uses the following expression:

```
new Date()
```

Figure 7-3 shows this column binding definition.

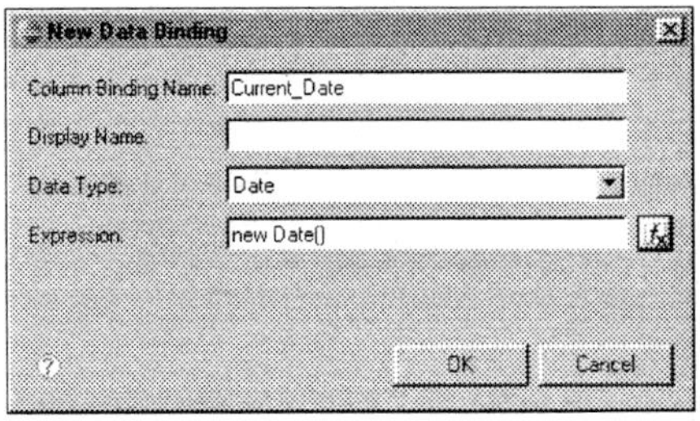

Figure 7-3 User-defined column binding

Descriptive names

One of the benefits of using column bindings is that you control the names used in the report. Instead of displaying data set field names, which are often not descriptive enough, or formulas, which can be long, you can specify short and descriptive names. If you share report designs with other report developers, descriptive names make that design much easier to understand. Modifying and maintaining a report design that has user-friendly names is easier. When deciding what names to use, consider that, in the layout editor, elements display up to 20 characters.

Dynamic updates of calculated data

Another advantage of column bindings becomes apparent when you work with calculated data. When a report needs to display a series of related calculated data, column bindings enable you to create and update calculations easily. For example, assume a report contains the following four data elements:

- The first data element uses column binding, Order_Total, which uses the SUM function, and the following expression to calculate the sum of all order line items:

      dataSetRow["pricequote"] * dataSetRow["quantity"]

- The second data element uses column binding, Sales_Tax, which refers to the previous column binding, Order_Total, to calculate the sales tax. The expression defined for the Sales_Tax column binding is

      row["Order_Total"] * 0.08

  Without using column bindings, the second data element must use the SUM function and the following longer expression to calculate sales tax:

      (dataSetRow["pricequote"] * dataSetRow["quantity"]) * 0.08

- The third data element uses column binding, Shipping_Charge, which also refers to the first column binding, Order_Total, to calculate the shipping charge. The expression defined for the Shipping_Charge column binding is

      row["Order_Total"] * 0.02

Again, without using column bindings, the third data element must use the SUM function, and the following lengthier expression to calculate the shipping charge:

```
(dataSetRow["pricequote"] * dataSetRow["quantity"]) * 0.02
```

■ The fourth data element uses column binding, Invoice_Total, which refers to all the previous column bindings to calculate the grand total. The expression defined for the Invoice_Total column binding is

```
row["Order_Total"] + row["Sales_Tax"] +
   row["Shipping_Charge"]
```

Without column bindings, the expression would be more complicated:

```
(dataSetRow["pricequote"] * dataSetRow["quantity"]) +
   ((dataSetRow["pricequote"] * dataSetRow["quantity"]) *
   0.08) +
   ((dataSetRow["pricequote"] * dataSetRow["quantity"]) *
   0.02)
```

You have already seen how column bindings make expressions shorter and more readable. Now, consider the case where you need to update one calculation that is used by other calculations. Suppose you need to change how Order_Total is calculated, from:

```
dataSetRow["pricequote"] * dataSetRow["quantity"]
```

to

```
(dataSetRow["pricequote"] * dataSetRow["quantity"]) -
   dataSetRow["discount"]
```

Because the second, third, and fourth data elements use Order_Total in their calculations, without using column bindings, you must manually edit those calculations as well. For example, without using column bindings, you would have to revise the expression for the fourth element as follows:

```
((dataSetRow["pricequote"] * dataSetRow["quantity"]) -
   dataSetRow["discount"]) +
   ((dataSetRow["pricequote"] * dataSetRow["quantity"]) * 0.08)
   + ((dataSetRow["pricequote"] * dataSetRow["quantity"]) *
   0.02)
```

By using column bindings, any change to the first calculation automatically applies to the second, third, and fourth calculations. Instead of modifying three expressions, you modify only one. Your work is faster and less error-prone.

Creating column bindings

As discussed previously, when you drag a data set field from Data Explorer to a table in the layout editor, BIRT creates the column binding. When you bind a table to a data set, BIRT automatically creates a column binding for each field in the data set.

For other cases, when you insert a dynamic text, text, image, or data element from the palette, you manually create the column binding if you want the element to display dynamic data. If the information to display is static—for example, a specific image stored in a file system, or literal text—then column binding is not applicable.

How to create a column binding

This procedure shows an example of creating a column binding for a data element.

1 Drag a data element from the palette and drop it in the report. New Data Binding appears.

2 Create a new column binding:

    1 In Column Binding Name, specify a unique name for the column binding.

    2 In Data Type, select a data type appropriate for the data returned by the expression you specify next. If you are not sure what the data type is, use the default type, Any.

    3 In Expression, specify the expression that indicates the data to return, using one of the following methods:

      ❑ Type the expression directly in the Expression field.

      ❑ If you need help constructing the expression, choose the expression builder button to launch the expression builder. Figure 7-4 shows an expression in the expression builder that combines the values of two data set fields selected from the Customers data set. Choose OK when you finish constructing the expression.

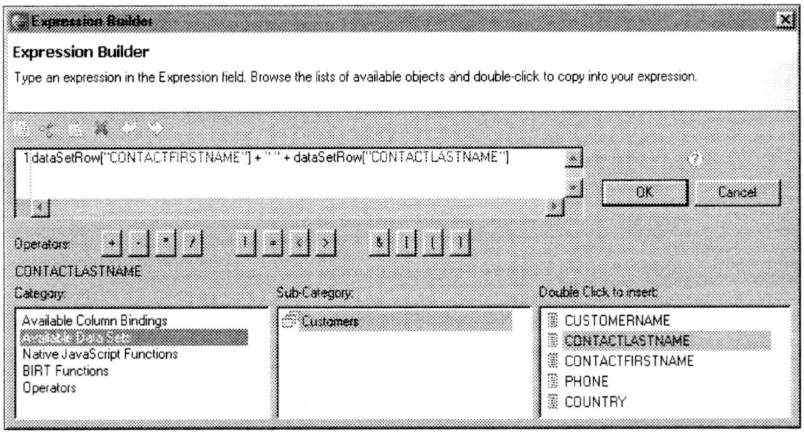

Figure 7-4   The expression builder showing a column-binding expression

Figure 7-5 shows an example of a column-binding definition.

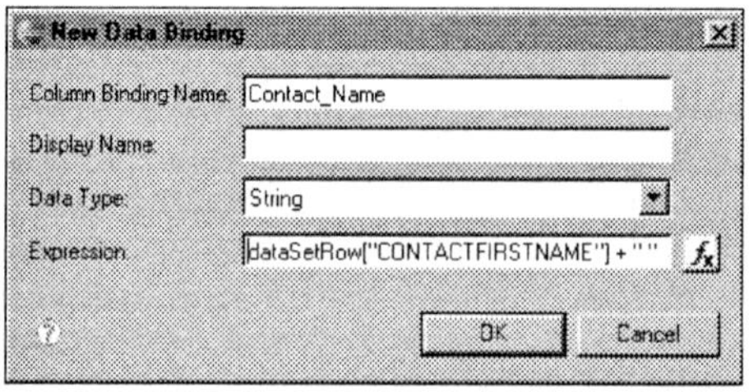

Figure 7-5   New column-binding definition

   4   Choose OK to save the column binding.

      In the layout editor, the report design displays [Contact_Name] in the
      location where you inserted the data element, indicating that the data
      element uses the column binding you defined.

 3   Preview the report. The data element displays the data defined in the
      column binding expression.

Editing and deleting column bindings

Be careful when editing or deleting column bindings. More than one element
can use a column binding, and a column binding can refer to other column
bindings. Earlier in this chapter, you saw examples of how a change to a
calculated-data expression cascaded to other expressions that used the
higher-level expression. The ease with which you can dynamically update
formulas that refer to column bindings also requires that you be aware of
those dependencies.

To minimize errors, BIRT allows you to edit the data type and the expression,
but not the name of the column binding. Figure 7-6 shows Edit Data Binding,
which opens when you double-click a data element on the report. The value in
Column Binding Name is read-only.

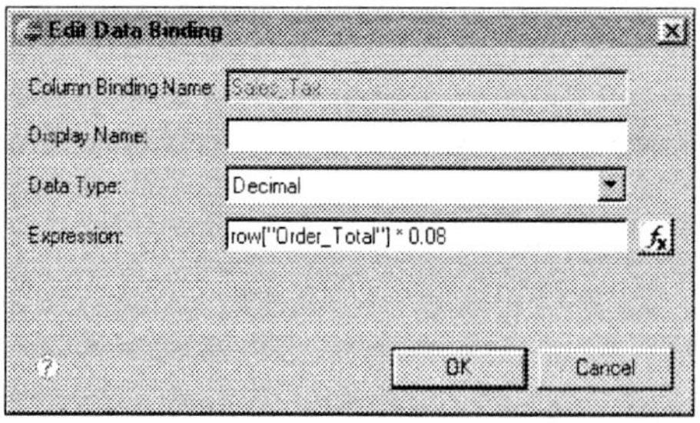

Figure 7-6   Edit Data Binding showing the definition of a column binding

If you could edit the name of the column binding, expressions in other column
bindings that refer to that column binding would no longer be valid, unless
you also update all expressions to refer to the renamed column binding. For

example, as Figure 7-6 shows, the expression in Sales_Tax refers to a column binding named Order_Total. If you could rename Order_Total, the expression in Sales_Tax, row["Order_Total"] * 0.08, would refer to a column binding that no longer exists.

Deleting a column binding that is used by multiple elements results in errors in the report design. Consider the following scenario:

You drop a data set field, COUNTRY, in a table. BIRT Report Designer creates a column binding named COUNTRY that refers to the data set field. You create a sort condition to display rows alphabetically by country names. The sort expression uses the COUNTRY column binding. Later, you decide that you do not want to display the COUNTRY values in the report. You delete the [COUNTRY] data element from the table. You want to maintain an accurate list of column bindings used in the table, so you also delete the COUNTRY column binding from the table's Binding page. When you run the report, you get an error message because the sort expression still refers to the COUNTRY column binding, which no longer exists.

Before you edit or delete a column binding, consider these guidelines:

- A change to a column binding's expression applies to other column bindings that refer to that column binding.

- A column binding can be used in a variety of expressions, not just by data elements that display field values in the report. For example, expressions used to sort, group, filter, or highlight data also refer to column bindings. If you delete a column binding, preview the report immediately to make sure you have not introduced any errors. If the report no longer generates, use the Undo functionality to restore the report to its previous state.

Copying data elements

Another action to be careful about is copying and pasting data elements. In a report that displays the same or similar data in multiple places, the natural inclination is to copy the data element and paste it elsewhere in the report. For example, you want to display the order ID in two places: the detail row and header row of a table. You already inserted the order ID data element in the detail row, so you copy the data element and paste it in the header row. When you run the report, the order ID appears in both places.

Later, you decide to add static text, Order Number:, to the order ID value that appears in the header row. You double-click the data element in the header row, and change the expression in the Edit Data Binding dialog from:

```
dataSetRow["ORDERNUMBER"]
```

to

```
"Order Number: " + dataSetRow["ORDERNUMBER"]
```

When you choose OK to save the change, BIRT prompts you to choose one of the following options:

- Create a new column binding for the selected data element. This option enables you to make changes only to the selected data element.

- Update both data elements to use the new expression.

Figure 7-7 shows the message that BIRT displays when you edit an expression for a column binding that is used by multiple data elements.

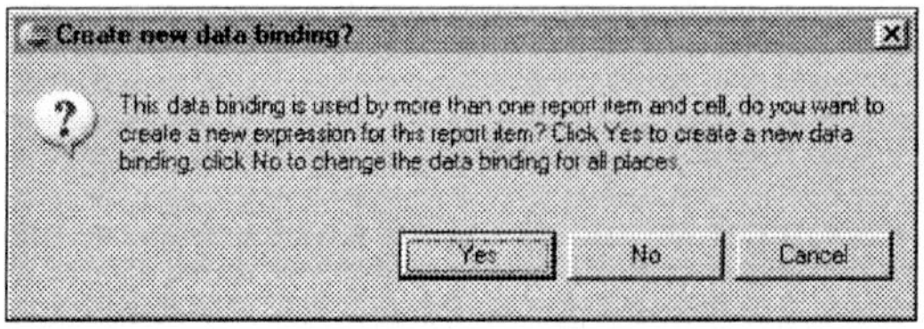

Figure 7-7   Options for editing a column-binding expression

When you copy and paste a data element, all the copies refer to a single instance of the column binding. Because this behavior is not apparent, BIRT asks you how you want a change in a column binding's expression or data type to be processed. Otherwise, you might assume that selecting a data element and editing its column binding information affects only the selected data element.

More about column-binding expressions

When you write an expression for a column binding, the expression can refer to data set fields, other column bindings, functions, and operators. Until you become familiar with writing expressions, you should use the expression builder to construct expressions. The expression builder displays the items—data set fields, column bindings, functions, and so on—that you can use in a column-binding expression.

The items available in the expression builder change depending on where you define the column binding. For example, if you insert a data element in a table that contains other column bindings, the data element can access those column bindings. If you insert a data element directly on the report page, the data element cannot access column bindings defined for the table or any other report element.

When you select an item in the expression builder, the expression builder adds the item to the expression with the proper syntax. When a column-binding expression refers to a data set field, the syntax is

```
dataSetRow["datasetField"]
```

When a column-binding expression refers to another column binding, the syntax is

```
row["columnBinding"]
```

If you use the expression builder to construct column-binding expressions, you do not need to remember what syntax to use. You will find it helpful, though, to understand what each syntax means because the expression examples that appear throughout the book use both syntaxes.

Designing Reports

Laying Out a Report

You can present information in a report in many ways. You can display information in a tabular list, a nested list, a chart, a series of text blocks, or a series of subreports. More complex report layouts can use a variety of these different presentations in a single report. Laying out a report entails placing data on the page and organizing the information in a way that helps a user to read and understand the information in the report.

Because there are infinite ways to lay out a report, it helps to work from a paper design. If you try to design and create the report layout at the same time, you can lose track of the data that you want to place in the report, or you can finish laying out one part of the report before you realize that you can better present the data using another layout.

Before you begin to lay out your report, verify in Data Explorer that your data set or data sets return the data that you want to use in your report. In many cases, the layout of a report is driven by the data.

Understanding the layout model

Like most documents, reports tend to be very structured. A report typically consists of distinct sections or a series of content blocks, as shown in Figure 8-1. BIRT Report Designer provides an intuitive way to lay out a report. A visual layout editor displays a page to which you add content, such as data fields, charts, pictures, or text blocks, in each section of the report.

A section can consist of one or multiple elements. The first section of a report, for example, is typically the report title. This section might contain just one text element. Another section, which displays a list of customer records, might contain four data fields and four column headings. More complex sections can contain multiple subsections to display items such as multiple lists that appear side by side or a combination of lists, charts, and text blocks. A key concept to understand about sections is that each section is a horizontal block of content.

You lay out the contents of each section of a report in the same way that you read a report—you start from the top of the report and go from left to right until the end of the report. By dividing a report into sections, you can manipulate each section independently. For example:

- Use a different set of data for each section.

- Size and format each section independently.

- Specify page breaks before or after each section.

- Conditionally show or hide each section.

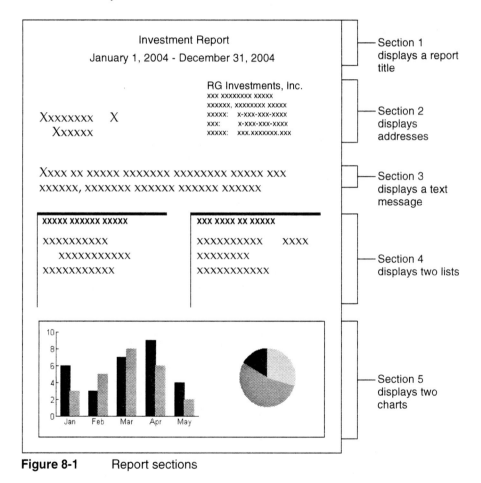

Figure 8-1   Report sections

About the report layout elements

BIRT Report Designer provides a variety of elements for building a report. To lay out a report, you drag report elements from the palette and drop them on the page in the layout editor. Report elements fall into two general categories:

- Elements that display information
- Elements that organize multiple elements in a section

Table 8-1 provides a summary of the report elements that you can use to lay out your report. Details about using these report elements appear later in this chapter or elsewhere in this book.

Table 8-1   Report layout elements

Report element	Description
Label	Displays a piece of static text.
Text	Displays text that can contain HTML formatting and dynamic values.
Dynamic text	Displays memo or CLOB (Character Large Object) data from a data set field. The data typically consists of large amounts of text.
Data	Displays a computed value or a value from a data set field.
Image	Displays any image that a web browser supports.
Grid	Organizes multiple report elements in a static table.
Table	Organizes data from a data set in a dynamic table.
List	Organizes data from a data set in a variety of layouts. By contrast, a table element organizes elements in a row-and-column format only.
Chart	Displays data from a data set in a variety of chart types, including pie charts, bar charts, and line charts.
Cross tab	Displays summary, or aggregate, data in a row-and-column matrix that is similar to a spreadsheet.

Overview of the layout process

To lay out a report, follow these general steps:

- Identify the sections in your report.
- For each section, insert either:
  - A single report element, such as a text element
  - A container element to organize multiple report elements in a section

- For sections that contain multiple elements, insert report elements in each container. You can insert containers within a container to create nested sections. Preview each section as you complete it. If you wait until you finish laying out the report before you verify the output, and there are errors, it can be difficult to determine which part of the report causes the problems.

Creating the sections of a report

Most sections in a report contain multiple elements. BIRT Report Designer provides three types of containers for organizing elements in a section:

- Grid
- Table
- List

The following sections describe each container element.

Organizing elements in a grid

Use a grid to arrange static elements, such as text and pictures, in a section. The grid is similar to the HTML table in a web page. It is ideal for creating report title sections and page headers and footers, as shown in Figure 8-2 and Figure 8-3.

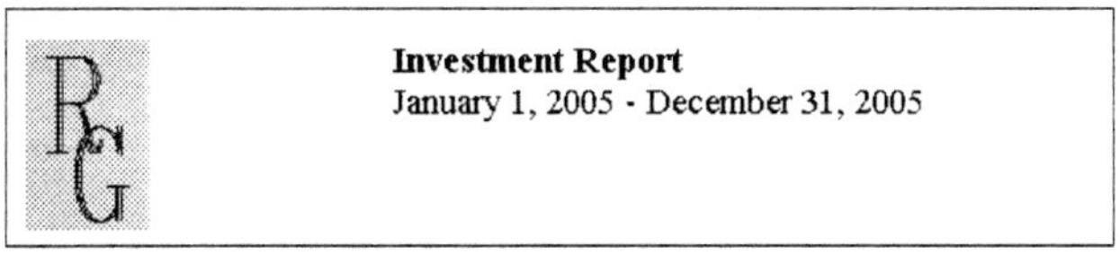

Investment Report
January 1, 2005 - December 31, 2005

Figure 8-2   Report title section

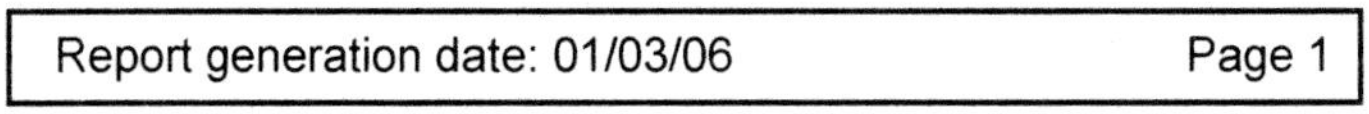

Report generation date: 01/03/06   Page 1

Figure 8-3   Report footer section

When you place a grid on the page, the layout editor displays a row-and-column structure, such as the one shown in Figure 8-4. By default, all the columns have the same width. All the rows have the same height.

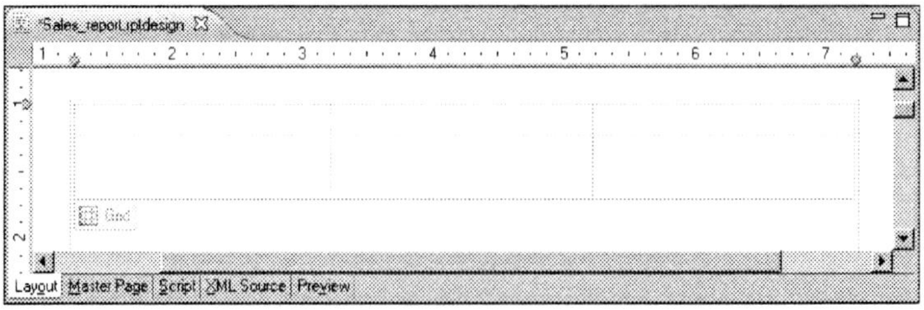

Figure 8-4   Row-and-column structure of a grid

The grid layout automates the task of aligning blocks of content. When you place report elements in the cells, the report elements are automatically aligned horizontally and vertically. If you have used other reporting tools that provide a free-form layout editor that lack this capability, you will appreciate the automatic alignment feature that the grid provides. Placing report elements and then aligning them manually is time-consuming.

Using BIRT Report Designer, you can add, delete, and resize rows and columns in the grid, as needed. Figure 8-5 shows a report title section that consists of a picture and two text elements, arranged in a grid with one row and two columns of different sizes.

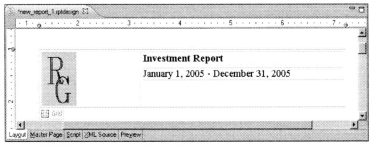

Figure 8-5   Grid displaying resized rows and columns

You can also format individual rows, columns, and cells to customize their size, color, borders, and text alignment. Chapter 10, "Formatting Report Content," describes these tasks.

Adding rows and columns

When you insert a grid, you specify the number of rows and columns that you want to start with. Depending on the number of report elements that you place in the grid, you might need to add rows or columns later.

How to add a row or column

1   In the layout editor, hover the mouse pointer over the bottom left corner of the grid until you see the Grid tab, then choose the tab. Guide cells appear at the top and left side of the grid, as shown in Figure 8-6.

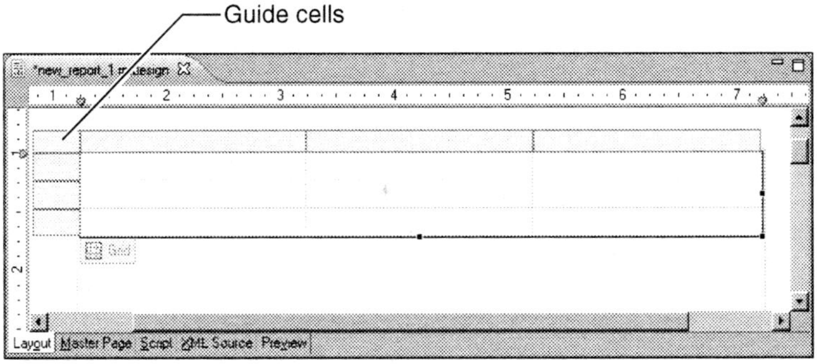

Figure 8-6   Guide cells support adding rows and columns

2 Right-click the guide cell next to where you want to add a row or column.

3 Choose one of the following items from the context menu to add a row or column in the desired location:

- Insert➤Row➤Above

- Insert➤Row➤Below

- Insert➤Column to the Right

- Insert➤Column to the Left

Deleting rows and columns

When you insert a grid, you specify the number of rows and columns that you want. If you do not place report elements in all the rows or columns, you can delete the empty rows and columns. Empty rows and columns have different effects on different output formats. By default, empty rows and columns do not appear as blank space in HTML and PDF formats. If you want an empty row or column to appear as blank space in these formats, set the row or column to a specific size. Empty rows and columns, however, appear as blank space in DOC, PPT, and XLS formats.

How to delete a row or column

1 In the layout editor, hover the mouse pointer over the bottom left corner of the grid until you see the Grid tab, then choose the tab. Guide cells appear at the top and left side of the grid.

2 Right-click the guide cell of the row or column that you want to delete, then choose Delete from the context menu. If the row or column contains elements, the elements are also deleted.

Organizing elements in a table

Use a table to display dynamic data in a row-and-column format. Dynamic data is data from a data source, such as a database or XML document. The data is dynamic because the values are not fixed in the report design. Instead, when the report runs, the report connects to the data source, retrieves the specified data, and displays the current data. Figure 8-7 shows an example table that displays customer names and phone numbers from a data source.

Customer	Phone
Alpha Cognac	61.77.6555
American Souvenirs Inc	2035557845
Amica Models & Co.	011-4988555
ANG Resellers	(91) 745 6555
Anna's Decorations, Ltd	02 9936 8555
Anton Designs, Ltd	+34 913 728555
Asian Shopping Network, Co	+612 9411 1555

Figure 8-7   Table data in a generated report

When you place a table on the page, the layout editor displays a row-and-column structure, such as the one shown in Figure 8-8.

Like the grid, the table layout automates the task of aligning report elements. Unlike the grid, the table iterates through all the data rows that a data set returns to display the dynamic list of data.

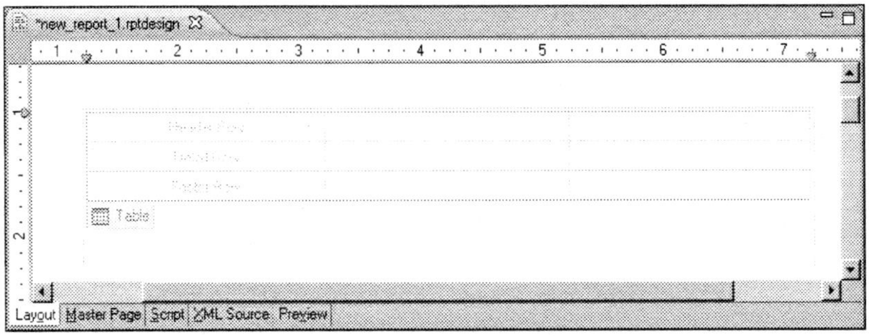

Figure 8-8   Row-and-column structure of a table

Note that a table can display data from one data set only. When you create a data set, ensure that it returns all the data that you want to display in a table. If the data that you need is stored in two database tables, write a query that joins the two tables. Alternatively, you can create two data sets and use two tables, one table for each data set.

Deciding where to place elements in a table

The table contains three types of rows in which you place report elements. Table 8-2 describes the types of information that you typically place in each row.

Table 8-2   Table row descriptions

Table row	Description
Header	Elements that you place in the header row appear at the beginning of the table. If the data in the table appears on multiple pages, the contents of the header display at the top of every page. You can display the header contents only once, at the beginning of the table, by turning off the table's Repeat Header property. Place elements in the header to display: ■ A title ■ Column headings, such as Customer Name, Address, and Phone, above the data in a customer list ■ Summary information, such as the number of customers in the list

(continues)

Table 8-2   Table row descriptions *(continued)*

Table row	Description
Detail	Elements that you place in the detail row represent the dynamic data in the table. The detail row displays each row from the data set. For example, display the main data, such as customer names, addresses, and phone numbers, in a customer list.
Footer	Elements that you place in the footer row appear once, at the end of the table. For example, display summary information, such as totals.

Figure 8-9 shows a table layout for displaying a list of customer names and their phone numbers. The finished report displays the list that appears in Figure 8-7.

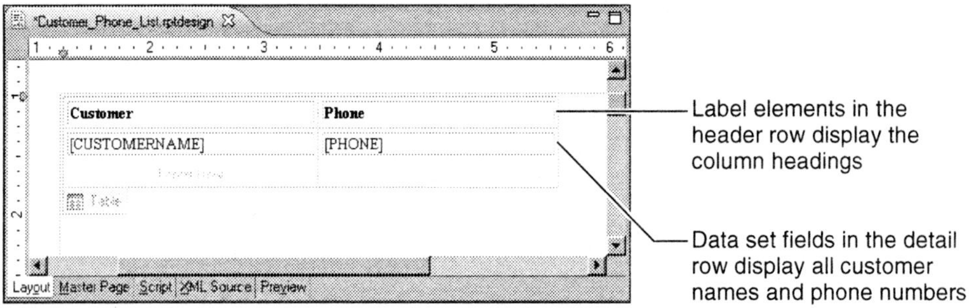

Label elements in the header row display the column headings

Data set fields in the detail row display all customer names and phone numbers

Figure 8-9   Table layout for customer names and phone numbers

Binding a table to a data set

When you place a data set field in a table, BIRT Report Designer:

- Binds, or associates, the data set with the table. By binding these items, the table has the information that it needs to iterate through the data rows that the data set returns.

- Creates a column binding, which binds the data set field with a named column.

- Creates a data element that uses the column binding to display data from the data set field.

You can view this binding information on the table's binding properties page. To do so, select the table, then choose the Binding tab at the top of Property Editor. Figure 8-10 shows the binding properties page.

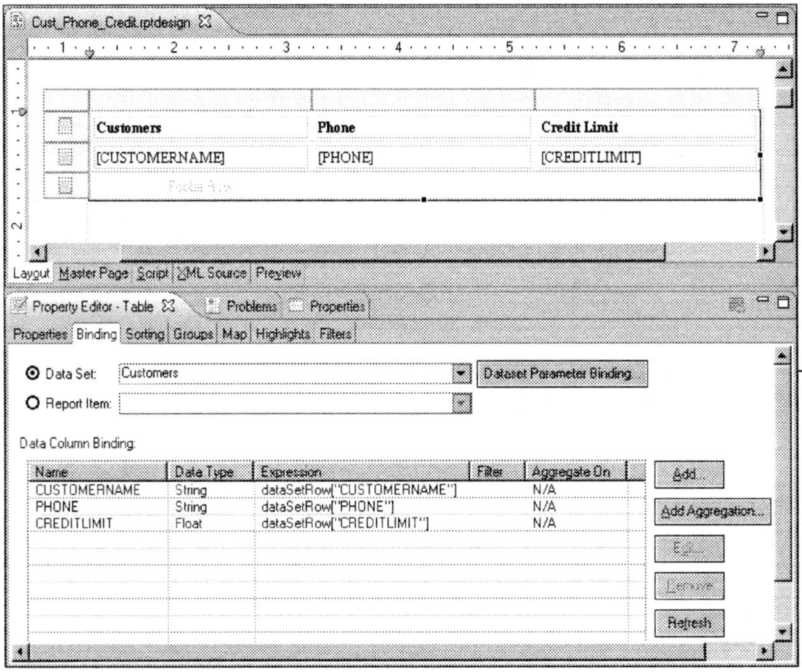

The Binding page shows which data set is bound to the table

Figure 8-10 Property Editor's Binding page for a selected table

You can also manually bind a table to a data set through this page. The easiest approach, however, is to place a data set field in the table and let BIRT Report Designer do the binding. If you are not placing data set fields in the table, but are inserting other types of elements, such as dynamic text elements or image elements that need to access data set data, then you need to manually bind the data set to the table before you insert those elements in the table.

A table can be bound to only one data set. BIRT Report Designer prevents you from inserting a field from a different data set. If you manually change the data set that is bound to a table after you place fields in the table, you need to delete the fields because the table no longer has information about them.

If, however, you do not change the data set binding, and you delete all the fields from a table, the table maintains its binding to the data set. To insert fields from a different data set into a table, you need to change the table's data set binding first. Deleting all the fields from the previous data set does not remove the original binding.

How to bind a data set to a table

1 In the layout editor, hover the mouse pointer over the bottom left corner until you see the Table tab, then choose the tab.

2 Choose the Binding tab at the top of Property Editor. The Data Set field shows either the name of the data set that is currently bound to the table or None if no data set is bound to the table.

3 From the Data Set drop-down list, select a data set. BIRT Report Designer binds the data set to the table. It also creates a column binding for each data set field. Now, elements placed in the table can access all the fields in the data set.

Adjusting table rows and columns

You can add, delete, and resize rows and columns in the table, as necessary. You add and delete table rows and columns in the same way that you add and delete grid rows and columns. These tasks are described earlier in this chapter.

A table can contain any number of header, detail, and footer rows. For example, you can add two header rows, one to display summary information and the other to display column headings.

Organizing elements in a list

Use a list element to display dynamic data in any format other than a table. For example, use the list element to create form letters, one for each customer in a data set. Figure 8-11 shows an example PDF report that displays a series of form letters. Each letter is the same except for the recipient's name, which is dynamically derived from a customer name field.

Figure 8-11 The list element supports the creation of form letters using dynamic data

When you place a list on the page, the layout editor displays the structure that appears in Figure 8-12.

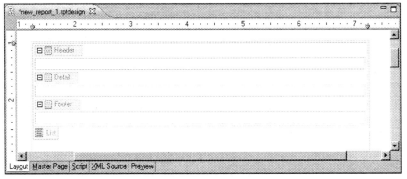

Figure 8-12 List structure

Deciding where to place elements in a list

Like the table, the list iterates through all the data rows that a data set returns to display data. Table 8-3 describes the three areas in a list.

Table 8-3 List area descriptions

List area	Description
Header	Elements that you place in Header appear once, at the beginning of the section. For example, display introductory information, such as a description of the report.
Detail	Elements that you place in Detail display dynamic data. The amount of data that appears is determined by the number of data rows that your data set returns. For example, print a letter for each customer in the data set.
Footer	Elements that you place in Footer appear once, at the end of the section. For example, display summary information, such as the number of records in the report.

Figure 8-13 shows a list layout that displays a form letter for each customer. The form letter is created using a text element that contains HTML formatting. The generated report displays the form letters that appear in Figure 8-11.

Figure 8-13 shows the most basic use of the list element. Typically, you use the list element to present data in more complex layouts. For example, you need a report that consists of many subreports. Each subreport goes to a single customer and consists of a cover letter, a summary account statement, and a detailed statement. To create this type of report, you define data sets that return each customer and the required account information, use grids and tables to create each section of the subreport, and place all the sections in a list element. For an example that shows the use of a list to organize subreports, see Chapter 16, "Building a Report That Contains Subreports."

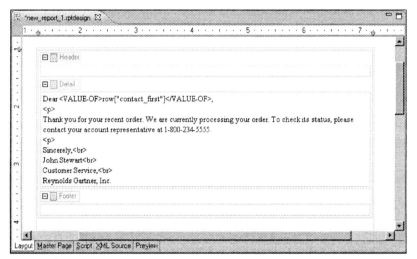

Figure 8-13   List element containing a text element in the detail area

Binding a list to a data set

Like the table, a list must be bound to a data set if the elements within the list need to access data set data. The binding principles and procedures for the table are the same for the list.

Placing report elements

You can place report elements in a page using one of the following techniques:

- Drag an element from the palette and drop it in the page.

- Use the Insert menu to place an element after a selected element. If none of the elements on the page are selected, the new element is added at the end.

- Drag a data set field from Data Explorer and drop it in a table, grid, or list. BIRT inserts a data element to display the contents of the data set field.

When you drag an element from the palette, two cursors appear in the layout editor. The arrow cursor tracks your mouse movement. The straight cursor, shown in Figure 8-14, moves to the left or bottom of an existing report element when you move the mouse pointer around on the page. Watch the straight cursor. It shows you where the element will be placed when you release the mouse button.

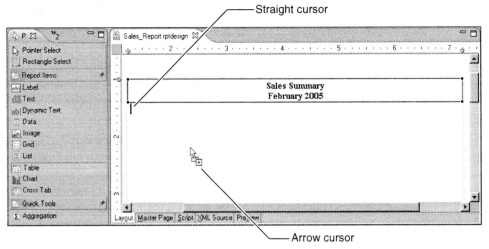

Figure 8-14   Straight cursor and arrow cursor indicate placement of an element

If you drop the element when the straight cursor is below an element, the new element appears on the next line, after the existing report element. Figure 8-15 shows the new element in the design.

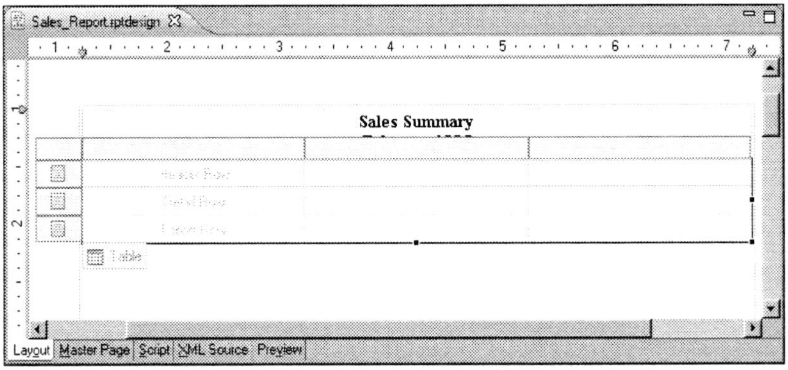

Figure 8-15   Inserted element placed beneath existing text element

Placing report elements side by side

The layout editor does not allow you to place report elements side by side directly on the page. For example, you cannot place two text elements, two tables, or a picture and a text element next to one another. The layout editor inserts the second element below the first one. To place multiple elements horizontally across the page, place them in a container element, such as a grid or table.

Inserting a data set field

Most of the information in a report is derived from data set fields. The report displays this data as it is stored in the data source. For example, in a customer orders report, you place customer name, order number, item, quantity, and price fields in the report.

To insert all the fields in a data set, choose Data Explorer, expand Data Sets, then drag the data set, and drop it in the page. BIRT Report Designer creates a table and the required column bindings, and places all the fields in the detail row of the table. The fields appear in the order in which they appear in the data set.

Often, however, you do not want to insert all the fields, or you want to insert them in a particular order. To place individual data fields, first insert a container element, typically a table, in which to place the fields. Although you can place data fields in a grid or directly on the page, you typically place fields in the detail row of a table or a list. If you place a field in a grid or in the page, only one value appears in the generated report. Unlike a table or list, the grid and page do not go through all the data rows in a data set.

To access and insert data set fields, choose Data Explorer, expand Data Sets, then select the data set. You can then drag data set fields from Data Explorer and drop them in the container, as shown in Figure 8-16.

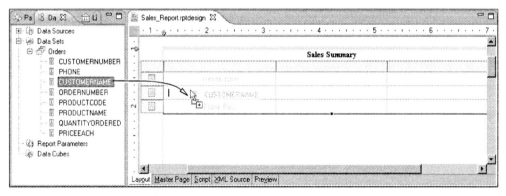

Figure 8-16   Use Data Explorer to insert data set fields in the report

Inserting a computed field

A computed field displays the result of an expression rather than stored data. For example, a database stores the prices of order items and the quantities that were ordered. To display the extended prices, you specify the following expression to calculate the values:

```
row["pricequote"] * row["quantity"]
```

Table 8-4 lists other examples of when to use computed fields and the types of expressions that you can specify.

Table 8-4   Examples of expressions in computed fields

Uses for computed fields	Examples of expressions

Display data that concatenates values from multiple fields	The following expression displays a customer's first and last names, which the data source stores in two fields:
	
	`row["firstname"] + " " + row["lastname"]`
	
	The following expression displays a full address by concatenating values from four fields in the data source:
	
	`row["address"] +", " + row["city"] + ", " +`
	`    row["state"] + " " + row["postalcode"]`

Display data that is calculated from multiple fields	The following expression calculates a customer's available credit: `row["creditlimit"] - row["balance"]`

Display data using a JavaScript or BIRT function	The following expression uses the JavaScript Date object to return the current date:
	
	`new Date( )`
	
	The following expression uses the BIRT DateTimeSpan.days( ) function to return the number of days between two dates:
	
	`DateTimeSpan.days(row["orderdate"],`
	`    row["shippeddate"])`

JavaScript is a case-sensitive language. You must type keywords, function names, and any other identifiers with the correct capitalization. You must, for example, type the Date( ) function as Date( ), not date( ) or DATE( ). If you need help constructing expressions with the correct syntax, choose objects, functions, and operators from the lower part of the expression builder. For more information about writing expressions or using the expression builder, see Chapter 13, "Writing Expressions."

You can create a computed field using either of the following techniques:

- Define the computed field in the data set.

- Define the computed field in the report layout.

The first technique is preferable because:

- You can test the results of the calculation by choosing Preview Results in the data set editor.

- The computed field is available to any table, list, or chart that uses the data set. It appears in the list of fields for that data set.

- BIRT Report Designer processes the computed values once, rather than multiple times, if the same computed field is used in multiple places in the report.

To create a computed field in the report layout, drag a data element from the palette, and drop it in the desired location. Then, in New Data Binding, create a column binding that defines the expression that returns the computed values. Figure 8-17 shows an example of a column binding that defines an expression, which uses the DateTimeSpan.days( ) function.

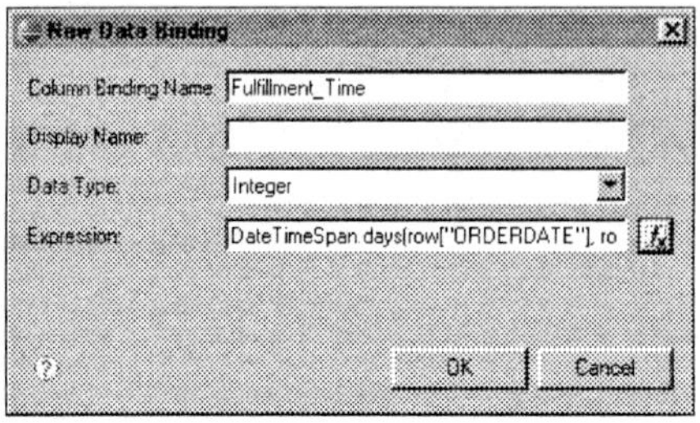

Figure 8-17   A column binding that defines an expression

If you insert the data element directly on the page or in a grid, and you want to write an expression that refers to a data set field, you must first bind the data element to the appropriate data set. On the other hand, if you insert the data element in a table or a list, the data element has access to the data set bound to the table or list.

Inserting an image

Images add visual appeal to reports. You can add a company logo and pictures of merchandise, and you can use icons instead of text labels. These images can originate from a file system, a web server, or a data source. Images are often used as decoration, but you can also use them as data. A product database, for example, might contain images of each item. If you create a report with product information, you can add product images to the report. Figure 8-18 shows a report that displays two types of images: a static image of a company logo, and dynamic images stored in a database.

BIRT supports the following types of image files: BMP, GIF, ICO, JFIF, JPE, JPEG, JPG, PNG, TIF, and TIFF. To display an image, insert the image element in your report. You have four choices when you insert an image. You can:

- Link the image from any location to the report.

- Link the image from the BIRT resource folder to the report. The resource folder is a central location for external files used by reports. Rather than link images from various locations, you may find it more convenient to store all image files in the resource folder because packaging files for deployment will be much easier.

- Embed the image in the report.

- Refer to the data set field that contains the images.

Use one of the first three methods to display a specific, or static, image. Typically, you display a static image once, so you insert the image directly on the report page, in a grid cell, or in the header row of a table. Use the fourth method to display a set of images returned by a data set. In this case, you typically want to display all the images in the data set field, so you insert the image element in the detail row of a table.

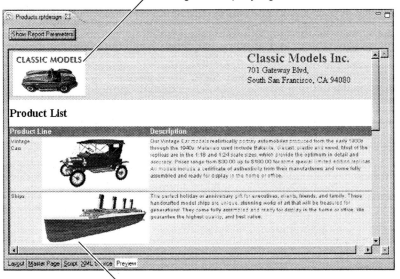

Figure 8-18   Report displaying two types of images

When displaying a static image, you need to decide whether to link or embed the image. Visually, there is no difference between a linked image and an embedded image. The difference is how changes to the image file affect what your report displays. If you link the image, any change you make to the original image file is reflected in the report. If you embed the image, changes to the original image file have no effect on the image that appears in the report. Use the guidelines in Table 8-5 to determine whether to link or embed an image in a report.

Table 8-5   Guidelines for linking and embedding images

When to link	When to embed
You expect to modify the original image, and you want the report to reflect future changes.	You expect to modify the original image, but you do not want the report to reflect future changes.
You do not expect to move or delete the original image file. Moving or deleting the image file breaks the link.	The original image file might be moved or deleted without your knowledge.

How to insert a linked image

1 Drag the image element from the palette, and drop it in the desired location on the page. Edit Image Item appears, as shown in Figure 8-19.

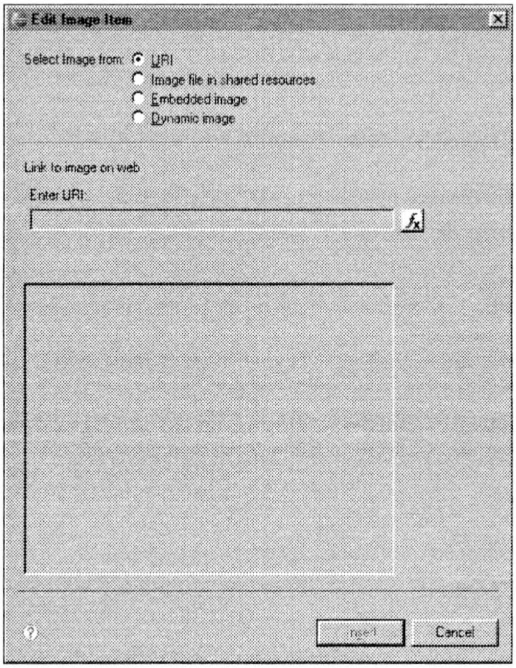

Figure 8-19   Edit Image Item dialog

2 To link to an image stored in the resource folder:

  1 In Select Image from, select Image file in shared resources.

  2 Choose Browse to find the image file in the designated resource folder.

  3 Select the image file, and choose OK.

  4 Choose Insert to insert the image in the report.

3 To link to images whose URIs are stored in a database, use the following procedure. The procedure assumes you have already created a data set that includes the field, which stores the URIs to the images.

  1 On Edit Image Item, in Select Image from, select URI.

  2 Under Enter URI, choose the expression builder button.

  3 In the expression builder, select the data set field that stores the locations of the images, then choose OK. Figure 8-20 shows an example of selecting a data set field named URL, which stores the URLs to images.

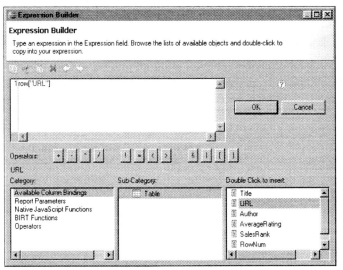

Figure 8-20   The expression builder showing a selected data set field that stores the URLs to images

Enter URI on Edit Image Item displays the expression that refers to the data set field.

4   Choose Insert to insert the image in the report.

4 To link to an image stored in any other location:

1   On Edit Image Item, in Select Image from, select URI.

2   Under Enter URI, choose the expression builder button.

3   In the expression builder, type the location of the image file. Enclose the URI in double quotation marks (" ").

The following expression is an example of a URL for a file in a remote location:

```
"http://mysite.com/images/companylogo.jpg"
```

The following expression is an example of a URI for a file that is on the local file system:

```
"file:///c:/myprojects/images/companylogo.jpg"
```

You would specify a local file system location only for testing in the early stages of report development. A deployed report cannot access resources on a local machine.

4   Choose Insert to insert the image in the report.

How to insert an embedded image

1 Drag the image element from the palette, and drop it in the desired location on the page.

2 On New Image Item, in Select Image from, select Embedded image. If you previously inserted images, New Image Item displays the names of those images, as shown in Figure 8-21.

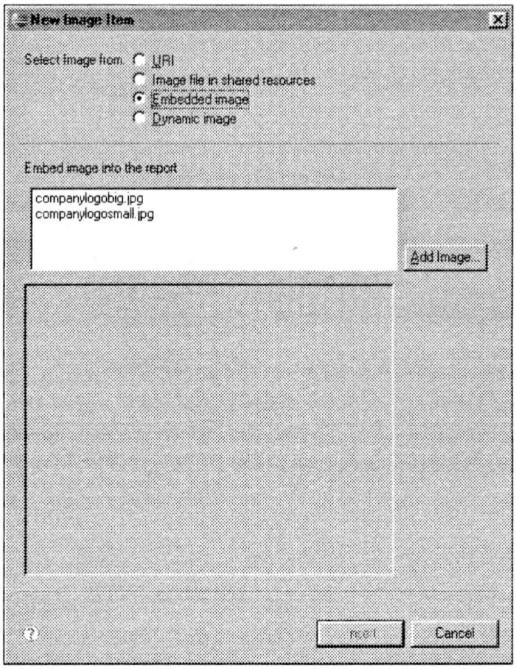

Figure 8-21 New Image Item showing embedded image names

3 To embed a new image, choose Add Image.

4 On Open Image File, find and select the image to embed, then choose Open. New Image Item displays the image.

5 Choose Insert. The image appears on the page.

How to insert images that are stored in a data source

1 In Data Explorer, create a data set that includes the image field.

2 In the layout editor, insert a table element on the page.

3 Bind the table to the data set in the following manner:

   1 Select the table and, in Property Editor, choose Binding.

   2 On the Binding page, in Data Set, choose the data set that contains the image field. BIRT creates a column binding for each field in the data set.

4 Drag the image element from the palette, and drop it in the detail row of the table.

5 On New Image Item, select Dynamic image.

6 Choose Select Image Data. Select Data Binding displays the column bindings available to the image element, as shown in Figure 8-22. The image element has access to all the column bindings defined for the table, its container.

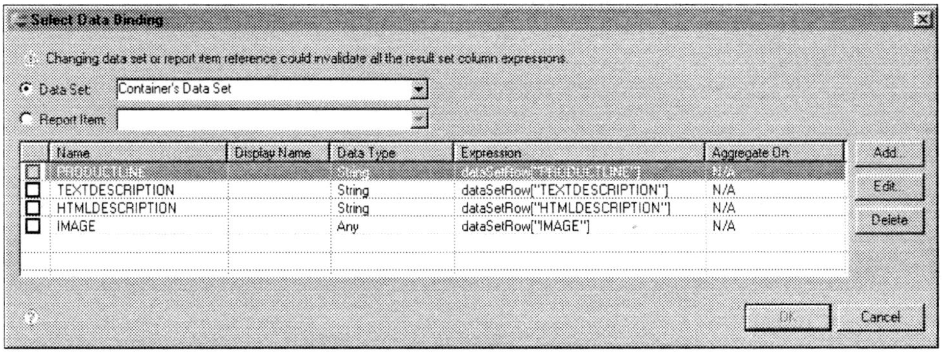

Figure 8-22   Select Data Binding showing column bindings

7 Select the column binding that references the image field by clicking the check box next to the column binding. Choose OK.

On New Image Item, under Enter dynamic image expression, an expression that refers to the selected column binding appears, as shown in Figure 8-23.

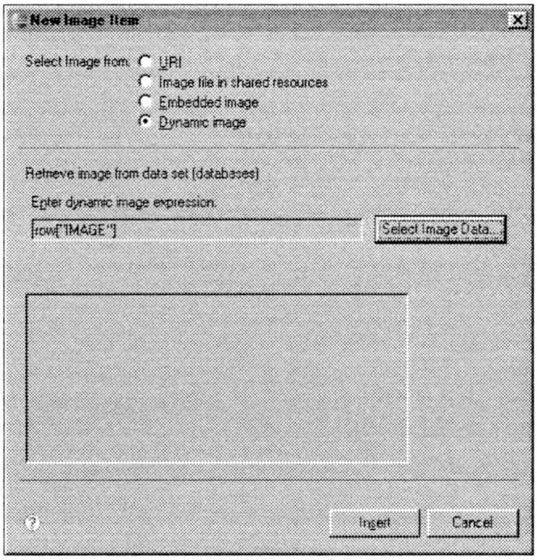

Figure 8-23   New Image Item showing the dynamic image expression

8 Choose Insert. The image element appears on the page in the layout editor. It shows an X. The actual images appear only when you preview the report.

Resizing an image

The image element displays an image at its actual size. If you cannot change the size of the original image, you can resize the image element in the report. Note, however, that images are designed to display optimally at a specific size. Resizing an image in the report typically results in the degradation of its appearance.

To resize an image, select the image element, then on Property Editor, select General. Specify a width and height for the image element. Typically, you want to resize an image so that its aspect ratio is maintained to avoid stretching the graphic out of proportion. To maintain an image's aspect ratio, specify the width and height as a percentage of the original size. For example, setting both the width and height to 80%, as shown in Figure 8-24, reduces the image size to 80% of the original size.

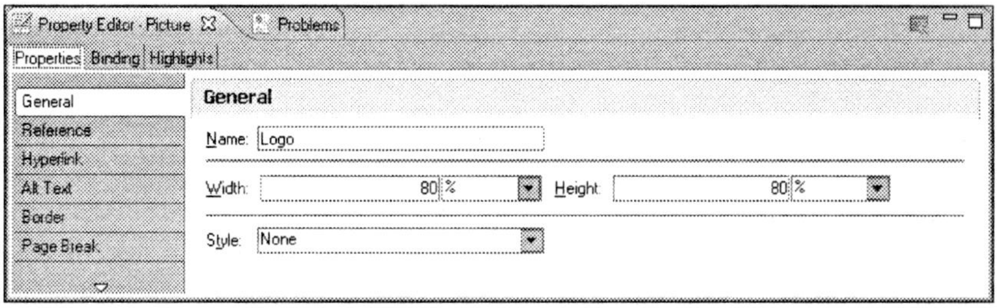

Figure 8-24   Setting the width and height of an image element

Providing a text alternative

A standard practice in HTML document design is to display a text alternative to an image. Sometimes, a document cannot access or display an image, or a user configures the browser to not display images. In these cases, rather than not display anything, the report should display a textual description of the missing image. The rule of thumb is that the text alternative should always describe the content of the image, but the description should also be short and succinct.

To specify a text alternative, select the image element, then on Property Editor, select Alt Text. Type the text you want to display in place of a missing image. For an image of a company logo, for example, type Company logo, as shown in Figure 8-25.

Figure 8-25   Providing a text alternative for an image

Displaying Text

A report typically presents most of its information in textual format. In fact, we can safely assume that all reports contain text. Even if a report consists primarily of charts or pictures, it still uses text to label charts, display titles, describe the charts or pictures, and so on.

Textual information can be

- Static text, which is text that you type in the report. You use static text in a report title, column headings, or to write a summary about the report.

- String, number, or date values that are derived from data set fields. The majority of information in a report typically comes from data set fields.

- String, number, or date values that are derived from JavaScript expressions. Reports often contain information that is calculated, such as the report-generation date, or the number of records in a report table.

Textual information can be as short as a single word, or span multiple paragraphs, even pages. BIRT Report Designer handles all lengths of text elegantly. When you insert a textual element, you do not need to worry about specifying an element size that is large enough to display all the text. BIRT Report Designer automatically adjusts the size of elements to accommodate their contents.

Types of textual elements

To support the wide variety of text that a report can display, BIRT Report Designer provides a rich set of textual elements. Table 9-1 describes these elements, and Figure 9-1 shows a report that displays the different types of textual information.

Table 9-1   Descriptions of BIRT textual elements

Textual element	Use to
Data	Display dynamic values that are derived from data set fields, computed fields, or JavaScript expressions. You can add literal, or static, text to the dynamic data. Doing so, however, changes the entire expression to a string, and, if the dynamic value is a number or a date, you can no longer format it as a number or a date.
Dynamic text	Display memo or Character Large Object (CLOB) data from a data set field. This type of data typically consists of large amounts of text.
Label	Display a small amount of static text, such as a report title or column heading.
Text	Display the following types of user-specified text: ■ Multiline text ■ HTML text that contains multiple style formats, for example, text with paragraph styles, such as bulleted lists and numbered lists, or text formats, such as bold or italics ■ Text that combines static text with dynamic values, such as a form letter that includes customer names and addresses that are stored in a data source ■ Interactive content driven by code, which you specify using the <script> tag

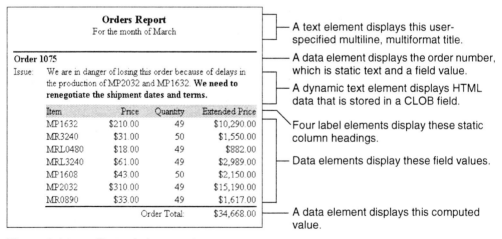

Figure 9-1   Textual elements in a report

Figure 9-2 shows how the report in the previous illustration appears in the layout editor.

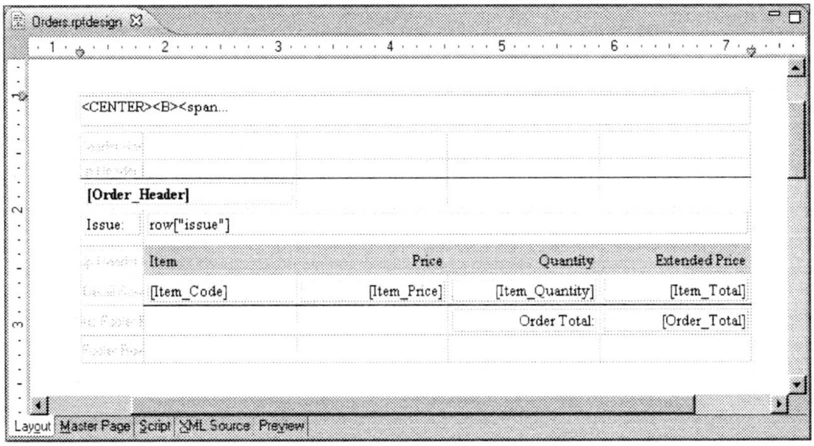

Figure 9-2   Textual elements in the report design

Deciding which textual element to use

In many cases, you can use several textual elements to accomplish the same task. For example, you can use a label element, a text element, or a data element to display a static report title like the one in the following example:

```
Sales Report for Quarter One, 2007
```

When you start applying complex formats or combining static text with dynamic data, you need to use the appropriate textual element to achieve the best results. This section provides guidelines and examples for determining the best textual element to use for different purposes. When you understand the differences among the textual elements, read the rest of this chapter for details about using each element.

Formatting words differently in a static string

The previous example showed how you can use a label, text, or data element to display a static title. If, however, you want to format words in the title differently, as shown in the following example, you can accomplish this task only by using the text element. With the label and data elements, formats apply to the entire string.

```
Sales Report for Quarter One, 2007
```

Combining static text with dynamic data

To display the following text, where Order Total: is static text, and the number is a dynamic, or calculated, value, you can use a text element or a data element:

```
Order Total: 74050
```

If, however, you want to format the dynamic value so that it appears as a currency value with comma separators and decimal places, as shown in the following example, use the text element. The text element enables you to format different parts of text differently.

```
Order Total: $74,050.00
```

Alternatively, you can use a label element and a data element to display the preceding text. Use the label element to display the static text portion, Order Total:, and the data element to display the dynamic portion, as shown in Figure 9-3. When the data element consists of just the number value, you can use the Format Number property to format the number.

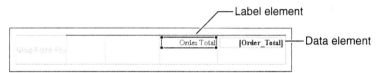

Figure 9-3   Label and data elements in the layout editor

Figure 9-4 shows the output of the preceding report design.

Order Total $59,664.00

Figure 9-4   Label and data elements in a report

The difference between using the label and data elements and using the text element is how you control the space between the static text and the dynamic value. Using the text element, you can easily specify one character space between the two. If you use the label and data elements, the spacing is determined by various factors, such as text alignment and column widths. In the previous example, the label element and data element are both right-aligned.

Displaying dynamic data that contains HTML tags

Many data sources store large amounts of text that contain internal formatting, as shown in the following example. Data like this is typically stored in CLOB fields.

```
<html><b>Customer log 04/12/05 13:45:00</b><br>Customer called
to enquire about order. He says order 2673-9890 was supposed
to arrive on 04/10/05. Records show that the order is on
backorder. Customer says he received no notification about the
status of his order. He wants to cancel the order if it is not
shipped by 04/15/05.<br><i>Action Items:</i><ul><li>Call
distributor about delivery status. <li>Send email to customer
about delivery status.</ul></html>
```

To display the text with the specified HTML formats, you can use the text element or the dynamic text element. If, however, you want to combine static text with dynamic text, use the text element. If you add static text to the dynamic text element, for example, "Customer Issue " + row["Issue"], the dynamic data appears in the report exactly as it appears in the field, including the HTML tags.

Figure 9-5 shows how the text element displays the static text, Customer Issue:, with the dynamic text. The text element converts the HTML tags to formatting and layout attributes. For example, text within the <b> and </b> tags appears in bold.

Static text
Customer Issue: **Customer log 04/12/05 13:45:00**
Customer called to enquire about order. He says order 2673-9890 was supposed to arrive on 04/10/05. Records show that the order is on backorder. Customer says he received no notification about the status of his order. He wants to cancel the order if it is not shipped by 04/15/05.
Action Items:
• Call distributor about delivery status.
• Send email to customer about delivery status.
Dynamic text

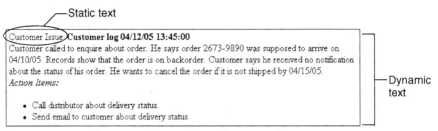

Figure 9-5 Static and dynamic text in a text element

Figure 9-6 shows how the dynamic text element displays the text when you add static text to the dynamic text. The HTML tags appear because the content is converted to string type.

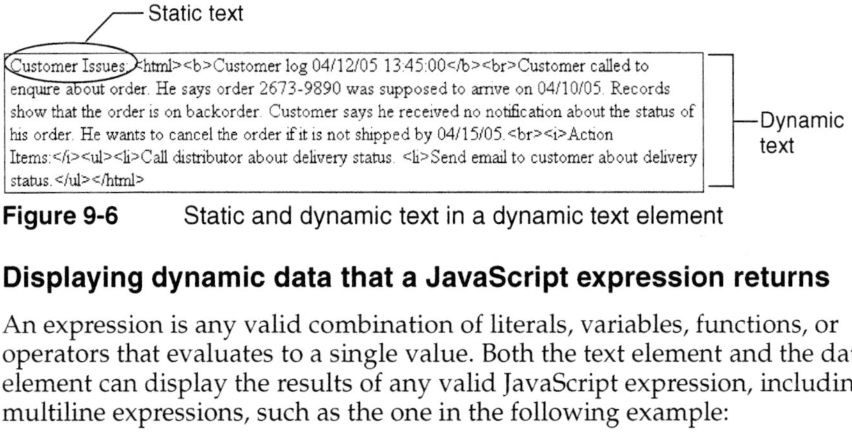

Static text
Customer Issues: <html><b>Customer log 04/12/05 13:45:00</b>
Customer called to enquire about order. He says order 2673-9890 was supposed to arrive on 04/10/05. Records show that the order is on backorder. Customer says he received no notification about the status of his order. He wants to cancel the order if it is not shipped by 04/15/05.
<i>Action Items:</i><ul><li>Call distributor about delivery status. <li>Send email to customer about delivery status.</ul></html>
Dynamic text

Figure 9-6 Static and dynamic text in a dynamic text element

Displaying dynamic data that a JavaScript expression returns

An expression is any valid combination of literals, variables, functions, or operators that evaluates to a single value. Both the text element and the data element can display the results of any valid JavaScript expression, including multiline expressions, such as the one in the following example:

```
if (row["creditScore"] > 700){
   displayString = "Your loan application has been approved."
   }
else{
   displayString = "Your loan application has been denied."
   }
```

The main difference is that it is easier to edit JavaScript expressions in a data element. When you double-click a data element, its value expression appears in the expression builder, which uses color for keywords and provides easy access to JavaScript functions and operators.

When you use a text element, its contents appear in the text editor. The first time that you specify a dynamic value in the text editor, the expression builder appears to help you construct the expression. When the expression is inserted in the text editor, you cannot relaunch the expression builder to edit the expression. You can edit the expression in the text editor, but the text editor does not provide color coding or access to JavaScript functions or operators.

Using a dynamic text element

You can place a dynamic text element directly on the page or in any of the container elements. Typically, you place it in a table or a list because the dynamic text element displays CLOB data from a data set field, and only the table and list elements iterate through the rows in a data set.

Unlike most data set fields, you do not simply drag a CLOB field from Data Explorer and drop it in the table or list. You can, but if the CLOB data is HTML text, the data element displays the contents of the field exactly as it appears, including the HTML tags. The dynamic text element, on the other hand, is designed to correctly display data that is stored as HTML.

As with any element that displays data set data, you must create a column binding that refers to the data set field. The column binding, in turn, needs access to the data set. If you insert the dynamic text element in a table or list that is already bound to a data set, the column binding has access to the data set. If the table or list is not bound with a data set, you must first bind the table or list with the data set.

How to use a dynamic text element

1 Make sure the table or list in which you want to insert a dynamic text element is bound to the data set that contains the CLOB data. To verify or create the data set binding, perform the following tasks:

   1 Select the table or list.

   2 Choose Binding on Property Editor.

   3 On the Binding page, in Data Set, select the data set. BIRT creates a column binding for each field in the data set.

2 Drag the dynamic text element from the palette, and drop it in the table or list.

3 On the expression builder, choose Available Column Bindings, choose the table under Sub-Category, then double-click the column binding that refers to the data set field that contains the CLOB data. Choose OK to save the expression.

4 In the layout editor, select the dynamic text element. Property Editor displays the properties of the dynamic text element.

5 Choose General properties, then choose one of the following values for Content type:

* Auto

  Choose this value if you do not know the format of the field contents. If the content contains HTML tags, BIRT Report Designer interprets it as HTML and displays the content correctly. If the content is plain text, BIRT Report Designer displays it correctly also.

* HTML

  Choose this value if you know that all the field contents are HTML.

* Plain

  Choose this value to display the field contents exactly as they appear in the data source. If the content contains HTML tags, BIRT Report Designer displays the HTML tags.

6 Preview the report to verify that the report displays the text from the specified data set field.

Using a label element

You can place a label directly on the page or in any of the container elements. When you insert a label, the layout editor displays an empty label with a cursor in it, as shown in Figure 9-7.

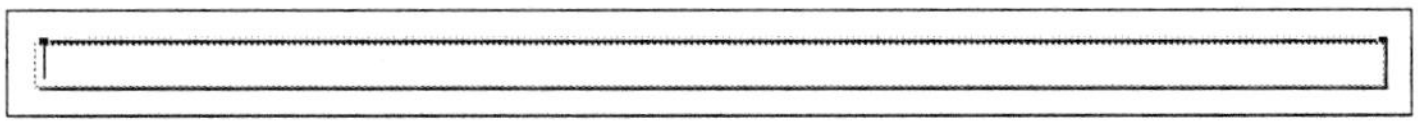

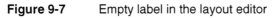

Figure 9-7 Empty label in the layout editor

Start typing the text that you want to display, then press Enter when you finish.

Figure 9-8 shows the result.

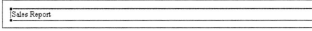

Figure 9-8 Label text in the layout editor

You can edit the text in the label by double-clicking the label or by selecting the label and pressing F2, then typing the new text.

You can change the format of the text by selecting the label, then setting the desired style properties in the property editor. You can, for example, specify a different font, text alignment, size, or color. These properties apply to the entire text string. You cannot, for example, set one word to bold and another to italic. If variable formats are a requirement, use a text element instead.

Using a text element

You can place a text element directly on the page or in any of the container elements. When you insert a text element, the layout editor displays the text editor, as shown in Figure 9-9.

First, decide what type of text you want to create. You have two choices:

- Plain text

- HTML

HTML enables you to create highly formatted text using HTML tags or CSS properties. The text can contain placeholders for data set field values and expressions, which enable you to mix static text with dynamically generated values. Plain text, on the other hand, cannot contain internal formatting or dynamic values. A text element that is set to plain text functions like a label element.

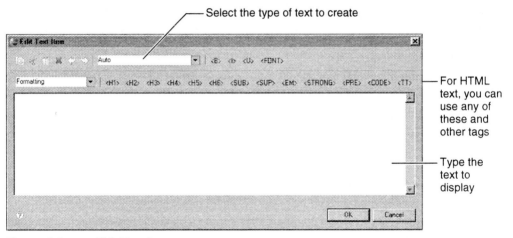

Figure 9-9   Edit Text Item

After you select the text type, type the text that you want to display in the report. If you selected HTML, you can use HTML tags or CSS properties in the text. You can type the tags manually, or you can insert the commonly used HTML tags that the text editor provides.

The following sections provide a few examples of text you can create using a text element of HTML type.

Applying multiple style formats in a text element

Using HTML, you can format individual words and lines in a text element. The following example shows two lines with different font sizes and styles.

Text that you supply:

```
<CENTER><B><span style="font-size: larger">
Shipped Orders Report
</B></span><BR>
<FONT size="small">For the month of March</FONT></CENTER>
```

Output:

Shipped Orders Report
For the month of March

Combining a JavaScript expression with static text in a text element

BIRT Report Designer provides a useful tag, VALUE-OF, which you can use to insert a dynamic value in a text element. Using the VALUE-OF tag, you can insert any JavaScript expression.

The following example shows static text combined with a value that a JavaScript function returns.

Text that you supply:

```
Report generated on <VALUE-OF>new Date()</VALUE-OF>
```

Output:

```
Report generated on Jan 19, 2006 12:30 PM
```

The following example shows static text combined with a conditional expression and a field value expression.

Text that you supply:

```
Dear <VALUE-OF>row["Sex"] == "M" ? "Mr." : "Ms."</VALUE-OF>
    <VALUE-OF>row["Name"]</VALUE-OF>,
```

Output:

```
Dear Mr. Scott Johnson,
Dear Ms. Ella Parker,
```

As the example shows, a conditional expression can have one of two values based on a condition. The syntax for this conditional expression is

```
condition ? value1 : value2
```

If the condition is true, the expression has the value of value1; otherwise, it has the value of value2.

Alternatively, you can use an if...else statement within the VALUE-OF tag. The following text displays the same results as the preceding conditional expression:

```
Dear <VALUE-OF>if(row["Sex"] == "M"){
Title = "Mr."
}
else{
Title = "Ms."
}</VALUE-OF>
<VALUE-OF>row["Name"]</VALUE-OF>,
```

Combining a value from a data set field with static text in a text element

The following example shows how to use the VALUE-OF tag to insert dynamic values that data set fields return.

Text that you supply:

```
Dear <VALUE-OF>row["contact_firstname"]</VALUE-OF>,
<p>
Thank you for your recent order. Order <VALUE-OF>
    row["orderID"]</VALUE-OF> will be shipped by <VALUE-OF>
    row["shipByDate"]</VALUE-OF>.
```

Output:

```
Dear Bob,

Thank you for your recent order. Order 1115 will be shipped by
Apr 17, 2005 12:00AM.
```

You can display field values in a text element only if the following two requirements are met:

- The text element has access to the data set that contains the fields.

  - If you place the text element directly on the page, you must bind the text element to the data set that contains the field value. To do so, select the text element, choose the Binding tab in the property editor, then select the data set to which to bind. Placing the text element directly on the page, however, displays only one occurrence.

  - If you place the text element in the detail row of a table or a list to display all values of a data set field, bind the table or list to the data set.

- A column binding is created for each data set field. The column binding refers to the data set field. The VALUE-OF tag, in turn, refers to the column binding.

Formatting dynamic values in a text element

The previous examples show how to use the VALUE-OF tag to insert dynamic values that a JavaScript function or a field returns. Sometimes the returned values are not in the format that you want. You can reformat the values using the format attribute, as shown in the following example.

Text that you supply:

```
<VALUE-OF format="MM-dd-yy">new Date()</VALUE-OF><br>
<VALUE-OF format="$#,###.00">row["orderTotal"]</VALUE-OF><br>
<VALUE-OF format="(@@@) @@@-@@@@">row["phone"]</VALUE-OF>
```

Output:

```
04-17-05
$321,000.00
(415) 123-5555
```

The format pattern must be enclosed in quotation marks. You can use any format pattern that the Format Number, Format DateTime, and Format String properties support. For information about these properties, see Chapter 10, "Formatting Report Content."

Displaying data set field values that are stored as HTML text

Sometimes values in a data set field contain HTML text. If you insert such a field in a report, BIRT Report Designer displays the content of the field exactly as it appears in the data source, including the HTML tags.

To display the text with its intended formatting, use a text element or a dynamic text element instead of a data element. As described earlier in this chapter, the text element enables you to add static text to the dynamic text, whereas the dynamic text element displays all the HTML tags if you add static text.

To use the text element, select HTML as the text type, then use the VALUE-OF tag to insert the value of the field, and set the format attribute to HTML, as shown in the following example.

Text that you supply:

```
Notes: <VALUE-OF format="html">row["CustomerNotes"]</VALUE-OF>
```

Formatting Report Content

Formatting is what you do to make a report visually appealing and effective. You format a report, for example, to highlight certain data, change the display of dates, numbers, or currency values, adjust the spacing between report elements, or display data based on a specified condition or output format.

BIRT Report Designer provides many options for customizing the appearance of report elements that you place in a report. Using various formatting properties, you can change the alignment, color, font, size, and other properties of these report elements. You also can add background colors, draw borders around elements, and so on.

If you are familiar with CSS, you can apply your knowledge of CSS properties because BIRT follows the CSS specification as closely as possible. Many of the formatting properties that you see in BIRT Report Designer are the same as CSS formatting properties.

The formatting options are available through the following views:

- Property Editor. This view organizes commonly used properties by functional categories. The properties that appear vary depending on which report element you are formatting. Figure 10-1 shows some of the categories of properties that are available through Property Editor.

- Properties. This view shows a list of the properties that you can set for an element, as shown in Figure 10-2. This view also shows more complex properties that are not available in Property Editor. The default application window layout does not display the Properties view. To display it, choose Window→Show View→Properties.

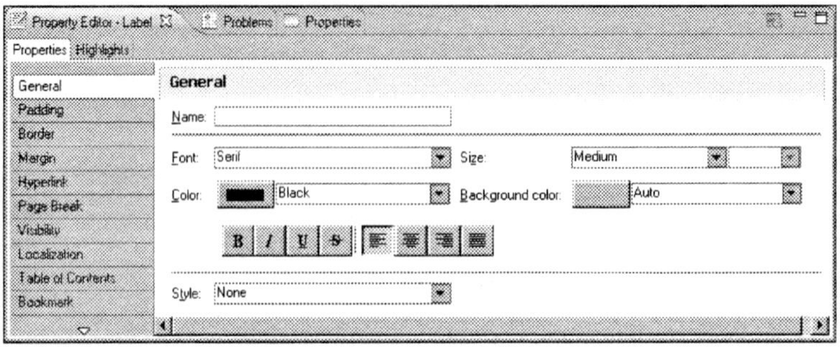

Figure 10-1   Property Editor showing categories of properties for a label element

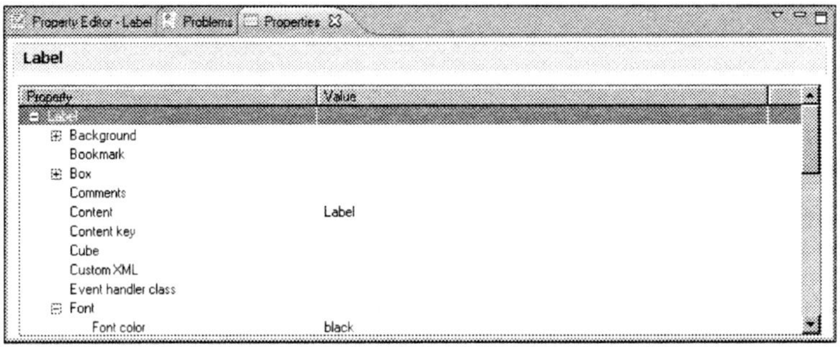

Figure 10-2   Properties view showing the properties for a label element

Formatting data

You format the data in a report element by selecting the element, then setting property values using Property Editor or the Properties view. If you apply a format using Property Editor, your format choices appear in the Properties view. Similarly, if you update a format using the Properties view, the change is reflected in Property Editor.

You can customize how data appears by modifying the following settings:

- Formats of numbers, text, dates, and times

  BIRT Report Designer provides common format styles in which to display numbers, currency, or date values. If you do not choose a format, BIRT Report Designer displays the data as it appears in the data source. If you want to use some combination of formatting that these styles do not provide, you can create a custom format.

- Font typeface, point size, and color

  When choosing fonts, remember that for the report user to view the report with the fonts that you choose, the fonts must be installed on the user's system. If your report will be distributed widely, select default fonts that are installed on all systems. You specify font attributes by setting the font properties in the General category of Property Editor.

- Text style as bold, italic, underline, or strike through

  These settings are available under the General category of Property Editor.

- Text justification as left, center, right, or justified

  These settings are available under the General category of Property Editor.

Formatting numeric data

You can apply number formats only to decimal, float, or integer data types. You can, for example, display integer-type numbers with decimal values, in scientific notation, or with a currency symbol.

Number formats have no effect on numbers that are string type. For example, a Customer_ID field can be defined as string type and display number values, such as 325. Number formats have no effect on these values.

You can display numeric data using either a text element or a data element, depending on what you want to accomplish. When you drag a data set field from Data Explorer and drop it on the report page in the layout editor, BIRT Report Designer automatically creates a data element to display the values of the data set field. The procedure for formatting data differs for a text element and a data element, as described in the following sections.

Formatting numeric data in a data element

You specify the format of numeric data in a data element by setting the data element's Format Number property, as shown in Figure 10-3.

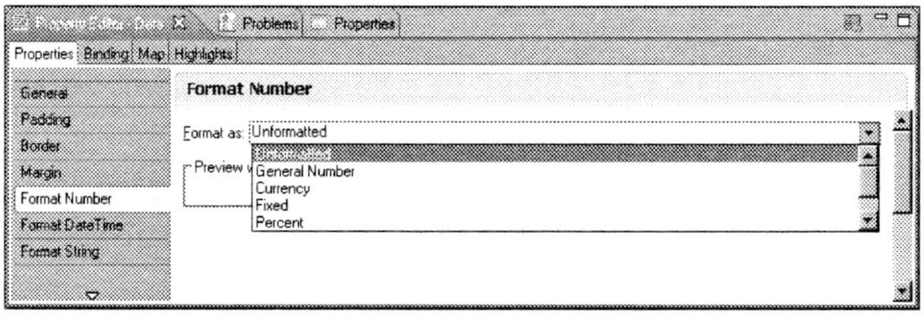

Figure 10-3   Format Number property values

Table 10-1 lists the types of number formats that you can choose and provides examples of how the formatted data appears.

Table 10-1   Examples of number formats

Format type	Example of data display
General Number	3000
Currency	$3,000.00

(continues)

Table 10-1 Examples of number formats *(continued)*

Format type	Example of data display
Fixed	3000.00
Percent	300000.00%
Scientific	3.00E03

You can also define your own formats. You can, for example, specify the number of digits after the decimal or add literal characters to the numbers. To define a custom format, you use special symbols to construct a format pattern. BIRT Report Designer supports the Java numeric formatting that is defined by the DecimalFormat class. For details about the supported formatting symbols, see the Javadoc for DecimalFormat.

Table 10-2 shows examples of custom format patterns and their effects on numeric data.

Table 10-2 Results of custom number format patterns

Format pattern	Data in the data set	Results of formatting
0000.00	12.5 124.5 1240.553	0012.50 0124.50 1240.55
#.000	100 100.25 100.2567	100.000 100.250 100.257
$#,###	2000.00 20000.00	$2,000 $20,000
ID #	15	ID 15

Formatting numeric data in a text element

When you insert dynamic data in a text element, you use the VALUE-OF tag. To format the dynamic data, include, within the VALUE-OF tag, a format attribute that specifies which format you want, as shown in the following examples. You must enclose the format value in double quotation marks (" ").

```
<VALUE-OF format="$#,###.00">row["orderTotal"]</VALUE-OF>
<VALUE-OF format="#.000">row["unitTotal"]</VALUE-OF>
```

You can use any format pattern that the Format Number property supports, as described in the preceding section.

Formatting date-and-time data

You can display date-and-time data in different formats. You can display dates and times in short, medium, or long formats. If the report runs on a machine that supports a different locale, the date data appears in the locale-appropriate format.

You can display date-and-time data using either a text element or a data element, depending on what you want to accomplish. When you drag a data set field from Data Explorer and drop it on the report page in the layout editor, BIRT Report Designer automatically creates a data element to display the values of the data set field. The procedure for formatting data differs for a text element and a data element, and is described in the following sections.

Formatting date-and-time data in a data element

You specify the format for date-and-time data in a data element by setting the element's Format DateTime property. As Figure 10-4 shows, BIRT Report Designer provides many common date-and-time formats from which to choose.

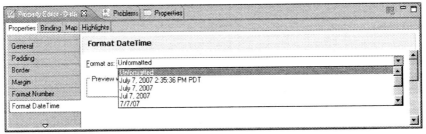

Figure 10-4   Format DateTime property values

You can also define your own date-and-time formats. You can, for example, specify two-digit months, use two digits for the year, or add the day of the week. To define a custom format, you use special symbols to construct a format pattern. BIRT Report Designer supports the Java formatting that is defined by the SimpleDateFormat class. For details about the supported formatting symbols, see the Javadoc for SimpleDateFormat.

Table 10-3 shows examples of custom format patterns and their effects on a date that is stored as 4/15/2005 in the data source.

Table 10-3   Results of custom date formats

Format pattern	Results of formatting
MM-dd-yy	04-15-05
E, M/d/yyyy	Fri, 4/15/2005
EEEE, M/dd/yy	Friday, 4/15/05
MMM d	Apr 15
MMMM	April
yyyy	2005
W	3 (the week in the month)
w	14 (the week in the year)
D	105 (the day in the year)

Specify custom formats if your report will be viewed in only one locale because custom formats always display date or time data in the specified format. For example, if you use the format MM-dd-yy, the date January 10, 2006, always appears as 01-10-06, regardless of the locale in which the report is viewed. For locales in which dates are displayed in date-month-year format, a 01-10-06 date is interpreted as October 1, 2006.

Formatting date-and-time data in a text element

When you insert dynamic data in a text element, you use the VALUE-OF tag. To format the dynamic data, include, within the VALUE-OF tag, a format attribute that specifies the format that you want, as shown in the following examples:

```
<VALUE-OF format="MM-dd-yyyy">row["orderDate"]</VALUE-OF>
<VALUE-OF format="M/d/yy hh:mm:ss">new Date()</VALUE-OF>
```

You can use any format pattern that the Format DateTime property supports, as described in the preceding section.

Formatting string data

Typically, you format string data to fix inconsistent or poorly formatted data that is retrieved from the data source. The data source, for example, can store names with inconsistent capitalization or phone numbers in 1234567890 format. To fix these problems, specify the desired string format.

You can display string data using either a text element or a data element, depending on what you want to accomplish. When you drag a data set field from Data Explorer and drop it on the report page in the layout editor, BIRT Report Designer automatically creates a data element to display the values of the data set field. The procedure for formatting data differs for a text element and a data element, and is described in the following sections.

Formatting text in a data element

You specify a text format by setting the data element's Format String property, as shown in Figure 10-5.

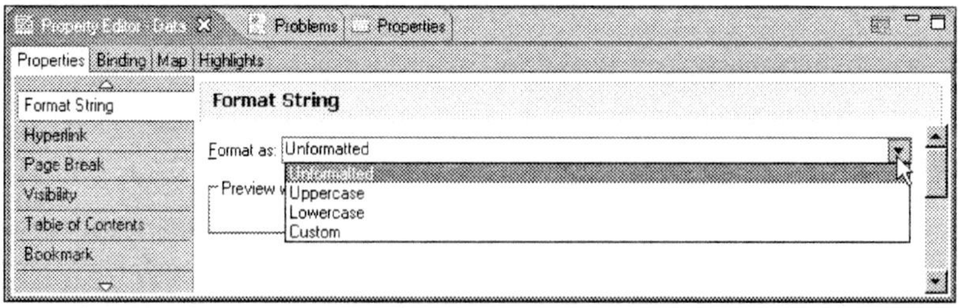

Figure 10-5   Format String property values

Table 10-4 lists the types of string formats that you can choose and provides examples of how the formatted data appears.

Table 10-4   Examples of string formats

Format type	Description	Example of data display
Lowercase	Converts the string to lowercase	smith
Uppercase	Converts the string to uppercase	SMITH

You can also define custom string formats using special symbols. Table 10-5 describes these symbols.

Table 10-5   Symbols for defining custom string formats

Symbol	Description
@	Character placeholder. Each @ character displays a character in the string. If the string has fewer characters than the number of @ symbols that appear in the format pattern, spaces appear. Placeholders are filled from right to left, unless you specify an exclamation point (!) at the beginning of the format pattern. See Table 10-6 for examples.
&	Same as @, except that if the string has fewer characters, spaces do not appear. See Table 10-6 for examples.
!	Specifies that placeholders are to be filled from left to right. See Table 10-6 for examples.
>	Converts string characters to uppercase.
<	Converts string characters to lowercase.

Table 10-6 shows examples of custom format patterns and their effects on text data.

Table 10-6   Results of custom string format patterns

Format pattern	Data in data source	Results of formatting
(@@@) @@@-@@@@	6175551007 5551007	(617) 555-1007 ( ) 555-1007
(&&&) &&&-&&&&	6175551007 5551007	(617) 555-1007 () 555-1007
!(@@@) @@@-@@@@	6175551007 5551007	(617) 555-1007 (555) 100-7
!(&&&) &&&-&&&&	6175551007 5551007	(617) 555-1007 (555) 100-7
!(@@@) @@@-@@@@ + ext 9	5551007	(555) 100-7 + ext 9
!(&&&) &&&-&&&& + ext 9	5551007	(555) 100-7 + ext 9
>&&&-&&&&&-&&	D1234567xy	D12-34567-XY
<&&&-&&&&&-&&	D1234567xy	d12-34567-xy

Formatting text data in a text element

When you insert dynamic data in a text element, you use the VALUE-OF tag. To format the dynamic data, include, within the VALUE-OF tag, a format attribute that specifies the format that you want, as shown in the following examples:

```
<VALUE-OF format="(@@@) @@@-@@@@">row["phone"]</VALUE-OF>
<VALUE-OF format=">">row["custName"]</VALUE-OF>
```

You can use any format pattern that the Format String property supports, as described in the preceding section.

Formatting with styles

You can customize the appearance of each report element by setting its visual properties using Property Editor. Depending on the number of elements that you want to format, this task can take a while, especially if you often change the appearance of elements. BIRT Report Designer solves this problem by providing a style mechanism that is similar to HTML CSS and Microsoft Word styles.

A style is a named set of formatting characteristics that you can apply to a report element to change its appearance quickly. When you apply a style, you apply an entire group of formats—font size, color, alignment, borders, and so on—in one step. For example, you want to format all the column headings in your report as Arial, small, blue, and center-aligned. Instead of formatting the column heading in four separate steps, you can achieve the same result in one step by applying a style.

Using styles, you can:

- Create a consistent appearance for similar report elements.

- Update the appearance of a set of report elements by changing a single style.

When you first create a report, it does not contain any styles. The report displays elements with default formatting values. To use styles to format report elements, you must first create the styles. If you have designed web pages and you use a CSS file that defines styles, you can reuse those styles in your reports.

Creating styles

BIRT Report Designer styles are a hybrid of CSS and Microsoft Word styles. You can:

- Create a named style, and apply it to a report element. For example, you can create a style called ColumnHeading, then apply the style to all column headings in your report. This approach is like using Microsoft styles in that you create a Body Text style then apply this style to selected paragraphs.

- Apply style properties to predefined style names, or selectors. These predefined style names correspond to the different types of report elements. For example, you can apply style properties to a style called table-header, and all table headers in your report will be formatted accordingly. This technique is like CSS in that you associate styles with HTML elements, such as <H1> or <P>.

You will find it useful to create styles using both techniques. The first technique is useful for creating specialized styles for different types of text content, such as important notes, offer notices, or copyrights. The second technique provides a powerful way to define style properties once for a container element and have those properties cascade to the container's contents. For example, if you want to apply a default format, such as the Arial typeface, to all elements in a report, you can apply the format to the predefined style name, report. After doing so, all text in the report appears in Arial.

Table 10-7 lists the predefined style names for which you can set style properties.

Table 10-7   Predefined style names

Predefined style name	Applies style properties to...
chart	All elements in a chart. Charts contain many elements that you can format individually in the chart builder. You typically use the predefined chart style to set general formats that you want to apply to all charts, such as boxes around all charts, or a particular font family to use as the default.
crosstab	All parts of a cross tab, and all elements in a cross tab.
crosstab-cell	Cross tab cells, including elements within them.
crosstab detail	The part of the cross tab that displays the aggregated values.
crosstab-header	The part of the cross tab that displays the row and column headings.
data	Data elements.
grid	Grids, including elements within them. For example, if you specify a background color, the entire grid displays the specified color. If you specify a font style, all textual elements in the grid display in the specified font style.
image	Image elements.
label	Label elements.
list	Lists, including elements in them.

(continues)

Table 10-7 Predefined style names *(continued)*

Predefined style name	Applies style properties to...
list-group-footer-n	A specific group footer (1–9) in lists that contain groups of data.
list-group-header-n	A specific group header (1–9) in lists that contains groups of data.
list-detail	Detail area of lists, including elements in that area.
list-footer	Footer area of lists, including elements in that area.
list-header	Header area of lists, including elements in that area.
page	The report's master page.
report	All elements in the report. The report is the topmost container. Any formatting you set for this style applies to everything in a report.
table	Tables, including elements in them.
table-detail	Detail rows of tables, including elements in the rows.
table-detail-cell	Cells in the detail rows of tables.
table-footer	Footer rows of tables, including elements in the rows.
table-footer-cell	Cells in the footer rows of tables.
table-group-footer-n	A specific group footer (1–9) in tables that contains groups of data.
table-group-footer-cell	Cells in the group footer rows of tables.
table-group-header-n	A specific group header row (1–9) in tables that contain groups of data.
table-group-header-cell	Cells in the group header row of tables.
table-header	Header rows of tables, including elements in the rows.
table-header cell	Cells in the header rows of tables.
text	Text elements.
TOC-level-n	A specific level (0–9) in a hierarchical table of contents. For reports that contain groups of data, BIRT automatically creates a table of contents, which users can use to jump to different parts of the report.

If you create styles using the cascading model, it is best to design a set of styles from the top-level container down. At the top level, define style properties that you want to apply to all elements, then add style properties at each successive level. For example, you can:

■ Use the report style to specify a default font family and font size for the entire report.

- Use the table style to specify a default font size and text alignment for all data in the table.

- Use the table-header style to specify bold font and a background color for table headers.

Any element that you insert in a table header inherits the style properties from the report, table, and table-header styles. Any element that you insert in a table detail inherits style properties from the report and table styles. Figure 10-6 shows the results of applying the cascading concept to styles.

Not all style properties cascade. For example, the background color, margins, borders, and padding properties do not cascade from a container to the elements within it. In these cases, cascading the style does not make good design sense. For example, it does not make sense to cascade border values because designs typically use different border values for different elements. A design might use a border around a table without using borders around rows, columns, cells, or elements in cells.

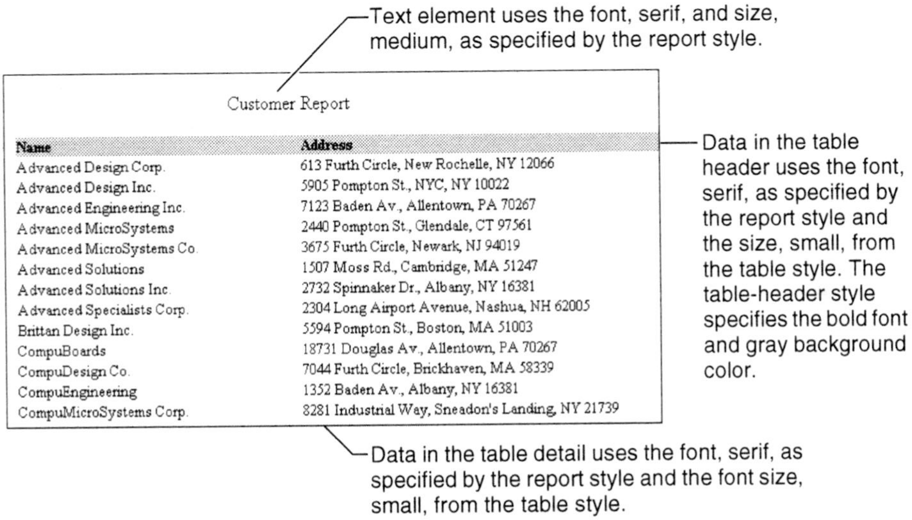

Figure 10-6   Report that shows the use of cascading styles

For details about each property, including the cascading rule, see the ROM Styles specification document, which is available at the following URL:

```
http://www.eclipse.org/birt/phoenix/ref/
```

How to create a style

1   In the layout editor, select the report element to which you want to apply a style. If you want to create a style but not apply it to any elements, click in an empty area on the report page.

2   Choose Element➤New Style. New Style appears, as shown in Figure 10-7. The left side displays the property categories. The right side displays the properties for the category that you select.

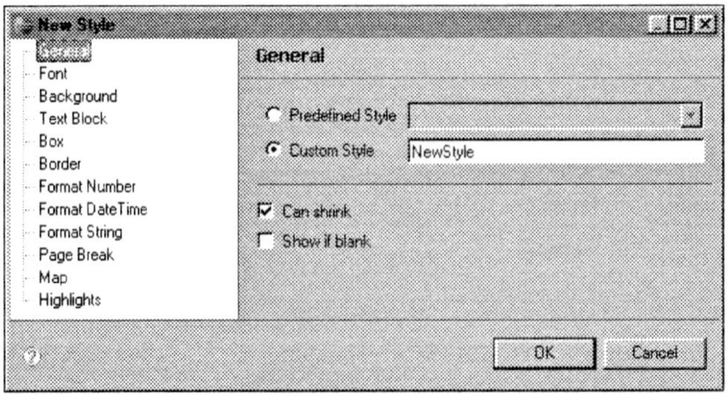

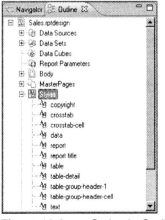

Figure 10-7 New Style

3 Specify one of the following settings:

- To apply style properties to a specific type of report element, select Predefined Style, and select a style from the drop-down list.

- To create a user-named style, specify a unique descriptive name for Custom Style. Ensure that the name is not the same as any of the predefined style names. If you specify a name that is the same as a predefined style, your custom style takes precedence, and you will no longer be able to use the predefined style to apply cascading styles.

4 Set the desired style properties by selecting a property category on the left and specifying property values.

5 When you finish setting style properties, choose OK to save the style. If you selected an element before you created the style, BIRT Report Designer applies the style to that element.

The custom styles and predefined styles that you define appear in Outline, as shown in Figure 10-8. Any time you want to change a style, you can access it from this view.

Figure 10-8 Styles in Outline

Reusing CSS styles

Most organizations maintain web sites, and most of the web pages on these sites use CSS to define the look and feel of the pages. As a report designer, you can reuse the styles from CSS files. The benefits of reusing styles are obvious—you save time by not having to reinvent the styles, and your reports reflect the standard style. You reuse CSS styles in two ways:

- Import the styles into your reports.
- Link the CSS file to your reports.

When you import styles from a CSS file, BIRT Report Designer copies the styles to your report. Subsequent changes to styles in the CSS file have no effect on the imported styles in the report. On the other hand, if you link a CSS file to your report, any change you make to the CSS file is reflected in the report.

Import styles if you expect the styles in the original CSS file to change, but you do not want your report to use the future style changes. If you do not have any control over the original CSS file, extensive style changes in the file, such as font sizes, line spacing, or text alignment, can alter a precisely designed report in unexpected ways.

Link a CSS file to your report if you are also the author of the CSS file, and you want to maintain and update the styles in all your reports by modifying a single CSS file.

BIRT Report Designer supports the CSS2 specification. Not all CSS2 properties, however, are supported. For a list of unsupported properties, see the Style and CSS specification document, which is available at the following URL:

```
http://www.eclipse.org/birt/
```

Styles that use unsupported properties are available to a report. The unsupported properties, however, do not have an effect when applied to a report element.

Importing styles

You can import any number of styles from a CSS file. If you import a style whose name matches the name of an existing style in the report, BIRT Report Designer appends a number to the name of the imported style. For example, if your report contains a style named TopLevelHeading, and you import a style with the same name, the imported style's name changes to TopLevelHeading1.

Imported styles appear in the list of available styles with all the styles that are created with BIRT Report Designer. You apply an imported style to a report element, edit the style's properties, or delete it in the same way that you do with a style that was created with BIRT Report Designer.

How to import styles

1 Select the layout editor.

2 Choose Element→Import CSS Style.

3 On Import CSS Styles, in File Name, specify the name of the CSS file whose styles you want to import. You can choose Browse to find the file. Import CSS Styles displays all the styles that are defined in the CSS file. Figure 10-9 shows an example of the styles in a CSS file named base.css.

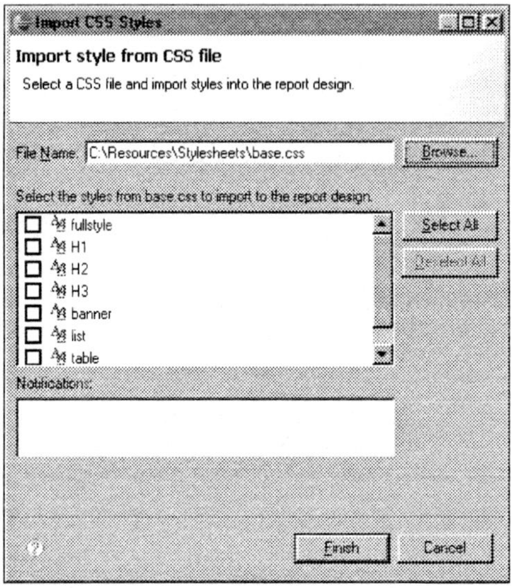

Figure 10-9   Examples of styles defined in a CSS file

4 Select the styles that you want to import. To import all the styles, choose Select All.

5 When you finish making your selections, choose Finish. BIRT Report Designer copies the styles to the report. The imported styles appear in the Styles list in Outline.

Linking a CSS file

Linking a CSS file to a report is a two-step process.

1 Place the CSS file in the BIRT resource folder. The resource folder is a central location for external files used by reports.

2 Link the CSS file in the resource folder to the report.

As with styles that you create or import, the styles in a linked CSS file also appear in the list of styles in Outline. The difference is that these styles are read-only. As you would expect, you cannot edit or delete these styles within BIRT Report Designer. Changes can be made only in the CSS file and these changes propagate to all reports linked to the CSS file.

If a style in a linked CSS file has the same name as a style that already exists (a style that you created or imported), the first style takes precedence. In the layout editor, the list of styles available to apply to a report element shows only the first instance of the style.

How to link a CSS file

1 In Library Explorer, right-click Shared Libraries, then choose Add CSS File, as shown in Figure 10-10.

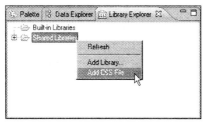

Figure 10-10   Choose Add CSS file

2 On Add CSS File, specify the CSS file to place in the resource folder.

  1 In Source File, type the path to the CSS file. You can choose Browse to locate and select the file.

  2 In File Name, optionally type a new name for the CSS file.

  3 In Folder, the read-only path value shows the location of the BIRT resource folder. You can add the CSS file to this root folder, or choose Browse to select a subfolder in which to place the CSS file.

  Figure 10-11 shows an example of values supplied in Add CSS File.

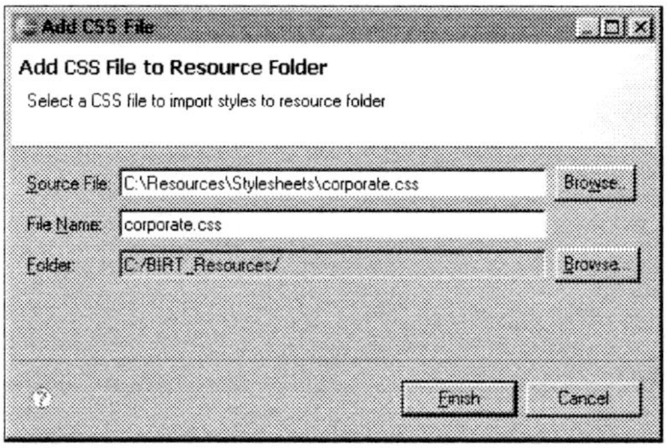

Add CSS File

Add CSS File to Resource Folder

Select a CSS file to import styles to resource folder

Source File: C:\Resources\Stylesheets\corporate.css   Browse

File Name: corporate.css

Folder: C:/BIRT_Resources/   Browse

Finish   Cancel

Figure 10-11   Add CSS File with values supplied

4 Choose Finish. The CSS file appears in Library Explorer, and it is available to any report design. Expand the file to display all styles, as shown in Figure 10-12.

Figure 10-12   Library Explorer showing a CSS file

3 Link the CSS file to the report by performing the following tasks:

   1 Choose Outline.

   2 Right-click Styles, then choose Use CSS File, as shown in Figure 10-13.

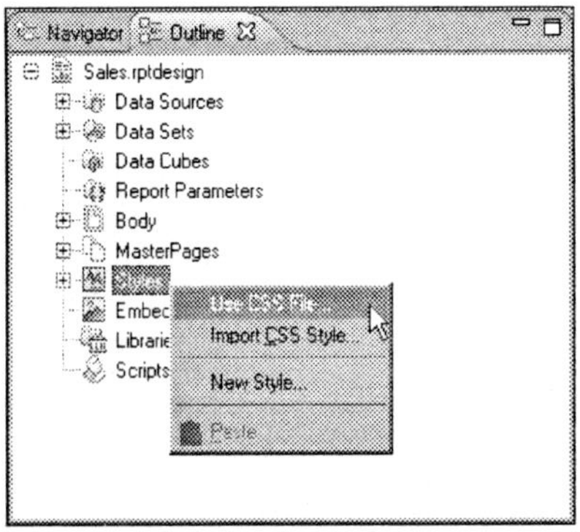

Figure 10-13   Choose Use CSS File

   3 On Use CSS, choose Browse to select the CSS file to link to the report. The Browse dialog, shown in Figure 10-14, displays the resource folder and the CSS files in the folder.

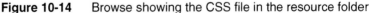

Figure 10-14   Browse showing the CSS file in the resource folder

   4 Select the CSS file, then choose OK. Use CSS displays the selected CSS file and the styles in that file, as shown in Figure 10-15.

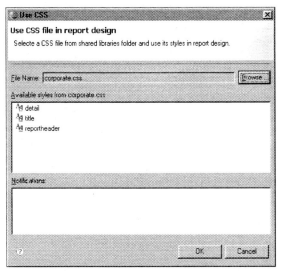

Figure 10-15　Use CSS showing the selected CSS file and its styles

5 Choose OK to confirm linking the CSS file in the resource folder to the report.

The linked CSS file and its styles appear under Styles in Outline, as shown in Figure 10-16. The style names appear in gray, indicating that they are not defined in the report design, but rather, are linked from an external file.

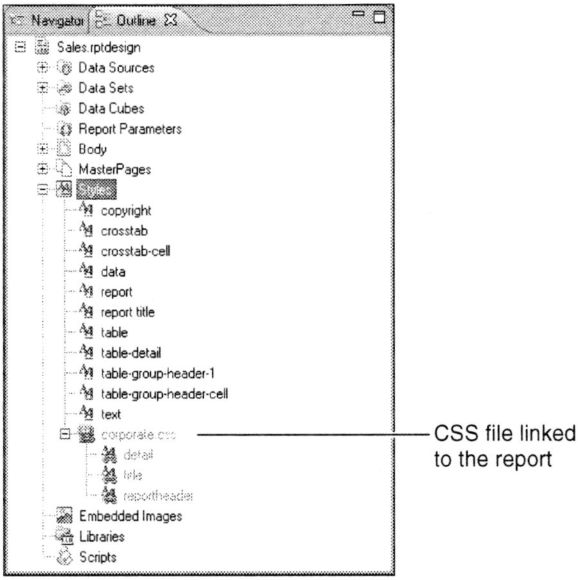

CSS file linked
to the report

Figure 10-16　Outline showing a linked CSS file and its styles

Applying a style

After you link a CSS file, or create or import styles for your report, you can apply styles to specific report elements. To apply a style to a report element, right-click the report element, choose Style➤Apply Style, then select one of the styles in the list. The list displays all the available styles. Choose None to remove the style that is currently applied to the report element.

If you set style properties to predefined style names, such as table-header or table-footer, BIRT Report Designer automatically applies the style properties to all those types of report elements. You cannot selectively apply predefined styles to only some elements of that type.

Modifying a style

One of the most powerful features of styles is the ease with which you can change the look of your report. If you decide to change fonts or font sizes in the entire report, all you do is modify the style that controls the font properties. To modify a custom or imported style, in Outline, expand Styles, right-click the style, then choose Edit Style. All report elements that use that style are automatically updated to use the new formatting.

To modify styles in a linked CSS file, edit the CSS file that resides in the BIRT resource folder. As soon as you save your edits, the report reflects the style changes.

Deleting a style

You can delete any style at any time. You should, however, delete only styles that you no longer need. If you delete a style that is applied to a report element or elements, the affected elements lose the formats that the style applied. Before you delete a style that is in use, BIRT Report Designer displays the names of the elements that are affected and prompts you to cancel or confirm the deletion.

To delete a style, choose Outline. Under Styles, right-click the style that you want to delete, then choose Delete.

You cannot delete individual styles in a linked CSS file. You can, however, unlink the CSS file from the report by right-clicking the file, then choosing Delete. BIRT unlinks the file without displaying a warning, even if there are report elements using styles in the CSS file. These report elements revert to their unformatted state.

Formatting data based on conditions

When you format a report element, the format applies to all instances of the element in the generated report. For example, if you specify that an item price appears in the Arial typeface and blue, all item prices in the generated report appear in Arial and blue. This type of formatting is called absolute formatting. The appearance of the element is set when you design the report.

You can, however, change the format of an element according to its value or the value of another element. For example, you can specify that item prices appear in green if the value exceeds $1,000.00 and in a default color if the value is equal to or less than $1,000.00. This type of formatting is called conditional formatting. Using conditional formatting, the appearance of the element is set when the report runs.

The following examples are some common uses of conditional formatting:

- Show numbers in a different color if they are negative.

- Highlight delinquent accounts by using a different typeface or font style.

- Highlight the top ten customers by displaying their names in a colored box.

Creating a formatting rule

BIRT Report Designer provides an easy way to apply conditional formatting to report elements. You use the Highlights page of Property Editor, where you create a formatting rule that defines when and how to change the appearance of an element. When you create a formatting rule, you specify the following information:

- The condition to meet in order to apply a format, for example, row["OrderTotal"] Greater than 50000.

- The format to apply, for example, font color = blue. You can also specify a style to apply.

Figure 10-17 shows an example of a formatting rule.

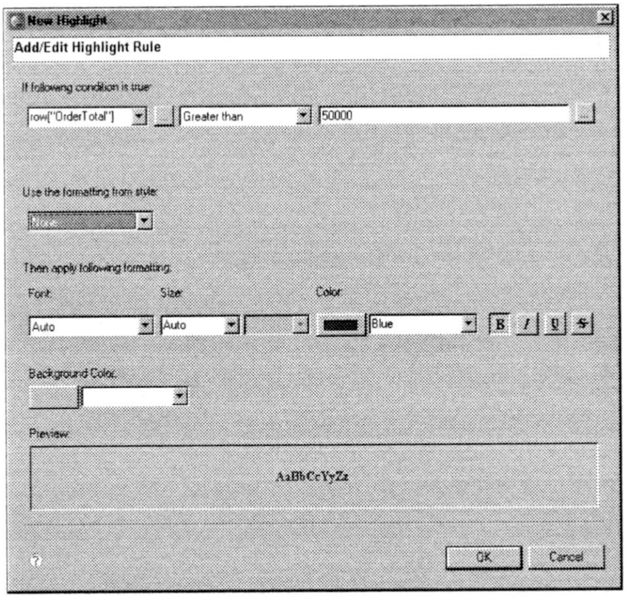

Figure 10-17 New Highlight showing a formatting rule

How to create a formatting rule

1 In the layout editor, select the report element that you want to format conditionally.

2 Choose the Highlights tab in Property Editor. The Highlights page appears, as shown in Figure 10-18. It is empty if you have not yet specified any formatting rules for the selected element.

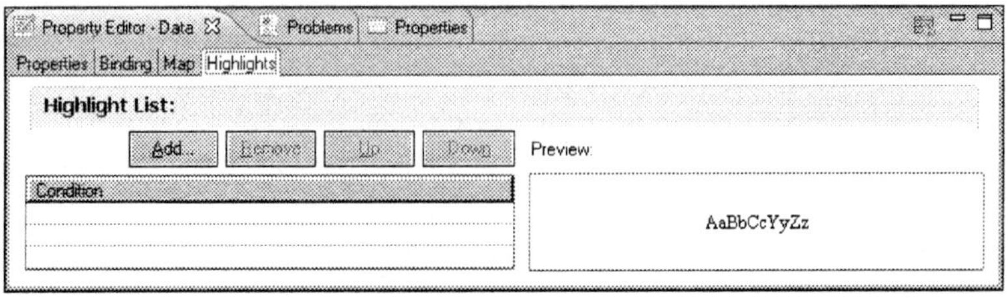

Figure 10-18   Highlights page

3 Choose Add to add a new formatting rule.

4 On New Highlight, create the rule for applying a particular format to the report element by completing the following steps:

    1 Think of the rule in plain English first. For example:

```
If the order total is greater than $50,000.00, then set
the font color to blue and the font style to bold.
```

    There are two parts to the rule: If and Then. The New Highlight dialog helps you specify the If and Then parts of the rule by breaking them down to more specific parts.

    2 Specify the If part of the rule by completing the following steps:

        1 In the first field, specify the first part of the If expression. Using the example rule, this part is order total:

            ❏ If the order total values come directly from the selected element, from the drop-down list, choose Value of this data item.

            ❏ If the order total values come from another data element, choose that element's column binding name from the drop-down list.

        2 In the second field, specify the second part of the If expression by selecting an option from the list. Using our example rule, this part is Greater than.

        3 In the third field, specify the third part of the If expression. Using our example rule, this part is a value of 50000, as shown in Figure 10-19.

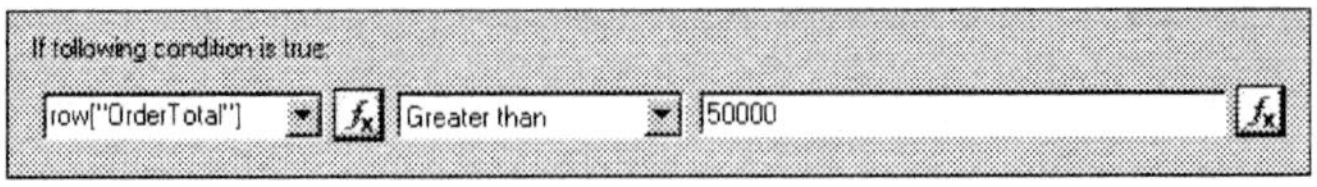

Figure 10-19   Elements of the If expression in New Highlight

You have now completed the If part of the rule, which specifies the following:

```
If row["OrderTotal"] is greater than 50000
```

3 Specify the Then part of your rule, which is "then set the font color to blue and the font style to bold," by completing the following steps:

   ❏ Choose Color, then select a color from the color picker.

   ❏ Choose B to select the Bold format, as shown in Figure 10-20.

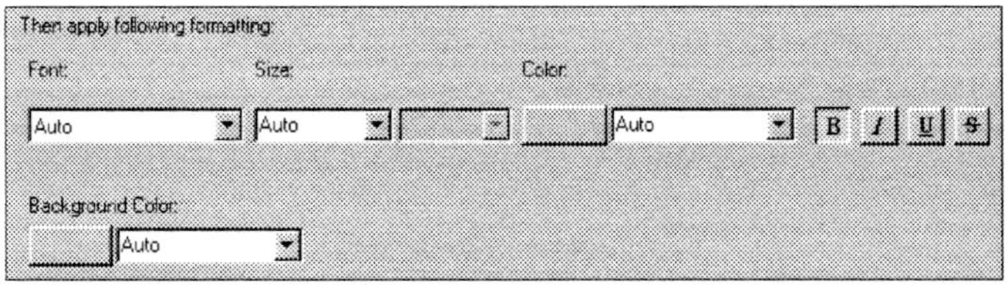

Figure 10-20   Elements of the Then expression in New Highlight

   ❏ Alternatively, if you created a style named order_data_highlight, for example, that specifies the formats, you can select the style from the list of styles under "Use the formatting from style:".

4 Choose OK to save the highlight rule.

The rule that you created appears in Highlight List, as shown in Figure 10-21. The rule takes effect the next time that you run the report.

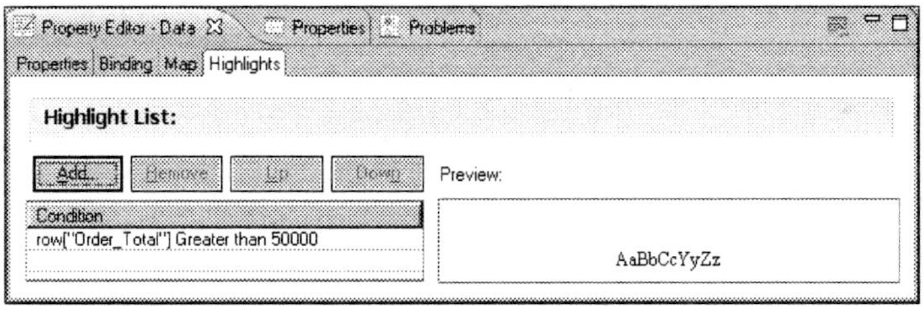

Figure 10-21   Highlight List

5 Preview the report to test your formatting rule.

Modifying a formatting rule

To modify a formatting rule, you use the same highlight tool that you use to create the rule. Select the element for which you want to modify the formatting rule, choose the Highlights tab in Property Editor, then double-click the rule to modify. You can change any part of the rule, such as the condition that triggers the formatting or the format properties to apply. The modified rule takes effect the next time that you run the report.

Creating multiple formatting rules

You can create multiple formatting rules for an element. You can, for example, create three rules to set the values of an order total data element to one of three colors, depending on the dollar amount. Figure 10-22 shows an example.

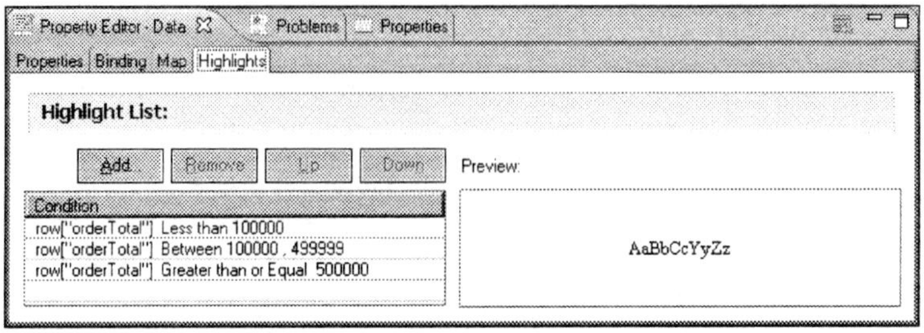

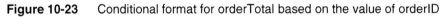

Figure 10-22   Highlights page showing multiple format rules for an element

You can create any number of rules, and you can base conditions on the value of the selected element or on the value of other elements. Using the previous example, you can also change the color of the order total value based on the value of another data element, such as order ID. Figure 10-23 shows this example.

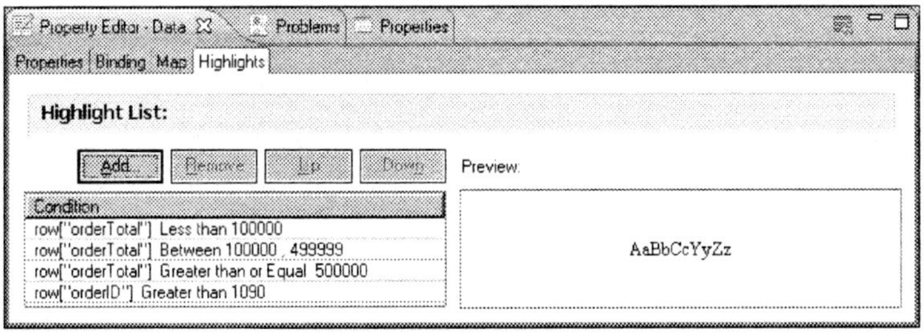

Figure 10-23   Conditional format for orderTotal based on the value of orderID

For each row of data, BIRT Report Designer evaluates the rules in the order in which they appear in the list of rules. As it evaluates each rule, BIRT Report Designer applies the specified format properties if the condition is met. If multiple rules with different conditions use the same format property, the later rule can override the format that the earlier rules specify.

Consider the following example:

- The first rule sets order total values to red if they are less than 100000.

- The fourth rule sets order total values to blue if the order ID is larger than 1090.

If an order total value is 50000 and the order ID is 2000 (the conditions in both rules are true), the order total value appears in blue, not red, because the fourth rule supersedes all rules before it. If, however, the fourth rule sets order total values to italics rather than to blue, the value appears in red and italics.

When you create multiple rules for an element, plan the rules carefully. Consider the effect of individual rules and how the order of the rules changes the results. Test thoroughly to verify that the report displays the results that you expect. If necessary, you can change the order of the rules by selecting a rule and moving it up or down the list using the Up or Down buttons on the Highlights page.

Deleting a formatting rule

All formatting rules that you create for an element take effect when you run the report. If you do not want a formatting rule to apply to an element, you must delete the rule from the Highlights page of the selected element.

Alternating row colors in a table

If a table displays many rows, it can be hard to read the data. A common solution is to use alternating colors for the rows, as shown in Figure 10-24.

Customer	Address	Phone
Atelier graphique	54, rue Royale, Nantes, 44000, France	40 32 2555
Signal Gift Stores	8489 Strong St., Las Vegas, NV 83030, USA	7025551838
Australian Collectors, Co.	636 St Kilda Road, Level 3, Melbourne, Victoria 3004, Australia	03 9520 4555
La Rochelle Gifts	67, rue des Cinquante Otages, Nantes, 44000, France	40.67.8555
Baane Mini Imports	Erling Skakkes gate 78, Stavern, 4110, Norway	07-98 9555
Mini Gifts Distributors Ltd.	5677 Strong St., San Rafael, CA 97562, USA	4155551450
Havel & Zbyszek Co	ul. Filtrowa 68, Warszawa, 01-012, Poland	(26) 642-7555
Blauer See Auto, Co.	Lyonerstr. 34, Frankfurt, 60528, Germany	+49 69 66 90

Figure 10-24   Conditional formatting that displays rows in alternating colors

To create this effect, use the conditional formatting feature, as described in the preceding section. The general condition that you specify is this: If the row number is even, set the row's background color to A; if the row number is odd, set the row's background color to B.

Note that BIRT counts the first row as 0, so what appears as the first row is actually row 0, what appears as the second row is actually row 1, and so on. In other words, the rows that appear to be odd-numbered rows in the generated report are technically even-numbered rows, and vice versa. In the report that appears in Figure 10-24, the gray color applies to even-numbered rows.

How to alternate row colors

1   Select the detail row in the table, as shown in Figure 10-25.

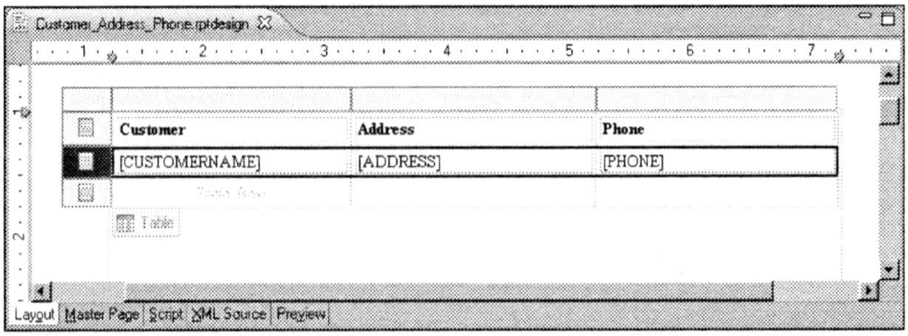

Figure 10-25 Detail row selected

2 In General properties in Property Editor, choose a color for Background Color, or use the default value, Auto. This color is the default color for the detail rows.

3 Choose the Highlights tab in Property Editor to create a formatting rule to apply a different color to alternate rows.

4 On the Highlights page, choose Add to create a formatting rule.

5 On New Highlight, specify an expression in the first field:

   1 Next to the first field, choose the expression builder button.

   2 In the expression builder, select Available Column Bindings, then select Table, then double-click RowNum. The following expression appears in the text area, as shown in Figure 10-26.

```
row.__rownum
```

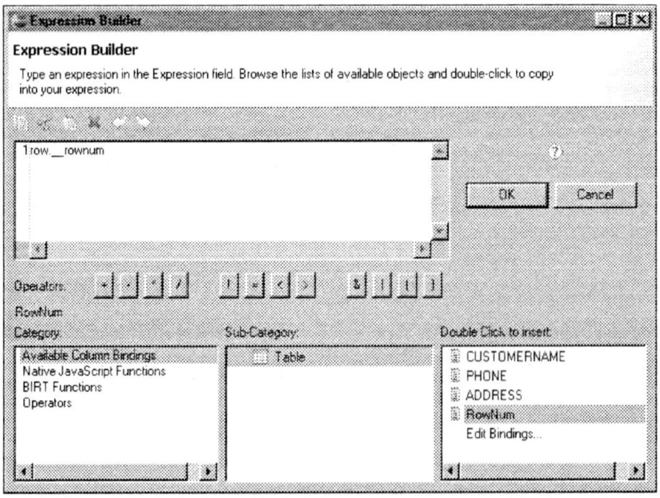

Figure 10-26 Expression Builder showing the row.__rownum expression

   3 Change the expression to:

```
row.__rownum % 2
```

row.__rownum represents the current row number. The modulus (%) operator returns the remainder of a division. 2 specifies the number by which to divide. Using this expression, even-numbered rows return 0, and odd-numbered rows return a non-zero value.

4 Choose OK to save the expression. The expression appears in the first field in New Highlight.

6 In the second field, choose either Equal to or Not Equal to:

- To apply the formatting rule to even-numbered rows, choose Equal to.

- To apply the formatting rule to odd-numbered rows, choose Not Equal to.

7 In the third field, type the following number:

0

0 specifies the value to compare to the result of the expression, row.__rownum % 2.

You just completed the If part of the formatting rule as follows:

```
If row.__rownum % 2 Equal (or Not Equal) 0
```

8 Specify the color to assign to the even- or odd-numbered rows by choosing a color for Background Color. Figure 10-27 shows an example of a completed format rule. The rule sets the background color of even-numbered rows to silver.

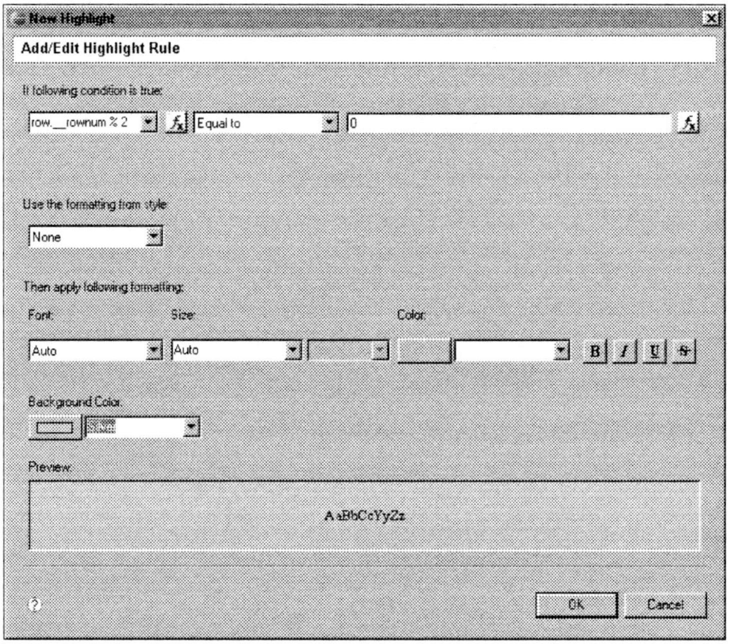

Figure 10-27   New Highlight dialog showing a complete format rule

Choose OK.

9 Preview the report. The detail rows should appear in alternating colors.

You can use row.__rownum and the % operator with different values to alternate colors for a different number of rows. For example, the following highlight expressions change the row color for every three and every five rows, respectively:

```
row.__rownum % 6 Greater than or Equal 3
row.__rownum % 10 Greater than or Equal 5
```

Specifying alignment of content in a table or grid

Content in a table or grid aligns horizontally and vertically. When you place elements in the cells of a table or grid, BIRT Report Designer, by default, aligns content as follows:

- Aligns text horizontally to the left
- Aligns content vertically to the cell's baseline

Aligning text horizontally

You can change the horizontal alignment of text by setting the text-alignment property to one of the following values: left, right, center, or justify. This property is equivalent to the CSS text-align property.

You can align content by applying the text-alignment property to individual data elements, to cells, to an entire row, or to the entire table or grid. To align all text in a table in the same way, set the text-alignment property at the table level. To align all text in a particular row, set the property at the row level.

Figure 10-28 shows the results of using the different property values.

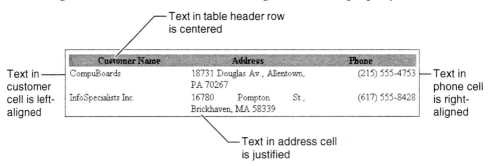

Figure 10-28   Text-alignment properties

Aligning content vertically

You can change the vertical alignment of content by setting the vertical-alignment property to one of the following values: top, middle, bottom. You can align content vertically by applying the vertical-alignment property to a row, to individual cells, or to a content element.

Set the vertical-alignment property on a row to align vertically all elements in the row at the same position. Figure 10-29 shows the results of setting a row's vertical-alignment property to middle. All the labels in the row, which has a specified height, appear in the center vertically.

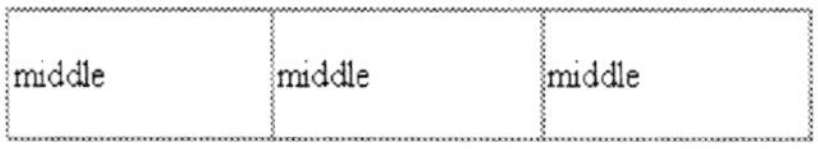

Figure 10-29   Vertical-alignment property setting for a row

Set the vertical-alignment property on a cell to control the vertical position of elements in the cell. Figure 10-30 shows the results of using a different vertical-alignment value for each grid cell that contains a label.

top		
	middle	
		bottom

Figure 10-30   Vertical-alignment property settings for cells that contain one element

Figure 10-31 shows the results of using a different vertical alignment value for each cell that contains two inline elements. An inline element is one that has no line break before or after it, and whose Display property is set to inline. Two inline elements in a cell appear side by side on a single line.

Figure 10-31   Vertical-alignment property settings for cells that contain multiple elements

Adjusting the spacing of content in a report

The default layout adds a minimum amount of space between elements in a report. After you lay out elements in your report, preview the report in the desired output format to see if you need to adjust the spacing between contents. Reports render differently in the different output formats.

One key difference is the effect of empty grid and table rows and columns in the generated report. In DOC, PPT, and XLS formats, empty rows and columns appear as blank space. For example, if a grid has three rows, but only one row contains content, the DOC, PPT, and XLS reports display two blank lines. In HTML and PDF, an empty row or column does not appear as blank space unless you set the row or column to a specific size.

Another key difference exists between HTML and page-based formats, such as PDF and DOC. In an HTML report, the contents, by default, adjust to the size of the window. In this default case, the page size and margin sizes specified in the report's master page have no effect on the HTML report. In page-based formats, such as PDF and DOC, the contents of table cells appear on one or multiple lines, depending on the sizes of the columns. The entire table occupies as much space horizontally as is available unless you specify a specific value for the table width. The available, or printable, area is determined by the page size and margin sizes of the master page.

Figure 10-32 shows the default spacing for report elements in a report design. As the figure shows, a table contains columns of equal width unless you specify explicit column widths.

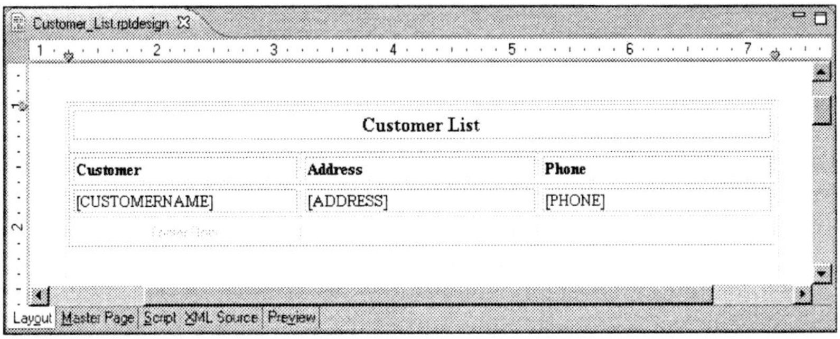

Figure 10-32   Default spacing in a report design

Figure 10-33 shows the report output in HTML. The default layout displays rows of content with very little space between them. You can resize a row to increase the space between rows and resize a column to adjust its width.

Customer List		
Customer	Address	Phone
Signal Engineering	149 Spinnaker Dr., New Haven, CT 97823	(203) 555-7845
Technical Specialists Co.	567 North Pendale Street, New Haven, CT 97823	(203) 555-9545
SigniSpecialists Corp.	5290 North Pendale Street, NYC, NY 10022	(212) 555-1957
Technical MicroSystems Inc.	4092 Furth Circle, NYC, NY 10022	(212) 555-7413
InfoEngineering	2678 Kingston Rd., NYC, NY 10022	(212) 555-1500
Advanced Design Inc.	5905 Pompton St., NYC, NY 10022	(212) 555-8493
Technical Design Inc.	897 Long Airport Avenue, NYC, NY 10022	(212) 555-7818
Design Solutions Corp.	7824 Baden Av., NYC, NY 10022	(212) 555-3675
TekniSystems	7476 Moss Rd., Newark, NJ 94019	(201) 555-9350

Figure 10-33   Default spacing in an HTML report

When the size of the browser window decreases, text in the table cells wraps, as shown in Figure 10-34. If you do not want the contents in the table to adjust to the browser window, you can specify a fixed width for the table. You can also change the report's layout from auto layout to fixed layout. These tasks are described later in this chapter.

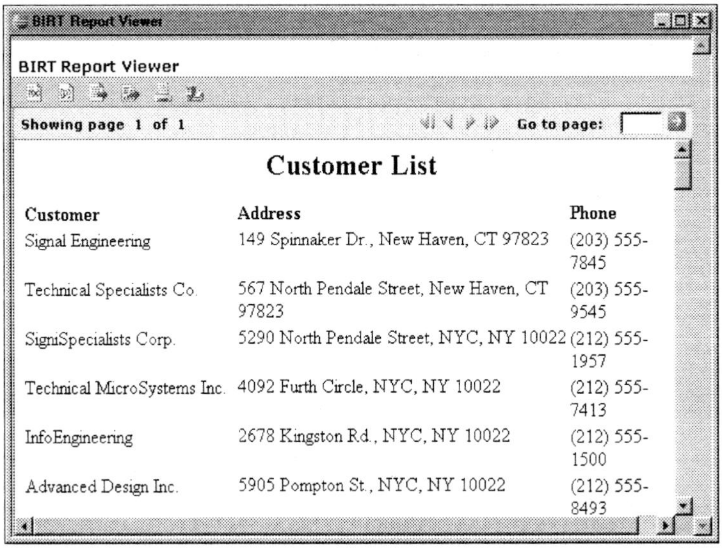

Figure 10-34 Report output in HTML when browser window size is reduced

Figure 10-35 shows the same report in PDF format. The data is left-aligned, and fits in three columns of equal size, which results in white space on the right. There is also very little space between the rows and columns.

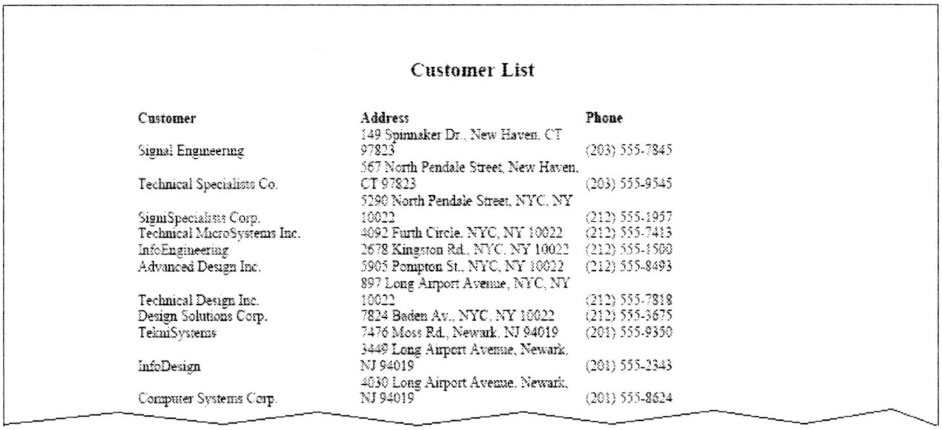

Figure 10-35 Default spacing in a PDF report

To adjust the spacing of content in a report, use one of the following techniques:

- Resize the rows or columns of a table or grid to adjust spacing of content in a table or grid.

- Insert an empty row or column in a table or grid, and specify a specific size for the row or column.

■ Resize the margins, borders, and padding of elements.

The first two techniques provide more predictable results. The padding and margin properties can yield varying results in different web browsers, depending on how the browser interprets these properties.

Resizing rows and columns

The quickest way to change the size of a row or column is to drag the row or column boundary to the desired height or width. You can also resize a row or column by setting a specific row height or column width.

You will find that setting a specific row height or column width is often preferable to dragging a row or column boundary because what you see in the layout editor is not what you get in the output. In the layout editor, the sizes of data, text, and label elements adjust to fit up to 20 characters.

The row height that you specify is the row's minimum height. It is not a fixed height. If it were, long content would be truncated. The column width that you specify, on the other hand, is a fixed width. Long blocks of content wrap to multiple lines.

How to resize a column or row by dragging its boundary

1 Select the tab at the bottom left corner of the grid or table. Guide cells appear at the top and left sides of the grid or table.

2 In the guide cell area, select a row or column boundary, and drag it until the row or column is the size that you want, as shown in Figure 10-36.

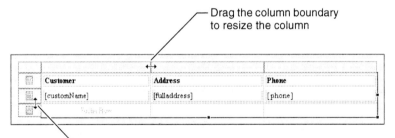

Figure 10-36   Resize rows or columns by dragging boundaries

How to specify a row height

1 Select the tab at the bottom left corner of the grid or table. Guide cells appear at the top and left sides of the grid or table.

2 Select the guide cell of the row that you want to resize.

3 In Property Editor, choose General. Property Editor displays the general properties of the row, as shown in Figure 10-37.

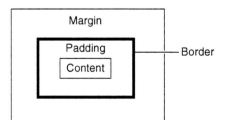

Figure 10-37   Property Editor showing row properties

4   Specify a value for Height. This value sets the minimum height for the row. You can specify different units of measurements, including inches, centimeters, millimeters, and points.

How to specify a column width

1   Select the tab on the bottom left corner of the grid or table. Guide cells appear at the top and left sides of the grid or table.

2   Select the guide cell of the column that you want to resize. Property Editor displays the column properties that you can set.

3   In the General category, specify a value for Width. This value sets a fixed width for the column. You can specify different units of measurements, including inches, centimeters, millimeters, and a percentage of the total grid width.

Resizing margins, borders, and padding of elements

As in CSS, BIRT Report Designer provides three properties to define the horizontal and vertical space between elements:

- Border is a visible or invisible line around the element.

- Padding is the space between the content of an element and the border.

- Margin is the space between the border and other elements.

Figure 10-38 shows how margins, borders, and padding work together.

Figure 10-38   Properties that define the space between elements

You can use the padding and margin properties of an element to adjust the horizontal and vertical spacing of content in a report. Figure 10-39 shows how to set a label element's Padding Bottom property to increase the space between the report title and the table below it.

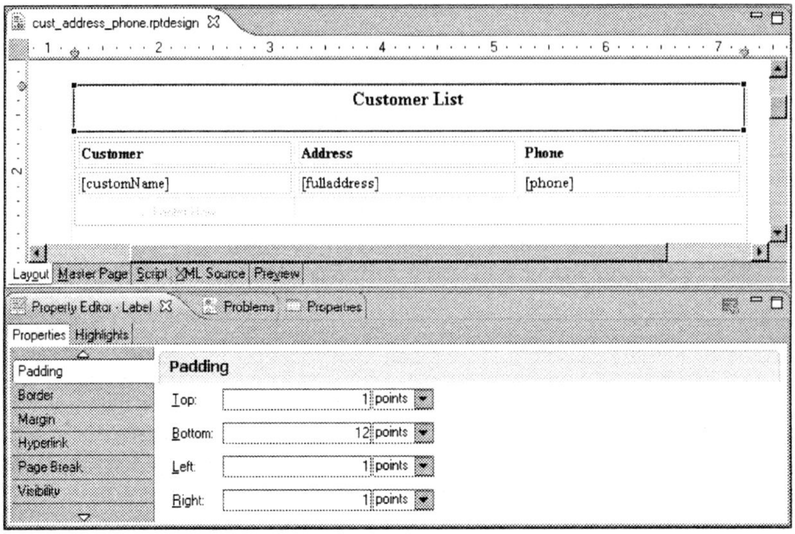

Figure 10-39 Use the Padding Bottom property to set the space below an element

Figure 10-40 shows the report output. You can get the same result by increasing the table's Margin Top property.

Customer List		
Customer	**Address**	**Phone**
Signal Engineering	149 Spinnaker Dr., New Haven, CT 97823	(203) 555-7845
Technical Specialists Co.	567 North Pendale Street, New Haven, CT 97823	(203) 555-9545
SigniSpecialists Corp.	5290 North Pendale Street, NYC, NY 10022	(212) 555-1957
Technical MicroSystems Inc.	4092 Furth Circle, NYC, NY 10022	(212) 555-7413
InfoEngineering	2678 Kingston Rd., NYC, NY 10022	(212) 555-1500

Figure 10-40 Report output showing the result of the Padding Bottom setting

Specifying fixed layout for HTML output

As described previously, by default, the contents of an HTML report adjust automatically to the size of the browser window. While this behavior is typical for many web pages, there are times when you want to deliver a highly formatted HTML document with a fixed layout because text-wrapping can make a report difficult to read.

You can specify a fixed layout for a report in the following two ways. Each option produces a different result.

- Set a specific width for the table or grid that contains the contents.

- Set the report's Layout Preference property to fixed layout. This option produces HTML output that is similar to PDF output. The page margins take effect, thus setting a fixed width in which to display the report content.

Compare the reports in Figure 10-41, Figure 10-42, and Figure 10-43. Figure 10-41 shows a report that contains a table with the default layout. The table does not have a fixed width, nor do the columns in the table.

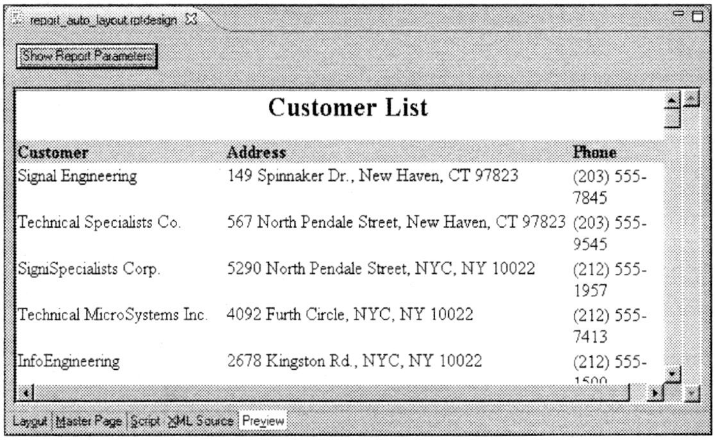

Figure 10-41　Report displaying default layout

Figure 10-42 shows the same report, but the table width is set to six inches. The columns also have specific widths set to accommodate the different amounts of data in each field. If you set only the table width, all the columns have the same width.

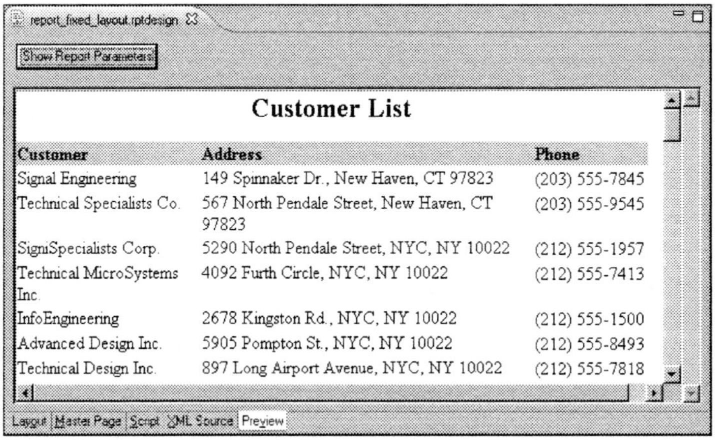

Figure 10-42　Report in which table and column widths are set

In Figure 10-43, the report again contains a table using the default layout, with no table or column widths set. This report design sets the Layout Preference property to fixed layout to control the appearance of the whole page. By default, reports use auto layout. When using fixed layout, the

HTML report uses the margins and page size set in the master page. In this case, the report shows 1.5-inch margins at the top and left side, similar to a PDF report. Unlike a PDF report, however, the HTML report still displays on a single page.

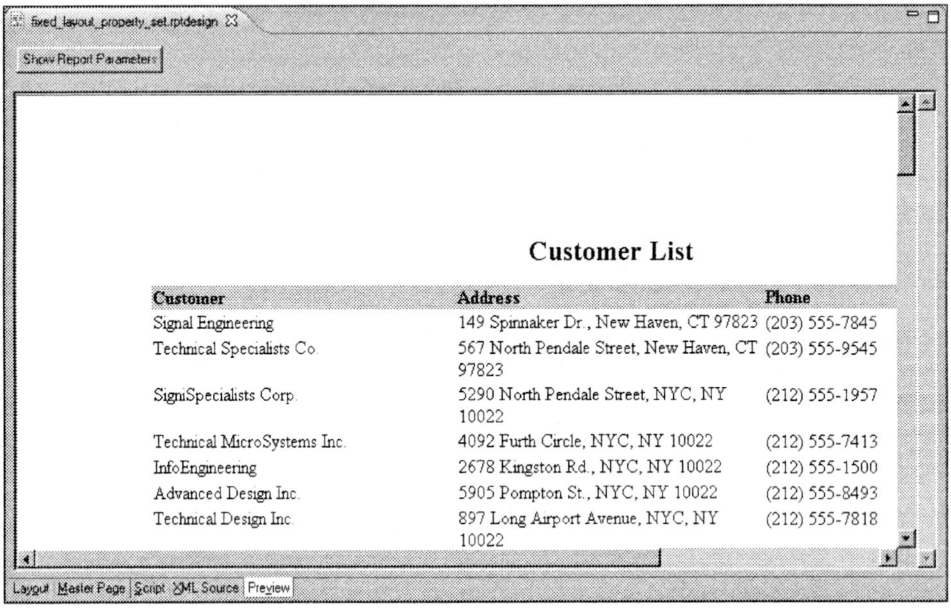

Figure 10-43 Report in which the Layout Preference property is set to fixed layout

To set the report's Layout Preference property, click in an empty area of the report page in the layout editor. Property Editor displays the properties of the report. In the report's general properties, change Layout Preference from Auto Layout to Fixed Layout, as shown in Figure 10-44.

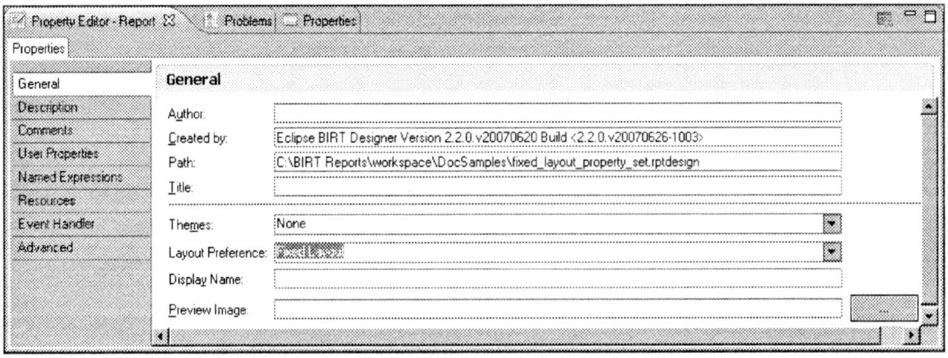

Figure 10-44 Property Editor showing the general properties of the report, including the Layout Preference property

Displaying content across multiple columns

Grid and table columns enable you to align report elements easily and neatly. Often, however, you need to display text or data across multiple columns to enhance the report's appearance. For example, compare the layout of the reports in Figure 10-45 and Figure 10-46.

Total Sales:
$37283510.00

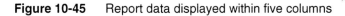

Customer total:
$954180.00

Order 1810

Item	Unit Price	Quantity	Extended Price
MDSPL04	$340.00	1728	$587520.00
MSL3280	$210.00	1746	$366660.00
		Order Total:	$954180.00

Figure 10-45   Report data displayed within five columns

Total Sales: $37283510.00

Brittan Design Inc.

Customer total: $954180.00

   Order 1810

Item	Unit Price	Quantity	Extended Price
MDSPL04	$340.00	1728	$587520.00
MSL3280	$210.00	1746	$366660.00
		Order Total:	$954180.00

Figure 10-46   Report data spans multiple columns

In the first report, data appears in a five-column table. The first column of the table contains the sales total, customer name, customer total, and order number. The order details occupy the rest of the columns. To fit five columns, each column is fairly narrow. Some of the content in the first column wraps onto two lines. If you increase the width of the first column, the second column moves too far to the right. Figure 10-47 shows the design for the first report.

In the second report, the sales total, customer name, and customer total span multiple columns, so that the text appears on one line. The second column starts farther to the left, eliminating extra space on the left of the detailed content.

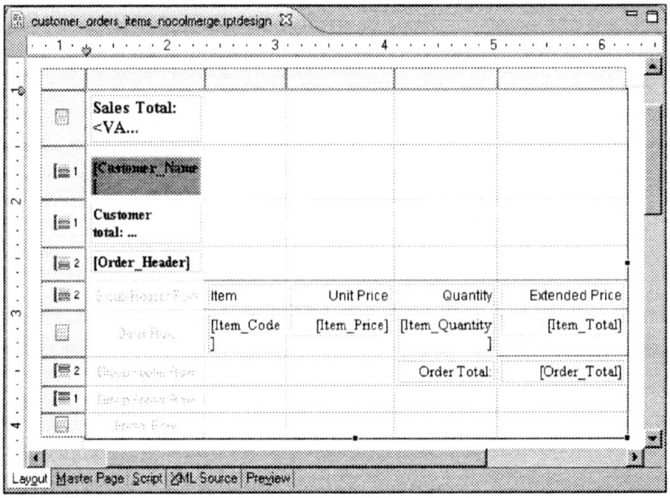

Figure 10-47 Report design without column spanning

Figure 10-48 shows the design for the second report.

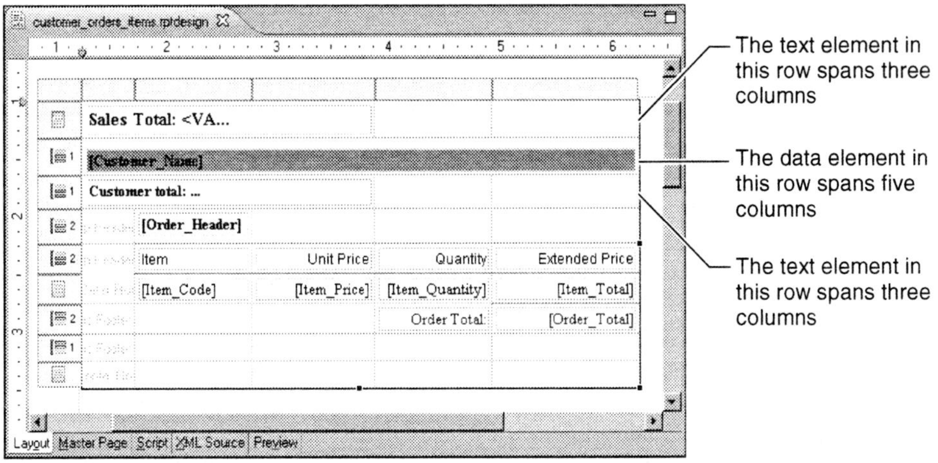

The text element in this row spans three columns

The data element in this row spans five columns

The text element in this row spans three columns

Figure 10-48 Report design that uses column spanning

To display table or grid content across multiple columns, you merge the cells.

How to merge table or grid cells

1 Select the cells that you want to merge by using Shift-click. A border appears around the cells that you select, as shown in Figure 10-49.

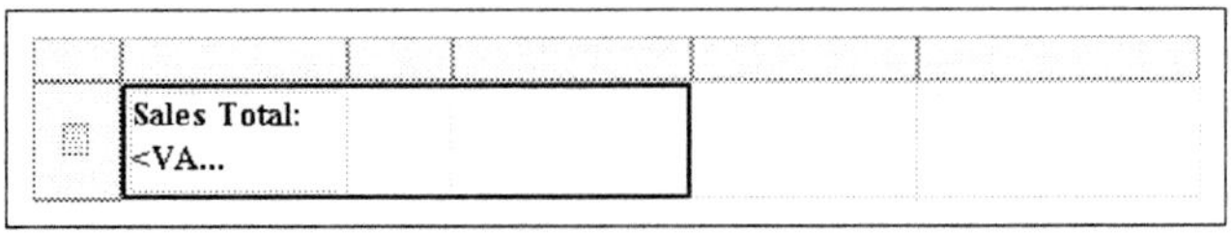

Figure 10-49 Cells selected for merging

2 Right-click within the border, then choose Merge Cells from the context menu. The cells merge into one, as shown in Figure 10-50.

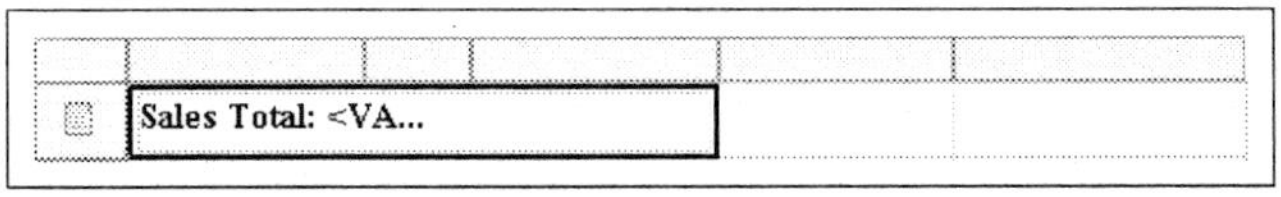

	Sales Total: <VA...

Figure 10-50 Merged cells

Specifying alternate values for display

Data in a data source can sometimes be cryptic or appear in abbreviated form. For example, gender values may be M or F rather than male or female. Credit rankings may be 1 to 5 rather than excellent, good, average, fair, or poor.

BIRT Report Designer enables you to specify alternate values to display if you do not want to use the original values in your report. You use a data element's map property to create rules for mapping data values. You create one map rule for each data value that you want to replace. For example, to map M and F to Male and Female, respectively, you create two map rules.

You can replace a data value with a literal text value. Alternatively, if you are creating a report that will be viewed in multiple locales, you can replace a data value with a resource key. A resource key is a text string in an external source that is translated, or localized, into different languages. Resource keys and localization are discussed in Chapter 24, "Localizing Text."

How to map data values to different display values

1 Select the data element for which you want to replace values. The property editor displays the properties for the data element.

2 Choose the Map tab at the top of Property Editor. Map List appears, as shown in Figure 10-51.

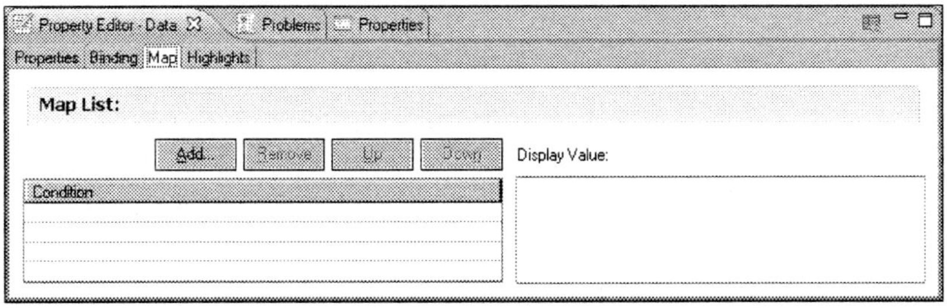

Figure 10-51 Map List

3 Choose Add to create a map rule.

4 On New Map Rule:

    1 In the first field, specify the expression that refers to the data set field for which you want to replace values. You can select, from the drop-down list, Value of this data item. The following is an example of an expression:

```
row["creditrank"]
```

    2 In the second field, select an operator from the list. For example:

```
Equal to
```

    3 In the third field, specify the value to replace. For example:

```
"A"
```

You must enclose string values in quotation marks (" ").

    4 Specify the value that you want to display. You have two options:

       ❑ Under "Then display following value:", type the text to display. For example:

```
Excellent
```

       ❑ Specify a resource key. Choose the ellipsis (...) button to select a resource key. You can access resource keys only if you have assigned a resource file to the report.

Figure 10-52 shows an example of a completed map rule, which replaces the value A with the value Excellent.

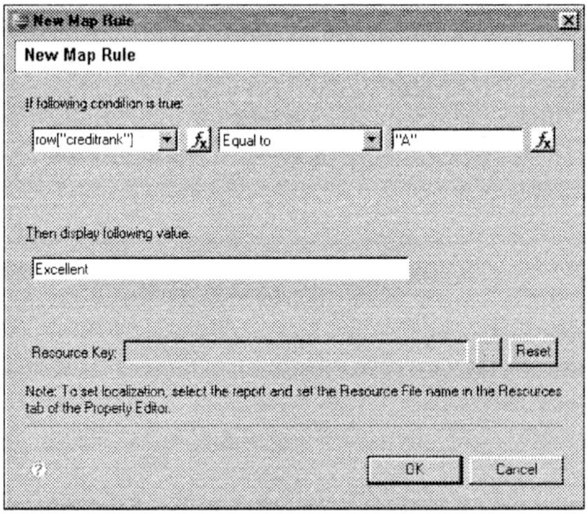

Figure 10-52   A map rule

    5 Choose OK. The rule that you created appears in Map List. When you select the rule, the display value appears in the box at the right, as shown in Figure 10-53.

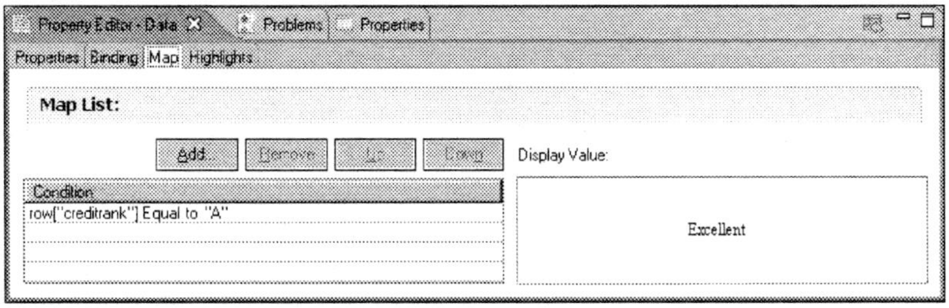

Figure 10-53 Map rule and its display value in Property Editor

6 Repeat steps 3 through 5 to create additional rules, one for each data value that you want to replace. Figure 10-54 shows an example of three map rules that were created for the selected data element.

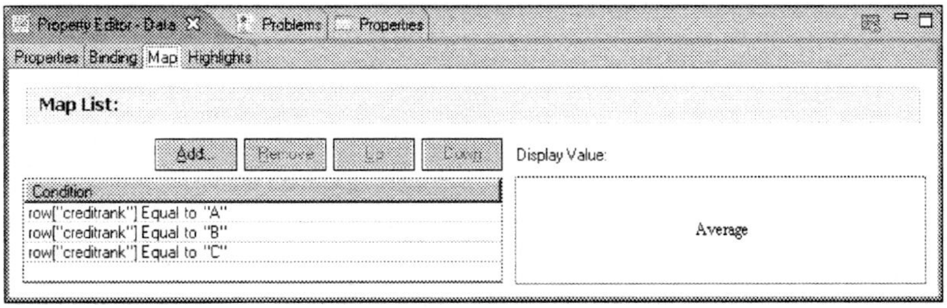

Figure 10-54 Three map rules for an element

5 Preview the report to check the results of your map rules.

Hiding elements based on conditions

In most cases, you add an element to a report because you want to display the contents of the element. There are many good reasons, however, for hiding report elements conditionally. Using an element's Visibility property, you can customize the information that your report displays. You can hide an element based on the output format or on a specific condition. You specify a condition by writing a Boolean expression that evaluates to either true or false.

The following examples describe cases for conditionally hiding an element. The examples also show the Boolean expressions to apply to the Visibility property.

- Display a text message only for certain records. You want your report to display a message when an account balance falls below a certain amount, such as $1,000.00. First, create a text element that displays something like "Your account balance is below the minimum balance required to waive the service fee." Then, conditionally hide the text element by setting its Visibility property to the following expression:

  ```
  row["accountbalance"] > 1000
  ```

When the expression returns true, the text element is hidden. Notice that you have to think the opposite when specifying the expression. You have to think about when you do not want the text to appear, rather than when you do. In this example, you want to display a message when the balance is less than $1,000.00. Therefore, you hide the text element when the balance is greater than $1,000.00.

- Display a text message if a report returns no data. If your report uses parameters to prompt users to specify the data that they want to view, and it is possible for the report to return nothing, you can display a message, such as "No records found." To accomplish this task, perform the following steps:

  1 Create a column binding, named Row_Count, for example, that uses the aggregate function, COUNT, to get the number of data rows in a table. Remember, for each piece of computed data to use or display in a report, there must be a column binding.

  2 Create a text or label element that displays the "No records found" message, then conditionally hide the element by setting its Visibility property to the following expression:

  ```
  row["Row_Count"] != 0
  ```

  The expression row["Row_Count"] refers to the Row_Count column binding that computes the number of rows. When Row_Count returns zero, the "No records found" message appears. Because an aggregate function processes all data rows in a table, you must place the text or label element in the header or footer row of the table. For more information about using aggregate functions, see Chapter 12, "Aggregating Data."

- Display different pictures, depending on the values of a field. To add visual interest to your report, you want to display two stars next to an order total that equals or exceeds $10,000.00, one star for totals between $5,000.00 and $10,000.00, and nothing for totals less than $5,000.00. Create two pictures—one with two stars and the other with one star—and insert them next to the element that displays the order number. Use the following expression to conditionally hide the two-star picture. The expression hides the two-star picture when the order total is less than $10,000.00.

  ```
  row["ordertotal"] <= 10000
  ```

  Use the following expression to conditionally hide the one-star picture. The expression hides the one-star picture if the order total is less than $5,000.00 or more than $10,000.00.

  ```
  row["ordertotal"] < 5000 || row["ordertotal"] > 10000
  ```

- Display different report sections, depending on the values of a field. For example, you want to display one set of information for full-time employees and different information for contractors. Create two report sections, one with full-time employee information and another with contractor information. Use the following expression to hide the section with full-time employee information conditionally. The expression hides the full-time employee information when the employee is classified as a contractor.

```
row["classification"] == "contractor"
```

Use the following expression to hide the section with contractor information conditionally. The expression hides the contractor information when the employee is classified as full-time.

```
row["classification"] == "fulltime"
```

The Visibility property also provides you with the option of:

- Hiding an element, depending on the output format. For example, you can hide an element for HTML output and display it for the other output formats (DOC, PPT, PDF, PS, XLS).

- Specifying different visibility conditions for different output formats. For example, you can hide an element in HTML if its value is x and hide an element in PDF if its value is y.

How to hide an element conditionally

1 Select the element to hide conditionally.

2 In Property Editor, choose Visibility. The Hide Element option appears, as shown in Figure 10-55.

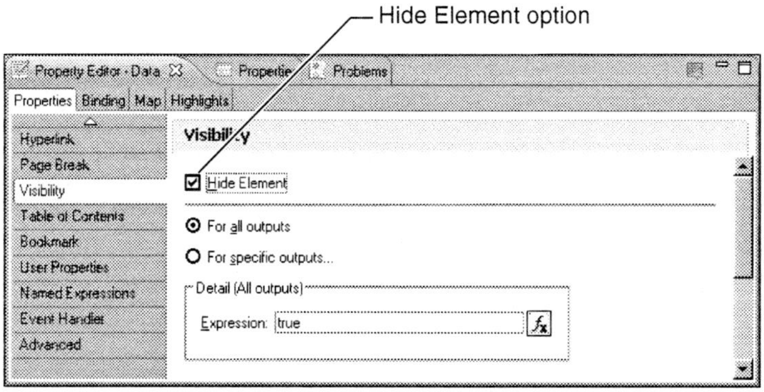

Figure 10-55   Hide Element option in Property Editor

3 Select Hide Element to specify that this element be hidden. If you want the element, such as an empty row, to always be hidden, this selection is all you need to do. If you want to hide the element conditionally, specify the condition as well.

4 Select the report format to which you want to apply the hide condition.

- To apply the hide condition for all report formats, select For all outputs.

- To apply the hide condition for certain report formats, select For specific outputs. Also select this option if you want to apply different conditions, depending on the report format.

5 Specify the hide condition by performing the following tasks:

1 Open the expression builder.

2 On the expression builder, create an expression that specifies the hide condition. Remember, you have to think about when you want to hide the element, not when you want it to appear.

For example, to display the text message, Jumbo, when a loan amount exceeds $363,000.00, conditionally hide the text element using the following expression:

```
row["ordertotal"] < 363000
```

This expression hides the text message when loan amounts are less than $363,000.00.

3 Choose OK.

6 Preview your report to test the conditional visibility.

Sorting and Grouping Data

When you first create a report and preview the data, the report displays the data in the order in which your data source returns it. The order varies, based on how data was entered in the data source and how you joined tables in the query.

In most cases, you will want to change the order in which data appears in the report. A customer phone list, for example, is easier to use if it is in alphabetical order. A sales report is more useful if it presents sales figures from highest to lowest, or the reverse, if you want to see low to top performers.

Compare the reports in Figure 11-1.

Report displays unsorted data

Customer	Phone
Signal Engineering	(203) 555-7845
Technical Specialists Co.	(203) 555-9545
SigniSpecialists Corp.	(212) 555-1957
Technical MicroSystems Inc.	(212) 555-7413
InfoEngineering	(212) 555-1500
Advanced Design Inc.	(212) 555-8493
Technical Design Inc.	(212) 555-7818
Design Solutions Corp.	(212) 555-3675
TekniSystems	(201) 555-9350
InfoDesign	(201) 555-2343
Computer Systems Corp.	(201) 555-8624
SigniDesign	(201) 555-5888
Advanced MicroSystems Co.	(201) 555-3722
TeleMicroSystems	(201) 555-5171

Report sorts data by customer name

Customer	Phone
Advanced Design Corp.	(914) 555-6707
Advanced Design Inc.	(212) 555-8493
Advanced Engineering Inc.	(215) 555-3197
Advanced MicroSystems	(203) 555-4407
Advanced MicroSystems Co.	(201) 555-3722
Advanced Solutions	(617) 555-3842
Advanced Solutions Inc.	(518) 555-9644
Advanced Specialists Corp.	(603) 555-8647
Brittan Design Inc.	(617) 555-2480
CompuBoards	(215) 555-4753
CompuDesign Co.	(617) 555-2663
CompuEngineering	(518) 555-3942
CompuMicroSystems Corp.	(914) 555-9081
CompuSolutions Co.	(201) 555-9867

Figure 11-1   Reports showing unsorted and sorted data

The report on the left displays customer names in the order the data set returns them, which is also called natural order. The report on the right displays customer names in alphabetical order. This report presents the data sorted by customer name.

Now, compare the reports in Figure 11-2. The report on the left sorts the data alphabetically by customer name. The report on the right also sorts the data alphabetically by customer name, but adds an additional sort criterion, by state. This report first groups the data by state. Within each state, the report sorts data by customer name.

Report sorts data by customer name

Report groups customers by state

Customer	Phone
Advanced Design Corp.	(914) 555-6707
Advanced Design Inc.	(212) 555-8493
Advanced Engineering Inc.	(215) 555-3197
Advanced MicroSystems	(203) 555-4407
Advanced MicroSystems Co.	(201) 555-3722
Advanced Solutions	(617) 555-3842
Advanced Solutions Inc.	(518) 555-9644
Advanced Specialists Corp.	(603) 555-8647
Brittan Design Inc.	(617) 555-2480
CompuBoards	(215) 555-4753
CompuDesign Co.	(617) 555-2663
CompuEngineering	(518) 555-3942
CompuMicroSystems Corp.	(914) 555-9081
CompuSolutions Co.	(201) 555-9867

Customer	Phone
CT	
Advanced MicroSystems	(203) 555-4407
Design Design	(203) 555-1450
Signal Engineering	(203) 555-7845
SigniSpecialists	(203) 555-2570
Technical Boards	(203) 555-2373
Technical Specialists Co.	(203) 555-9545
MA	
Advanced Solutions	(617) 555-3842
Brittan Design Inc.	(617) 555-2480
CompuDesign Co.	(617) 555-2663
Computer MicroSystems Corp.	(508) 555-7307
Design Engineering Corp.	(617) 555-6274

Figure 11-2   Reports showing two different sorting techniques

As you can see from the examples, sorting and grouping are two essential ways to organize data for more effective viewing and analysis.

Sorting data

As the previous section describes, you sort data to display report data in a more meaningful order. Without sorting, a report can be much less usable. For example, it often displays data in seemingly random order because that was the way the data was entered into the data source.

You can sort data in ascending or descending order, and you can sort by as many fields as you like. For example, you can sort a list of customers by credit rank, then by customer name.

Figure 11-3 shows the first six data rows in three lists. The first list is unsorted, the second sorts data by credit rank, and the third sorts data first by credit rank, then by customer name.

A field that you use to sort data is called a sort key. For example, if you sort data by customer name, then the customer name field is a sort key.

Data unsorted

Credit	Customer
B	Signal Engineering
A	Technical Specialists Co.
C	SigniSpecialists Corp.
A	Technical MicroSystems Inc.
A	InfoEngineering
A	Advanced Design Inc.

Data sorted by credit rank

Credit	Customer
A	Technical Specialists Co.
A	Technical MicroSystems Inc.
A	InfoEngineering
A	Advanced Design Inc.
A	Technical Design Inc.
A	Design Solutions Corp.

Data sorted by credit rank,
then by customer name

Credit	Customer
A	Advanced Design Inc.
A	Advanced MicroSystems
A	Advanced MicroSystems Co.
A	Advanced Solutions
A	Advanced Solutions Inc.
A	Advanced Specialists Corp.

Figure 11-3   Three examples of sorting list data

Ways to sort data

You sort data in one of two ways:

- Specify sorting in the data set query so that the database processes the data before sending the results to BIRT. Specify sorting in the query whenever possible. Databases are efficient at sorting data, especially if they have indexes to optimize sorts.

- Sort data in BIRT. Use this method if your data source, such as a text file, does not support sorting. If you group data, BIRT handles all sorting automatically.

How to sort data through the query

1   In Data Explorer, create a new data set, or edit an existing one.

2   In the query text area, write an ORDER BY clause in the SELECT statement. For example, the following statement returns customer information and sorts rows by credit rank, then by customer name:

```
SELECT Customers.customerName,
Customers.phone,
Customers.creditRank
FROM Customers
ORDER BY Customers.creditRank, Customers.customerName
```

3   Choose Preview Results to verify the data that the query returns. The rows should be sorted by the fields in the ORDER BY clause.

4   Choose OK.

How to sort data in BIRT

The instructions in this section assume that you already inserted data in a report.

1   In the layout editor, select the table element or list element that contains the data that you want to sort. Property Editor displays the properties for the table or list.

Figure 11-4 shows an example of a selected table and the table's properties.

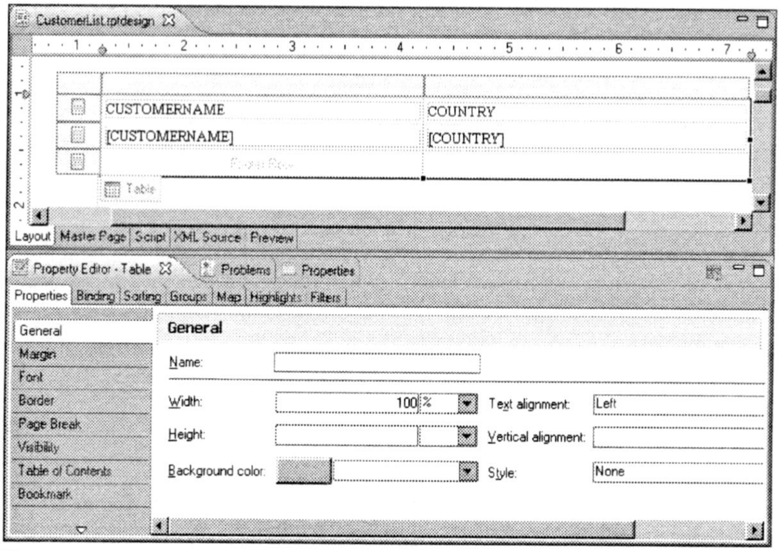

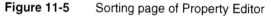

Figure 11-4   Properties for a selected table

2   Choose the Sorting tab in Property Editor.

3   On the sorting page, shown in Figure 11-5, choose Add to specify the field on which to sort the rows.

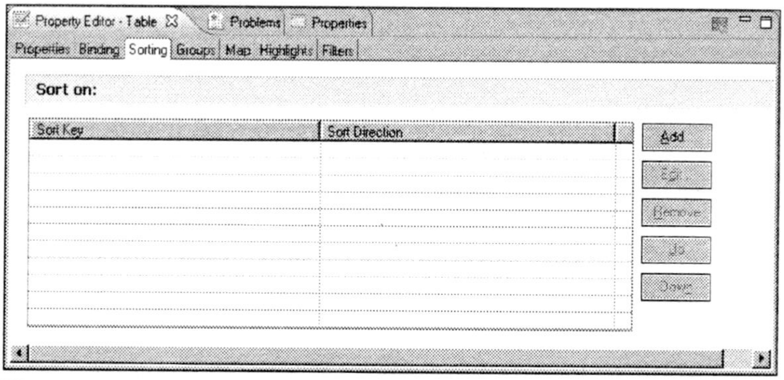

Figure 11-5   Sorting page of Property Editor

4   On New Sort Key:

- In Key, complete one of the following steps:

  □ To specify a field to sort by, select a field from the drop-down list.

  □ To specify an expression by which to sort the data, choose the expression builder button, then provide an expression in the expression builder.

- In Direction, specify the sort order by selecting Ascending or Descending.

Figure 11-6 shows an example of a sort definition.

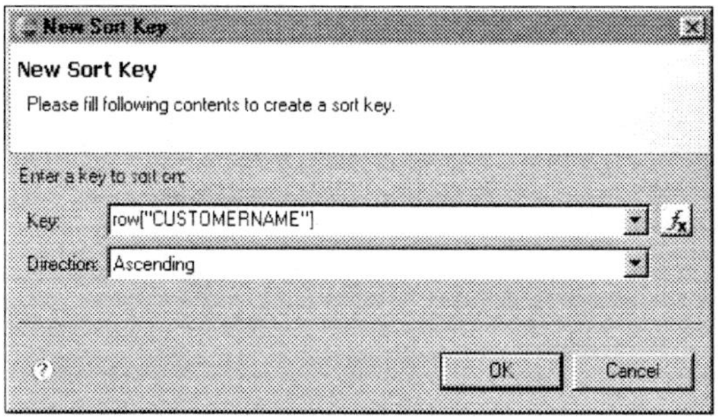

Figure 11-6   Sort expression in New Sort Key

Choose OK. The Sorting page displays the sort key that you defined for the selected table or list.

5   Preview the report. The data in the details section appears in a different order.

Sorting string data case-insensitively

BIRT and some databases sort string data according to UCS2 code point values, so uppercase letters precede lowercase letters. For example, "Z" appears before "a." The following list of values is an example of how BIRT sorts string data:

```
ANG Resellers
AV Stores, Co.
Alpha Cognac
American Souvenirs Inc
Anna's Decorations, Ltd
abc Shops
```

Most of the time, report users prefer to view a list of names in simple alphabetical order, without regard to capitalization. To display string values in case-insensitive alphabetical order, use JavaScript's toUpperCase( ) or toLowerCase( ) function to convert the values to all uppercase or all lowercase before sorting.

The following expression is an example of a sort key expression that you specify:

```
row["CUSTOMERNAME"].toUpperCase()
```

Using this expression, the previous list of values appears alphabetically as:

```
abc Shops
Alpha Cognac
American Souvenirs Inc
ANG Resellers
Anna's Decorations, Ltd
AV Stores, Co.
```

Grouping data

It is common for reports to present data that is organized into meaningful groups. For example, rather than displaying a basic list of orders, an orders report can group orders by customers, then group customers by state. In addition to providing a more effective way to view data, grouped reports have other advantages over reports that are not grouped.

When you group data, you can:

- Add titles or other text at the beginning of each group.

- Add subtotals, counts, averages, or other summary information at the beginning or end of each group.

- Insert a page break before or after each group.

- Automatically generate a table of contents that displays the values of every group. The table of contents supports navigating to specific locations in the report.

- Remove duplicate field values.

Compare the reports in Figure 11-7 and Figure 11-8. The report in Figure 11-7 displays customer order information in a simple list. The data rows are sorted by customer name, then by order number. Notice the repeated customer name and order ID information.

Customer	Order ID	Item	SKU Price	Quantity	Total Price
Brittan Design Inc.	1810	MSL3280	$210.00	1746	$366,660.00
Brittan Design Inc.	1810	MDSPL04	$340.00	1728	$587,520.00
CompuBoards	1075	MP2032	$310.00	49	$15,190.00
CompuBoards	1075	MP1632	$210.00	49	$10,290.00
CompuBoards	1900	MP2032	$310.00	13	$4,030.00
CompuBoards	1900	MP1632x	$221.00	13	$2,873.00
CompuBoards	1900	MSL3290	$300.00	13	$3,900.00
CompuBoards	1900	MDSPL04	$340.00	13	$4,420.00
CompuBoards	1900	MPL1632	$303.00	13	$3,939.00
CompuBoards	1900	MVL1664	$320.00	13	$4,160.00
CompuBoards	1900	MPL2032	$650.00	13	$8,450.00
CompuDesign Co.	1615	MSL3290	$300.00	386	$115,800.00
CompuDesign Co.	1615	MPL1632	$610.00	384	$234,240.00
CompuDesign Co.	1660	MP1632s	$290.00	306	$88,740.00

Figure 11-7   Report showing data in a simple list

The report in Figure 11-8 shows data from the same data set. Unlike the first report, it groups the data rows by customers and order numbers, removing the repeated customer names and order numbers. The customer name and order totals appear at the beginning of each customer group. The order number appears at the beginning of each order group, and a subtotal appears at the end of each order. When the report is displayed in the BIRT report viewer or in PDF format, a table of contents appears to the left of the report.

To create the report in Figure 11-8, you use the customer and order ID fields to create two groups. The customer group is the outer, or top, group. The orders group is within the customer group. You can create as many groups as you want. In the example report, you could, for example, create a third group to organize customers by state. You could also add a fourth group to organize states by region. Practically, however, a report that contains too many groups can make the report difficult to read.

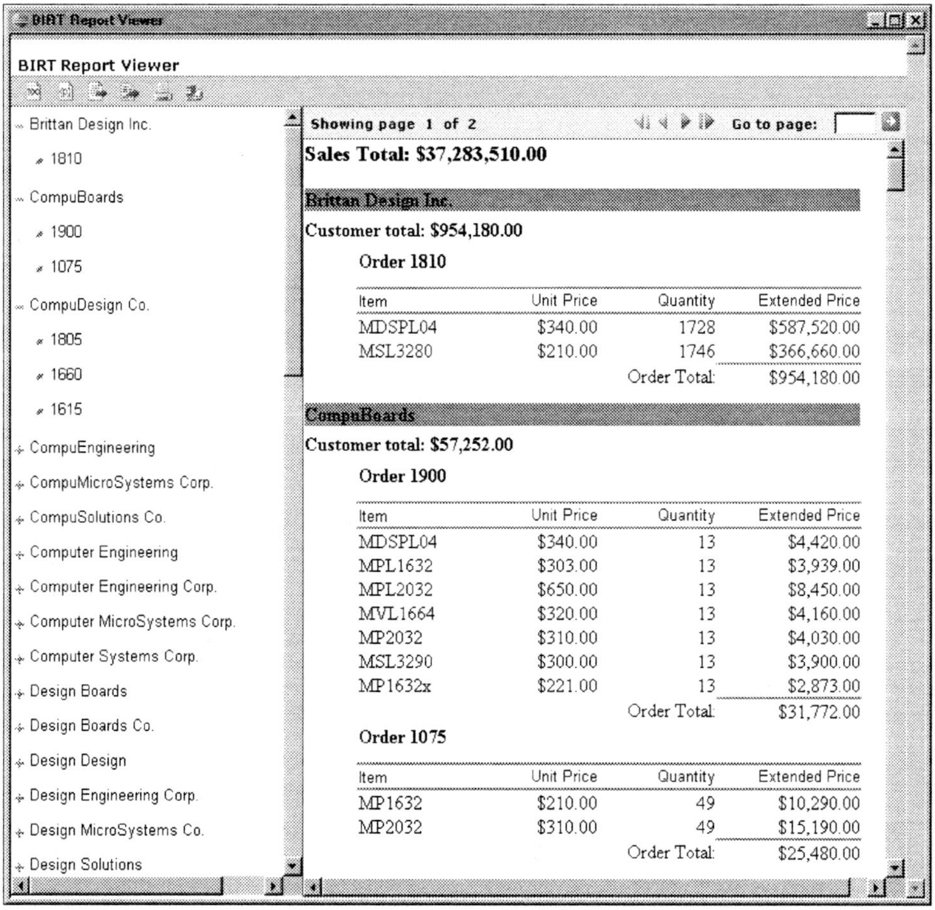

Figure 11-8 Viewing a report that shows customers, orders, and items

How to group data

The instructions in this section assume that you already inserted data in your report.

1 In the layout editor, select the table element or list element that contains the data that you want to group.

2 On Property Editor, choose the Groups tab, then choose Add. New Group, shown in Figure 11-9, displays the properties you can set for the group.

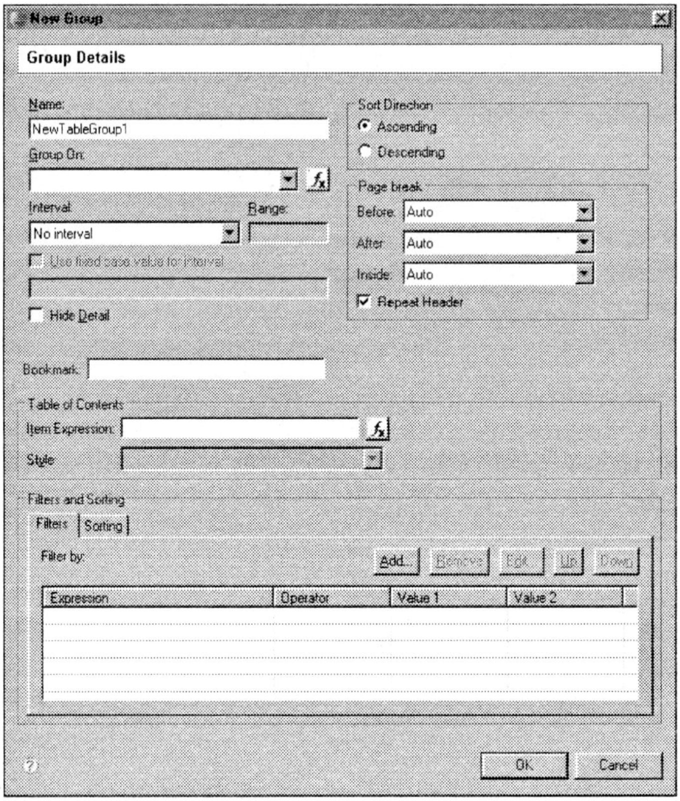

Figure 11-9 New Group

3 Specify the properties of the group.

* For Name, type a name for the group. The name identifies the group and appears in the Edit Group context menu, so you can easily find a specific group for editing later.

* For Group On, select the field on which you want to group. The drop-down list displays all the fields associated with the table. You can group on a field in the table or a field that you have not used in the table. To group on a field that you have not used in the table, you must first create the column binding. Column binding is described in Chapter 7, "Binding Data."

* For Interval, you can select a grouping interval, then specify a range. You can also specify the initial value to use for calculating numeric intervals. For information about grouping by intervals, see "Grouping data by intervals," later in this section.

- For Hide Detail, specify whether or not to display the detail rows. Select this option to display only summary data in the group's header or footer rows.

- For Table of Contents—Item Expression, specify the expression that returns the values to display in the auto-generated table of contents. By default, the group values appear in the report's table of contents.

- For Table of Contents—Style, select a style to apply to the values in the table of contents. For information about styles and how to create them, see Chapter 10, "Formatting Report Content."

- For Sort Direction:

  ❏ Select Ascending to sort the group values in ascending order.

  ❏ Select Descending to sort the group values in descending order.

- For Page Break, you can control where page breaks occur. If you want to display each group of data on its own page, you can insert a page break before or after each group. For more information about setting page breaks, see Chapter 21, "Designing a Multipage Report."

- For Filters, you can specify a filter condition to select group values that meet a certain criteria. For information about filtering group values, see Chapter 14, "Filtering Data."

- For Sorting, you can specify that the group values be sorted by a field other than the field on which the data is grouped. For information about sorting group values, see "Sorting data at the group level," later in this chapter.

Choose OK to save the group.

The table shows two new rows, group header and group footer. Figure 11-10 shows the new rows. BIRT Report Designer places a data element in the group header automatically. This data element displays the values of the field (PRODUCTCODE, in this example) on which the group is based.

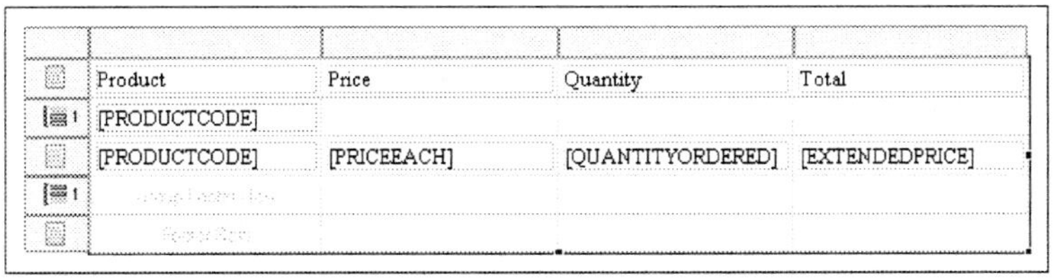

Figure 11-10 Group header and group footer rows in a table

4 Preview the report. The data is organized in groups.

5 To create additional groups, repeat all the previous steps.

Grouping data by intervals

When you create a group, BIRT's default behavior is to group data by a single value, such as a customer name, an order ID, or a date. In the detailed orders report shown earlier in this chapter, each customer name starts a new group, and each order ID starts a new group within the customer group.

Sometimes, it is more useful to group data by a specific interval. A sales report, for example, can present sales by quarters, rather than by dates. Similarly, you can group data in a shipping report by weeks or months, rather than by dates.

Compare the reports in Figure 11-11 and Figure 11-12. The report in Figure 11-11 groups shipping information by dates.

Shipping Schedule		
Ship by	Order ID	Customer name
01/02/2006	1440	Advanced Engineering
01/02/2006	1445	Technical Design Corp.
01/03/2006	1355	Signal MicroSystems
01/04/2006	1400	InfoSpecialists Inc.
01/05/2006	1320	CompuDesign Co.
01/09/2006	1410	Brittan Design Inc.
01/10/2006	1420	Exosoft Corp
01/11/2006	1250	Technical Solutions Inc.
01/11/2006	1325	SigniMicro Systems
01/12/2006	1500	CompuBoards

Figure 11-11   Dates grouped by single date values

The report in Figure 11-12 groups the same shipping information by weeks.

Weekly Shipping Schedule		
Week of 01/02/2006		
Ship by	Order ID	Customer name
01/02/2006	1440	Advanced Engineering
01/02/2006	1445	Technical Design Corp.
01/03/2006	1355	Signal MicroSystems
01/04/2006	1400	InfoSpecialists Inc.
01/05/2006	1320	CompuDesign Co.
Week of 01/09/2006		
Ship by	Order ID	Customer name
01/09/2006	1410	Brittan Design Inc.
01/10/2006	1420	Exosoft Corp
01/11/2006	1250	Technical Solutions Inc.
01/11/2006	1325	SigniMicro Systems
01/12/2006	1500	CompuBoards

Figure 11-12   Dates grouped into weekly intervals

As the reports show, grouping by interval provides the following benefits:

- Organizes a long report into shorter, more readable pieces
- Summarizes data further for more effective analysis

The following sections describe in more detail how to group string, numeric, and date-and-time data by intervals.

Grouping string data by intervals

When you group string data by interval, the interval that you specify is a prefix of a particular length. For example, if a customer group sorts customers by name, you can group customers by the first letter of their names, or the first two letters, or the first three letters, and so on.

You typically group by the first letter to group names by letters of the alphabet. In a customer list, for example, you might want to group all customers whose names begin with A under the heading A, all customers whose names begin with B under the heading B, and so on.

You can group by multiple letters to group items whose names contain special prefixes for classification or categorization. A computer parts vendor, for example, might use the prefix ME for all memory chips, CP for CPU boards, MO for monitors, and so on. In this case, creating a computer parts list that groups names by the first two letters lends itself to logical groupings by part type.

Figure 11-13 shows the results of grouping names by the first letter, the first two letters, and the first three letters. Lines separate the groups.

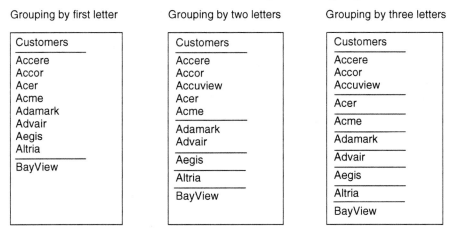

Figure 11-13   Results of grouping string data by intervals

How to group string data by intervals

1   Create a group using the instructions in "How to group data," earlier in this chapter.

2 Set the Interval field in the group editor to Prefix.

3 Set Range to the number of characters by which to group.

Grouping numeric data by intervals

When you group numeric data by intervals, you group by a range of numbers. For example, if an order group sorts orders by numeric ID, you can group the orders by intervals of 10, 50, 100, 1000, and so on.

The interval that is best for any set of numeric data depends on the range of numeric values. If the numbers range from 100 to 200, it makes sense to group in intervals of 10. If the numbers range from 100 to 1000, you might want to group in intervals of 100.

Figure 11-14 shows the results of grouping numbers by intervals of 10, 100, and 1000. Lines separate the groups.

Grouping by 10s	Grouping by 100s	Grouping by 1000s

Order ID	Order ID	Order ID
1070	1070	1070
1080	1080	1080
1085	1085	1085
1095	1095	1095
1340	1340	1340
1345	1345	1345
1405	1405	1405
2005	2005	2005
2030	2030	2030
3015	3015	3015
3020	3020	3020
3025	3025	3025

Figure 11-14   Results of grouping numeric data by intervals

Groups are calculated from the first value in the data set. If the first number is 1070, and you use an interval of 10, the first group contains values from 1070 to 1079, the second group contains values from 1080 to 1089, and so on. In the example report that shows a grouping interval of 1000, the numbers 2005 and 2030 are not in a separate group, which is what you might expect, because the first group contains numbers from 1070 to 2069. The second group contains numbers from 2070 to 3069.

Rather than using the first data set value as the starting, or base, value for determining the grouping of numbers, you can specify a different base value to group numbers in more predictable ranges. Compare the two reports in Figure 11-15.

Grouping by 1000s
No base value specified

Grouping by 1000s
Base value of 1000

Order ID
1070
1080
1085
1095
1340
1345
1405
2005
2030
3015
3020
3025

Order ID
1070
1080
1085
1095
1340
1345
1405
2005
2030
3015
3020
3025

Figure 11-15   Comparison of grouping using no base value and using a base value of 1000

A base value of 1000 provides better results than a base value of 1070 when grouping by intervals of 1000. Rather than grouping numbers in groups of 1070–2069 and 2070–3069, the second report uses more logical groups of 1000–1999 and 2000–2999.

How to group numeric data by intervals

1   Create a group using the instructions in "How to group data," earlier in this chapter.

2   Set the Interval field in the group editor to Interval.

3   Set Range to the desired grouping interval.

4   If you want to specify a starting value to use for calculating groups, select Use fixed base value for interval, and specify a number.

Grouping date-and-time data by intervals

When you group date-and-time data by intervals, you group data by time periods, such as hours, days, weeks, months, and so on. Grouping by time periods is useful for reports that display information that has a time or schedule focus, such as weekly shipping schedules or quarterly sales figures.

The reports in Figure 11-16 show the results of grouping dates by weeks, months, and quarters. The lines separate the groups. Weekly groups start on Mondays, monthly groups start on the first date of the month, and quarterly groups are January 1–March 31, April 1–June 30, July 1–September 30, and October 1–December 31. If you group by year, the groups start on January 1 and end on December 31.

Grouping by weeks	Grouping by months	Grouping by quarters
Ship Dates	**Ship Dates**	**Ship Dates**
January 9, 2006 January 15, 2006	January 9, 2006 January 15, 2006 January 30, 2006	January 9, 2006 January 15, 2006 January 30, 2006 February 5, 2006 March 7, 2006
January 30, 2006 February 5, 2006	February 5, 2006	
March 7, 2006	March 7, 2006	April 5, 2006 April 12, 2006 June 18, 2006 June 30, 2006
April 5, 2006	April 5, 2006 April 12, 2006	
April 12, 2006	June 18, 2006 June 30, 2006	July 7, 2006
June 18, 2006		October 1, 2006
June 30, 2006	July 7, 2006	
July 7, 2006	October 1, 2006	
October 1, 2006		

Figure 11-16   Results of grouping date-and-time data by intervals

If you do not want to use the default start value for date-and-time groups, you can specify a different base value to group dates in different ranges. For example, an organization's fiscal year is October 1 to September 30, and you want to group ten years worth of data into yearly groups by fiscal year rather than by calendar year. To do so, set the interval to month and the range to 12, then specify a base value such as 1995-10. You must use the year-month format. The report will display the data in the following groups: October 1, 1995–September 30, 1996; October 1, 1996–September 30, 1997; October 1, 1997–September 30, 1998; and so on.

How to group date-and-time data by intervals

1   Create a group using the instructions in "How to group data," earlier in this chapter.

2   Set the Interval field in the group editor to one of the time period values, such as Year, Month, Week, Day, or Hour.

3   Set Range to the number of units to include in each group. For example, if you selected Week as the interval, specify 2 as the range to group data in two-week periods.

4   If you want to specify a different starting value to use for calculating groups, select Use fixed base value for interval, then specify a date.

Sorting data at the group level

When you create a group, the default setting specifies sorting the group values by the grouping field in ascending order. For example, if you create an order ID group, the default setting is to sort order ID values in ascending order. You can, however, sort the group values by a different field. For example, rather than sort group values by order ID, you can sort by order total.

Sorting at the group level is different from sorting at the detail row level. When you sort at the detail row level, you specify the sorting criteria on the Sorting page in Property Editor. When you sort at the group level, you specify the sorting criteria through the Groups page.

The report in Figure 11-17 groups sales data by product code. The group header, highlighted with a gray background, displays the product code and the sales total. The product code group uses the default sorting, which sorts by product code in ascending order, such as S10_1678, S10_1949, S10_2016, and so on.

S10_1678			$6,702.15
Order Number	Quantity Sold	Price Per Unit	Order Total
10211	41	$90.92	$3,727.72
10223	37	$80.39	$2,974.43
S10_1949			**$16,769.28**
Order Number	Quantity Sold	Price Per Unit	Order Total
10206	47	$203.59	$9,568.73
10215	35	$205.73	$7,200.55
S10_2016			**$7,996.11**
Order Number	Quantity Sold	Price Per Unit	Order Total
10201	24	$116.56	$2,797.44
10223	47	$110.61	$5,198.67

Figure 11-17 Results of sorting group values in ascending order

The report in Figure 11-18 contains the same data as the report in Figure 11-17, but rather than sorting by product code, it sorts by the product sales total in ascending order.

S10_1678			$6,702.15
Order Number	Quantity Sold	Price Per Unit	Order Total
10211	41	$90.92	$3,727.72
10223	37	$80.39	$2,974.43
S10_2016			**$7,996.11**
Order Number	Quantity Sold	Price Per Unit	Order Total
10201	24	$116.56	$2,797.44
10223	47	$110.61	$5,198.67
S10_1949			**$16,769.28**
Order Number	Quantity Sold	Price Per Unit	Order Total
10206	47	$203.59	$9,568.73
10215	35	$205.73	$7,200.55

Figure 11-18 Results of changing the sort order of groups

By changing the field on which groups are sorted, you can choose the information to emphasize. As Figure 11-18 shows, the report can group sales data by product code but list them in order of sales total, which is often a more useful way to present sales information.

How to sort data at the group level

1 Create a group using the instructions in "How to group data," earlier in this chapter. Figure 11-19 shows the group editor. You can specify sorting in two ways. The first way is to specify sorting by the grouping field. The second way enables you to specify a different field by which to sort and also enables you to specify a sort expression.

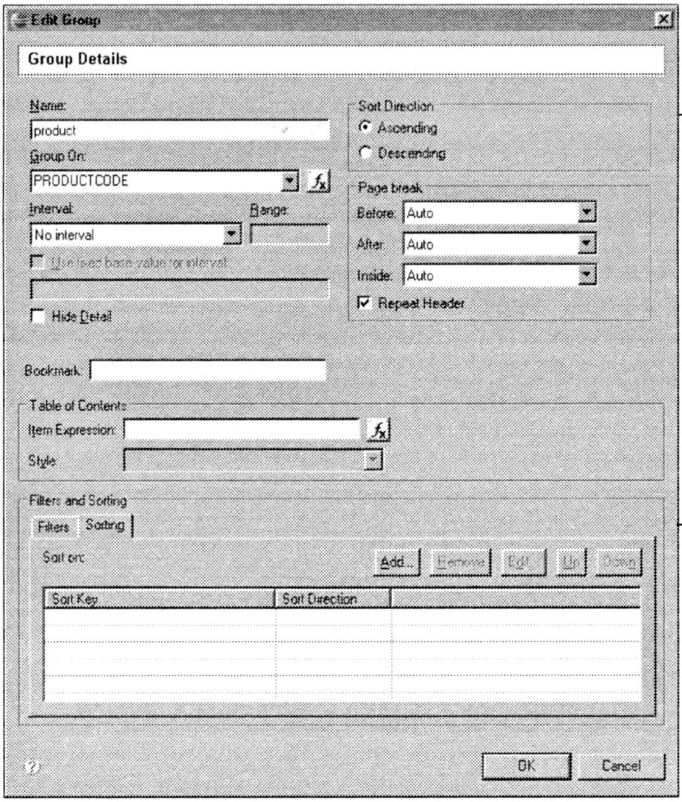

This Sort specifies sorting by the Group On value

This Sort specifies sorting by a different field or on an expression

Figure 11-19 Sorting options in Edit Group

2 In Filters and Sorting, choose Sorting.

3 Choose Add to specify a sort key.

4 On New Sort Key:

    1 In Key, complete one of the following steps:

        ❑ To specify a field to sort by, select a field from the drop-down list.

        ❑ To specify an expression by which to sort the data, choose the expression builder button, then provide an expression in the expression builder.

    2 In Direction, specify the sort order by selecting Ascending or Descending.

Figure 11-20 shows an example of a sort definition that sorts group values by sales totals in ascending order.

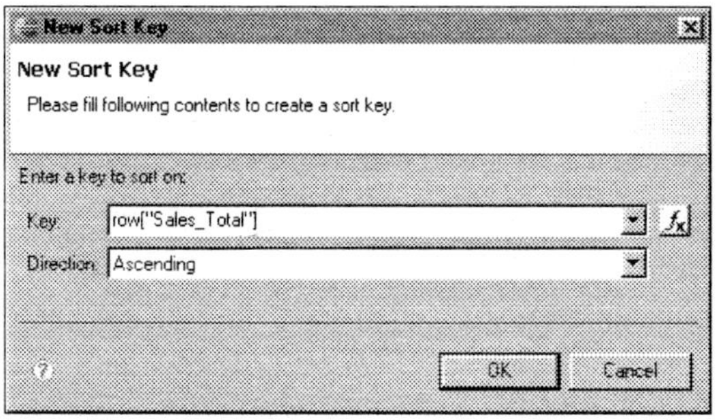

Figure 11-20   New Sort Key, displaying a sort definition

3   Choose OK to save the sort definition.

The sort definition appears in Edit Group, as shown in Figure 11-21.

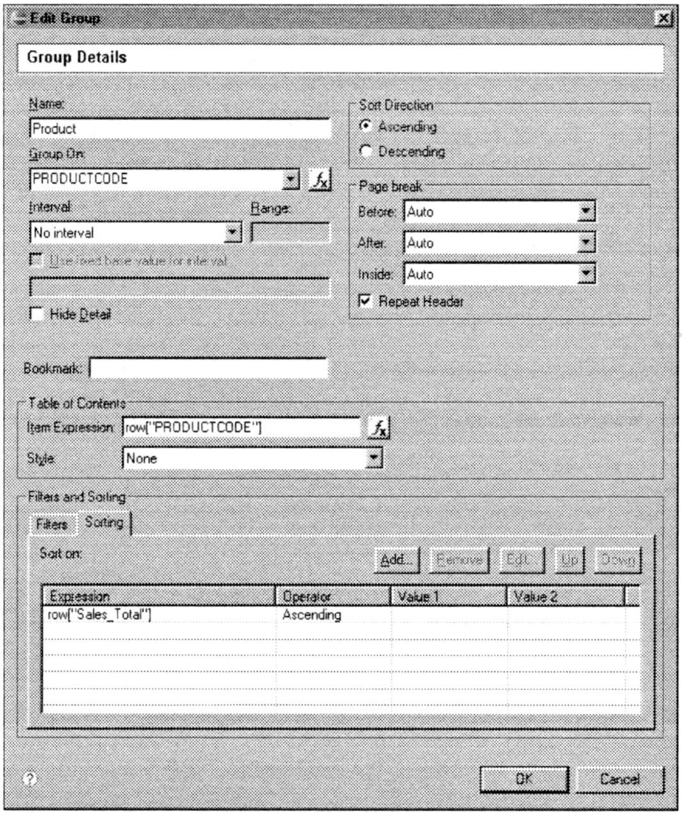

Figure 11-21   Sorting expression in Edit Group

5   Preview the report.

Creating multiple groups

When you create multiple groups, the order in which you create them determines how the report groups data. Before you create groups, think about their order. For example, if you want to group data by state, then by city, create the groups in that order. In other words, state is the table or list element's first, or top-level, group, and city is the second, or inner, group.

The reports in Figure 11-22 show the results of creating the state and city groups in different orders. The first report shows the output when the state group is the top-level group. The second report shows the output when the city group is the top-level group.

Data in the first report is organized logically. The report shows each state in alphabetical order, then the cities are sorted alphabetically within each state. On the other hand, data in the second report is sorted by city first, which results in repeated state headings that are organized in seemingly random order.

Report groups data by state, then by city   Report groups data by city, then by state

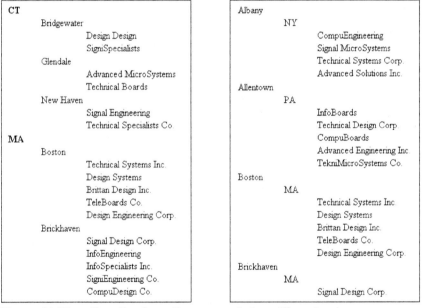

Figure 11-22   Results of creating groups in two different orders

Figure 11-23 shows the report design for the first report. The state field appears in the group header 1 row, and the city field appears in the group header 2 row.

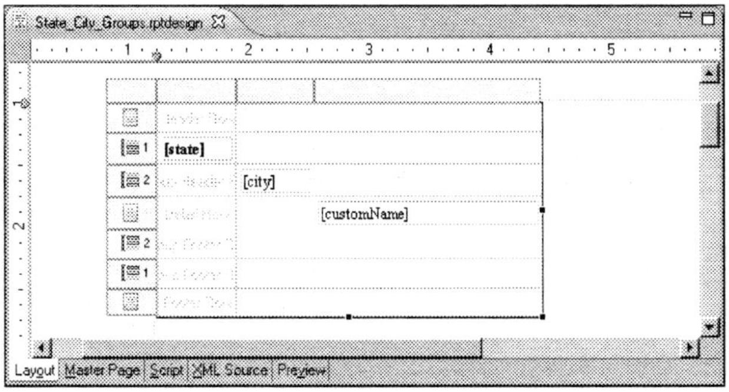

Figure 11-23   Report design grouping data by state, then by city

You can create groups using any of the following procedures. The procedure
you use depends on your preference and whether you are creating all the
groups for the first time or adding groups to an existing group structure.

- To create groups that follow the order in which you create them, use one
  of the following procedures:

  - Select the table or list, then choose Element➤Insert Group➤Below
    from the main menu to create each group. For example, if you create a
    state group first and a city group second, the state group is the top-
    level group, and the city is the inner group.

  - Select the table or list, then choose the Groups tab on Property Editor.
    Like the previous technique, the order in which you create the groups
    determines the order in which data is grouped.

- To add a group at the top level, select the table or list, then choose Insert
  Group➤Above from the context menu. For example, if you already
  created a city group, use Insert Group➤Above to add a state group as the
  top-level group.

- To add a group at the lowest level, right-click the table or list, then choose
  Insert Group➤Below from the table or list's context menu. For example, if
  you already created a state group, choose Insert Group➤Below to add a
  city group as the inner group.

- To add a group between two existing groups, use one of the following
  procedures:

  - Right-click the group row above which to create the new group, then
    choose Insert Group➤Above.

  - Right-click the group row below which to create the new group, then
    choose Insert Group➤Below.

All the techniques display the Edit Group dialog box, where you define the
properties of a group. If you inadvertently create groups in the wrong order,
you can easily change the order of the groups. You do not have to delete and
recreate the groups.

Changing the order of groups

The Groups page in Property Editor shows all the groups that you create for a particular table or list. You must use this page, shown in Figure 11-26, to change the order of groups. You can also add, edit, and delete groups using this page.

You cannot change the order of groups by moving data elements in the layout editor. This action affects only the display position of the data values. Compare the report designs in Figure 11-24. The state and city data elements are transposed by dragging and dropping in the layout editor.

State data element placed in group header 1
City data element placed in group header 2

State data element moved to group header 2
City data element moved to group header 1

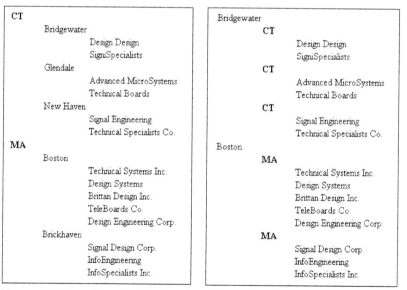

Figure 11-24   Report designs with transposed state and city elements

Now, compare the corresponding report output, shown in Figure 11-25. The first report shows data sorted by state, then by city. The second report displays the city values above the state values. The report data, however, is still sorted by state first, then by city.

CT	Bridgewater
Bridgewater	CT
Design Design	Design Design
SigniSpecialists	SigniSpecialists
Glendale	CT
Advanced MicroSystems	Advanced MicroSystems
Technical Boards	Technical Boards
New Haven	CT
Signal Engineering	Signal Engineering
Technical Specialists Co.	Technical Specialists Co.
MA	Boston
Boston	MA
Technical Systems Inc.	Technical Systems Inc.
Design Systems	Design Systems
Brittan Design Inc.	Brittan Design Inc.
TeleBoards Co.	TeleBoards Co.
Design Engineering Corp.	Design Engineering Corp.
Brickhaven	MA
Signal Design Corp.	Signal Design Corp.
InfoEngineering	InfoEngineering
InfoSpecialists Inc.	InfoSpecialists Inc.

Figure 11-25   Reports showing the effects of transposing state and city elements

How to change the order of groups

1 Select the table or list whose groups you want to re-order.

2 In Property Editor, choose the Groups tab. The Groups page displays the groups defined in the table or list, as shown in Figure 11-26.

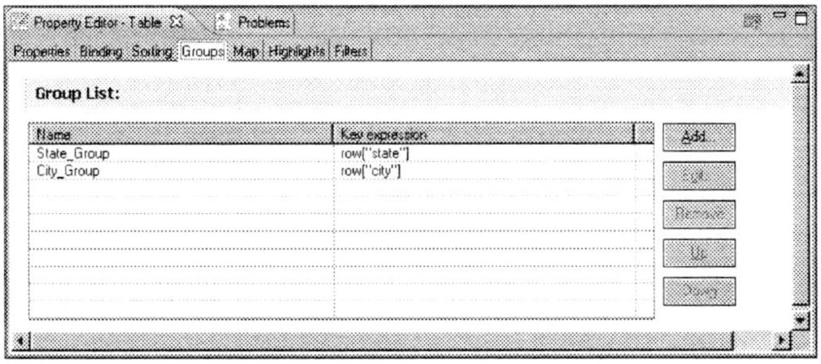

Figure 11-26 Groups page

This page displays the group names in the order in which the report currently groups the data.

3 Select a group from the list, then use the Up or Down button to move the selected group up or down the list. In the layout editor, the data elements change positions to reflect the new grouping order.

4 Repeat the previous step until you finish changing the order of groups.

Adding group headings

If your report contains groups, you typically add a descriptive heading that appears at the beginning of each group to identify the data within the group. When you create a group, BIRT Report Designer automatically inserts a data element in the group header row to serve as the group heading. This data element displays the values of the field on which the group is based. For example, if you group data by state, the data element displays a state name for each group.

Unlike column headings, which are static, group headings change based on the content of the group. If a report groups data by customers, for example, you can display the customer name at the beginning of each group. For a customer list that groups names by the first letter, the titles for the groups are A, B, C, and so on. For a shipping schedule that groups data by weeks, the titles for the groups could be Week of 01/02/06, Week of 01/09/06, and so on.

The reports in Figure 11-27 show examples of headings that change with each group. Bold text highlights the group headings. If you do not use group headings, it is unclear where one group ends and another begins. Remove the A and B headings from the Customers report, for example, and the report looks like a list sorted alphabetically. You can add a line or space between groups to indicate a change in group, but a descriptive heading makes it easier for users to find information in the report.

Customer Orders	Customers	Weekly Shipping Schedule

<table>
<tr><td>Advanced Design</td><td>A</td><td>Week of 01/02/06</td></tr>
</table>

Customer Orders

Advanced Design
Order 1010

Item	Quantity	Price
M12	2	$60.00
M15	1	$55.00

Order 1015

Item	Quantity	Price
R50	1	$20.00

...

Advantix Inc
Order 1050
...

Customers

A

Accere
Accor
Acer
Acme
Adamark
Advair

B

BayView
Beaucoup
...

Weekly Shipping Schedule

Week of 01/02/06

Ship date	Order ID
01/02/06	1015
01/03/06	1025
01/03/06	1026
01/04/06	1020
01/05/06	1022
01/06/06	1030

Week of 01/09/06

Ship date	Order ID
01/09/06	1029

Figure 11-27   Examples of group headings that change

Inserting group header rows

If you deleted a group header row from a table, you can re-insert the row. You can also insert additional group header rows, if you want to display header information on two lines, for example, a group title on the first line, and summary information on the next line.

How to insert a group header row

1   Select the table in which you want to insert a group header row.

2   Right-click the Table tab, then choose Insert Group Header or Footer→<group>→Header, as shown in Figure 11-28.

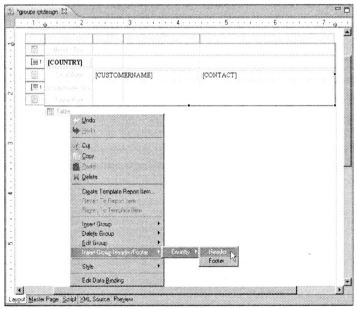

Figure 11-28   Inserting a group header row

Displaying group headings in the detail row

Headings that are in a group header row appear above the detail rows. Sometimes, a report looks better if the headings appear in the first detail row of each group. Compare the examples in Figure 11-29. The example on the left shows the group headings, which are order numbers, in a row above the detail rows. The example on the right shows the group headings in the detail row.

Group headings (order numbers) appear above the detail rows

Group headings (order numbers) appear in the first detail row

Order 10200		
	S24_1785	$3,285.81
	S32_1374	$2,831.85
	S32_4289	$1,764.45
		$7,882.11
Order 10202		
	S32_2206	$901.53
	S32_4485	$2,530.84
		$3,432.37

Order 10200	S24_1785	$3,285.81
	S32_1374	$2,831.85
	S32_4289	$1,764.45
		$7,882.11
Order 10202	S32_2206	$901.53
	S32_4485	$2,530.84
		$3,432.37

Figure 11-29 Two ways to display group headings

To display group headings on the same line as the first detail row, you drop the cell that contains the heading, using the Drop property. You cannot just move the group heading to the detail row because it would be repeated for every row. To drop a cell, you must observe the following rules:

- There must be an empty cell below the cell that contains the group heading. Otherwise, the cell content overwrites the content in the cell below it.

- If a table contains multiple group header rows, you can drop only cells in the group header row directly above the detail row.

- You can only drop cells in a group header row. You cannot drop cells in a detail or group footer row.

You can drop a group header cell so that it spans the detail rows, or all the rows in the group, including the group footer row. You see a difference only if the group header cell has a border or background color. Compare the examples in Figure 11-30. The example on the left drops the group header cell to the detail rows. The example on the right drops the group header cell to all the rows in the group.

Notice that the cell color in the example on the left extends to the last detail row, whereas the cell color in the example on the right extends to the group footer row. If the cell did not have a background color, the output would look the same whether you set the cell's Drop property to Detail or All. The order numbers always appear in the first detail row of each group.

Group header cell (shown with gray background) dropped to the detail rows

Group header cell dropped to all rows in the group

Order 10200	S24_1785	$3,285.81
	S32_1374	$2,831.85
	S32_4289	$1,764.45
		$7,882.11
Order 10202	S32_2206	$901.53
	S32_4485	$2,530.84
		$3,432.37

Order 10200	S24_1785	$3,285.81
	S32_1374	$2,831.85
	S32_4289	$1,764.45
		$7,882.11
Order 10202	S32_2206	$901.53
	S32_4485	$2,530.84
		$3,432.37

Figure 11-30   Reports showing different settings for the Drop property

Figure 11-31 shows the portion of the report design that generates the previous example output.

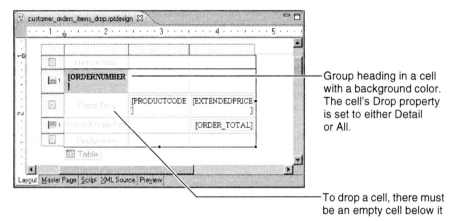

Group heading in a cell with a background color. The cell's Drop property is set to either Detail or All.

To drop a cell, there must be an empty cell below it

Figure 11-31   Report design that generates a dropped cell

How to drop a group heading to the detail row

1 Select the cell that contains the group heading you want to drop. The cell directly below it must be empty.

2 On Property Editor, choose General from the list of properties.

3 For Drop, select one of the following values:

- Detail—Select this value to drop the group heading so that it spans only the detail rows.

- All—Select this value to drop the group heading so that it spans all the rows in the group, including the group footer row.

These values display a difference in the generated report only if the cell has borders or background color.

4 Preview the report. The group heading appears in the first detail row of each group.

Specifying expressions for group headings

Unlike column headings, which you create using static text, you specify expressions for group headings because the heading values are dynamic. In other words, the value changes based on the group's content. You can use a data set field, a computed field, or a text element with dynamic values, depending on the value that you want to display.

Typically, you use a computed field to combine a field value and static text. Sometimes, you use a JavaScript function to display the values you need. The following list shows some examples of expressions that you can use for group headings:

- To display the customer name as the group heading, use the customer name field as the expression. For example:

  ```
  dataSetRow["customerName"]
  ```

- To display a group heading that combines static text with a field, insert a data element, and use an expression like the following example:

  ```
  "Order " + dataSetRow["orderID"]
  ```

- To create headings (A, B, and so on) for a customer list that is grouped by the first letter, insert a data element, and use the JavaScript charAt( ) function to get the first letter of the name in each group. For example:

  ```
  dataSetRow["customerName"].charAt(0)
  ```

- To create headings that display the names of months (January, February, and so on) for each group of dates, insert an HTML text element, and use the following expression:

  ```
  <VALUE-OF format="MMMM">row["shipByDate"]</VALUE-OF>
  ```

Tutorial 2: Grouping report data

This tutorial provides instructions for grouping customer data by credit limit. It uses the report that you built in Tutorial 1: "Building a simple listing report," in Chapter 3, "Learning the Basics." In the first tutorial, you built a simple report that listed customers in alphabetical order. In this report, you organize customers into credit limit groups of $50,000.00, such as 0–49999, 50000–99999, 100000–149999, and so on.

Before you begin this tutorial, you must complete the first tutorial. In this second tutorial, you perform the following tasks:

- Open the report design.

- Save the report as a new file.

- Add the credit limit field to the data set.

- Add credit limit data to the report.

- Group customer data by credit limit.

- Display credit limit ranges in the group header.

- Display aggregate information.

- Format the report.

- Preview the report in the BIRT report viewer.

- Display credit limit ranges in the table of contents.

Task 1: Open the report design

In the first tutorial, you created Customers.rptdesign in a project folder named My Reports. Open Customers.rptdesign using one of the following procedures:

- If you are using BIRT Report Designer, open the file through Navigator, using the following steps:

  1 Open Navigator by choosing Window→Show View→Navigator. Navigator shows all the project folders and report files you create.

  2 Navigate to the My Reports folder, then double-click Customers.rptdesign.

- If you are using BIRT RCP Report Designer, use the main menu to open the file.

  1 Choose File→Open File.

  2 Navigate to and select Customers.rptdesign, then choose Open.

The file opens in the layout editor, as shown in Figure 11-32.

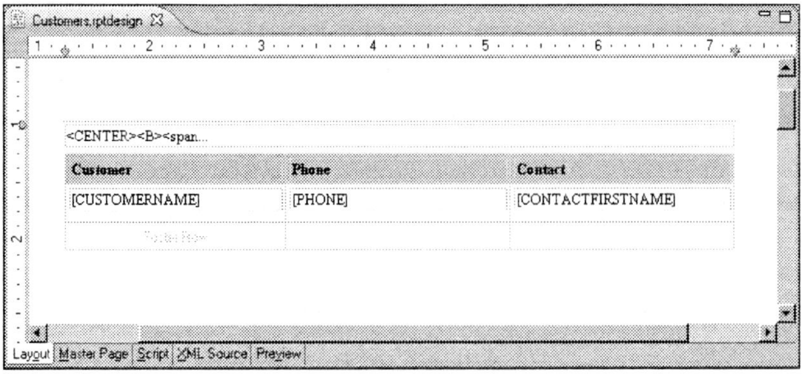

Figure 11-32   Customer report design in the layout editor

Task 2: Save the report as a new file

Rather than editing directly the report that you created in the first tutorial, save Customers.rptdesign as a new file.

1 Choose File→Save As. Save As displays the file's current name and location.

2 For File name, change Customers.rptdesign to Customers_grouped.rptdesign, then choose Finish. BIRT Report Designer makes a copy of Customers.rptdesign. The new file appears in the layout editor.

Task 3: Add the credit limit field to the data set

In order for the report to display credit limit data, you must add the CREDITLIMIT field to the data set.

1 Choose Data Explorer, expand Data Sets, then double-click Customers. Edit Data Set displays the SQL query for the Customers data set.

2 In the query, add a comma (,) after phone.

3 On the next line, add the following text:

```
creditLimit
```

The modified query should look like the one shown in Figure 11-33.

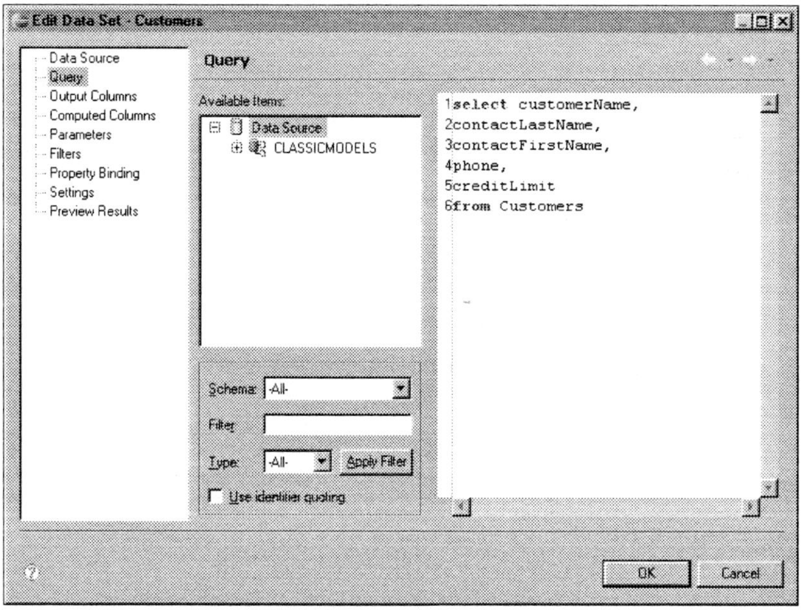

Figure 11-33   Query with creditLimit field added

4 Choose Preview Results to verify that the query returns rows with credit limit information.

5 Choose OK to save the data set.

Task 4: Add credit limit data to the report

In this procedure, you insert the credit limit field in the existing table.

1 In the layout editor, select the table. Guide cells appear at the top and left side of the table.

2 Right-click the guide cell above the first column, then choose Insert➤Column to the Left, as shown in Figure 11-34.

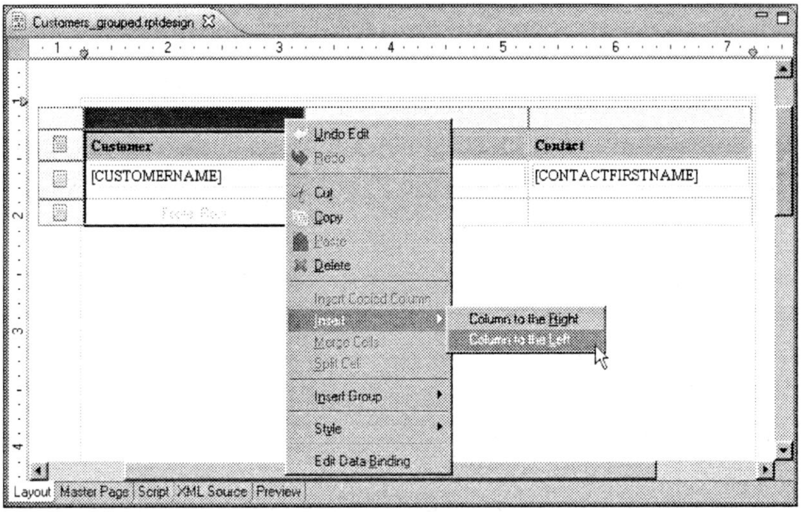

Figure 11-34 Inserting a column to the left of an existing column

A new column appears.

3 In Data Explorer, expand Data Sets, then expand Customers. The Customers data set displays the fields specified in the query.

4 Drag the CREDITLIMIT field from Data Explorer, and drop it in the detail row cell next to [CUSTOMERNAME].

In the layout editor, the table displays the field that you added. The table also shows the label element that the layout editor automatically added to the header row. This label serves as the column heading and displays the field name as static text. The report should look like the one shown in Figure 11-35.

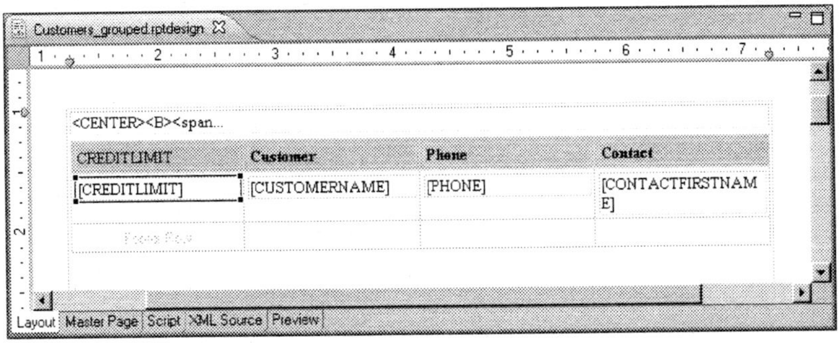

Figure 11-35 Result of adding the credit limit field in the layout editor

5 Edit the CREDITLIMIT label so that it appears as **Credit Limit**.

6 Preview the report. The report should look like the one shown in Figure 11-36.

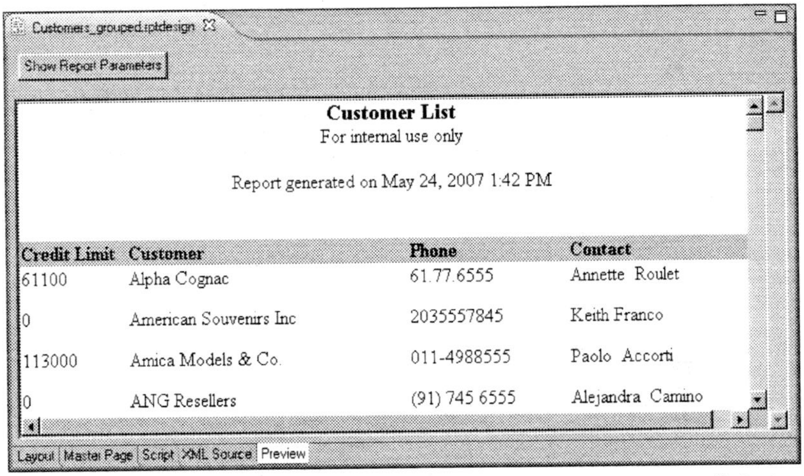

Figure 11-36 Report preview showing the result of adding credit limit

Some of the customers have a credit limit of 0. These are new customers who have not yet been approved for a line of credit.

Task 5: Group customer data by credit limit

The report is currently sorted alphabetically by customer name. Recall that in the first tutorial, you specified that the rows in the table be sorted by customer name. In this procedure, you group the data by credit limit in intervals of 50,000. When you group data, BIRT sorts the rows into groups first, then it sorts the rows within each group, assuming that you also specify a sort condition at the table level. As you will see when you complete this task, the data rows within each credit limit group will be sorted by customer name.

1 Choose Layout to return to the layout editor.

2 Right-click the table, and choose Insert Group➤Above. New Group, shown in Figure 11-37, displays the group properties you can set.

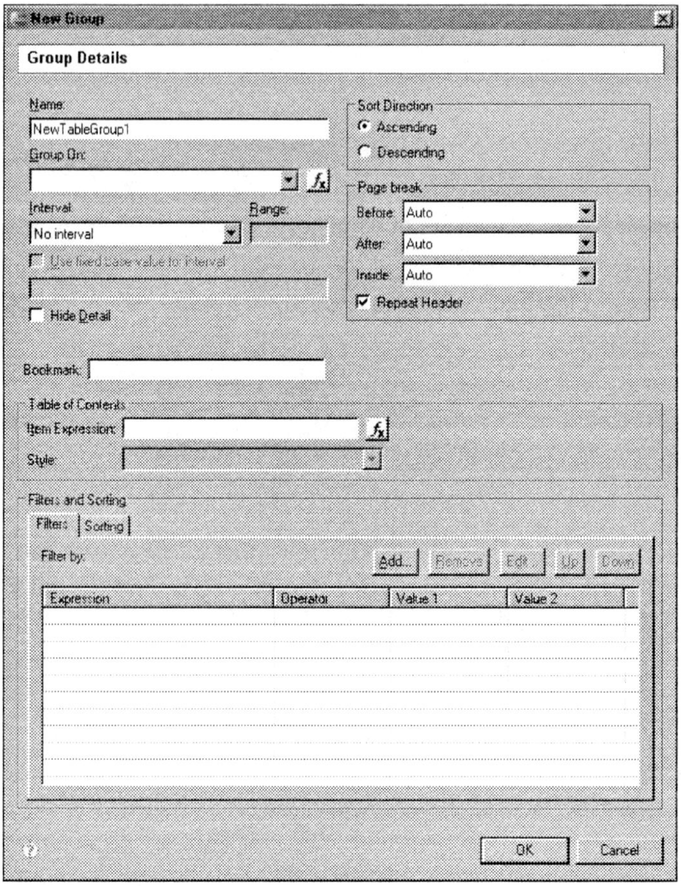

Figure 11-37 New Group

3 Follow these steps to specify grouping by credit limit in intervals of 50000:

    1 For Name, type the following text as the group name:

        `credit_group`

    2 For Group On, select CREDITLIMIT from the drop-down list.

    3 For Interval, select Interval from the drop-down list.

    4 For Range, type 50000.

    5 Use the default values for the other options. Choose OK.

The table in the report design displays a group header and a group footer row, as shown in Figure 11-38. The table also shows the data element that the layout editor automatically added to the group header row. This data element serves as the group heading and, in the generated report, displays the first credit limit value of each group.

Customers_grouped.rptdesign
Credit Limit
Customer
Phone
Contact
[CREDITLIMIT]
[CREDITLIMIT]
[CUSTOMERNAME]
[PHONE]
[CONTACTFIRSTNAM E]
Layout
Master Page
Script
XML Source
Preview

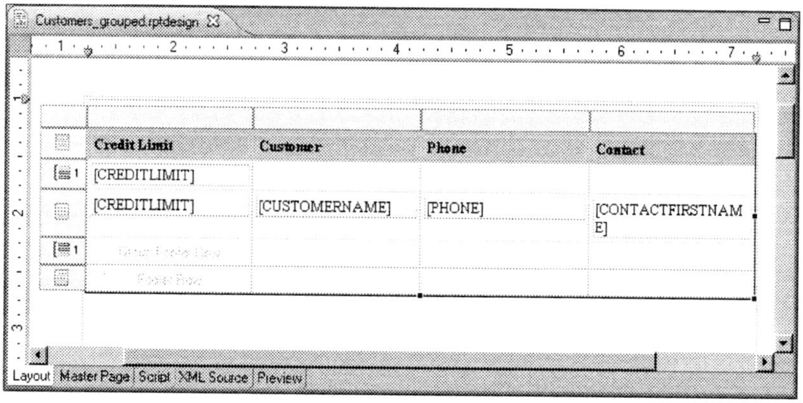

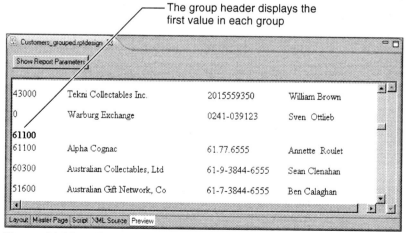

Figure 11-38 Group header and group footer rows in a report design

4 Select the [CREDITLIMIT] data element that appears in the group header row. Do not select the [CREDITLIMIT] data element that appears in the detail row.

5 In Property Editor, choose General, then choose B to format the group heading as bold text.

6 Preview the report. Scroll down the report to view all the data. The report organizes data into four credit limit groups. At the beginning of each group, you see the following numbers in bold: 0, 61100, 113000, 227600. These numbers match the first credit limit value of each group. Within each group, customer names are sorted in alphabetical order. Figure 11-39 shows one of the four credit limit groups.

The group header displays the first value in each group
Customers_grouped.rptdesign
Show Report Parameters
43000
Tekni Collectables Inc.
2015559350
William Brown
0
Warburg Exchange
0241-039123
Sven Ottlieb
61100
61100
Alpha Cognac
61.77.6555
Annette Roulet
60300
Australian Collectables, Ltd
61-9-3844-6555
Sean Clenahan
51600
Australian Gift Network, Co
61-7-3844-6555
Ben Calaghan
Layout
Master Page
Script
XML Source
Preview

Figure 11-39 Report preview showing one of the four credit limit groups

Task 6: Display credit limit ranges in the group header

Rather than display the first value of each group in the group header, the report is easier to navigate if it displays the credit limit range for each group, as follows:

```
0 - 49999
50000 - 99999
100000 - 149999
```

This procedure shows how to write a JavaScript expression to display these credit limit ranges. The procedure also shows how to create a column binding with which to associate the JavaScript expression.

1 Choose Layout to return to the layout editor.

2 Delete the [CREDITLIMIT] data element in the group header, and insert a new data element in its place.

New Data Binding, shown in Figure 11-40, prompts you to create a column binding for the new data element.

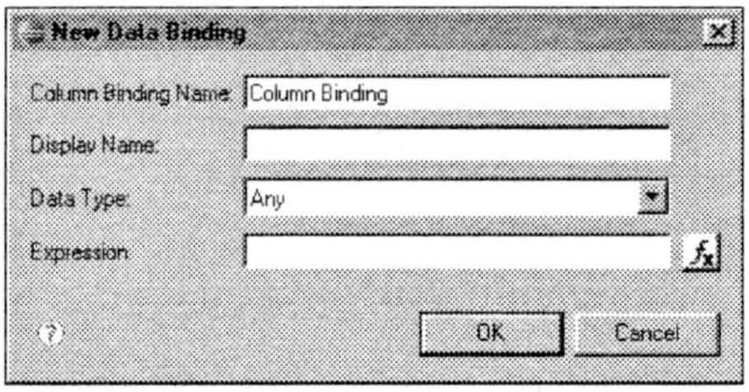

Figure 11-40   New Data Binding

3 On New Data Binding, provide a name and expression for the column binding.

1 In Name, type the following name:

```
CREDIT_GRP_HEADER
```

2 Open the expression builder to write a JavaScript expression.

3 In the expression builder, type the following expression:

```
for(i=50000; i<300000; i+=50000){
    if( row["CREDITLIMIT"] < i ){
        rangeStart = i-50000;
        rangeEnd = i-1;
        break;
    }
}
displayString = rangeStart + " - " + rangeEnd;
```

Choose OK. The expression appears in the Expression field on New Data Binding, as shown in Figure 11-41.

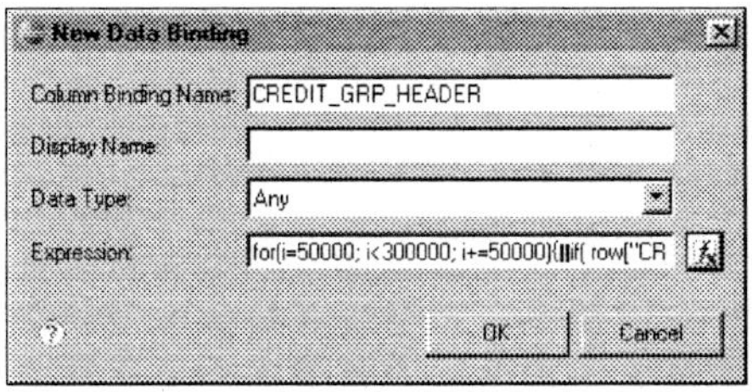

Figure 11-41 Column binding defined

4   Choose OK to save the column binding for the data element.

In the layout editor, the data element displays the column binding name, [CREDIT_GRP_HEADER].

4   Select the data element. In Property Editor, choose General, then choose B to format the group heading as bold text.

5   Preview the report. The group headers display the credit limit ranges. Figure 11-42 shows the 50000 - 99999 group header.

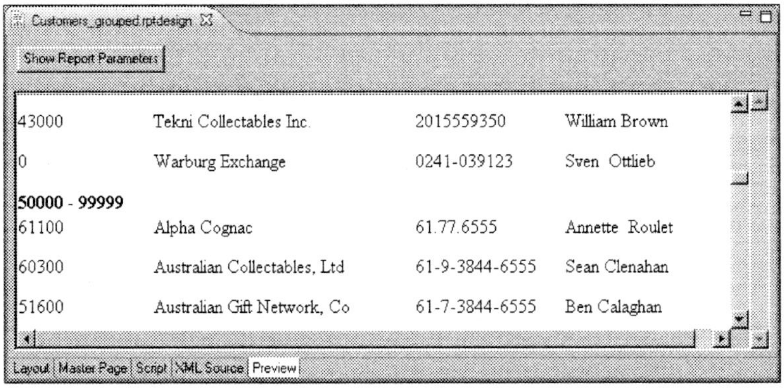

Figure 11-42 Report preview showing credit limit ranges

Task 7:   Display aggregate information

One of the benefits of grouping data is that you can add summary, or aggregate, information at the beginning or end of each group. In this procedure, you add the following aggregate information to the report:

■   The number of customers in each group

■   The number of all customers that are listed in the report

Display the number of customers in each group

1   Choose Layout to return to the layout editor.

2   In the palette, under Quick Tools, drag an aggregation element and drop it in the second cell in the group footer row. Elements that are in the group footer appear at the end of every group.

3 On Aggregation Builder:

  1 In Column Binding Name, type the following name:

    GRP_TOTAL_CUSTOMERS

  2 In Function, select COUNT.

  3 In Aggregate On, select Group and credit_group. This value indicates that the COUNT function returns the number of rows in each credit limit group.

  Figure 11-43 shows the complete definition for the aggregation element.

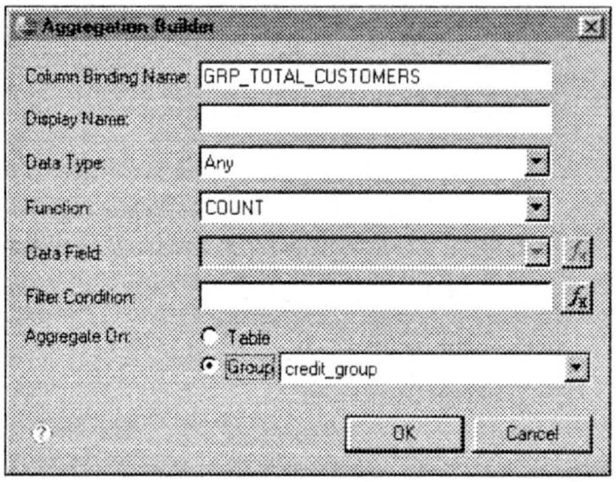

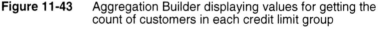

Figure 11-43   Aggregation Builder displaying values for getting the count of customers in each credit limit group

4 Choose OK. In the report design, shown in Figure 11-44, the aggregation element displays the sigma symbol followed by the column binding name.

    Σ [GRP_TOTAL_CUSTOM...]

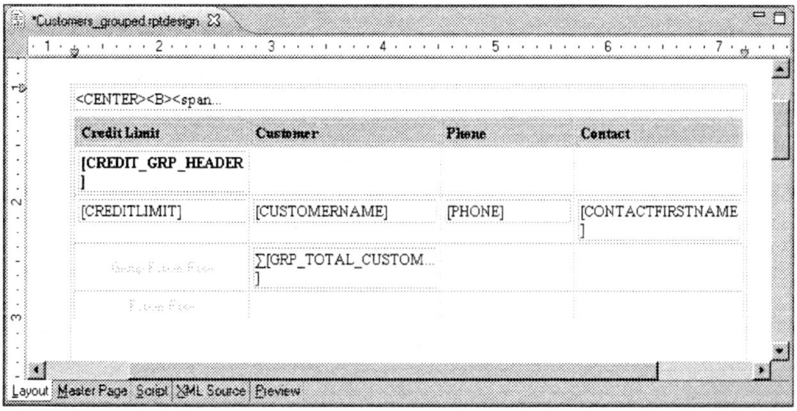

Figure 11-44   Report design displaying the aggregation element

4 Preview the report. The report displays the number of customers at the end of each group. Figure 11-45 shows the number of customers, 37, for the first credit limit group.

Customers_grouped.rptdesign ☒			
Show Report Parameters			
0	Stuttgart Collectable Exchange	0711-555361	Rita Müller
43000	Tekni Collectables Inc.	2015559350	William Brown
0	Warburg Exchange	0241-039123	Sven Ottlieb
	37		
50000 - 99999			
61100	Alpha Cognac	61.77.6555	Annette Roulet
60300	Australian Collectables, Ltd	61-9-3844-6555	Sean Clenahan

Layout | Master Page | Script | XML Source | Preview

Figure 11-45   Report preview showing a count for each group

5 Choose Layout to return to the layout editor.

6 Instead of displaying just the number of customers in each group, display the following text before the total:

    `Customers:`

  1 Drag a text element from the palette, and drop it in the first cell in the group footer row.

  2 On Edit Text Item, select HTML from the drop-down list that displays Auto.

  3 Specify the following text in the text area, shown in Figure 11-46:

    `Customers: <VALUE-OF>row["GRP_TOTAL_CUSTOMERS"]</VALUE-OF>`

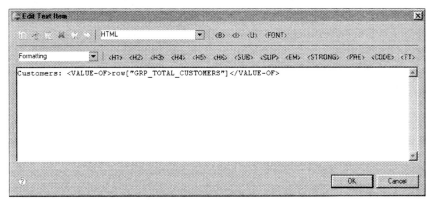

Figure 11-46   Text specified for the text element

In a text element, the <VALUE-OF> tag supports the display of dynamic data. The expression, row["GRP_TOTAL_CUSTOMERS"], is a reference to the column binding you created to return the number of customers in each credit limit group.

    4 Choose OK to save your edits to the text element.

7 Preview the report.

8 Scroll to the bottom of the first credit limit group. The report should look like the one in Figure 11-47.

0	Stuttgart Collectable Exchange	0711-555361	Rita Müller
43000	Tekni Collectables Inc.	2015559350	William Brown
0	Warburg Exchange	0241-039123	Sven Ottlieb
Customers: 37	37		
50000 - 99999			
61100	Alpha Cognac	61.77.6555	Annette Roulet
60300	Australian Collectables, Ltd	61-9-3844-6555	Sean Clenahan

Figure 11-47   Report preview showing the text displayed by the text element

The group footer displays the following information:

```
Customers: 37        37
```

9 Choose Layout to return to the layout editor.

10 Delete the aggregation element from the second cell in the group footer row to remove the second total, which is now redundant.

Display the number of customers in the report

In the previous procedure, you added aggregate data by inserting the aggregation element from the palette. This time, you add aggregate data by creating a column binding through the table's Binding page.

1 Select the table.

2 On Property Editor, choose the Binding tab.

The Binding page, shown in Figure 11-48, displays all the column bindings used by elements in the table. The right side of the page displays buttons that represent the actions you can perform with each column binding.

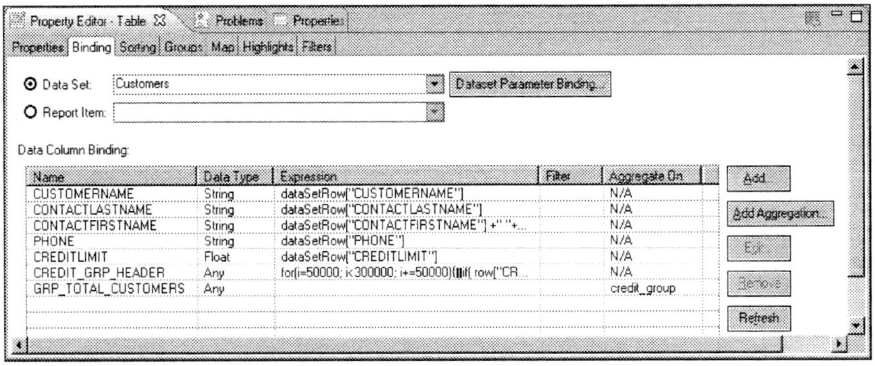

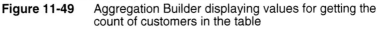

Figure 11-48   Binding page displaying the column bindings

3 Choose Add Aggregation to create a new column binding that defines an aggregate expression.

4 On Aggregation Builder, specify the values shown in Figure 11-49.

  1 In Column Binding Name, type the following name:

   TOTAL_CUSTOMERS

  2 In Function, select COUNT.

  3 In Aggregate On, select Table. This value indicates that the COUNT function returns the number of rows in the table.

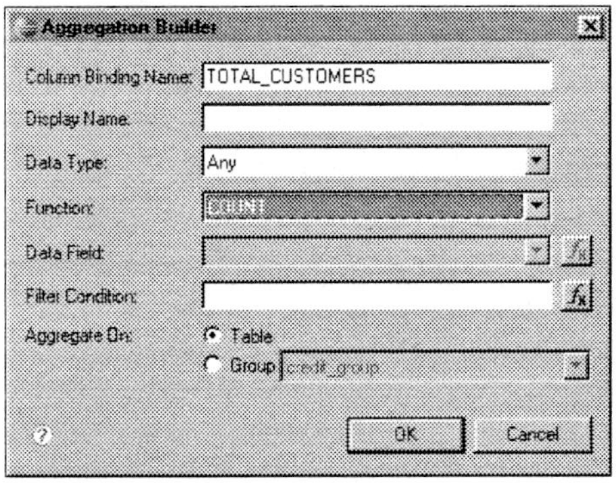

Figure 11-49   Aggregation Builder displaying values for getting the count of customers in the table

  4 Choose OK.

The new column binding, TOTAL_CUSTOMERS, appears on the Binding page, and is available for use by any element in the table.

5 Select the table. Guide cells appear at the top and left side of the table.

6 Right-click the guide cell on the left of the first row, Table - Header, then choose Insert➤Row➤Above.

A new table header row appears above the row that displays the column headings. The new row appears in color because it inherited the properties of the row below it.

7 Select the new row. In Property Editor, choose General, and set Background color to white.

8 Drag a data element from the palette, and drop it in the first cell in the new table header row. Elements that are in the table header appear at the beginning of the section.

9 On New Data Binding, create a new column binding:

    1 In Column Binding Name, type the following name:

        CUSTOMER_TOTAL

    2 Use the default data type, Any.

    3 In Expression, choose the expression builder button.

    4 In the expression builder:

       1 Type the following text:

          "Number of customers: " +

       2 In the lower pane of the expression builder, select Available Column Bindings, select Table, then double-click TOTAL_CUSTOMERS, the column binding you created to get the number of customers in the table.

         The expression, row["TOTAL_CUSTOMERS"] appears after the text you typed in the text area, as shown in Figure 11-50.

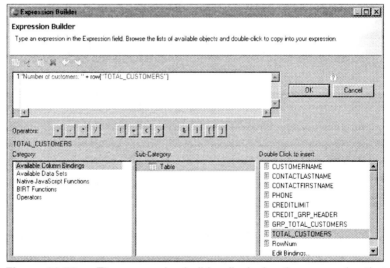

Figure 11-50 The expression builder displaying the expression that refers to the TOTAL_CUSTOMERS column binding

3 Choose OK. The expression appears in the Expression field on New Data Binding, shown in Figure 11-51.

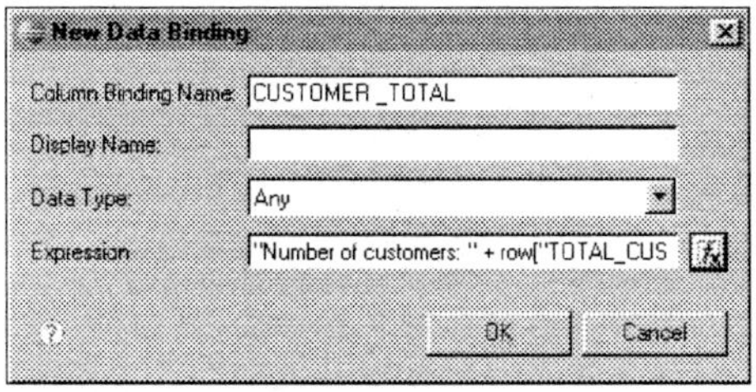

Figure 11-51   Column binding defined

5 Choose OK to save the column binding. The report design should look like the one shown in Figure 11-52.

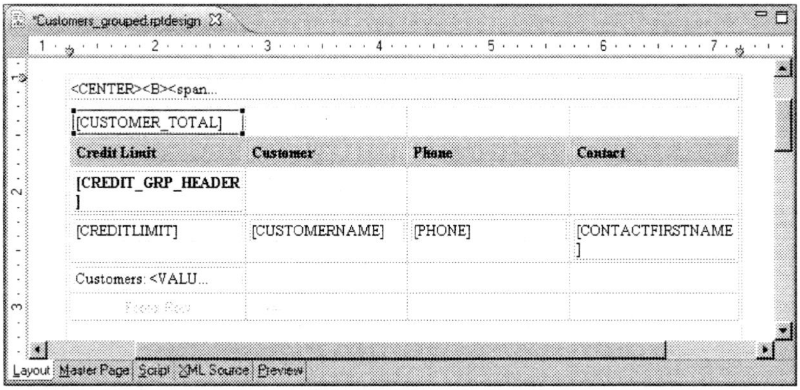

Figure 11-52   Report design showing a total count for customers

10 Preview the report. The report displays the number of customers at the beginning of the table, as shown in Figure 11-53.

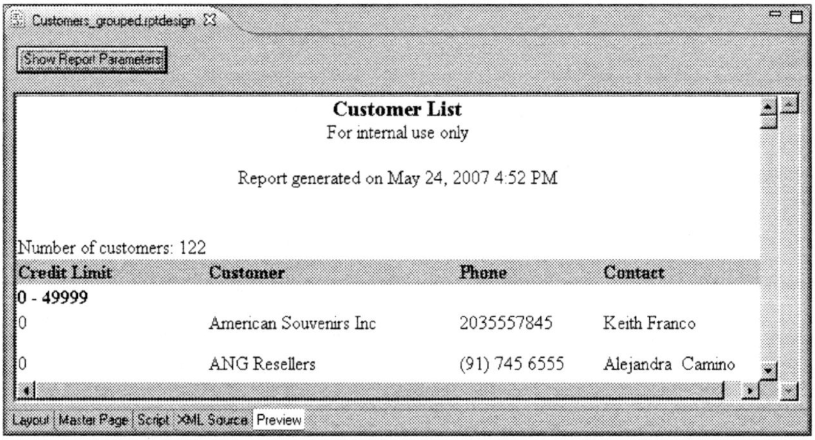

Figure 11-53   Report preview showing a total number of customers

Task 8: Format the report

Now that the report displays the correct data, you can focus on improving the report's appearance. You perform the following tasks in this section:

- Remove credit limit data from the detail rows.

- Display group headings on the first row of each group.

- Separate each group with a line.

Remove credit limit data from the detail rows

To verify that data appears in the correct credit limit groups, it is useful to display each customer's credit limit. Now that we have verified the data, we can delete the individual credit limit information from the report.

1 Choose Layout to return to the layout editor.

2 Delete the [CREDITLIMIT] data element from the detail row.

3 Preview the report. It should look like the one shown in Figure 11-54.

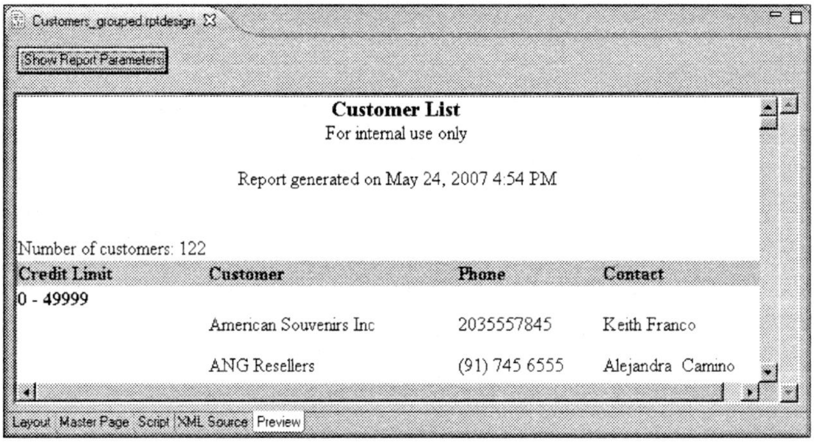

Figure 11-54   Report preview without credit limit data for each row

Display group headings on the first row of each group

The credit limit group headings appear in their own rows, above the detail rows of each group. In this procedure, you drop the group headings so that they appear in the first detail row of each group.

1 Choose Layout to return to the layout editor.

2 Select the cell that contains the group heading, as shown in Figure 11-55. Be sure to select the cell and not the data element in the cell.

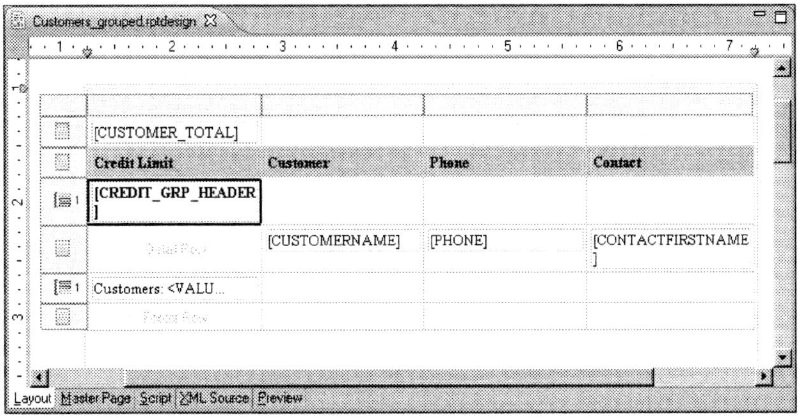

Figure 11-55 Group heading cell selected

3 In the general properties of Property Editor, set Drop to Detail. In the report design, the group heading still appears above the detail row because technically the element is still in the group header row.

4 Preview the report. The group headings appear in the first row of each group, as shown in Figure 11-56.

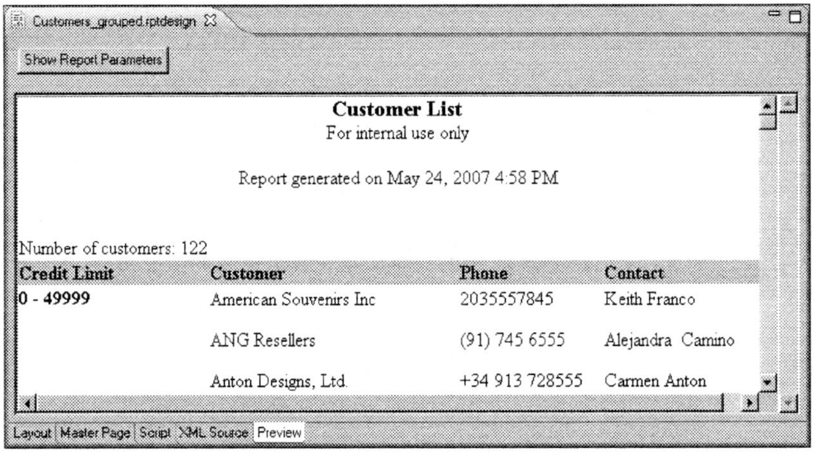

Figure 11-56 Report preview showing dropped group headings

Separate each group with a line

Drawing a line to separate each group makes it easier to see the groups of data.

1 Choose Layout to return to the layout editor.

2 Select all the cells in the group footer row. To select multiple cells, use Shift-click.

3 Choose Border in Property Editor, then set the border properties, as follows:

■ Set Style to a solid line.

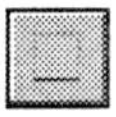

■ Choose the button that shows the bottom border.

4 Add more space between the line and text above it. While the cells are still selected, choose the Padding properties in Property Editor, and set Bottom to 6.0 points, as shown in Figure 11-57.

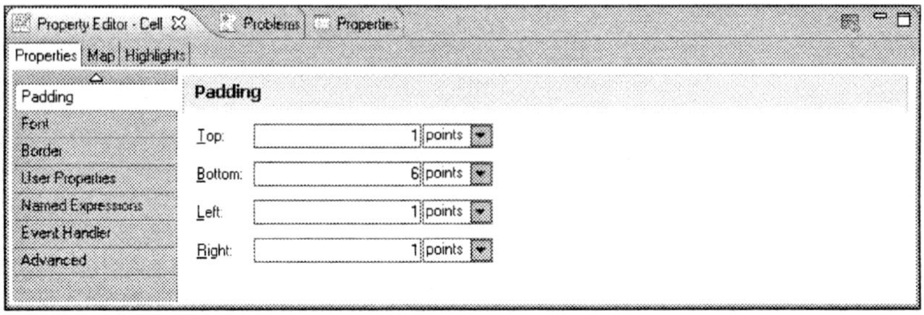

Figure 11-57   Property Editor showing padding values for selected cells

5 Preview the report. A line appears at the end of each group, as shown in Figure 11-58.

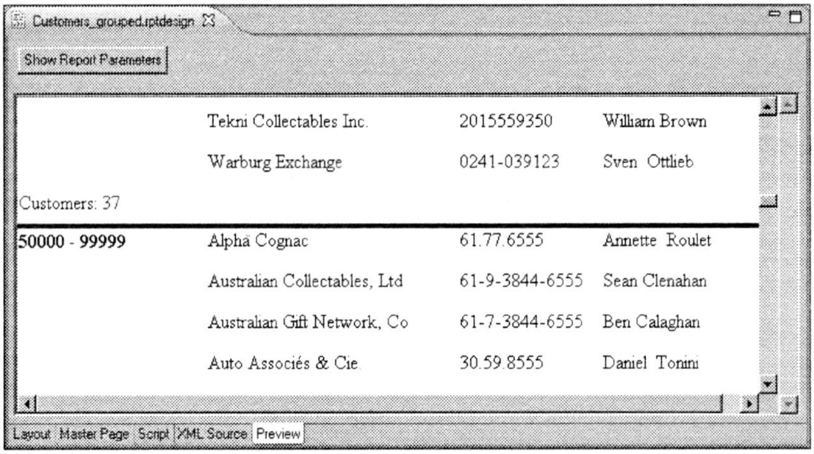

Figure 11-58   Report preview showing a line between groups

Task 9:   Preview the report in the BIRT report viewer

So far, you have been checking the report output in the BIRT Report Designer previewer. This time, you will use the report viewer to see what the report looks like when it is deployed. The report viewer provides additional functionality, including the capability to navigate to specific sections of a report using a table of contents. When you create groups in a report, BIRT automatically generates a table of contents, using the group values to show the hierarchy of the report.

1 Choose File➤View Report➤View Report in Web Viewer. The report appears in the report viewer.

2 Choose the table of contents button in the toolbar to display the table of contents. The table of contents displays the first value in each of the four credit limit groups. When you select a value, the report displays the corresponding section of the report. If you select 61100, for example, the report shows the customer rows in the 50000 - 99999 credit limit range, as shown in Figure 11-59.

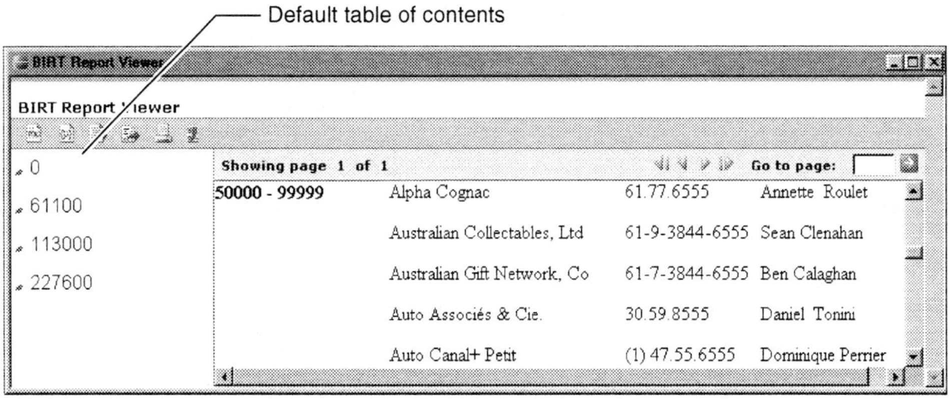

Default table of contents

Figure 11-59 Select a value in the table of contents to view the corresponding data

Task 10: Display credit limit ranges in the table of contents

Rather than display the first value of each credit limit group, the table of contents makes more sense if it displays the same credit limit range values as the report. You accomplish this task by using the same JavaScript expression that you used previously to display credit limit ranges (0 - 49999, 50000 - 99999, and so on) in the group header.

1 Return to BIRT Report Designer.

2 In the layout editor, select the table, then choose the Groups tab in Property Editor.

3 Double-click credit_group in the list of groups.

Edit Group, shown in Figure 11-60, displays the properties of the group. Under Table of Contents, Item Expression is set, by default, to the grouping field, row["CREDITLIMIT"].

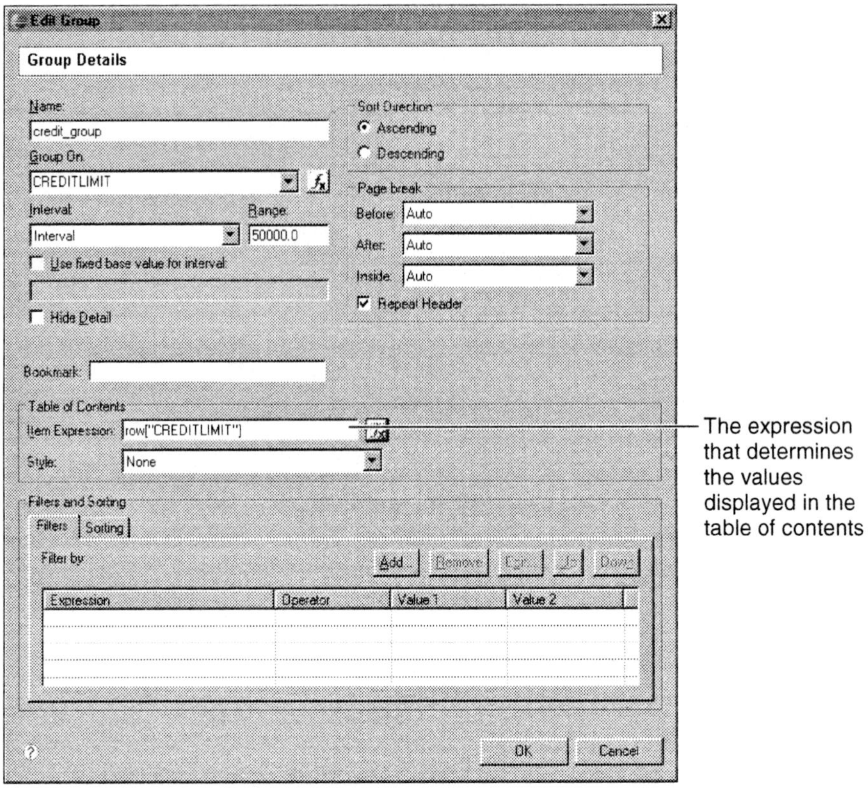

Figure 11-60   Edit Group displaying the properties of credit_group

The expression that determines the values displayed in the table of contents

4   Choose the expression builder button, and in the expression builder, replace the row["CREDITLIMIT"] expression with the following expression. This expression is the same column-binding expression that is used by the data element, [CREDIT_GRP_HEADER], in the group header. Rather than typing the expression again, you can copy it from the data element and paste it here.

```
for(i=50000; i<300000; i+=50000){
    if( row["CREDITLIMIT"] < i ){
        rangeStart = i-50000;
        rangeEnd = i-1;
        break;
    }
}
displayString = rangeStart + " - " + rangeEnd;
```

5   Choose OK.

6   Preview the report in the report viewer to verify the change in the table of contents. The table of contents displays the credit limit ranges, as shown in Figure 11-61.

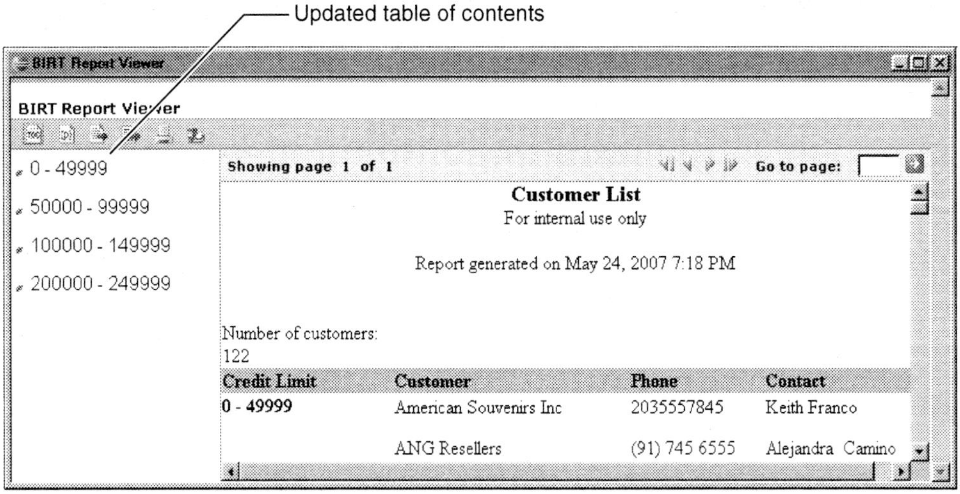

Updated table of contents

Figure 11-61   Updated table of contents displaying credit limit ranges

Aggregating Data

One of the key features of any report is the ability to display summary, or aggregate, information. For example, a sales report can show the overall sales total; sales subtotals by product type, region, or sales representatives; average sales figures; or the highest and lowest sales figures.

Aggregating data involves performing a calculation on a set of values rather than on a single value. For a simple listing report, aggregate calculations are performed on values in a specific field, over all the data rows in the report. The listing report in Figure 12-1 displays aggregate data at the end of the report.

Customer	Payment Date	Check Number	Amount
Saveley & Henriot, Co.	16 January 2004	FU793410	$49,614.72
Men 'R' US Retailers, Ltd.	18 January 2004	DG700707	$21,053.69
Osaka Souveniers Co.	19 January 2004	CI381435	$47,177.59
Auto Canal+ Petit	28 January 2004	HJ217687	$49,165.16
Euro+ Shopping Channel	30 January 2004	HJ32686	$59,830.55
Double Decker Gift Stores, Ltd	31 January 2004	PO860906	$7,310.42
Corrida Auto Replicas, Ltd	06 February 2004	NA377824	$22,162.61
Auto Associés & Cie.	10 February 2004	EP227123	$5,759.42
West Coast Collectables Co.	13 February 2004	PB951268	$36,070.47
Frau da Collezione	17 February 2004	LL427009	$7,612.06
Handji Gifts& Co	28 February 2004	LA318629	$22,474.17
Signal Collectibles Ltd.	29 February 2004	PT550181	$12,573.28
Clover Collections, Co.	01 March 2004	NM916675	$32,538.74

Summary Information
Number of records: 13
Average payment: $28,718.68 ⎱ Aggregate
Largest payment: $59,830.55 ⎰ data
Smallest payment: $5,759.42

Figure 12-1   A simple listing report that displays detail and aggregate data

In the example, BIRT calculates the average payment in the report by adding the values in the Amount field in every row, then dividing the total by the number of rows. Similarly, BIRT returns the largest and smallest payment amounts by comparing the amount values in every row in the report.

For a report that groups data, as shown in Figure 12-2, you can display aggregates for each group of data rows, as well as for all the data rows in the report.

Sales Report

Total Sales: $37,283,510.00

Average Order Amount: $155,997.95

— Aggregate data that is calculated over all data rows in the report

Brittan Design Inc.

Customer total: $954,180.00

— Aggregate data for the customer group

Order 1810

Item	Unit Price	Quantity	Extended Price
MDSPL04	$340.00	1728	$587,520.00
MSL3280	$210.00	1746	$366,660.00
		Order Total:	$954,180.00

— Aggregate data for the order group

CompuBoards

Customer total: $57,252.00

Order 1900

Item	Unit Price	Quantity	Extended Price
MDSPL04	$340.00	13	$4,420.00
MPL1632	$303.00	13	$3,939.00
MPL2032	$650.00	13	$8,450.00
MVL1664	$320.00	13	$4,160.00
MP2032	$310.00	13	$4,030.00
MSL3290	$300.00	13	$3,900.00
MP1632x	$221.00	13	$2,873.00
		Order Total:	$31,772.00

Order 1075

Item	Unit Price	Quantity	Extended Price
MP1632	$210.00	49	$10,290.00
MP2032	$310.00	49	$15,190.00
		Order Total:	$25,480.00

Figure 12-2   A grouped report that displays detail and aggregate data

Types of aggregate calculations

BIRT provides a wide range of functions that perform aggregate calculations. Table 12-1 describes these functions.

Table 12-1   Aggregate functions

Aggregate function	Description
AVERAGE	Returns the average (mathematical mean) value in a set of values. For example, if a set contains values 5, 2, 7, and 10, AVERAGE returns 6.

Table 12-1   Aggregate functions *(continued)*

Aggregate function	Description
COUNT	Counts the number of rows. If a set contains values 5, 2, 7, and 10, COUNT returns 4.
COUNTDISTINCT	Counts the number of unique values in a set of values. If a set of values contains values 5, 2, 5, 7, and 10, COUNTDISTINCT returns 4.
FIRST	Returns the first value in a set of values. If a set of values contains values 5, 2, 7, and 10, FIRST returns 5.
IS-BOTTOM-N	Returns a Boolean value that indicates if a value is one of the bottom n values. If a set of values contains 5, 2, 7, and 10, and you specify 2 as the n value, IS-BOTTOM-N returns true for values 5 and 2, and false for values 7 and 10.
IS-BOTTOM-N-PERCENT	Returns a Boolean value that indicates if a value is one of the bottom n percent values. If a set of values contains 5, 2, 7, and 10, and you specify 25 (percent) as the n value, IS-BOTTOM-N-PERCENT returns true for 2, and false for 5, 7, and 10.
IS-TOP-N	Returns a Boolean value that indicates if a value is one of the top n values. If a set contains values 5, 2, 7, and 10, and you specify 2 as the n value, IS-TOP-N returns false for 2 and 5, and true for 7 and 10.
IS-TOP-N-PERCENT	Returns a Boolean value that indicates if a value is one of the top n percent values. If a set of values contains 5, 2, 7, and 10, and you specify 25 (percent) as the n value, IS-TOP-N-PERCENT returns false for 5, 2, and 7, and true for 10.
LAST	Returns the last value in a set of values. If a set of values contains values 2, 5, 7, and 10, LAST returns 10.
MAX	Returns the largest value in a set of values. If a set of values contains values 5, 2, 7, and 10, MAX returns 10. For string values, MAX returns the last value alphabetically. For date values, MAX returns the latest date.
MEDIAN	Returns the median, or mid-point, value in a set of values. If a set of values contains values 5, 2, 7, and 10, MEDIAN returns 6.
MIN	Returns the smallest value in a set of values. If a set of values contains values 5, 2, 7, and 10, MIN returns 2. For string values, MIN returns the first value alphabetically. For date values, MIN returns the earliest date.
MODE	Returns the mode, which is the value that occurs most often in a set of values. If a set of values contains values 5, 2, 5, 7, and 10, MODE returns 5.

(continues)

Table 12-1   Aggregate functions *(continued)*

Aggregate function	Description
MOVINGAVE	Returns the moving average for a set of values over a specified interval or number of values. This type of calculation is typically used for analyzing trends of stock prices. You can, for example, display the moving average of stock prices over three days. If a set of values contains values 5, 2, 5, 7, and 10, and you specify 3 as the interval, MOVINGAVE returns null, null, 4, 4.66, and 7.33 for each row, respectively.
PERCENTILE	Returns the percentile value in a set of values, given a specified percent rank. For example, you can get the score that represents the 50th percentile of all scores on a test. If a set of values contains 50, 75, 80, 90, and 95, and you specify a percent rank of 0.9 (to get the 90th percentile value), PERCENTILE returns 93.
PERCENT-RANK	Returns the rank of a value as a percentage of all the values in a set. The return value ranges from 0 to 1. If a set of values contains 50, 75, 80, 90, and 95, PERCENT-RANK returns 0, 0.25, 0.5, 0.75, and 1 for each row, respectively.
PERCENT-SUM	Returns the percentage of a total. If a set of values contains 50, 75, 80, 90, and 95, the sum of the values is 390. PERCENT-SUM returns 0.128 (50/390), 0.192 (75/390), 0.205 (80/390), 0.231 (90/390), and 0.244 (95/390) for each row, respectively.
QUARTILE	Returns the quartile value in a set of values, given a specified quart (0 - 4). MIN, MEDIAN, and MAX return the same value as QUARTILE when quart is equal to 0, 2, and 4, respectively. If a set of values contains 50, 75, 80, 90, and 95, and you specify a quart of 2, QUARTILE returns 80.
RANK	Returns the rank of a value in a set of values. The rank of a value ranges from 1 to the number of values in the set. If two values are identical, they have the same rank. If a set of values contains 50, 75, 80, 90, and 95, RANK returns 5, 4, 3, 2, and 1 for each row, respectively.
RUNNINGCOUNT	Returns the row number, up to a given point, in the report. If a set of values contains 50, 75, 80, 90, and 95, RUNNINGCOUNT returns 1, 2, 3, 4, and 5 for each row, respectively.
RUNNINGSUM	Returns the total, up to a given point, in the report. If a set of values contains 50, 75, 80, 90, and 95, RUNNINGSUM returns 50, 125, 205, 295, and 390 for each row, respectively.

Table 12-1   Aggregate functions *(continued)*

Aggregate function	Description
STDDEV	Returns the standard deviation of a set of values. Standard deviation is a statistic that shows how widely values are dispersed from the mean value. If a set of values contains 50, 75, 80, 90, and 95, STDDEV returns 17.536.
SUM	Adds all the values in a set of values. If a set of values contains 50, 75, 80, 90, and 95, SUM returns 390.
VARIANCE	Returns the variance of a set of values. Variance is a statistical measure that expresses how large the differences between the values are. The variance increases as the differences between the numbers increase. If a set of values contains 50, 75, 80, 90, and 95, VARIANCE returns 307.5. If a set of values contains 5, 2, 5, 7, and 10, VARIANCE returns 8.7.
WEIGHTEDAVE	Returns the weighted average value in a set of values, given weights specified in another set of values. In a weighted average, some numbers carry more importance (weight) than others. Grades are often computed using a weighted average. For example:

Score   Weight (counts toward n% of grade)
50   10
75   25
80   15
90   30
95   20

Given this set of scores and weights, WEIGHTEDAVE returns 81.75.

Placing aggregate data

Where you place aggregate data is essential to getting the correct results. For aggregate calculations, such as SUM, AVERAGE, MAX, and MODE, which process a set of values and return one value, you typically insert the aggregate data in the following places in a table:

- At the beginning of a group, in the group header row

- At the beginning of a table, in the header row

- At the end of a group, in the group footer row

- At the end of the table, in the footer row

You can place this type of aggregate data in a table's detail row, but the data would not make much sense because the same aggregate value would appear repeatedly for every row in the group. On the other hand, you insert aggregate calculations, such as RUNNINGSUM, MOVINGAVE, PERCENT-RANK, and RANK, in the detail row of a table. These functions process a set of values and return a different value for each row.

The report in Figure 12-3 groups data rows by customer, then by order ID. It displays totals for each order, totals for each customer, and a grand total of all sales. At the detail level, the report displays the running total for each line item.

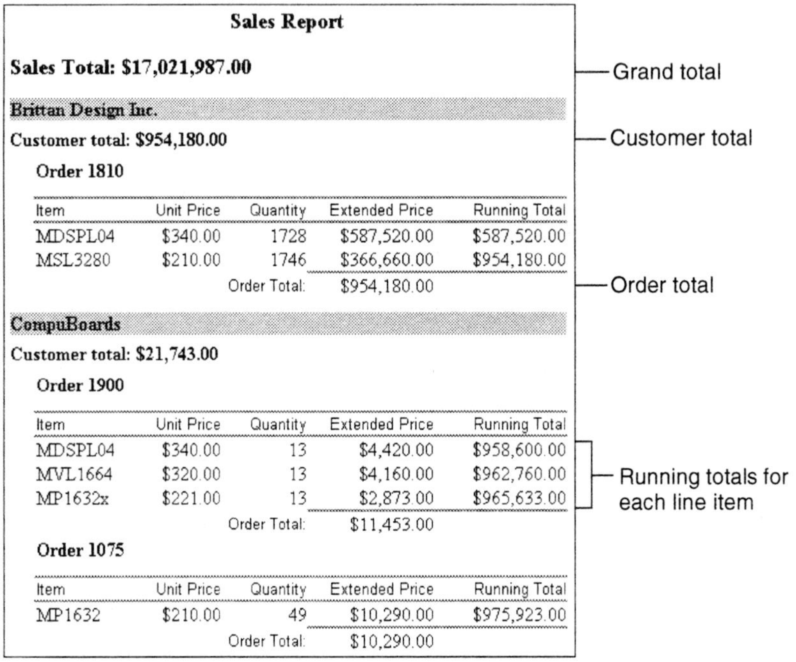

Figure 12-3   Report showing totals for groups and running totals for detail rows

To display the aggregate data as shown in the preceding report example, place the aggregate data in these locations:

■ To display the grand total at the beginning of the report, place the aggregate data in the table's header row.

■ To display the customer total at the beginning of each customer group, place the aggregate data in the customer group's header row.

■ To display the order total at the end of each order group, place the aggregate data in the order group's footer row.

■ To display the running totals, place the aggregate data in the table's detail row.

Figure 12-4 shows the report design.

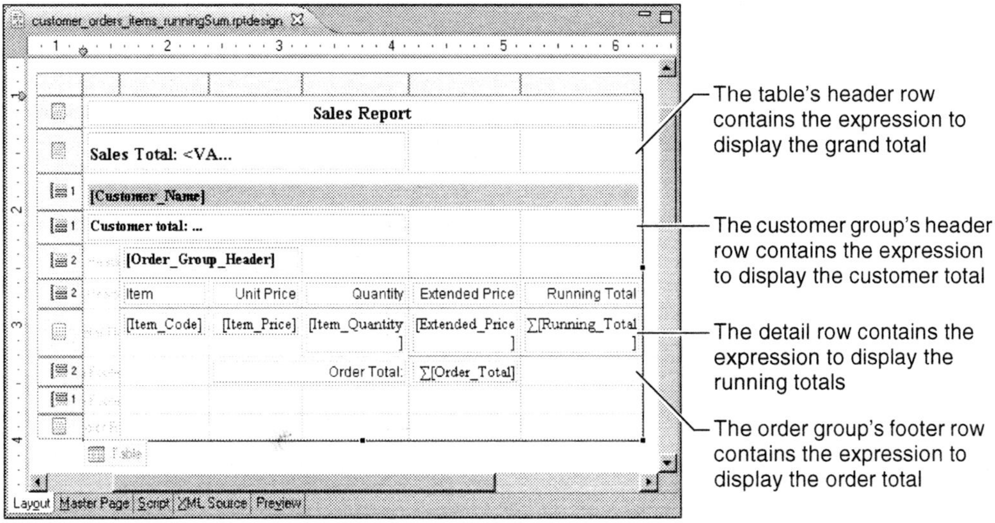
customer_orders_items_runningSum.rptdesign
Sales Report
Sales Total: <VA...
[Customer_Name]
Customer total: ...
[Order_Group_Header]
Item
Unit Price
Quantity
Extended Price
Running Total
[Item_Code]
[Item_Price]
[Item_Quantity]
[Extended_Price]
∑[Running_Total]
Order Total:
∑[Order_Total]
Layout
Master Page
Script
XML Source
Preview
The table's header row contains the expression to display the grand total
The customer group's header row contains the expression to display the customer total
The detail row contains the expression to display the running totals
The order group's footer row contains the expression to display the order total

Figure 12-4 Aggregate calculations in a report design

Creating an aggregation

As with all dynamic or computed data, you must create a column binding for each aggregation. To display the aggregate data, you use a text element or a data element that refers to the column binding. BIRT Report Designer provides a tool, Aggregation Builder, to help you create the column binding and the aggregation. Figure 12-5 shows Aggregation Builder displaying default values.

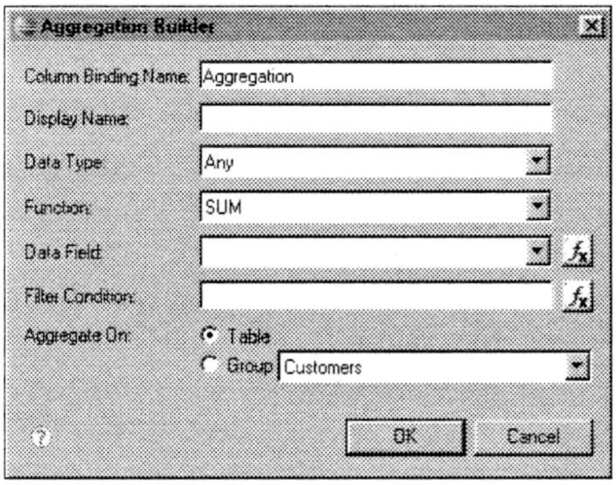
Aggregation Builder
Column Binding Name:
Aggregation
Display Name:
Data Type:
Any
Function:
SUM
Data Field:
Filter Condition:
Aggregate On:
Table
Group
Customers
OK
Cancel

Figure 12-5 Aggregation Builder showing default values

You access Aggregation Builder, using one of the following procedures:

- On the palette, under Quick Tools, drag the aggregation element and drop it in the desired location in a table. Use this procedure when you want to display just the aggregate value, for example, 55. The aggregation element is a shortcut to inserting a data element and associating it with a column binding that defines the aggregation.

- Select the table in which to place aggregate data, choose the Binding tab in Property Editor, then choose Add Aggregation. Use this procedure when you want to use the aggregate value within another expression, for example, to:

  - Display the aggregate value with static text, as shown in the following example:

    ```
    Number of rows: 55
    ```

  - Use the aggregate value in a conditional expression, as shown in the following example:

    ```
    row["Order_Total"] Greater Than or Equal 10000
    ```

When you define an aggregation in Aggregation Builder, take care to provide the required information properly, or the report will generate unexpected results. Table 12-2 describes the information you must supply for all aggregations you create.

Table 12-2   Required information for defining an aggregation

Property	Description
Column Binding Name	Use a short but descriptive name that describes the aggregate value that is returned by the column binding, for example, Grand_Total, Customer_Total, and Order_Total. Every column binding in a report must have a unique name.
Data Type	Most aggregate values are numbers, so you typically select either decimal, float, or integer as the data type. The type you select depends on the type of the values being aggregated, and on the level of precision your report requires. For example, the decimal type is typically used for money values. If you select integer type for money values, the numbers are rounded, which is less precise.
Function	Select the function that performs the aggregate calculation you want. The functions are described in Table 12-1.
Data Field	Select the data set field whose values you want to aggregate. The COUNT function, which returns the number of rows, is the only function that does not require the data field argument.

Table 12-2 Required information for defining an aggregation *(continued)*

Property	Description
Aggregate On	Select the data rows to include in the aggregate calculation.
	■ Select Table to perform the calculation over all the data rows in the table.
	■ Select a specific group to perform the calculation over the data rows in that group.
	Selecting the wrong item produces incorrect results. For example, if you place aggregate data in a customer group header, but you select Table as the Aggregate On value, the customer group header displays the aggregate value for the table, not the aggregate value for the customer group.

Most aggregate functions require only the information described in Table 12-2. Some functions, such as IS-TOP-N, MOVINGAVE, QUARTILE and WEIGHTEDAVE, require additional information, which appears in Aggregation Builder after you select the function. For information about the additional information you supply for these functions, read the function descriptions in Table 12-1.

The rest of this section describes how to create the aggregations to calculate the subtotals and totals that appear in the report example in the previous section.

Displaying the grand total in the table's header row

In the report example, a text element displays the sales grand total, using the following combination of static text and dynamic data:

```
Sales Total: $17,021,987.00
```

First, calculate the sales grand total by defining the aggregation in a column binding. Then, insert a text element that uses this column binding.

How to calculate the grand total

1 Select the table that contains the report data.

2 In Property Editor, choose the Binding tab. The Binding page displays all the column bindings defined and used by elements in the table.

3 On the Binding page, choose Add Aggregation.

4 On Aggregation Builder:

   1 In Column Binding Name, type the following name for the column binding:

   ```
   Grand_Total
   ```

   2 In Data Type, select Decimal as the type of the aggregate value.

3 In Function, use the default, SUM.

4 In Data Field, select the data set field, dataSetRow["extendedPrice"], whose values you want to sum.

5 In Aggregate On, select Table to perform the aggregate calculation over all the rows in the table. Figure 12-6 shows the complete definition.

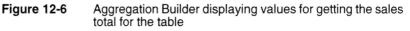

Figure 12-6   Aggregation Builder displaying values for getting the sales total for the table

6 Choose OK. The Grand_Total column binding is now available to any report element you place in the table.

How to use the column binding in a text element

1 Drag a text element from the palette and drop it in the table header row.

2 On Edit Text Item, select HTML from the drop-down list that displays Auto.

3 Type the following text, as shown in Figure 12-7:

```
Sales Total: <VALUE-OF format=$#,####.00>row["Grand_Total"]
    </VALUE-OF>
```

Figure 12-7   Text, containing static text and dynamic data, specified for the text element

The expression, row["Grand_Total"], refers to the column binding you created to calculate the sales grand total.

4 Choose OK to save the expression specified for the text element.

Displaying the customer total in the customer group header

In the report example, a text element displays the customer total, using the following combination of static text and dynamic data:

```
Customer Total: $954,180.00
```

Just as you did to calculate and display the sales grand total, first, calculate the customer total by defining the aggregation in a column binding. Then, insert a text element that uses this column binding.

Figure 12-8 shows the definition of the column binding and aggregation in Aggregation Builder. The aggregation uses the SUM function to add all the values in the extendedPrice field, for all rows in each customer group.

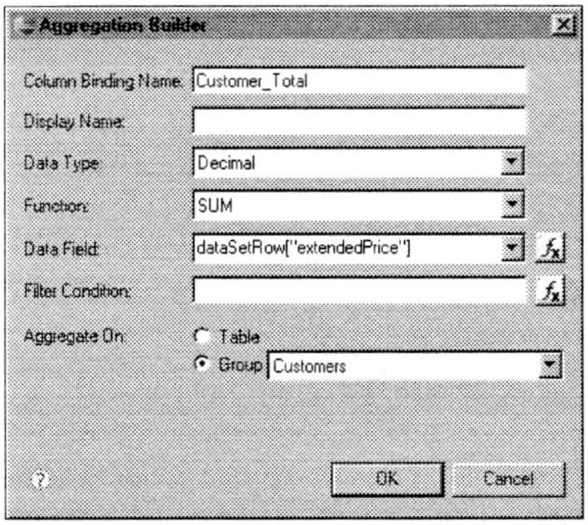

Figure 12-8   Aggregation Builder displaying values for getting the sales total for each customer group

The text element you insert in the customer group header row to display the customer totals contains the following expression:

```
Customer Total: <VALUE-OF format=$#,####.00>
    row["Customer_Total"]</VALUE-OF>
```

Displaying the order total in the order group footer

In the report example, a data element displays the order total. Unlike the previous procedures in which text elements are used to display static text with the aggregate value, the data element is used to display just the order total value.

In this case, drag the aggregation element from the palette, and drop it in the order group footer. On Aggregation Builder, specify the values as shown in Figure 12-9. The aggregation uses the SUM function to add all the values in the extendedPrice field, for all rows in each order group.

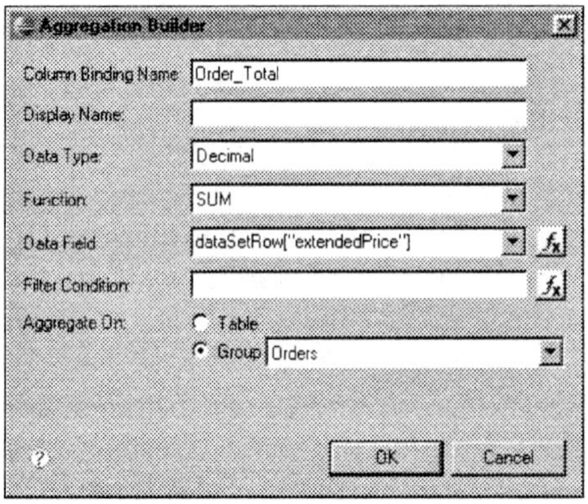

Figure 12-9   Aggregation Builder displaying values for getting the total for each order group

In the report design, the data element displays the sigma symbol followed by the column binding name, as shown in the following example:

Σ [Order_Total]

Displaying the running total in the detail rows

In the report example, a data element displays the running total. Drag the aggregation element from the palette, and drop it in the detail row. On Aggregation Builder, specify the values as shown in Figure 12-10. This time, you use the RUNNINGSUM function, rather than the SUM function, and you aggregate on all the rows in the table.

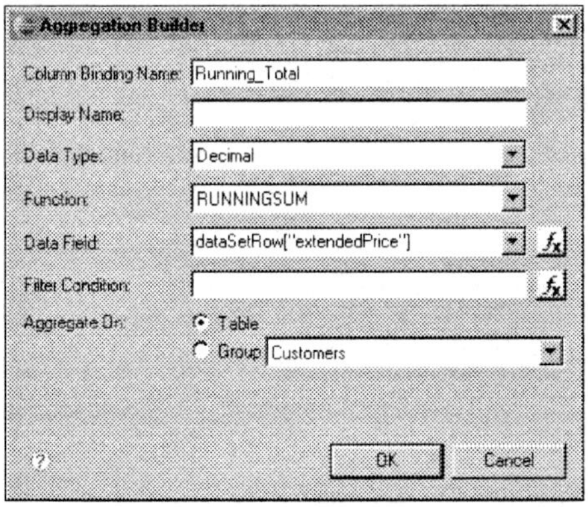

Figure 12-10   Aggregation Builder displaying values for getting the running total for each detail row

Viewing the column bindings for the report

Figure 12-11 shows the column bindings defined for the table that contains all the report data. The four column bindings that define aggregations appear at the bottom of the list.

The Aggregate On values indicate the level at which aggregate calculations apply. The ALL value indicates that the aggregate calculation is applied to all rows in the table. The Orders and Customers values indicate that the aggregate calculations are applied to rows in the Orders group and to rows in the Customers group, respectively. The N/A value indicates that the expression is not an aggregate expression.

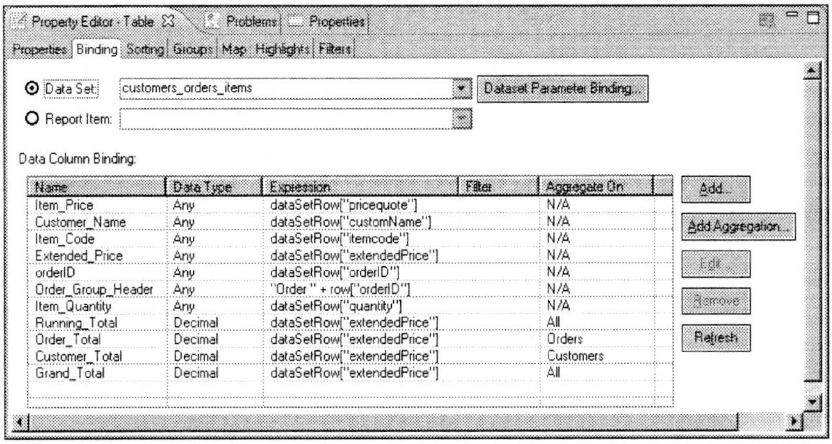

Figure 12-11   Column bindings used by elements in the table

Filtering aggregate data

When you calculate aggregate data, you can specify a filter condition to determine which rows to factor in the calculation. For example, you can exclude rows with missing or null credit limit values when you calculate an average credit limit, or include only deposit transactions when you calculate the sum of transactions.

To specify a filter condition when you aggregate data, in Aggregation Builder, specify a filter expression that evaluates to true or false. The following examples of aggregations include filter conditions:

- If summing the values in the extendedPrice field, adding the following filter expression returns the sum of extended prices for item MSL3280 only:

  ```
  row["itemCode"] == "MSL3280"
  ```

- If averaging the values in the orderAmount field, adding the following filter expression returns the average order amount for closed orders only:

  ```
  row["orderStatus"] == "Closed"
  ```

Figure 12-12 shows an example of an aggregation in Aggregation Builder that includes a filter condition. The aggregation returns the sales total for item MSL3280.

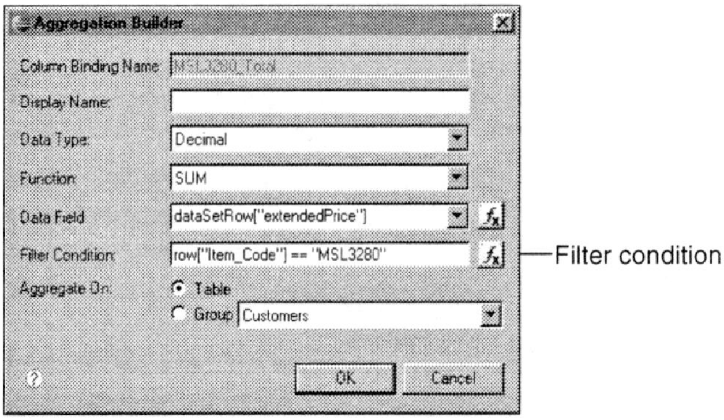

— Filter condition

Figure 12-12 Aggregation definition that includes a filter condition

Excluding null values from an aggregate calculation

When you calculate the sum of a numeric field, it does not matter if some of the rows contain null values for the specified numeric field. The results are the same, regardless of whether the calculation is 100 + 75 + 200 or 100 + 75 + 0 (null) + 200. In both cases, the result is 375. Note that null is not the same as zero (0). Zero is an actual value, whereas null means there is no value.

Some aggregate calculations, however, return different results when null values are included or excluded from the calculation. The average value returned by the calculation without the null value in the previous example is 125, which is calculated as (100 + 75 + 200)/3. The average value of the calculation with the null value, however, is 93.75, which is calculated as (100 + 75 + 0 + 200)/4. Similarly, COUNT returns a different number of total rows, depending on whether you include or exclude rows with null values for a specified field.

By default, aggregate functions include all rows in their calculations. To exclude rows in which a specified field contains null values, you must specify a filter condition, as described in the following examples:

- If averaging the values in a transactionAmount field, adding the following filter condition performs the aggregate calculation on rows where the transaction amount is not null:

      row["transactionAmount"] != null

- If counting the number of new customers in a report, adding the following filter condition counts only rows in which the creditLimit field has no value (indicating new customers):

      row["creditLimit"] == null

Counting rows that contain unique values

When you use COUNT to return the number of rows in a group or table, BIRT counts all rows. Sometimes, you want to get the count of distinct values. For example, a table displays a list of customers and their countries, as shown in Figure 12-13. The table lists 12 customers from 4 different countries.

Customers with orders over 10K	
Customer	Country
American Souvenirs	USA
Land of Toys Inc.	USA
Porto Imports	
La Rochelle Gifts	France
Gift Depot	USA
Dragon Souvenirs	Singapore
Saveley & Henriot, Co.	France
Technics Stores Inc.	USA
Osaka Souvenirs Co	Japan
Diecast Classics Inc	USA
Collectable Mini Designs	USA
Mini Wheels Co	USA

Figure 12-13   A table that lists customers and their countries

If you insert a data element that uses COUNT in the header or footer row of the table, COUNT returns 12, the number of rows in the table. If, however, you want to get the number of countries, use COUNTDISTINCT instead.

In the example report, COUNTDISTINCT returns 5, not 4 as you might expect, because like the other aggregate functions, COUNTDISTINCT counts rows with null values. The third row in the table contains a null value for country. To get the real count of countries that are listed in the table, add a filter condition to the aggregation, as follows:

```
row["country"] != null
```

This condition counts only rows in which the country value is unique and not null.

Calculating percentages

To provide more meaningful analysis, reports that display subtotals and totals frequently also display percentages. For example, if a report groups revenues by regions for a given quarter, it is useful to know both the actual revenue for each region and the percentage of revenues generated by each region.

Some percentages are calculated at the detail level, where each number in a row is calculated as a percentage of the total of all rows in a group. Some percentage calculations require aggregate values from two different groups of data. For example, a report displays each regional sales total as a percentage of the total national sales. To calculate this aggregate data for each region, two totals are required:

- The total of all sales in each region
- The overall total of sales across all regions

Figure 12-14 shows an example of a report that displays sales data that is grouped by state, then by product.

Sales By State and Product

Total Sales: $149,833.76

California — 34.15%

Product Code	Total Units	Amount	% of Total Amount	
S10_1678	152	$12,652.59		24.73%
Order 10145	45	$3,445.20	27.25%	
Order 10159	49	$3,986.15	31.50%	
Order 10168	36	$3,410.64	26.96%	
Order 10201	22	$1,810.60	14.31%	
S10_2016	125	$13,044.24		25.49%
Order 10145	37	$3,872.79	29.69%	
Order 10159	37	$3,740.70	28.68%	
Order 10168	27	$2,633.31	20.19%	
Order 10201	24	$2,797.44	21.45%	
S10_4698	146	$25,475.89		49.78%
Order 10145	33	$5,112.69	20.07%	
Order 10159	22	$3,749.24	14.72%	
Order 10168	20	$3,214.80	12.62%	
Order 10201	49	$9,394.28	36.88%	
Order 10362	22	$4,004.88	15.72%	
Totals:		$51,172.72		

Massachusetts — 17.19%

Product Code	Total Units	Amount	% of Total Amount	
S10_1678	78	$6,821.58		26.48%
Order 10285	38	$3,445.20	50.50%	
Order 10388	40	$3,376.38	49.50%	
S10_2016	97	$11,145.67		43.27%
Order 10285	47	$5,198.67	46.64%	
Order 10388	50	$5,947.00	53.36%	
S10_4698	48	$7,790.91		30.25%
Order 10285	27	$4,496.85	57.72%	
Order 10388	21	$3,294.06	42.28%	
Totals:		$25,758.16		

This aggregate value displays a state's total sales as a percentage of the overall sales

This aggregate value displays a product's total sales as a percentage of the state's total sales

These aggregate values display each order's sales as a percentage of the product's total sales

Figure 12-14 Percentage calculations in a grouped report

The report shows the following three percentage calculations:

- A state's total sales as a percentage of the overall sales
- A product's total sales as a percentage of the state's total sales
- An order's sales as a percentage of the product's total sales

Figure 12-15 shows the report design.

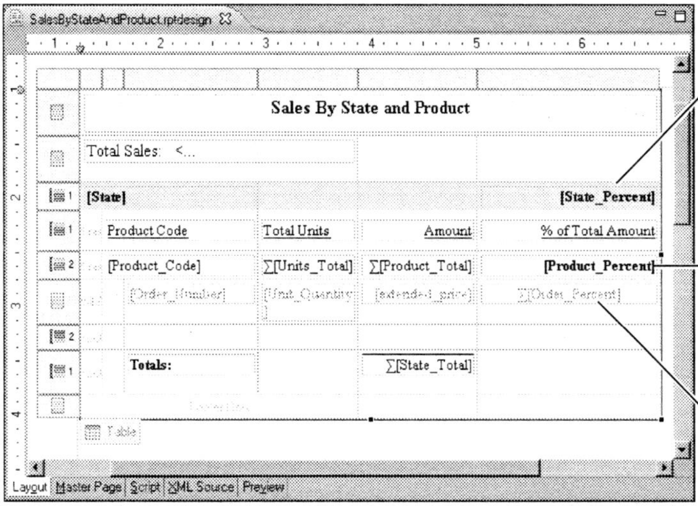

The table's group 1 header contains the expression to display the state's total sales as a percentage of the overall sales

The table's group 2 header contains the expression to display the product's total sales as a percentage of the state's total sales

The table's detail row contains the expression to display the order total as a percentage of the product total

Figure 12-15   Percentage calculations in a report design

Calculating each order total as a percentage of the product sales total

As the report in Figure 12-14 shows, orders whose information appears in the report's detail rows are grouped by product code. The amount of each order is displayed in the Amount column. The percent number that appears next to each amount represents that order's total as a percentage of the product's sales total. To get that value for each order, the report uses the PERCENT-SUM function, as shown in Figure 12-16. Insert an aggregation element in the detail row, then define the aggregation. Notice that the Aggregate On value is Product group, which indicates that each aggregate value is a percentage of the total of the rows in a product group.

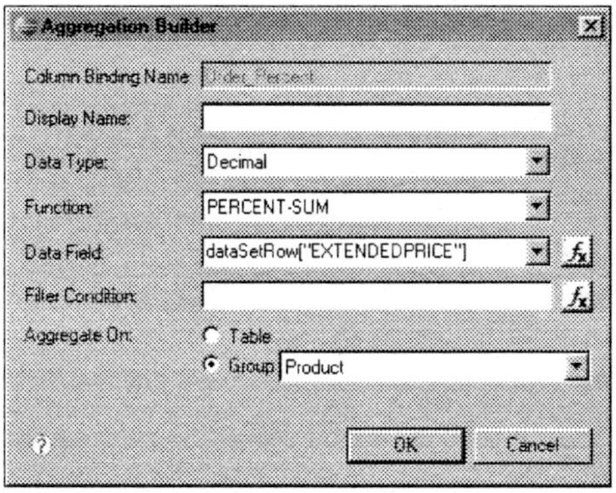

Figure 12-16   The Order_Percent column binding uses the PERCENT-SUM function

Calculating the product's sales total as a percentage of a state's sales total

Unlike the previous percentage calculation, the example report does not use the PERCENT-SUM function to calculate the product's sales total as a percentage of a state's sales total. You use PERCENT-SUM only for values in the detail row. You cannot use this function to calculate percentage values that require data from two different groups, which, in this example, are the product and state groups.

The report shown in Figure 12-15 uses two column bindings, Product_Total and State_Total, to calculate a product's sales total and a state's sales total, respectively. These column bindings are then used in an expression in another column binding, Product_Percent, to calculate the product's sales total as a percentage of a state's sales total. Insert a data element, then specify the expression. As Figure 12-17 shows, the expression in Product_Percent is

```
row["Product_Total"]/row["State_Total"]
```

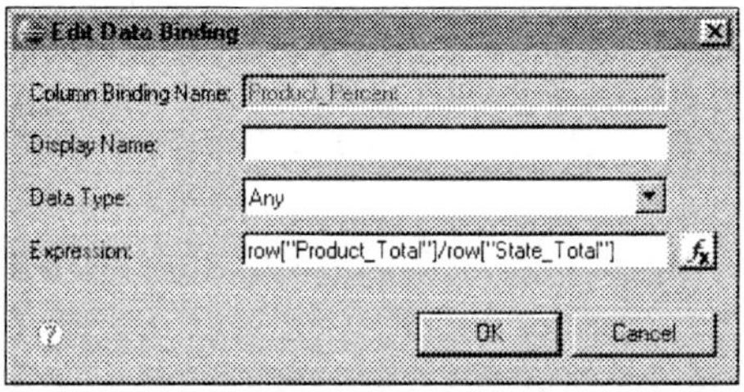

Figure 12-17   The Product_Percent column binding uses the Product_Total and State_Total column bindings in an expression

Calculating the state's sales total as a percentage of the overall sales total

The report shown in Figure 12-15 uses two column bindings, Grand_Total and State_Total, to calculate the overall sales and a state's sales total, respectively. These column bindings are used in an expression in another column binding, State_Percent, to calculate the state's sales total as a percentage of the overall sales total. As Figure 12-18 shows, the expression in State_Percent is

```
row["Product_Total"]/row["State_Total"]
```

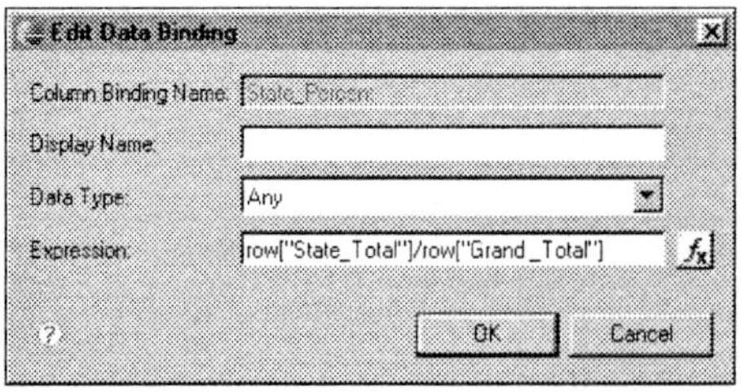

Figure 12-18   The State_Percent column binding uses the State_Total and Grand_Total column bindings in an expression

Displaying the percentage values in the correct format

The values returned by the previous calculations range from 0 to 1. To display a value, such as 0.8, as 80%, use the following procedure:

1 Select the data element that displays the percentage value.

2 In Property Editor, choose Format Number, then choose the Percent format.

3 Choose the settings that you want, including the number of decimal places and the placement of the percent symbol. Figure 12-19 shows an example of specifying the percent format for numbers in a data element.

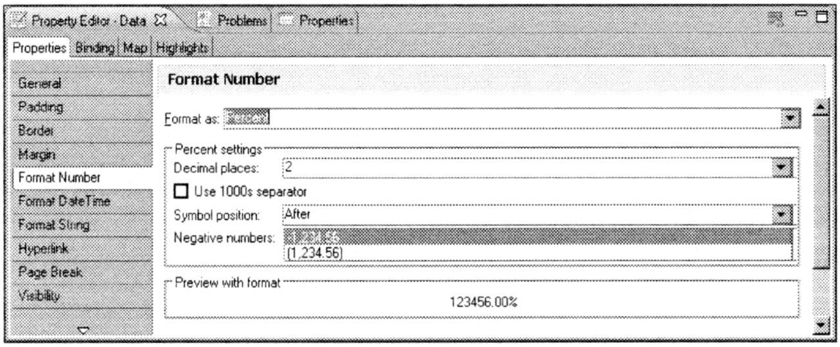

Figure 12-19   Percent format specified for numbers in a data element

Creating a summary report

Reports typically display both detail and aggregate data. A summary report is a report that shows only aggregate data. Summary reports, such as the top ten products or sales totals by state, provide key information at a glance and are easy to create. Figure 12-20 shows an example of a report that displays sales data by state. This report is the summary version of the report shown in Figure 12-14.

Sales By State

Total Sales: $149,833.76

California	$51,172.72	34.15%
Massachusetts	$25,758.16	17.19%
New Jersey	$18,021.37	12.03%
New York	$37,053.19	24.73%
Pennsylvania	$17,828.32	11.90%

Figure 12-20   Summary report showing sales data by state

Hiding details

When you create a report that contains data in detail rows and aggregate data in header or footer rows, you can change such a report to a summary report by hiding the contents in the detail rows. To hide these contents, you can use one of the following techniques:

- Choose the group whose details you want to hide, and in the group editor, select the Hide Detail option.

- Select the row that contains the details, and use the Visibility property to hide the contents of the row.

While both techniques provide the flexibility of maintaining two versions of a report, the first technique is more intuitive. However, in a report that contains more than one group, using the Visibility property gives you more control over which group details to hide.

Consider the example sales report that groups order data by state and product. If you want to show only the state totals, as shown in Figure 12-20, you choose the top-level group, state, then select the Hide Detail option, as shown in Figure 12-21.

Select this option to hide detail rows

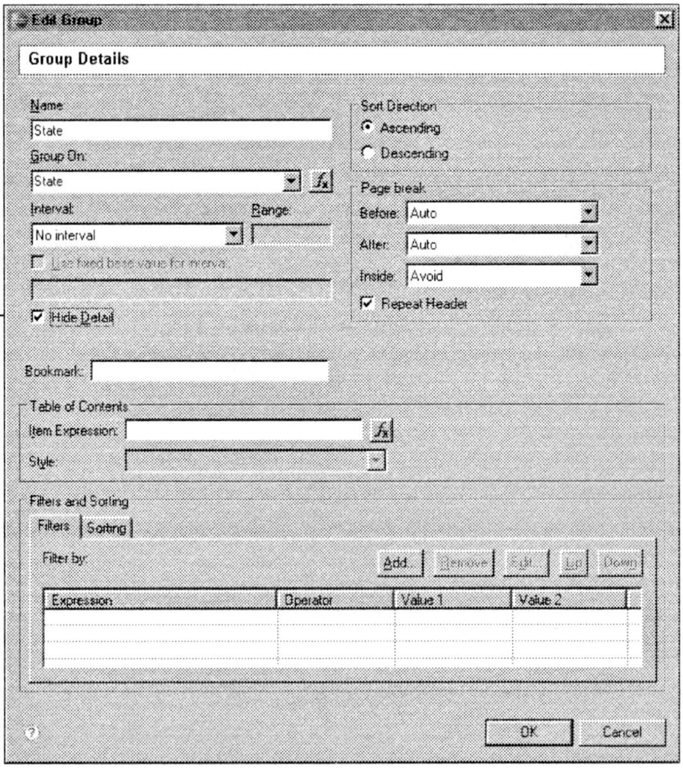

Figure 12-21   Select Hide Detail to hide all data within the state group

Hiding the details from the state group recursively hides all data within the state group; the report hides product groups and the order details within each product group. If, however, you want to hide only the product groups, but still show the order details within the product groups, as shown in Figure 12-22, you can get this output only by selecting specific sections and using the Visibility property to hide the selected sections.

Sales By State

Total Sales: $149,833.76

California		$51,172.72	34.15%
Order 10145	45	$3,445.2?	
Order 10159	49	$3,980.15	
Order 10168	36	$3,410.64	
Order 10201	22	$1,910.60	
Order 10145	37	$3,872.79	
Order 10159	37	$3,740.70	
Order 10168	27	$2,633.31	
Order 10201	24	$2,797.44	
Order 10145	55	$5,113.69	
Order 10159	22	$3,749.24	
Order 10168	2?	$3,214.80	
Order 10201	49	$9,394.28	
Order 10362	22	$4,004.88	
Massachusetts		$25,758.16	17.19%
Order 10285	36	$5,445.20	
Order 10388	42	$5,376.58	
Order 10285	47	$5,190.07	
Order 10388	54	$5,947.00	
Order 10285	27	$4,496.85	
Order 10388	21	$3,294.00	
New Jersey		$18,021.37	12.03%
Order 10251	59	$5,533.61	
Order 10251	44	$5,076.20	
Order 10251	43	$7,411.48	
New York		$37,053.19	24.73%
Order 10107	30	$2,440.50	
Order 10237	23	$2,113.01	
Order 10329	42	$3,276.30	
Order 10107	29	$4,126.54	
Order 10308	34	$3,922.58	
Order 10329	20	$2,188.4?	

Figure 12-22 Report showing the top-level state data and the order details, but not the product groups

Figure 12-23 shows the report design that generates the output in Figure 12-22. In the design, the following rows have their Visibility property set to hide the rows:

- Group 1 header row, which displays the column headings for the product summary data

- Group 2 header row, which displays the product summary data

Figure 12-23 shows the group 2 header row selected in the layout editor, and the Hide Element option selected for the Visibility property in Property Editor.

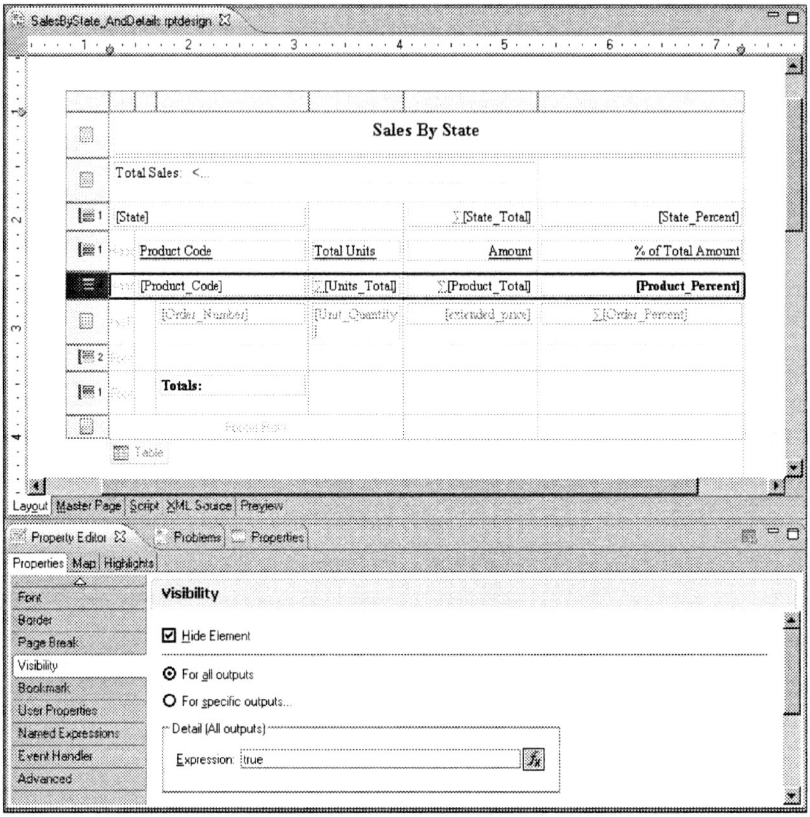

Figure 12-23   Report design with the product group row selected, and the row's Visibility property set to hide the row

Creating a top *n* report

To create a top *n* or bottom *n* summary report, insert the aggregate data in the header or footer row. Then create a filter for the group that contains the data, and use a filter condition, as shown in the following examples:

```
//Show only the top ten orders
row["Total_Sales"] Top n 10
```

```
//Show only orders in the top ten percent
row["Total_Sales"] Top Percent 10
```

```
//Show only the lowest five orders
row["Total_Sales"] Bottom n 5
```

```
//Show only orders in the bottom one percent
row["Total_Sales"] Bottom Percent 1
```

Figure 12-24 shows a top ten report. Figure 12-25 shows the report design.

Top 10 Sales Representatives	
Gerard Hernandez	$1,258,577.81
Leslie Jennings	$1,081,530.54
Pamela Castillo	$868,220.55
Larry Bott	$732,096.79
Barry Jones	$704,853.91
George Vanauf	$669,377.05
Peter Marsh	$584,593.76
Loui Bondur	$569,485.75
Andy Fixter	$562,582.59
Steve Patterson	$505,875.42

Figure 12-24   Top ten report

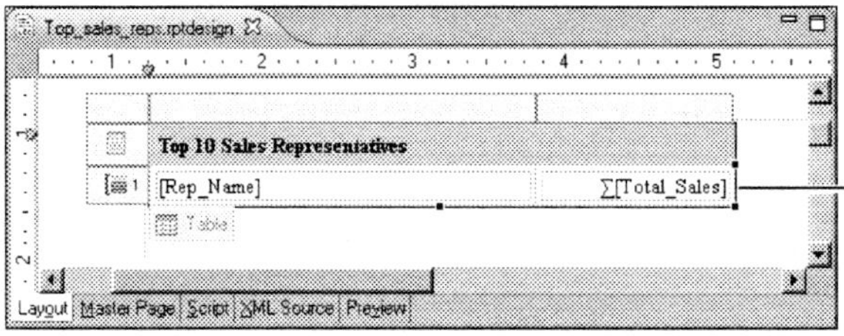

Figure 12-25   Top ten report design

The data elements that display the sales representative names and their sales totals are in a group header row. This report groups sales data rows (not shown in the report) by sales representatives. To display only the top ten sales representatives, a filter is specified in the group definition, as shown in Figure 12-26.

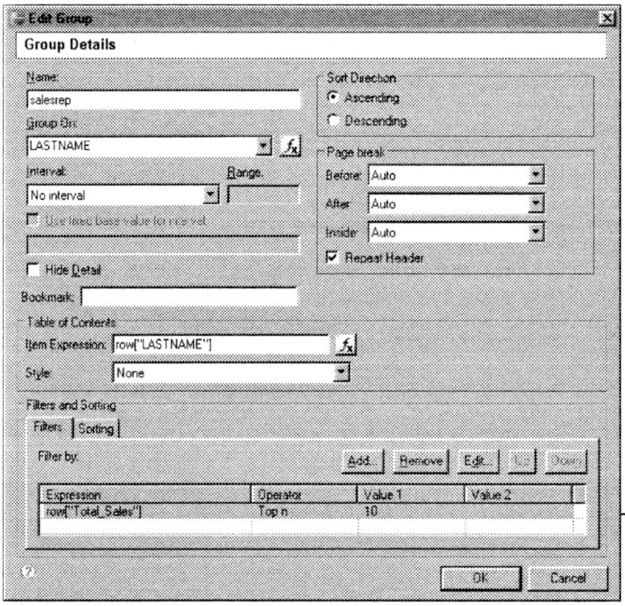

Figure 12-26   Top ten filter, defined in the group

Writing Expressions

You can create many reports using data that comes directly from a data source simply by dragging the data set fields from Data Explorer to the report. Sometimes, however, you want to display information that is not in the data source, or you want to display data differently than it appears in the data source. You might also want to sort data using a formula, rather than sorting on an existing field. For these cases, and many others, you write expressions using JavaScript.

An expression is a statement that produces a value. An expression can be a literal value, such as:

```
3.14
"It is easy to create reports with BIRT"
```

When you drag a field into the report, BIRT Report Designer creates a column binding with the correct expression for you. The expression specifies the name of the field whose values the report displays. For example, the following expressions get values from the customerName field and the phone field, respectively:

```
dataSetRow["customerName"]
dataSetRow["phone"]
```

An expression can contain any combination of literal values, fields, operators, variables, and functions, as long as it evaluates to a single value. In the following examples, the first expression combines static text with a field, the second expression uses a JavaScript function, and the third expression multiplies the values of two fields:

```
"Order Total: " + row["orderTotal"]
row["orderDate"].getYear()
row["itemQuantity"] * row["itemPrice"]
```

This chapter describes some common uses and examples of expressions in reports. This chapter does not describe all the functions, objects, or operators that you can use in expressions. If you are new to JavaScript, you will find it useful to read a book about JavaScript.

Basic concepts

This section describes some of the basic concepts that you need to understand and remember when writing JavaScript expressions. Understanding these concepts helps you avoid some common mistakes.

Data types

One of the fundamental concepts to understand is data types. Data types are the types of values—numbers, strings, and Booleans, for example—that can be represented and manipulated in any programming language. Every database field has a certain data type, every piece of report data has a certain data type, and every expression that you create returns a value of a particular data type.

This concept is important because, if the expression that you write does not handle data types properly, you get errors or the results are not what you want. For example, you cannot perform mathematical calculations on numbers if they are of string type, and you cannot convert values in a date field to uppercase characters.

If you write an expression to manipulate a data set field, verify its type, particularly if the field values are numbers. Numbers can be of string or numeric type. For example, databases typically store zip codes and telephone numbers as strings. Item quantities or prices are always of numeric type so that the data can be manipulated mathematically. IDs, such as customer IDs or order IDs are usually of numeric type so that the data can be sorted in numeric order, such as 1, 2, 3, 10, 11, rather than in alphanumeric order, such as 1, 10, 11, 2, 3.

To see the data type of a field, open the data set in Data Explorer, and choose Output Columns. Output Columns displays the fields in the data set and their types, as shown in Figure 13-1.

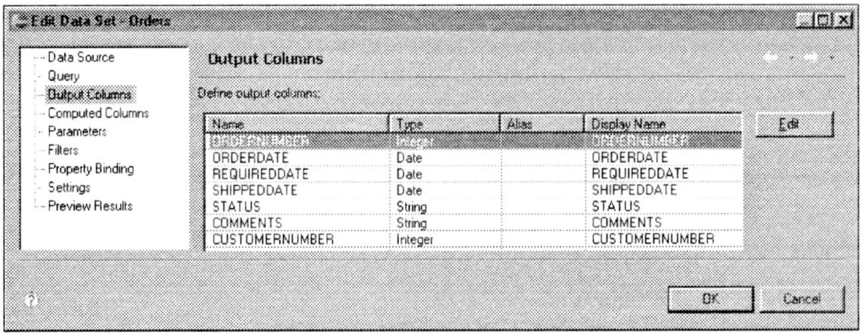

Figure 13-1   Output Columns

Case sensitivity

JavaScript is a case-sensitive language. This feature means that a keyword, a function name, a variable name, or any other identifier must always be typed with the correct capitalization. You must, for example, type the getDate( ) function as getDate( ), not as GetDate( ) or getdate( ). Similarly, myVar, MyVar, MYVAR, and myvar are four different variable names.

Data set field names are case-sensitive. If you refer to a data set field in an expression, specify the field name with the same capitalization that the data source driver uses to identify the field. As mentioned previously, Output Columns in the data set editor shows the fields. If you use the expression builder to write an expression, selecting a field to insert in the expression ensures that the correct field name is used.

Multiline expressions

You can write an expression that contains multiple lines, as shown in the following example:

```
firstInitial = row["customerFirstname"].charAt(0);
firstInitial + ". " + row["customerLastname"];
```

The expression looks like lines of program code because it is. Expressions can be small pieces of code that do something. The expression in the previous example does the following tasks:

- It extracts the first character of a string value in a customerFirstname field and assigns the value to a variable named firstInitial.

- Then, it combines the firstInitial value, a period, a space, and the value in a customerLastname field.

An expression can contain as many lines as you need. Just remember that an expression returns a single value. If an expression contains several lines, it returns the results of the last line. The previous expression returns a value, such as T. Rae.

The lines are called statements, and they are separated from each other by semicolons. If you place each statement on a separate line, as shown in the example, JavaScript allows you to leave out the semicolons. It is, however, good practice to use semicolons to separate statements.

Using the expression builder

The expression builder is a tool that you use to create, modify, and view expressions. It provides a list of the objects, functions, and operators that you can include in expressions. The expression builder is particularly useful when you are learning how to write expressions in JavaScript and discovering which BIRT and JavaScript functions you can use.

The expression builder is available when you need to specify an expression, such as when you create a computed field in Data Explorer, when you filter data, when you insert a data element, when you specify a data series for a chart, or when you want to display dynamic data in a text element. Figure 13-2 shows the expression builder.

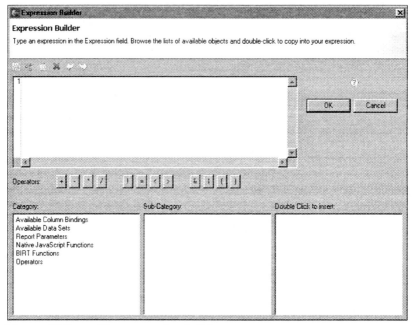

Figure 13-2   The expression builder

You open the expression builder by choosing one of the buttons that appear in Figure 13-3.

Figure 13-3   The expression builder access buttons

The expression builder consists of two parts:

- The top part of the expression builder is where you create or edit an expression. When you choose objects from the bottom part, they appear in this area. You can also type an expression directly here.

- The bottom part provides a hierarchical view of the column bindings, report parameters, JavaScript functions, BIRT functions, operators, and data set fields that you can select to build an expression. The items that appear under Category vary, depending on the context of the expression. When you select an item in Category, its contents appear in Sub-Category. When you select an item in Sub-Category, its contents—which you insert in an expression—appear in the box that is the farthest to the right. Figure 13-4 shows an example.

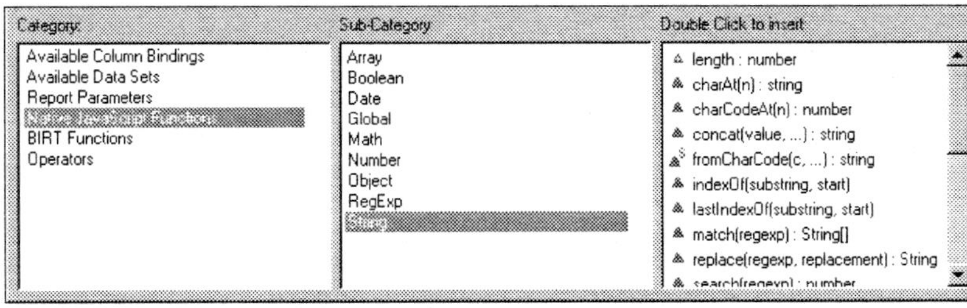

Figure 13-4   Functions for String class

Table 13-1 provides detailed descriptions of the items in the expression builder's Category column.

Table 13-1   Categories in the expression builder

Item	Description
Available Column Bindings	Displays the column bindings—references to data set fields—that are available to the current report element. An element can access column bindings that are defined on the element itself and on the element's container.
Report Parameters	Displays the report parameters that you created using Data Explorer. Report parameters are typically used to get input from users when they run the report.
Native JavaScript Functions	Displays native JavaScript functions by objects, such as String, Date, Math, and so on. Use these functions to manipulate or calculate data.
	For summary information about a function, hover the mouse over the item to display a Tooltip. For detailed information, see a JavaScript book.
BIRT Functions	Displays the JavaScript functions that are defined by BIRT. The functions are categorized in these objects: DateTimeSpan and Finance. Use these functions to calculate data.
	For summary information about a function, hover the mouse over the item to display a Tooltip. For detailed information, see "Scripting Reference" in BIRT's online help.
Operators	Displays types of JavaScript operators, such as Assignment, Comparison, Computational, and Logical.
Available Data Sets	Displays the data set or data sets that are available to the current report element. Expand the data sets to select fields to use in an expression. You can access data set fields only when you create a column-binding expression or when you create a computed field in the data set editor.

Manipulating numeric data

Numeric data is probably the most commonly manipulated type of data. Expressions can perform a basic operation, such as multiplying a price field by a quantity field to calculate an extended price, or more complex calculations, such as a financial calculation that returns the depreciation value of an asset. You can use Aggregation Builder to calculate aggregate information, such as totals, averages, medians, modes, and so on, as discussed in Chapter 12, "Aggregating Data."

Both JavaScript and BIRT provide a wide range of functions for manipulating numeric data. In the expression builder, look under Native JavaScript Functions—Number and Math, and under BIRT Functions—Finance. The following sections describe common number-manipulation tasks and provide examples of expressions.

Computing values from multiple numeric fields

If your report primarily displays values from numeric fields, it most likely contains computed values as well. An invoice, for example, typically shows the following computed values:

- Extended prices that display the result of unit price * quantity for each line item

- Sales tax total that displays the sum of extended prices * tax rate

- Invoice total that displays the sum of extended prices + shipping + sales tax

Order of precedence

When a calculation involves more than two numbers and different operators, remember the order of precedence, which is the order in which operators are evaluated. Consider the following math expression:

```
55 + 50 + 45 * 2
```

If you did each operation from left to right in these steps:

```
55 + 50 = 105
105 + 45 = 150
150 * 2 = 300
```

your answer would be 300.

If you specify the math expression in a data element, BIRT Report Designer returns 195, which is the correct answer. The difference in answers lies in the order of precedence. This concept is one that you might remember from math class. Multiplication and division are evaluated first from left to right across the expression. Then, addition and subtraction are evaluated from left to right across the expression. Using the previous example, the expression is evaluated as follows:

```
45 * 2 = 90
55 + 50 = 105
105 + 90 = 195
```

If you want the addition performed first, instead of the multiplication, enclose the addition part within parentheses, as follows:

```
(55 + 50 + 45) * 2
```

The following list describes examples of expressions that compute values from multiple numeric fields:

- The following expression calculates a total price after deducting a discount and adding an 8% tax that applies to the discounted price:

```
(row["extendedPrice"] - row["discount"]) +
    (row["extendedPrice"] - row["discount"]) * 0.08
```

- The following expression calculates an invoice total, which includes the total of all extended prices, an 8% sales tax, and a 10% shipping and handling charge:

```
row["salesTotal"] +
    (row["salesTotal"] * 0.08) +
    (row["salesTotal"] * 0.10)
```

- The following expression calculates a gain or loss in percent:

```
(row["salePrice"] - row["unitPrice"])/row["unitPrice"] * 100
```

Division by zero

If you divide the value of one numeric field by another and the denominator value is 0, the result is infinity (∞).

For example, if the following expression:

```
row["total"]/row["quantity"]
```

evaluates to:

```
150/0
```

the data element that contains the expression displays ∞.

The return value is infinity because dividing a number by zero is an operation that has no answer. Mathematicians consider this operation undefined, illegal, or indeterminate.

If you do not want the infinity symbol to appear in the report, you can replace it with a string value, such as Undefined, or replace it with an empty string ("") to display nothing. The infinity symbol is a numeric value, therefore, you must convert it to a string before replacing it with a different string.

The following expression replaces ∞ with Undefined:

```
// Convert number to a string
x = row["total"]/row["quantity"] + ""
// Replace ∞ with the word Undefined
x.replace("Infinity", "Undefined")
```

Converting a number to a string

You can convert a number to a string using one of the following techniques:

- Use the JavaScript toString( ) function.

- Add an empty string ("") to the number.

The following expressions yield the same result. If the value of orderID is 1000, both expressions return 10005.

```
row["orderID"].toString( ) + 5
row["orderID"] + "" + 5
```

Any time that you combine a literal string with a number, JavaScript converts the number to a string. Be aware of this fact, especially if you want to also manipulate the number mathematically. For example, the following expression changes orderID to a string:

```
"Order ID: " + row["orderID"]
```

If you want to perform a calculation and also add a literal string, do them in separate steps. Perform the calculation first, then append the string, as shown in the following example:

```
orderIDvar = row["orderID"] + 10;
"Order ID: " + orderIDvar;
```

If the value of orderID is 1000, the expression returns

```
Order ID: 1010
```

Manipulating string data

Often, a data source contains string or text data that is not in the right form for your reporting needs. For example, you want to sort a report by last name, but the data source contains last names only as part of a full name field. Or, conversely, you want to display full names, but the data source stores first names and last names in separate fields.

JavaScript provides a wide range of functions for manipulating strings. In the expression builder, look under Native JavaScript Functions—String. The following sections describe some of the common string-manipulation tasks and provide examples of expressions.

Substituting string values

Sometimes, you need to substitute one string value for another. Perhaps data was added to the data source inconsistently. For example, some addresses contain "Street," and some contain "St.". You can replace entire string values or just parts of a string by using the replace( ) function in JavaScript.

The replace( ) function searches for a specified string and replaces it with another string. It takes two arguments: the string to replace, and the new string. The following expression searches for "St." in an address field and replaces it with "Street":

```
row["address"].replace("St.", "Street")
```

What if you need to search for and replace multiple strings in a single field? Add as many replace( ) functions as you need to the expression, as shown in the following example:

```
row["address"].replace("St.", "Street").replace("Ave.",
    "Avenue").replace("Blvd", "Boulevard")
```

As with any global search-and-replace operation, be aware of unintended string replacements. For example, the row["address"].replace("St.", "Street") expression replaces St. Mary Road with Street Mary Road. In this case, rather than just searching for "St.", you need to search for "St." at the end of a line. To specify this type of search, you need to specify a string pattern to search, rather than a literal string. For more information about searching for patterns, see "Matching string patterns," later in this chapter.

If you need to replace entire strings, rather than just a part of the string, you can use the mapping feature instead. The mapping feature is ideal for replacing known sets of values. For example, a gender field contains two values, M or F. You can map the M value to Male, and F to Female. For more information about mapping values, see "Specifying alternate values for display" in Chapter 10, "Formatting Report Content."

Combining values from multiple fields

Each field in a database often represents a single piece of information. A customer table, for example, might contain these fields: customerFirstname, customerLastname, addressLine_1, addressLine_2, city, state, zip, and country.

You can create a customer report that uses data from all these fields by dragging each field to a table cell. The generated report, however, does not look professional because the space between each piece of data is uneven, as shown in Figure 13-5. The spacing is uneven because the size of each table column adjusts to fit the longest string.

Name		Address					
Jean	King	8489 Strong St		Las Vegas	NV	83030	USA
Susan	Nelson	5677 Strong St		San Rafael	CA	97562	USA
Julie	Murphy	5557 North Pendale Street		San Francisco	CA	94217	USA
Kwai	Lee	897 Long Airport Avenue		NYC	NY	10022	USA
Jeff	Young	4092 Furth Circle	Suite 400	NYC	NY	10022	USA

Figure 13-5   Report with separate field values

The solution is to combine, or concatenate, the first and last names and place the concatenated name in a single table cell. Similarly, concatenate all the address-related fields and place the full address in a single table cell. In JavaScript, you concatenate string values using the + operator.

For the name, add a literal space (" ") between the name fields so that the first and last name values do not run together. For the address, add a comma and space between all the fields, except between state and zip. For these fields, add only a space between them.

For this example, you would use the following expression to display the full customer name:

```
row["customerFirstname"] + " " + row["customerLastname"]
```

You use the following expression to display the full address:

```
row["addressLine1"] + ", " + row["addressLine2"] + ", " +
    row["city"] + ", " + row["state"] + " " + row["zip"] + ", "
    + row["country"]
```

The report now looks like the one shown in Figure 13-6.

Name	Address
Jean King	8489 Strong St , null, Las Vegas, NV 83030, USA
Susan Nelson	5677 Strong St , null, San Rafael, CA 97562, USA
Julie Murphy	5557 North Pendale Street, null, San Francisco, CA 94217, USA
Kwai Lee	897 Long Airport Avenue, null, NYC, NY 10022, USA
Jeff Young	4092 Furth Circle, Suite 400, NYC, NY 10022, USA

Figure 13-6   Report with combined field values

Several addresses display the word null because the addressLine2 field contains no data. In a database, a null value means no value was supplied. In cases where you concatenate fields that might contain no data, you need to remove the word null from the returned string value. This task is described in the next section.

Removing null values from combined fields

When you concatenate string values, JavaScript converts null values to the word null. The example report in the previous section displayed addresses with the word null when the addressLine2 field did not contain a value, for example:

```
8490 Strong St., null, Las Vegas, NV 83030, USA
```

You can remove the word null by using the replace( ) function. In this example, use replace( ) in the expression to search for "null, " and replace it with an empty string. You should also search for the comma and space after null to remove the extra comma and space that is added after the addressLine2 field. If you search only for "null" you get the following results:

```
8490 Strong St., , Las Vegas, NV 83030, USA
```

You use the following expression to remove null values from a concatenated address:

```
(row["addressLine1"] + ", " + row["addressLine2"] + ", " +
   row["city"] + ", " + row["state"] + " " + row["zip"] + ", "
   + row["country"]).replace("null, ","")
```

Searching for and replacing "null, " does not, however, take into account missing values in the state and country fields. The state value does not have a comma after it, so you need to search for "null ". The country value does not have a comma or space after it, so you need to search for "null".

To replace null values in the state and country fields, add two more replace( ) functions to the expression, as follows:

```
(row["addressLine1"] + ", " + row["addressLine2"] + ", " +
   row["city"] + ", " + row["state"] + " " + row["zip"] + ", "
   + row["country"]).replace("null, ","").replace("null ","")
   .replace("null","")
```

Getting parts of a string

Sometimes, you want to display only a portion of a string. For example:

- An address field stores a full address, but you want to display only the zip code or the state.

- A name field stores a full name, and you want only the first or last name.

- An e-mail field stores e-mail addresses, and you want only the user name that precedes the @ symbol.

Depending on the content of the string and which part of a string you need— the first part, the last part, or a part after or before a particular character—the expression that you specify varies. The JavaScript functions that you are likely to use in the expression include the functions shown in Table 13-2.

Table 13-2   Getting information about a string

JavaScript	Use to
charAt( )	Get the character at the specified position of a string. Note that in JavaScript, the first character starts at 0, not 1.
indexOf( )	Find the first occurrence of a specified character and return its position in the original string.

(continues)

Table 13-2   Getting information about a string *(continued)*

JavaScript	Use to
lastIndexOf( )	Find the last occurrence of a specified character and return its position in the original string.
length	Get the length of a string. Note that length is a property of a string, not a function, so you do not use parentheses, ( ), after the keyword, length.
substr( )	Return a substring of a specified length, starting from a particular position in the original string.

The following examples show how to get different parts of a string. Assume a customerName field stores names in first name and last name format, such as Robert Allen.

- To get the first name:

  - Use indexOf( ) to get the position of the space character that separates the first name from the last name.

  - Use substr( ) to get the first name, starting from the first character and for a specified length. The first character for JavaScript starts at 0, not 1. The length that you need to specify is equal to the position of the space character, and not the position of the space character minus 1, as you might think. Consider the name Robert Allen. Logically, the space between the first and last names is the seventh character, but JavaScript counts its position as six. To return the first name, Robert, excluding the space, you want substr( ) to return six characters.

  The following expression returns the first name:

  ```
  spaceCharPosition = row["customerName"].indexOf(" ");
  newStringtoDisplay =
      row["customerName"].substr(0, spaceCharPosition);
  ```

- To get the last name, you use indexOf( ) and substr( ) again. The difference is the arguments that you specify for substr( ). To get the last name, you want to start from the character after the space, and the number of characters that you want is the length of the entire string minus the length up to the space.

  The following expression returns the last name:

  ```
  spaceCharPosition = row["customerName"].indexOf(" ");
  newStringtoDisplay =
      row["customerName"].substr(spaceCharPosition + 1,
      row["customerName"].length - spaceCharPosition);
  ```

- To get the first name initial and the last name to display, for example, R. Allen:

  - Use the expression in the previous example to get the last name.

- Add a statement that gets the first letter in the customerName field. You can use substr(0,1) to get only the first character. You can also use charAt(0), which returns a character in a specified position of a string.

- Add a statement to combine the first name initial, a period, a space, and the last name.

The following expression returns the first name initial and last name:

```
firstNameInitial = row["customerName"].charAt(0);
spaceCharPosition = row["customerName"].indexOf(" ");
lastName = row["customerName"].substr(spaceCharPosition + 1,
    row["customerName"].length - spaceCharPosition);
newStringtoDisplay = firstNameInitial + ". " + lastName;
```

Matching string patterns

The previous section described some techniques for getting parts of a string for display. Sometimes you need to match patterns, rather than literal substrings, in string values. You can, for example, use pattern-matching to:

- Filter rows to display only customers whose last names start with a particular string pattern.

- Search for string patterns, using wildcard characters, and replace with a different string.

To perform pattern-matching, you use regular expressions. A regular expression, also known as regexp, is an expression that searches for a pattern within a string. Many programming languages support regular expressions for complex string manipulation. JavaScript regular expressions are based on the regular expression features of the Perl programming language with a few differences.

In JavaScript, a regular expression is represented by the RegExp object, which you create by using a special literal syntax. Just as you specify a string literal as characters within quotation marks, you specify a regular expression as characters within a pair of forward slash (/) characters, as shown in the following example:

```
var pattern = /smith/;
```

This expression creates a RegExp object and assigns it to the variable pattern. The RegExp object finds the string "smith" within strings, such as smith, blacksmith, smithers, or mark smith. It would not match Smith or Mark Smith because the search is case sensitive.

You can perform complex pattern-matching by using any number of special characters along with the literal string to search for, as shown in Table 13-3.

Table 13-3   Examples of regular expressions

Regular expression	Description
/y$/	Matches any string that contains the letter "y" as its last character. The $ flag specifies that the character to search for is at the end of a string. Matches: Carey, tommy, johnny, Fahey. Does not match: young, gayle, faye.
/^smith/i	Matches any string that starts with "smith". The ^ flag specifies that the string to search for is at the beginning of a string. The i flag makes the search case insensitive. Matches: Smith, smithers, Smithsonian. Does not match: blacksmith, John Smith.
/go*d/	Matches any string that contains this pattern. The asterisk (*) matches zero or any number of occurrences of the character previous to it, which is "o" in this example. Matches: gd, god, good, goood, goodies, for goodness sake. Does not match: ged, gored.
/go?d/	Matches any string that contains this pattern. The question mark (?) matches zero or one occurrence of the character previous to it, which is "o" in this example. Matches: gd, god, godiva, for god and country. Does not match: ged, gored, good, for goodness sake.
/go.*/	Matches any string that contains "go" followed by any number of characters. The period (.) matches any character, except the newline character. Matches: go, good, gory, allegory.
/Ac[eio]r/	Matches any string that contains "Ac" followed by either e, i, or o, and r. Matches: Acer, Acir, Acor, Acerre, National Acer Inc. Does not match: Aceir, Acior, Aceior.

There are many more special characters that you can use in a regular expression, too many to summarize in this section. In addition, the RegExp object provides several functions for manipulating regular expressions.

The following is an example of using a regular expression with the test( ) function to test for customer names that start with "national":

```
var pattern = /^national/i;
var result = pattern.test(row["customerName"]);
```

The first statement specifies the string pattern to search. The second statement uses the test( ) function to check if the string pattern exists in the customerName field value. The test( ) function returns a value of true or false, which is stored in the result variable.

If you are familiar with regular expressions in other languages, note that some of the syntax of JavaScript regular expressions differs from the syntax of Java or Perl regular expressions. Most notably, JavaScript uses forward slashes (/ /) to delimit a regular expression, and Java and Perl use double quotation marks (" ").

Using pattern-matching in filter conditions

In BIRT Report Designer, regular expressions are particularly useful when creating filter conditions. For example, a filter condition can contain a regular expression that tests whether the value of a string field matches a specified string pattern. Only data rows that meet the filter condition are displayed. You can, for example, create a filter to display only rows where a memo field contains the words "Account overdrawn", where a customer e-mail address ends with ".org", or where a product code starts with "S10".

When you use the filter tool in BIRT Report Designer to specify this type of filter condition, use the Match operator, and specify the regular expression, or string pattern, to match. Figure 13-7 shows an example of specifying a filter condition that uses a regular expression.

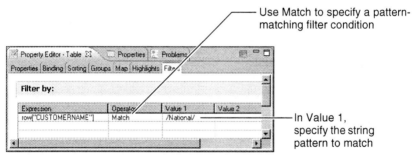

Figure 13-7   Example of regular expression

In this example, the filter condition is applied to a table in the report design. In the generated report, the table displays only customers whose names contain the word National. You can learn more about filtering data in the next chapter.

Using pattern-matching to search for and replace string values

So far, this chapter has described some of the syntax that is used to create regular expressions. This section discusses how regular expressions can be used in JavaScript code to search for and replace string values. Recall that in "Substituting string values," earlier in this chapter, we used replace( ) to search for a specified string and replace it with another.

Sometimes, you need the flexibility of searching for a string pattern rather than a specific string. Consider the example that was discussed in that earlier section. The row["address"].replace("St.", "Street") expression replaces St. Mary Road with Street Mary Road. To avoid these types of erroneous search-and-replace actions, use the following expression to search for "St." at the end of a line. The $ flag specifies a match at the end of a string.

```
row["address"].replace (/St.$/, "Street")
```

Consider another example: In your report, you display the contents of a memo field. You notice that in the content, the word JavaScript appears as javascript, Javascript, and JavaScript. You want JavaScript to appear consistently in the report. To do so, you can write the following expression to search for various versions of the word and replace them with JavaScript:

```
row["memoField"].replace("javascript",
    "JavaScript").replace("Javascript", "JavaScript")
```

This expression searches for the specified strings only. It would miss, for example, JAVASCRIPT or javaScript. You can, of course, add as many versions of the word you can think of, but this technique is not efficient.

An efficient and flexible solution is to use a regular expression to search for any and all versions of JavaScript. The following expression replaces all versions of JavaScript with the correct capitalization, no matter how the word is capitalized:

```
row["memoField"].replace(/javascript/gi, "JavaScript")
```

The g flag specifies a global search, which means that all occurrences of the pattern are replaced, not just the first. The i flag specifies a case-insensitive search.

Converting a string to a number

A data source can store numbers as strings. Telephone numbers, zip codes, user IDs, and invoice numbers are some of the numbers that might be stored as strings. If you want to manipulate these numbers mathematically, you need to convert them to a numeric type using the parseInt( ) or parseFloat( ) JavaScript function. The following example converts an invoice ID to an integer and adds 10 to it:

```
parseInt(row["invoiceID"]) + 10
```

If the invoiceID is 1225, this expression returns 1235. If you did not convert invoiceID to a real number, the result of adding 10 to invoiceID is 122510.

Manipulating date-and-time data

Both JavaScript and BIRT provide a wide range of functions for manipulating dates. In the expression builder, look under Native JavaScript Functions—Date, and under BIRT Functions—DateTimeSpan. The following sections describe some of the common date-manipulation tasks and provide examples of expressions.

Displaying the current date

A report typically displays the date on which it is generated, so that users can tell if the data in the report is up-to-date. To display the current date, use the following expression in a data element:

```
new Date( )
```

When the report is run, the current date appears in the format that is determined by the locale setting on the user's system. If, for example, the locale is English (United States), the date appears as follows:

```
6/18/05 12:30 PM
```

If you want to display the date in a different format, such as June 18, 2005, use Property Editor to set the data element's Format DateTime property to the desired format.

Getting parts of a date or time as a number

You can use the JavaScript date functions, such as getDay( ), getMonth( ), and getYear( ), to get the day, month, or year of a specified date field. Similarly, with the getHours( ), getMinutes( ), and getSeconds( ) functions, you can get the hour, minute, or second of a specified time field. All these functions return values as numbers. For example, getDay(row["orderDate"]) returns 1 for a date that falls on Monday. Except for getDate( ), which returns the day of the month, the range of return values for the other functions start at 0. The return values for getMonth( ), for example, are between 0, for January, and 11, for December. Similarly, getDay( ) returns 0 for Sunday and 6 for Saturday.

If you want to display parts of a date in a different format, for example, display the month as a word such as January, February, and so on, use Property Editor to set the data element's Format DateTime property to the desired format.

Calculating the time between two dates

It is often useful to calculate and display the number of days, months, or years between two dates. For example, a data source might store two dates for each order record—the date on which the order was placed and the date on which the order was shipped. To provide information about order fulfillment trends, you can use BIRT's DateTimeSpan functions to calculate and display the number of days between the order date and the ship date, as follows:

```
DateTimeSpan.days(row["orderDate"], row["shippedDate"])
```

You can also display the number of hours between the two dates, using the following expression:

```
DateTimeSpan.hours(row["orderDate"], row["shippedDate"])
```

Use a different DateTimeSpan function, depending on the range of time between two dates. For example, you would not use DateTimeSpan.month( ) to calculate the amount of time between order dates and ship dates because, if orders are usually shipped within two weeks, DateTimeSpan.month( ) will often return 0.

Calculating a date

You can add or subtract a specified amount of time to, or from, a date to calculate a new date. For example, the following information is stored for each order record: the date on which the order was placed and the shipment time in days. You want to calculate the date that customers can expect to receive their orders. Given those two fields, you can calculate the new date by adding the number of shipping days to the date on which the order was placed. You use BIRT's DateTimeSpan.addDate( ) function to calculate the new date. The addDate( ) function takes four arguments: the starting date, the number of years, the number of months, and the number of days.

The following expression shows how to calculate the expected delivery date:

```
DateTimeSpan.addDate(row["orderDate"], 0, 0, row["shipTime"])
```

Another function that you can use to calculate a new date is DateTimeSpan.subDate( ). Use this function to subtract days, months, or years to arrive at a new date. It takes the same four arguments as addDate( ).

Using Boolean expressions

A Boolean expression returns one of two values: true or false. The following expressions are basic Boolean expressions:

```
row["sales"] > 5000
row["state"] == "CA"
row["orderDate"] >= new Date(2005, 4, 30)
```

The first expression tests if the sales value is greater than 5000. If the value is greater than 5000, the expression returns true. If it is not, the expression returns false.

The second expression tests if the state value is equal to CA. If the value is CA, the expression returns true; if not, the expression returns false. For Boolean expressions, you must use comparison operators. As the second expression shows, you use ==, not the assignment operator, =. The expression row["state"] = "CA" returns CA. It does not return a true or false value.

The third expression tests if the order date is greater than or equal to the date May 30, 2005. Note that months in a JavaScript Date object start at zero, so January is month 0 and December is month 11.

A Boolean expression can be as complex as you need. It can contain a combination of And (&&) and Or(| |) operators, along with the comparison operators. The following expressions are examples of complex, or compound, Boolean expressions:

- The following expression returns true if an order total is greater than or equal to 5000 and an order ID is greater than 2000. Both conditions must be true.

  ```
  row["orderTotal"] >= 5000 && row["orderID"] > 2000
  ```

- The following expression returns true if the state is CA or WA. Only one condition needs to be true.

  ```
  row["state"] == "CA" || row["state"] == "WA"
  ```

- The following expression returns true if three conditions are true:

  - The state is CA or WA.

  - The order total is greater than 5000.

  - The order ID is greater than 2000.

    ```
    (row["state"] == "CA" || row["state"] == "WA") &&
        (row["orderTotal"] > 5000 && row["orderID"] > 2000)
    ```

You use a Boolean expression to:

- Conditionally display a report element.

- Specify conditions with which to filter data.

- Specify conditions with which to perform particular tasks. You can, for example, use a Boolean expression in an if statement to do something when the expression is true and to do something else when the expression is false.

  ```
  if (row["creditScore"] > 700) {
      displayString = "Your loan application has been
      approved."
      }
  else{
      displayString = "Your loan application has been denied."
      }
  ```

You seldom use a Boolean expression on its own unless you want to display true or false in the report.

Filtering Data

Data sources typically contain large amounts of data. Reports usually need only a specific subset of data that meets certain conditions. You can select specific records to use in a report by using filters. For example, rather than get information about all customers, you can create filters to select customers in a certain region or customers with a certain credit rank. You can also design filters that provide the report user with the opportunity to specify the filter conditions when the report runs. This chapter discusses creating filters for which you specify the conditions at design time.

Filtering opportunities

Generally, one goal in developing reports with acceptable performance is to limit the amount of data in a report to just the data that meets the report users' requirements. You can limit, or filter, data in different ways depending on the type of data source you are using and the type of report you are creating.

The first opportunity you have for filtering is to use any filtering techniques provided by your data source. For example, JDBC-compliant databases allow users to run SQL queries that use restrictive WHERE clauses. In fact, best practices recommend designing databases with filtering in mind. You can achieve optimal report performance by filtering data while it is still in the database.

After BIRT retrieves the data from the data source, there are several more opportunities for filtering. Base the decision on where and when to filter on efficiency. For example, instead of creating two data sets that return similar data, one for populating a table and another for populating a list, you can create one data set for use by both the table and the list.

You can use a combination of filtering techniques. For example, if you are accessing data from a database, you can write a query that filters some rows and use other techniques to filter additional rows. Figure 14-1 shows the effects of using various filtering techniques at different points in processing data.

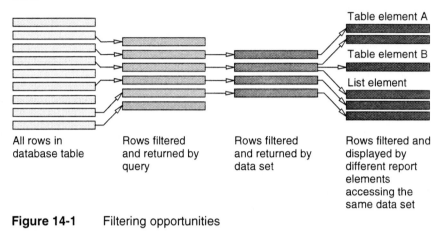

| All rows in database table | Rows filtered and returned by query | Rows filtered and returned by data set | Rows filtered and displayed by different report elements accessing the same data set |

Figure 14-1   Filtering opportunities

Specifying conditions on row retrieval

If your report accesses data from a database or an XML data source, you can specify filter conditions to retrieve a certain set of data from the data source. By filtering at the data source level and retrieving a limited number of rows, you improve performance. The larger the number of rows a data set returns, the more memory and resources BIRT uses to store and process the rows. This section covers some typical ways to filter data in a database or XML data source.

Filtering database data

When you create a JDBC data set, you use a SQL SELECT statement to specify which rows to retrieve from the database. To select only rows that meet certain criteria, add a WHERE clause to the SELECT statement. The WHERE clause consists of the keyword WHERE, followed by a search condition that specifies which rows to retrieve.

For example, the following statement returns only customers from the USA:

```
SELECT customerName
FROM Customer
WHERE country = 'USA'
```

As another example, the following statement returns only customers from USA and whose credit limit exceeds $10,000.00:

```
SELECT customerName
FROM Customer
WHERE country = 'USA'
AND creditLimit > 10000
```

In the following example, the statement returns all customers from USA or Canada:

```
SELECT customerName
FROM Customer
WHERE country = 'USA'
OR country = 'Canada'
```

How to filter the rows to retrieve from a JDBC data source

This procedure assumes that you have already created a JDBC data set using a SQL query or stored procedure.

1 In Data Explorer, double-click the data set to which to add a filter condition.

2 On Edit Data Set, add a WHERE clause to the SELECT statement to specify a filter condition.

For examples and information about the types of filter conditions that you can specify, see the next section.

3 Choose Preview Results to verify that the query returns only the rows that meet the filter condition.

Types of SQL filter conditions

Table 14-1 describes the types of SQL filter conditions and provides examples of filter conditions that are used in WHERE clauses.

Table 14-1   Examples of filter conditions in the WHERE clause

Type of filter condition	Description	Examples of WHERE...

Comparison	Compares the value of one expression to the value of another expression	`quantity = 10`
		`custName = 'Acme Inc.'`
		`custName > 'P'`
		`custState <> 'CA'`
		`orderDate > {d '2005-06-30'}`

(continues)

Table 14-1   Examples of filter conditions in the WHERE clause *(continued)*

Type of filter condition	Description	Examples of WHERE...

Range	Tests whether the value of an expression falls within a range of values. The test includes the endpoints of the range.	`price BETWEEN 1000 AND 2000`
		
		`custName BETWEEN 'E' AND 'K'`
		
		`orderDate BETWEEN`
		`     {d '2005-01-01'}`
		`     AND {d '2005-06-30'}`

Membership	Tests whether the value of an expression matches one value in a set of values	`officeCode IN (101,103,104)`
		
		`itemType IN ('sofa',`
		`     'loveseat', 'endtable',`
		`     'clubchair')`
		
		`orderDate IN`
		`     ({d '2005-10-10'},`
		`     {d '2005-10-17'})`

Pattern-matching	Tests whether the value of a string field matches a specified pattern	`custName LIKE 'Smith%'`
		(% matches zero or more characters)
		
		`custName LIKE 'Smiths_n'`
		(_ matches one character)
		
		`custState NOT LIKE 'CA%'`

Null value	Tests whether a field has a null, or missing, value	`manager IS NULL`
		`shipDate IS NULL`
		`shipDate IS NOT NULL`

SQL provides many other operators and options that you can use to create more complex search conditions. For more information about the WHERE clause, see the SQL documentation for your JDBC database.

Filtering XML data

When you create an XML data set, you specify what data to retrieve from an XML data source by mapping XML elements and attributes to data set tables and columns. To map an XML element to a table or to a column, you specify an XPath expression. If you are not familiar with XML, XPath is a query language for accessing parts of an XML document. Figure 14-2 shows an example of a table mapping defined in an XML data set. The XPath expression is /library/book.

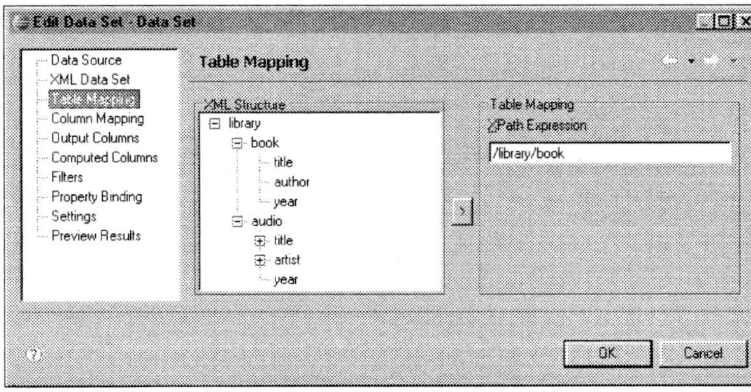

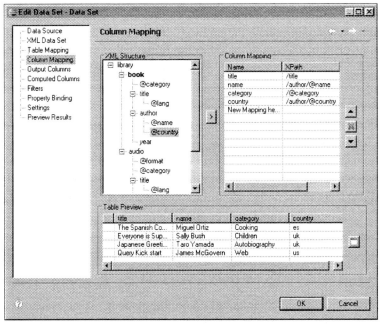

Figure 14-2   Table mapping for an XML document

Figure 14-3 shows an example of column mappings defined in an XML data set. The XPath expressions define the paths to the elements or attributes, which are relative to the table mapping path.

Figure 14-3   Column mappings and the data rows returned by the XML data set

To retrieve only data rows that meet certain criteria, specify the value to search for in the table mapping XPath expression. The following XPath expression, for example, specifies that only rows where the book category is Children should be retrieved:

```
/library/book[@category="Children"]
```

When filtering data with an XPath expression, observe the following limitations:

- You can specify only one value on which to search. You cannot, for example, search for categories Children and Cooking.

- You can filter only on XML attributes, not XML elements. The XML structure in the Column Mapping page displays XML attributes with the @ symbol. In the Column Mapping page shown in Figure 14-3, for example, @category, @lang, @name, and @country are attributes, whereas title, author, and year are elements.

If you need more advanced filtering capabilities, use BIRT Report Designer's filter tool, which is described later in this chapter.

How to define a filter on row retrieval for XML data sets

1 In Data Explorer, double-click the XML data set to which you want to add a filter condition.

2 On Edit Data Set, choose Table Mapping.

3 Modify the XPath expression to specify the filter condition. The following expressions are examples of XPath filtering expressions:

```
/library/book[@category="Children"]
/library/book/author[@country="uk"]
```

The value you specify within the double quotation marks (" ") must match exactly the value in the XML document.

4 Choose Column Mapping, and edit the column mappings so that the paths are compatible with the modified table mapping. Rather than directly edit the XPath expressions, you may find it easier to delete the existing column mappings, then create new ones by selecting the element or attribute in the XML data structure and choosing the right arrow.

5 Choose Preview Results to confirm that the filter returns only rows that match the value that you specified.

Filtering data after row retrieval

BIRT provides options for filtering data that complement, and in some cases, replace filtering provided by data sources. It is recommended to filter at the data source when possible. There are cases, however, when you cannot. For example, if you use flat file data sources and you want to filter data, you must filter data in BIRT.

In addition, if using SQL to modify an existing database query is problematic, you can specify the filter conditions using JavaScript expressions instead of SQL. BIRT Report Designer provides a graphical tool to help you build these filter conditions.

Deciding where to filter in BIRT

There are three places in BIRT you can filter data. You can create a filter in any or all of the following places:

- The data set
- A report element, such as a table, list, or cross tab
- A group

The first opportunity to filter data in BIRT is on the data set level. Use this technique if only one report element uses the data set or if you want all report elements that use the data set to use the same set of rows.

Next, you can filter on a report element. You can edit the report element filter properties to specify conditions for displaying only certain data rows. Use this technique if multiple tables, lists, and charts use the same data set, but you want each report element to display a different set of rows.

For example, you create a data set that returns data for all customers in the USA. You use this data set for two elements, such as a table and a list. You can specify a different filter condition for each element to limit further the rows to display. The table element, for example, can filter the rows to display only customers from California. The list element can filter the rows to display only customers from New York. Figure 14-4 illustrates this concept.

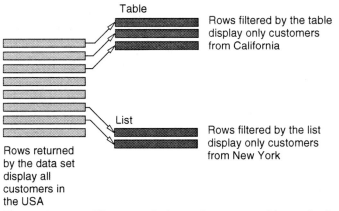

Figure 14-4   Filters applied to a data set, a table, and a list

Finally, you can filter on a group of data. If you group data in a table or list, you can edit the filter properties of each group. Filter at the group level if a table or list displays rows in groups and you want to display only certain groups. For example, a sales report groups orders by customer. Rather than showing data for all customers, you can specify a filter to display only customers that have order totals above a certain amount, or specify a filter to display only the top three customers.

Figure 14-5 compares three reports that use the same data set but different group filters. The first report shows all customer groups. The second report uses a filter at the customer group level to show only customers whose order totals exceed $100,000.00. The third report uses a filter at the customer group level to show the top three customers with the highest order totals.

Report shows all customer groups

Corporate Gift Ideas Co.	$102,908.44
Order 10159	$37,872.32
Order 10162	$25,345.98
Order 10381	$28,734.69
Order 10384	$10,955.45
Gift Depot Inc.	$83,274.15
Order 10172	$19,318.08
Order 10263	$40,618.93
Order 10413	$23,337.14
Land of Toys Inc.	$105,499.28
Order 10107	$9,347.60
Order 10248	$34,077.36
Order 10292	$23,510.33
Order 10329	$38,563.99
Muscle Machine Inc	$146,063.02
Order 10127	$45,049.74
Order 10204	$47,609.95
Order 10267	$20,314.44
Order 10349	$33,088.89
Online Diecast Creations Co.	$93,495.72
Order 10100	$8,563.71
Order 10192	$40,586.41
Order 10322	$44,345.60
The Sharp Gifts Warehouse	$133,390.92
Order 10250	$40,517.12
Order 10400	$29,589.38
Order 10407	$48,904.14

Report applies a filter on the customer group to show customers whose order totals exceed $100,000.00

Corporate Gift Ideas Co.	$102,908.44
Order 10159	$37,872.32
Order 10162	$25,345.98
Order 10381	$28,734.69
Order 10384	$10,955.45
Land of Toys Inc.	$105,499.28
Order 10107	$9,347.60
Order 10248	$34,077.36
Order 10292	$23,510.33
Order 10329	$38,563.99
Muscle Machine Inc	$146,063.02
Order 10127	$45,049.74
Order 10204	$47,609.95
Order 10267	$20,314.44
Order 10349	$33,088.89
The Sharp Gifts Warehouse	$133,390.92
Order 10250	$40,517.12
Order 10257	$14,380.28
Order 10400	$29,589.38
Order 10407	$48,904.14

Report applies a filter on the customer group to show customers with the top three order totals

Land of Toys Inc.	$105,499.28
Order 10107	$9,347.60
Order 10248	$34,077.36
Order 10292	$23,510.33
Order 10329	$38,563.99
Muscle Machine Inc	$146,063.02
Order 10127	$45,049.74
Order 10204	$47,609.95
Order 10267	$20,314.44
Order 10349	$33,088.89
The Sharp Gifts Warehouse	$133,390.92
Order 10250	$40,517.12
Order 10257	$14,380.28
Order 10400	$29,589.38
Order 10407	$48,904.14

Figure 14-5   Three reports that apply filters on the group level to display different results from the same data set

You can specify filter conditions at all three levels if your report design needs it. Filtering at each level serves a different purpose, can yield different results, and can have different rules. Use the following guidelines to help you decide where to filter data for a report:

- When you filter at the data set level, BIRT filters all rows that are retrieved from the data source.

- When you filter at the report element level, BIRT filters all rows that are returned by the data set that is bound to the report element.

- When you filter at the group level, BIRT filters only rows in that particular group. In the reports shown in Figure 14-5, you can filter on customer names and order totals only. You cannot, for example, filter on order number because that data is in a different group. Typically, a filter at the group level uses an aggregate expression.

- Filters that use aggregate data can be specified only at the group level. The second report shown in Figure 14-5 uses the following filter condition:

```
row["Customer_Total"] Greater than 100000
```

The third report uses the following filter condition:

```
row["Customer_Total"] Top n 3
```

In these filter conditions, row["Customer_Total"] refers to a column binding that calculates customer order totals, using the SUM aggregate function. If you use aggregate data in a filter at the data set or report element level, BIRT Report Designer displays an error message.

- Some filter conditions provide the same results whether they are applied at the data set, report element, or group level. In the reports shown in Figure 14-5, if you want to display only customers whose names start with M or a later letter, you can specify the following filter condition at the data set, table, or group level, and the reports display the same data:

```
row["customerName"] Larger Than "M"
```

Types of BIRT filter conditions

Just as with the data source filtering, you can design different types of BIRT filter conditions depending on how you want to search for data rows. For example, you can specify that BIRT returns rows when the value of a particular field matches a specific value, when the field value falls within a range of values, when the field value matches a string pattern, or when the field value is null.

The filter tool displays operators as English words instead of the actual operators. For example, the tool displays Equal, Greater than, Greater than or Equal, and Not Equal, instead of ==, >, >=, and !=. Table 14-2 describes the types of filter conditions that you can create with the filter tool. The table also contains numerous examples of expressions you can create using the operators. Most operators can be used with different data types. You should be aware that the filter tool provides two pattern-matching operators: Like and Match. The Like operator enables users who are familiar with SQL to specify pattern-matching expressions using SQL syntax. The Match operator enables users who are familiar with JavaScript to specify pattern-matching expressions using JavaScript's regular expression syntax.

Table 14-2   Examples of BIRT filter conditions

Type of filter condition	Description	Example as it appears in the filter tool

Comparison	Compares the value of a field to a specified value.	`row["quantity"] Less than 10`
		`row["custName"] Equal "Acme Inc."`
		`row["custName"] Greater than or`
		`    Equal "P"`
		`row["custState"] Not Equal "CA"`
		`row["orderDate"] Less than or Equal`
		`    "06/30/05"`

Null value	Tests whether a field has a value or not.	`row["manager"] Is Null` `row["shipDate"] Is Not Null`

Range	Tests whether the value of a field falls within a range of specified values. The test includes the endpoints of the range.	`row["quantity"] Between 50 and 100`
		(returns all quantities between 50 and 100, including 50 and 100)
		`row["custName"] Between "A" and "B"`
		(returns all names that start with A)
		`row["custName"] Not Between "A" and`
		`    "M"`
		(returns all names that start with M and later letters)
		`row["orderDate"] Between`
		`    "06/01/05" and "06/30/05"`
		(returns all dates between these dates, including 06/01/05 and 06/30/05)

Conditional logic	Tests if a complete filter condition evaluates to true or false. Use to create a single filter condition that consists of multiple conditions.	`row["country"] == "USA"||`
		`    row["country"] == "Canada"`
		`    Is False`
		(returns all countries except the USA and Canada)
		`row["orderStatus"] == "Open"||`
		`    row["orderTotal"] > 100000`
		`    Is True`
		(returns all orders with open status and all orders with totals exceeding 100000)

Table 14-2 Examples of BIRT filter conditions *(continued)*

Type of filter condition	Description	Example as it appears in the filter tool
Pattern-matching test, using JavaScript syntax	Tests whether the value of a string field matches a specified pattern called a regular expression. For more information about matching patterns with regular expressions, see "Matching string patterns" in Chapter 13, "Writing Expressions."	row["custName"] Match /Smith/ (returns names that contain the substring Smith) row["creditRank"] Match /[AB]/ (returns credit ranks A or B) row["productCode"] Match /^S10/ (returns product codes that begin with S10)
Pattern-matching test, using SQL syntax	Tests whether the value of a string field matches a specified pattern that uses SQL syntax.	row["custName"] Like '%Smith%' (returns names that contain the substring Smith) row["productCode"] Like 'S10%' (returns product codes that begin with S10)
Top or bottom *n* logic	Tests if the value of a specified field is within the top or bottom *n* values.	row["age"] Top Percent 5 (returns ages in the top five percent) row["age"] Bottom Percent 5 (returns ages in the bottom five percent) row["orderTotal"] Top n 10 (returns the top ten orders) row["orderTotal"] Bottom n 10 (returns the bottom ten orders)

Creating a filter condition

The procedure for creating a filter condition is the same whether you create it at the data set, report element, or group level. The difference is how you access the filter tool.

When you create a filter condition, you specify the following information:

- The expression to evaluate, typically the field to search, such as row["grade"]

- The operator that specifies the type of filter test, such as Equal to

- The value for which to search, such as "A"

You can create more complex filter conditions that include JavaScript functions or scripts. For example, you can specify computed values for the expression and value portions of the filter. The following example shows a multiline expression in the expression part. The expression returns a customer's first name from the customerName field, which stores full names.

```
spaceCharPosition = row["customerName"].indexOf(" ");
stringToGet = row["customerName"].substr(0, spaceCharPosition);
```

If you combine this expression with the Equal to operator and specify a value of "John", the filter condition extracts the first name from the customerName field, compares the first name to John, and returns only rows where this condition is true.

The expressions and values that you specify in a BIRT filter condition must use JavaScript syntax, unless you use the LIKE operator. As described in Table 14-2 in the previous section, when you supply a value for a filter condition that uses the LIKE operator, you specify a string pattern that uses SQL syntax.

If you filter data using both the SQL query and BIRT Report Designer's filter tool, be careful not to confuse SQL syntax with JavaScript syntax when specifying the filter condition. It is easy, for example, to confuse the use of single quotation marks (' ') and double quotation marks (" "). SQL requires single quotation marks for string and date constants, but JavaScript requires double quotation marks. Another example is the comparison operator. You use = for SQL and == for JavaScript.

How to filter at the data set level

1   In Data Explorer, right-click the data set whose rows you want to filter, then choose Edit. Edit Data Set displays the query for the data set, as shown in Figure 14-6.

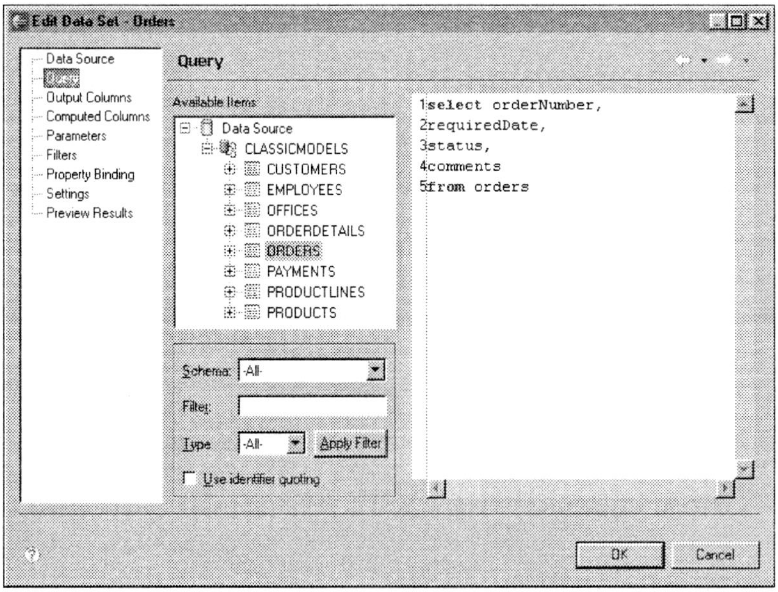

Figure 14-6   Edit Data Set displaying the query

2 Choose Filters from the left side of the window. Edit Data Set displays filter information, as shown in Figure 14-7.

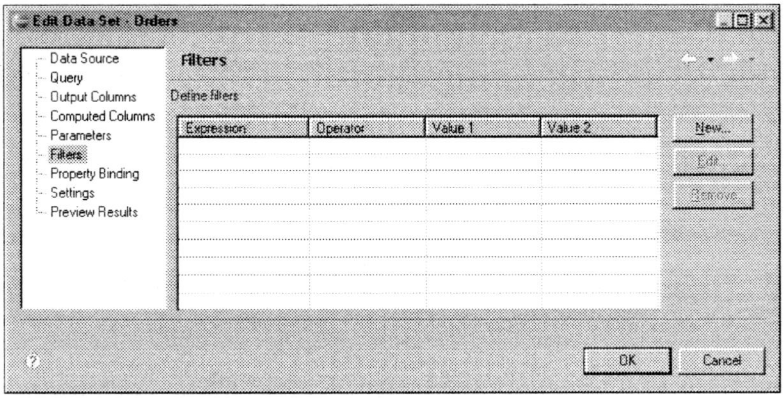

Figure 14-7   Edit Data Set displaying filtering information

3 Choose New to create a filter condition.

4 On New Filter, specify the following values:

- In Expression, select a field from the drop-down list. Alternatively, open the expression builder to create a more complex expression.

- In Operator, select an operator from the drop-down list.

- In Value 1, specify the value to search. You can type the value, select from the list of values, or use the expression builder to create a more complex value expression. If you select the Is True, Is False, Is Null, or Is Not Null operator, you do not specify a value.

- In Value 2, specify a value only if you select the Between or Not Between operator. Figure 14-8 shows an example of a filter condition.

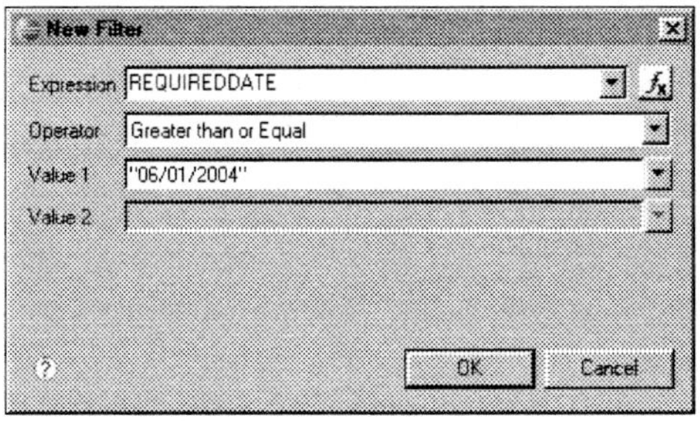

Figure 14-8   New Filter displaying a filter condition

Choose OK to save the new filter condition.

5 To create additional filter conditions for the data set, repeat steps 3 and 4. Figure 14-9 shows two examples of filter conditions created for a data set. Figure 14-10 shows the rows that the data set returns.

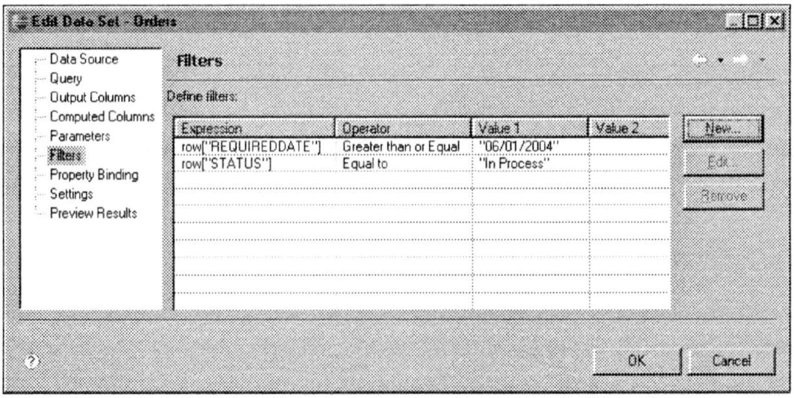

Figure 14-9   Edit Data Set displaying the filter conditions for the data set

6   Choose Preview Results to verify the results that filtering the data set
    returns. If you specified multiple filter conditions, the data set returns
    only rows that match all filter conditions, as shown in Figure 14-10. To
    return rows that match any one of the filter conditions, create a single
    filter condition that contains an OR expression, then select the Is True
    operator. This task is described later in this chapter.

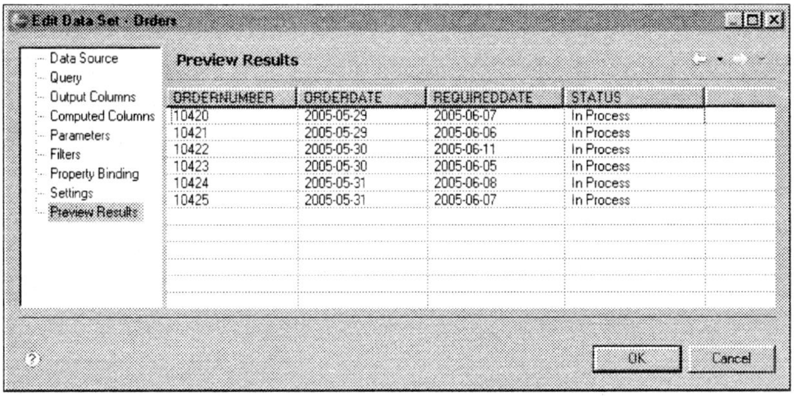

Figure 14-10   Preview Results shows only rows that meet both filter
                    conditions

How to filter at the report element level

These instructions assume you already created a report that uses a table to
display data from a data set.

1   Open Property Editor.

2   In the layout editor, select the table or list whose data you want to filter.
    Property Editor displays the properties of the table or list, as shown in
    Figure 14-11.

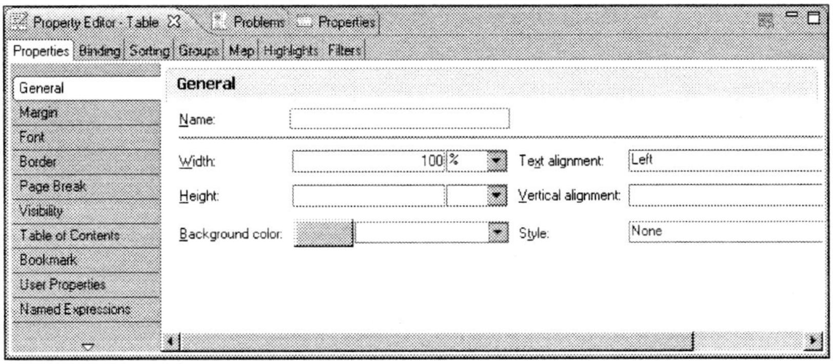

Figure 14-11 Table properties

3 Choose the Filters tab. Property Editor displays the Filters page.

4 Choose Add to create a filter condition.

5 On New Filter Condition, specify the filter condition, then choose OK. For detailed steps, see the previous section.

6 Figure 14-12 shows some examples of filter conditions specified for a table.

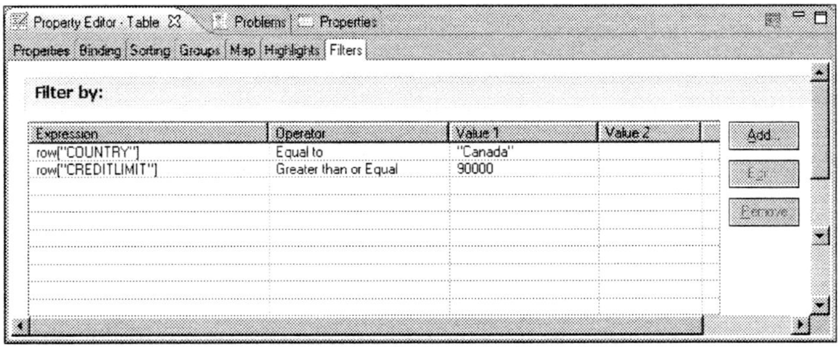

Figure 14-12 Filter conditions for a table

7 Preview the report to verify the results. If you specified multiple filter conditions, the report displays only rows that match all filter conditions.

How to filter at the group level

These instructions assume that you have already created a table that displays data from a data set, and created a group or groups to organize the data.

1 In the layout editor, select the table that contains the data to filter.

2 In Property Editor, choose the Groups tab. Property Editor displays the groups that you defined for the table.

3 Double-click the group whose data you want to filter. Edit Group displays the properties of the group. Figure 14-13 shows an example.

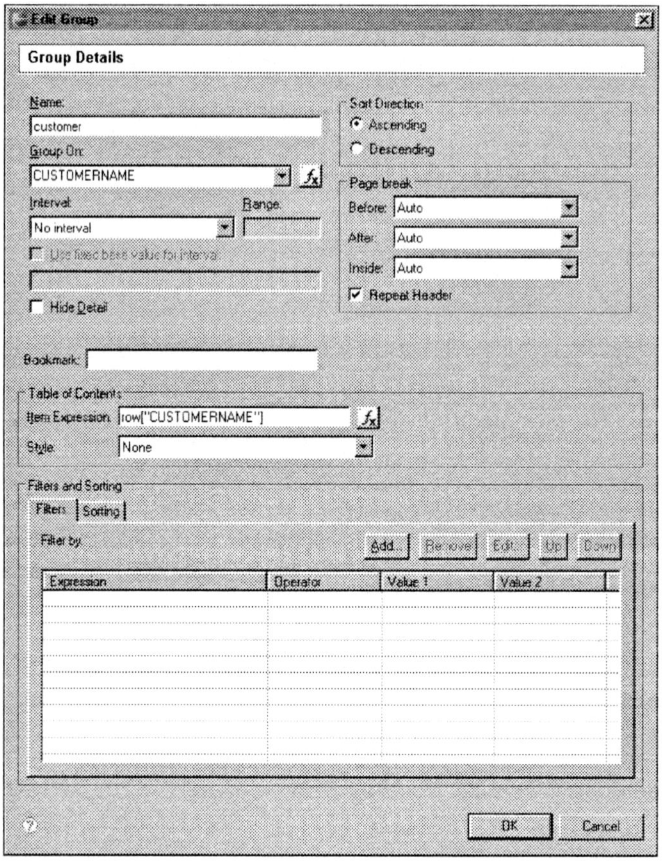

Figure 14-13   Edit Group

4   Under Filters and Sorting, choose the Filters tab.

5   Choose Add to create a filter condition.

6   On New Filter Condition, specify the filter condition, then choose OK.
Figure 14-14 shows an example of a filter condition defined for a group.

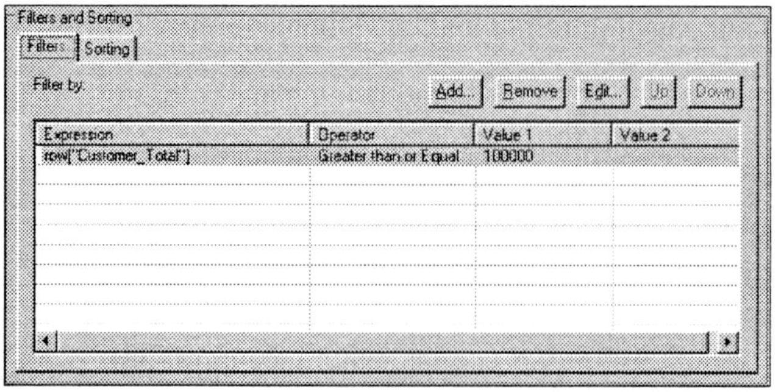

Figure 14-14   Filter condition for a group

7 Choose OK.

8 Preview the report to verify the results. The report displays a different set of group values.

Creating multiple filter conditions

The filter tool enables you to create any number of conditions for filtering data. BIRT evaluates each condition and includes only data rows that meet all the conditions. For example, assume the following two conditions were created with the filter tool:

```
row["orderTotal"] Larger Than 10000
row["country"] Equal "USA"
```

In this example, BIRT includes a row only if the value in the orderTotal field is greater than 10000 and the value in the country field is equal to USA. In other words, creating two filter conditions is equivalent to specifying the following JavaScript expression:

```
row["orderTotal"] > 10000 && row["country"] == "USA"
```

The following rows meet the specified filter conditions:

Country	Order ID	Order Total
USA	1010	15000
USA	1035	18500
USA	1155	25000
USA	1200	12000
USA	1455	20500

If you want to return a row if it meets any one of multiple conditions, create a single filter condition that uses the OR (| |) operator to combine multiple conditions. For example, to include a row where either orderTotal exceeds 10000 or country is USA, create an expression that compares to true, as follows:

```
row["orderTotal"] > 10000 || row["country"] == "USA" Is True
```

For expressions that compare to true or false, you must use the comparison operator. As the previous example shows, you use ==, not the assignment operator, =. Figure 14-15 shows how the filter condition appears in the filter tool. Note that you select Is True as the operator.

Expression	Operator	Value 1
row["orderTotal"] > 10000 || row["country"] == "USA"	Is True	

Figure 14-15   Filter condition that uses the OR and Is True operators

In this example, the following rows meet the specified filter condition:

Country	Order ID	Order Total
Belgium	1020	21000
France	2005	14500
USA	1425	5000
USA	1750	7500
USA	1010	15000
USA	1035	18500
USA	1155	25000
USA	1200	12000
USA	1455	20500

Enabling the User to Filter Data

When you create a report, you build a data set and typically specify filter criteria to display specific data in the report. When a user views the report, the user sees the information that you selected. As users become familiar with the report and recognize its potential as an analytical tool, they may want to view the data in different ways. For example, in a sales report, a user may want to view only sales in California, or sales over a certain amount, or sales that closed in the last 30 days.

The solution for this type of ad hoc reporting requirement is for the report to prompt the user to provide information that determines what data to display. Report developers make this solution available by using report parameters.

About report parameters

Report parameters collect information that determines the data to display in the report when the report runs. Typically, you use report parameters to prompt a report user to specify what data to display before BIRT generates the report. You can also use report parameters in more creative ways. For example, a web application can use a user's login information to programmatically set the value of an account number report parameter. Then the web application can generate a report for that particular account.

Using report parameters, you can:

- Generate on-demand reports.

  By using report parameters in a report design, you can create a single report design that generates specialized reports, on demand, to meet the different needs of report users.

- Design a report once, and use the same design to display different data that is based on specific criteria.

  Report parameters are essential tools for time-sensitive reports. Consider a monthly sales report. A report developer generates and publishes a report each month. When the report developer first creates the report, she builds a query to show sales data for the month of January only. To generate a report for February's numbers, she must modify the query to get data for February only. Without using report parameters, the report developer must modify the query manually every month. By creating a report parameter that prompts for the month for which to display sales information, the report developer can create one report and run it each month to refresh its data. The report user gets exactly what he needs to see.

- Manage large reports.

  Report parameters are also useful for managing large reports. Consider a report design that generates a detailed report that is several hundred pages long. It displays, for example, all itemized sales orders for all customers in all cities in every state. That report is comprehensive but includes more information than most users want. To reduce the size of the report and let the user select only the data that he wants to view, you can use report parameters to generate specific parts of the original report. You can, for example, provide report parameters that ask the user to specify a customer name, a city, or a state for which to display sales orders.

Enter Parameters, shown in Figure 15-1, displays the available parameters to a report user when the user runs the report. The user chooses the parameter values, and BIRT generates a report according to the user's choices.

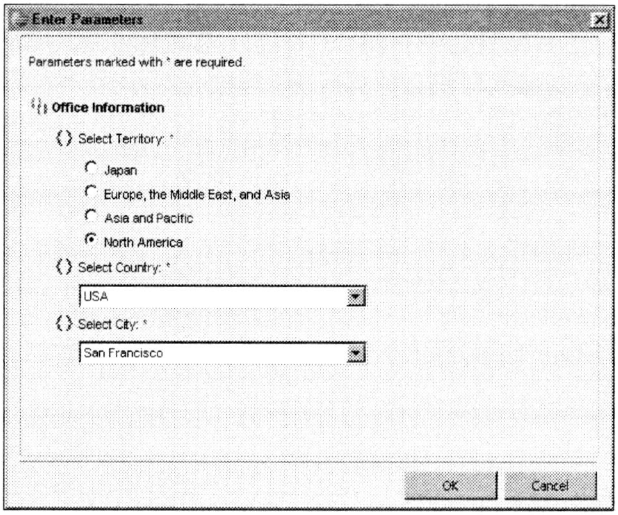

Figure 15-1   Enter Parameters

Planning to use report parameters

Before you create parameters for a report, decide what field values you want the report user to specify and how to prompt the user for those values.

- Think of the different ways in which a user may need to filter the information. You create one report parameter for each question that you want the user to answer. Theoretically, you can create a parameter for each discrete piece of data in the data source. To ensure that report parameters are not overwhelming for the user, limit the available parameters to important fields.

- If you create more than one report parameter, consider the interaction of the values. For example, if you create two parameters to get the values of state and sales total, decide whether to return rows only if both values in the row match or if either value matches.

- If you create many report parameters, organize them in logical groups. For example, you can create two groups of parameters to organize customer parameters, such as customer name, city, and state, in one group and order parameters, such as order ID, order date, and order amount, in another group.

- Use short, descriptive text prompts, but ensure the text is not ambiguous. For example, Customer State is clearer than State.

- Do not assume that the report user knows how the data is stored in the data source. For example, a user might not know that an order-status field takes three values: Open, Closed, and In Evaluation. Without this knowledge, the user does not know what value to enter for an order-status parameter. To improve usability, create a drop-down list or radio buttons for the user to select a value instead of requiring the user to type a value. Figure 15-1 provides an example of a simple, but effective, parameter presentation.

Ways to enable user filtering

Filtering on user-specified values can occur either at query run time, or after running the query. To enable a user to filter at query run time, you must use a JDBC data source. If the report uses a text file or XML data source, you must define filters at the table-element or list-element level.

Enabling the user to filter at query run time

As described previously, a report parameter enables or requires users to specify a value that determines the data to include in a report. When they run a report that uses a JDBC data source, BIRT updates the SQL query with these values before it retrieves any data. The data source then returns only the rows that match the user-specified values.

To enable users to filter database data, you complete the following tasks in the recommended order. For detailed information about these tasks, see the corresponding topics later in this section.

- Create report parameters to prompt the user to specify values that determine what rows to retrieve.

- Insert parameter markers in the SQL query.

- Create a data set parameter to supply a value for each parameter marker in the SQL query.

- Bind the data set parameter to the report parameter, so that the data set parameter gets the user-specified value from the report parameter and passes it to the SQL query.

- Determine how to present the report parameters to a user.

- Test the report parameters.

Creating a report parameter

Report parameters provide a mechanism for passing values into a report. You can create a report parameter to prompt the report user to specify a value for a particular field, or you can use a hidden report parameter to pass a value into the report on a programmatic basis. For instance, a hidden parameter might be used to pass a customer's account code into a report if you did not want a customer to look at any account data but her own.

Report parameters have global scope, which means they are available to the entire report and any report element can access a report parameter's value. To enable user filtering, you typically bind the report parameter to a corresponding data set parameter.

When you create a report parameter, you perform two main tasks:

- Define the basic properties of the parameter: its name and data type.

- Design the presentation of the parameter to the report user. The tasks you should consider include the following:

  - Specifying whether users type a value or select a value from a list box or radio buttons

  - Providing a default value

  - Displaying a descriptive text prompt

  - Organizing report parameters in logical groups

How to create a basic report parameter

1 In Data Explorer, right-click Report Parameters, and choose New Parameter.

New Parameter appears, as shown in Figure 15-2.

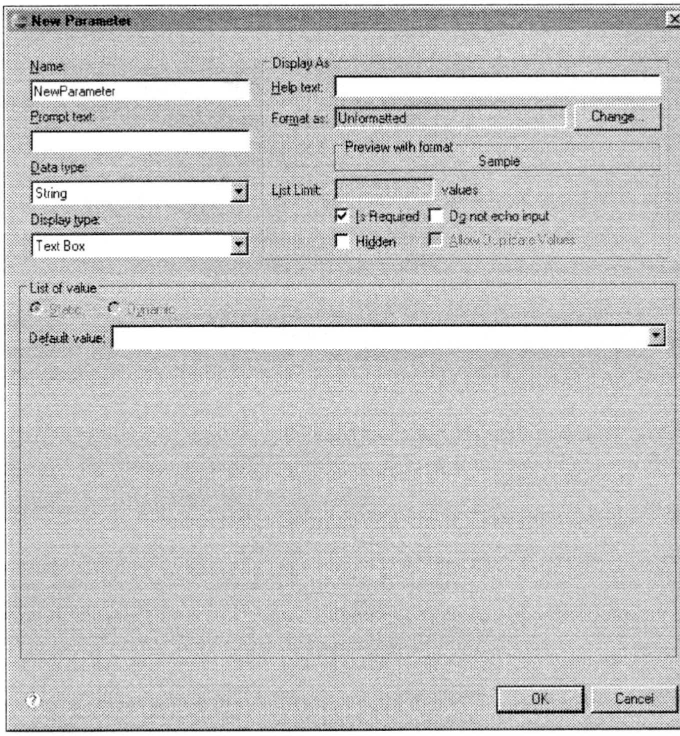

Figure 15-2   New Parameter

2 Specify the following basic properties:

   1 In Name, type a name for the parameter. It is good practice to use a prefix, such as RP, in the name to help distinguish report parameters from other parameter types, such as data set parameters. For example, a report parameter used to filter on a quantityinstock field might be named RP_quantityinstock. The value you specify in Name appears as the prompt to the report user if you do not specify a value for the next property, Prompt text. Rather than specify only a Name value for the parameter, you should use a technically descriptive value in Name, and provide a user-friendly value in Prompt text.

   2 In Data type, select a data type for the parameter.

     The data type that you select does not have to match the data type of the field in the data source. Values in an orderID field, for example, can be stored as integers in the database, but the report parameter that is associated with this field can be of decimal or string type. The data type that you select for the report parameter determines the formatting options that are available if you choose to provide a default value or a list of values for the report parameter.

3 Choose OK.

The parameter appears under Report Parameters in Data Explorer.

Inserting a parameter marker in the SQL query

After you create your report parameter, insert a parameter marker in the WHERE clause of the SQL query of the data set that you want to filter with the value of the report parameter. The parameter marker, represented by a question mark (?), indicates where you want BIRT to insert the parameter value.

For example, to ask the user to specify the threshold inventory quantity for a restocking report, insert the ? parameter marker in the WHERE clause, as shown in the following example:

```
WHERE quantityinstock < ?
```

When the report runs, if the user specifies 500 for quantityinstock, BIRT replaces ? with 500 and sends the following filter condition to the data source:

```
WHERE quantityinstock < 500
```

If you write a filter condition that uses more than one field, think about the interaction of the field values. Each of the following WHERE clauses, for example, returns a different set of rows:

```
WHERE quantityinstock < ? AND productvendor = ?
WHERE quantityinstock < ? OR productvendor = ?
```

The first clause returns only those rows in which both the quantityinstock and the productvendor values match the values that replace the ? markers. The second clause returns more rows. It returns rows in which the quantityinstock value is less than the value that replaces the quantityinstock ? marker and rows in which the productvendor value matches the value that replaces the productvendor ? marker.

Write filter conditions that make sense for your report. Before you complete all steps to enable filtering, you should test your filter conditions by specifying actual values in the WHERE clause to verify that the results meet your expectations.

SQL supports many options and operators for specifying filter conditions. For complete information about writing WHERE clauses and SQL statements in general, consult a book about SQL.

How to insert a parameter marker in the SQL query

This procedure assumes that you already created a data set.

1 In Data Explorer, right-click the data set whose query you want to edit, then choose Edit. Edit Data Set displays the query.

2 Add a WHERE clause with one or more parameters, as shown in the following examples:

```
WHERE quantityinstock < ?

WHERE quantityinstock <= ? AND productvendor = ?

WHERE quantityinstock <= ? OR productline LIKE ?
```

Figure 15-3 shows an example of a query with two parameter markers.

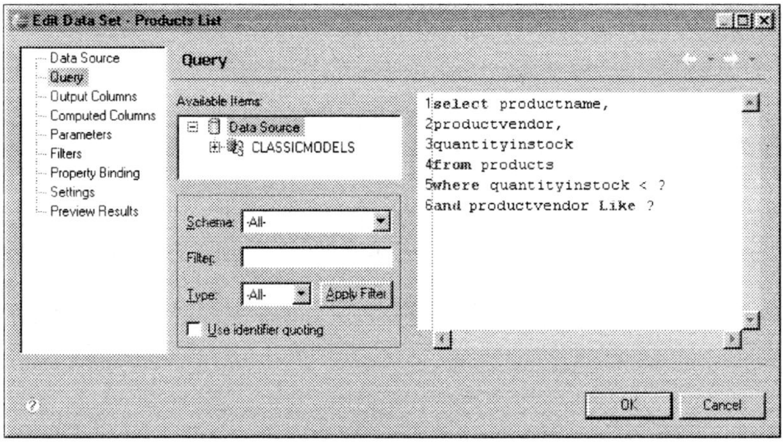

Figure 15-3   Query with two parameter markers

At this point, you are ready to create a data set parameter for each ? parameter marker. The next section describes this task.

Creating a data set parameter and binding it to the report parameter

A data set parameter passes a value that replaces the ? parameter marker in the WHERE clause of the query when the query is run. You must create one data set parameter for each parameter marker in the query's WHERE clause. If you do not, BIRT displays an error.

SQL uses the positions of the ? parameter markers in the WHERE clause to determine which data set parameter matches which ? marker. Therefore, the order of the data set parameters is critical. For example, you must create two data set parameters if you specify the following WHERE clause:

```
WHERE quantityinstock < ? and productvendor LIKE ?
```

The first parameter in the list of data set parameters must pass a value to quantityinstock < ?, and the second parameter must pass a value to productvendor LIKE ?. Figure 15-4 shows these two data set parameters. The order of these parameters matches the order of the parameter markers' appearance in the example WHERE clause. If you change the WHERE clause in the query, you must update the data set parameters accordingly.

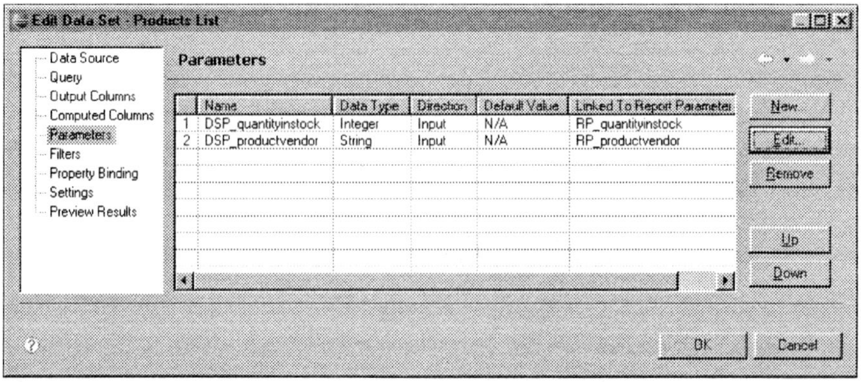

Figure 15-4   Edit Data Set with two data set parameters

A data set parameter replaces a parameter marker in the query with a value from another part of the report design. Think of the data set parameter as an intermediary—it gets a value from a report element, then it passes the value to the query. To enable users to filter data, you use a data set parameter to get a value from a report parameter. When you create the data set parameter, you bind it to the appropriate report parameter, so that the data set parameter value is set to the report parameter value at report run time.

How to create a data set parameter

This procedure assumes that you already inserted a parameter marker in the SQL query, as described previously. If you use multiple data set parameters, create them in the order in which their corresponding parameter markers appear in the WHERE clause.

1   In Data Explorer, choose the data set for which you want to create parameters. Edit Data Set displays the query for the data set.

2   Choose Parameters. Edit Data Set displays the Parameters page.

3   Choose New.

4   On New Parameter:

    1   In Name, type a name for the data set parameter. It is good practice to use a prefix, such as DSP, to differentiate the parameter from other parameter types, such as report parameters.

    2   In Data type, select a data type for the parameter.

    3   In Direction, choose Input. This value means that the parameter is an input parameter.

    4   In Linked To Report Parameter, select the report parameter to bind to this data set parameter.

Figure 15-5 shows an example of a data set parameter definition where the data set parameter, DSP_quantityinstock, is linked to a report parameter, RP_quantityinstock.

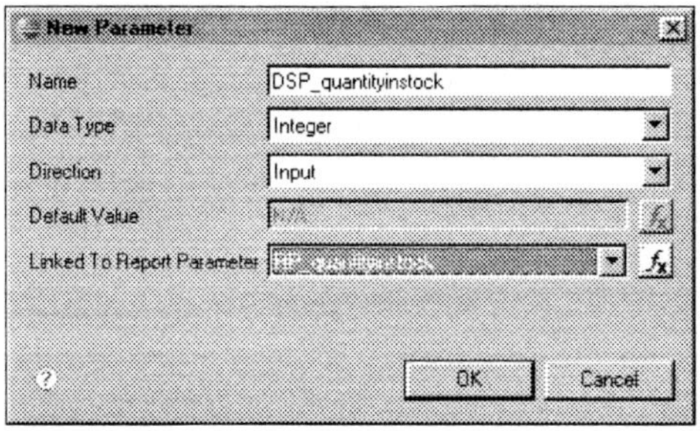

Figure 15-5   Data set parameter definition

  5   Choose OK.

5 Repeat steps 3 and 4 to create additional data set parameters for any other parameter markers that you inserted in your SQL query.

6 To save the changes to the data set, choose OK.

7 Test the parameters to verify that the query is updated with user-specified values and that the report shows the results you expect.

  1   Choose Preview.

  2   If Enter Parameters does not appear, choose Show Report Parameters.

Enter Parameters displays all the report parameters that you created. Figure 15-6 shows example report parameters, RP_quantityinstock and RP_productvendor. The parameter names are displayed because values were not supplied for the Prompt text property.

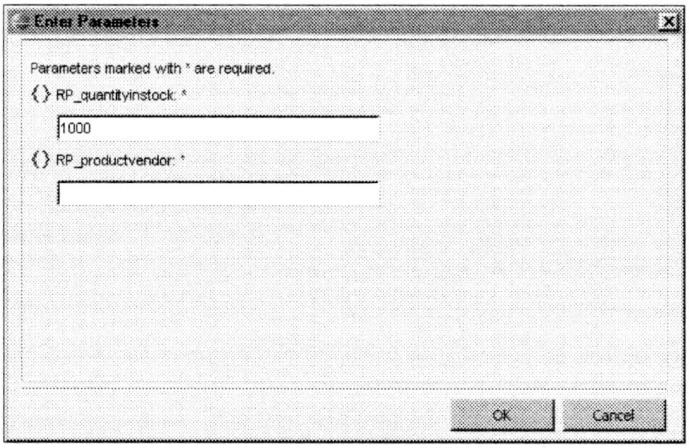

Figure 15-6   Enter Parameters

  3   Specify a value for each parameter, then choose OK.

If you completed all the tasks that were described earlier in this chapter, the WHERE clause of your query incorporates the specified values, and the report displays the rows that match the WHERE clause.

Creating a SQL query at run time

The previous sections described how to create a report parameter and a data set parameter, and how to bind both types of parameters to replace a ? marker in the WHERE clause of a SQL query with a user-specified report parameter value. This technique works well when the WHERE clause uses a filter condition that substitutes one value for each ? marker.

You cannot, however, use this technique for a WHERE clause that uses a membership filter condition, as shown in the following example:

```
WHERE city IN ('San Francisco', 'San Jose', 'Los Angeles')
```

The following WHERE clause accepts only one value to replace the ? marker:

```
WHERE city IN (?)
```

For cases such as this, where you need to update a WHERE clause with multiple report parameter values for a single ? marker, you use the data set's property binding feature to update the entire query at run time.

How to update a query at run time

1 On the Query page of a data set, define a SQL query, such as:

```
SELECT CustomerName FROM customers
```

2 Create three report parameters, for example, City1, City2, and City3.

3 In Edit Data Set, choose Property Binding, and define the following query text to use the values from the three report parameters, as shown in Figure 15-7:

```
"SELECT CustomerName from customers where customers.City IN
    ( " +  "'"+params["City1"]+"' , '" + params["City2"] +
    "' , '" + params["City3"] + "' )"
```

Figure 15-7   Property Binding showing the dynamic query

The query you specify in Property Binding replaces the query you specified on the Query page.

4 Choose OK to save the changes to the data set.

Enabling the user to filter after running the query

An alternative to enabling filtering at query run time is to enable filtering at the time the report is rendered. This option is available for all data sources, including JDBC, XML, and text file, but filtering at query run time through the use of data set parameters is usually the preferred approach for JDBC for performance reasons.

Though the goal in enabling users to filter at query run time and after the query runs is the same, the steps are different. To enable users to filter after running the query, you complete the following tasks in the recommended order. For detailed information about these tasks, see the corresponding topics later in this section.

- Create report parameters to prompt a user to specify field values that determine what data to display.

- Create one filter condition for each field for which you want the report user to supply a value. Set the value of each filter condition to a report parameter to dynamically update the filter condition with the parameter value.

- Determine how to present the report parameters.

- Test the report parameters.

Creating a report parameter

Just as you create a report parameter to enable user filtering at query run time, you create a report parameter to enable user filtering after the query is executed. As report parameter creation is covered earlier in this chapter, it is not repeated here.

Updating a filter condition when the report runs

Typically, when you specify a filter condition to display only certain data in a report, you specify the value on which to search, as in these examples:

```
row["quantityinstock"] Less than 500
row["productvendor"] Equal to "Exoto Designs"
```

To enable a user to filter data when the report runs, specify the report parameter as the filter value. The following expressions are examples of filter conditions whose values are set to report parameters:

```
row["quantityinstock"] Less than params["RP_quantityinstock"]
row["productvendor"] Equal to params["RP_productvendor"]
```

When the user runs the report and supplies a value for the report parameter, BIRT dynamically updates the filter condition with the parameter value and generates a report that displays only the specified data.

How to update a filter condition dynamically when the report runs

This procedure assumes that you already created a report design that contains a table or list to display data from a data set and uses one or more report parameters. This procedure uses the parameter to filter the values that the table displays.

1 In the layout editor, select the table element or list element to filter. The property editor displays the properties of the selected table or list.

Figure 15-8 shows an example of a selected table and its properties.

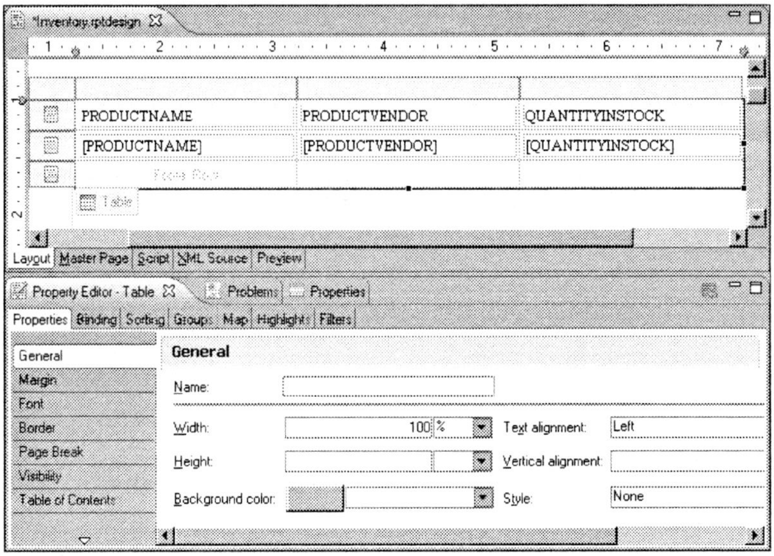

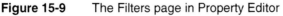

Figure 15-8   Table properties

2 Choose the Filters tab. Property Editor displays the Filters page, as shown in Figure 15-9.

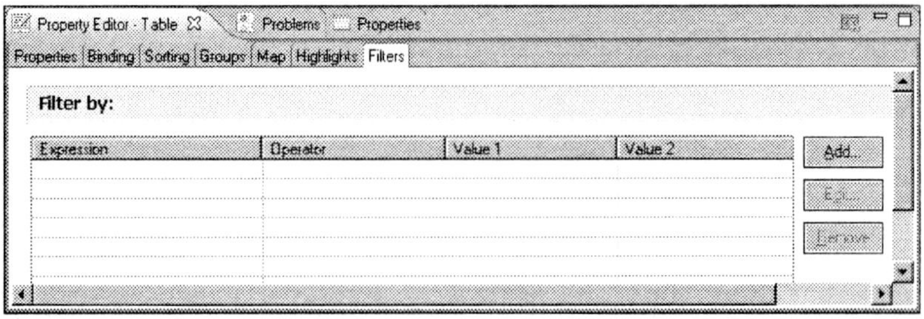

Figure 15-9   The Filters page in Property Editor

3 Choose Add to create a new filter condition.

4 On New Filter Condition, specify the filter condition.

    1 In the first field, select a field from the drop-down list. Alternatively, open the expression builder to create a more complex expression.

    2 In the second field, select an operator from the drop-down list.

    3 In the third field, specify the name of the report parameter that you created. You can use the expression builder to select the report parameter from the list of report parameters in the report design, as shown in Figure 15-10.

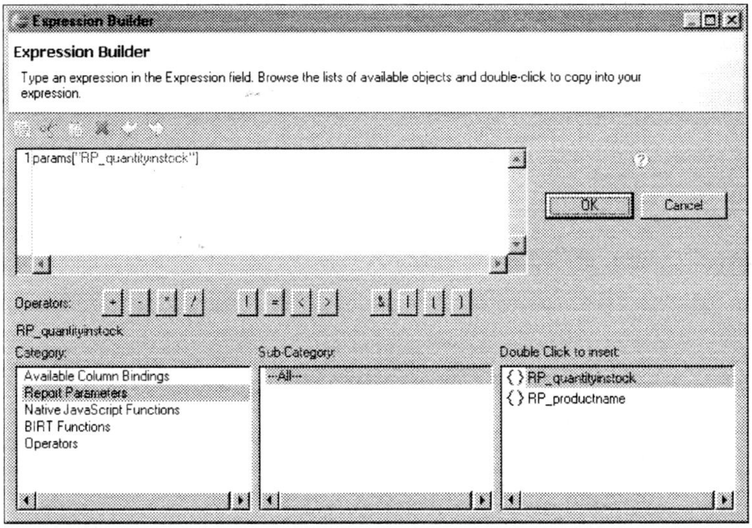

![Expression Builder dialog showing expression params["RP_quantityinstock"], operators, categories including Available Column Bindings, Report Parameters, Native JavaScript Functions, BIRT Functions, Operators, and insert list with RP_quantityinstock and RP_productname]

Figure 15-10   Using the expression builder to select a report parameter

Choose OK to apply the expression to the filter condition. New Filter Condition displays the completed filter condition, as shown in Figure 15-11.

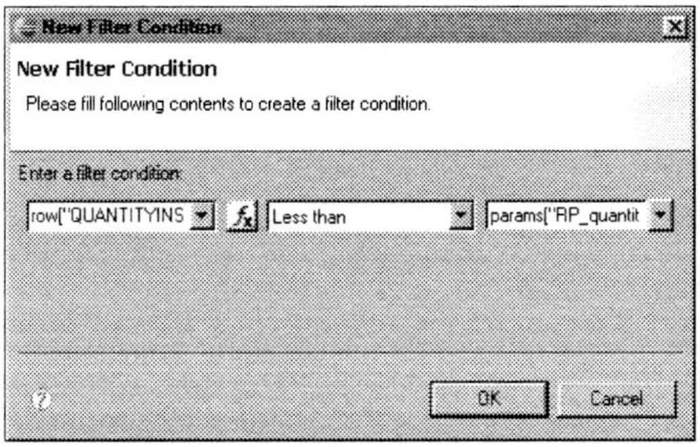

![New Filter Condition dialog with fields row["QUANTITYINS], Less than, params["RP_quantit]]

Figure 15-11   A filter condition

    4 Choose OK to save the filter condition.

The filter condition appears on the Filters page in Property Editor, as shown in Figure 15-12.

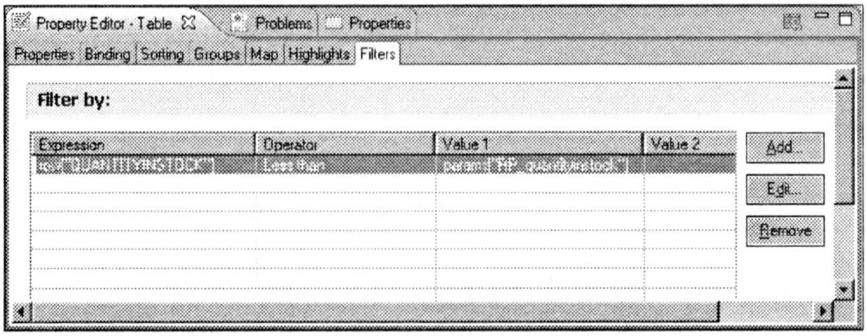

Figure 15-12   Filter condition set to a report parameter

5 Preview the report.

Enter Parameters appears and displays the report parameters that you created. Figure 15-13 shows an example.

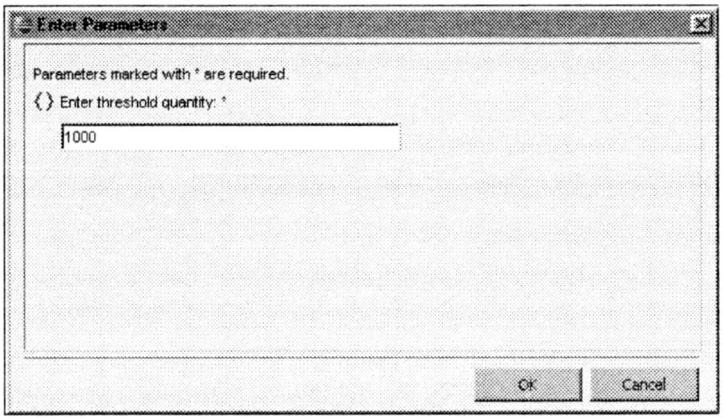

Figure 15-13   Enter Parameters showing a report parameter

6 Specify values for the report parameters, then choose OK.

The report displays data that matches the values that you specified.

Designing the presentation of report parameters

After you verify that your report parameters generate the report that you expect, remember to improve the presentation of the parameter information. If you used the default options when you created the report parameter, you can make the parameters more user-friendly by setting their display properties when you edit the report parameters. You access these properties by double-clicking a report parameter in Data Explorer. Table 15-1 lists the ways in which you can enhance the usability and appearance of report parameters. Details about each technique are presented in subsequent sections.

Table 15-1 Techniques for enhancing report parameter usability

Technique	Property to set
Use a prompt that describes clearly what values a user can enter. For example, you can display text, such as: `Enter the state's abbreviation`	Prompt text
Provide a default value that results in a well-presented report in the event that a user does not supply a value. A default value also functions as an example.	Default value
Provide helpful information about a report parameter. A user sees this information when he hovers the mouse over the parameter. For example, for a customer ID parameter, you can provide information, such as: `Type a number between 100 and 500`	Help text
Rather than requiring the user to type a value in a text box, create a list box, a combo box, or a set of radio buttons that provide values that a user can select.	Display type
If a report parameter displays a default value or a list of values in a list box, a combo box, or radio buttons, display those values in a suitable format. For example, if values for sales totals are stored in #### format in the data source, you can change the display format to $#,###.00.	Format

Providing a default value

Although BIRT does not require you to specify a default value for each report parameter, typically, you should provide one. If you do not, the user must specify a value to generate the report. It is particularly important to specify a default value if you present the report parameter as a text box in which the user has to type a value, rather than a list box from which the user can select a value.

The default value can be any value from the data set field that is bound to the report parameter. You should, however, specify a value that most users would select, such as Active for an account status. Another option is to specify a value that appears most often. If the field contains unique values, such as an order ID or a customer ID, it is typical to specify the first ID as the default value, particularly when using a list box or combo box to display a list of values.

How to provide a default value for a report parameter

This procedure assumes that you already created at least one report parameter in your report design.

1 In Data Explorer, expand Report Parameters, then choose the report parameter to edit.

   Edit Parameter displays the current property settings for the selected report parameter. Figure 15-14 shows an example of a report parameter with no value specified for Default value.

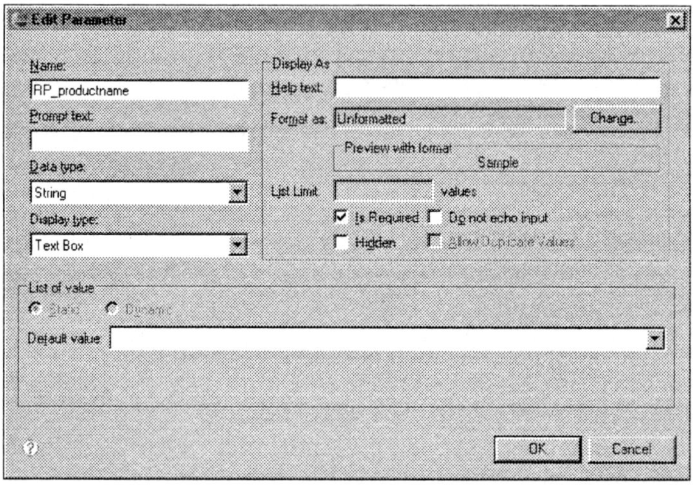

Figure 15-14 Property settings for a report parameter

2 Depending on the display type that you select, complete one of these tasks:

   ▧ If the display type is text box, for Default value, type a value. Use a value that exists in the data set field that is bound to this report parameter.

   ▧ For all other display types, specify a list of values to display, then select one value as the default value.

3 Choose OK.

Providing the user with a list of values

List boxes, combo boxes, and radio buttons are ideal mechanisms for providing a list of choices to a user. A user can make only one selection from multiple choices. The differences between these user interface elements are as follows:

■ Radio buttons occupy as many lines in the Enter Parameters dialog as there are choices, and you must specify one button as a default value. For ease of use, a set of radio buttons should contain fewer than 10 entries.

■ The list box and combo box appear similar to the user. Both save space in the Enter Parameters dialog. The list box takes up only one line, and the combo box takes up two lines in Enter Parameters. For ease of use, a list box or combo box should contain fewer than 100 values.

- In addition to presenting a list of choices, the combo box also supports the user typing a value. This feature is useful if the user wants to supply a string pattern. For example, instead of selecting a specific name for a customer name parameter, the user can type M% to get all customers whose names start with M. This technique assumes that the user is familiar with SQL pattern-matching syntax.

- The combo box requires you to specify a default value when you create it. A list box does not.

Figure 15-15 shows an example of an Enter Parameters dialog that displays a list box, combo box, and radio buttons.

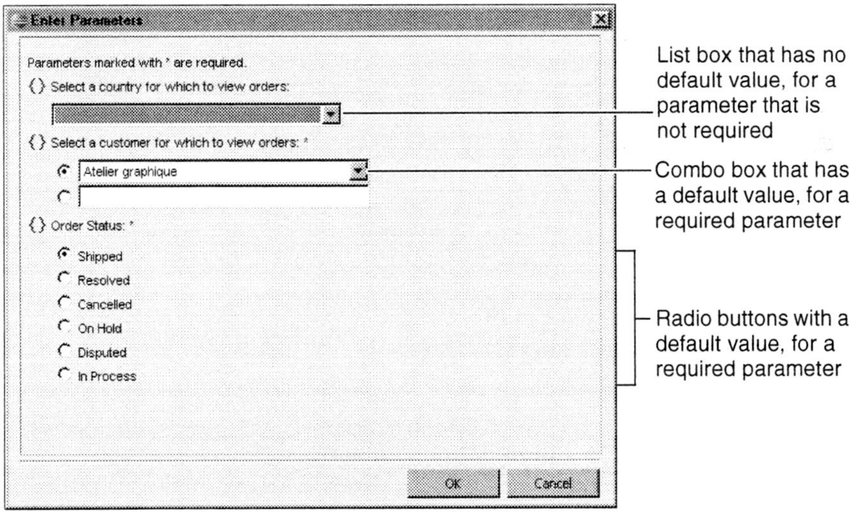

List box that has no default value, for a parameter that is not required

Combo box that has a default value, for a required parameter

Radio buttons with a default value, for a required parameter

Figure 15-15   Three types of selection elements in Enter Parameters

You create a list of values for a list box or a combo box using one of the following techniques:

- Create a static list of values.

- Create a dynamic list of values.

For radio buttons, you can only create a static list of values. In a static list, you specify the values to display to the report user during report design. In a dynamic list, BIRT retrieves the values from the data source when the report runs.

Create a dynamic list for values that are frequently updated in the data source. New customer names or product names, for example, are often added to a data source. If you create a static list of these values, you have to update the list manually to match the values in the data source.

Creating a static list, however, provides more control over the list of values to display to the report user. For example, you might want to present only certain values to the user, or localize the values.

Creating a static list of values

You can create a static list of values for a list box, combo box, or a set of radio buttons using one or both of the following techniques:

- Import values from a data set field.
- Type each value to display.

To display all the unique values in a data set field, which is the typical case, import the values from the data set field. You can type the values, but this task would be tedious. Type a value only to display a value that is not in the data set field, such as ranges of values (0–100, 101–200, and so on).

To import all values from a data set field, you first create a data set that retrieves the values. The query in the following example retrieves all the values from the country field. You would specify this simple query to populate a parameter list with all the country names.

```
SELECT DISTINCT country
FROM Customers
```

Sometimes, the values in a data set field are not in a suitable form or descriptive enough for report users. For example, the values in a territory field might use abbreviations, such as NA, EMEA, or APAC. For such cases, it is preferable to display the full names to the user. You do so by providing alternate values in the Display Text property.

If you are creating a report that will be viewed in multiple locales, you can localize each value by providing a resource key in the Display Text Key property. A resource key is a text string in an external source that is translated, or localized, into different languages. Resource keys and localization are discussed in Chapter 24, "Localizing Text."

How to specify static report parameter values for users to select

This procedure assumes that you already created at least one report parameter in your report design.

1 In Data Explorer, expand Report Parameters, then choose the report parameter to edit.

   Edit Parameter displays the property settings for the report parameter.

2 For Display type, choose Combo Box, List Box, or Radio Button.

   Edit Parameter displays the Selection values table and the Import Values button, as shown in Figure 15-16. The Selection values table is where you specify the values to display in the list box, combo box, or radio buttons.

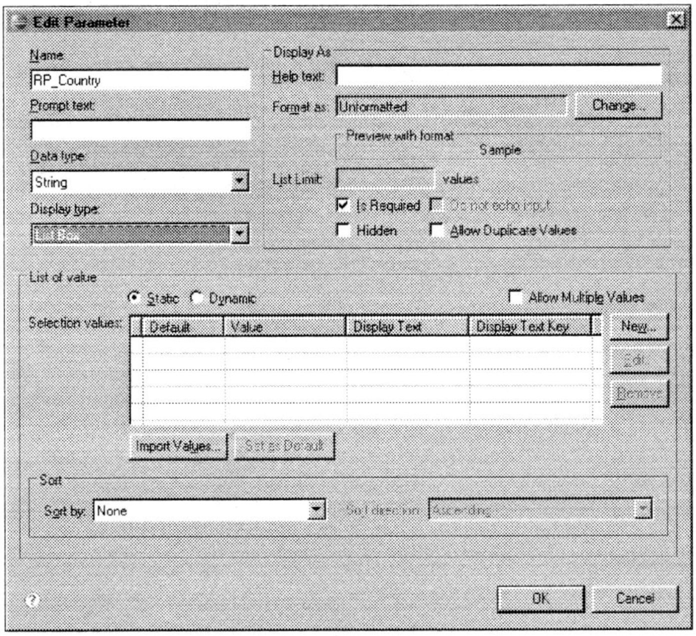

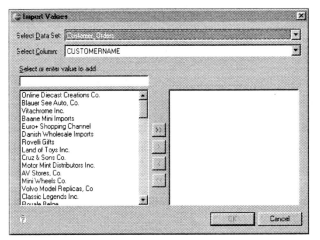

Figure 15-16   Selection values table and Import Values button in Edit
Parameter

3   In List of value, use the default value, Static.

4   To import values from a data set field, perform the following tasks:

1   Choose Import Values. Import Values displays the first data set in the
report and the values of the first field in the data set, as shown in
Figure 15-17.

Figure 15-17   Import Values

2   In Select Data Set, choose the data set that has the field values you want to display in the list box, combo box, or radio buttons. Typically, this data set is one that you create specifically for populating the parameter's list of values.

3   In Select Column, choose the field that contains the values to use. Import Values displays the values for the selected field.

4   Select the values to import.

❑   To import all values, choose the double right arrow (>>) button.

❑   To import a particular value, select the value, and choose the right arrow (>) button.

Choose OK. Edit Parameter displays the imported values in the Selection values table, as shown in Figure 15-18.

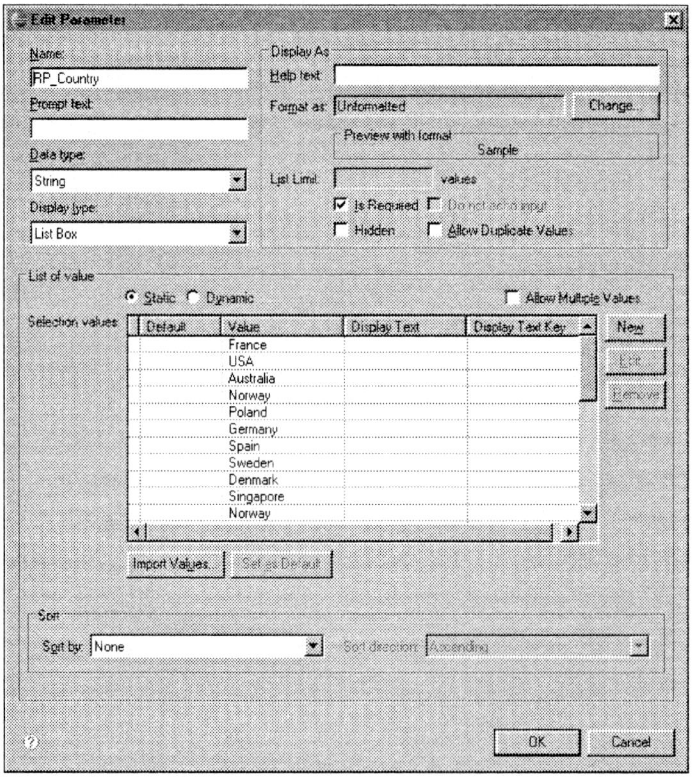

Figure 15-18   Imported values in Edit Parameter

5   To add values manually, complete the following steps for each value:

1   Next to the Selection values table, choose New.

2 In New Selection Choice:

  1 In Display Text, type the text prompt to display to the user.

  2 In Value, type the value to pass to the SQL query or the filter condition. Figure 15-19 shows an example of a user-defined value that appears as All Customers on the Enter Parameter dialog when the user runs the report. When the user selects this value, % is passed to the SQL query.

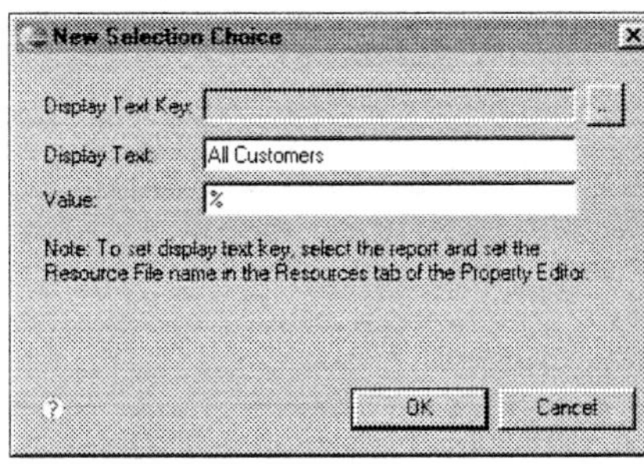

Figure 15-19   Creating a new value

3 Choose OK. The new value is added to the Selection values table.

6 To provide descriptive labels for users to choose, other than the value in Value, perform the following steps:

  1 Double-click the item in the Selection values table.

  2 On Edit Selection Choice, in Display Text, type the text that you want to display to the user. Figure 15-20 shows an example of displaying United Kingdom instead of UK.

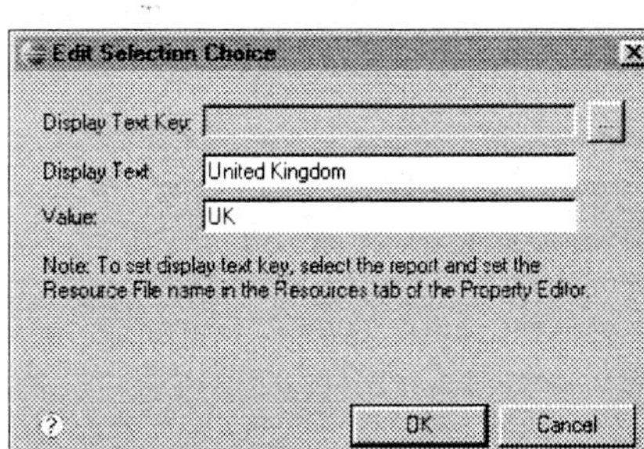

Figure 15-20   Specifying the text to display

3 Choose OK to save the change. The item is updated in the Selection values table.

7 To designate a value as the default value, select the value, then choose Set as Default. A default value is required for a combo box or a set of radio buttons. For these items, the OK button is not available until you select a default value.

8 To specify how the values should be sorted when presented to the user:

   1 Under Sort, in Sort by, select one of the following values:

   ❑ Select None, the default, to display the values in natural order, which is the order of items in the Value column of the Selection values table.

   ❑ Select Display Text to display in ascending or descending order the values in the Display Text column.

   ❑ Select Value Column to display in ascending or descending order the values in the Value column.

   2 In Sort direction, select either Ascending or Descending.

9 Choose OK to save your changes to the report parameter.

Creating a dynamic list of values

You can create a dynamic list of values for a list box or a combo box. In the same way as you create a static list, you first create a data set that retrieves the values with which to populate the list. The query in the following example retrieves all the unique values from the customername field in the Customers table. You specify this simple query in a data set to populate a parameter list with all the customer names.

```
SELECT DISTINCT customername
FROM Customers
```

For a report design using dynamic lists, values are retrieved from the data source when the report runs. You cannot tell during the design process how many values the list box or combo box displays when the user runs the report. If you are concerned about the list getting too long, you can specify a maximum number of values to display. This solution, however, is not practical because the list would display the first value up to the specified maximum number, and omit the rest of the values.

Just as you can with a static list of values, you can display alternate values if you do not want to display the actual field values. You cannot, however, specify an alternate display value for each individual value because you do not know at design time the precise list of values. Instead, you specify an expression that applies to all the values. For example, you can prepend values with static text by using an expression, such as:

```
"Order " + dataSetRow["Ordernumber"]
```

How to specify dynamic report parameter values for users to select

This procedure assumes that you are editing a report parameter that you have already created.

1 In Data Explorer, expand Report Parameters, then choose the report parameter to edit. Edit Parameter displays the property settings for the report parameter.

2 In Display type, choose Combo Box or List Box.

3 In List of value, choose Dynamic. Edit Parameter displays additional fields, as shown in Figure 15-21.

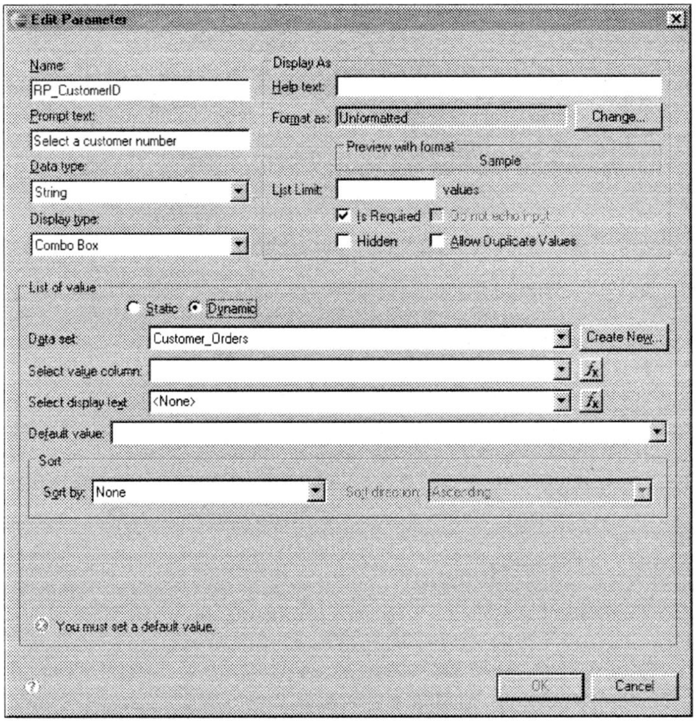

Figure 15-21　Dynamic parameter options in Edit Parameter

4 In Data set, select the data set from which you want to display the field values in the list box or combo box.

5 In Select value column, select the field that contains the values that you want to pass to the SQL query or filter condition at run time.

6 In Select display text, optionally select a field that contains the values that you want to display to the user. For example, the values to pass to the SQL query or filter condition are from the customernumber field, but you want to display values from the customername field to the user. You can also use the expression builder to specify an expression to display custom values. The following example shows how you can use an expression to combine values from two fields:

```
dataSetRow["ORDERNUMBER"] + "--" +
    dataSetRow["CUSTOMERNAME"]
```

From this expression, BIRT provides meaningful values to the user, such as:

```
10100--Online Diecast Creations, Co.
10101--Blauer See Auto, Co.
```

7 In Default value, select a value to use as the default value. A default value is required for a combo box.

8 Optionally, in List Limit, specify the maximum number of values to display.

9 Choose OK to save your changes to the report parameter.

Formatting report parameter values

By default, the default values you specify and the values that you import to display in a list box, combo box, or radio buttons appear exactly as they are stored in the data source. Sometimes, the values are not in a format that is appropriate for display. For example, US telephone numbers might be stored in ########## format. It is preferable to display these values in another format, such as (###) ###-####. International telephone numbers, however, do not display correctly using this format.

You can specify a different format using the Format property. You format a report parameter value in the same way that you format a value that a data element displays. You select from a list of common formats, or you specify a custom format pattern.

Note that you can reformat values for display purposes only. You cannot use the Format property to require a user to type values in a particular format. In addition, the property setting does not affect the format of the data in the report.

How to format a report parameter value

This procedure assumes that you already created at least one report parameter in your report design.

1 In Data Explorer, expand Report Parameters, then choose the report parameter to edit. Edit Parameter displays the current property settings for the selected report parameter.

2 In Format as, choose Change. Change is not available for report parameters of Boolean type. Format Builder appears. Its contents differ, depending on the data type of the report parameter. Figure 15-22 shows Format Builder for string data.

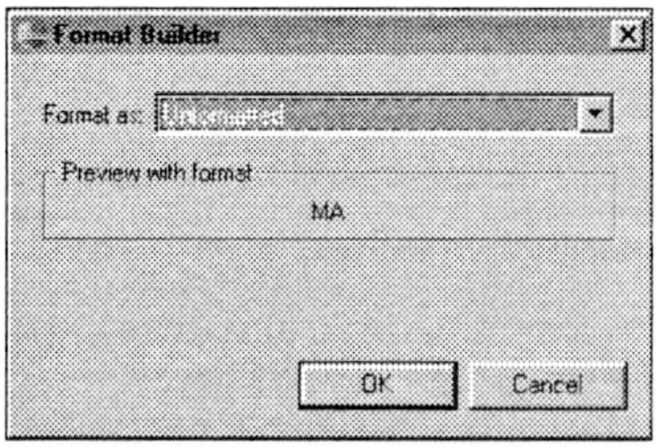

Figure 15-22   Format Builder for string data

3 Specify the format to use. The format choices that are available vary according to the data type of the parameter.

   1 For Format <data type> as, choose one of the predefined formats, or choose Custom to define your own format pattern.

   Additional fields may appear, depending on the data type and format that you selected. A sample formatted value appears in Preview with format. Figure 15-23 shows the additional fields that are available for a report parameter of decimal type when Currency format is selected.

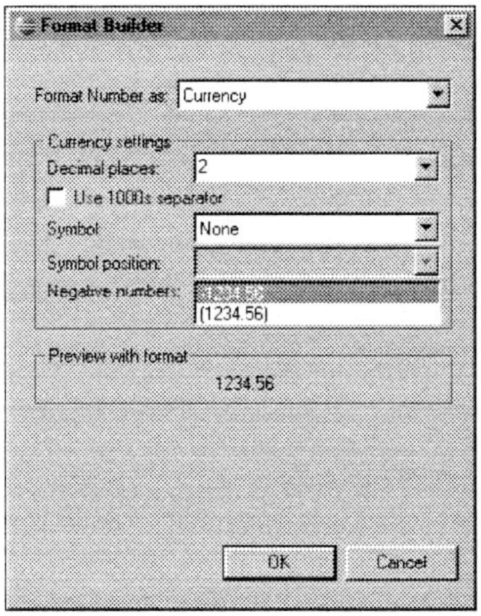

Figure 15-23   Format Builder for currency data

   2 Type or select values for any additional fields that are available for that parameter data type and format.

   3 When you finish specifying the format, choose OK. Edit Parameter appears. Format shows the format that you specified.

Organizing report parameters in groups

If you create many parameters or want to provide the user with a prompt for certain sets of parameters, consider using parameter groups. Typically, you create parameter groups to organize report parameters logically. For example, you could create a parameter group to contain the report parameters for a specific table or data set.

When prompting the user to supply parameter values, the Enter Parameters dialog displays the parameter group name and the parameters within that group. Figure 15-24 shows two parameter groups, Office Information and Product Information. Each group contains multiple report parameters.

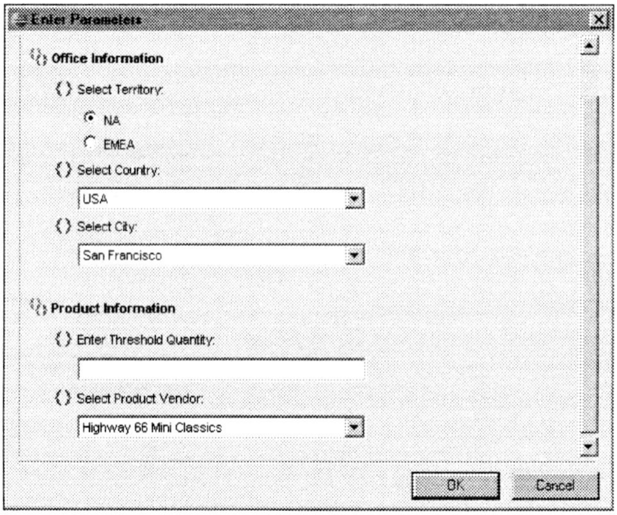

Figure 15-24 Parameter groups with multiple parameters in each group

You can create a parameter group before or after you create the report parameters. If you create the report parameters first, you can drag them from the report parameters list to the parameter group. If you create the parameter group first, you create the report parameters in the parameter group.

How to create a parameter group

1 In Data Explorer, right-click Report Parameters, and choose New Parameter Group. New Parameter Group appears.

2 In Name, specify a unique name for this parameter group.

3 In Display Name, specify the name that the Enter Parameters dialog displays when it prompts a user for parameter values.

Figure 15-25 shows an example.

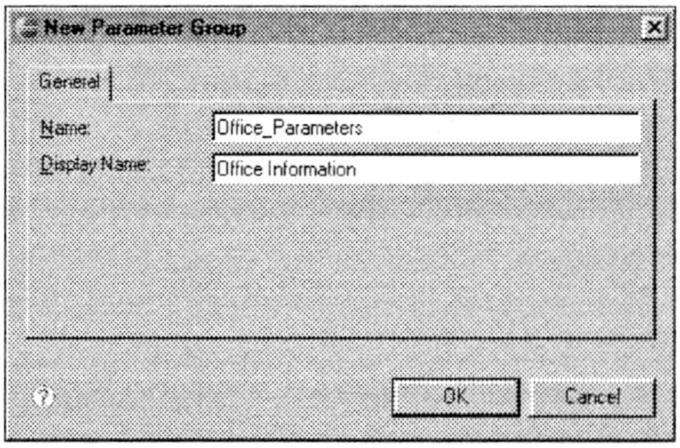

Figure 15-25 Create a display name for a parameter group

4 Choose OK. BIRT Report Designer creates the new parameter group and displays it in Report Parameters in Data Explorer, as shown in Figure 15-26.

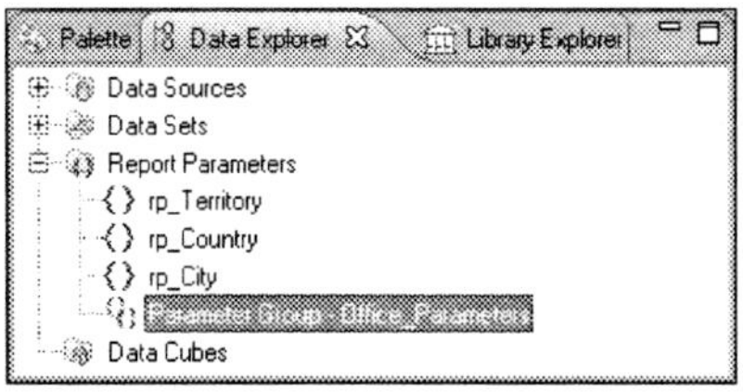

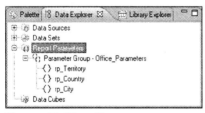

Figure 15-26   New parameter group in Data Explorer

5 Add report parameters to the parameter group. You can add parameters to a parameter group in two ways:

- Move an existing parameter to the parameter group. From the report parameters list in Data Explorer, drag an existing parameter, and drop it in the parameter group.

- Create a new parameter in the parameter group. In Report Parameters, right-click the parameter group name, and choose New Parameter.

Figure 15-27 shows Data Explorer after you move three report parameters to a parameter group called Office_Parameters.

Figure 15-27   Parameter group containing three parameters

Figure 15-28 shows the Enter Parameters dialog, which displays the new parameter group and its three report parameters.

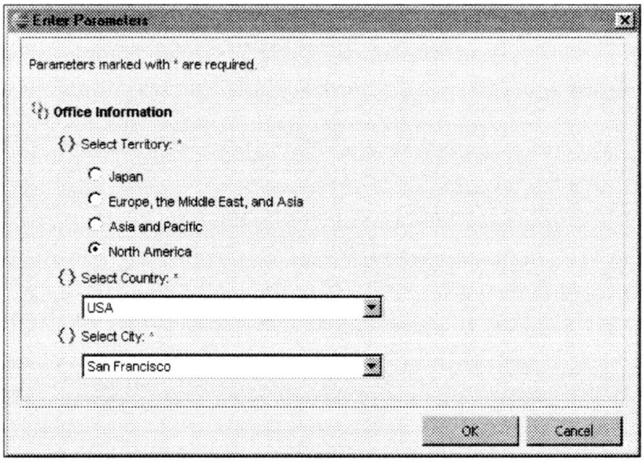

Figure 15-28   Office Information parameter group on Enter Parameters

Enter Parameters displays parameter groups and report parameters in the order in which they appear in the report parameters list. To display the groups or report parameters in a different order, change the order in Data Explorer.

Creating cascading report parameters

Cascading parameters are report parameters that have a hierarchical relationship, as shown in the following three examples:

Product Type	Territory	Mutual Fund Type
Product	Country	Fund Class
	City	Fund

In a group of cascading parameters, each report parameter displays a set of values. When the report user selects a value from the top-level parameter, the selected value determines the values that the next parameter displays, and so on.

The advantages of cascading parameters are obvious when you compare the alternative technique, which is the creation of separate and independent parameters. Consider the Territory-Country-City example. If you create three separate parameters, the territory parameter displays a list of all territories, the country parameter displays all countries, and the city parameter displays all cities. Figure 15-29 shows independent parameters as they appear to the report user.

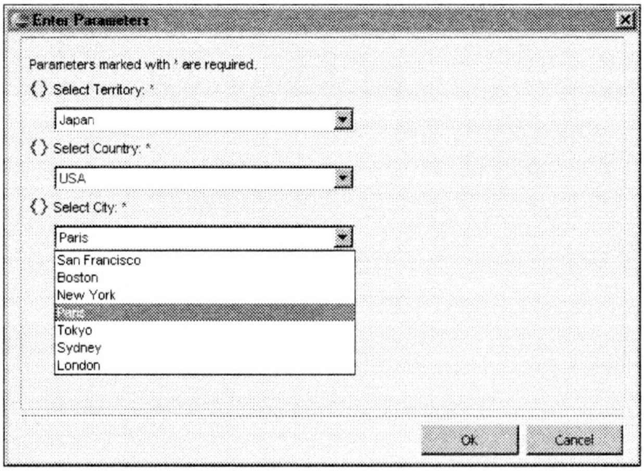

Figure 15-29 Independent parameters

The user has to traverse three long lists to select the values, and there is a potential for user errors. The user can inadvertently select invalid combinations, such as Japan, USA, Paris.

Cascading parameters, on the other hand, display only relevant values based on user selections. For example, the territory parameter displays all the territories, and when the report runs, the user selects a territory, such as NA (North America), then the country parameter displays only countries in the sales territory of North America. Similarly, when the user selects USA, the city parameter displays only cities in the USA. Figure 15-30 shows cascading parameters as they appear to the report user.

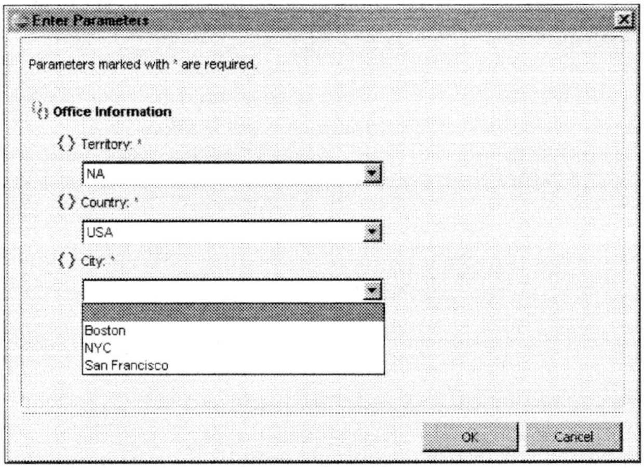

Figure 15-30   Cascading parameters

Before you create cascading report parameters, you must first create the data set or data sets that return the values to display in the cascading parameter lists. The query in the following example retrieves all the values from the territory, country, and city fields of the Offices table. You specify this query in a data set used to populate the Territory-Country-City parameter lists.

```
SELECT Offices.territory,
Offices.country,
Offices.city
FROM Offices
```

In this example, the Territory-Country-City cascading parameter uses a single data set to populate all the parameter lists because the fields are in the same table.

If, however, the fields are in different tables or different data sources, you can create multiple data sets, where each data set provides the values for each report parameter in the cascading parameter group. When you create multiple data sets for cascading parameters, you must link the data sets through a common field to create the appropriate dependency relationships.

For example, the data set for the top-level report parameter contains the following query to retrieve all the values from the productline field in the Productlines table:

```
SELECT Productlines.productline
FROM Productlines
```

The data set for the second report parameter contains the following query to retrieve the values from the productname field in the Products table. The product name values to get depend on the product line value that the user selects at run time. The WHERE clause gets the value of the product line value at run time.

```
SELECT Products.productname
FROM Products
WHERE Products.productline = ?
```

In this second data set, you must also create a data set parameter and bind it to the product line report parameter.

How to create cascading parameters that use a single data set

1 In Data Explorer, right-click Report Parameters, and choose New Cascading Parameter.

2 On New Cascading Parameter, in Cascading Parameter Name, you can specify a different name. The name that you specify appears only in the list of report parameters in Data Explorer.

3 For Prompt text, specify the name for the parameter group that appears in the Enter Parameters dialog.

4 Select Single Data Set.

5 Create the report parameters for this group of cascading parameters.

   1 In Parameters, choose Add. On Add Cascading Parameter, specify the following values:

      1 In Name, type the parameter name.

      2 In Data Set, select the data set that returns the values for populating all the parameter lists.

      3 In Value, select the field that contains the values that you want to pass to the SQL query or filter condition at run time.

      4 In Display Text, optionally select a field that contains the values that you want to display to the user. For example, the values to pass to the SQL query or filter condition are from the productcode field, but you want to display values from the productname field to the user.

      5 Choose OK.

   2 In Properties, set the other properties for this report parameter, including the prompt text, display type, and default value.

   3 To create the next report parameter, choose Add, and follow the same steps until you set up all levels of the cascading parameter group. Figure 15-31 shows sample values in New Cascading Parameter.

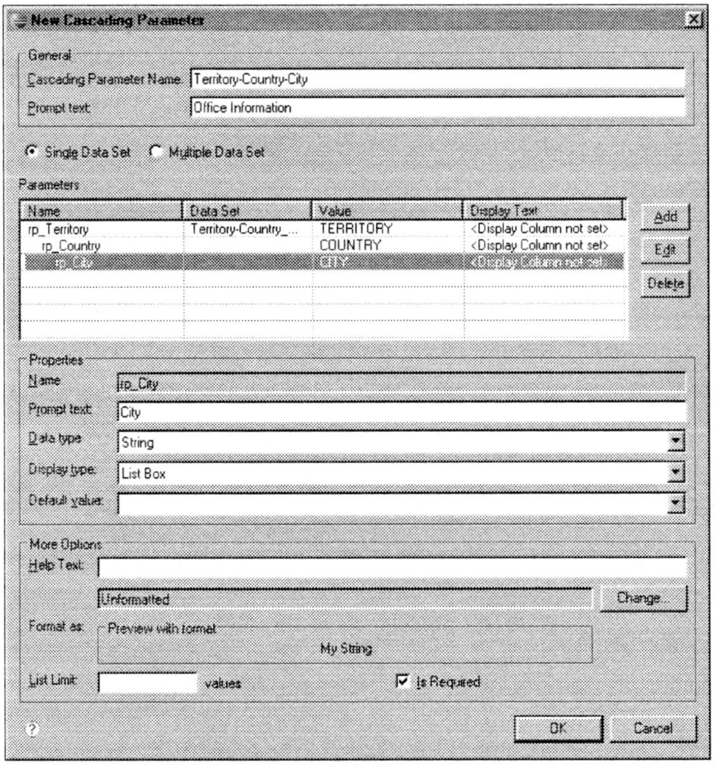

Figure 15-31 A cascading parameter that uses a single data set

6 When you finish creating all the report parameters in the group, choose OK. The cascading parameters appear in Report Parameters in Data Explorer.

How to create cascading parameters that use multiple data sets

This procedure assumes that you created all the data sets that return the values to display in the cascading parameter lists.

1 In Data Explorer, right-click Report Parameters, and choose New Cascading Parameter.

2 On New Cascading Parameter, in Cascading Parameter Name, you can specify a different name. The name that you specify appears only in the list of report parameters in Data Explorer.

3 For Prompt text, specify the name for the parameter group that appears in the Enter Parameters dialog.

4 Select Multiple Data Set.

5 Create the report parameters for this group of cascading parameters.

1 In Parameters, choose Add. On Add Cascading Parameter, specify the following values:

   1 In Name, type the parameter name.

   2 In Data Set, select the data set that returns the values for populating the top-level parameter.

   3 In Value, select the field that contains the values that you want to pass to the SQL query or filter condition at run time.

   4 In Display Text, optionally select a field that contains the values that you want to display to the user. For example, the values to pass to the SQL query or filter condition are from the productcode field, but you want to display values from the productname field to the user.

   5 Choose OK.

2 In Properties, set the other properties for this report parameter.

3 To create the next report parameter, choose Add, and follow the same steps until you set up all the levels in the cascading parameter group. Figure 15-32 shows sample values in New Cascading Parameter.

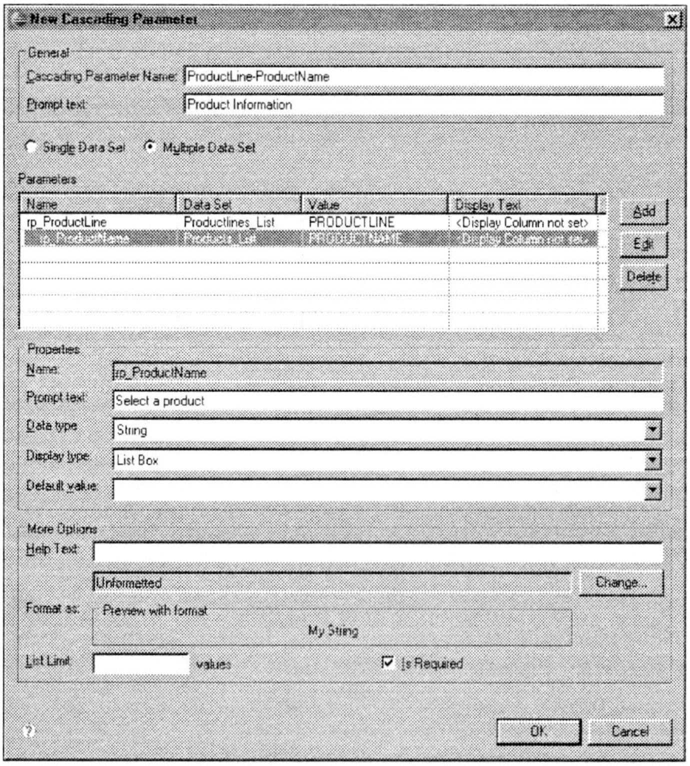

Figure 15-32   Example of a cascading parameter that uses multiple data sets

6 When you finish creating all the report parameters in the group, choose OK. The cascading parameters appear under Report Parameters in Data Explorer.

7 Add data set parameters to the dependent data sets and bind them to the appropriate report parameters from the cascading parameter group.

　1 In Data Explorer, right-click the data set that supplies the values for the second parameter in the cascading parameter group, then choose Edit. Edit Data Set displays the query.

　2 Add a WHERE clause to the SQL query to filter the values of the data set based on the value of the top-level parameter. Figure 15-33 shows an example.

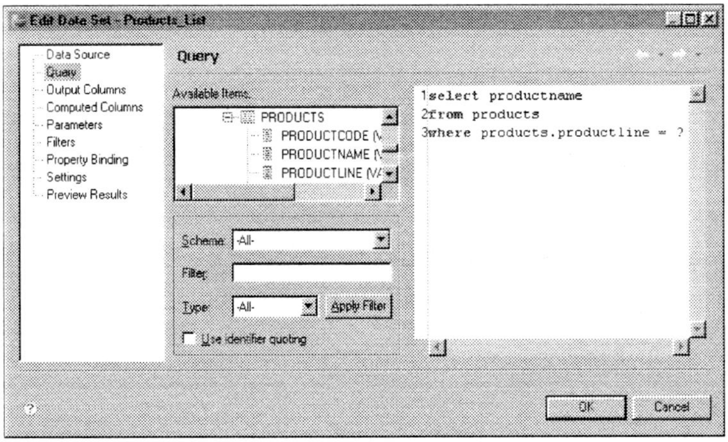

Figure 15-33　Query using WHERE clause to get a value at run time

3 Create a data set parameter to supply a value for the parameter marker in the SQL query.

　1 Choose Parameters.

　2 Select the placeholder data set parameter, then choose Edit.

　3 On Edit Parameter, specify a name for the data set parameter, and link it to the top-level report parameter, as shown in the example in Figure 15-34.

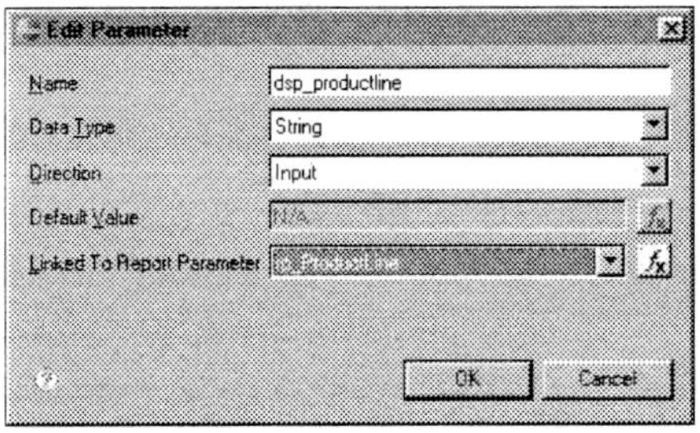

Figure 15-34　Linking a data set parameter to a report parameter

4　Choose OK to save your edits to the data set parameter.

4　On Edit Data Set, choose OK to save your changes to the data set.

5　Follow the same steps for subsequent data sets in the cascading parameter group until you establish dependencies for all levels in the group.

Figure 15-35 shows an example of cascading parameters based on the product line and product data sets.

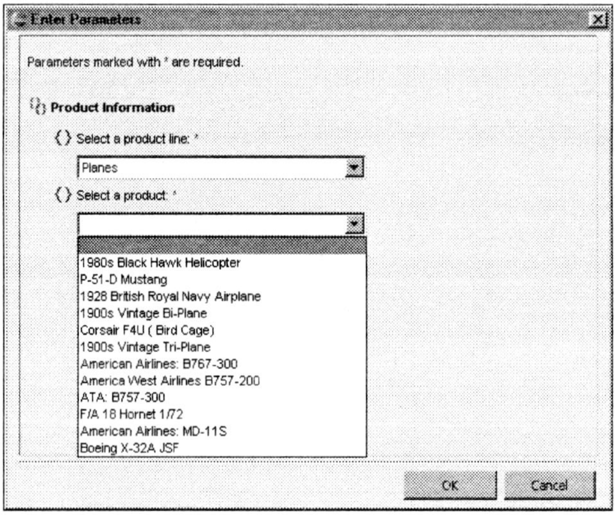

Figure 15-35　　Product line and product cascading parameters

Changing the order in which report parameters appear

By default, report parameter groups and report parameters are displayed to the user in the order in which they appear under Report Parameters in Data Explorer. The groups and parameters in the report parameters list, in turn, appear in the order in which you created them. You can change the order of groups and report parameters.

How to change the order in which report parameters appear

1　Choose Data Explorer.

2　Expand the report parameters list to display the list of parameter groups and report parameters.

3　Select a report parameter group or a report parameter, and drag it to a new position in the list. Figure 15-36 shows an example of moving the rp_State report parameter to the top of the list.

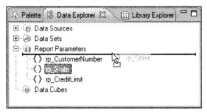

Figure 15-36   Moving a report parameter

4 Repeat step 3 until all the report parameter groups and report parameters appear in the desired order.

Testing the report parameters

It is important to test all the report parameters that you create to verify that they work the way that you intend and that they meet user needs. Testing entails running the report, supplying different report parameter values, and checking the generated report carefully. You can test parameters using the following guidelines:

- Test each report parameter as you create it.

  If you create many report parameters, it is best to test each parameter as you create it. If you wait until you create all the report parameters before you begin testing, it is much harder to debug errors in the output because it is not immediately clear which parameter causes the problem.

- Run the report without specifying any parameter values.

  The result of running a report without specifying any parameter values should be a report with information in it. If the OK button on the Enter Parameters dialog is unavailable, at least one report parameter that is currently empty requires the user to specify a value. Ensure that you provide a default value for each required parameter. A report parameter requires a value unless you deselect the Is Required option.

- Test each value in a list box, combo box, or series of radio buttons.

  If you manually created the values that these items display, rather than importing values from the data set field, test each value to confirm that the output is correct. If the report appears with no data, it means that no records matched your selection, which indicates one of three possibilities:

  - There are no rows that contain the value that you selected.

  - The value that you created is not valid. For example, you might have created the value Closed for an order-status field, but the value in the data source is actually Shipped.

  - Another parameter causes the problem.

To debug the first two possibilities, review the data in the data source. Debugging the third possibility requires more effort if the report contains many other report parameters. As suggested earlier, you can avoid this situation if you always test parameters, one at a time, as you create them.

How to test report parameters

1 In the layout editor, choose Preview. Enter Parameters displays the report parameters that you created.

2 Specify a value for the report parameters. Choose OK. The report appears.

3 Review the report data carefully.

4 Test each report parameter with a different value by first choosing Show Report Parameters, then providing another value.

5 Repeat step 4 until you are certain that the report displays the correct data.

Tutorial 3: Creating and using report parameters

This tutorial provides instructions for building a report that lists products, their vendors, and quantities in stock. Rather than display all the products in stock, the report shows only products that need to be re-stocked. Because the number at which inventory is considered low can change with time, the report uses a report parameter that prompts the user to specify the minimum stock threshold when the user runs the report. The report also uses a report parameter that lets the user select a particular vendor or all vendors for the products that need re-stocking.

In this tutorial, you perform the following tasks:

- Create a new report.
- Build a data source.
- Build a data set.
- Lay out the data.
- Create a report parameter that prompts for a minimum product quantity.
- Create a report parameter that prompts for a vendor name.
- Edit the query.
- Create data set parameters and bind them to the report parameters.
- Test the report parameters.
- Provide the option to select all vendors.
- Create a title that uses the report parameter values.

Task 1: Create a new report

1 In Navigator, right-click the My Reports project you created in the first tutorial, then choose New→Report.

2 On New Report, type the following text as the file name:

```
Inventory.rptdesign
```

3 Choose Finish. The layout editor displays a blank report.

Task 2: Build a data source

Before you begin designing your report in the layout editor, create a data source to connect your report to the Classic Models sample database.

1 Choose Data Explorer.

2 Right-click Data Sources, and choose New Data Source from the context menu.

3 Select Classic Models Inc. Sample Database from the list of data sources. Use the default data source name, then choose Next. Connection information about the new data source appears.

4 Choose Finish. BIRT creates a new data source that connects to the sample database. It appears within Data Sources in Data Explorer.

Task 3: Build a data set

In this procedure, you build a data set to retrieve data from the Products table in the Classic Models database.

1 In Data Explorer, right-click Data Sets, and choose New Data Set.

2 On New Data Set, type the following text for Data Set Name:

```
Products
```

3 Use the default values for the other fields, then choose Next.

4 On Query, type the following query. Alternatively, drag the fields from the Products table, and drop them in the text area.

```
select productname,
productvendor,
quantityinstock
from Products
```

5 Choose Finish to save the data set. Edit Data Set displays the columns you specified in the query, and provides options for editing the data set.

6 Choose Preview Results to confirm that the query is valid and that it returns the correct data. You should see the results that appear in Figure 15-37.

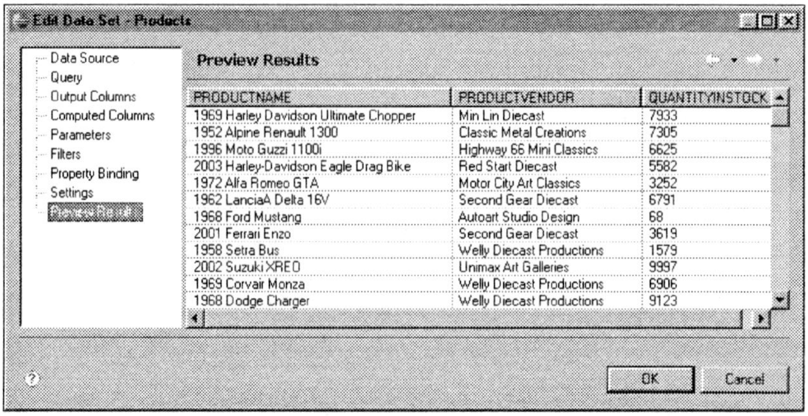

Figure 15-37 Data rows returned by the Products data set

7 Choose OK to save the data set.

Task 4: Lay out the data

In this procedure, you create a layout that displays the data in a simple row-and-column format.

1 Drag the Products data set from Data Explorer, and drop it in the layout editor. BIRT Report Designer creates a table that contains all the data set fields and corresponding labels, as shown in Figure 15-38.

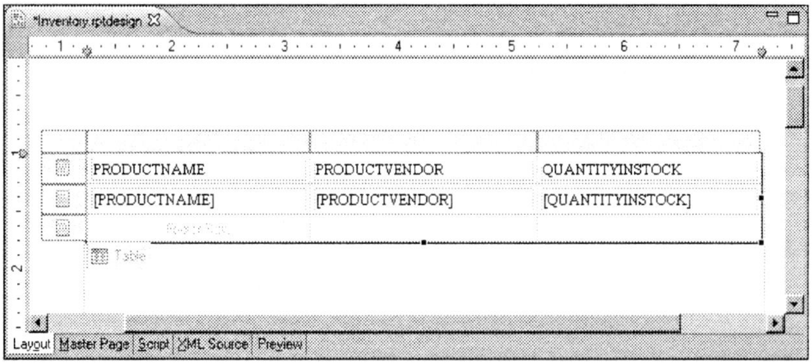

Figure 15-38 Layout editor displaying product data in a table

2 Edit and format the labels in the table's header row (the first row).

1 Double-click PRODUCTNAME. Change the text to:

    Product Name

2 Press Enter to accept the change.

B

3 In Property Editor, in General properties, choose B to format the label text as bold text.

4 Similarly, edit the PRODUCTVENDOR and QUANTITYINSTOCK labels so that they appear as follows:

```
Vendor
Quantity In Stock
```

3 Preview the report. It should look like the one in Figure 15-39.

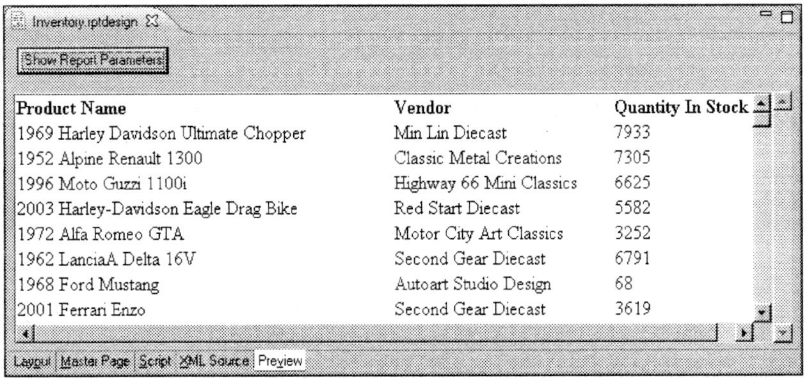

Product Name	Vendor	Quantity In Stock
1969 Harley Davidson Ultimate Chopper	Min Lin Diecast	7933
1952 Alpine Renault 1300	Classic Metal Creations	7305
1996 Moto Guzzi 1100i	Highway 66 Mini Classics	6625
2003 Harley-Davidson Eagle Drag Bike	Red Start Diecast	5582
1972 Alfa Romeo GTA	Motor City Art Classics	3252
1962 LanciaA Delta 16V	Second Gear Diecast	6791
1968 Ford Mustang	Autoart Studio Design	68
2001 Ferrari Enzo	Second Gear Diecast	3619

Figure 15-39 Report preview

Task 5: Create a report parameter that prompts for a minimum product quantity

In this procedure, you create a report parameter that prompts the user to specify a minimum quantity of stock. The report will display only rows where the quantity in stock is less than or equal to the user-specified value.

1 Choose Layout to resume editing the report.

2 In Data Explorer, right-click Report Parameters, then choose New Parameter.

3 Specify the following property values for the report parameter:

1 In Name, type the following text:

```
RP_quantityinstock
```

2 In Prompt text, type the following text:

```
Display products whose quantity in stock is less than or
   equal to this number
```

3 In Data type, select Integer.

4 In Display type, use the default, Text box.

5 In Default value, type the following amount:

```
1000
```

Figure 15-40 shows the complete parameter definition.

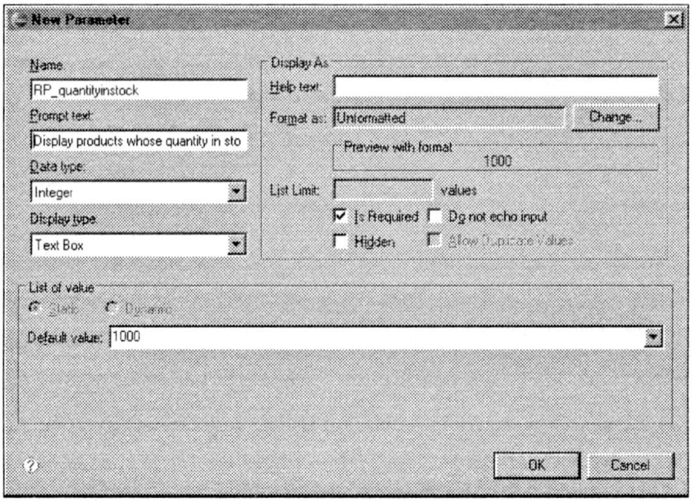

Figure 15-40 Properties for RP_quantityinstock report parameter

4 Choose OK to save the report parameter.

5 In the layout editor, choose Preview. As shown in Figure 15-41, Enter Parameters appears, displaying the prompt text and the default parameter value that you specified when you created the report parameter.

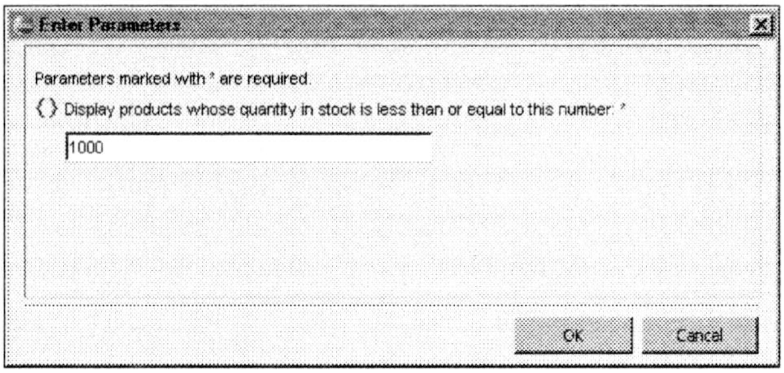

Figure 15-41 Enter Parameters displaying the RP_quantityinstock parameter

Choose OK. The report output shows all products. The report does not display only products with quantities less than or equal to 1000 because you have not yet bound the report parameter to the data set.

Task 6: Create a report parameter that prompts for a vendor name

In this procedure, you create a report parameter that asks the user to select a particular vendor or all vendors for the products whose quantity in stock matches the user-specified value. You create a report parameter that appears as a list box, which displays all the vendor names.

1 Choose Layout to resume editing the report.

2 In Data Explorer, right-click Report Parameters, then choose New Parameter.

3 Specify the following property values for the report parameter:

1 In Name, type the following text:

   RP_productvendor

2 In Prompt text, type the following text:

   Display products for this vendor

3 In Data type, select String.

4 In Display type, select List Box.

On New Parameter, List of value displays options for providing a list of values to the user, as shown in Figure 15-42. The figure also shows the properties you have specified for the report parameter so far.

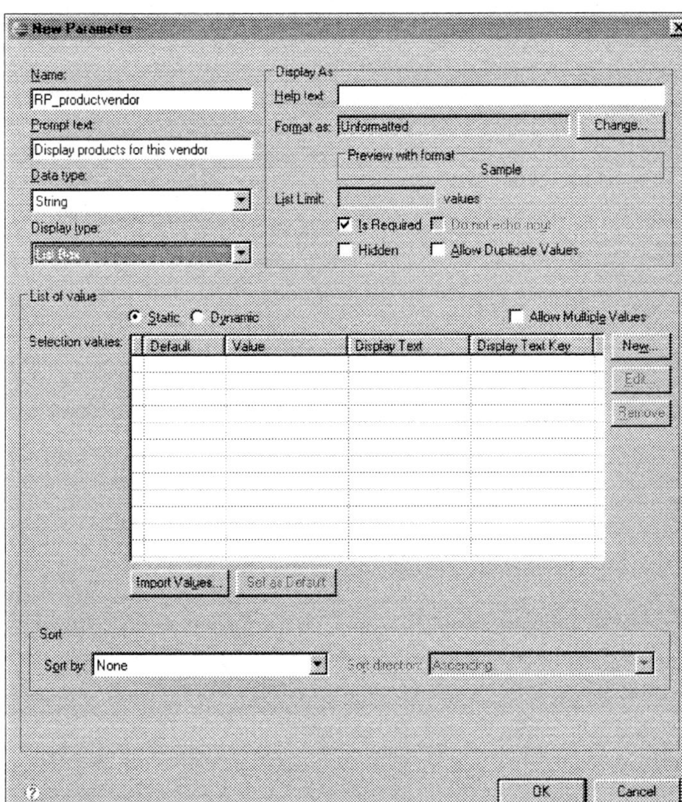

Figure 15-42 Properties for RP_productvendor report parameter

4 Under List of value, choose Dynamic.

This option creates a list of values dynamically. BIRT retrieves the values from the data source when the report runs, which ensures that the values displayed are always current.

Under List of value, Data Set displays Products, which is the only data set created for the report so far.

5 Create a new data set to retrieve the vendor names to display in the list box's list of values.

  1 Choose Create New, next to the Data set field.

  2 On New Data Set, in Name, type the following name:

    Vendors

    Choose Next.

  3 On Query, type the following query:

    ```
    select productvendor
    from Products
    ```

  4 Choose Finish to save the data set. Edit Data Set displays the columns you specified in the query, and provides options for editing the data set.

  5 Choose Preview Results to confirm that the query is valid and that it returns the correct data. You should see the results that appear in Figure 15-43. Notice that some vendor names are listed multiple times.

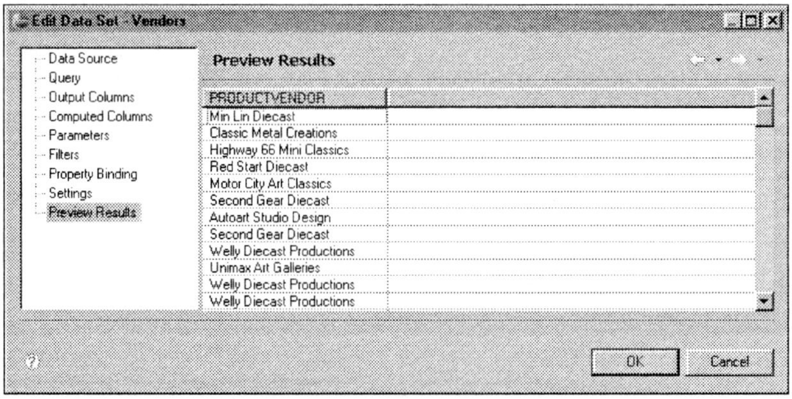

Figure 15-43 Data rows returned by the Vendors data set

  6 Choose OK to save the data set.

6 Specify the values to display in the list box.

  1 On New Parameter, in Data set, choose Vendors, the data set you created in the previous step.

    2 In Select value column, select PRODUCTVENDOR.

    3 In Select display text, select PRODUCTVENDOR.

7 Specify how the values should be sorted.

    1 Under Sort, in Sort by, select either Value Column or Display Text. In this tutorial, both provide the same values.

    2 In Sort direction, select Ascending.

8 Deselect Allow Duplicate Values. Remember that the Vendors data set returned some vendor names multiple times. Deselecting the Allow Duplicate Values option displays each name once in the list box.

Figure 15-44 shows the complete definition of the RP_productvendor report parameter.

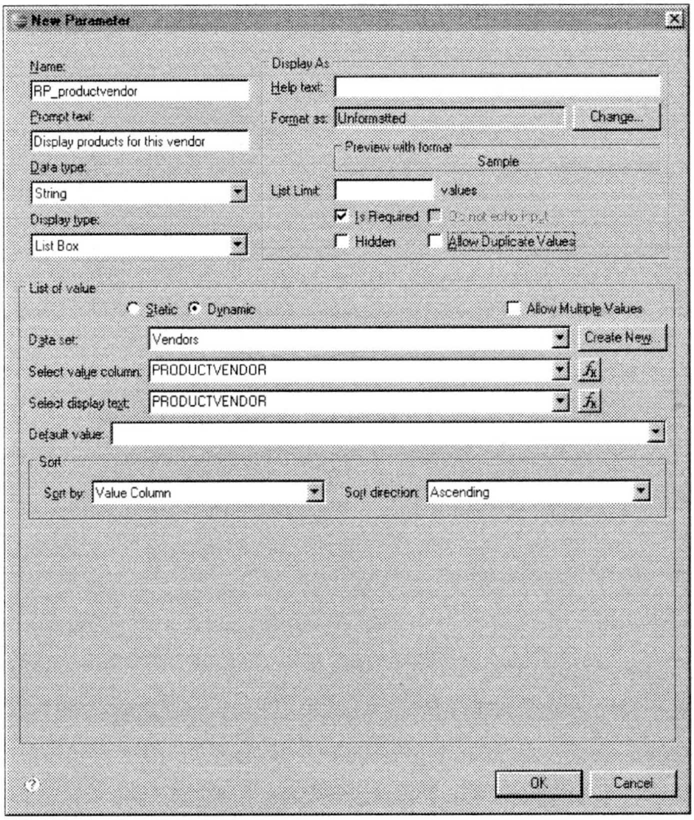

Figure 15-44   Complete definition of the RP_productvendor report parameter

9 Choose OK to save the report parameter.

10 In the layout editor, choose Preview. Enter Parameters appears, as shown in Figure 15-45. The RP_productvendor parameter appears as a list box with the first value in the list selected by default.

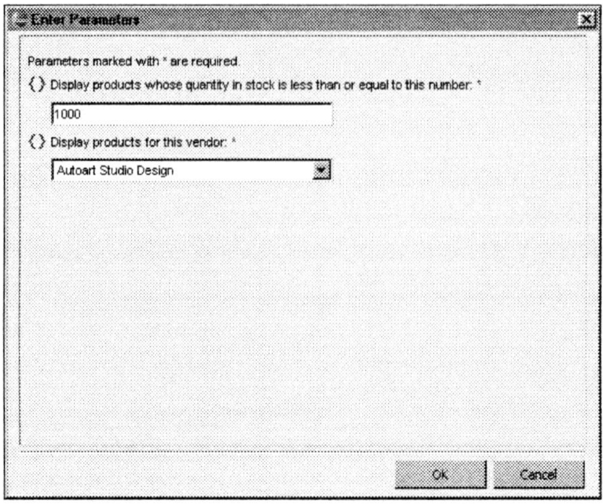

Figure 15-45   Enter Parameters displaying both report parameters

11 View the values in the list box. The values are sorted in ascending alphabetical order, and there are no duplicate values.

Choose OK. The report output still shows all products because you have not yet bound the report parameters to the Products data set.

Task 7:   Edit the query

In this procedure, you edit the query in the Products data set so that it is dynamically updated at run time to use the values of the report parameters.

1 Choose Layout to resume editing the report.

2 In Data Explorer, right-click the Products data set, and choose Edit.

3 Edit the query to add a WHERE clause as follows:

```
select productname,
productvendor,
quantityinstock
from Products
where quantityinstock <= ?
and productvendor Like ?
```

The WHERE clause contains two parameter markers, ?, which indicate where you want BIRT to insert the report parameter values at report run time. The Like operator is a SQL pattern-matching option. Using Like, you can replace the parameter marker with a value, such as A%, to return rows where the vendor name starts with A. In a later procedure, you see the flexibility of using the Like operator instead of the = operator.

Task 8: Create data set parameters and bind them to the report parameters

In this procedure, you define two data set parameters that correspond to the ? markers in the query. You then bind each data set parameter to the appropriate report parameter. At run time, the data set parameters get the values from the report parameters, and pass the values to the query.

1 In Edit Data Set, choose Parameters. The Parameters page displays two placeholder data set parameters, which BIRT Report Designer created when you modified the query.

2 Define the first data set parameter.

   1 Select the first parameter, then choose Edit.

   2 On Edit Parameter, specify these values:

      ❑ In Name, type the following text:

        `DSP_quantityinstock`

      ❑ In Data Type, select Integer.

      ❑ In Direction, select Input.

      ❑ In Linked to Report Parameter, select RP_quantityinstock. This option binds the data set parameter to the RP_quantityinstock report parameter.

   Figure 15-46 shows the complete data set parameter definition.

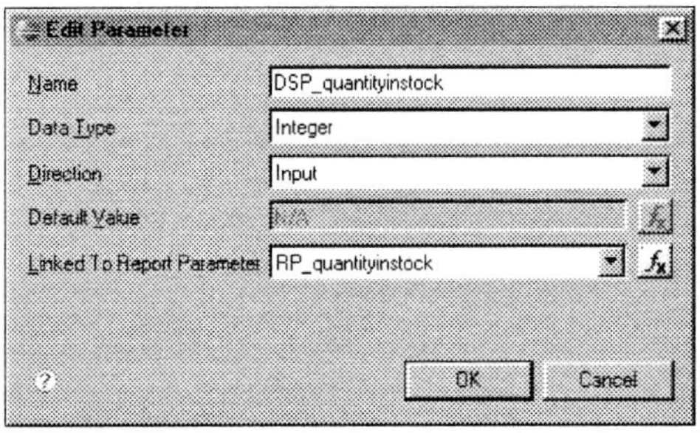

Figure 15-46   Definition of the first data set parameter

   3 Choose OK to save the data set parameter. The Parameters page displays the edited data set parameter.

3 Define the second data set parameter.

   1 Select the second parameter, then choose Edit.

   2 On Edit Parameter, specify these values:

      ❑ In Name, type the following text:

        `DSP_productvendor`

❏ In Data Type, select String.

❏ In Direction, select Input.

❏ In Linked to Report Parameter, select RP_productvendor.

Figure 15-47 shows the complete data set parameter definition.

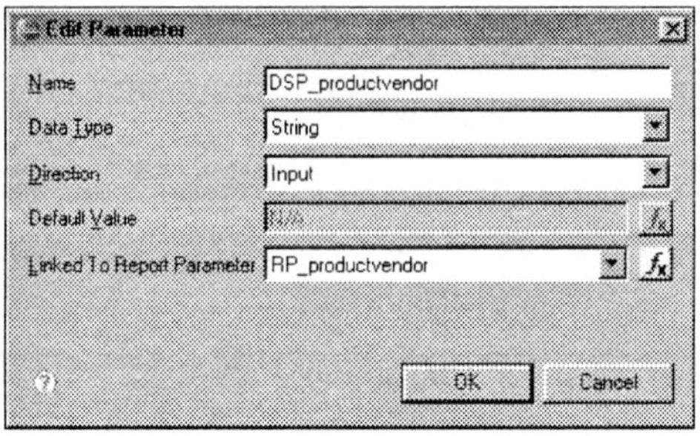

Figure 15-47   Definition of the second data set parameter

3 Choose OK to save the data set parameter.

The Parameters page, shown in Figure 15-48, displays the edited data set parameter.

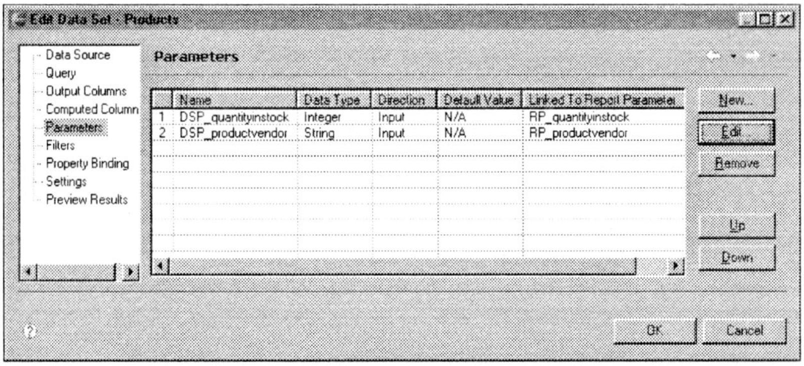

Figure 15-48   Parameters page displaying the two data set parameters

4 Choose OK to save your changes to the Products data set.

Task 9: Test the report parameters

In this procedure, you test that the query is properly updated with the report parameter values.

1 Choose Preview. Figure 15-49 shows the report output. This time, BIRT uses the default report parameter values, and generates the report without displaying Enter Parameters.

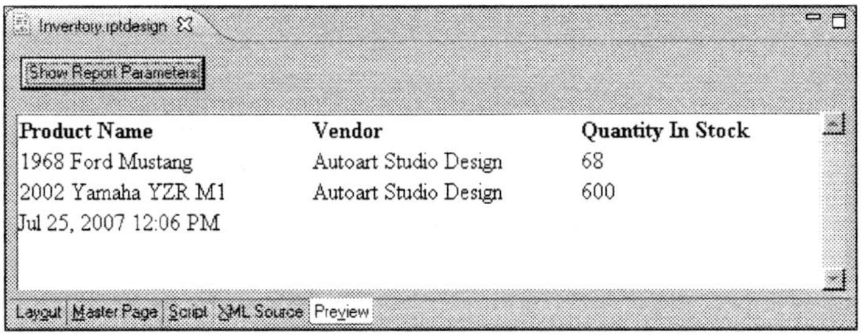

Figure 15-49 Report displays rows that match the default report parameter values

2 Choose Show Report Parameters to run the report with different parameter values. The report does not display any rows if none of the rows match the values you supply.

Task 10: Provide the option to select all vendors

The query and the design of the report parameters require the user to specify a minimum stock quantity and a specific vendor. The report displays only products with the specified minimum stock quantity and for the selected vendor. In this procedure, you provide the user with the option of selecting all vendors, so that the report displays all products—supplied by any vendor—with the specified minimum quantity. To provide this option, you modify the RP_productvendor report parameter to display an All Vendors value, and to send the appropriate value to the query.

1 In Data Explorer, expand Report Parameters, right-click RP_productvendor, then choose Edit.

2 On Edit Parameter, under List of value, choose Static. This option lets you create user-defined values, whereas the dynamic option does not.

The properties under List of Value change to reflect the change from dynamic to static values.

3 Specify the values to display in the list box.

    1 Choose Import Values. Import Values displays the first data set in the report, Products, and the values of the first field in the data set, PRODUCTNAME.

    2 In Select Data Set, select Vendors.

    3 In Select Column, select PRODUCTVENDOR. Import Values displays the values for the field.

    4 Choose >> to import all values from the field.

    Figure 15-50 shows the selections you make in Import Values.

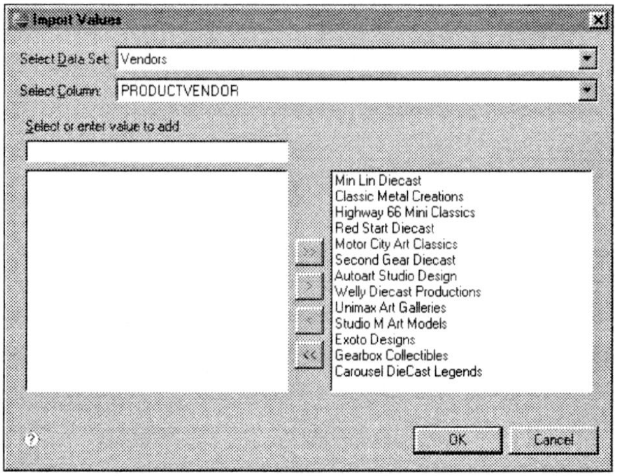

Figure 15-50 Import Values showing the data set field values to import

5 Choose OK. Edit Parameter displays the imported values in the Selection values table, as shown in Figure 15-51.

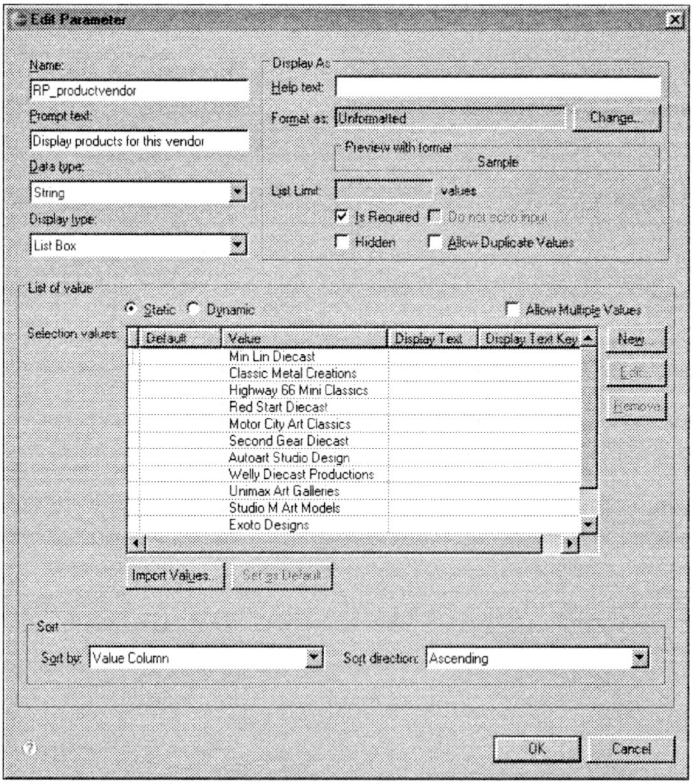

Figure 15-51 Edit Parameter displaying the values that appear in the list box

4 Add a new value to display in the list box.

   1 Choose New next to the Selection values table.

   2 On New Selection Choice, as shown in Figure 15-52:

      1 In Display Text, type the following text:

         `All Vendors`

      2 In Value, type the following character:

         `%`

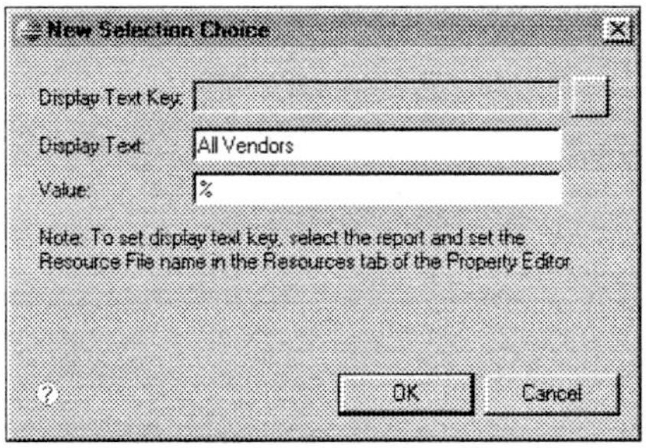

Figure 15-52   Definition of a new value

In SQL, % is a wildcard character that matches any sequence of characters. When the user selects All Vendors, the WHERE clause in the Products query is updated as:

```
WHERE ...
and productvendor Like %
```

This query returns all rows with any productvendor value.

      3 Choose OK to save the new value definition.

On Edit Parameter, the new value appears at the bottom of the Selection values table.

5 Designate the new value as the default value.

   1 In the Selection values table, scroll to the bottom of the list.

   2 Select the % value.

   3 Choose Set as Default.

6 Specify how the values should be sorted when presented to the user.

   1 Under Sort, in Sort by, select Value Column. This sort displays All Vendors at the top of the list in the list box because the value % appears before A.

   2 In Sort direction, select Ascending.

   3 Deselect Allow Duplicate Values.

7 Choose OK to save your changes to the report parameter.

8 Test the report parameter.

1 Choose Preview. Enter Parameters appears, as shown in Figure 15-53. All Vendors is the first value in the list, and this value is selected by default.

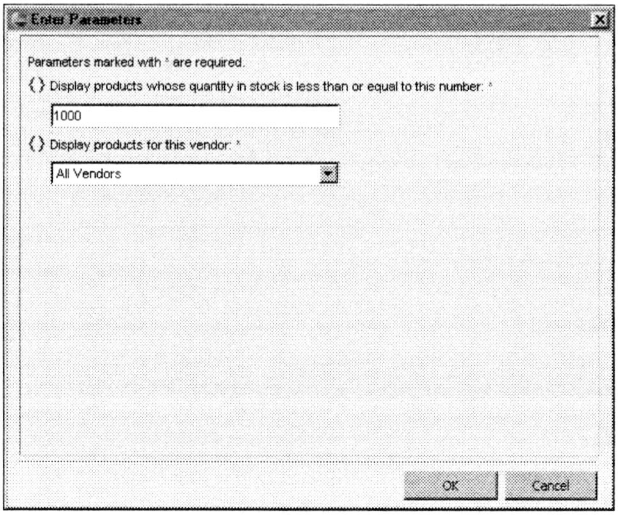

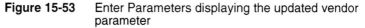

Figure 15-53   Enter Parameters displaying the updated vendor parameter

2 Provide values for the parameters.

❏ For the first parameter, type the following number:

500

❏ For the second parameter, use All Vendors.

Choose OK.

The generated report should look like the one shown in Figure 15-54. The report displays products, supplied by any vendor, where the quantity in stock is less than or equal to 500.

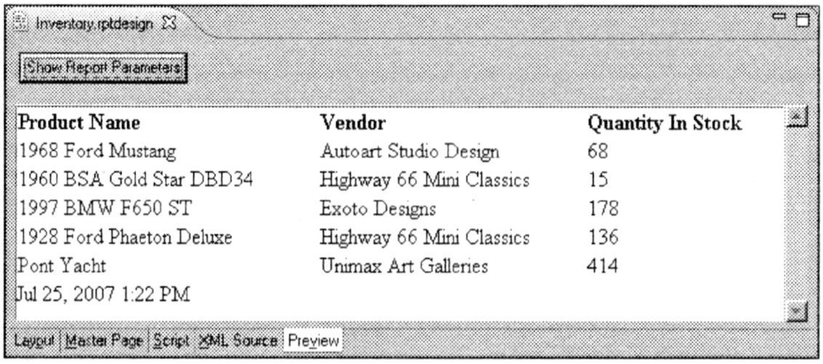

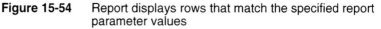

Figure 15-54   Report displays rows that match the specified report parameter values

Task 11: Create a title that uses the report parameter values

Report parameters can be used for purposes other than filtering data. In this procedure, you add a report title that displays a report parameter value.

1 Choose Layout to resume editing the report.

2 Insert a text element at the top of the report.

3 On Edit Text Item, in the field with the value Auto, select HTML from the drop-down list.

4 Type the following text:

```
Products with inventory less than
    <VALUE-OF>params["RP_quantityinstock"]</VALUE-OF>
```

The <VALUE-OF> tag supports displaying a dynamic value. The expression params["RP_quantityinstock"] refers to the RP_quantityinstock report parameter.

5 Choose OK to save your edits to the text element.

6 Preview the report. The report title displays the following text:

```
Products with inventory less than 500
```

Building a Report That Contains Subreports

You can build a report that contains multiple reports, called subreports, and you can lay out the subreports in a variety of configurations. BIRT supports many ways of arranging subreports within a single report, such as:

- Displaying multiple reports, one after another. For example, you can display the top ten customers, top ten sales representatives, and top ten products.

- Displaying multiple reports next to one another. For example, you can display general employee information and employee salary history.

- Displaying one report within another. For example, you can display detailed mutual fund performance within general fund information.

Also, you can combine any of the report configurations that are in the preceding list.

A subreport is simply a report that appears inside another report. You already know how to create a report. Basically, it takes one additional step to create a report that contains subreports. You must set up the structure of the main report to organize the subreports.

Each subreport can access a different data source, its own set of tables and fields, and specify its own data selection criteria. Subreports can be linked to one another or be independent of each other. Two reports are linked when the data of one report determines what data appears in another.

Always create, lay out, and test each subreport before you create the next one, and verify that the subreport displays the correct data. If you skip intermediate testing, it can be difficult, if you have problems, to determine which subreport causes errors.

Creating the report structure

This section describes some general principles and provides a few examples for organizing subreports in a report. The three report elements that you use to organize subreports are the table, list, and grid. Reports with complex layouts typically use all three of these container elements.

- The table iterates through the rows in a data set and displays the data in row and column format. For some reports, a subreport consists of data that is organized in a table.

- The list also iterates through the rows in a data set. The list, however, provides much greater flexibility for arranging data. A report that contains multiple linked subreports typically uses a list as the top-level container. Within the list, subreport data can be organized in tables.

- The grid is a static table that organizes elements in rows and columns. In a report with subreports, you can use a grid to align multiple tables horizontally or to add space between tables. For example, to display two subreports next to one another, you can create two tables to display the data for the subreports then insert both tables in a grid to align the subreports.

Building a report with independent subreports

Figure 16-1 shows an example of a report with four unlinked subreports. Each Top 10 subreport displays a different set of data. Each subreport is a table with data elements. The tables are arranged in a grid so that they can appear side by side.

Top 10 Products	
1992 Ferrari 360 Spider red	$276,839.98
2001 Ferrari Enzo	$190,755.86
1952 Alpine Renault 1300	$190,017.96
2003 Harley-Davidson Eagle Drag Bike	$170,686.00
1968 Ford Mustang	$161,531.48
1969 Ford Falcon	$152,543.02
1980s Black Hawk Helicopter	$144,959.91
1998 Chrysler Plymouth Prowler	$142,530.63
1917 Grand Touring Sedan	$140,535.60
2002 Suzuki XREO	$135,767.03

Top 10 Sales Representatives	
Gerard Hernandez	$1,258,577.81
Leslie Jennings	$1,081,530.54
Pamela Castillo	$868,220.55
Larry Bott	$732,096.79
Barry Jones	$704,853.91
George Vanauf	$669,377.05
Peter Marsh	$584,593.76
Loui Bondur	$569,485.75
Andy Fixter	$562,582.59
Steve Patterson	$505,875.42

Top 10 Customers	
Euro+ Shopping Channel	$820,689.54
Mini Gifts Distributors Ltd	$591,827.34
Australian Collectors, Co.	$180,585.07
Muscle Machine Inc	$177,913.95
La Rochelle Gifts	$158,573.12
Dragon Souveniers, Ltd	$156,251.03
Down Under Souveniers, Inc	$154,622.08
Land of Toys Inc	$149,085.15
AV Stores, Co.	$148,410.09
The Sharp Gifts Warehouse	$143,536.27

Top 10 Cities	
Madrid	$979,880.77
San Rafael	$591,827.34
NYC	$497,941.50
Auckland	$292,082.87
Singapore	$263,997.78
Paris	$240,649.68
San Francisco	$199,051.34
New Bedford	$190,500.01
Nantes	$180,887.48
Melbourne	$180,585.07

Figure 16-1   Unlinked subreports

Figure 16-2 shows the design for the report that appears in Figure 16-1.

A fixed-width empty grid column adds
space between the subreports

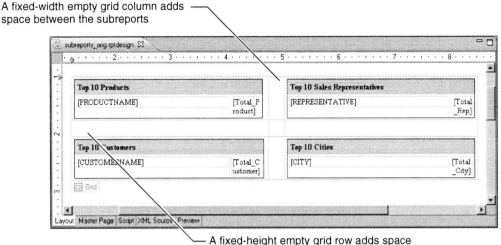

A fixed-height empty grid row adds space
between the top and bottom subreports

Figure 16-2   Report design for unlinked subreports

Building a report with linked subreports

The preceding section described creating subreports that are not linked to
each other. The subreports run independently and do not coordinate their
data. Sometimes, however, you need to create reports that coordinate data,
such as a detailed customer-issues report in a customer report, or a list of
top ten stocks in a fund report. Figure 16-3 shows these two example reports.

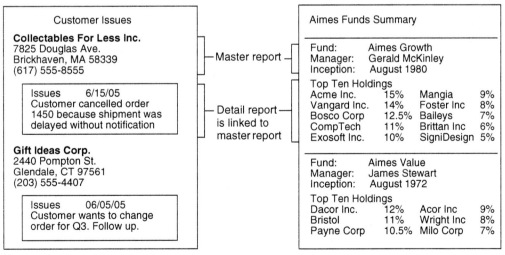

Figure 16-3   Linked subreports

As the example shows, one report is nested in another, creating a master report and detail report relationship. Each report accesses data from a different table or data source, and the reports are linked by a common field value, such as customer ID or mutual fund name. The value of the linking field in the master report determines the data that appears in the detail report. For example, if the customer ID in the master report is 112, the detail report displays the issues for the customer whose ID is 112.

Creating the structure of a report with linked subreports

The master-detail report examples in the previous section use the list element as the primary organizational structure. The list iterates through the data rows that the data set returns, and it supports the structure of nested reports.

Within the list, a grid aligns the data in both reports. The data for the master report is placed in the grid in the detail area of the list. The grid aligns the data in a column, and the list iterates through the master report's data rows. The detail report uses a table to iterate through its data rows.

This structure assumes that the master and detail reports use different data sets and that each data set accesses data from a different table or data source. Figure 16-4 shows the report design for the customer-issue master-detail report that appears in the previous section.

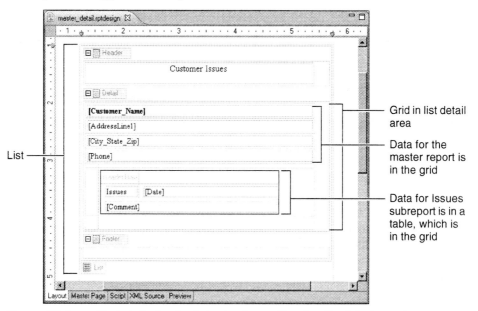

Figure 16-4   Report design for linked subreports using the list element

An alternate design is to use two tables, one nested in the other. Place data for the master report in the detail rows of the outer table. Place data for the detail report in a table, and place the table in the detail row of the outer table. Figure 16-5 shows this alternate report design.

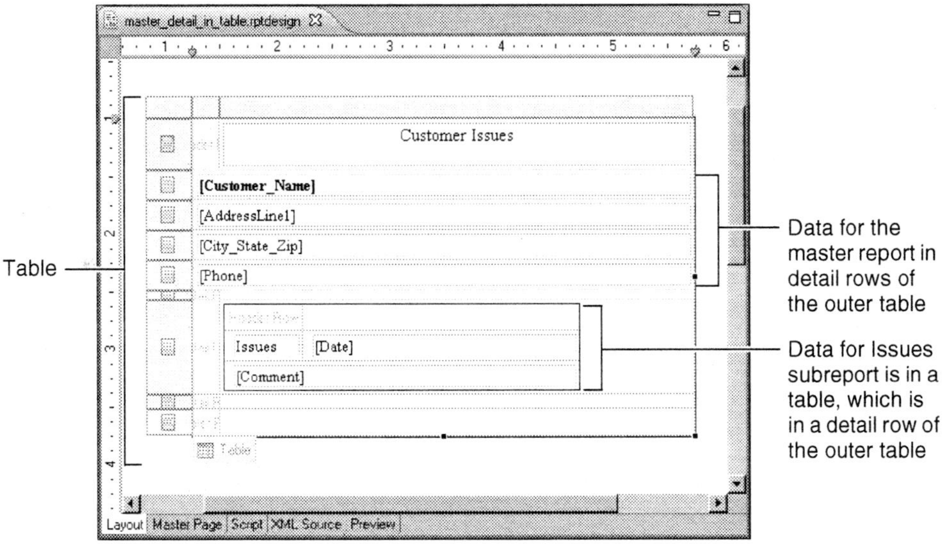

Figure 16-5   Report design for linked subreports using nested tables

Linking master and detail reports

Master and detail reports must be linked by a common field. In the customer-issue example report, the linking field is the customer ID. To link the reports, perform the following tasks:

1 For the detail report's data set, create a SELECT statement with a parameter marker in a WHERE clause. For example:

```
SELECT *
FROM issues
WHERE issues.customerNumber = ?
```

2 Create a data set parameter. Figure 16-6 shows the definition of a parameter in the data set that the detail report uses. You must supply a specific value as the parameter's default value so that the query works properly during the report design process.

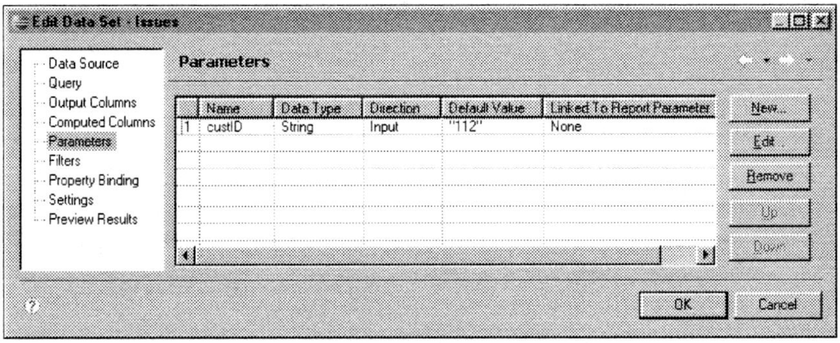

Figure 16-6   Data set parameter definition

3 In the layout editor, bind the detail report's data set parameter to the linking field in the master report. Figure 16-7 shows an example of this binding, which you perform using the property editor for the detail table.

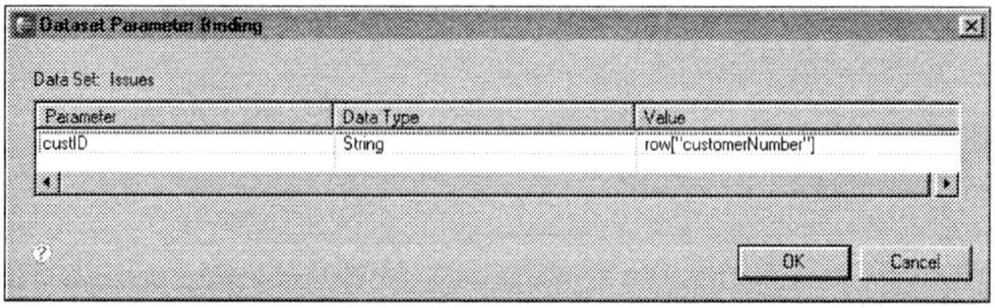

Figure 16-7   Data set parameter bound to the linking field

When the report runs, BIRT performs the following tasks:

- When the master report processes a customer row, it passes the customer number value to the data set parameter that you defined for the detail report.

- The data set parameter passes this customer number value to the detail report's query and dynamically updates the WHERE clause.

- The detail report displays the issues data for that customer number.

The previous steps repeat until the master report processes all its customer rows.

Tutorial 4: Building a report containing side-by-side subreports

This section provides step-by-step instructions for building a report that displays a list of customers. For each customer, the report displays order and payment information. The order information and payment information are in separate, adjacent subreports. The customer report is the master report, which is also called the outer report. The orders and payments subreports are the detail reports, which are also called the inner reports.

Each report accesses data from a different table in the sample database, Classic Models. The customer report, orders subreport, and payment subreport use data from the Customers, Orders, and Payments tables, respectively.

A common field, CUSTOMERNUMBER, links the reports. The value of the linking field in the master report determines what data appears in the detail reports. For example, if the customer number in the master report is 173, the detail reports display the order and payment information for the customer whose ID is 173.

Figure 16-8 shows a portion of the finished report.

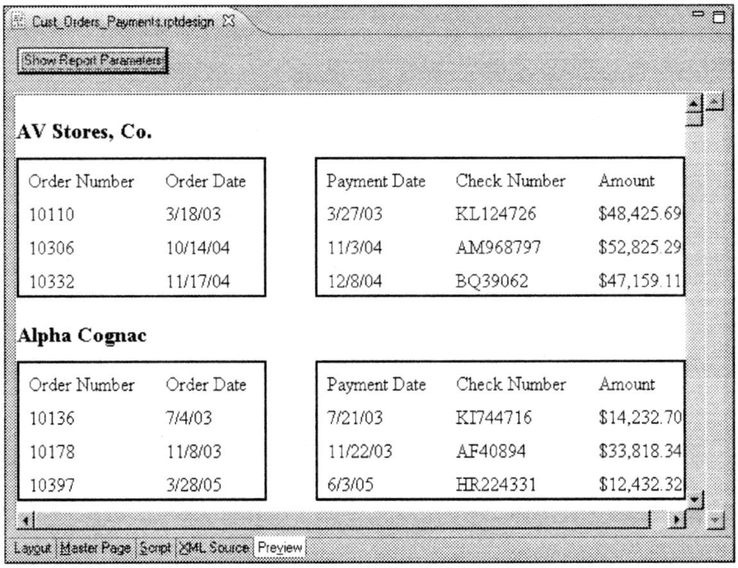

Figure 16-8   Customers master report including orders and payments subreports

In this tutorial, you perform the following tasks:

- Create a new report.

- Build a data source.

- Build a data set for the customer report.

- Build a data set for the orders subreport.

- Build a data set for the payments subreport.

- Create the customer master report.

- Create the orders subreport.

- Link the orders subreport to the customers master report.

- Create the payments subreport.

- Link the payments subreport to the customers master report.

- Display only customers that have orders or payments.

- Display the subreports next to one another.

- View the outline of the report.

- Format the report.

Task 1: Create a new report

If you are using BIRT Report Designer, this task assumes you have already created a project for your reports. If you are using BIRT RCP Report Designer, there is no requirement for a project.

1 Choose File➤New➤Report.

2 On New Report, select a project in which to store your report.

3 Type the following text as the file name:

    Cust_Orders_Payments.rptdesign

4 Choose Finish. A blank report appears in the layout editor.

Task 2: Build a data source

Before you begin designing your report in the layout editor, you create a data source to connect your report to the Classic Models database.

1 Choose Data Explorer.

2 Right-click Data Sources, and choose New Data Source from the context menu.

3 Select Classic Models Inc. Sample Database from the list of data sources, use the default data source name, then choose Next. Connection information about the new data source appears.

4 Choose Finish. BIRT Report Designer creates a new data source that connects to the sample database. The new data source appears within Data Sources in Data Explorer.

Task 3: Build a data set for the customer report

In this procedure, you build a data set to indicate what data to extract from the Customers table. The customer report that you create later uses this data set.

1 In Data Explorer, right-click Data Sets, and choose New Data Set.

2 On New Data Set, type the following text for data set name:

    Customers

3 Use the default values for the other fields.

   ▪ Data Source shows the name of the data source that you created earlier.

   ▪ Data Set Type specifies that the data set uses a SQL SELECT query.

4 Choose Next. Query displays the information to help you create a SQL query. The text area on the right side shows the required keywords of a SQL SELECT statement.

5 In Available Items, expand CLASSICMODELS, then expand the Customers table. The columns in the Customers table appear.

6 Use the following SQL SELECT statement to indicate what data to retrieve. You can type the column and table names, or you can drag them from Available Items to the appropriate location in the SELECT statement.

```
SELECT Customers.customerName,
Customers.customerNumber
FROM Customers
```

This statement that you created, which is shown in Figure 16-9, gets values from the CUSTOMERNAME and CUSTOMERNUMBER columns in the Customers table.

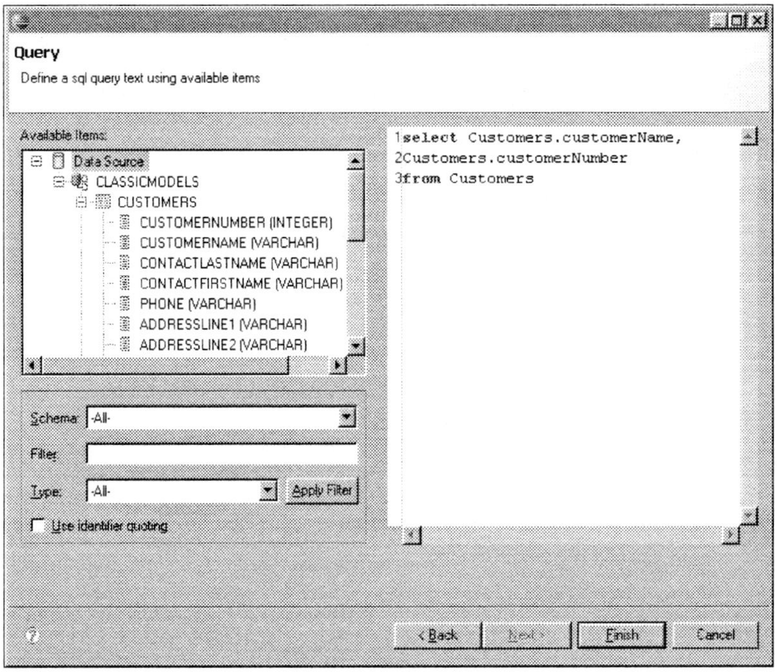

Figure 16-9   Query for Customers data set

7 Choose Finish to save the data set. Edit Data Set displays the columns specified in the query, and provides options for editing the data set.

8 Choose Preview Results to confirm that the query is valid and that it returns the correct data. If you created the SELECT statement correctly, you should see the results that appear in Figure 16-10. These are the data rows that the query returns.

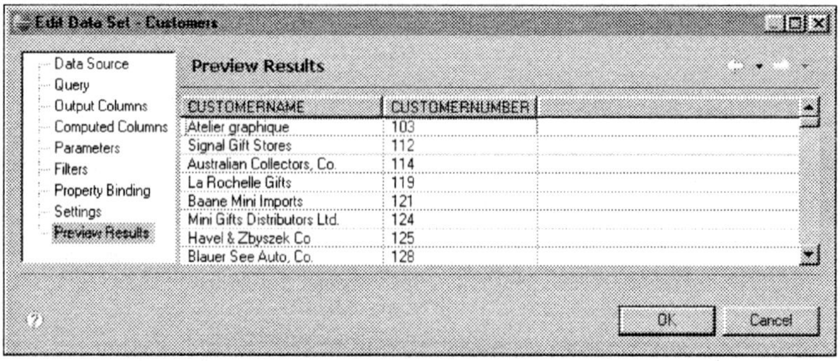

Figure 16-10 Data preview

9 Choose OK to save the data set.

Task 4: Build a data set for the orders subreport

In this procedure, you build a data set to indicate what data to extract from the Orders table. The orders subreport that you create later uses this data set.

1 In Data Explorer, right-click Data Sets, and choose New Data Set from the context menu.

2 On New Data Set, type the following text for the data set's name:

    Orders

3 Use the default values for the other fields, then choose Next.

4 On Query, in Available Items, expand CLASSICMODELS, then expand the Orders table to display the columns in the table.

5 Use the following SQL SELECT statement to indicate what data to retrieve:

```
SELECT Orders.orderNumber,
Orders.orderDate
FROM Orders
WHERE Orders.customerNumber = ?
```

This statement selects the ORDERNUMBER and ORDERDATE columns from the Orders table. The WHERE clause has a parameter marker for the value of CUSTOMERNUMBER. When the report runs, the orders subreport gets the current CUSTOMERNUMBER value from the customers report.

6 Choose Finish to save the data set. Edit Data Set displays the columns specified in the query, and provides options for editing the data set.

7 Create a data set parameter to supply the CUSTOMERNUMBER value in the WHERE clause.

   1 Choose Parameters from the left side of the window. Edit Data Set displays a default parameter definition.

2 Choose Edit to modify the parameter definition.

3 On Edit Parameter, specify the following values, as shown in Figure 16-11:

❑ Name: CustID

❑ Data Type: Integer

❑ Direction: Input

❑ Default value: 103

103 is one of the values in the CUSTOMERNUMBER column. A default value is required for BIRT Report Designer to run the query for testing purposes.

❑ Linked To Report Parameter: None

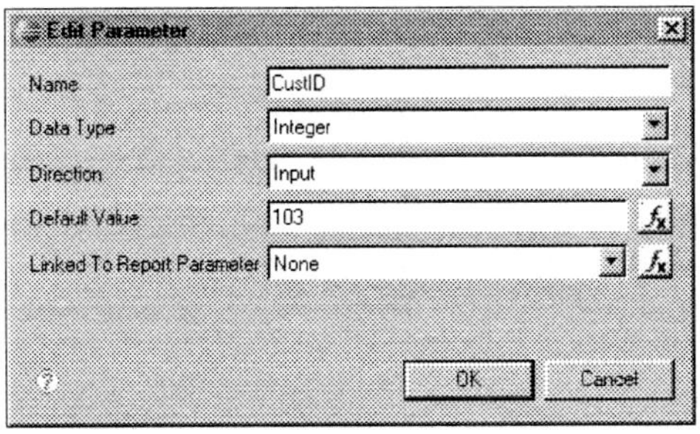

Figure 16-11   Edited parameter definition

4 Choose OK to confirm your edits to the parameter definition. The parameter definition appears in Edit Data Set, as shown in Figure 16-12.

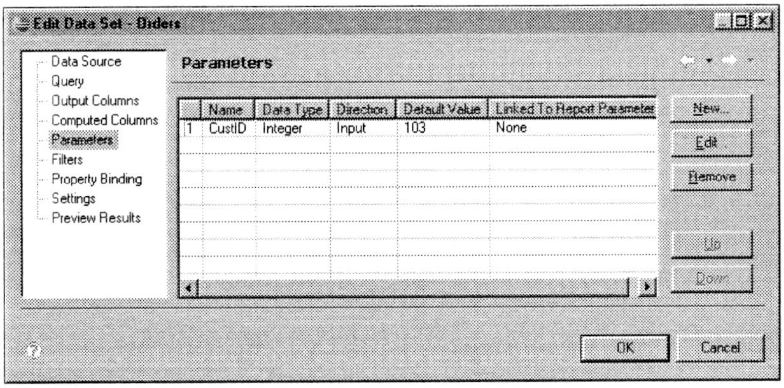

Figure 16-12   Parameter definition in the Orders data set

8 Choose Preview Results to confirm that the query is valid and that it returns the correct data. If you created the SELECT statement and created the data set parameter correctly, you should see the results that appear in

Figure 16-13. These are the data rows that the query returns for customer number 103.

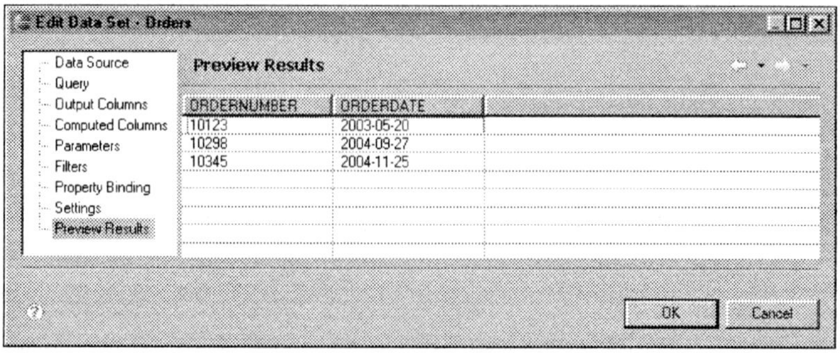

Figure 16-13   Data preview for the orders subreport

9 Choose OK to save the changes to the data set.

Task 5: Build a data set for the payments subreport

In this procedure, you build a data set to indicate what data to extract from the Payments table. The payments subreport that you create later uses this data set.

1 In Data Explorer, right-click Data Sets, and choose New Data Set from the context menu.

2 On New Data Set, type the following text for the data set's name:

Payments

3 Use the default values for the other fields, then choose Next.

4 On Query, in Available Items, expand CLASSICMODELS, then expand the Payments table to display the columns in the table.

5 Use the following SQL SELECT statement to indicate what data to retrieve:

```
SELECT Payments.paymentDate,
Payments.checkNumber,
Payments.amount
FROM Payments
WHERE Payments.customerNumber = ?
```

This statement selects the PAYMENTDATE, CHECKNUMBER, and AMOUNT columns from the Payments table. The WHERE clause has a parameter marker for the value of CUSTOMERNUMBER. When the report runs, the payments subreport gets the current CUSTOMERNUMBER value from the customers report.

6 Choose Finish to save the data set. Edit Data Set displays the columns specified in the query, and provides options for editing the data set.

7 Create a data set parameter to supply the CUSTOMERNUMBER value for the WHERE clause.

    1 Choose Parameters. Edit Data Set displays a default parameter.

    2 Choose Edit to modify the parameter definition.

    3 On Edit Parameter, specify the following values:

        ❏ Name: CustID

        ❏ Data Type: Integer

        ❏ Direction: Input

        ❏ Default value: 103

        ❏ Linked To Report Parameter: None

    4 Choose OK to confirm your edits to the parameter definition.

8 Choose Preview Results to confirm that the query is valid and that it returns the correct data. If you created the SELECT statement and created the data set parameter correctly, you should see the results that appear in Figure 16-14. These are the data rows that the query returns for customer number 103.

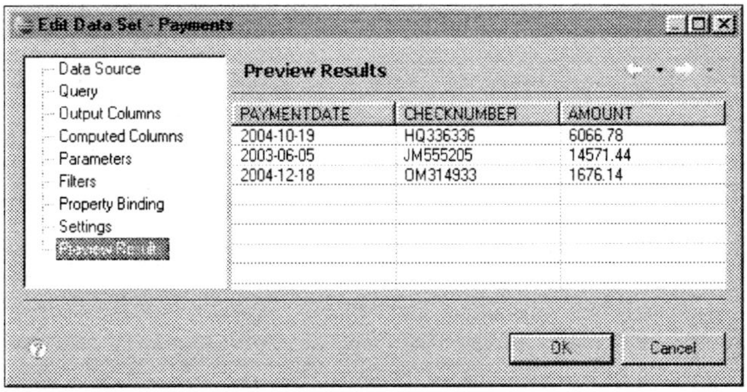

Figure 16-14   Data preview for the payments subreport

9 Choose OK to save the changes to the data set.

Task 6: Create the customer master report

You use a list element to create the master report and organize the orders and payments subreports within it. The list iterates through the customer data rows and creates the related orders and payments subreports for each record. For the sake of simplicity, the customer report displays just the customer name. It can, of course, display additional data, such as customer address, phone number, and credit limit.

1 Choose Palette.

2 Drag a list element from the palette, and drop it in the report. The list element appears in the report, as shown in Figure 16-15.

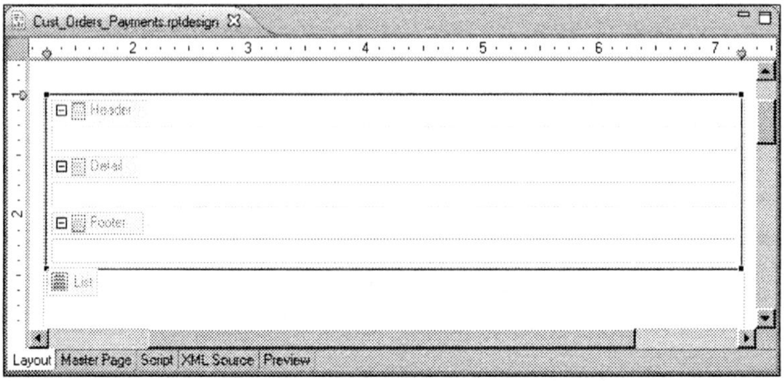

Figure 16-15 List element

3 Associate, or bind, the list with the Customers data set.

   1 In Property Editor, choose the Binding tab.

   2 In Data Set, select Customers from the drop-down list.

BIRT creates a column binding for each column in the Customers data set. Figure 16-16 shows the binding information for the list.

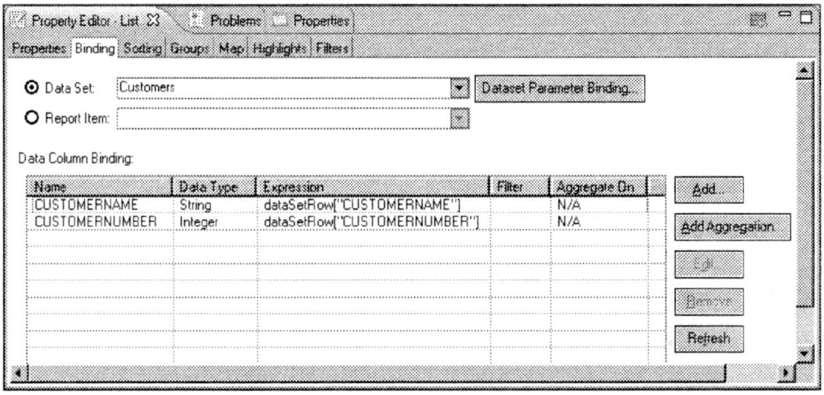

Figure 16-16 Binding information for the list element

4 Choose Data Explorer, expand Data Sets, then expand Customers. The columns that you specified in the query appear below Customers.

5 Drag CUSTOMERNAME from Data Explorer, and drop it in the detail area of the list. Figure 16-17 shows what the report design looks like so far.

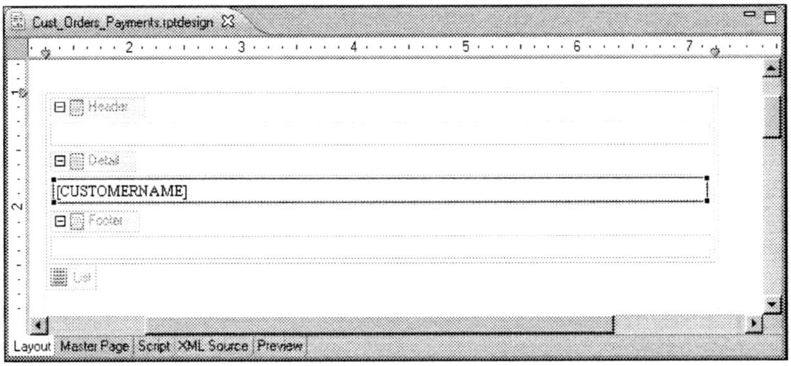

Figure 16-17 Data set field in the list element

6 Choose Preview to preview the report. The report should look like the one shown in Figure 16-18. The report lists all the customer names in the order in which the query returns them.

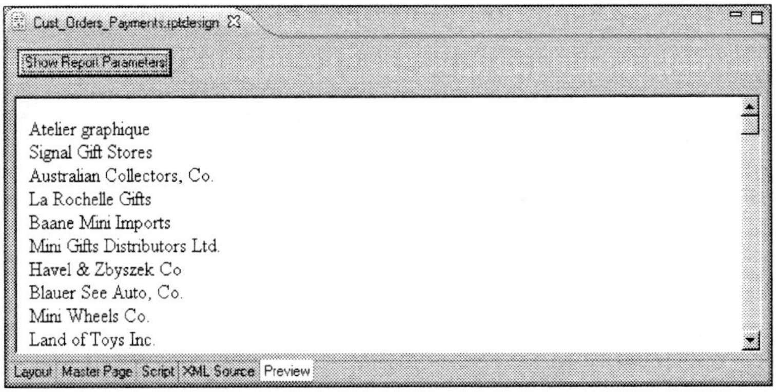

Figure 16-18 Data preview for the master report

7 Sort the customer names in ascending order.

   1 Choose Layout to return to the layout editor.

   2 In the layout editor, select the list element. Hover the mouse pointer over the bottom left corner until you see the List tab, then choose the tab.

   3 In Property Editor, choose the Sorting tab.

   4 On the Sort page, choose Add to create a sort expression.

   5 On New Sort Key, specify the following values, as shown in Figure 16-19:

       ❑ In Key, select CUSTOMERNAME from the drop-down list.

       ❑ In Direction, use the default value, Ascending.

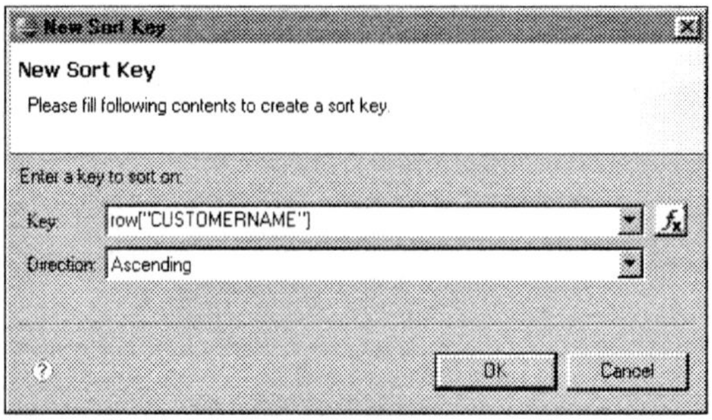

Figure 16-19   Sort definition

Choose OK. The Sort page displays the sort expression that you
defined for the list.

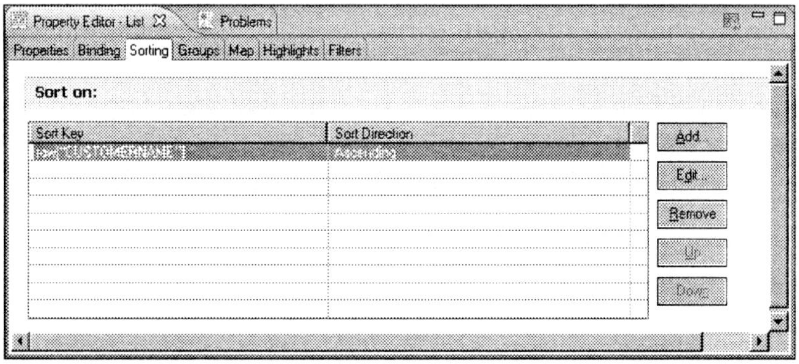

Figure 16-20   Sort expression

8 Preview the report. Customer names appear in ascending order.

Task 7: Create the orders subreport

The orders subreport lists the orders for each customer in a row and column
format. It displays the order number and date of each order. To iterate
through the Orders data set rows and display them in a row and column
format, you use the table element.

1 Choose Layout to return to the layout editor.

2 Drag a table element from the palette, and drop it below the
[CUSTOMERNAME] data element, in the detail area. Insert Table
prompts you to specify the number of columns and detail rows to create
for the table. The dialog also prompts you to select a data set to bind with
the table.

3 On Insert Table, specify the following values, as shown in Figure 16-21:

   ❋ In Number of columns, type 2.

   ❋ In Number of details, type 1.

* In Data Set, select Orders from the drop-down list.

Figure 16-21   Properties specified for the table

Choose OK. A table appears in the detail area of the list, as shown in Figure 16-22.

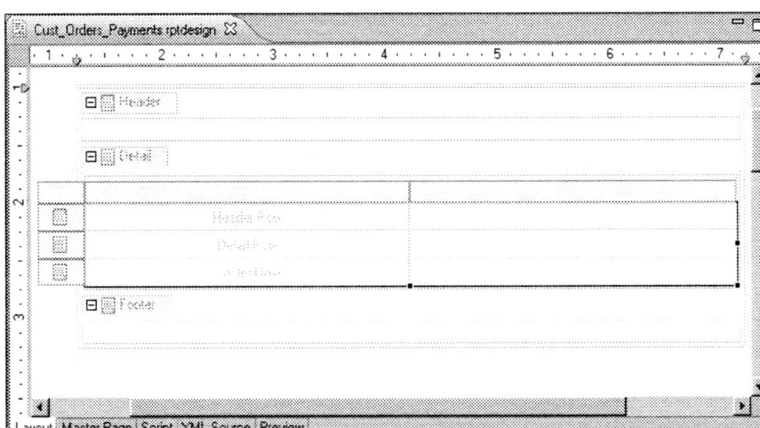

Figure 16-22   Table inserted in the detail area of the list

4 Choose Data Explorer, expand Data Sets, then expand Orders. The columns that you specified in the query appear below Orders.

5 Drag ORDERNUMBER from Data Explorer, and drop it in the first cell of the table's detail row.

In the layout editor, the table cell in which you dropped the data set field contains a data element that displays [ORDERNUMBER]. Above this data element is a label element that the layout editor automatically adds to the header row. This label displays the field name as static text and serves as the column heading.

6 Drag ORDERDATE from Data Explorer, and drop it in the second cell in the detail row. The report page should look like the one shown in Figure 16-23.

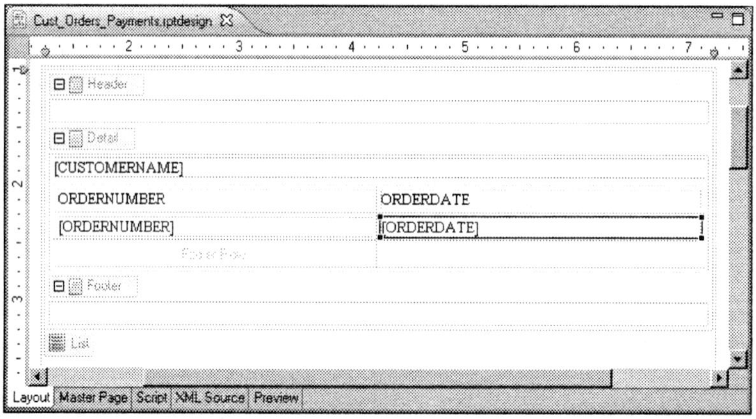

Figure 16-23 Report design includes the orders subreport

7 Sort the order rows by order number.

   1 Select the Orders table.

   2 In Property Editor, choose Sorting.

   3 On the Sort page, choose Add to create a sort expression.

   4 On New Sort Key, specify the following values, then choose OK:

      ❑ In Key, select ORDERNUMBER from the drop-down list.

      ❑ In Direction, use the default value, Ascending.

8 Preview the report. The report should look like the one shown in Figure 16-24.

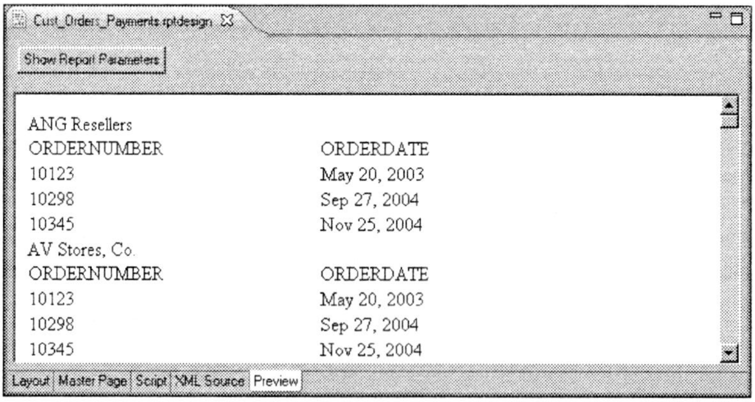

Figure 16-24 Preview of the report shows repeated order records

The same order records appear for every customer because you specified a default value of 103 for customerNumber when you created the data set parameter, CustID. Because of this default value, the orders subreport always displays the order records for customer 103. The solution is to update the value of the CustID parameter dynamically each time the customer row in the master report changes. This procedure is described in the next task.

Task 8: Link the orders subreport to the customers master report

You link the orders subreport to the customers master report by binding the CustID parameter to the CUSTOMERNUMBER data set field in the customers report. Each time the customers report reaches a new customer row, the CustID parameter is updated with the new CUSTOMERNUMBER value.

1 Choose Layout to return to the layout editor.

2 Select the Orders table.

3 In Property Editor, choose Binding.

4 On the Binding page, choose Dataset Parameter Binding. Dataset Parameter Binding displays the CustID parameter, as shown in Figure 16-25. Its value is set to the default, 103, which you specified when you created the data set parameter.

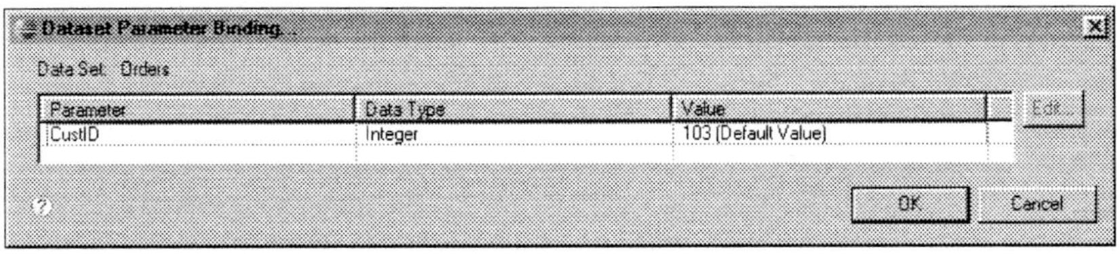

Figure 16-25   Dataset Parameter Binding for the Orders table

5 Change the parameter value to the CUSTOMERNUMBER field in the customers report.

1 Select the parameter, then choose Edit. Edit data set parameter binding, shown in Figure 16-26, prompts you to specify a new parameter value.

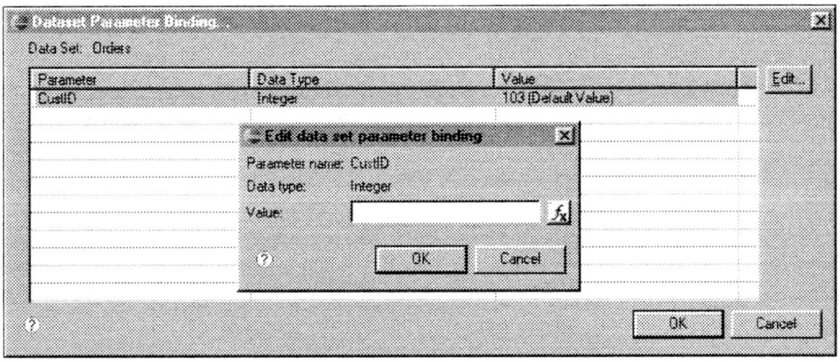

Figure 16-26   Edit data set parameter binding

2   Choose the expression builder button that appears to the right of the Value field.

3   On the expression builder, choose Available Column Bindings, choose List, then double-click CUSTOMERNUMBER. The expression builder displays the expression, row["CUSTOMERNUMBER"], as shown in Figure 16-27.

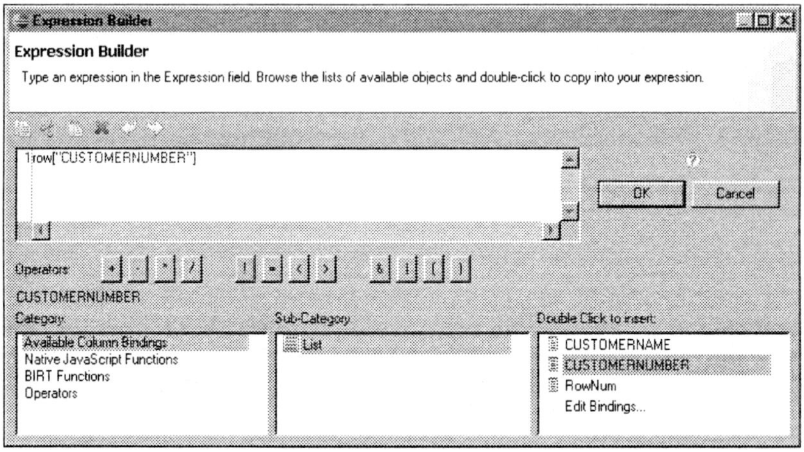

Figure 16-27   CUSTOMERNUMBER field in the expression builder

Choose OK to save the expression and close the expression builder.

4   On Edit data set parameter binding, choose OK to accept the new parameter value. Dataset Parameter Binding displays the new value of row["CUSTOMERNUMBER"] for the CustID parameter.

6   Choose OK to save the changed data set parameter binding.

7   Preview the report, which should look like the one shown in Figure 16-28.

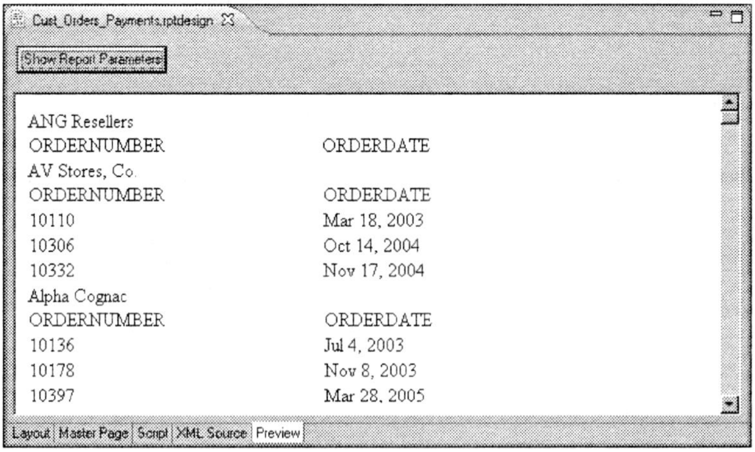

Figure 16-28   Preview of the report shows correct orders data

Now different order records appear for different customers. Not all customers have order records. To display only customers that have orders, you change the query for the customers report. This task is described later in Task 11: "Display only customers that have orders or payments."

Task 9:   Create the payments subreport

The payments subreport shows, in a row and column format, the payments that each customer made. It displays the payment date, check number, and amount of each order. To iterate through the Payments data set rows and display them in a row and column format, you use a table element. This time, you use an alternate and quicker method to insert the table and the data set fields in the table.

1   Choose Layout to return to the layout editor.

2   Choose Data Explorer, and expand Data Sets.

3   Drag the Payments data set, and drop it below the orders subreport, in the detail area of the list.

BIRT Report Designer inserts a table in the report, and places all the data set fields in the detail row of the table. BIRT Report Designer also inserts labels in the header row of the table. The labels display the field names as static text and serve as the column headings. The report design should look like the one shown in Figure 16-29.

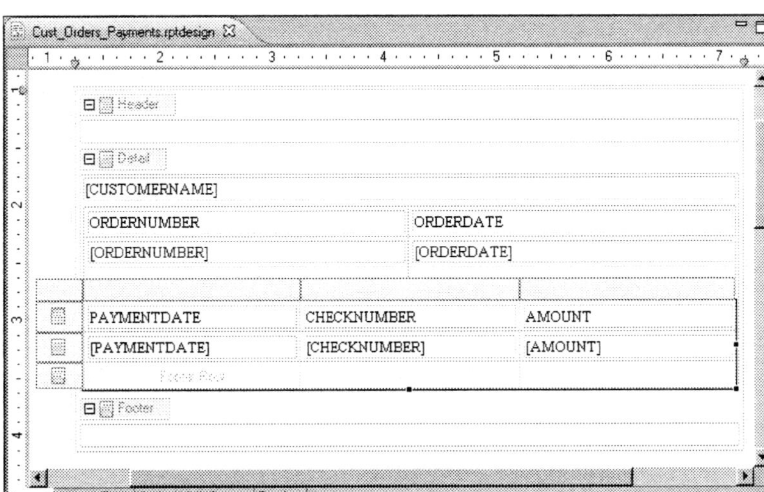

Figure 16-29   Report design includes the payments subreport

4   Sort the payment rows by payment date.

   1   Select the Payments table.

   2   In Property Editor, choose Sorting.

3   On the Sort page, choose Add to create a sort expression.

4   On New Sort Key, specify the following values, then choose OK:

❑   In Key, select PAYMENTDATE from the drop-down list.

❑   In Direction, use the default value, Ascending.

5   Preview the report. The report should look like the one shown in
Figure 16-30.

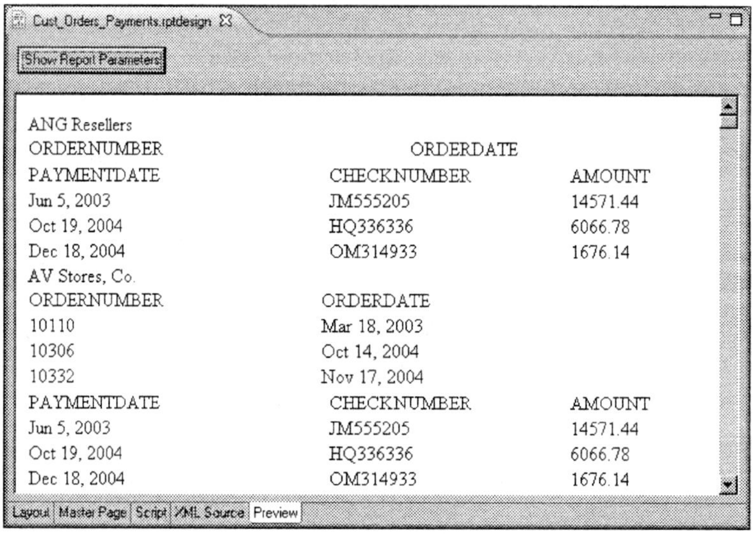

Figure 16-30   Report preview shows repeated payment records

As with the orders subreport when you first created it, the same payment
records repeat for every customer because you specified a default value of
103 for customerNumber when you created the parameter, CustID, for the
Payments data set. Because of this default value, the payments subreport
always displays the payment records for customer 103. Just as you did for
the orders subreport, you need to dynamically update the value of the
CustID parameter for each customer in the master report.

Task 10: Link the payments subreport to the customers master report

You link the payments subreport to the customers master report by binding
its CustID parameter to the CUSTOMERNUMBER field in the customers
report.

1   Choose Layout to return to the layout editor.

2   Select the Payments table.

3   In Property Editor, choose the Binding tab.

4 On the Binding page, choose Dataset Parameter Binding. Dataset Parameter Binding displays the CustID parameter. Its value is set to the default, 103, which you specified when you created the data set parameter.

5 Change the parameter value to the CUSTOMERNUMBER field in the customers report.

1 Select the parameter, then choose Edit. A dialog prompts you specify a parameter value.

2 Choose the expression builder button that appears on the right of the Value field.

3 On the expression builder, choose Available Column Bindings, choose List, then double-click CUSTOMERNUMBER. The expression builder displays the expression row["CUSTOMERNUMBER"]. Choose OK to save the expression and close the expression builder.

4 On Edit data set parameter binding, choose OK to accept the new parameter value. Dataset Parameter Binding displays the new value of row["CUSTOMERNUMBER"] for the CustID parameter, as shown in Figure 16-31.

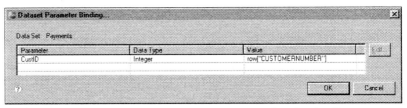

Figure 16-31   Modified data set parameter binding for the Payments
table

6 Choose OK to save the changed data set parameter binding.

7 Preview the report. Now the report displays different payment records for different customers. Not all customers have payment records. To display only customers that have payments or orders, you change the query for the customers report.

Task 11: Display only customers that have orders or payments

The database contains customers that do not have orders or payments. The query for the customers report returns all customers. When you run the report, there are customer rows that show only the column headings for the Orders and Payments tables, as shown in Figure 16-32.

ANG Resellers		
ORDERNUMBER	ORDERDATE	
PAYMENTDATE	CHECKNUMBER	AMOUNT

Figure 16-32   Report shows no order or payment data for one customer

You can exclude customers that do not have orders or payments by changing the query for the customers report.

1 Choose Layout to return to the layout editor.

2 In Data Explorer, expand Data Sets, right-click Customers, then choose Edit.

3 Add the following SQL lines to the end of the existing query:

```
WHERE
EXISTS
(SELECT Orders.customerNumber
FROM Orders
WHERE Customers.customerNumber =
Orders.customerNumber)
OR
EXISTS
(SELECT Payments.customerNumber
FROM Payments
WHERE Customers.customerNumber =
Payments.customerNumber)
```

The WHERE EXISTS clause checks the Orders and Payments tables for customerNumber values that match the customerNumber values in the Customers table. Only rows that have matching customerNumber values are selected. The complete query should look like the one shown in Figure 16-33.

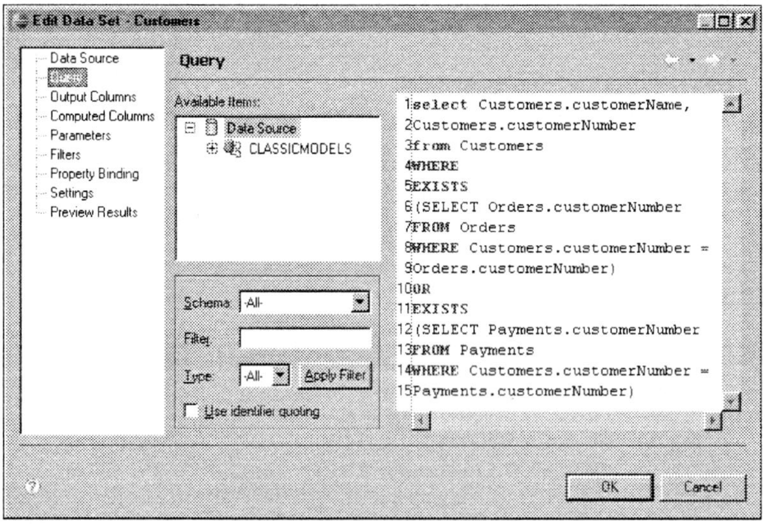

Figure 16-33   Updated SELECT query in Edit Data Set

4 Choose Preview Results to verify that the query returns rows, then choose OK to save the change to the data set.

5 Preview the report. Scroll down the report to check the output. The report no longer displays customers that do not have orders or payments.

Task 12: Display the subreports next to one another

Now that the subreports display the correct data, you can focus on laying out the subreports next to one another. You cannot place two tables next to one another because BIRT Report Designer creates block-level elements, which means that each element starts on a new line. To display side-by-side tables, you insert the tables in a grid. The grid enables you to align elements easily.

1 Choose Layout to return to the layout editor.

2 Drag a grid element from the palette, and drop it into the Detail row, between the [CUSTOMERNAME] data element and the Orders table. Before you drop the grid, verify that the straight cursor appears on the left side of the Orders table.

Insert Grid prompts you to specify the number of columns and rows for the grid.

3 In Number of columns, type 2 and in Number of rows, type 1, then choose OK. A grid using two columns and one row appears in the layout editor.

4 Move the Orders table to the first grid cell. To do this, select the Table tab in the bottom left corner of the table, then drag the table and drop it in the grid cell.

5 Move the Payments table to the second grid cell. The report layout should look like the one shown in Figure 16-34.

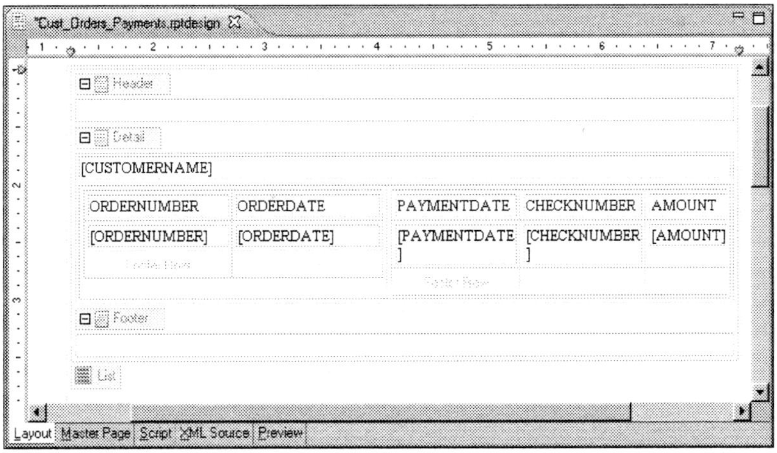

Figure 16-34　Side-by-side subreports in the report design

6 Preview the report. The report should look like the one shown in Figure 16-35.

Cust_Orders_Payments.rptdesign ☒

Show Report Parameters

AV Stores, Co				
ORDERNUMBER	ORDERDATE	PAYMENTDATE	CHECKNUMBER	AMOUNT
10110	Mar 18, 2003	Mar 27, 2003	KL124726	48425.69
10306	Oct 14, 2004	Nov 3, 2004	AM968797	52825.29
10332	Nov 17, 2004	Dec 8, 2004	BQ39062	47159.11
Alpha Cognac				
ORDERNUMBER	ORDERDATE	PAYMENTDATE	CHECKNUMBER	AMOUNT
10136	Jul 4, 2003	Jul 21, 2003	KI744716	14232.7
10178	Nov 8, 2003	Nov 22, 2003	AF40894	33818.34
10397	Mar 28, 2005	Jun 3, 2005	HR224331	12432.32

Layout | Master Page | Script | XML Source | Preview

Figure 16-35   Report preview showing side-by-side subreports

Task 13: View the outline of the report

This report contains several levels of nested elements. At the top-most level is the list element. Within the list is a grid, which contains two tables. Within each table are data elements. The layout editor shows the borders of container elements and data elements, but for a container using several levels of nested elements, it can be difficult to see and select individual elements.

To get a clear view of the hierarchy of elements, use the Outline view. Figure 16-36 shows the outline of the report. Select Body, then expand each item to view all the elements in the report.

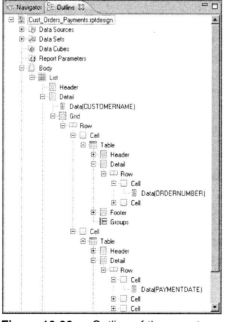

Figure 16-36   Outline of the report

If you have difficulty selecting an element in the layout editor, select the element in the Outline view. When you select an element in Outline, the element is selected in the layout editor.

Task 14: Format the report

Now that the report displays the correct data and layout, you can turn your attention to improving the report's appearance. You perform the following tasks in this section:

- Highlight the customer names.

- Edit the column headings.

- Change the date formats.

- Change the number formats.

- Increase the vertical space between elements.

- Increase the horizontal space between the Orders and Payments tables.

- Add borders around the tables.

- Increase the space between the table borders and contents.

Highlight the customer names

1 Choose Layout to return to the layout editor.

2 In the layout editor, select the [CUSTOMERNAME] data element.

3 Choose the Properties tab of Property Editor.

4 Select General from the list under Properties. Property Editor displays the general formatting properties of the data element.

5 For Size, choose Large to display the element's text in a larger size.

B 6 Choose B to format the data as bold text.

Edit the column headings

When you insert a data set field in a table, BIRT Report Designer automatically adds a label with the data set field name in the header row. Often, data set field names are not in a form that is appropriate for reports, and need to be changed.

1 Double-click the first column heading in the Orders table. The text is highlighted.

2 Replace ORDERNUMBER with the following text, then press Enter:

```
Order Number
```

3 Repeat the previous steps to change the rest of the column headings to the following text:

```
Order Date
Payment Date
Check Number
Amount
```

The report layout should look like the one shown in Figure 16-37.

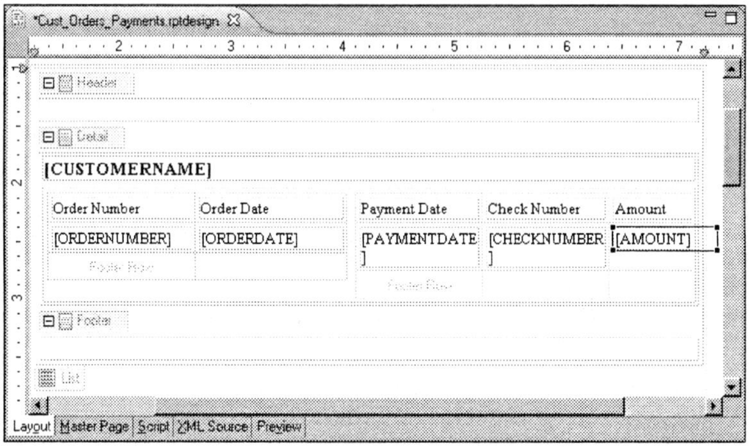

Figure 16-37   Edited column headings in the report design

4 Preview the report. The report should look like the one shown in Figure 16-38.

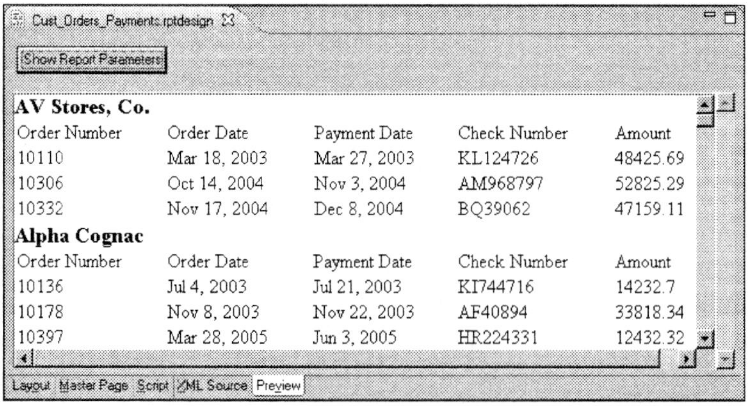

Figure 16-38   Edited column headings in the report preview

Change the date formats

When you insert a data element of date data type, BIRT Report Designer displays dates according to your system's locale setting. BIRT Report Designer provides many different date formats that you can select if you do not want to use the default format. In this procedure, you create a style that changes the format of ORDERDATE and PAYMENTDATE values from Jun 3, 2005 to 6/3/05.

1   Choose Layout to return to the layout editor.

2   Select the data element that displays [ORDERDATE].

3   Choose Element➤New Style from the main menu. New Style displays the properties you can set for a style, as shown in Figure 16-39.

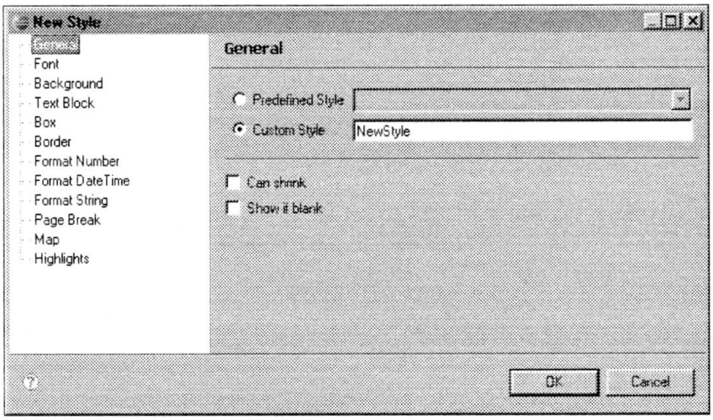

Figure 16-39   New Style

4   For Custom Style, type the following name:

    Date_data

5   Choose Format DateTime from the list of style properties on the left.

6   Choose the m/d/yy format from the drop-down list, as shown in Figure 16-40. The values in the drop-down list dynamically update with the current date.

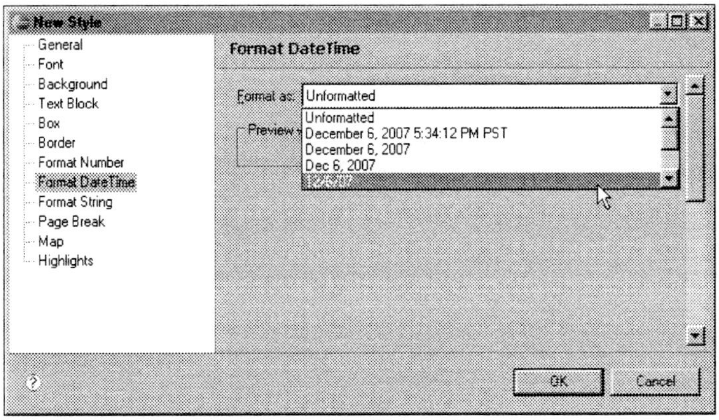

Figure 16-40   DateTime formats

7 Choose OK.

The Date_data style is applied to the [ORDERDATE] data element, as shown in Figure 16-41.

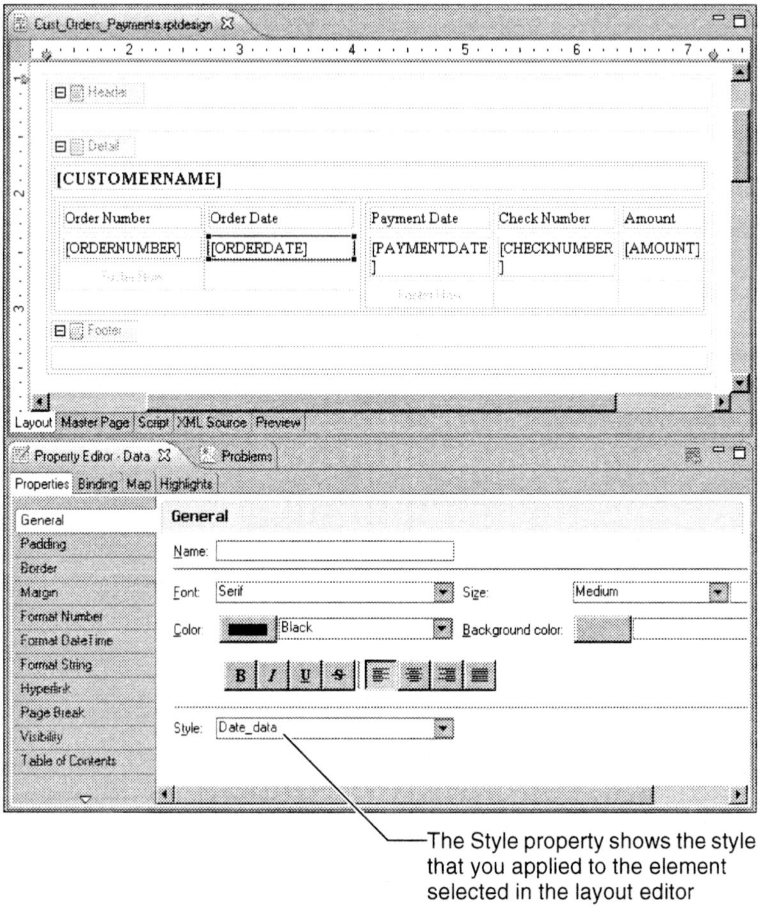

The Style property shows the style that you applied to the element selected in the layout editor

Figure 16-41 Date_data style applied to a data element

8 Apply the Date_data style to the payment date data element.

1 Select the data element that displays [PAYMENTDATE].

2 Right-click the selected element, then choose Style➤Apply Style➤ Date_data.

9 Preview the report. The dates have changed from Mar 18, 2003 format to 3/18/03 format, as shown in Figure 16-42.

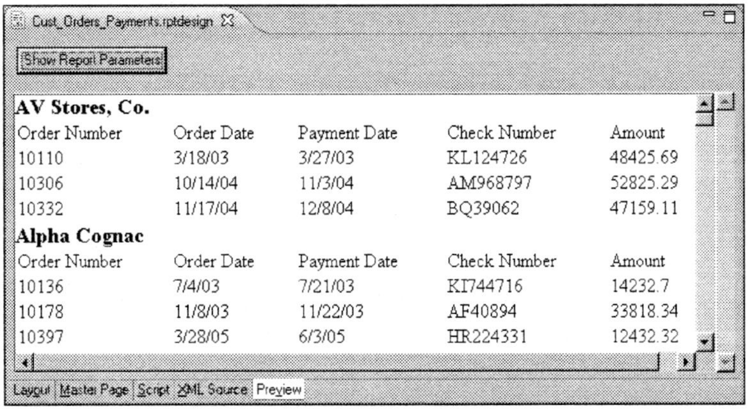

Figure 16-42 Changed date formats in the report preview

Change the number formats

When you insert a data element of integer data type, BIRT Report Designer displays numbers according to your system's locale setting. BIRT Report Designer provides many different number formats that you can select if you do not want to use the default format. In this procedure, you create a style that changes the amount values format from 48425.69 to $48,425.69.

1 Choose Layout to return to the layout editor.

2 Select the data element that displays [AMOUNT] in the Payments table.

3 Choose Element→New Style from the main menu. New Style displays properties in the general category.

4 For Custom Style, type the following name:

```
Currency_data
```

5 Choose Format Number from the list of style properties on the left.

6 Specify the following formatting attributes:

- For Format as, select Currency from the drop-down list.

- For Decimal places, use the default value of 2.

- Select Use 1000s separator.

- For Symbol, select $ from the drop-down list.

- Use the default values for the other attributes.

Figure 16-43 shows the specified currency format.

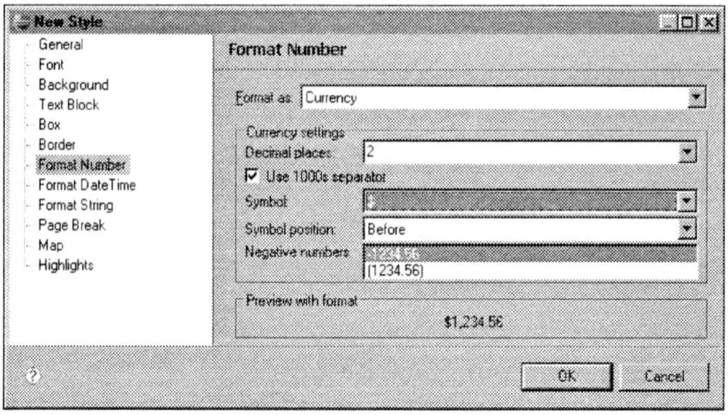

Figure 16-43   Format Number properties

7 Choose OK to save the style. The Currency_data style is applied to the [AMOUNT] data element, as indicated by the element's Style property in Property Editor.

8 Preview the report. The numbers appear in the currency format, as shown in Figure 16-44.

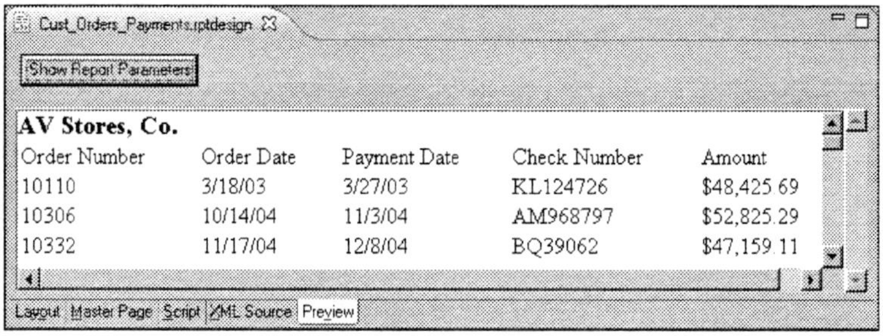

Figure 16-44   Currency format in the report preview

Increase the vertical space between elements

In this procedure, you increase the space between each customer name and the lines before and after it. To adjust the vertical space between elements, you can use any of the following techniques:

- Increase the top or bottom padding or margins of elements.

- Organize the elements in a grid and adjust the heights of the grid rows.

- Organize the elements in a grid and use empty rows with specified heights to provide space between elements.

Padding and margins property values can yield different results in different web browsers. Using a grid to format the layout is easier and provides more predictable results. In this procedure, you use the third technique.

1 Choose Layout to return to the layout editor.

2 Place the [CUSTOMERNAME] data element in the grid that contains the two tables by completing the following steps:

1 Select the grid. Hover the mouse pointer over the bottom left corner until you see the Grid tab, then choose the tab. Guide cells appear at the top and left of the selected grid.

2 Right-click the guide cell on the left of the grid's first row, then choose Insert➤Row➤Above, as shown in Figure 16-45.

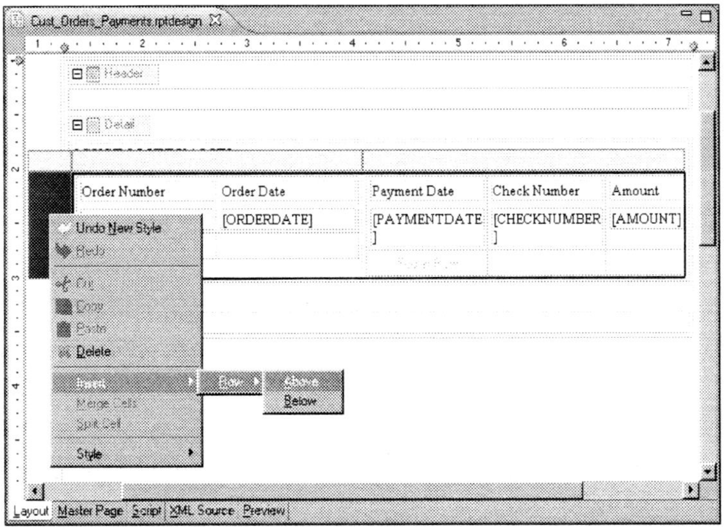

Figure 16-45   Inserting a new row

A new row appears above the selected row.

3 Move the [CUSTOMERNAME] data element from its current location to the first cell of the new grid row. Figure 16-46 shows the [CUSTOMERNAME] data element in the new location.

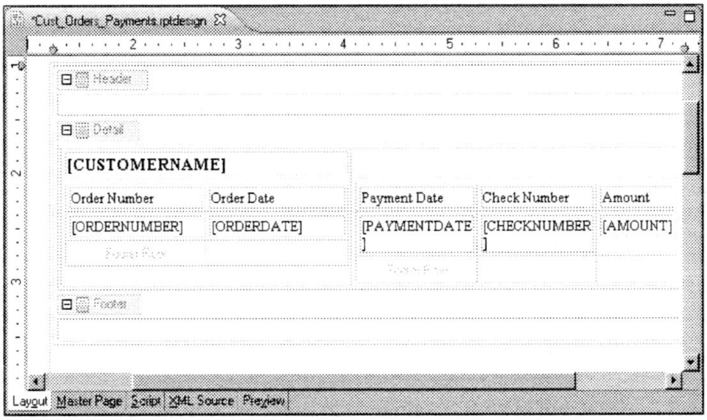

Figure 16-46   Data element moved to the new row

3 Using the procedures for adding a row that were described earlier, complete the following tasks:

- Add a new grid row above the row that contains the [CUSTOMERNAME] data element.

- Add a new grid row below the row that contains the {CUSTOMERNAME] data element.

4 Select the grid, then select the first row in the grid, as shown in Figure 16-47.

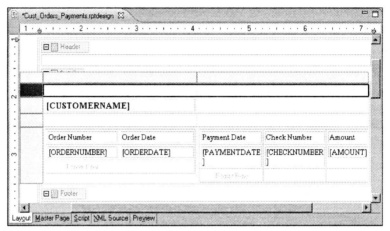

Figure 16-47 Selecting the first row

5 In General properties, set the row's height to 0.2 in, as shown in Figure 16-48.

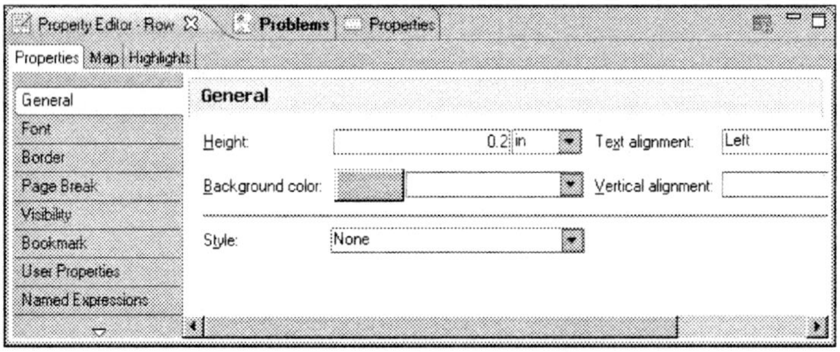

Figure 16-48 Setting the row height property

6 Select the third row in the grid, and set its height to 0.1 in. The report design should look like the one shown in Figure 16-49.

The custom row heights provide the exact amount of space you need between elements. If you prefer to work with a unit of measurement other than inches, you can select mm, points, or even pixels for very precise sizing control.

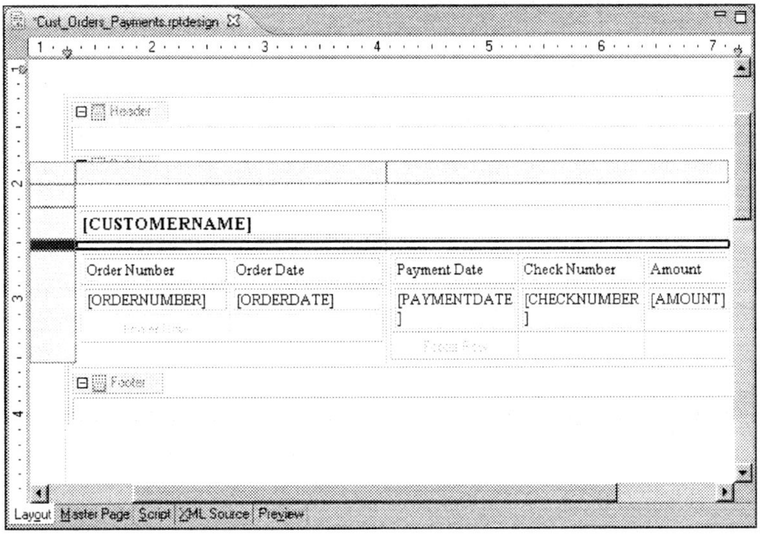

Figure 16-49 New row heights in the report design

7 Preview the report. There is more space above and below the customer name. The report should look like the one shown in Figure 16-50.

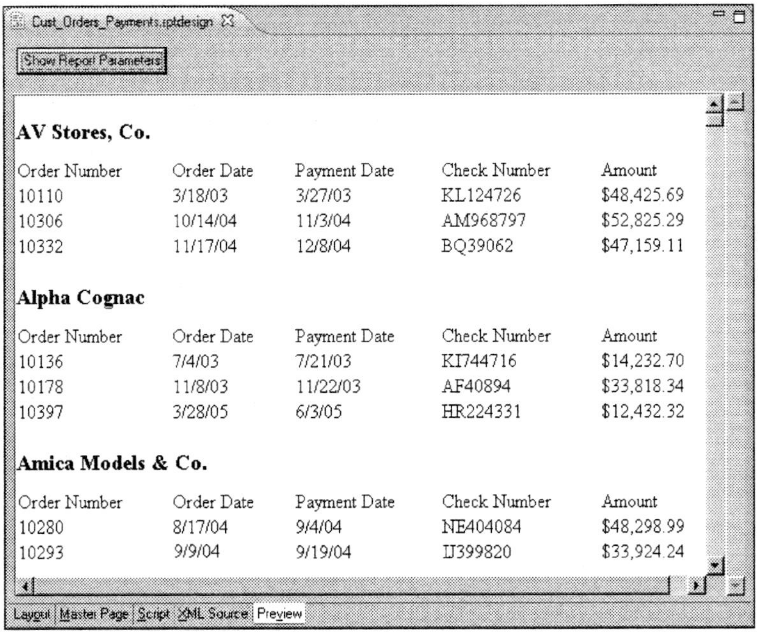

Figure 16-50 Report preview, showing added space

Increase the horizontal space between the Orders and Payments tables

In this procedure, you increase the space between the Orders and Payments tables. As with vertical spacing, you can adjust the horizontal space between elements in the following ways:

- Increase the left or right padding or margins of elements.

- Organize the elements in a grid and adjust the widths of the grid columns.

- Organize the elements in a grid and add empty columns using specified widths to provide space between elements.

Again, padding and margins property values can yield different results in different web browsers. Using a grid to format the layout is easier and provides more predictable results. In this procedure, you use the third technique.

1 Choose Layout to return to the layout editor.

2 Select the grid. Hover the mouse pointer over the bottom left corner until you see the Grid tab, then choose the tab.

Guide cells appear at the top and left of the selected grid.

3 Right-click the guide cell above the first column, then choose Insert➤Column to the Right, as shown in Figure 16-51.

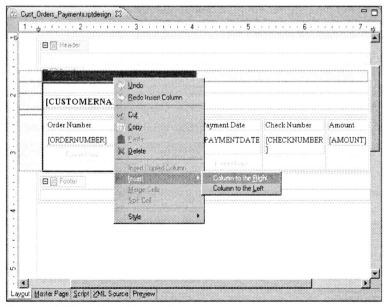

Figure 16-51   Inserting a column

A new column appears between the first and third columns.

4 Select the column that you just added, and use Property Editor to set the column width to 0.4 in, as shown in Figure 16-52.

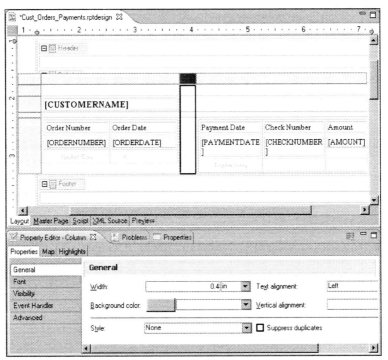

Figure 16-52 Setting a column width

The width of the second column decreases.

5 Preview the report. There is more space between the Orders and Payments tables, as shown in Figure 16-53.

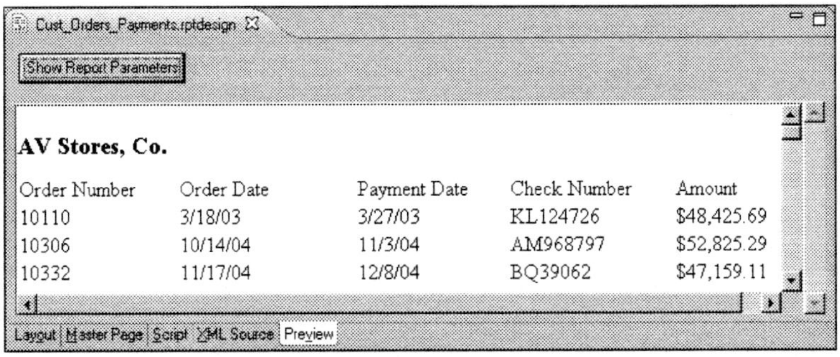

Figure 16-53 Report preview, showing added space between tables

Add borders around the tables

In this procedure, you add a box around the Orders and Payments tables to clearly identify them as two separate subreports.

1 Choose Layout to return to the layout editor.

2 Select the Orders table. Hover the mouse pointer over the bottom left corner until you see the Table tab, then choose the tab. Guide cells appear at the top and left of the selected table.

3 Choose Border in Property Editor, then set the border properties as follows:

* Set Style to a solid line, the default option.

* Set Color to black, the default color.

* Set Width to the thinnest line.

* Choose the All Borders button to add borders to all sides of the table, as shown in Figure 16-54.

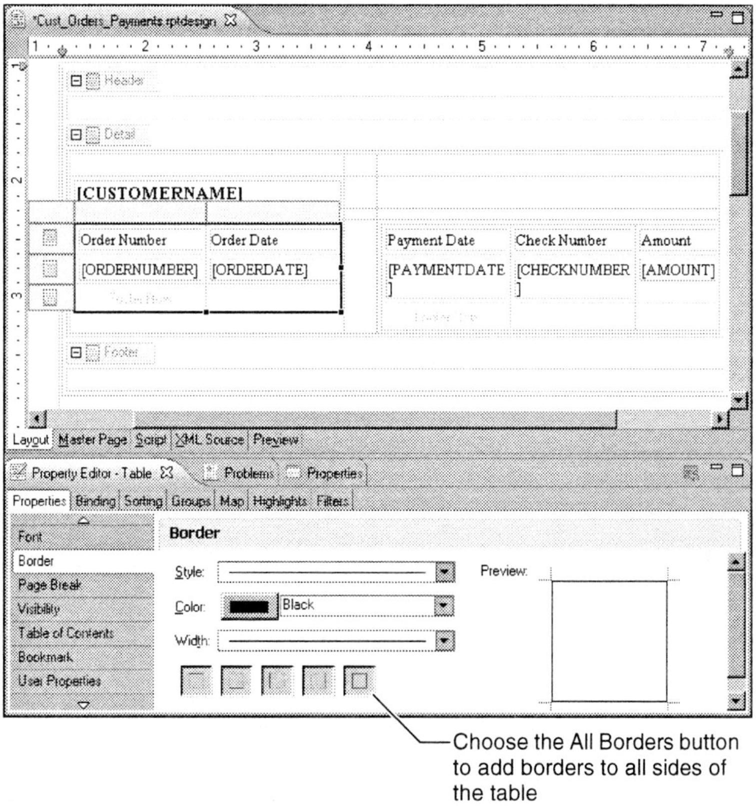

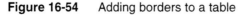

Choose the All Borders button to add borders to all sides of the table

Figure 16-54 Adding borders to a table

4 Repeat the previous steps to draw a border around the Payments table.

5 Preview the report. The report should look like the one shown in Figure 16-55.

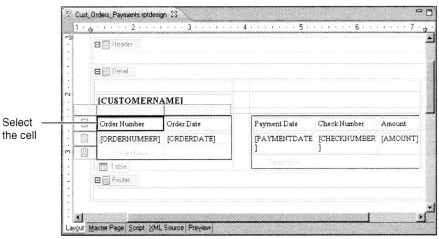

Figure 16-55 Borders around tables in report preview

Increase the space between the table borders and contents

The top and left borders of the tables are too close to the table content. In this procedure, you increase the space between the top and left borders and the content.

1 Choose Layout to return to the layout editor.

2 Select the first cell in the group header row of the Orders table. Be careful to select the cell, as shown in Figure 16-56, and not the data element in the cell.

Figure 16-56 Selecting a cell

The title bar of Property Editor shows the type of the element that you selected. Verify that it displays the following text:

```
Property Editor - Cell
```

3 Choose the Padding properties in Property Editor, then set Top and Left to 6 points. Use the default values for Bottom and Right. Figure 16-57 shows these property settings.

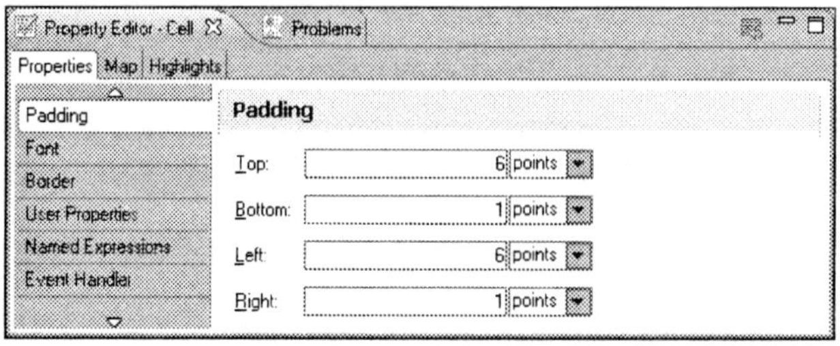

Figure 16-57   Cell padding properties in Property Editor

In the layout editor, extra space appears at the top and left of the cell, as shown in Figure 16-58.

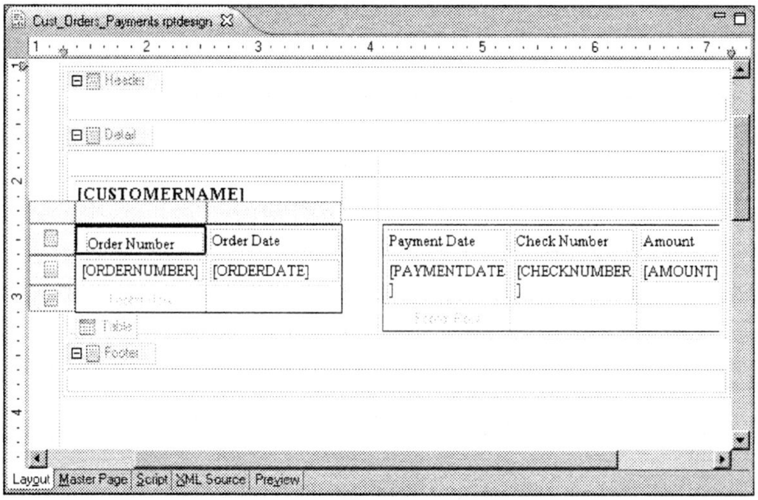

Figure 16-58   Cell padding in the report design

4 In the Orders table, select the other cells that contain elements, and set the Top and Left padding properties to 6 points.

5 Similarly, in the Payments table, select all the cells that contain elements, and set the Top and Left padding properties to 6 points.

6 Preview the report. The report should look like the one shown in Figure 16-59.

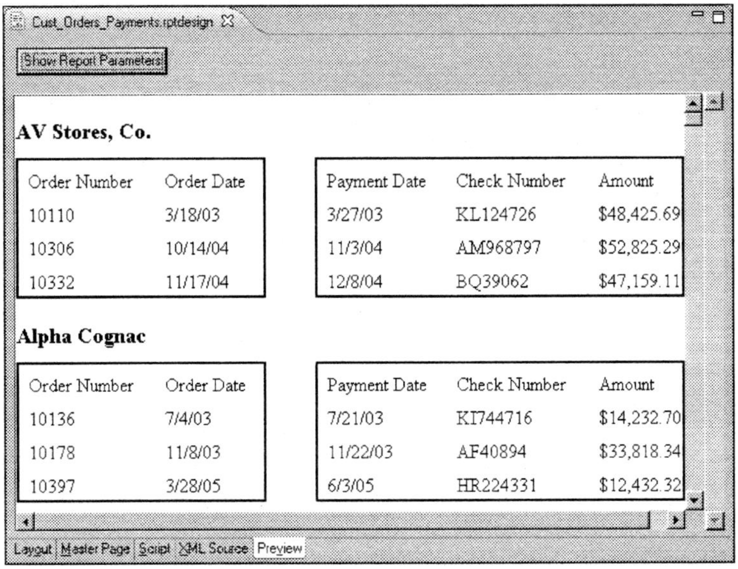

Figure 16-59 Report preview shows more space within the tables

Using a Chart

A chart is a graphical representation of data or the relationships among sets of data. Charts display complex data in an easy-to-assimilate format. You can use a chart as a report in itself or combine a chart with other report elements to enhance or highlight related information. The BIRT Report Designer chart builder facilitates selecting a chart type, organizing the data into visual elements, and formatting the elements. Visual elements can include bars in a bar chart, points and trend lines in a line chart, and dials in a meter chart to name a few.

The guidelines for planning a chart and a report are similar. To create an effective chart, you must decide what data to display, then you select the chart type that best presents that data. For example, to show the growth of a company's business units over time, you use a chart that tracks data along an axis, such as a line chart or a bar chart. To show scientific X-Y data, you use a scatter chart.

This chapter discusses the types of charts available in the BIRT Report Designer, provides a tutorial in which you use the BIRT sample database, Classic Models, and includes a tour of the design interface. As you complete the tutorial, you learn about the essential chart-building tasks.

Surveying the types of charts

BIRT supports a number of different types of charts. Some chart types, such as bar and line charts, use axes to arrange data. You learn more about how axes work in charts in the next chapter.

The following sections describe the main chart types.

About area charts

An area chart displays data values as a set of points that are connected by lines. If you include several series on an area chart, the chart displays filled areas that overlap. The area chart in Figure 17-1 shows the percentage of orders and the corresponding unit volume for trains, ships, and planes over three months.

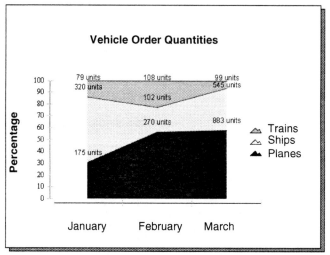

Figure 17-1   Area chart

The area chart emphasizes change along the category axis. A stacked or percent stacked area chart also shows the relationship of parts to a whole. In Figure 17-1, a percent stacked area chart shows how percentages of order quantities of different vehicles relate to each other over time.

About bar charts

A bar chart typically displays data values as a set of vertical columns, but you can flip the axis to display horizontal bars, as shown in Figure 17-2.

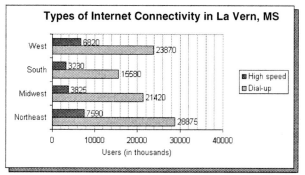

Figure 17-2   Bar chart

When you flip the axes to create vertical instead of horizontal columns, the layout of the information changes such that the eye can easily compare the value differences between two types of internet connectivity.

A bar chart is useful to show data changes over a period of time or to illustrate comparisons among items. Like an area chart, stacked and percent stacked bar charts can also show the relationship of individual items to a whole.

About tube, cone, and pyramid charts

Tube, cone, and pyramid charts are variations of the bar chart that use tubular, conical, and pyramid-shaped risers instead of bars. You can specify different types of risers within the same chart to distinguish types of data, as shown in Figure 17-3. The bar riser represents unit volume and the pyramid riser represents dollar volume.

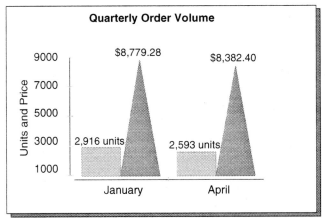

Figure 17-3   Bar-pyramid chart

Use a bar, tube, cone, or pyramid chart when you want to display data values as a set of vertical or horizontal columns. Use a combination of risers to differentiate information.

About line charts

A line chart displays data as a sequence of points, connected by a line. For example, the line chart in Figure 17-4 shows sales values for chips and boards over time. Figure 17-4 also shows trends in data over four quarters.

In addition to the main chart types, you can choose a number of subtypes. The area, bar, cone, line, pyramid, and tube are main chart types that have a stacked subtype and a percent stacked subtype. After selecting one of the main chart types, you can choose its stacked subtype to position positive or negative values above or below the origin of the chart. Alternatively, you can choose its percent stacked subtype to show the contribution of individual items to the whole.

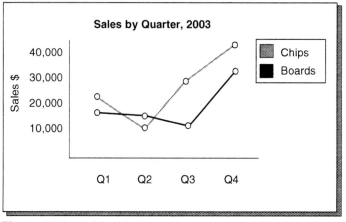

Figure 17-4   Line chart

About meter charts

A meter chart uses a needle to point to values on a circular or semicircular dial. You use a meter chart to create a gauge or dashboard display. You can emphasize settings on the dial by dividing the meter background into sections called dial regions. You can adjust the dial settings the same way you adjust an axis, giving you many options for arranging and emphasizing the dial data. Figure 17-5 shows a meter chart that contrasts the speed of two products.

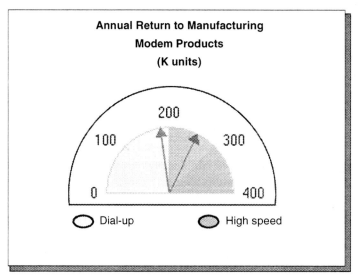

Figure 17-5   Meter chart

A meter chart is best used to show a small number of values in a prominent way.

About pie charts

You use a pie chart to show the relationships of parts to the whole. For example, the chart in Figure 17-6 shows revenue for different product lines. Each sector shows revenue for an item as a percentage of the total revenue. In this example, DSP is the smallest sector, accounting for only eight percent of total revenue.

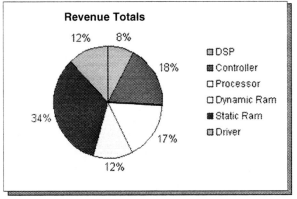

Figure 17-6   Pie chart

Like the line chart, a pie chart shows the relationship of parts to a whole.

About scatter charts

A scatter chart shows data as points. Scatter charts display values on both axes. For example, the chart in Figure 17-7 compares two sets of numerical data for certain sports cars: the top speed and the price. You can see from the chart how performance increases in relation to price.

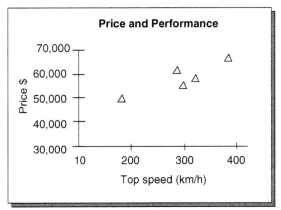

Figure 17-7   Scatter chart

A scatter chart shows the relationships among the numeric values of multiple data series. Scatter charts typically display scientific data.

About bubble charts

A bubble chart resembles a scatter chart, but it uses bubbles instead of data points. You choose a bubble chart instead of a scatter chart if you have three values per data point. For example, the bubble chart in Figure 17-8 plots the retail against the wholesale prices of products, calculates the discount, and uses the size of the bubbles to show the amount of the discount. The color-coding of the bubble identifies the product type.

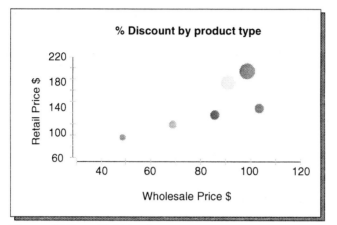

Figure 17-8   Bubble chart

Bubble charts typically describe financial data. Use a bubble chart when you want to express data using more than two values.

About stock charts

A stock chart shows data as points on a time continuum, such as days of the week. Figure 17-9 shows a sample stock chart.

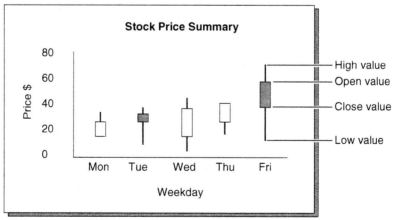

Figure 17-9   Stock chart

Stock values appear as a candlestick, a box with lines extending up and down from the ends. Open and close values mark the upper and lower edges of the box. High and low values mark the upper and lower points of the line. The default appearance of the bar depends on the chart values. If the open value is higher than the close value, the box is shaded. If the close value is higher than the open value, the box is white. You can change the color of the shaded boxes.

Although a stock chart typically displays stock price data, you can also use a stock chart to show scientific data, such as temperature changes over time.

About difference charts

A difference chart typically shows variation between two sets of data by shading the areas between points of comparison. You can format the series of values to display positive areas in one color and negative areas in another, as shown in Figure 17-10. The dark-shaded spike in the chart represents an unusual delay beyond the request date for shipment of order 10165. The light-shaded areas represent shipments made earlier than requested.

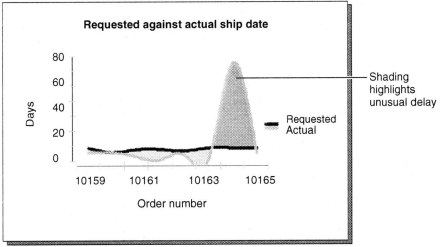

Figure 17-10   Difference chart

Use a difference chart when you want to use shading and multiple graphs to accentuate the deviation between data variables.

About Gantt charts

A Gantt chart graphically presents project scheduling information by displaying the duration of tasks. One axis contains the time series, and the other shows progress by task. Figure 17-11 uses color-coded bars to show the status of tasks in various stages. The bars use the palette of each series, Stage 1 and Stage 2, as the line color.

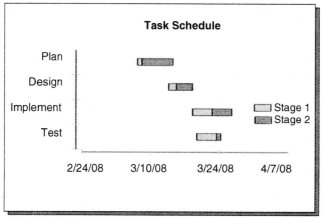

Figure 17-11   Gantt chart

Gantt charts use symbols and colors on bars to mark beginning and ending dates and status, respectively.

Tutorial 5: Creating a standalone chart

This tutorial covers the following topics:

- Using the chart builder. You use the chart builder to create or modify a chart. The chart builder organizes tasks, so you can easily find the settings that you need and preview your progress as you build a chart. The tutorial explores the chart builder and its most common settings.

- Providing data for a chart. In addition to stand-alone charts like the pie chart that you create in this tutorial, you can use charts with other report elements, such as lists or tables. The position of a chart in a report with other elements can affect the data that the chart displays. You can set up a data set and apply filters from within the chart builder.

- Selecting a chart type. You review the types and subtypes, so you know the different presentation possibilities for displaying your data.

- Setting chart output formats. By default, the chart builder creates a chart in Scalable Vector Graphics (SVG) format. You can also create a chart in a static image file format, such as BMP or PNG.

- Plotting chart data. The various types of charts use data differently. You can drag and drop columns from the Chart Preview to areas of the Select Data page to define how to plot the data.

- Formatting a chart. In the tutorial, you format some parts of a pie chart, such as leader lines and data labels, using settings such as text style, position, and visibility. Other chart types offer different formatting options. You can manipulate the scale or placement of data on an axis or in a pie or meter to show information effectively.

The tutorial provides step-by-step instructions for building a report that displays order totals organized by product line. The report presents information graphically in a pie chart. In this case, the chart is the entire report.

To create a chart, you complete the following tasks:

- Set up the report design file and data. You create a new report, data source, and data set.

- Add the chart element to the report design. You insert a chart element into a report and select a chart type.

- Provide data for the chart. You link the chart to a data set and build the expressions that the chart uses.

- Change the chart title.

- Refine the chart appearance. You remove the chart legend and modify the labels that identify each sector.

- Preview the chart using the report previewer.

Task 1: Set up and query the data source

Before you start to design a chart, you must create a report design file for the chart, then set up the data source and data set that the chart uses. These tasks are discussed in detail in earlier sections of this book and in a tutorial in which you build a sample report. This tutorial builds on that knowledge, explaining how to select the data from the database that you use to build a sample pie chart.

1 Choose File➤New➤Report and name the new report design Chart.rptdesign. Choose Blank Report when the new report wizard displays the list of report templates.

2 Build a data source for the report design file using the sample database, Classic Models.

3 Build a data set for the chart. Use the following data set name:

    ChartData

Use the following SQL SELECT statement:

```
SELECT Products.ProductLine,
sum(OrderDetails.QuantityOrdered)
FROM OrderDetails,
Products
WHERE Products.ProductCode=OrderDetails.ProductCode
GROUP BY Products.ProductLine
ORDER BY Products.ProductLine
```

This SELECT statement gets values from the ProductLine column in the Products table, groups the results by product line, and calculates the sum of the order quantities for each group.

4 Preview the results of the query to validate it. If you created the SELECT statement correctly, you should see the data shown in Figure 17-12.

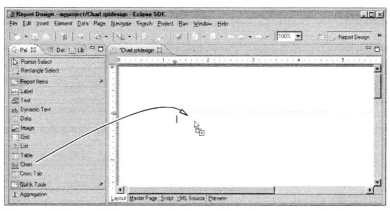

PRODUCTLINE	2
Classic Cars	35,582
Motorcycles	12,778
Planes	11,872
Ships	8,532
Trains	2,818
Trucks and Buses	11,001
Vintage Cars	22,933

Figure 17-12 Previewing the data set

The first column lists product-line names. The second column shows the total orders for each product line. By default, BIRT uses sequential numbers to name generated columns, such as the sum column named 2 in Figure 17-12.

5 To rename the sum column to something more descriptive, choose Output Columns from the list in the left pane. Use the following text for the alias for the 2 column:

```
TotalOrders
```

Use the following text for the display name for the 2 column:

```
TOTALORDERS
```

6 To close Edit Data Set and open the layout editor, choose OK.

Task 2:   Add the chart to the report

You use the palette to add a chart element, and then select a chart type. In this tutorial, you select a pie chart.

1 Choose Palette, then drag the chart element from the palette to the blank report design, as shown in Figure 17-13.

Figure 17-13   Adding a chart element to a blank report design

The chart builder, shown in Figure 17-14, appears.

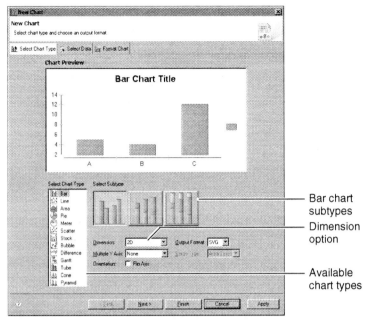

Figure 17-14   Select Chart Type

The lower part of the Select Chart Type page displays the different types of charts that you can create. Some chart types include several subtypes, giving you a wide range of available types. Choosing a chart type on Select Chart Type displays the available subtypes for that type of chart. By default, these subtypes create two-dimensional charts. Later in this chapter, you learn how to use the Dimension option, which can affect the available subtypes.

2 In the Select Chart Type list, select Pie. The chart builder shows a symbol of a pie chart in the Subtype area, as shown in Figure 17-15. Pie charts have only one subtype, regardless of the Dimension setting, so you see only one option in the Subtype area.

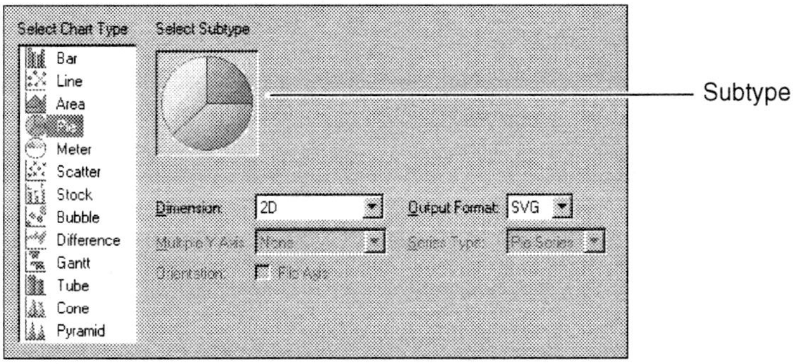

Figure 17-15   Two-dimensional subtype for a pie chart

Task 3: Provide data for a chart

In task one, you created the data source connection and data set that you need. After selecting the data set to use, you must set up the expressions that the chart uses to represent the data graphically. Each type of chart uses data differently. For a pie chart, you must select data expressions that specify

- The data values represented by sectors in the pie. In this tutorial, you use an expression that creates one sector for each product line value.

- The size of each sector. In this tutorial, the number of orders determines the size of each product-line sector.

You can use different techniques to provide a data expression in a chart. The easiest way to specify the data to use is to drag a column from Data Preview to a field. You can also type the expression or use expression builder to create an expression.

1 To navigate to the page you use to provide data, choose Next. The upper half of Select Data, shown in Figure 17-16, provides a chart preview.

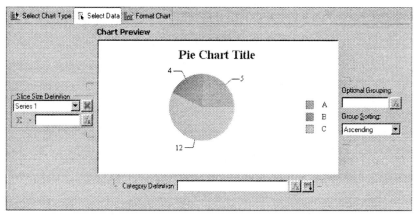

Figure 17-16   Previewing the chart in the upper section of Select Data

Chart Preview displays a rough sketch of the chart for design purposes. For example, if you change the color of the pie chart sectors or replace the default title text with a new title, Chart Preview reflects your changes.

The final published version looks more elaborate and complete, particularly if you choose to use live data for previews. In Chart Preview, the chart builder uses either live data from your data set or randomly generated sample data, depending on how you have set the Enable Live Preview preference.

2 In the lower half of the Select Data page, choose Use Data Set, as shown in Figure 17-17.

This report file includes only one data set. Select ChartData from the drop-down list.

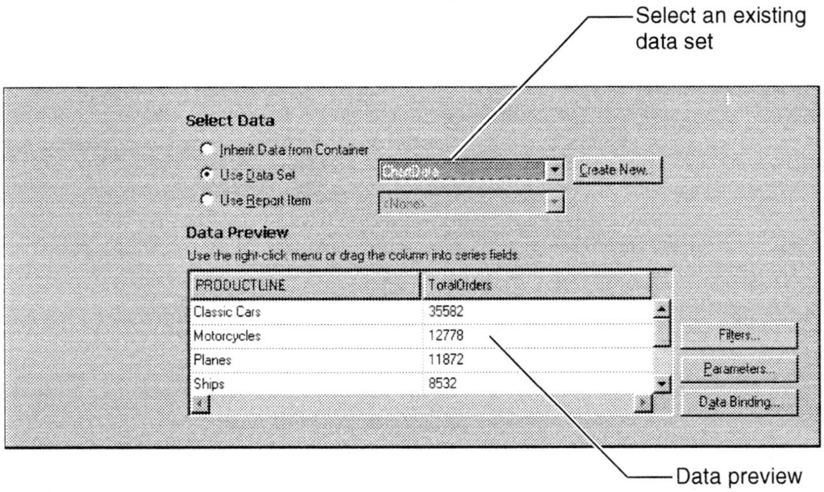

Select an existing data set

Data preview

Figure 17-17   Selecting a data set in the lower section of Select Data

In the lower half of the chart builder, Data Preview displays some of the data from the data set that you are using. You can see the product line and total orders columns. By default, Data Preview shows six data rows.

3 First, to determine which sectors the pie chart displays, you provide a category definition. In Data Preview, select the PRODUCTLINE column heading, and drag it to the empty field to the right of Category Definition, as shown in Figure 17-18.

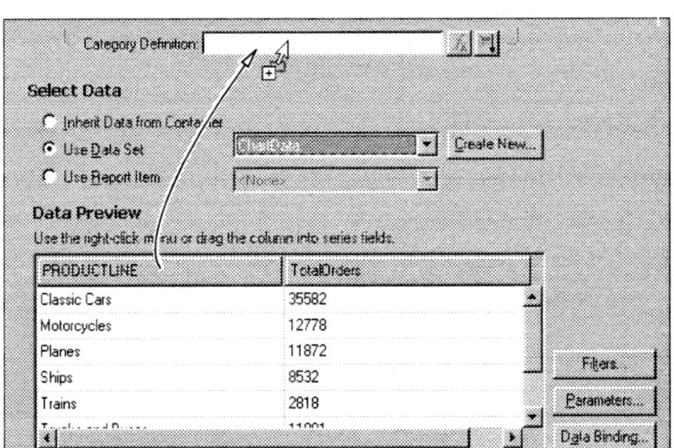

Figure 17-18   Supplying a category series expression

The following expression appears in Category Definition:

```
row["PRODUCTLINE"]
```

4 To set the size of each sector, select the TotalOrders column header, and drag it to the empty field in Slice Size Definition, as shown in Figure 17-19.

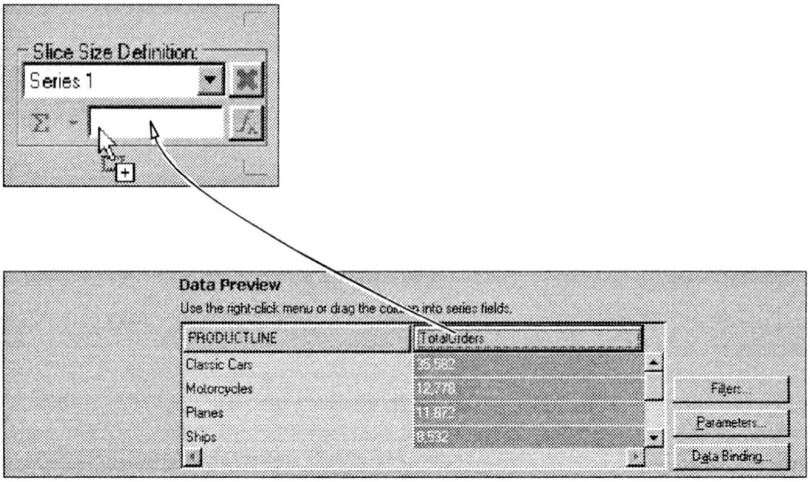

Figure 17-19   Supplying a value series expression

The following expression appears in Slice Size Definition:

```
row["TOTALORDERS"]
```

In Data Preview, the total orders column now appears colored to indicate that the column is used in the chart. The image in Chart Preview also changes to use the data you specified. The product lines have become the chart categories. Each sector represents one product line. The size of each sector represents the total orders for that product-line category.

Task 4: Enlarge the report design and preview the report

In earlier sections of this book, you enlarged the size of the report layout to accommodate your report elements. You usually need to perform this task after you create a report that contains a chart. The size of the default pie chart cannot accommodate all the Classic Model data, so you grab the middle handle and stretch the report in the Layout editor.

In earlier sections of this book, you also used the previewer in the report editor to preview how reports will look when you publish them. The Chart Preview in chart builder serves only as a guide for designing the chart and is not intended to show you exactly how your chart will look as a published report. You need to look at a preview in the report editor to ensure that the size of the report layout accommodates the chart you designed.

1 To close the chart builder, choose Finish. The chart element appears in the layout editor, shown in Figure 17-20.

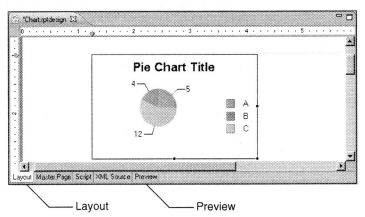

Layout　　　Preview

Figure 17-20　Chart element displayed in the layout editor

2 Choose Preview to preview the report in the report editor. The chart appears small, relative to the report page. Also in this case, the layout is too small to accommodate all the data, which includes Vintage Cars. The preview truncates the data and you cannot see Vintage Cars.

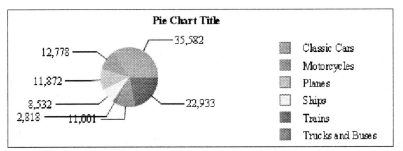

Figure 17-21　Preview of cramped chart before enlargement

3 To make the chart bigger so that all the data is visible and not so cramped, choose Layout, and enlarge the chart element to approximately 5 inches wide and 3 inches tall. To enlarge the chart, select it, then drag the handles that appear in the borders of the chart element, as shown in Figure 17-22.

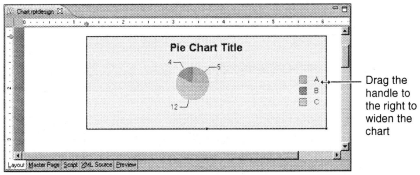

Drag the handle to the right to widen the chart

Figure 17-22　Enlarging a chart element

4 Choose Preview to show the chart in the previewer again. The chart looks like the one shown in Figure 17-23. Compare the preview in Figure 17-23 with the preview in Figure 17-21, where Vintage Cars data is not visible.

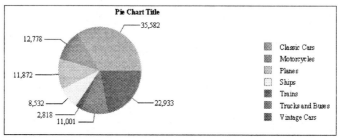

Figure 17-23   Preview of chart after enlargement

The chart now uses the correct data, but the layout is not very attractive. You need to format the chart to make it visually appealing and to emphasize the points that you want. The remaining procedures in this tutorial help you to modify the chart. Some of the changes that you make include creating a new title, adjusting the data labels, and removing the legend.

Task 5: Change the chart title

Currently, the chart displays a default title. You provide new text for the title.

1 Choose Layout to return to the layout editor, then double-click the chart design to open the chart builder.

2 Choose Format Chart. Figure 17-24 shows the Format Chart page of the chart builder. Choose Title from the list at the left.

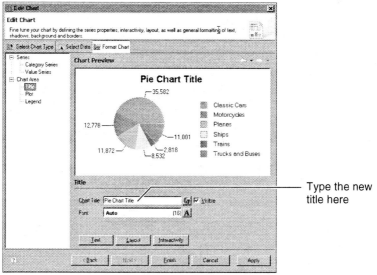

Type the new title here

Figure 17-24   Adding a title in the chart area section

3 In Chart Title, type

> Orders by Product Line

Choose Finish.

Task 6: Refine the chart appearance

The chart includes labels that identify the data value being presented in each sector. A legend identifies which product line each sector represents. Though the legend includes useful information, it also takes up space and reduces the size of the pie, so you may have to make a trade-off. One possibility is to remove the legend and use sector labels to display the product line information. Using the sector labels instead of a legend is a better choice when report users cannot easily distinguish colors. Each data label displays category information (the sector name) and value information (the total number of orders for the sector). For example, the following label identifies the motorcycles sector:

> Motorcycles: 12,778

1 To navigate to the legend section of the chart builder, choose Legend from the navigation list at the left.

2 Deselect Visible, as shown in Figure 17-25.

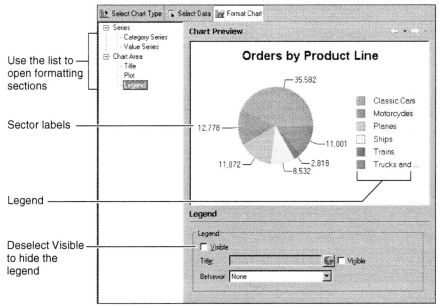

Figure 17-25   Legend section of Format Chart

3 Now you can add the legend information to the sector labels. Navigate to the value series formatting section, then choose Labels.

Figure 17-26 shows Series Labels.

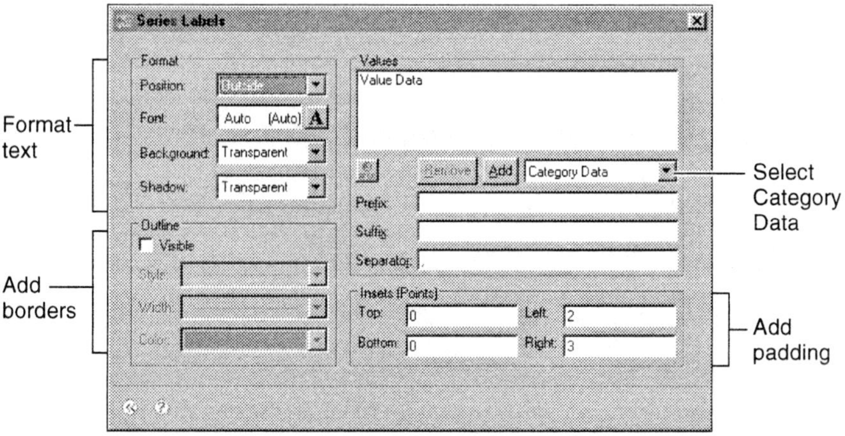

Figure 17-26   Series Labels formatting options

4 To add the section name to the label, ensure that Category Data appears in the drop-down list in the Values area, then choose Add. Category Data appears below Value Data in the list, as shown in Figure 17-27.

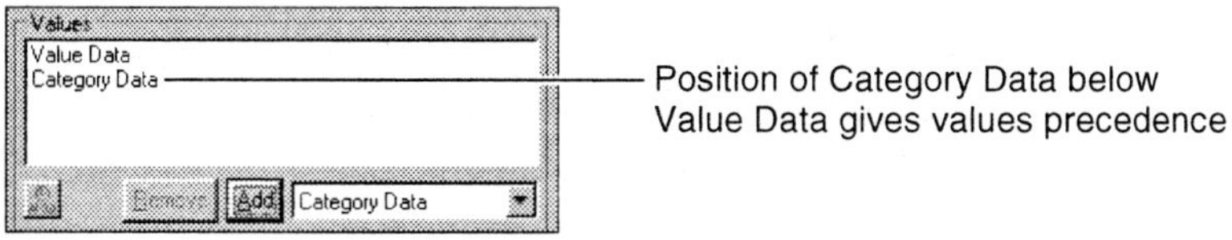

Position of Category Data below Value Data gives values precedence

Figure 17-27   Adding category data to a label

You need to rearrange the label data, so the Category Data, which are the product line names, appear before the values in the chart labels. For example, you want the label to read Classic Cars, 35,582 instead of 35,582, Classic Cars.

5 Select Value Data, and choose Remove, then, in the drop-down list, select Value Data again, and choose Add. Value Data now appears below Category Data in the list, as shown in Figure 17-28.

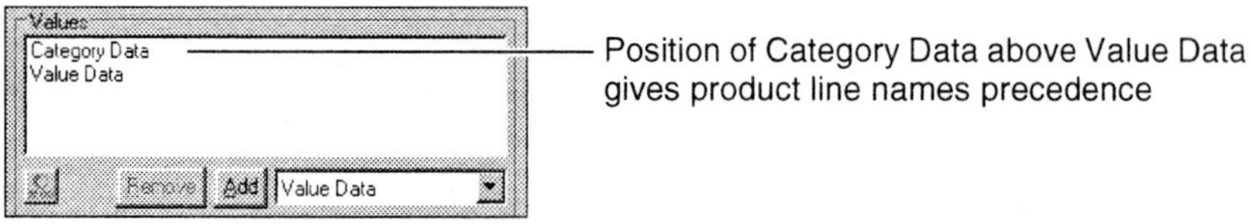

Position of Category Data above Value Data gives product line names precedence

Figure 17-28   Category data precedes value data

Now the labels display information in the correct order, but you still need to change the label appearance. When you use more than one kind of information in a label, you can use a separator between the different sections. The default separator is a comma.

6 To change the separator, in Separator, type a colon (:) then a space, as shown in Figure 17-29.

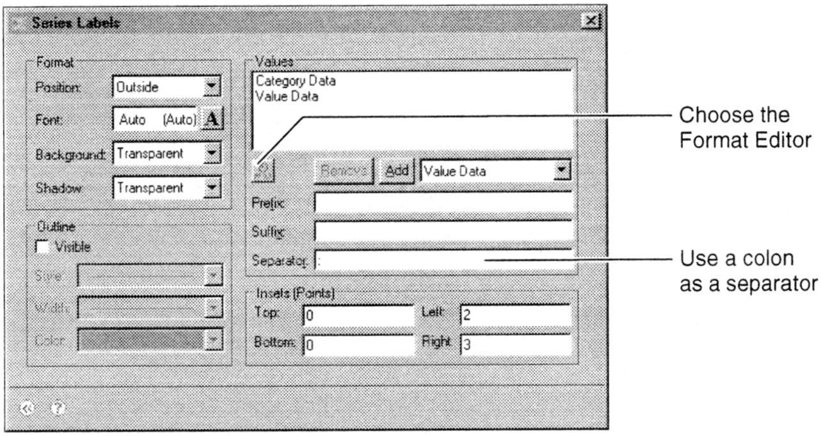

Choose the Format Editor

Use a colon as a separator

Figure 17-29   Adding a label separator

To change the number format of the value part of the label, select Value Data in the list, then choose the Format Editor. In Edit Format, you can change the format of date-and-time or numerical data.

7 Select Standard, then change the value in Fraction Digits to 0, as shown in Figure 17-30.

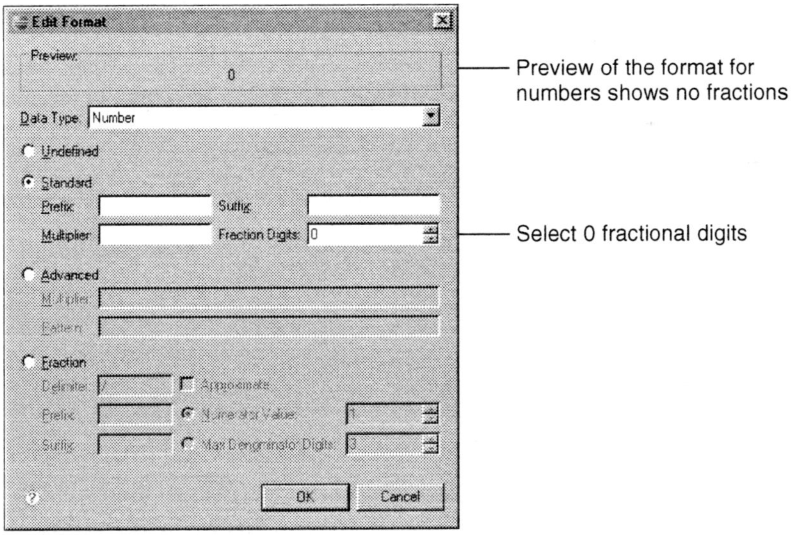

Preview of the format for numbers shows no fractions

Select 0 fractional digits

Figure 17-30   Edit Format

Choose OK to close Edit Format.

A **8** To change the formatting attributes of the label text, choose Font Editor, as shown in Figure 17-31.

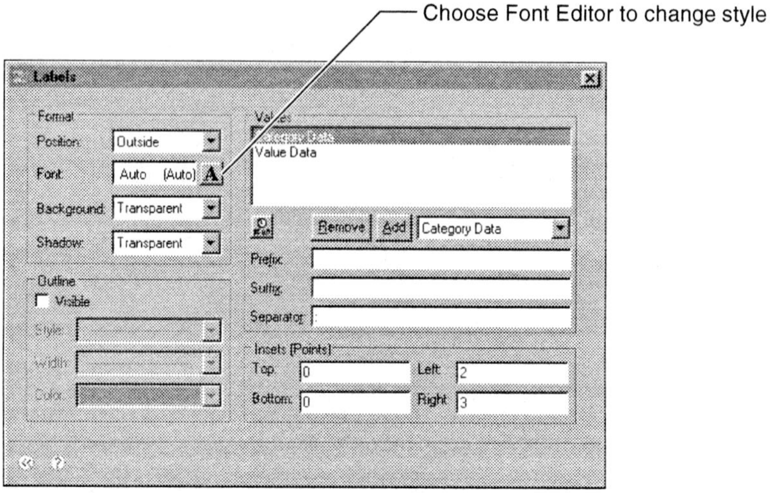

Figure 17-31 Opening Font Editor from Labels

Edit Font appears.

1 Change the font to Tahoma and the size to 11, as shown in Figure 17-32.

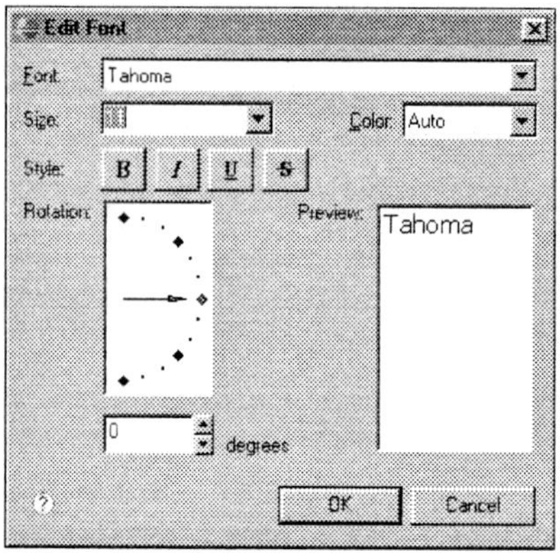

Figure 17-32 Edit Font

2 Choose OK, and close Series Labels.

9 Now you set a consistent length for the leader lines that connect the labels to the sectors. Figure 17-33 shows where to find the leader line settings.

1 In Leader Line Style, accept the default, Fixed Length. Change Leader Line Length to 20.

2 Explode the sectors, so there is space between them. In Slice, set By Distance to 3.

To make the chart more useful to the report users, you can add interactive features, such as hyperlinks and highlighting, as described in later sections of this book. You can add interactive features to the chart area, legend, marker lines, and to other parts of the chart.

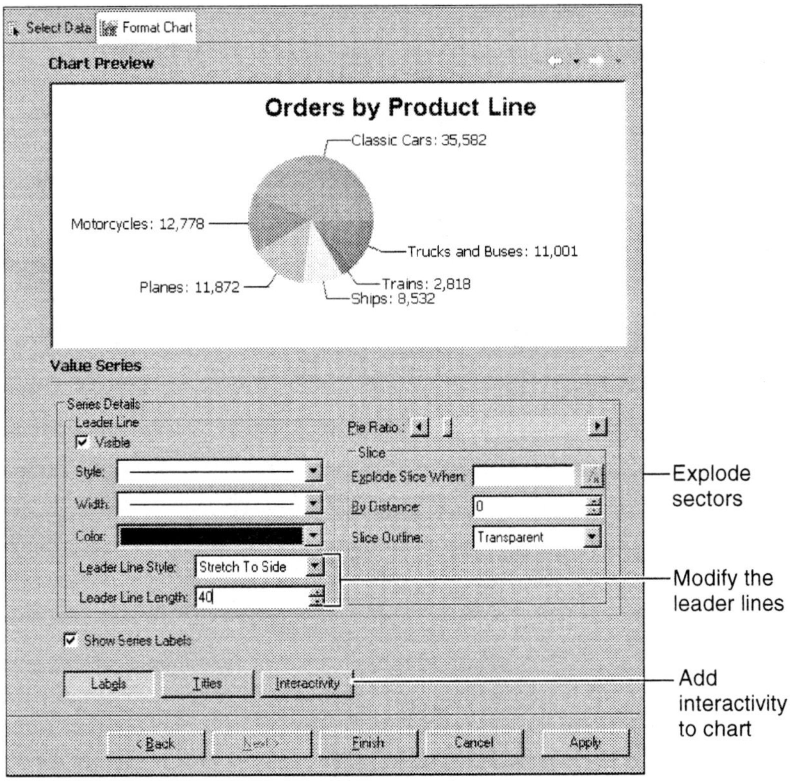

Figure 17-33   Editing leader lines and exploding sectors

You have finished creating and formatting the chart.

10 To close the chart builder and see the chart element in the layout editor, choose Finish. Then, for the last time, choose Preview to preview the chart.

The chart looks like the one shown in Figure 17-34.

The completed chart shows the category names for each sector as well as the sector values. The size and organization of the chart make quick analysis possible, while still providing detailed data.

For example, the user can immediately see that the largest pie sector is Classic Cars, which has 35,582 orders, followed by Vintage Cars, which has 22,933. The two car sectors are larger than all other sectors combined. Other product-line groups, such as Trains, do not contribute significant numbers of orders.

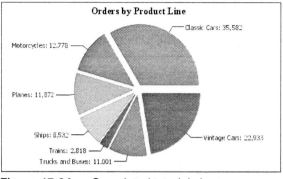

Figure 17-34   Completed tutorial chart

Exploring the chart builder

The tutorial that you just completed introduced the chart builder. As you saw in the tutorial, the chart builder has the following main pages:

- Select Chart Type

    In this page, you determine the type of chart and basic structural attributes such as orientation and the dimension of the chart.

- Select Data

    In this page, you specify the data that the chart displays.

- Format Chart

    In this page, you modify the appearance of the data that the chart displays, such as the range of values an axis displays, or the visual elements of the chart, such as the color of the lines in a line chart.

You access these pages by choosing the buttons at the top. You then complete the mandatory tasks, as well as some tasks that are optional, such as formatting the labels. This section describes the chart builder pages.

The most common task that you complete on Select Chart Type is selecting a chart type and subtype, as you did in the tutorial. You can also use Select Chart Type to modify the subtype you choose. You can show some charts in two dimensions, two dimensions with depth, or three dimensions, and you can flip the axes of some charts to a horizontal position. Select Chart Type is also where you can determine the output format of the chart. Figure 17-35 shows the options that appear on Select Chart Type.

Creating a chart with depth or three-dimensions

All chart types offer two-dimensional subtypes in which the chart shape appears flat against the chart background. Some BIRT charts have subtypes with depth, which use the appearance of depth to enhance a chart. Finally, some charts have three-dimensional subtypes, which arrange series elements along a third axis in addition to the typical x- and y-axes.

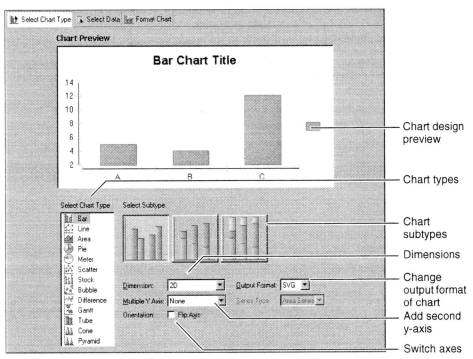

Figure 17-35 Select chart type and subtype

Figure 17-36 shows the difference between a bar chart with depth and a three-dimensional bar chart. In the first chart, the bars have the appearance of three-dimensional objects, but they are arranged on the x- and y-axes only. Three-dimensional charts show how an object on the z-axis changes according to the two other axes. For example, a three-dimensional map can reveal altitude changes on z according to longitude and attitude on x and y. The second chart in Figure 17-36 uses the z-axis as well as the x- and y-axis, plotting a Z data point value for each X-Y data point pair.

A chart with depth plots data on two axes, x and y

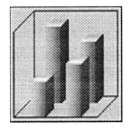

A three-dimensional chart uses an x-, a y-, and a z-axis

Figure 17-36 Depth and three-dimensional bar charts

These charts show each value as a separate bar. The following 2D with Depth subtypes present data by stacking the elements of an area, bar, or line chart to show series data as it contributes to a category total:

- A stacked chart arranges the data points from one series on top of the data points of another series.

- A percent stacked chart is similar to a stacked chart, except the total of the data points in a category fills the entire plot area for a category. The value of each data point is a percentage of the total of all data points for that category.

Figure 17-37 shows examples of a stacked bar chart series and a percent stacked bar chart series.

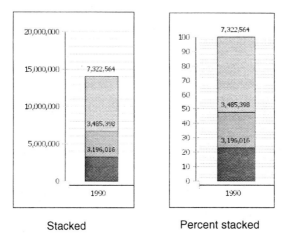

      Stacked   Percent stacked

Figure 17-37   Stacked and percent stacked bar charts

Understanding chart output formats

There are four output formats available: BMP, JPEG, PNG, and SVG. By default, the chart builder creates a chart in SVG format. SVG is a language that is used to describe two-dimensional graphics and graphical applications in XML. SVG enables report developers to include more accessible, searchable, and interactive images in their reports. For example, the legend interactive features that BIRT charts include use the SVG format to enable highlighting and hiding series data.

SVG files are typically smaller than image files in other formats and produce high-resolution images. You can also produce a chart in other image formats, such as PNG or BMP. For example, if your chart uses a photograph as a background image, you will likely want to use JPEG or PNG format, because those formats display photographic images particularly well. Some web browsers, for example, Mozilla, are in the process of adding support for SVG images. Internet Explorer requires a plug-in to support SVG. You must use the SVG format if you want your chart to be interactive.

The following procedure explains how to change the chart output format.

How to change the chart output format

1   On the chart builder, choose Select Chart Type. Select Chart Type appears as shown in Figure 17-38.

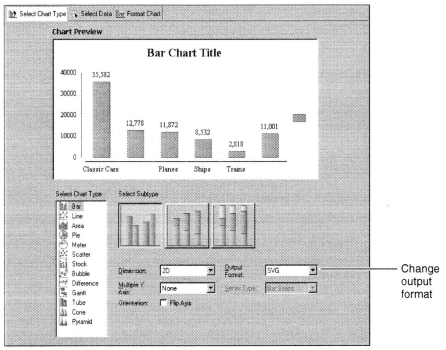

Figure 17-38   Output format option on Select Chart Type

2   In Output Format, select an option, such as PNG or BMP.

Choose Finish.

Now you have created a sample chart and become familiar with the different types of charts and the output formats a chart can use. Subsequent chapters describe in detail how to use and format data in a chart.

Using a chart as part of a report

There are two ways to use the charting capabilities in BIRT. You can include a chart in a report with other elements, such as tables, lists, and images, or you can create a report like the one in the tutorial that consists entirely of a chart. You can specify a chart data set that is different from the data set that you use for the rest of the report. For example, a chart that you place in a customer list could show the total sales for each customer. The customer list might use one set of data, such as customer names and addresses, whereas the chart uses a data set that returns the sales totals.

A chart that you place in a table typically uses the same data set as the table. In a table that groups data, you would usually want the chart to use the same grouping setup as the table. You usually place a chart element in the following places:

- A table header or footer. The chart displays data for the entire data set.

- A group header or footer. Each group section includes a chart, and each chart displays data for its group section.

- A detail row. Each detail row in the completed report includes a chart, and each chart displays data for its detail row.

For example, Figure 17-39 shows the design for a report that includes Classic Models database order information that is grouped by product line, such as ships, vintage cars, and motorcycles. The report uses a chart to present the order totals graphically.

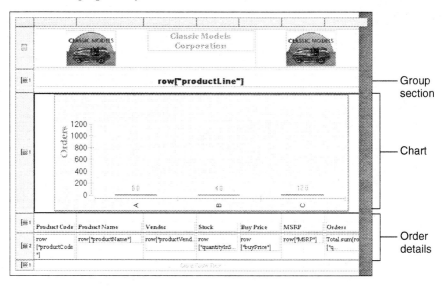

Figure 17-39   Report design including a chart in a group section

Figure 17-39 shows that the group section uses a header, row["productLine"]. The report positions the chart above the order details.

When you preview the chart, the data for a productLine group consists of one section. Each group provides a chart before listing the order details. Figure 17-40 shows the order details for the product line, ships. Details include ship product codes, names, vendors, and other details.

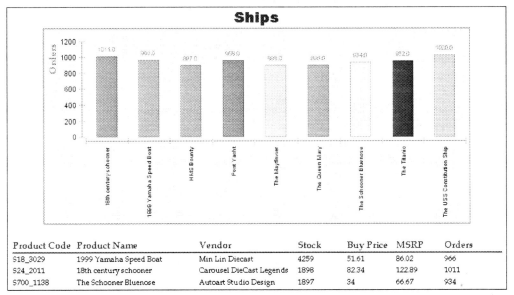

Figure 17-40   Report including a chart in a group section

Displaying Data in Charts

You use the same kind of data sources for a chart as you do for other report items. You can open a connection to a data source and create the data set for a chart from the Data Explorer. The procedure for creating a data set for a chart is basically the same as that for a report. You learned to create a data set in Task 4:, "Build a data set" of the tutorial at the beginning of this book.

How you retrieve and arrange data in a chart can be different from the way that you use data elsewhere in BIRT. As you saw in the chart tutorial, you provide expressions that organize the data into visual elements, such as bars or lines. After you preview the chart, you may think that you need additional or different data to make the meaning of the chart complete or clear. For example, you can group data values or use chart axis settings to modify the range, scale, or formatting of the data that the chart displays.

Linking a data set to a chart

Generally, you define the data source and create a data set, using the Data Explorer before you start building a chart or a report. It is a best practice to use the Data Explorer to set up the data source, data set, and any filters of the data before creating the chart element. Performing these tasks in the Data Explorer gives you optimal control and performance.

After you create a data set in the Data Explorer, you open the chart builder and select the chart type, as you did in the tutorial in "Using a Chart." Now, you are ready to link the data set you created to the chart. Choose Select Data.

In the middle of the Select Data page of the chart builder, shown in Figure 18-1, select Use Data Set to link data to the chart.

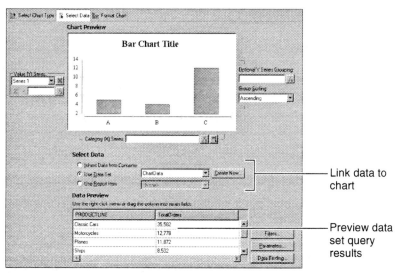

Link data to chart

Preview data set query results

Figure 18-1   Select Data page of the chart builder

In Use Data Set, you open the list of existing data sets and select one. If your existing data sets do not suffice, and you do not want to exit the chart builder and start over, you can also choose Create New to create a new data set from any of the existing data sources that you connected to your report.

After selecting a data set for the chart, Data Preview displays actual data rows, six by default. From the data preview, you can see if you want to exclude values by filtering data or by using a parameter to return only certain data. You drag and drop data columns from the data preview to the upper half of the Select Data page to specify expressions that the chart builder uses for creating visual chart elements.

Understanding the axes of a chart

In most charts with axes, the x-axis is a category axis, and the y-axis is a value axis. There is one noteworthy exception. By default, the x-axis of a scatter chart is a value axis, but you can make it a category axis by navigating to the x-axis section of Format Chart and selecting Is Category Axis.

About the axes

You often place text and date-and-time data on the category axis, which has regular segments that do not correspond to numerical values. If you have too many categories to fit within the finite limitations of the chart, you can use grouping. By default, category values appear in the same order as they occur in the data source, unless sorted in another order by the query. You can sort the values in ascending or descending order, and you can also group category data, using Edit Group and Sorting.

A value axis positions data relative to the axis marks. The value of a data point determines where it appears on a value axis. You can plot numeric and date-and-time data on a value axis. You do not plot text data on a value axis.

Defining the axes

After you select the data set, you define how the chart builder uses data from the data set to plot the chart. The options you use in the upper half of the Select Data page, shown in Figure 18-2, define the axes.

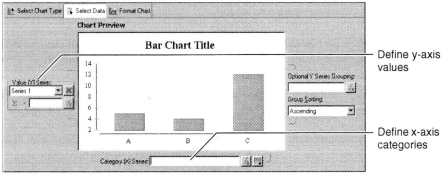

Figure 18-2   Upper half of Select Data page

Plotting different chart types

In the Select Data page, the category series, or category definition, option plots data on the x-axis. The value series option plots data on the y-axis. The options differ slightly in name and function, depending on the chart type. For example, when you create a meter chart, which has no axes, you define the position of a needle on the dial instead of defining a y-axis. When you create a pie chart, you define the size of the slices instead of the y-axis. In the chart builder, these options are appropriately named meter definition and slice size, respectively. Table 18-1 describes the differences in plotting options in the Select Data page for chart types.

Table 18-1   Differences in x- and y-axis plotting options for chart types

Chart type	Option name	Description
Area, bar, cone, difference, line, pyramid	Category X series	Arranges data on x-axis. Can group, sort, and aggregate data.
	Value Y series	Plots values on y-axis.
Bubble	Category X series	Plots values on the x-axis. Can group, sort, and aggregate data.
	Y value and size	Plots values on y-axis and defines the size of the bubbles.

(continues)

Table 18-1   Differences in x- and y-axis plotting options for chart types *(continued)*

Chart type	Option name	Description
Meter	Category definition	Requires a blank string " ": quotation mark, space, quotation mark.
	Meter value definition	Defines values of the dial and position of the needle. Creates multiple meters
Alternate meter subtype	Category definition	Requires a blank string " ": quotation mark, space, quotation mark.
	Meter value definition	Defines values of the dial and position of the needle.
Pie	Category definition	Defines what slices represent.
	Slice size definition	Defines size of sectors. Creates multiple pies.
Scatter	Category X series	Plots markers along x-axis. Groups data along x-axis.
	Value Y series	Defines intersection of x-y value pairs. Defines multiple x-y value pairs.
Stock	Category X series	Plots values along x-axis.
	Value Y series	Defines four levels of data: high, low, open, close. Defines multiple sets of candlesticks.

Plotting the x- and y-axes

You can drag and drop the data columns from Data Preview to the category and value axes definition areas to plot the axes. The chart builder writes expressions for creating visual chart elements based on the data columns you drag and drop. You can then enhance the expressions to plot computed or filtered data. For example, you plot dates along the x-axis by dragging and dropping the ORDERDATE column from the data preview to Category X Series, as shown in Figure 18-3.

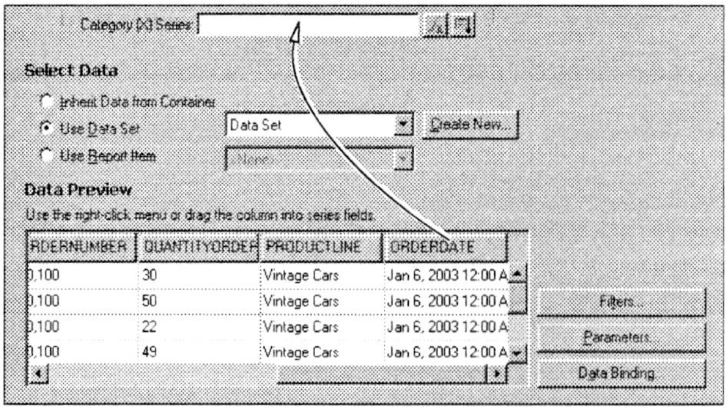

Figure 18-3   Defining the x-axis expression

You can specify that the chart builder plot X-Y data points using one column of data, such as order quantity, multiplied by another column, such as price. You plot these data points by first dragging and dropping the order quantity column from Data Preview to Value Y Series, as shown in Figure 18-4.

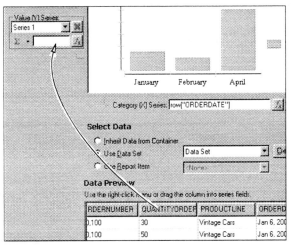

Figure 18-4   Defining the y-axis expression

Next, you open the expression builder to enhance the expression, as shown in Figure 18-5.

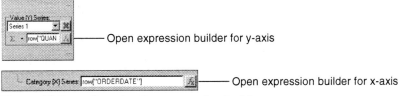

Figure 18-5   Opening the expression builder

In the expression builder, which is described earlier in this book, you can view and click the available column bindings to add code for the bindings to your expression. You can also add operators, JavaScript functions, and BIRT functions.

You need to type the portions of the following expression that you cannot drag and drop. For example, the first line of the following expression applies a filter to the query of the Classic Models database to return only classic car data. The second line computes the revenue for each order.

```
if(row["PRODUCTLINE"] == "Classic Cars"){
row["QUANTITYORDERED"] * row["PRICEEACH"]}
```

Using this expression to define the Value (Y) Series expression plots data points using order quantities times price.

Figure 18-6 shows the expression builder and available column bindings.

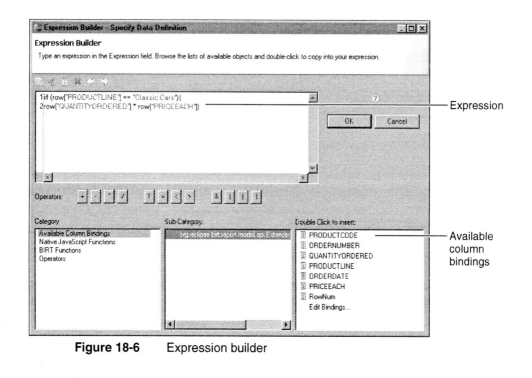

Figure 18-6   Expression builder

Grouping and sorting category data

When your expression returns too many categories to fit on the x-axis, on the dial or a meter, or in a pie, you need to use the grouping functionality in the chart builder as shown in Figure 18-7.

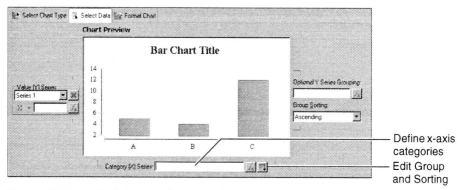

Figure 18-7   Defining x-axis categories and grouping and sorting

You can group text, numeric, or date-and-time data. For example, the Classic Models database includes the daily order information shown in Figure 18-8.

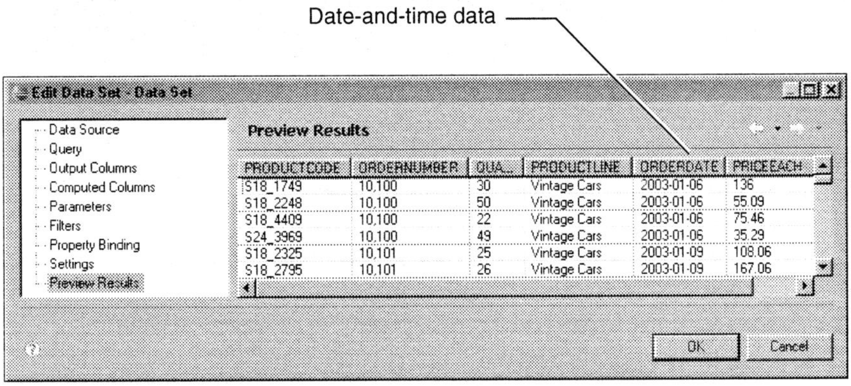

Date-and-time data ───

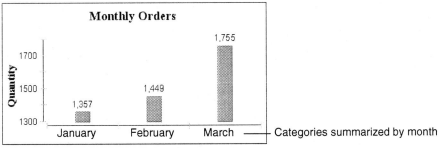

Figure 18-8   Date-and-time data in the Classic Models database

Plotting every single order across the x-axis creates such clutter that you cannot read the chart. You need to summarize the data to make the chart readable. Figure 18-9 shows the categories, summarized by month, on the x-axis.

Monthly Orders

```
                                              1,755
1700
                                               ▊
1500                      1,449
                           ▊
       1,357
1300    ▊

     January           February          March  ── Categories summarized by month
```

Quantity (y-axis label)

Figure 18-9   X-axis categories grouped by month

How to group categories on the x-axis

1   In the chart builder, on Select Data, choose Edit Group and Sorting. Figure 18-7 shows the location of Edit Group and Sorting.

2   In Grouping, select Enabled to see the grouping options shown in Figure 18-10.

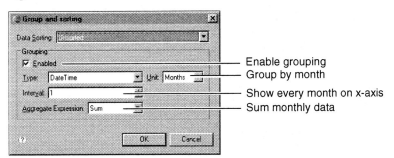

— Enable grouping
— Group by month
— Show every month on x-axis
— Sum monthly data

Figure 18-10   Grouping category data by month

3 Use the following options to set up a group:

- In Type, select Text, Numeric, or DateTime. If you select DateTime, you can specify the units to use to form the groups, such as Minutes.

- In Interval, select a number that represents the size of the groups to create. For example, to group three-row sequences of text data, select 3. To group numeric data in sections of four, select 4.

- In Aggregate Expression, select the function to use to aggregate the data in the group. You can select Average, Sum, Count, Distinct Count, First, Last, Minimum, and Maximum.

Grouping date-and-time data

You can group date-and-time data by seconds, hours, minutes, days, weeks, months, or years. Using the interval option, you can perform selective plotting of members of the group. For example, if you want to plot data for every other month, use an interval of 2.

Grouping textual data

You group textual data using an interval. The interval determines how many rows compose each group. For example, if you use an interval of 20, each group contains 20 rows of text from the database.

Grouping numeric data

You group numeric data by specifying the rows of data that compose the group. The chart builder uses a base value of 1 to create numeric groups. If you change the setting to 20, the first group contains rows with values between 1 and 20, the second group contains rows with values between 21 and 40, and so on. If the chart does not include a value in a group section, that section does not appear in the report. If you group order numbers 150–300 using a value of 20, the first group section that appears in the chart is 141–160.

For example, Table 18-2 displays budget data for three cities.

Table 18-2   Data for a chart that uses category series grouping

Year	City	Budget
2008	Los Angeles	3485398
2008	Chicago	2783726
2008	New York	7322564
2009	Los Angeles	4694820
2009	Chicago	3196016
2009	New York	8008278
2010	Los Angeles	6819951

Table 18-2   Data for a chart that uses category series grouping *(continued)*

Year	City	Budget
2010	Chicago	2569121
2010	New York	8085742

To group data using the Year field, you enable grouping, specify the data type of the field, and define a grouping interval. The data type that you select determines how the chart builder creates the groups as follows:

- If Year is a text field, selecting an interval value of 3 creates three groups. The first group includes the first three rows in the table, the second group contains rows four through six, and the third group contains the last three rows.

  When you group text values, you must use a regular grouping interval. You cannot create groups of varied sizes or use a field value to create a group. To create sensible groups in the chart, you must arrange the data in your data source before you create the chart. To use more complicated grouping, you should use your query to group data, then you can use those grouped values in the chart.

- If Year is a numeric field, selecting an interval value of 3 creates two groups. The first group includes the 1998 rows, because grouping by three from a base value of 1 creates one group that ends with 2008. The second group contains the 2009 and 2010 rows.

After you define how to create the groups, you must select an aggregate function that determines how the chart builder combines the values in each group.

Sorting category data

The category values appear in the chart in the order that the query returns them. You can sort the data so that it appears in a different order on an axis, in a dial, or in a pie. For example, you can show cities along the x-axis in alphabetical order. You can show customer ranks in descending numeric order around a pie. You can sort the data in an ascending or a descending sort order. To sort data, choose Data Sorting, shown in Figure 18-11.

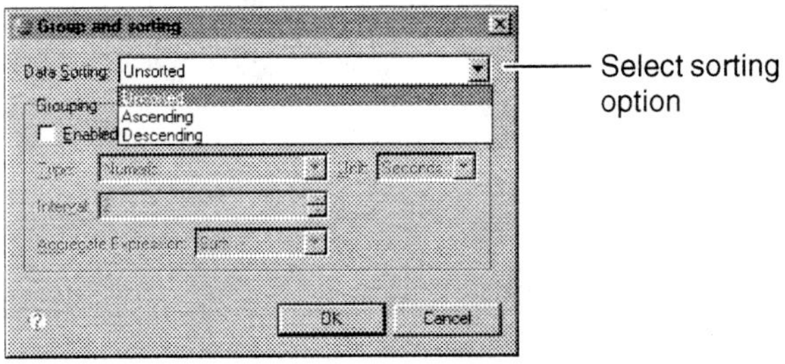

Figure 18-11   Selecting a sorting option and enabling grouping

After choosing Edit Group and Sorting in the Select Data page, you can set sorting options in Group and sorting.

Grouping optional Y value data

You group Y values for different reasons, depending on the chart type, as described in Table 18-3.

Table 18-3   Differences in optional grouping options for chart types

Chart type	Reason for using optional Y grouping
Bar, cone, line, pyramid, tube	To summarize data into multiple sets of risers in the chart.
Area, difference	To summarize data into multiple areas in the chart.
Bubble	To identify bubbles using the legend.
Meter	To plot multiple meters.
Alternate meter subtype	To plot multiple dials.
Pie	To plot multiple pies.
Scatter	To plot multiple x-y value pairs.
Stock	To plot multiple sets of candlesticks.

To group y-axis values, you use Optional Y Grouping in the Select Data page of the chart builder.

Grouping Y values in a bar chart

The chart in Figure 18-12 groups Y values to plot multiple sets of bars representing the monthly sum of orders for three types of vehicles.

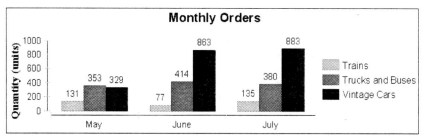

Figure 18-12   Bar chart that plots multiple sets of bars by grouping

Figure 18-13 shows the axes and grouping definitions used to create this chart.

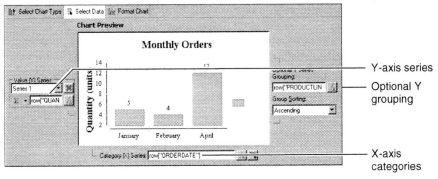

Figure 18-13 — Y-axis series — Optional Y grouping — X-axis categories

Figure 18-13 Axes and grouping definitions for plotting multiple sets of bars

You build the expressions shown in Table 18-4 by dragging and dropping columns from the data preview in the Select Data page to the three areas shown in Figure 18-13.

Table 18-4 Definitions of series in bar chart that uses grouping

Series	Expression
Value Y series	`row["ORDERQUANTITY"]`
Category X series	`row["ORDERDATE"]`
Optional Y series grouping	`row["PRODUCTLINE"]`

Grouping multiple y-axis values in a stock chart

In a stock chart, four different value series expressions provide the high, low, open, and close data. The category series expression arranges the values along the x-axis, typically along a date or time scale. To set up multiple sets of candlesticks, you can either define multiple value series definitions or use optional grouping. For example, the stock chart in Figure 18-14 shows stock data for two companies.

The data for the chart appears in Table 18-5.

Table 18-5 Data for a stock chart that uses grouping

Symbol	Date	High	Close	Low	Open
MIVA	3/1/2008	23.77	22.73	22.00	22.10
MIVA	3/2/2008	23.10	23.04	22.60	22.71
HOMS	3/1/2008	116.41	115.28	115.13	115.19
HOMS	3/4/2008	116.30	115.13	115.13	116.21
HOMS	3/2/2008	116.48	116.26	115.16	115.19
MIVA	3/4/2008	23.86	23.56	22.74	22.79
HOMS	3/3/2008	116.31	116.17	115.14	116.30

(continues)

Table 18-5   Data for a stock chart that uses grouping *(continued)*

Symbol	Date	High	Close	Low	Open
MIVA	3/3/2008	22.80	22.78	22.65	22.66

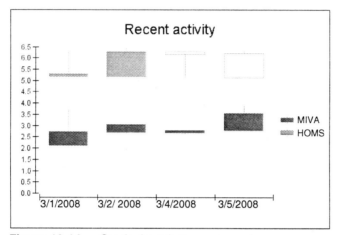

Figure 18-14   Stock chart that uses grouping

Figure 18-15 shows the expressions to use to create the chart. The chart uses the Y-value expressions to set up the candlesticks and the category X expression to arrange the candlesticks in chronological order along the x-axis. The expression, row["Symbol"], which you drag and drop in Optional Y Series Grouping, creates one set of candlesticks for each ticker symbol.

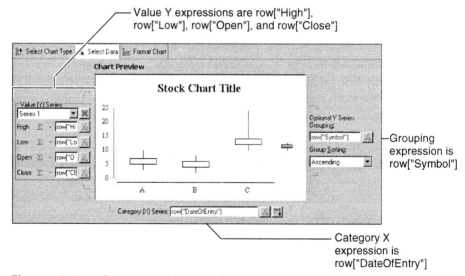

Figure 18-15   Data expressions for the stock chart

You can also use multiple sets of value series expressions to create multiple sets of candlesticks. For example, you can create the same chart using joined data from Table 18-6 and Table 18-7.

Table 18-6   Data for a stock chart that uses two sets of value series expressions

DateOfEntry	HOMSHigh	HOMSLow	HOMSOpen	HOMSClose
3/1/2008	116.41	115.13	115.19	115.28
3/2/2008	116.48	115.16	115.19	116.26
3/3/2008	116.31	115.14	116.30	116.17
3/4/2008	115.30	115.13	115.13	116.21

Table 18-7   More data for a stock chart that uses two sets of value series expressions

DateOfEntry	MIVAHigh	MIVALow	MIVAOpen	MIVAClose
3/1/2008	23.77	22.00	22.10	22.73
3/2/2008	23.10	22.60	22.71	23.04
3/3/2008	22.80	22.65	22.66	22.78
3/4/2008	23.86	22.74	22.79	23.56

To define multiple sets of candlesticks, you use the value series drop-down list. Select New Series, shown in Figure 18-16, and then either drag and drop columns from Chart Preview to the expression fields, or type code to create the series expressions. After you add one or more sets of expressions, you can use the drop-down list to navigate among them.

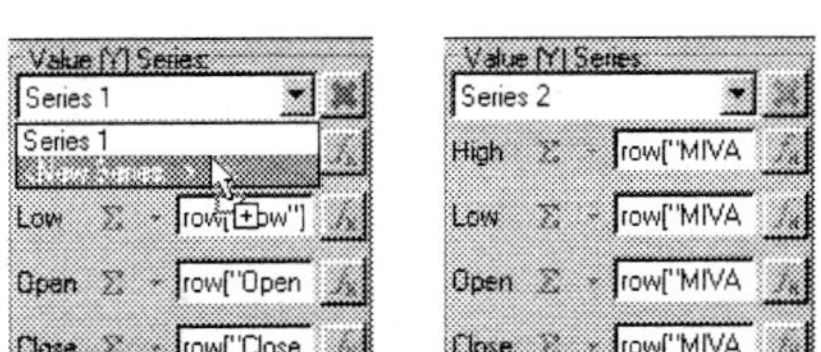

Figure 18-16   Adding a stock chart value series

To create multiple sets of candlesticks, you use the following expressions to define the category and value series in the stock chart:

- The category series definition is row["DateOfEntry"].

- The first set of value series expressions uses row["HOMSHigh"], row["HOMSLow"], row["HOMSOpen"], and row["HOMSClose"].

- The second set of value series expressions uses row["MIVAHigh"], row["MIVALow"], row["MIVAOpen"], and row["MIVAClose"].

Using multiple y-axes

You can use more than one y-axis in a chart. Additional y-axes can use a different scale from the first y-axis. After you add the second axis, you must define the data for it. To create a second y-axis, you use the Select Chart Type page. In Multiple Y Axis, select More Axes. Figure 18-17 shows Select Chart Type.

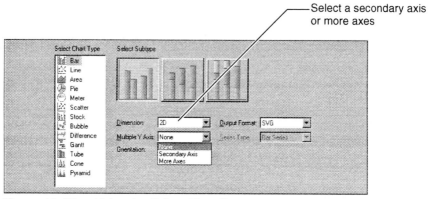

Select a secondary axis or more axes

Figure 18-17   Using the Select Chart Type page to add a y-axis

After you enable multiple axes, you must specify the data for the additional axes. You define the y-, but not the x-axis, of each additional axis. The category x-axis and optional grouping definitions apply to all y-axes. In Select Data, you provide the expression for the second y-axis, as shown in Figure 18-18.

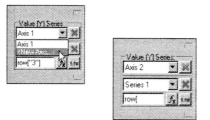

Figure 18-18   Using Chart Data to add data for a second y-axis

Transposing the chart axes

You can switch the chart axes, so the x-axis is vertical and the y-axis is horizontal. Figure 18-19 shows a bar chart with transposed axes.

You can transpose the axes of two-dimensional charts and charts using depth. You cannot transpose the axes in a three-dimensional chart. To transpose axes, navigate to the Select Chart Type page, then select Flip Axis.

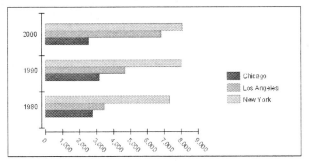

Figure 18-19   Bar chart with transposed axes

Filtering data

You can limit the data that the chart displays by applying a filter. Usually, you filter data as you create a data set in Data Explorer, but if you already started designing a chart, you can filter the data in the chart builder to prevent losing work on the chart. You choose Filters in the Select Data page, as shown in Figure 18-20.

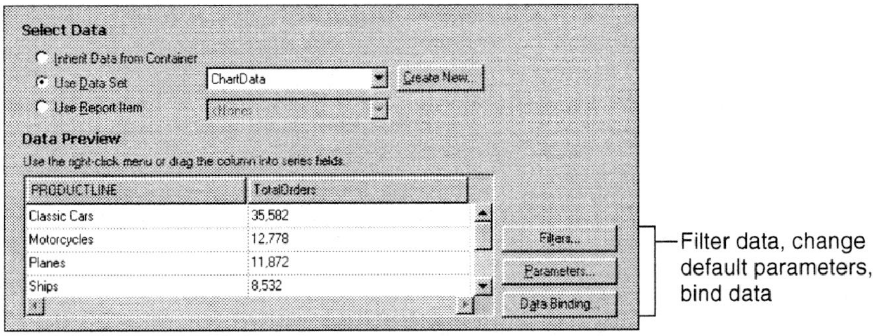

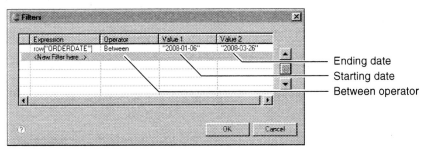

Figure 18-20   Options for filtering data from the chart builder

In Filters, shown in Figure 18-21, you construct the expression to filter the data. As you learned earlier in this book, you select the expression, operator, and values from the drop-down list, which contains only valid options.

Figure 18-21   Filtering data by date

You can define multiple filters by clicking an empty row in filters and selecting another set of options. Using the up and down arrows, you can prioritize the filters by moving their position in the list.

Changing default report parameters

Earlier in this book, you learned how to include a parameter marker, ?, in the query defined for a data set. The marker specifies how BIRT dynamically updates the query when the user supplies a report parameter. If the data set linked to the chart includes a parameter marker in the query, you can review or change the default parameter value from the chart builder. From the Select Data page, choose Parameters. From Parameters, shown in Figure 18-22, you select Value to change the default value of the parameter.

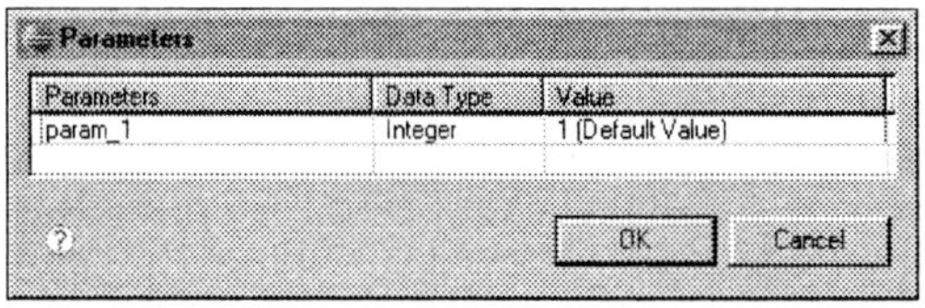

Figure 18-22   Changing the default parameter value from the chart builder

Creating data bindings

Data binding establishes a relationship between chart or report items and the underlying data source. When a user types a parameter in response to a prompt from the report, the data values of the chart or report item changes, and BIRT updates the chart or report.

From within the chart builder, you can add, edit, and delete data bindings using the data set linked to the chart. From the Select Data page, choose Data Binding. Select Data Binding, shown in Figure 18-23, is displayed.

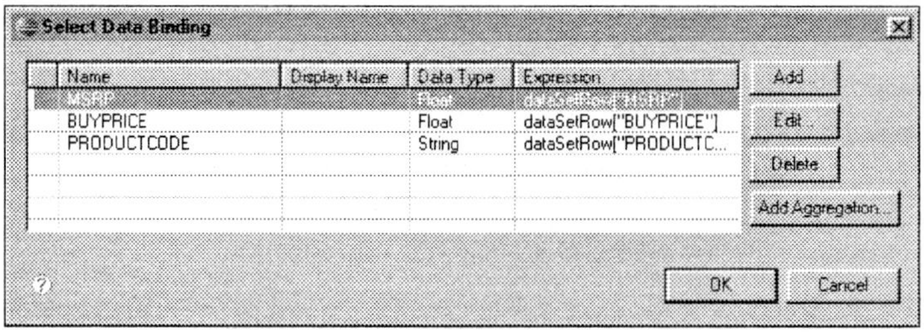

Figure 18-23   Creating data bindings

Use Add, Edit, or Delete to perform the data binding tasks. Choose Add Aggregation to create a computed column using the aggregate functions described earlier in this book.

Previewing data and chart

From within the chart builder, you can see some of the data in the data set linked to the chart. Previewing sample data can help you decide which column to use to plot the x- and y-axis. For example, in Figure 18-24, Data Preview shows several columns of data from the Classic Models database that ships with BIRT.

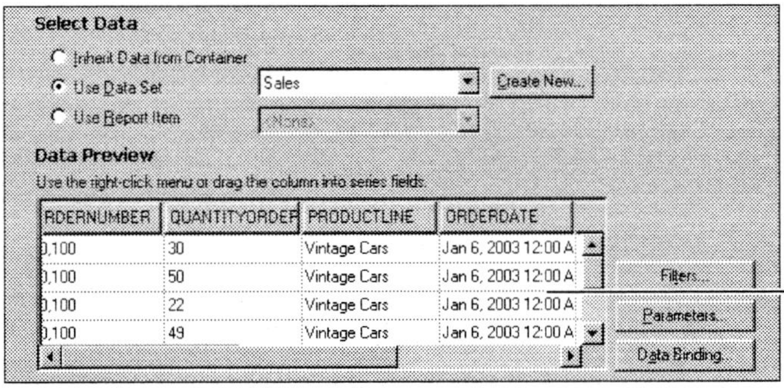

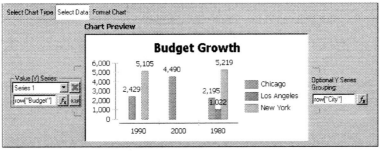

Figure 18-24   Previewing the data in the chart builder

Data Preview serves another important purpose as you define charts. You can drag and drop the columns from Data preview to the value, category, and optional Y grouping definitions in the upper portion of Select Data.

As you set up the expressions that specify the data for your chart, Chart Preview presents a rough idea of how your published chart will look. Figure 18-25 shows the chart preview for a bar chart.

Figure 18-25   Previewing chart data on Select Data

You can change some characteristics of chart previews to improve performance. As you design a chart, the chart preview uses either live data, as shown in Figure 18-25, or randomly generated sample data, as shown in Figure 18-26.

You can also change the number of data rows that appear in chart builder. By default, the data preview section shows six rows of data. You can display more or fewer rows.

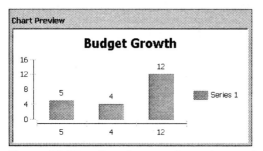

Figure 18-26   Bar chart preview using random data

How to change chart preview preferences

1 Choose Window➔Preferences.

2 Expand the Report Design list item, then choose Chart to see the options shown in Figure 18-27.

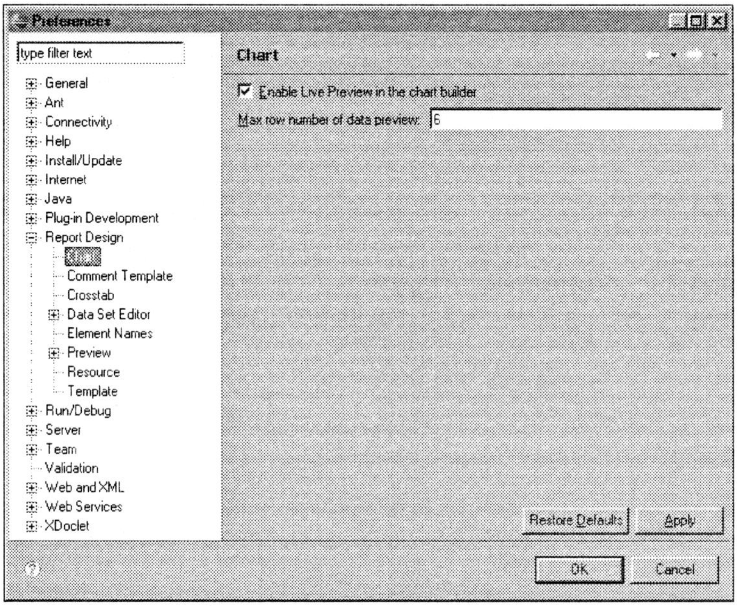

Figure 18-27   Chart page of Preferences

3 To have the chart builder use randomly selected data in the chart preview window, deselect Enable Live Preview.

4 To set the number of rows that Data Preview displays, type a value in the field.

5 Choose Finish.

Now you understand how to set up and manipulate the data that you use in a chart. The next chapter describes how to customize the appearance of a chart.

Creating a combination chart

A combination chart is a chart that incorporates two different chart types. You can combine the following chart types: area, bar, cone, pyramid, stock, tube, or line. You must use at least two value series. Using multiple value series expressions, you can present more data on the chart. For example, Figure 18-28 shows a chart with one value series, the bar, for order quantity and another, the pyramid, for revenue.

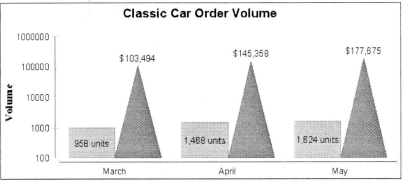

Figure 18-28   Combination bar and pyramid chart

The chart groups the dates by month and shows the unit order volume and revenue for classic cars over a three-month period.

To provide more than one value series expression, you use the value series drop-down list. Select New Series, then use the expression field to supply the series expression, as shown in Figure 18-29.

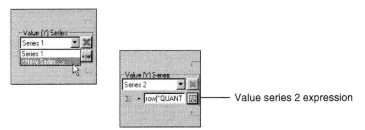

Figure 18-29   Adding a value series expression

After you add one or more series, you use the drop-down list to navigate among the value series definitions.

To create the combination chart, you first create a chart of one type, such as a bar chart. Next, you define the series expressions. Finally, navigate to the Series section of Format Chart, and select a chart of another type, such as pyramid, as shown in Figure 18-30.

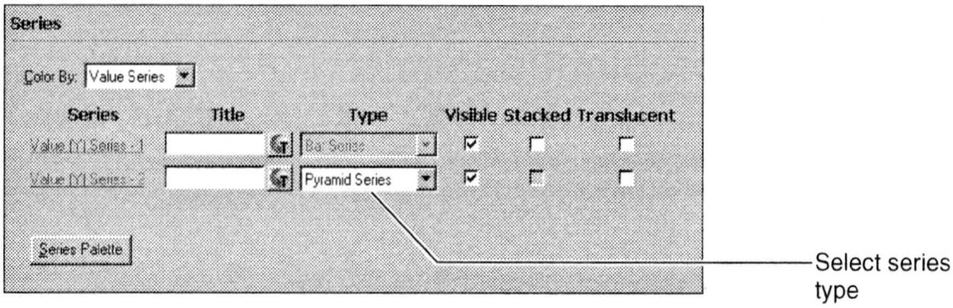

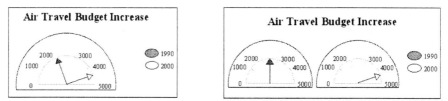

Series
Color By: Value Series
Series
Title
Type
Visible Stacked Translucent
Pyramid Series
Series Palette
Select series type

Figure 18-30 Creating a combination chart

Defining a meter chart

A meter chart shows a data value as a needle that marks a position on a dial. You can create a chart that shows one or more needles on one dial or one that shows multiple dials, each displaying one needle. You cannot use multiple needles on multiple dials. Figure 18-31 shows two sample meter charts.

Air Travel Budget Increase
0
1000
2000
3000
4000
5000
1990
2000
Air Travel Budget Increase
0
1000
2000
3000
4000
5000
0
1000
2000
3000
4000
5000
1990
2000

Figure 18-31 Meter charts using one and two meters

The meter value series specifies the needle value. The expression that you choose determines where on the dial the needle appears. To show multiple needles or meters, you can either use multiple meter value series expressions or optional grouping.

A category definition is not essential to a meter chart. You must, however, provide an expression in the category definition field. You can type a space that is enclosed by quotation marks in this field to satisfy this requirement. The chart selects the first row returned by the meter value definition and uses the data from that row in the chart.

Using multiple meters in a chart

The meter value definition specifies the dial values and position of the needle. To show multiple meters, you can use either multiple meter value definitions or grouping. For example, Figure 18-32 is a standard meter chart. Standard meter charts use only one needle for each meter. The chart uses population as the needle value and city as a grouping field. Because the chart builder requires a value in the category field, you must provide a blank string, " ", for the category definition.

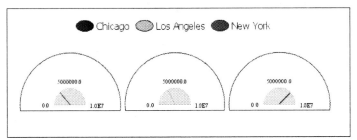

Figure 18-32   Meter chart that uses multiple meters

The chart in Figure 18-32 uses the data in Table 18-8.

Table 18-8   Data for a meter chart that uses grouping

City	Population
Chicago	2783726
Los Angeles	3485398
New York	7322564

The chart builder uses the expressions to position the needles and plot each population value as the position of a needle on the dial. The chart builder uses the values to position the dials, one for each meter, in the chart. The grouping sets up a meter for each city. The legend identifies the meters.

Using multiple dials in a chart

To show multiple dials, select the alternate subtype when you choose the chart type, as shown in Figure 18-33.

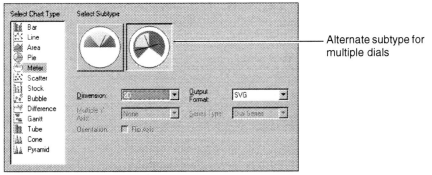

Alternate subtype for multiple dials

Figure 18-33   Selecting the subtype, meter chart that uses multiple dials

You can also use multiple series definitions to create multiple meters or a meter with multiple needles. For example, the chart in Figure 18-34 is a superimposed meter chart that shows multiple needles in one meter. One needle shows interior temperature, and the other needle shows exterior temperature.

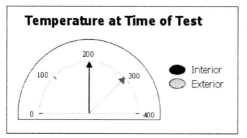

Figure 18-34   Super-imposed meter chart

The chart in Figure 18-34 uses the data in Table 18-9.

Table 18-9   Data for a meter chart that uses two meter value expressions

InteriorTemp	ExteriorTemp
201	303

The first meter value series expression is row["InteriorTemp"]. The second meter value series expression is row["ExteriorTemp"]. The chart does not use optional grouping. The category definition is a blank string, " ".

To provide more than one meter value series expression, you use the meter value series drop-down list. Select New Series, then use the expression field to supply the series expression. After you add one or more series, you use the drop-down list to navigate among the meter value series definitions.

Laying Out and Formatting a Chart

Charts include many different visual elements. You can customize the appearance of most chart elements. To clarify the presentation of data or to create a more pleasing composition, you can rearrange the chart layout. For example, you can change where the chart title appears or add padding between a series of bars and the axis on which they are arranged.

You can also change the color and style of the chart elements. For example, you might need to modify a chart to use your company's standard color scheme. You can outline or add a background color to the plot, legend, or labels. You can also change the color and shape of the series elements, such as the sectors in a pie chart or the candlesticks in a stock chart.

Figure 19-1 identifies parts of a basic bar chart.

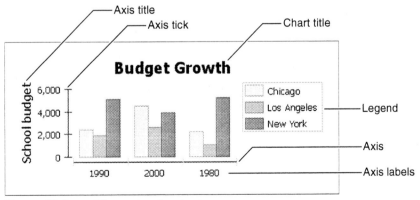

Figure 19-1   Elements of a chart

You can add gridlines that extend across the plot or data point labels to show the exact value of each bar. Generally, you can make the following types of changes to charts:

- Laying out and formatting the chart. You can change the background color or outline of different chart areas or modify the padding between chart areas.

- Formatting numbers, dates, and times. You can customize the appearance of dates and numbers in a chart, and add a prefix or suffix to numbers.

- Formatting the chart legend, plot, and title. You can add color, an outline, and a shadow to highlight the plot, title, or legend.

- Formatting axis titles, markers, lines, and labels. You can adjust the line style of an axis. You can also modify the text style, position, coloring, or outline of axis labels or titles.

- Formatting a series. You can change the type of a series, such as line or bar, and the color or style of the series markers. You can also change attributes that are specific to each series type.

Formatting specific types of charts

In addition to formatting options that apply to charts in general, the chart builder includes unique formatting options for specific chart types.

Formatting an area chart

You can change the style or color of the area borders or hide them.

For example, Figure 19-2 shows a chart with standard lines bordering the areas on the left and curved lines bordering the areas on the right.

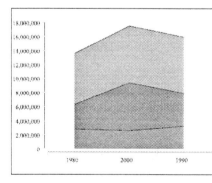
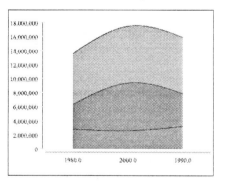

Area chart using default lines   Area chart using a curved line

Figure 19-2   Area chart using different border line options

You can also add point markers that identify the data points that an area encloses. The legend uses the markers to identify the areas. In a chart without markers, the legend uses lines. Figure 19-3 shows one area chart that has markers and one that does not.

Area chart using markers   Area chart using no markers

Figure 19-3   Area chart with and without markers

To format an area, line, or scatter chart, navigate to the Value Series section of Format Chart, then modify the area chart lines or markers, as shown in Figure 19-4.

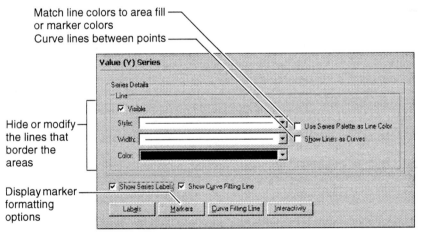

Figure 19-4   Format options for an area, line, or scatter

Formatting a line or a scatter chart

Line and scatter charts use the same formatting attributes. By default, a line chart shows lines between data points, but a scatter chart does not.

To format a line or scatter-chart series, navigate to the Value Series section of Format Chart. Use the settings to modify the chart lines and markers, as shown in Figure 19-4.

Sometimes, line charts include categories for which no data exists. You can define how the chart treats the empty values. By default, the chart connects the line between the existing points, but you can set an option to hide the connecting line. In Figure 19-5, the chart is missing the data for four dates. That point is made clearer in the second chart where the line breaks whenever there is missing data.

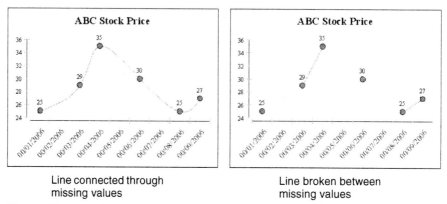

Line connected through
missing values

Line broken between
missing values

Figure 19-5   Charts using connected and broken lines

To break the line, navigate to the Value Series section of Format Chart, then deselect Connect Missing Values.

Formatting a bar chart

By default, bars appear as rectangles without outlines, but you can change the bars to cones, tubes, or pyramids, or add a bar outline. To format a bar chart, navigate to the Series section of Format Chart. Use the settings to modify the bars, as shown in Figure 19-6.

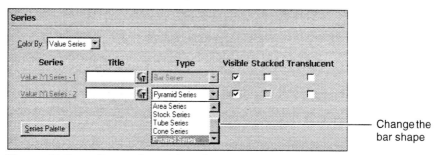

Change the
bar shape

Figure 19-6   Formatting options for a bar chart series

To add an outline to the bars or other risers, navigate to the Value (Y) Series section of Format Chart, and select a color in Series Outline.

Formatting a bubble chart

You can add acceleration lines to bubble charts to emphasize their y-axis value, as shown by the dashed acceleration lines in Figure 19-7. You can also add various styles and colors of lines around the bubbles. In Figure 19-7, a thick black line encircles the bubbles to accentuate them.

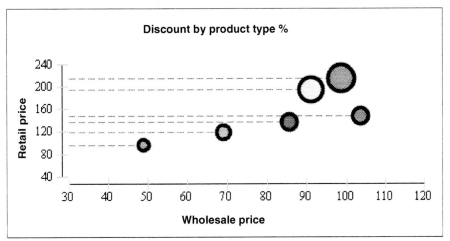

Figure 19-7   Using acceleration lines in a bubble chart

You use the Value (Y) series to access these capabilities. Navigate to the Value (Y) Series section of Format Chart. Use Series Details to add and format acceleration lines, or to add lines around the bubbles, as shown in Figure 19-8.

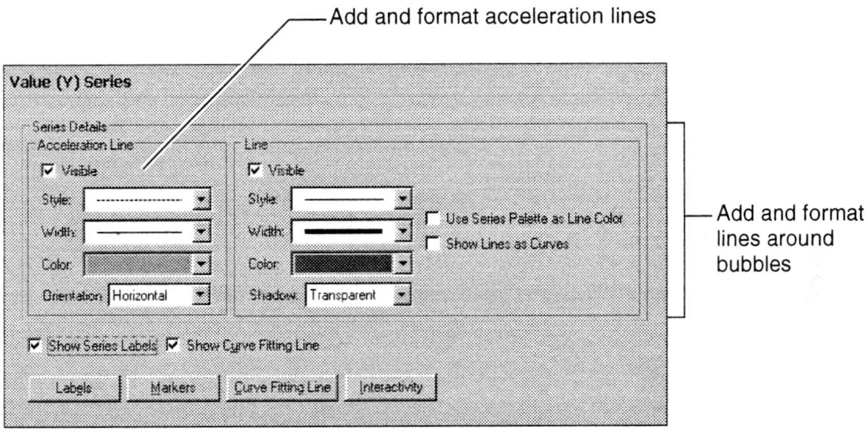

Add and format acceleration lines

Add and format lines around bubbles

Figure 19-8   Bubble chart formatting options

Formatting a difference chart

Difference charts highlight differences in data using fill areas. The chart can display positive differences in one color and negative differences in another. For example, you can use a difference chart to show how sales compare to quota over a period of time, where the positive value represents sales in excess of quota while the negative value shows sales below quota.

To show positive and negative differences, navigate to the Value (Y) Series section of Format Chart. Use Value (Y) Series to add and format positive and negative areas to the difference chart, as shown in Figure 19-9.

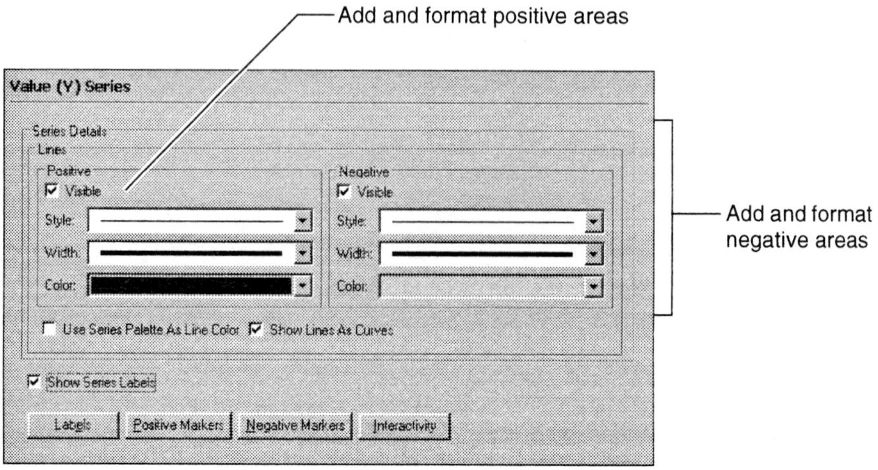

Figure 19-9 Adding positive and negative fills to a difference chart

Formatting a Gantt chart

Gantt charts reflect project schedules and represent tasks using bars that show beginning and ending dates. The bars are filled with colors representing the task status.

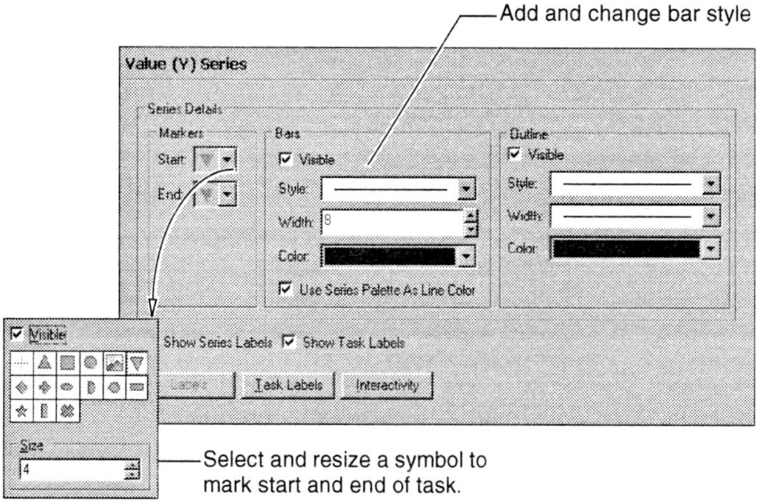

Figure 19-10 Formatting a Gantt chart

To add and format task markers and bars, navigate to the Value (Y) Series section of Format Chart. Use Value (Y) Series to change and resize the symbols that mark the start and end of a task. You can also specify the color, style, and size of symbol markers and task bars, as shown in Figure 19-9.

Formatting a meter chart

When you format a meter chart series, you work with the chart elements shown in Figure 19-11.

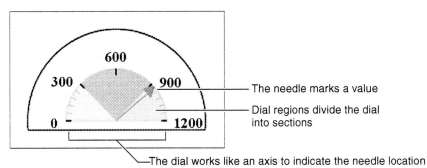

The needle marks a value

Dial regions divide the dial into sections

The dial works like an axis to indicate the needle location

Figure 19-11   Elements of a meter chart

You can modify the following meter chart attributes:

■ Dial size. You can determine the radius of the dial. You can also use start- and stop-angle settings to determine if the dial is circular or semicircular.

■ Dial scale and tick marks. Working with the dial scale and tick settings is similar to working with the same settings on an axis.

■ Needle formatting. You can modify the style and width of the needle or change how the pointer end of the needle appears.

■ Dial placement. If you create a chart that displays multiple dials, you can arrange the dials in a row or in columns.

■ Label settings. You can show or hide labels for regions and for the chart data point, which is where the needle falls on the meter.

■ Dial-region size, color, and placement. Working with dial-region settings is similar to working with axis-marker settings.

Working with the dial size

To change the distance between the center of the chart and the outside of the dial, you change the dial radius. Use percentage settings to size the dial relative to the meter. For example, a setting of 50 creates a dial radius that is half the distance from the center of the meter to its outer boundary. In a chart that uses more than one value-series definition, you set a single dial radius that applies to all series. If different series contain different dial radius values, the dial uses the larger value.

To change the shape of a dial, you change the dial start- and stop-angle settings. The angles are measured counter-clockwise from the right. For example, in Figure 19-12, the dial uses a start setting of 20 and a stop setting of 160.

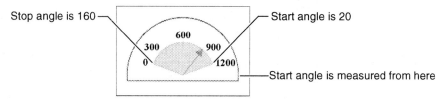

Figure 19-12 Start- and stop-angle settings in a semicircular meter

You can create a full circle, instead of the default semicircle meter. For example, the chart shown in Figure 19-13 uses a start angle of –90 and a stop angle of 270. The first value in the dial, 0, appears at –90 degrees, and the last, 1200, is not labeled but appears at 270 degrees.

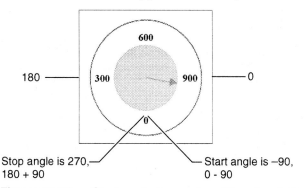

Figure 19-13 Start- and stop-angle settings in a full meter and full dial

The start and stop settings of the dial define the size of the meter that surrounds it. If you use an angle setting that is less than 0 degrees or greater than 180 degrees, the chart displays a full circle. If you use angle settings between 0 and 180, the chart displays a half-circle.

To set the size of a dial, navigate to the Value Series section of Format Chart. Use the settings to modify the dial size, as shown in Figure 19-14.

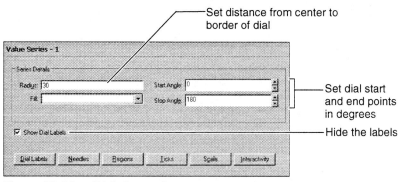

Figure 19-14 Dial size settings

Working with the dial scale and markings

The chart builder uses the available data to set a span for the dial, then it places tick marks at appropriate intervals along it. The dial scale determines the span of the data.

To change the scale of a dial, navigate to the Value Series section of Format Chart, then choose Scale. Use the Scale settings to change the range or spacing of the data the dial displays, as shown in Figure 19-15.

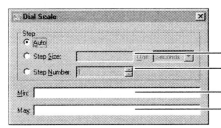

Set interval between major dial values
Set number of minor grid marks between two major grid marks
Set minimum value of dial
Set maximum value of dial

Figure 19-15   Dial scale options

To modify the tick marks on a dial, navigate to the Value Series section of Format Chart, then choose Ticks. Use the settings to modify the major or minor grid ticks, as shown in Figure 19-16.

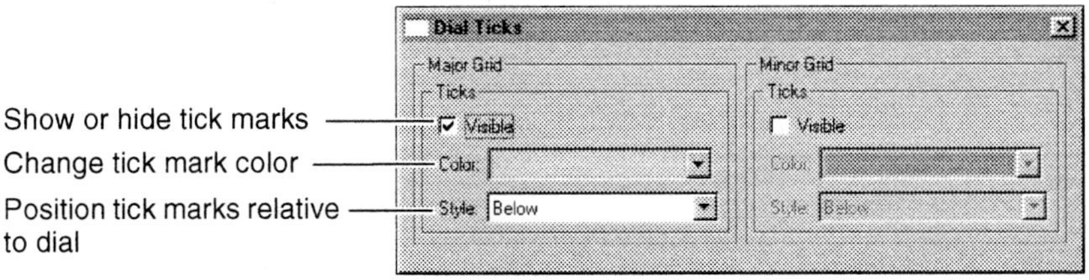

Show or hide tick marks
Change tick mark color
Position tick marks relative to dial

Figure 19-16   Dial tick mark options

Working with needle settings

You can change the line style, width, and head style of a needle. Navigate to the Value Series section of Format Chart, then choose Needles to modify the needle appearance, as shown in Figure 19-17. To change the color of a needle, change the value series palette, as shown in Figure 19-18.

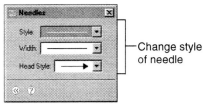

Change style of needle

Figure 19-17   Needle style options

Figure 19-18   Changing needle color

Arranging multiple meters

In a chart with multiple meters, you can position the meters by specifying
how many columns to use to display them. For example, you want to use
three meters to contrast the performance of two managers in one territory
and one manager in another territory, so you specify a two-column grid for
displaying the meters. Using a two-column grid that has three meters
produces the chart shown on the left in Figure 19-19. To arrange the meters
vertically, as shown on the right, you specify using a three-column grid.

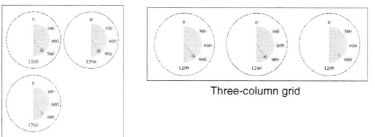

Figure 19-19   Using two- and three-column grids in a meter chart

To layout the meters, navigate to the Chart Area section of Format Chart,
then choose General Properties. In Grid Column Count, select the number of
columns the chart uses to display the meters, as shown in Figure 19-20.

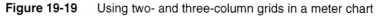

Figure 19-20   Grid Column Count option

Specifying a grid column count of 1 positions multiple meters vertically. Specifying a grid column count equal to the number of meters positions meters horizontally.

Working with meter chart labels

To format the labels that identify points on the dial, navigate to the Value Series section of Format Chart and choose Dial Labels. Use the settings shown in Figure 19-21 to outline, pad, or format the labels.

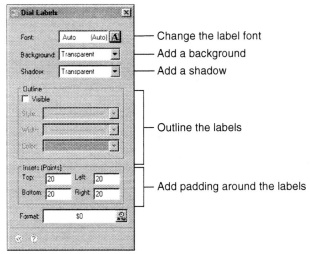

Figure 19-21   Dial label options

Working with dial regions

To highlight the values on the dial, you use dial regions. Dial regions are similar to axis markers. You determine a start and an end value for each region. After you set up the regions, you can change the region color or outline. If regions overlap, the last region that you create takes precedence in formatting. You can also change the radius of a region to determine where it starts or ends in relation to the position of the dial. For example, Figure 19-22 shows a chart with two regions. The region on the left has an outer radius of 50. The region on the right has an outer radius of 75.

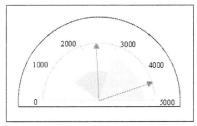

Figure 19-22   Regions in a dial

To add and format a dial region, navigate to the Value Series section of Format Chart, then choose Regions to add or format a region using the options shown in Figure 19-23.

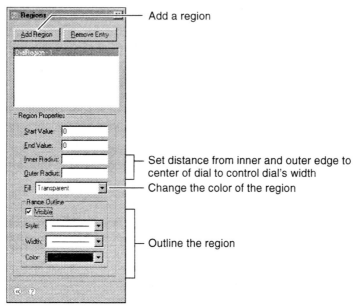

Regions
Add Region
Remove Entry
Region Properties
Start Value: 0
End Value: 0
Inner Radius:
Outer Radius:
Fill Transparent
Range Outline
Visible
Style:
Width:
Color
Add a region
Set distance from inner and outer edge to center of dial to control dial's width
Change the color of the region
Outline the region

Figure 19-23 Formatting regions

Choose Add Region. The region appears in the list at the top of the window. Provide a start and an end value for the region, as shown in Figure 19-24.

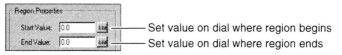

Region Properties
Start Value: 0.0
End Value: 0.0
Set value on dial where region begins
Set value on dial where region ends

Figure 19-24 Choosing dial region settings

Formatting a pie chart

You can change the aspect ratio of the pie chart, making it circular or oval, as shown in Figure 19-25.

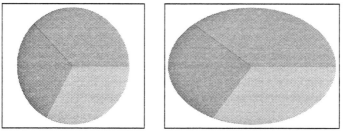

Figure 19-25 Pie chart displayed as a circle and an oval

To make an oval-shaped pie, navigate to the Value Series section of Format Chart, shown in Figure 19-26, then select 0.5 in Pie Ratio. Select 1 in Pie Ratio to make the pie a circle.

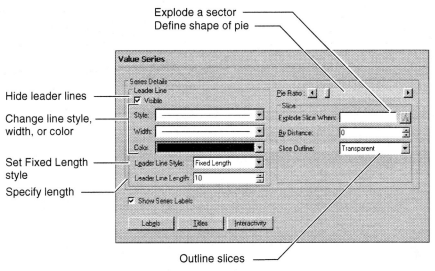

Figure 19-26   Formatting a pie chart

Working with leader lines

As shown in Figure 19-26, you can modify the line style, width, or color of leader lines in the same way as you modify the formatting attributes of other lines in a chart. If you select the leader-line style Fixed Length, you can modify the length of the leader lines by changing the style of the leader line. You can also hide the leader lines.

Working with pie sectors

You can outline each sector and change the outline properties. You can also select a color palette for the sectors. To outline pie-chart sectors, navigate to the Value Series section of Format Chart, then use Slice Outline to select an outline color, as shown in Figure 19-26.

You can set a minimum value for pie sectors. A sector with a value equal to or greater than the minimum appears as usual. Sectors with values below the minimum are combined in a new remainders sector. You can create a label for the remainders sector to display in the legend.

You can set the minimum as a static value or as a percentage of the pie value. For example, you can show sales totals for a group of customers and combine customers with sales below $1,000,000.00 in a sector called Infrequent Orders, or you can combine customers with sales below two percent of the total sales.

To specify a minimum sector size, navigate to the Category Series section of Format Chart, then set up a minimum sector size equal to either a value related to slice size or to a percentage of the pie, as shown in Figure 19-27. The chart builder combines slices smaller than the minimum into another category.

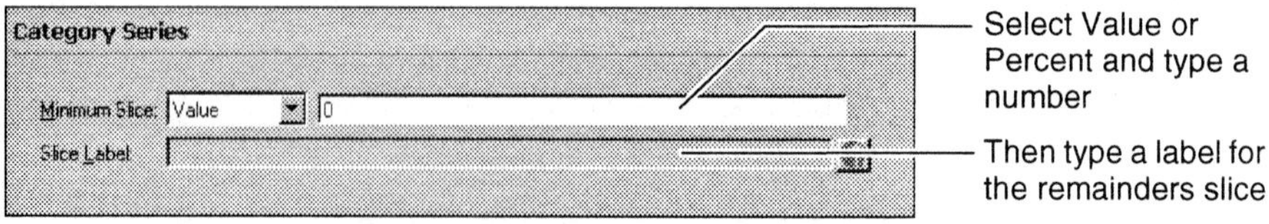

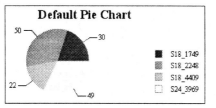

Select Value or Percent and type a number

Then type a label for the remainders slice

Figure 19-27   Minimum sector settings

Exploding sectors of a pie chart

By default, pie sectors appear joined to one another, not pulled away from the pie, and leader lines connect sectors and associated data labels, as shown in Figure 19-28.

Figure 19-28   Pie chart using default settings

You can explode sectors, which adds space between them, to emphasize particular sectors. You can specify how far from the center of the pie the exploded sectors appear. First, you decide how a pie selects sectors to explode, or you explode all sectors. You can also explode the pie based on an expression. For example, you can explode only those sectors that compose more than 20 percent of the pie. To explode all pie chart sectors, provide a number in By Distance and do not provide an explosion expression.

You can use Edit Expression, which includes a Chart Variables category, as shown in Figure 19-29, to create the expression. You use this category to add elements such as Value Data or Category Data to your expression. For example, you can use an expression such as ValueData > 200 to explode sectors that have a value greater than 200.

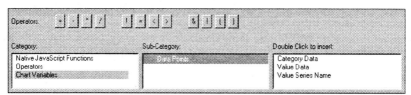

Figure 19-29   Edit Expression that explodes pie sectors

To explode pie sectors based on an expression, navigate to the Value Series section of Format Chart. In Explode Slice When, shown in Figure 19-26, provide an expression. When the expression is true for a sector, that sector pulls away from the pie.

For example, to explode sectors for which the category value is California, use the following expression:

```
CategoryData="California"
```

To set the explosion distance, navigate to the Value Series section of Format Chart. In By Distance, provide the percentage of separation of the sectors from the pie center. For example, an explosion value of 50 pulls out exploded sectors half the distance of the original pie.

Arranging multiple pies

When you use multiple pies, you can specify how many columns to use to display them. For example, in Figure 19-30, the chart on the left uses one column, so the chart builder positions the pies vertically, one below the other, within the column. The chart on the right uses two columns, so the chart builder positions pies in each of two columns.

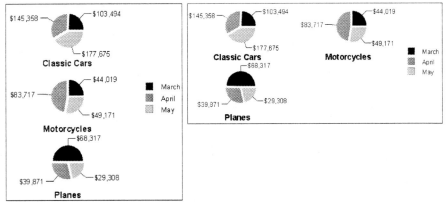

Figure 19-30   Pie charts using different column-count settings

To arrange multiple pies in a pie chart, navigate to the Chart Area section of Format Chart, then choose General Properties. In Grid Column Count, select how many columns to use to display the pies.

Formatting a stock chart

A stock chart uses a candlestick, a box with lines extending up and down from the ends. The upper and lower edges of the box are the stock open and close values. The upper and lower points of the line are the high and low values.

If the open value is higher than the close value, the box is shaded. If the close value is higher than the open value, the box is transparent. For example, in the chart in Figure 19-31, the marker for 03/01/2005 indicates that day's close value was lower than the open value.

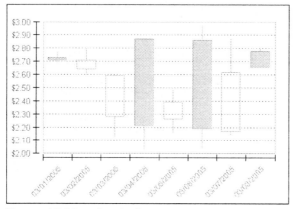

Figure 19-31   Stock chart

When you format a stock chart, you can change the color of the shaded boxes using the Series Palette. You can also change the color and style of the box outline and the candlestick lines.

To format a stock-chart series, navigate to the Value Series section of Format Chart, then use the settings, shown in Figure 19-32, to format the candlesticks for a stock series, to display series labels, or to add a curve-fitting line.

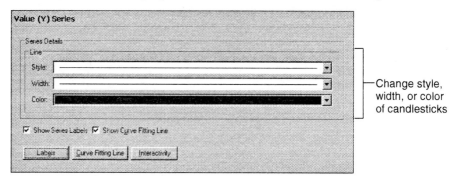

Figure 19-32   Stock-chart series options

Formatting a three-dimensional chart

When you format a three-dimensional chart, you can use axis rotation to change the orientation of the chart or use unit spacing to set the space between series.

Working with chart rotation

You can rotate the axes of a three-dimensional chart. When you rotate axes, you use the following settings:

- The x-axis rotation controls how the chart tilts toward or away from the viewer.

- The y-axis rotation controls how the chart pivots left and right on the y-axis in the center of the chart.

- The z-axis rotation controls how the chart tilts up and down on the central z-axis.

By default, a three-dimensional chart uses an x-axis rotation of –20, a y-axis rotation of 45, and a z-axis rotation of zero. A chart that uses default rotation settings appears oriented like the one shown in Figure 19-33.

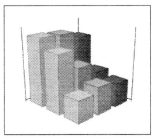

Figure 19-33   Three-dimensional chart using default axis rotation

Figure 19-34 shows the effects of changing each setting in the sample chart.

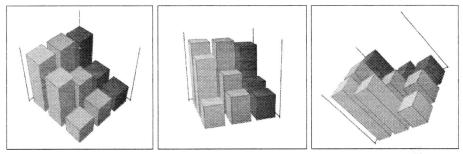

X rotation set to –45   Y rotation set to –45   Z rotation set to –45

Figure 19-34   Three-dimensional charts using different rotation settings

To change the rotation of an axis, navigate to the Chart Area section of Format Chart, then provide a rotation value, as shown in Figure 19-35.

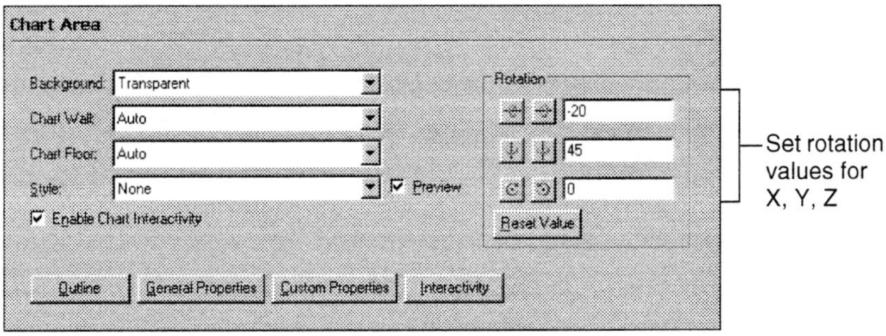

Figure 19-35   Rotation options in the Axis section

Working with the space between elements

To control the space between the series in a three-dimensional chart, you use unit spacing. The unit-spacing value is the percentage of the series width that appears between each series. For example, the default unit spacing is 50. Consequently, the space between two series elements in the chart, such as two sets of bars, is approximately 50 percent of the width of one series element. For example, Figure 19-36 shows the difference between two unit-spacing settings in a sample three-dimensional bar chart.

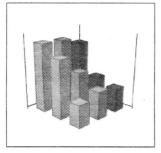 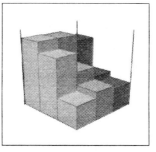

Unit spacing set to 100   Unit spacing set to 0

Figure 19-36   Charts using different unit-spacing settings

To change the spacing, navigate to the Chart Area section of Format Chart, then choose General Properties. In Unit Spacing, provide a value. The value indicates the percentage of the series width to use to separate series elements.

Setting the wall or floor color

In a chart that has depth or a three-dimensional chart, you can modify the color of the chart wall or floor. The default wall and floor color setting is transparent. Figure 19-37 shows where the wall and floor appear in a sample bar chart using depth.

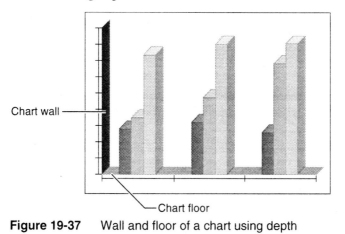

Figure 19-37   Wall and floor of a chart using depth

Figure 19-38 shows where the wall and floor appear in a three-dimensional chart.

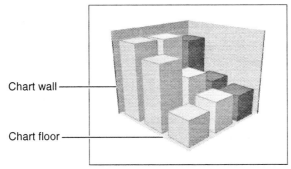

Figure 19-38   Walls and floor of a three-dimensional chart

To set the wall or floor color of a chart using depth or a three-dimensional chart, navigate to the Chart Area section of Format Chart. Use the settings shown in Figure 19-39 to set a wall or floor color.

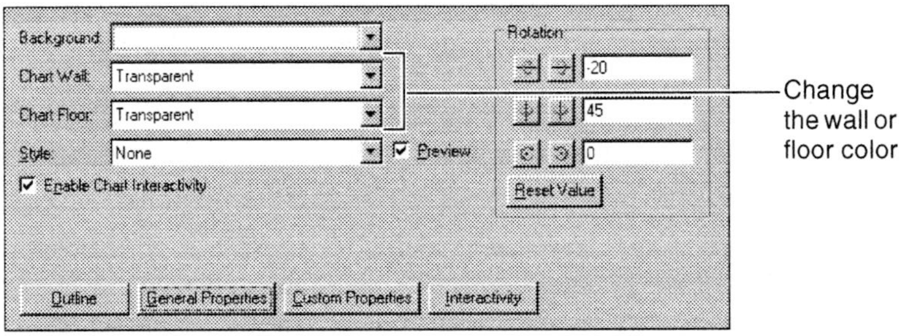

Figure 19-39   Wall and floor color options

Setting the series depth of a chart

In a chart using depth or in a three-dimensional chart, you can specify how deep the chart markers stretch. For example, you can specify the depth of lines in a two-dimensional with depth pie chart. The units of measurement, such as points, for the series depth is the same as the chart uses.

To set the depth of series elements in a chart with depth, navigate to the Chart Area section of Format Chart, then choose General Properties. Provide a value in Series Depth.

Laying out and formatting the chart

You can add background color, an outline, and change the line style of the chart components shown in Figure 19-40.

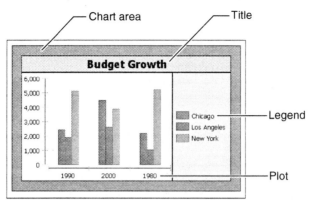

Figure 19-40 Parts of the chart included in Chart Area

To change the size and placement of the chart area, the title, the legend, and the plot, you can adjust the inset spaces between them. For example, you can add padding between the title and the plot or increase the size of the chart area without increasing the size of the other areas.

Setting the background color for a chart

The background color of the chart can be a standard color, a custom color, or a color gradient. You can also use an image in the background. You can also use a transparent background. A transparent background displays the background color of the report page on which it appears.

How to set a chart's background color

1 In the chart builder, choose Format Chart, then navigate to the Chart Area section. Use the list on the left to navigate among sections. Figure 19-41 shows the Chart Area section.

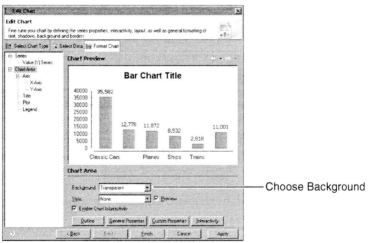

Figure 19-41 Background option in the Chart Area section

2 Choose Background to open the color picker.

Figure 19-42 shows the color picker.

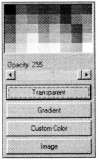

Figure 19-42   Color picker

3 Use the color picker to select a background color or image as follows:

- To use one of the basic colors, select a colored square.

- To use a transparent background, use the Opacity scroll tool to set the opacity to 0, then press Enter.

- To use a gradient color, choose Gradient, then use Gradient Editor to select a start color, end color, and rotation for the gradient pattern. Figure 19-43 shows the gradient editor.

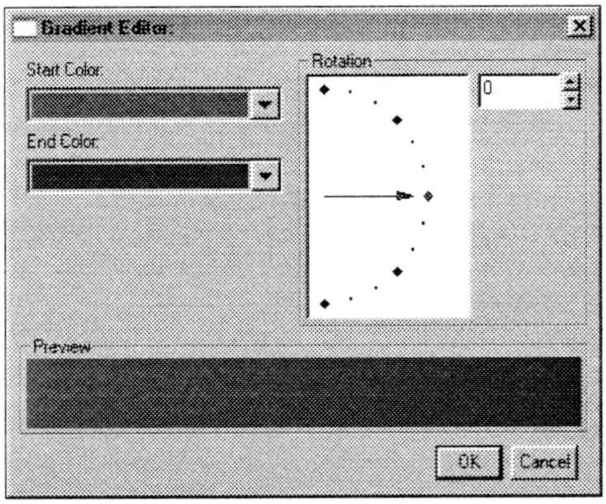

Figure 19-43   Setting colors and rotation for a gradient color

- To use a custom color, choose Custom Color to show the custom color list, then select a color.

- To use a background image, choose Image, then use Open to navigate to and select the image to use.

    The background color or image appears in Background on the chart builder.

4 To apply the color to the chart, choose Finish.

To define a custom color, on the color picker, choose Define Custom Colors to show the custom color picker, as shown in Figure 19-44.

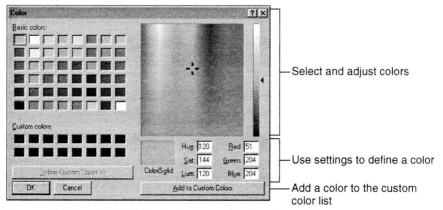

Select and adjust colors

Use settings to define a color

Add a color to the custom color list

Figure 19-44   Color picker including custom color options

Use the color picker options to select or define a custom color. When you finish, choose Add to Custom Colors, then choose OK.

Outlining a chart

An outline can distinguish the chart area from the rest of a report. To add an outline, navigate to the Chart Area section of Format Chart, then choose Outline to see the outline options, as shown in Figure 19-45.

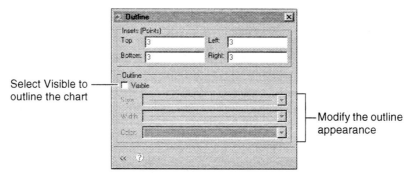

Select Visible to outline the chart

Modify the outline appearance

Figure 19-45   Setting a chart outline

Select Visible to add the outline, then use the Style, Width, and Color fields to change the appearance of the outline.

Adding padding around the chart

You can change the spacing around a chart and within the chart. The settings around and within the chart are called inset settings. To add more space, use a higher inset setting. For example, Figure 19-46 shows the effect of using two different chart top inset settings. In the second chart, the top section of the chart area is larger.

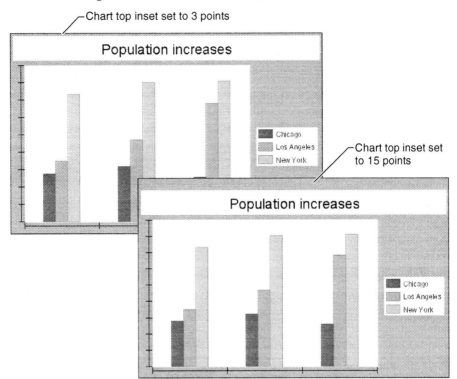

Figure 19-46   Charts using different inset settings

By default, inset values appear in points. To specify different units, such as pixels, inches, or centimeters, use Property Editor, as shown in Figure 19-47 to select the chart unit. The unit that you choose applies to chart settings, such as insets, or the width of series in three-dimensional charts and charts with depth.

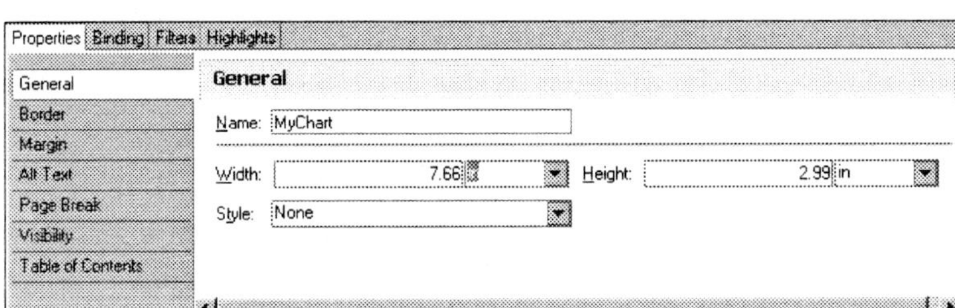

Figure 19-47   Changing units of measurement for the chart

To increase or decrease the number of units between chart elements, navigate to the Chart Area section of Format Chart, then choose General Properties and change the number of units, as shown in Figure 19-48.

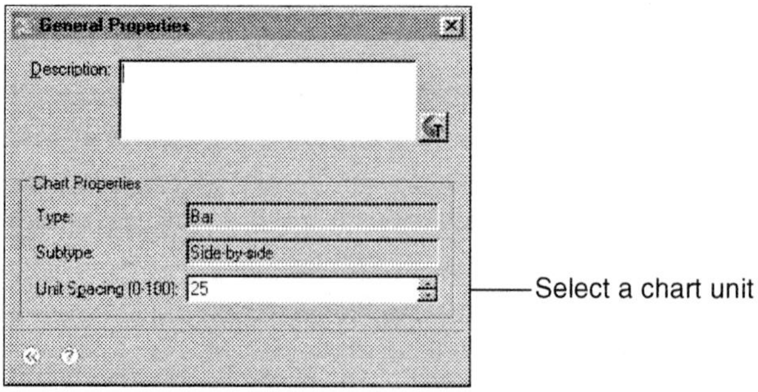

Select a chart unit

Figure 19-48   Setting the chart unit option

To set chart area insets, navigate to the Chart Area section of Format Chart, then choose Outline to see inset options, as shown in Figure 19-49. Type a value in one or more of the Insets fields.

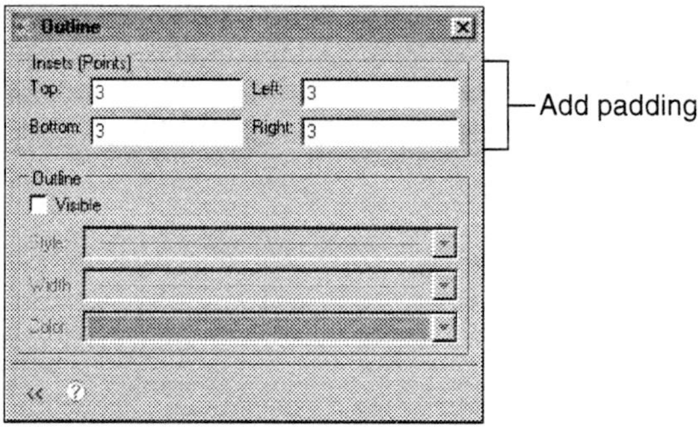

Add padding

Figure 19-49   Setting the inset options

Formatting numbers, dates, and times

You can format numbers, dates, or times that the chart displays in a number of ways. You can format numbers and produce multiples of them in the following ways:

- Add a prefix, such as a currency symbol.

- Multiply values by a number, such as 100.

- Add a suffix to a number value, such as the word million.

- Determine the number of decimal places that numbers include.

- Specify a number format pattern, such as #.###, which formats numbers using a point as the thousands separator.

You can format the following attributes of dates and times:

- Type. You can use a standard format, including Long, Short, Medium, and Full.

- Details. You can specify that the format is Date or DateTime.

- Pattern. You can specify a pattern, such as MMMM to show only the month value or dddd to show only the day value, such as Wednesday.

How to format a number

1 In the chart builder, either navigate to Legend in Format Chart and choose Entries, or navigate to Values Series and choose Labels. Choose Edit Format.

2 From the Data Type drop-down list, choose Number to see the number format options. Figure 19-50 shows the options.

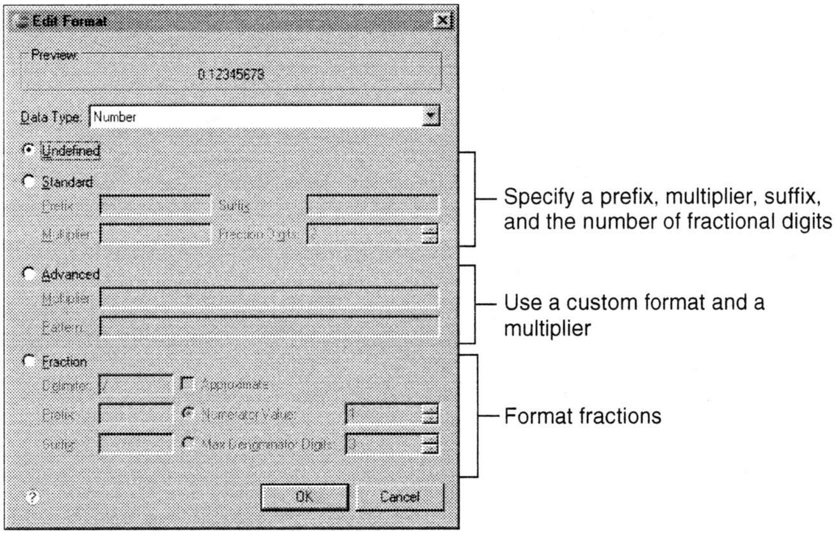

Figure 19-50 Format options for numeric data

3 To add a prefix, multiplier, or suffix, or to specify the number of decimal places, select Standard, then specify the following format settings:

- To add a number prefix, type the value in Prefix.

- To multiply values by a number, type the number by which to multiply expression values in Multiplier.

- To add a number suffix, type the value in Suffix.

- To specify the number of decimal places to use, select the number in Fraction Digits.

4 To use a custom number pattern, select Advanced, then specify the following format settings:

- To multiply values by a number, type the number by which to multiply expression values in Multiplier.

- To specify a number format pattern, type the pattern string in Pattern.

5 To use a custom fraction format, select Fraction, then specify the following format settings:

- Specify a delimiter symbol, such as slash (/).

- To add a prefix, type the value in Prefix.

- To add a suffix, type the value in Suffix.

- To define guidelines for representing fractions rather than using the default, select Approximate, then provide a suggested numerator or the suggested maximum number of denominator digits. For example, to show fractions with single-digit denominators, such as 1/2 or 3/8, supply 1 as the maximum number of denominator digits.

6 When you finish defining the format, choose OK.

How to format a date and time

1 In the chart builder, to the right of Type, choose Edit Format.

2 From the Data Type drop-down list, choose DateTime to see the format options. Figure 19-51 shows the options.

3 To use a predefined format type, select Standard, then specify the following format options:

- Select a format value in Type.

- In Details, select Date or DateTime.

4 To use a custom format pattern, select Advanced, then type the custom format string in Pattern.

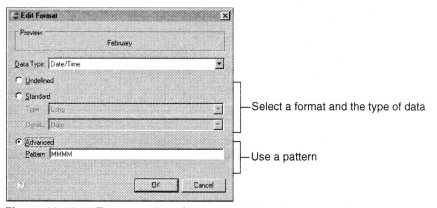

Figure 19-51 Format options for date-and-time data

5 When you finish defining the format, choose OK.

Formatting the chart legend, plot, and title

When you create a chart, the chart builder inserts the legend, plot, and title using default placement and size. You can rearrange or format the legend, plot, or title. Each area includes a client area outside the axes in which data or text appears. For example, Figure 19-52 shows an outline around the legend. The text area in the legend uses a colored background.

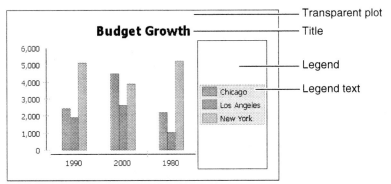

Figure 19-52   Legend areas

To highlight the plot, legend, or title, you can add a shadow behind that area. For example, Figure 19-53 shows a shadow behind title text. A shadow uses basic or custom colors. You cannot use a gradient color as a shadow.

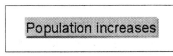

Figure 19-53   Title using shadow

You can change the location of these chart elements, add inset padding to separate a part from another part, or change the way a part resizes when the chart expands or contracts. You adjust the layout using the following settings:

■ Visibility

You can hide the title and legend of a chart, as shown in Figure 19-54.

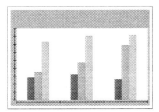

Figure 19-54   Chart not using a title or legend

■ Anchoring

To change where the plot, legend, or title appears, change the anchoring. For example, Figure 19-55 shows some of the different anchoring options for the legend text area within the legend area.

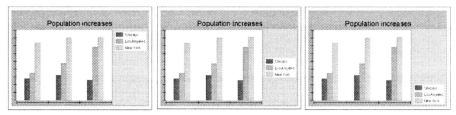

Figure 19-55   Charts using different legend anchor settings

Anchor positions are based on directions. For example, the first example chart in Figure 19-55 uses North_East.

■ Insets

To adjust the padding around a chart area, modify the inset settings. For example, Figure 19-56 shows the effect of increasing the top inset setting for the plot. The chart on the right uses a higher inset setting, so there is more space between the top of the plot and other chart elements, such as the title.

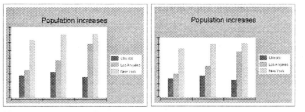

Figure 19-56   Charts using different plot inset settings

You also use inset settings to modify where the client area or text area appears within a chart area. For example, to change where series markers, such as bars in a bar chart, appear within the plot, change the plot client area insets. Figure 19-57 shows the effect of increasing the left inset for a bar chart plot client area. The chart on the right uses a higher inset setting, so more space appears between the plot client area, where the bars appear, and the edge of the rest of the plot.

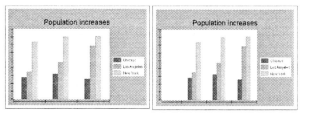

Figure 19-57   Charts using different plot client area inset settings

The following sections describe how to arrange and format the chart plot, legend, and title.

Working with the plot area

When you adjust the plot area, you can modify the entire plot area, which includes the axes, or only the area that appears within the axes. Figure 19-58 shows the two sections of the plot in a sample bar chart. The lighter area shows the area including axes. The smaller, darker area shows the area within the axes. To use one color across the entire plot, you must select that color in both areas.

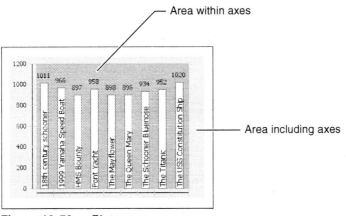

Figure 19-58   Plot areas

Setting the color, outline, or shadow for the plot

The default background color for the plot is transparent. You can also use a standard color, a custom color, a color gradient, or an image. Also, you can outline the plot and change the line color, style, and width. To highlight the plot area within the axes, you can use a shadow, similar to the one in Figure 19-59. You add a shadow by setting the Shadow option in Area Format, as shown in Figure 19-64.

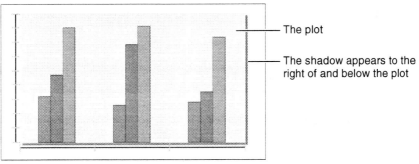

Figure 19-59   Plot using a shadow

Placing and adding space around the plot

You can use anchor settings to modify where the plot appears within the chart and inset settings to determine how much padding appears between the plot and other chart features. You can use plot spacing settings to modify the space between the plot area and the chart axes. Plot spacing includes horizontal and vertical settings. For example, Figure 19-60 shows the effect of increasing the horizontal spacing in a bar chart. In the second chart, the space between the horizontal axis and the bottom edge of the plot is much larger. To change the spacing around the plot, you set inset and spacing options in Area Format, as shown in Figure 19-64.

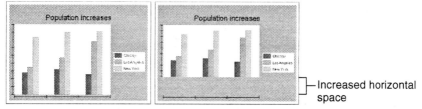

Figure 19-60   Charts using different horizontal plot spacing

Specifying the plot size

You can use the height hint and width hint settings to suggest a minimum height and width for the plot. In most cases, BIRT Report Designer uses the values you supply to size the plot. If you set a plot size that is too large to fit in the total design space, or if other chart elements such as the legend or a title are too large to accommodate the suggested plot size, BIRT Report Designer ignores the settings.

A height or width hint is most useful in a report that uses multiple charts, such as a report with different chart elements or a report that includes a chart element in a group section. Because chart sizing is dynamic, one chart element can produce multiple charts with plots of different sizes, as shown in Figure 19-61.

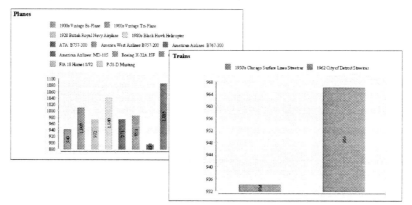

Figure 19-61   Charts created not using a height hint

Height and width hints help you to regulate the plot sizes in a group of charts. For example, the illustrations in Figure 19-62 show the result of setting the Height Hint parameter in a bar chart.

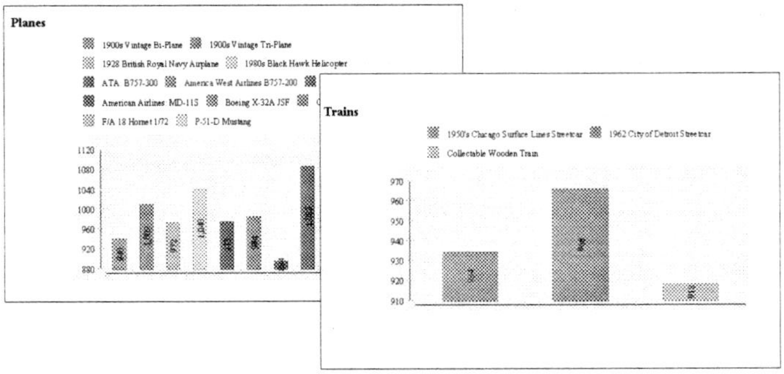

Charts from a design using a height hint maintain the same height

Figure 19-62 Effect of setting a height hint

The following procedures describe how to set the background color for a plot and how to include an outline or shadow and make adjustments in the size and placement of the chart.

To set a background color for the plot navigate to the Plot section of Format Chart, shown in Figure 19-63. Choose Background for either Area Including Axes or Area Within Axes, then use the color picker to select a background color. To apply the color to the plot, choose Finish.

How to modify the plot area

1 Navigate to the Plot section of Format Chart.

You see one of the two types of plot sections, as shown in Figure 19-63, depending on the type of chart.

Plot section of pie and meter charts   Plot section of other charts

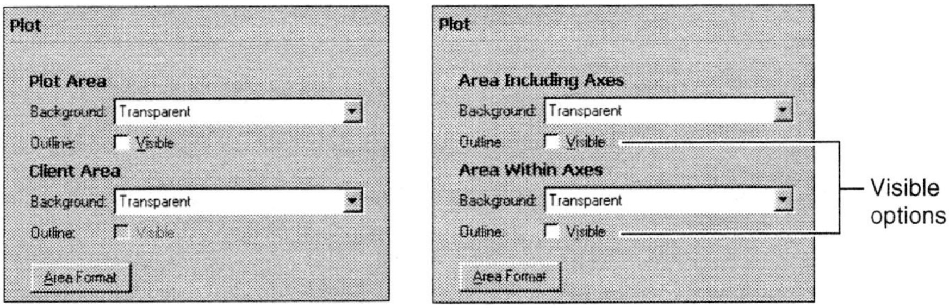

Figure 19-63 Plot section options in Format Chart

2 To make an outline of an area visible, select Visible in Outline for one or both areas.

3 To make other modifications to the area, choose Area Format.
Figure 19-64, shows the options you can set. Area Format exhibits the

same nomenclature differences, depending on the type of chart you are building, as shown in Figure 19-63.

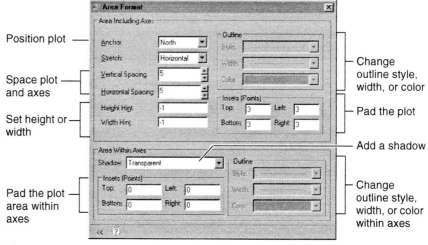

Figure 19-64   Options in Area Format

4 Modify any of the following options:

※ Modify the outline style, width, or color.

※ Set padding to add space on any or all sides of the plot.

※ Choose Shadow, then use the color picker to select a shadow color.

※ Set where the plot appears in the chart.

※ Add space between the vertical edge of the plot and the vertical axis.

※ Add space between the horizontal edge of the plot and the horizontal axis.

※ Set padding around the plot area enclosed by the 2D axes.

※ Constrain the height or width of the plot block.

5 When you are done, close Area Format, then choose Finish on the chart builder to save your changes.

Formatting the chart title text

You can modify the appearance of the title text in the expected ways. For example, you can change the font, size, color, style, or alignment of the text. You can also set the format to strike through or to rotate the title.

How to modify title text

1 Navigate to the Chart Area section of Format Chart.

2 To format the title, choose Title , then choose Font Editor to open the font editor.

3 Use the font editor settings shown in Figure 19-65 to modify the font.

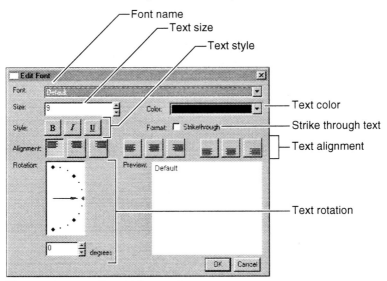

Figure 19-65   Font Editor options

4 To accept your changes, choose OK, and choose Finish on the chart builder.

Formatting the title area

When you apply a background color or outline to a chart title, you can work with the entire title area or with only the text area. Figure 19-66 shows the difference between the two areas in a sample chart. If you apply a background color to the title area, the same color appears in the text area unless you set a new background color for the text. You can add a shadow only to the text area. You cannot shadow the entire title area.

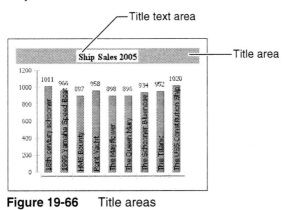

Figure 19-66   Title areas

To add a background color, outline, or shadow to the chart title text area, navigate to Title in the Chart Area section of Format Chart, then choose Text to see the options that are shown in Figure 19-67. Use the settings to modify the title text.

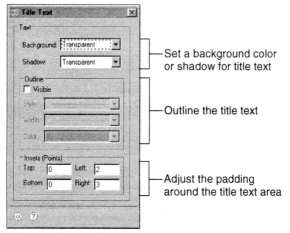

Set a background color or shadow for title text

Outline the title text

Adjust the padding around the title text area

Figure 19-67   Formatting options for the text of the title

To add a background color or outline to the title area of the chart, or to position the title area, navigate to Title in the Chart Area section of Format Chart, then choose Layout to see the options shown in Figure 19-68.

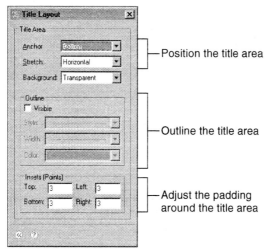

Position the title area

Outline the title area

Adjust the padding around the title area

Figure 19-68   Formatting options for the title area

You can use anchor settings to modify where the title appears within the chart. To determine how much padding appears between the title or title text areas and other chart features, use the inset settings.

Working with the legend

By default, a chart displays a legend. The legend uses a transparent background and does not include an outline or a shadow. To highlight the legend area, you can add a background color, outline, or shadow. You can hide the legend or change its position in the chart area, and you can add a legend title or modify legend-text properties, such as the font size.

Setting the color, outline, or shadow for the legend

When you apply a background color or outline to a chart legend, you can work with the entire legend area or with the text area only. Figure 19-69 shows the difference between the two areas in a sample chart. If you apply a background color to the legend area, the color also appears in the text area, unless you set a background color in the text area that overrides the legend area settings. You can add a shadow only to the text area. You cannot shadow the entire legend area.

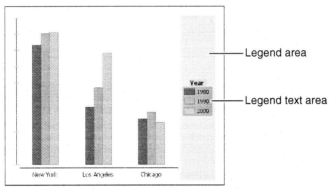

Figure 19-69   Legend areas

To format the legend, navigate to the Chart Area section of Format Chart, and select Legend. First, select Visible in both places in the Legend section, as shown in Figure 19-70 to make the legend area and legend title visible, and then choose either Title, Layout, or Entries.

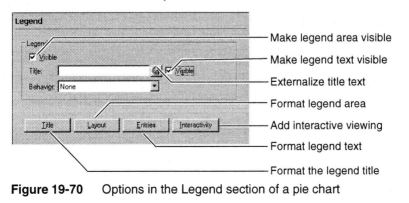

Figure 19-70   Options in the Legend section of a pie chart

To format the legend area, choose Layout from the Legend section, then use Layout Legend, shown in Figure 19-71.

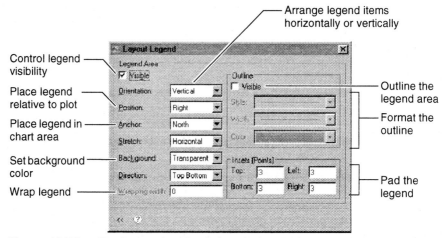

Arrange legend items horizontally or vertically

Control legend visibility

Place legend relative to plot

Place legend in chart area

Set background color

Wrap legend

Outline the legend area

Format the outline

Pad the legend

Figure 19-71   Background option in Layout Legend

You can prevent truncation of the legend by increasing the wrapping width. Specify a maximum width for legend items. Items that extend beyond the wrapping width appear on multiple lines in the legend.

Placing and adding space around a legend

You use anchor settings to modify where the legend appears within the chart. To determine how much padding appears between the legend or legend text areas and other chart features, use the inset settings.

To adjust the position of the entire legend area, rather than the client area where the legend items appear, change the legend-position setting. You position a legend relative to the plot. For example, Figure 19-72 shows different legend positions in a sample chart.

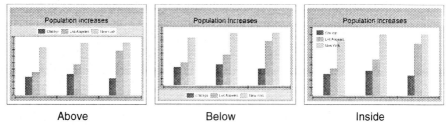

Above   Below   Inside

Figure 19-72   Legend positions

You can also organize legend items within the legend client area. For example, in Figure 19-73, the chart on the left shows legend items arranged horizontally. The chart on the right shows legend items arranged vertically. To adjust the positions of legend items in the legend-client area, set the legend orientation.

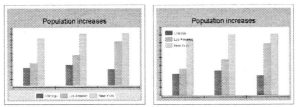

Figure 19-73   Horizontal and vertical legend orientation

Showing series item values in a legend

In a legend, you can display the value of a series item as well as the item name. To display values in the legend, navigate to the Legend area of Format Chart, then select Show Value, as shown in Figure 19-74.

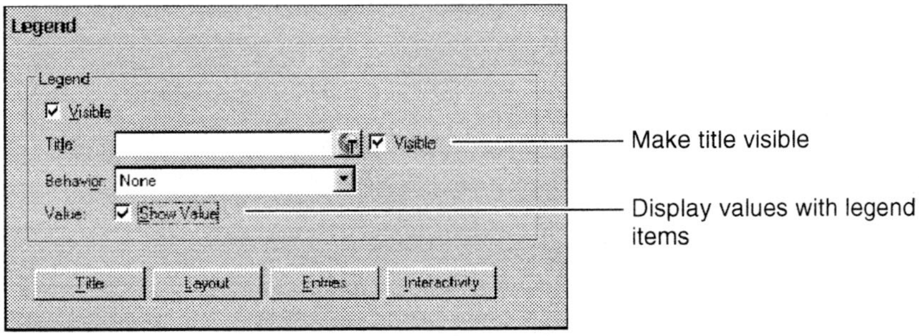

Make title visible

Display values with legend items

Figure 19-74   Displaying values in the legend

A pie chart always shows the legend values, so the Legend section of a pie chart does not include Show Value.

Formatting the legend text

You can change the font style and size of the legend text. If you use more than one series, you can add a separator line between the items in one series and the items in the next.

To format the legend text, navigate to the Legend section of Format Chart and choose Entries, then choose Font Editor, shown in Figure 19-75. Use the font editor to modify the font attributes.

Adding a legend title

You can use a title for the chart legend. When you first add the title, it uses default font settings and appears above the list of legend items. You can change the font style and color of the title. You can also add a title outline, background color, or shadow, or position the title below, to the left, or to the right of the legend text.

To add and format the title of the legend, navigate to the Legend section of Format Chart. Figure 19-70 shows the Legend section options. Select Visible to show the title, then type the title text.

To format the title, choose Title. Then use the settings shown in Figure 19-75 to format the title.

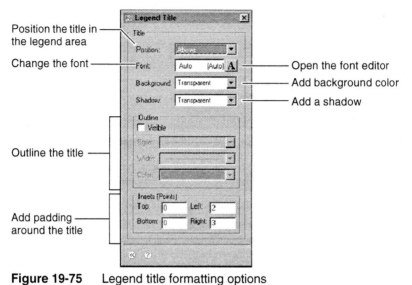

Position the title in the legend area

Change the font

Outline the title

Add padding around the title

Open the font editor

Add background color

Add a shadow

Figure 19-75   Legend title formatting options

Formatting axis titles, markers, lines, and labels

In earlier sections you learned how to format the titles of the chart itself and of the legend. You can also entitle the x- and y-axis, use markers to highlight points on the chart, modify the style and color of axis lines, and label the axis.

You can hide or reposition an axis element and change the default appearance of it in Format Chart. For example, you can delete the title for an axis or move the axis tick marks. You can also change the color or style of an element, add an outline, or change the padding.

Working with an axis title

Charts other than pie and meter can have x-axis or y-axis titles. To add and format an axis title, you navigate to the Format Chart section. Select Visible, shown in Figure 19-76, type the title text, and then navigate to either the X-Axis or Y-Axis section in the Chart Area. Choose Title to modify the title position, outline, padding, or font style of the axis title. Toggle between the x-axis and y-axis to make title changes to one or the other by navigating to X-Axis or Y-Axis in the Chart Area, and then choosing Title.

In Axis Title, shown in Figure 19-77, you can position the title above or below an x-axis, or you can position the title to the left or right of a y-axis. You can outline the title, and add padding around it using Insets. You can change the size and style of the font, and add a shadow or a background color.

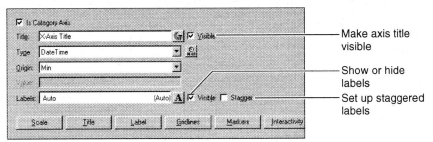

Figure 19-76   Title field and labels in an axis section

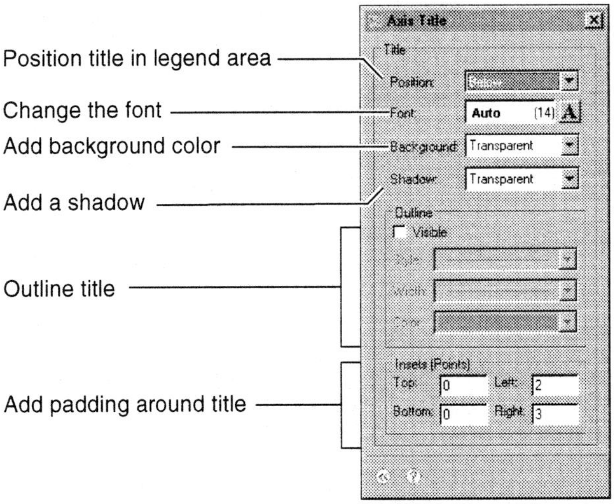

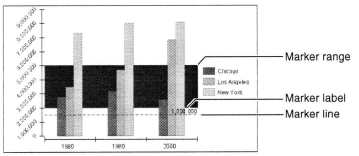

Figure 19-77   Formatting options for an x-axis title

Working with axis markers

Axis markers highlight numbers or ranges on two-dimensional charts or charts with depth. Figure 19-78 shows a chart with a marker line and range.

Figure 19-78   Chart using a marker line and a marker range

You can use the following types of markers:

- A marker line is a line that extends across the plot from a point on the axis. You specify the axis and value from which to draw the line.

- A marker range is a rectangular area that highlights a range of values. You specify between which values and from which axis to draw the rectangle.

For example, Figure 19-78 shows a marker line and a marker range. Both markers highlight points on the y-axis. The marker line uses a label to show the marker value. You can change the style or color of the marker, change label text, or hide labels. You should only add a marker to an x-axis if it shows numeric or date-and-time data. Adding a marker to an axis that shows text values as categories generally does not help users read the chart.

Adding an axis marker

To create and format an axis marker, navigate to the Format Chart section for the axis to which you want to add a marker, then choose Axis Markers to see the options shown in Figure 19-79.

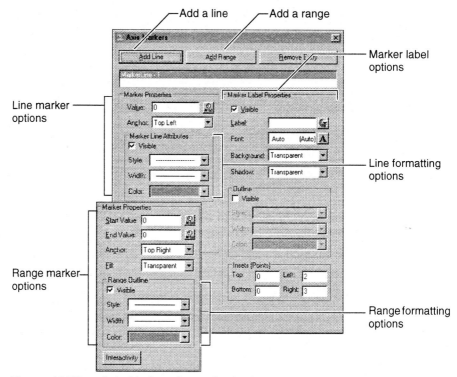

Figure 19-79   Axis Markers formatting options

To create a marker line, choose Add Line. The marker appears in the marker list. In Value, type the value at which the line should start. To create an axis marker range, choose Add Range. When you add a range instead of a line marker, Marker Properties shows options for a range. Set the span of values the range marker covers. In Start Value, type the value at which to begin the range. In End Value, type the value at which to end the range.

Formatting axis markers

A marker displays a label to identify the axis point or range that the marker highlights. You can adjust the line style, width, and color of a marker line, or change the range fill color or outline of a marker range. You can also hide or format the label. To format a marker line or range, use the line format options, which are shown in Figure 19-79.

To hide or format a marker label, select the name of the line or range to format in the marker list, then set the corresponding properties, as shown in Figure 19-80.

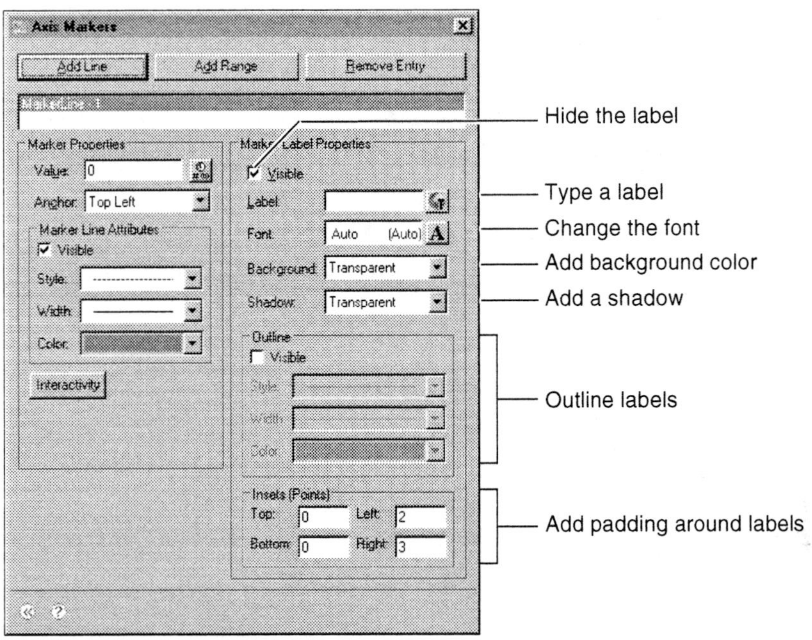

Figure 19-80   Axis Markers label options

Working with an axis line

You can modify the line style and of an axis and its tick marks. Major and minor tick marks highlight large and small intervals in the axis. Typically, when you first create a chart, the axes use major tick marks that are positioned across an axis. You can also position tick marks to the left or right of a vertical axis or above or below a horizontal axis. Figure 19-81 shows different tick mark settings for a y-axis.

You can also add gridlines, which extend from an axis and span the plot area. For example, Figure 19-82 shows a chart that uses y-axis gridlines to clarify the data points. When you add major or minor gridlines to an axis, the chart includes a gridline for each major or minor interval on the axis.

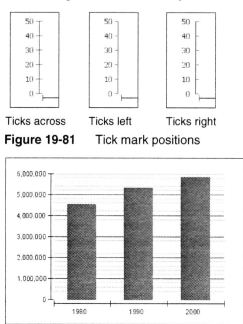

50
40
30
20
10
0
Ticks across
Ticks left
Ticks right

Figure 19-81 Tick mark positions

6,000,000
5,000,000
4,000,000
3,000,000
2,000,000
1,000,000
0
1980
1990
2000

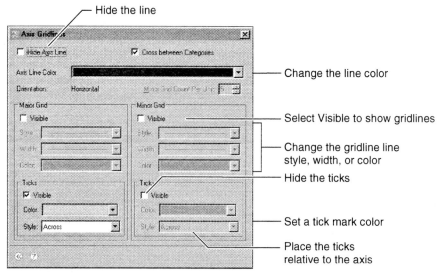

Figure 19-82 Y-axis gridlines

To modify an axis line, navigate to the Format Chart section for the axis, then choose Gridlines. Use the Gridlines settings to format the axis line. Figure 19-83 shows the gridline options for the x-axis of a 2D chart.

Hide the line
Hide Axis Line
Cross between Categories
Axis Line Color
Orientation:
Horizontal
Major Grid
Minor Grid
Visible
Ticks
Visible
Color
Style:
Across
Change the line color
Select Visible to show gridlines
Change the gridline line style, width, or color
Hide the ticks
Set a tick mark color
Place the ticks relative to the axis

Figure 19-83 Axis Gridlines tick marks formatting options

To modify axis tick marks, navigate to the Format Chart section for the axis, then choose Gridlines. Use the Gridlines settings to format the tick marks, as shown in Figure 19-83. You can modify major or minor tick mark settings.

To add or modify gridlines, navigate to the Format Chart section for the axis, then choose Gridlines. Use the settings to add or change the axis gridlines, as shown in Figure 19-83. You can modify major or minor division settings.

Working with axis labels

By default, a chart displays labels to the left of a vertical axis and below a horizontal axis, as shown in Figure 19-84.

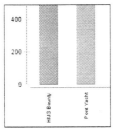

Figure 19-84   Default axis label positions

You can hide or reposition the labels on an axis. For example, you can show the labels on the y-axis to the right of the axis rather than the left, or rotate the labels on the x-axis so that they are easier to read. You can also modify the label font; add a background color, shadow, or outline; or change the padding around the labels.

Sometimes, a chart displays so many values on an axis that the label text overlaps and becomes illegible. In this case, the chart builder drops some of the axis labels. Figure 19-85 shows a chart in which labels have disappeared. In the chart, only three of four x-axis labels appear. The chart dropped the second label because it overlapped the neighboring labels.

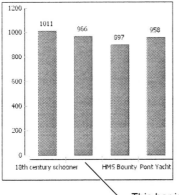

Figure 19-85   Chart displaying a missing x-axis label

To fix this problem, you can rotate the labels or stagger them, so they do not overlap. Figure 19-86 shows the two solutions on an x-axis. In the chart on the left, rotation of x-axis labels makes all the labels fit into the space. On the right, staggering labels displays all axis categories.

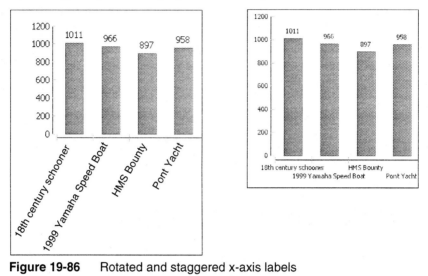

Figure 19-86   Rotated and staggered x-axis labels

You can also skip labels. For example, in Figure 19-87, the chart on the left shows all labels. The chart on the right skips every other label. To skip labels, set the interval at which labels should appear. For example, to show every other label, use an interval of 2. To show every fifth label, use an interval of 5.

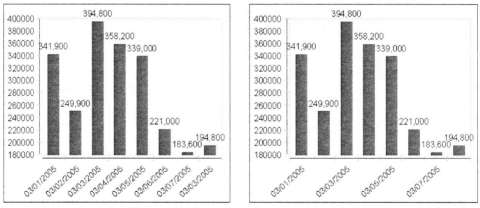

Figure 19-87   Charts showing all labels and skipped labels

To format axis labels, navigate to the Format Chart section for the axis, then choose Label. Use the Axis Label options to update the axis label options, as shown in Figure 19-88.

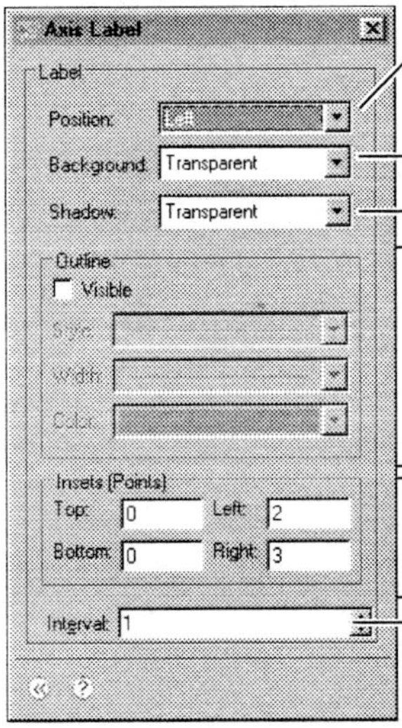

Figure 19-88   Axis Label formatting options

Defining the axis data type and number format

The axis data type and format determine how the chart builder arranges the data that appears on the axis. To set the axis type, you select one of the following settings:

- Linear. This axis type spaces values evenly.

- Logarithmic. This axis type spaces values on a scale that is based on multiples of 10.

- DateTime. This axis type shows data on a date or time scale.

- Text. This axis type displays text only and spaces words evenly. The location of a data point on a text axis does not indicate its size. Typically, a text axis is a category axis.

How to set the data type and format of an axis

1   On Format Chart, navigate to the axis section, then use the Type settings to change the data type of the axis. Figure 19-89 shows axis options.

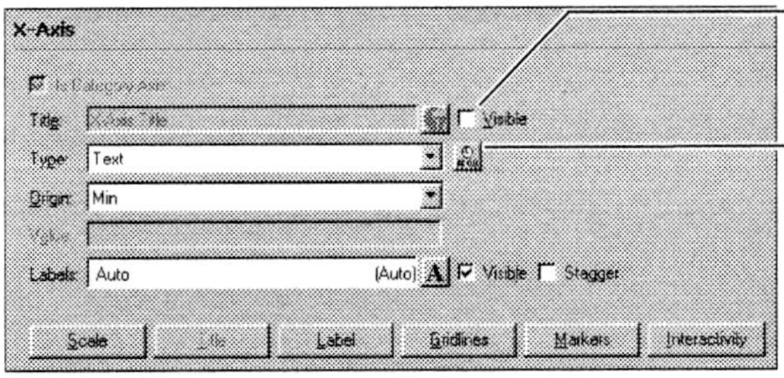

Figure 19-89   X-axis section of Format Chart

2 Choose Open Edit Format.

The Edit Format dialog box displays options for the data type of the axis. Figure 19-90 shows options for the DateTime data type.

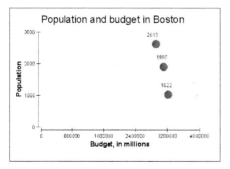

Pattern MMMM displays name of month

Figure 19-90 Editing the format of a date

Defining where one axis intersects the other

When you set an axis intersection setting, you define at what value the axis meets the opposing axis. You can select one of the following values:

- Select Min to have the axis intersect the opposing axis at the opposing axis's minimum value.

- Select Max to have the axis intersect the opposing axis at the opposing axis's maximum value.

- Select Value to have the axis intersect the opposing axis at a value that you specify.

Typically, a chart displays each axis intersecting the opposing axis at the minimum value. Figure 19-91 and Figure 19-92 show the results of selecting Min, Max, and Value for the y-axis of a scatter chart.

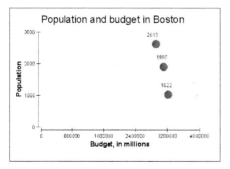
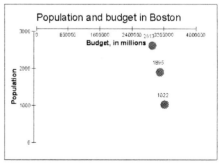

X-axis intersects y-axis at minimum value   X-axis intersects y-axis at maximum value

Figure 19-91 Y-axis Min and Max intersection options

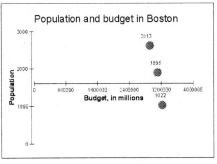

Population and budget in Boston

X-axis intersects y-axis at 1500

Figure 19-92 Y-axis Value intersection option

To set the intersection of an axis, on Format Chart, navigate to the page for that axis. In Origin, select Min, Max, or Value as the intersection setting. If you select Value, you must provide a value at which to join the axes.

Defining the scale of an axis

The scale of an axis determines the range of values displayed on a linear, logarithmic, or date-and-time axis. When you first create a chart, the chart builder selects a maximum and a minimum axis value to fit the data that the axis displays. Typically, the chart builder selects a minimum value that is just below the lowest axis value and a maximum value that is just higher than the highest axis value, rounding down or up to the nearest major unit, so the markings on the axis span the range of data that it displays.

You can use axis scale to change the following settings:

- The minimum and maximum values for an axis.

- The span between major grid values and the number of minor grid marks between major grid values on the axis. The distance between major grid marks is the step value. The number of minor grid marks is the minor grid count.

For example, in Figure 19-93, the axis on the left shows values from 0 to 1200. The step value is 200, so the major grid marks indicate values of 200, 400, and so on. The minor grid count is five grid marks for each major unit. The axis on the right shows values from 0 to 800. The step value is 100, so the major grid marks indicate 100, 200, and so on. The minor grid count is two grid marks for each major unit.

You can set the scale of value axes only. Category axes do not support scale changes. The following procedures describe how to set the scale of an x-axis. To set the scale of a y-axis, complete the same steps on the y-axis page. Most scale items appear in the Scale dialog. To set the number of minor grid marks per major unit, you use the Gridlines dialog.

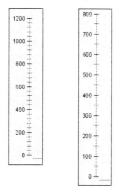

Figure 19-93   Axes using different scale options

To define the scale of an axis, on Format Chart, navigate to the section for the axis to modify, then choose Scale. Use the Scale options to change the range and divisions of data on an axis. Figure 19-94 shows the scale options for a y-axis that uses a linear data type.

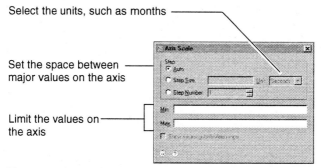

Select the units, such as months

Set the space between major values on the axis

Limit the values on the axis

Figure 19-94   Scale options

To define the minor grid count, on Format Chart, navigate to the axis to modify, then choose Gridlines. Use Minor grid count per unit to set the number of minor grid marks between two major grid marks, as shown in Figure 19-95.

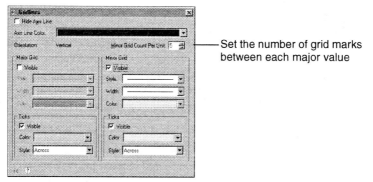

Set the number of grid marks between each major value

Figure 19-95   Setting the minor grid count

Formatting a series

You can format the color of value or category series elements by moving colors to the top of the color palette. You can add a trendline to value series of many chart types. You can also add a trendline to the category series in a scatter chart, because a scatter chart category series displays values. Generally, the type of series determines what formatting options you can apply for that series.

Stacking series

You can stack the value series that you display in a chart. In a stacked chart, the data points from one value series are arranged on top of the data points of another series. Stacking helps to show each data point's contribution to the total of all the data points in a category.

You can stack only area, bar, cone, pyramid, tube, and line series. To stack a series, navigate to the Series section of Format Chart, then select Stacked for the series.

Hiding a series

You can hide a series in a chart. A hidden series contributes data, but does not appear in the chart. For example, you might want to use a series to contribute to a trendline without displaying the series data points. Typically, you hide a value series rather than a category series.

To hide a series, navigate to the Series section of Format Chart, and deselect Visible for the series.

Making a series translucent

You can make a chart series translucent so you can see an image or color behind the chart data. For example, Figure 19-96 shows two versions of a chart that uses an image as the plot background. The chart on the left uses a solid series. The chart on the right uses a translucent series.

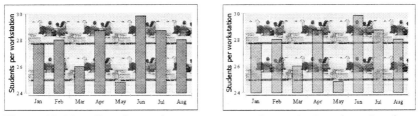

Figure 19-96   Bar chart using an opaque series and a translucent series

To make a series translucent, navigate to the Series section of Format Chart, and select Translucent for the series.

Setting the color palette for a series

You can specify which colors a series uses. Charts that have axes, such as line and stock charts, use varied colors to distinguish between different value series. When a bar chart uses more than one set of bars, the default behavior is to show each set in a different color. If a bar chart uses only one set of bars, the bars are the same color. Figure 19-97 shows charts using the default settings.

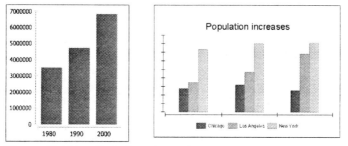

Figure 19-97   Default series colors

In charts that have axes, you can choose to color the chart by category series instead. This approach is useful when you have only one value series, but you want to show variously colored series elements, as in the chart in Figure 19-98. The chart uses one value series, but shows each bar in the series in a different color. Coloring the chart by category series also displays the category series items, rather than the value series items, in the legend.

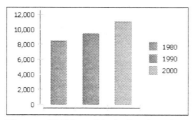

Figure 19-98   Varied colors in a chart using one value series

Pie charts and meter charts work differently. By default, a bar or a meter chart varies the category series colors to show each pie sector or needle in a different color, as shown in Figure 19-99.

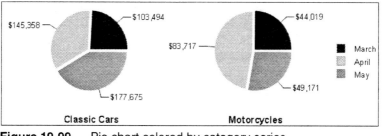

Figure 19-99   Pie chart colored by category series

You can color by value series to show all the sectors in a pie or all the needles on a meter in the same color. For example, Figure 19-100 shows the same pie chart, colored by value series.

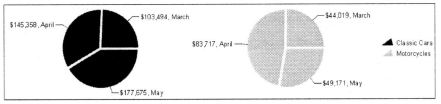

Figure 19-100   Pie chart colored by value series

To determine which data the legend displays, navigate to the Series section of Format Chart, then use Color By to select Value Series or Categories.

When you create a chart, it uses default colors for series elements. To select different colors, you modify the series palette. The chart uses the colors that you select in the order in which you select them in the palette list. If the chart displays more series elements than there are colors in the palette, it uses some colors more than once.

To specify the colors used in the chart, navigate to the Series section of Format Chart, then choose Series Palette to see the options shown in Figure 19-101.

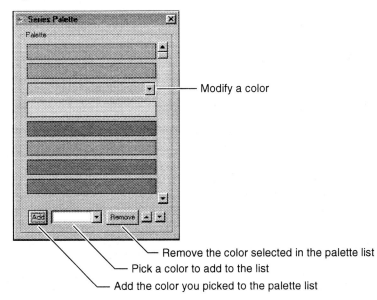

Figure 19-101   Series Palette

Use the following settings to modify the series palette:

- To set an element in the chart to use particular colors, find the color in the palette, and move that color to the top of the palette.

- To add a new color, select the color drop-down list to the right of Add, and use the color picker to select or create a color. When you finish, choose Add.

- To remove a color, select the color in the list, and choose Remove.

- To modify a color, select it, then use the color picker to select or create a color.

When you finish adjusting the color palette, close Series Palette, then choose Finish in the chart builder.

Working with data points and data point labels

By default, a chart displays labels that identify value-series values, such as the height of a bar in a bar chart or the size of a sector in a pie chart.

To display different data in the labels, you change the data point settings. The data point settings determine what text each label displays. Typically, the label shows the value-series value, such as the highest point of a line chart on the y-axis. You can also show where the point appears on the x-axis, use the series value to show to which group of data points a point belongs, or display the value as a percentage of the total value of all points in the chart.

For example, in Figure 19-102, the first chart uses a legend to show which bar represents each series. The second chart labels each bar with the city name.

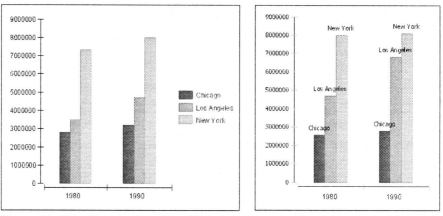

Figure 19-102   Bar charts using different label settings

After you decide what data to show in the labels, you can change the number format of the data points or add a prefix or a suffix to the label expression. You can also use a separator between values.

For example, in the chart in Figure 19-102, you can display the city value and the year value, separated by a comma, such as Chicago, 1980. In a different chart, you could add a currency symbol before a value or append text, such as Orders.

To modify the data a label displays, navigate to the Value Series section of Format Chart, then choose Labels. Use the settings in Values, shown in Figure 19-103, to set up the data the label displays.

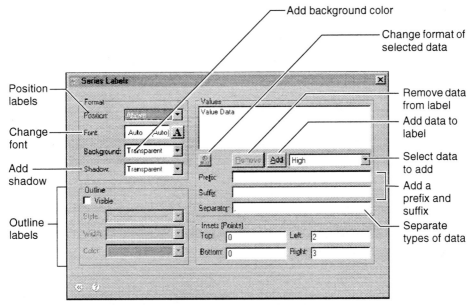

Figure 19-103   Label data settings

To format data point labels, navigate to the Value Series section of Format Chart, then choose Labels. Use the settings in Values to set up the data the label displays, as shown in Figure 19-103.

Adding and formatting a curve-fitting line

A curve-fitting line is a graphical representation of a trend in data. You can use a curve-fitting line to detect patterns in data or to predict future values. For example, the chart in Figure 19-104 uses curve-fitting lines to highlight population trends in several cities. You can use the trendlines to estimate population in the years after 2000. The population for Los Angeles, for example, is growing sharply, while the population in New York has increased less dramatically.

You use curve-fitting lines in two-dimensional and two-dimensional with depth area, bar, bubble, line, scatter, and stock charts. You cannot use curve fitting with a three-dimensional chart. A curve-fitting line in a BIRT chart places each curve-fitting point based on the following factors:

- The location of the neighboring data points
- A weight function that takes into account all the data points that the curve-fitting line includes

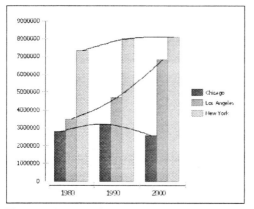

Figure 19-104   Chart using curve-fitting lines

A curve-fitting line can look very different depending on the span and amount of data that you use. Before adding curve fitting to your chart, ensure you have enough data to show a meaningful trend.

To display a curve-fitting line, navigate to the Value Series section of Format Chart, then select Show Curve Fitting Line, as shown in Figure 19-105. By default, a curve-fitting line uses a thin black line. You can change the line style or color.

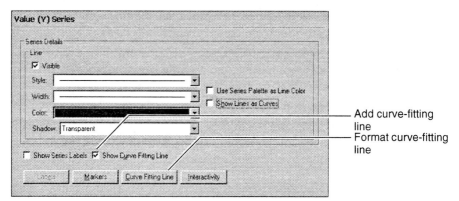

Figure 19-105   Show curve-fitting line option

To format a curve-fitting line, navigate to the Value Series section of Format Chart, and choose Curve Fitting Line, then use the settings to change the style, width, or color of the line, as shown in Figure 19-106.

To add labels to a curve-fitting line, navigate to the Value Series section of Format Chart, and choose Curve Fitting Line. In Label, select Visible, then use the settings on Curve Fitting Line to format the labels, as shown in Figure 19-106.

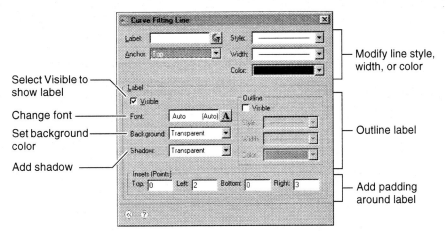

Select Visible to show label

Change font

Set background color

Add shadow

Modify line style, width, or color

Outline label

Add padding around label

Figure 19-106   Labeling and formatting options for a curve-fitting line

Presenting Data in a Cross Tab

A cross tab displays data in a row-and-column matrix that looks similar to a spreadsheet. Like a spreadsheet, the cross tab is ideal for summarizing data in a compact and concise format. It displays summary, or aggregate, values such as sums, counts, or averages. The cross tab groups these values by one set of data listed down the left side of the matrix and another set of data listed across the top of the matrix.

Figure 20-1 shows a cross tab that displays sales totals by state and by product line. The cross tab uses data from three fields: state, productline, and extendedprice.

Values in the productline field form the columns

	Classic Cars	Motorcycles	Planes	Ships	Trains	Grand Total
CA	$458,563.64	$162,710.57	$108,632.26	$66,758.95	$17,965.32	$814,630.74
CT	$89,671.28	$39,699.67	$41,142.34	$5,936.68	$9,548.53	$185,998.50
MA	$223,366.59	$91,024.09	$51,924.57	$71,419.40	$9,695.99	$447,430.64
NH	$69,150.35	--	--	--	--	$69,150.35
NJ	--	$35,116.44	$33,308.49	$4,346.26	--	$72,771.19
NV	$58,718.89	--	--	--	--	$58,718.89
NY	$260,619.73	$99,514.87	$24,647.66	$36,219.65	$15,033.47	$436,035.38
PA	$102,856.24	$39,025.09	$15,889.79	$4,983.38	$4,862.02	$167,616.52
Grand Total	$1,262,946.32	$467,090.73	$275,545.11	$189,664.32	$57,105.33	$2,252,352.21

Values in the state field form the rows

Each cell is an intersection of a row and column field, and displays the sales total by state and product line. Sales totals are calculated by summing values in the extendedprice field.

Figure 20-1   Cross tab displaying sales totals by state and product line

As Figure 20-1 shows, a cross tab has the following characteristics:

■ It requires at least three fields.

■ One field populates the column headings in the cross tab. There is one column for each unique value in the field. In the example shown in Figure 20-1, there are five unique values in the PRODUCTLINE field: Classic Cars, Motorcycles, Planes, Ships, and Trains.

■ One field populates the row headings in the cross tab. There is one row for each unique value in the field. In the example, there are eight unique values in the state field: CA, CT, MA, NH, NJ, NV, NY, and PA.

■ One field's values are aggregated, and these values populate the cells of the cross tab. In the example, each cell displays a sales total by product line and by state. The sales total is calculated using the SUM function on the values in the extendedprice field.

This chapter begins with a tutorial in which you build a cross tab similar to the one shown in Figure 20-1. The tutorial leads you through the essential tasks. The rest of the chapter expands on some of the concepts, such as data cubes, which are unique to cross tabs.

Tutorial 6: Creating a cross tab

This tutorial provides instructions for creating a cross tab that displays sales totals by state and product line. The cross tab uses data from the Customers, OrderDetails, and Products tables in the sample database, Classic Models.

In this tutorial, you perform the following tasks:

■ Create a new report

■ Build a data source

■ Build a data set

■ Add a cross tab to the report

■ Organize data for the cross tab

■ Insert data in the cross tab

■ Add grand totals

■ Format the cross tab

Task 1: Create a new report

1 Choose File➤New➤Report.

2 On New Report, select a project in which to save your report.

3 Type the following text as the file name:

```
SalesByStateAndProductLine.rptdesign
```

4 Choose Finish. A blank report layout appears in the layout editor.

Task 2: Build a data source

Before you begin designing your report in the layout editor, you create a data source to connect your report to the Classic Models database.

1 Choose Data Explorer.

2 Right-click Data Sources, and choose New Data Source from the context menu.

3 Select Classic Models Inc. Sample Database from the list of data sources, use the default data source name, then choose Next. Connection information about the new data source appears.

4 Choose Finish. BIRT Report Designer creates a new data source that connects to the sample database. It appears within Data Sources in Data Explorer.

Task 3: Build a data set

In this procedure, you build a data set to indicate what data to extract from the Customers, OrderDetails, and Products tables.

1 In Data Explorer, right-click Data Sets, and choose New Data Set.

2 On New Data Set, type the following text for data set name:

```
Sales
```

3 Use the default values for the other fields.

- Data Source shows the name of the data source that you created earlier.

- Data Set Type specifies that the data set uses a SQL SELECT query.

4 Choose Next. Query displays the information to help you create a SQL query. The text area on the right side shows the required keywords of a SQL SELECT statement.

5 Use the following SQL SELECT statement to indicate what data to retrieve. You can type the column and table names, or you can drag them from Available Items to the appropriate location in the SELECT statement.

```
SELECT Customers.state,
Orderdetails.quantityOrdered,
Orderdetails.priceEach,
Products.productline
```

```
FROM Customers INNER JOIN Orders ON Customers.customerNumber
    = Orders.customerNumber
INNER JOIN Orderdetails ON Orders.orderNumber =
    Orderdetails.orderNumber
INNER JOIN Products ON Orderdetails.productCode =
    Products.productCode

WHERE Customers.country = 'USA'
```

This SELECT statement joins four tables to get the required data.

6 Choose Finish to save the data set. Edit Data Set displays the columns specified in the query, and provides options for editing the data set.

7 Choose Computed Columns, then choose New to create a computed field that calculates extended prices by multiplying values from the QUANTITYORDERED and PRICEEACH fields.

8 On New Computed Column, specify the following values, as shown in Figure 20-2:

1 In Column Name, type

```
EXTENDED_PRICE
```

2 In Data Type, select Decimal.

3 In Expression, type

```
row["QUANTITYORDERED"] * row["PRICEEACH"]
```

Alternatively, you can open the expression builder to construct the expression by selecting the appropriate data set fields. Note that unlike the SELECT statement where you can type table field names in any case, data set field names are case-sensitive. If, in Expression, you typed row["quantityOrdered"], BIRT displays an error when you preview the results returned by the data set.

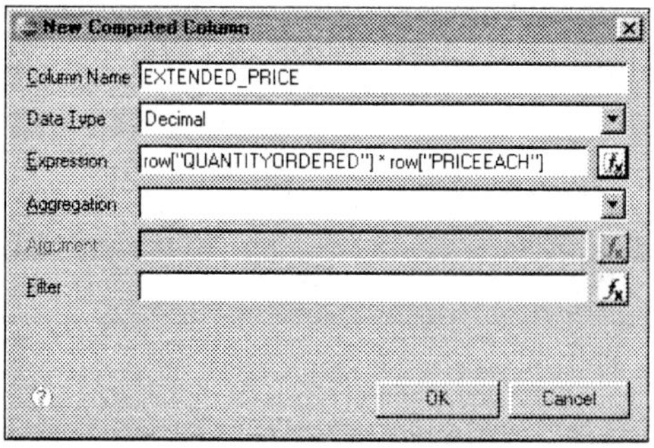

Figure 20-2 Computed field EXTENDED_PRICE

4 Choose OK to save the computed field.

9 Choose Preview Results to confirm that the query is valid and that it returns the correct data. If you created the SELECT statement and computed field correctly, you see the results that appear in Figure 20-3. These are the data rows that the query returns.

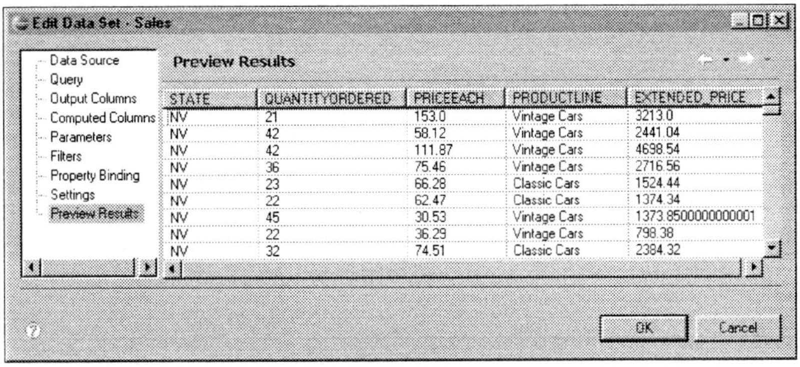

Figure 20-3   Preview of rows returned by the Sales data set

10 Choose OK to save the data set.

Task 4: Add a cross tab to the report

You use the palette to add a cross tab.

1 Choose the palette, then drag a cross-tab element from the palette to the report. A cross tab appears in the report, as shown in Figure 20-4.

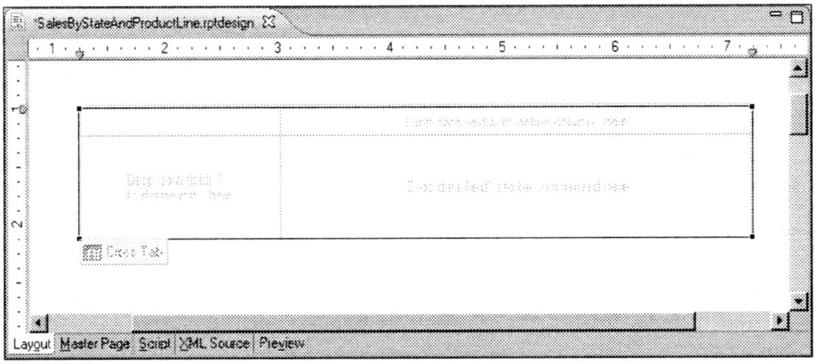

Figure 20-4   Cross tab inserted in the report

The cross tab displays instructions for adding data to specific areas in the cross tab.

2 Choose Data Explorer, expand Data Sets, then expand Sales to display the fields in the data set. Drag STATE into the cell that displays Drop data field(s) to define rows here.

Cross Tab Cube Builder appears, as shown in Figure 20-5.

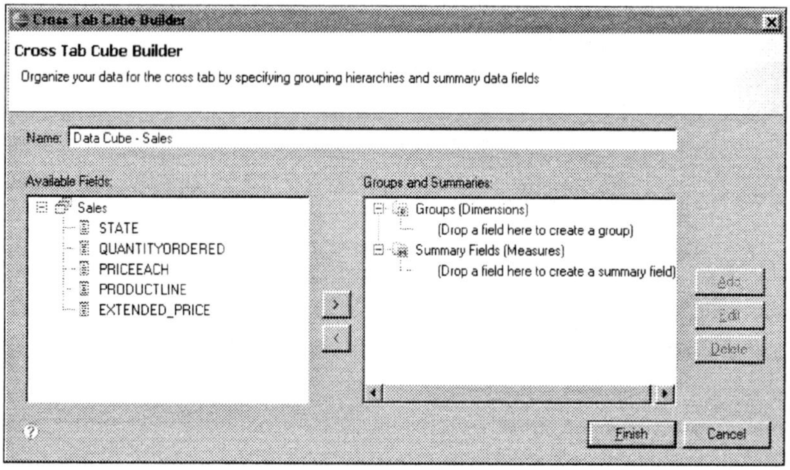

Figure 20-5 Cross Tab Cube Builder

Task 5: Organize data for the cross tab

In this procedure, you set up the following items:

- A data group, or dimension, containing values to use as the row headings
- A data group, or dimension, containing values to use as the column headings
- A summary field, or measure, whose aggregate values to use in the cells of the cross tab

Data that you set up for a cross tab is stored in an entity called a cube.

1 On Cross Tab Cube Builder, in Available Fields, drag STATE and drop it on (Drop a field here to create a group), as shown in Figure 20-6.

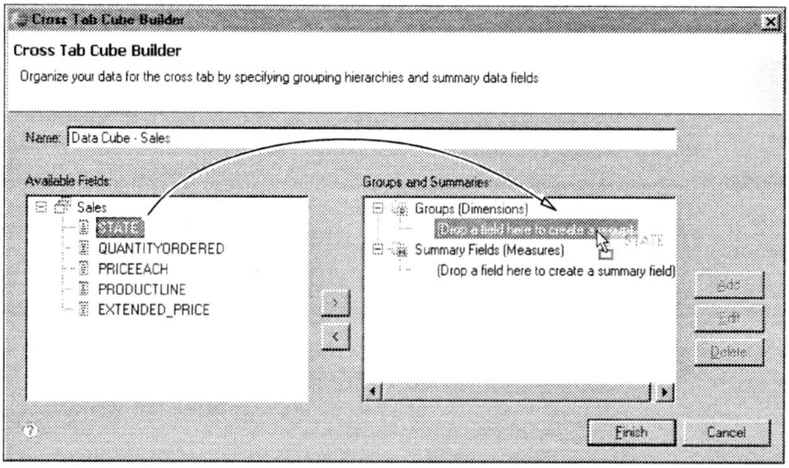

Figure 20-6 Adding a state group to the cube

2 Drag PRODUCTLINE from Available Fields and drop it on (Drop a field here to create a group). Cross Tab Cube Builder shows the STATE and PRODUCTLINE groups you created, as shown in Figure 20-7.

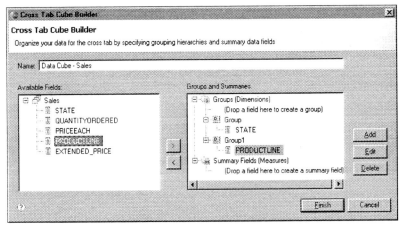

Figure 20-7   Cross Tab Cube Builder displaying two groups

3 Drag EXTENDED_PRICE from Available Fields and drop it on (Drop a field here to create a summary field).

EXTENDED_PRICE(SUM) appears under Summary Field. SUM indicates that the SUM aggregate function is used to calculate the totals of the EXTENDED_PRICE values. The cube builder selects the SUM function by default. You can, however, select a different function to apply to a summary field by selecting the measure, then choosing Edit.

Figure 20-8 shows the dimensions and measure you defined.

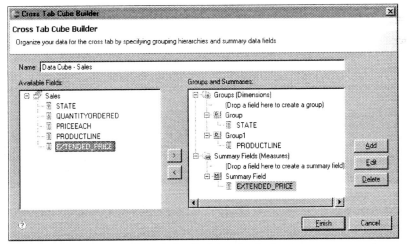

Figure 20-8   Cross Tab Cube Builder displaying two groups and a summary field

4 Choose Finish to save the cube. The Sales cube appears under Data Cubes in Data Explorer, as shown in Figure 20-9.

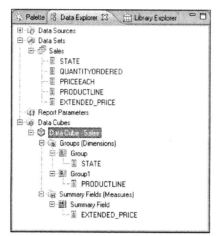

Figure 20-9　　Data Explorer showing the Sales cube

Task 6:　Insert data in the cross tab

You insert data from the cube into the row, column, and detail areas of the cross tab.

1 From Data Explorer, under the first group in the Sales cube, drag STATE and drop it in the cross-tab area that displays Drop data field(s) to define rows here, as shown in Figure 20-10.

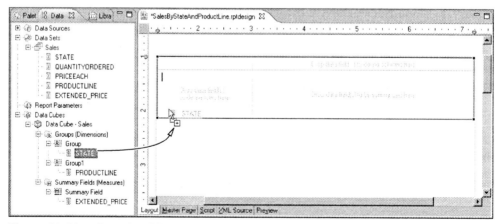

Figure 20-10　　Inserting STATE data in the cross tab

2 From the Sales cube, under Group1, drag PRODUCTLINE and drop it in the cross-tab area that displays Drop data field(s) to define columns here.

3 From the Sales cube, under Summary Field, drag EXTENDED_PRICE and drop it in the cross-tab area that displays Drop data field(s) to be summarized here.

The cross tab should look like the one shown in Figure 20-11.

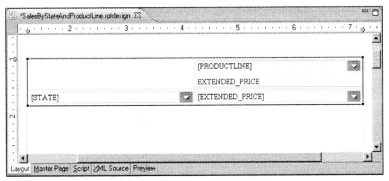

Figure 20-11   Cross tab design

4 Choose Preview to preview the cross tab output. Figure 20-12 shows a portion of the data that the cross tab displays.

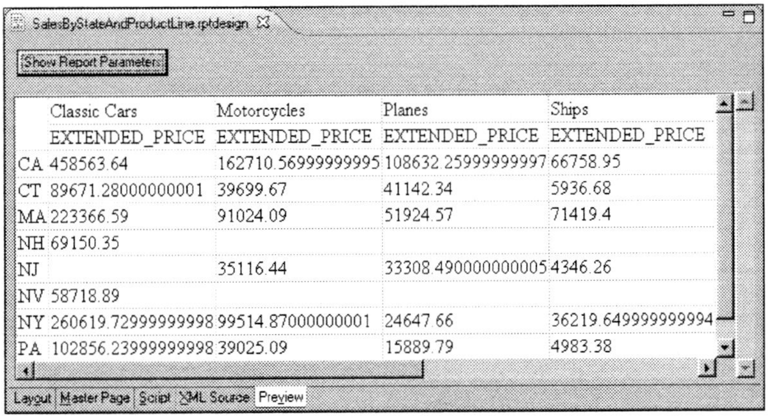

	Classic Cars	Motorcycles	Planes	Ships
	EXTENDED_PRICE	EXTENDED_PRICE	EXTENDED_PRICE	EXTENDED_PRICE
CA	458563.64	162710.56999999995	108632.25999999997	66758.95
CT	89671.28000000001	39699.67	41142.34	5936.68
MA	223366.59	91024.09	51924.57	71419.4
NH	69150.35			
NJ		35116.44	33308.490000000005	4346.26
NV	58718.89			
NY	260619.72999999998	99514.87000000001	24647.66	36219.649999999994
PA	102856.23999999998	39025.09	15889.79	4983.38

Layout Master Page Script XML Source Preview

Figure 20-12   Preview of the cross tab data

The row headings display the states, the column headings display product lines, and the cells display the sales totals. The first cell displays 458563.64, which is the sales total of classic cars sold in California.

Task 7: Add grand totals

Each number that is displayed in the cross tab represents the sales total of a particular product for a particular state. In this procedure, you add grand totals to display the total sales of all products for each state, the total sales of each product, and the total of all sales across products and states.

1 Choose Layout to return to the layout editor.

2 Select the cross tab by clicking on the tab in the lower left corner of the cross tab. Make sure you select the entire cross tab, not just a part of it. Property Editor displays the properties of the cross tab, as shown in Figure 20-13.

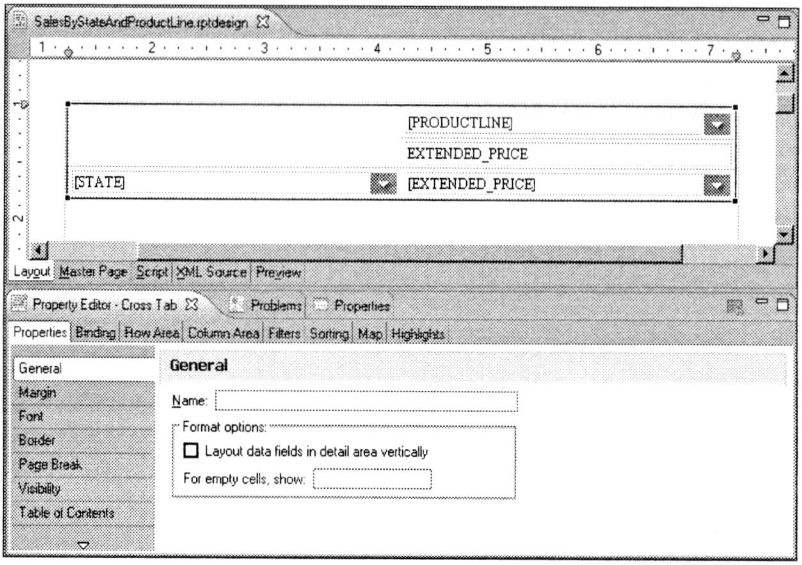

Figure 20-13   Property Editor displays the general properties of the selected cross tab

3 In Property Editor, choose the Row Area tab.

4 Choose Grand Totals, then choose Add.

5 On Grand Total, shown in Figure 20-14, use the default values, then choose OK.

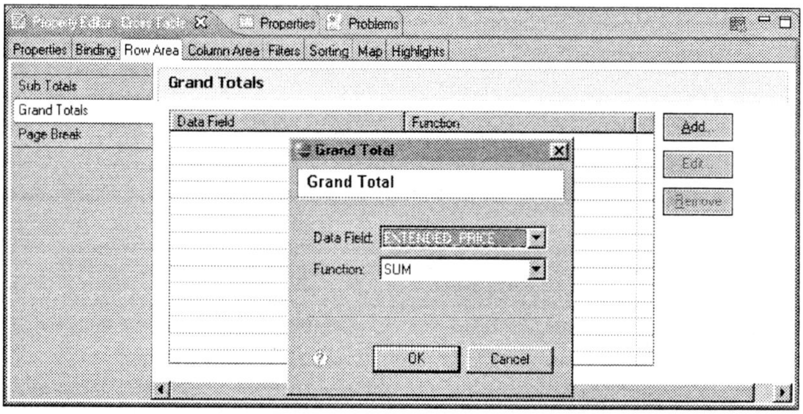

Figure 20-14   Creating grand totals in the cross-tab row area

A new row is added to the cross tab, as shown in Figure 20-15. In this row is a label that displays Grand Total and a data element that displays Σ [EXTENDED_PRICE].

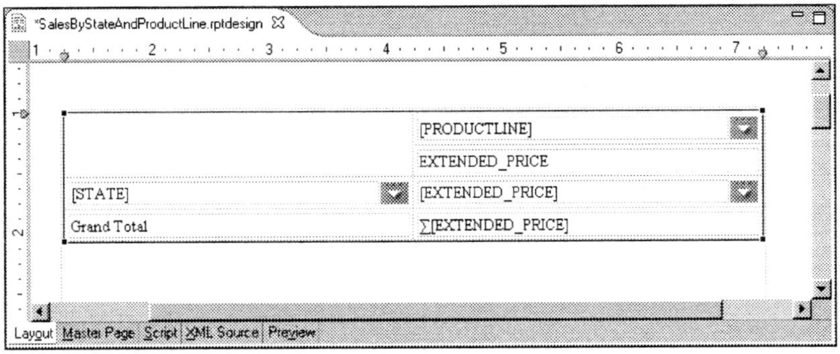

Figure 20-15   Cross tab including a new row to display grand totals

6   In Property Editor, choose the Column Area tab.

7   Choose Grand Totals, then choose Add.

8   On Grand Total, use the default values, then choose OK.

A new column is added to the cross tab, as shown in Figure 20-16.

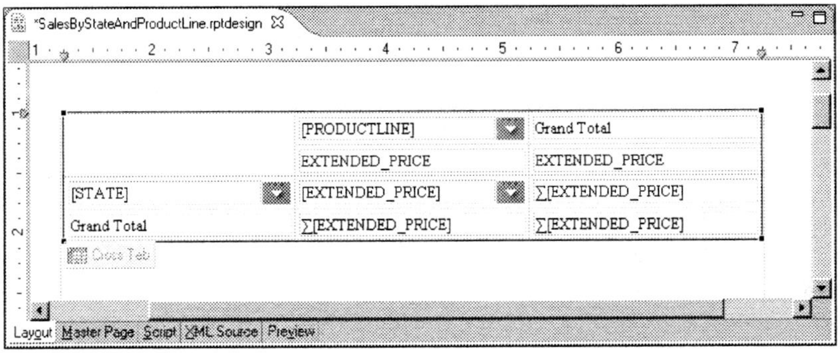

Figure 20-16   Cross tab with a new column to display grand totals

9   Preview the report. Grand totals appear in the last row and last column of the cross tab.

Task 8: Format the cross tab

Now that the cross tab displays the correct data, you can focus on improving the presentation of data in the cross tab. You perform the following tasks in this section:

■   Display a string in empty cells.

■   Change the format of the numbers.

- Edit the column headings.

- Use darker lines around the cross tab and the cells.

Display a string in empty cells

If there are no sales for a particular product in a particular state, the cell displays nothing. Because an empty cell can be interpreted as missing data, you can display a string, such as 0.00 or --, to indicate that the value is zero.

1 Choose Layout to return to the layout editor.

2 Select the cross tab. Select the entire cross tab by clicking on the tab in the lower left corner of the cross tab.

3 In Property Editor, choose the Properties tab, then choose General.

4 In For empty cells, show:, type --, as shown in Figure 20-17.

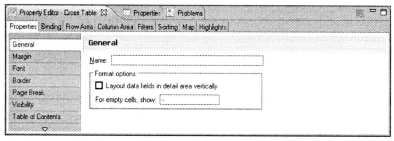

Figure 20-17　General properties of the cross tab

5 Preview the report. Cells that were previously empty now display --, as shown in Figure 20-18.

	Classic Cars	Motorcycles	Planes	Ships
	EXTENDED_PRICE	EXTENDED_PRICE	EXTENDED_PRICE	EXTENDED_PRICE
CA	458563.64	162710.56999999995	108632.25999999997	66758.95
CT	89671.28000000001	39699.67	41142.34	5936.68
MA	223366.59	91024.09	51924.57	71419.4
NH	69150.35	--	--	--
NJ	--	35116.44	33308.490000000005	4346.26
NV	58718.89	--	--	--
NY	260619.72999999998	99514.87000000001	24647.66	36219.649999999994
PA	102856.23999999998	39025.09	15889.79	4983.38

SalesByStateAndProductLine.rptdesign

Show Report Parameters

Layout　Master Page　Script　XML Source　Preview

Figure 20-18　Preview of the cross tab showing -- to indicate no data

Change the format of the numbers

To indicate that the numbers displayed in the cross tab are dollar amounts, use the currency format. It is also easier to read the numbers if they are aligned to the right.

1 Choose Layout to return to the layout editor.

2 Click in an empty area on the report page.

3 Choose Element→New Style.

4 In Custom Style, type the following name for the new style:

crosstab_currency

5 Choose Format Number from the list of property categories.

6 In Format As, select Currency from the drop-down list.

7 In Currency Setting, specify the following values:

1 Set Decimal places to 2.

2 Select Use 1000s separator.

3 In Symbol, select $.

4 Use the default values for the other currency settings.

Figure 20-19 shows the currency values you set.

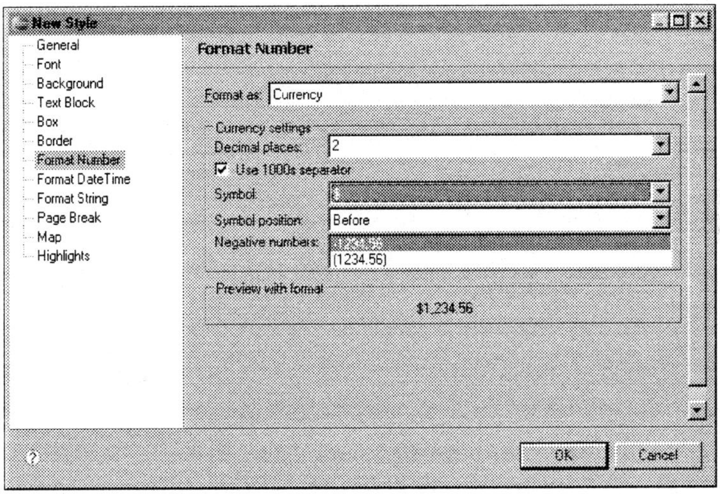

Figure 20-19　Format Number showing the currency settings

8 Choose Text Block from the list of property categories.

9 In Text alignment, select Right, as shown in Figure 20-20.

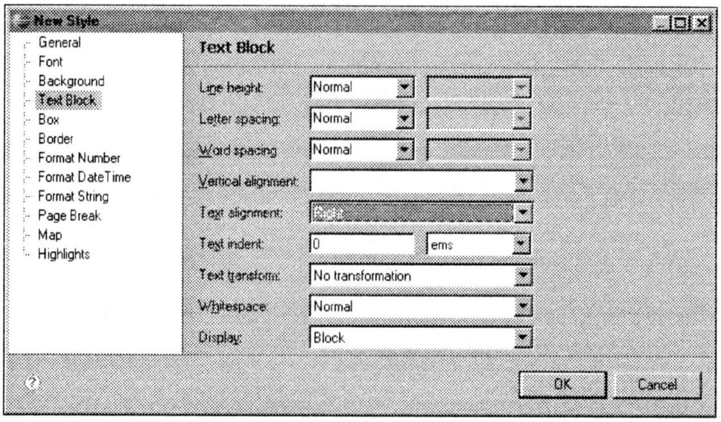

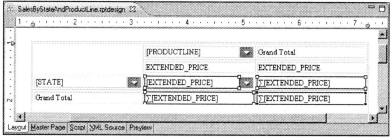

Figure 20-20   Text Block showing the change in text alignment

10 Choose OK to save the crosstab_currency style.

11 In the layout editor, select the four [EXTENDED_PRICE] data elements, as shown in Figure 20-21.

Figure 20-21   Data elements selected

12 In General properties of Property Editor, in Style, select crosstab_currency from the drop-down list, as shown in Figure 20-22.

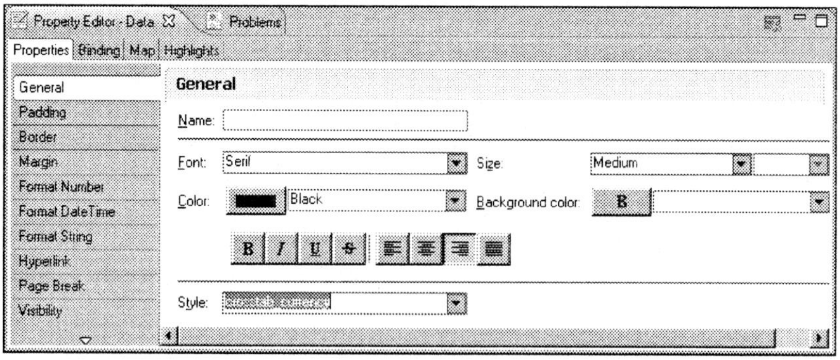

Figure 20-22   Select the crosstab_currency style to apply to the data elements

13 Preview the report to verify the formatting change.

Edit the column headings

When you insert a summary field, BIRT adds a label that displays the field name as a column heading. In the generated cross tab, the heading EXTENDED_PRICE appears in every column below the product line names. Because the cross tab displays values from one summary field only, the label is not necessary.

1 Choose Layout to return to the layout editor.

2 Select the two labels that display EXTENDED_PRICE, as shown in Figure 20-23. These labels are directly below [PRODUCTLINE] and Grand Total.

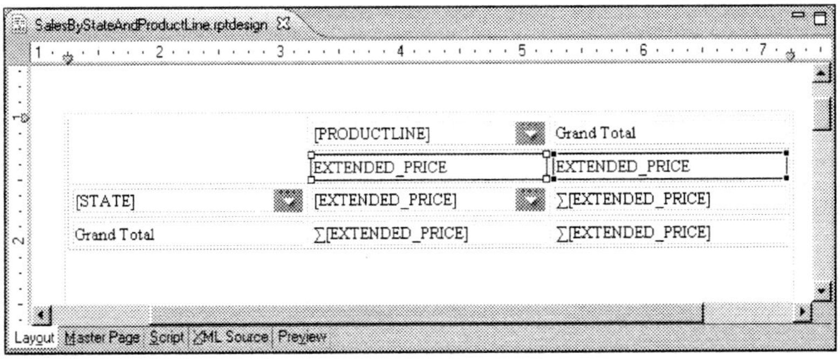

Figure 20-23   EXTENDED_PRICE labels selected

3 Press Delete.

4 Preview the report. Figure 20-24 shows a portion of the generated cross tab.

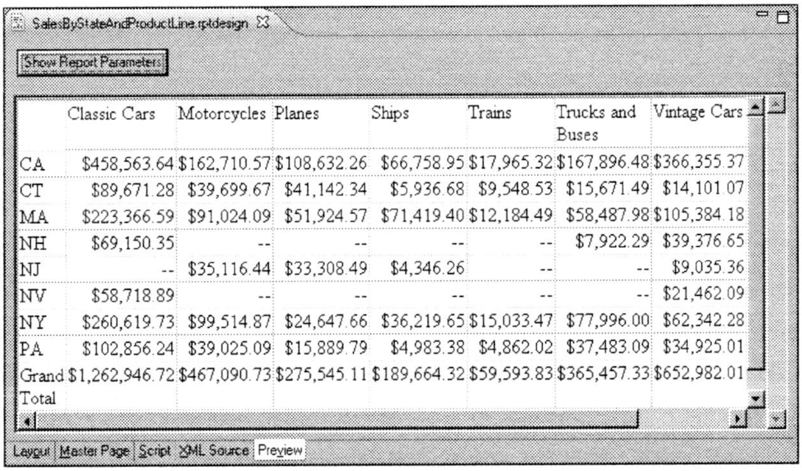

	Classic Cars	Motorcycles	Planes	Ships	Trains	Trucks and Buses	Vintage Cars
CA	$458,563.64	$162,710.57	$108,632.26	$66,758.95	$17,965.32	$167,896.48	$366,355.37
CT	$89,671.28	$39,699.67	$41,142.34	$5,936.68	$9,548.53	$15,671.49	$14,101.07
MA	$223,366.59	$91,024.09	$51,924.57	$71,419.40	$12,184.49	$58,487.98	$105,384.18
NH	$69,150.35	--	--	--	--	$7,922.29	$39,376.65
NJ	--	$35,116.44	$33,308.49	$4,346.26	--	--	$9,035.36
NV	$58,718.89	--	--	--	--	--	$21,462.09
NY	$260,619.73	$99,514.87	$24,647.66	$36,219.65	$15,033.47	$77,996.00	$62,342.28
PA	$102,856.24	$39,025.09	$15,889.79	$4,983.38	$4,862.02	$37,483.09	$34,925.01
Grand Total	$1,262,946.72	$467,090.73	$275,545.11	$189,664.32	$59,593.83	$365,457.33	$652,982.01

Figure 20-24   Preview of the cross tab

Use darker lines around the cross tab and the cells

BIRT uses two predefined styles, crosstab and crosstab-cell, to set the default appearance of the overall cross tab and the cells, respectively.

1 Choose Layout to return to the layout editor.

2 Choose the Outline view.

3 Expand the Styles item to show the crosstab and crosstab-cell styles, as shown in Figure 20-25.

Figure 20-25 Outline view displaying the cross-tab styles

4 Right-click the crosstab style, then choose Edit Style.

5 On Edit Style, choose Border. The colors of the borders are set to Gray.

6 Change the color of all the borders to Black, as shown in Figure 20-26.

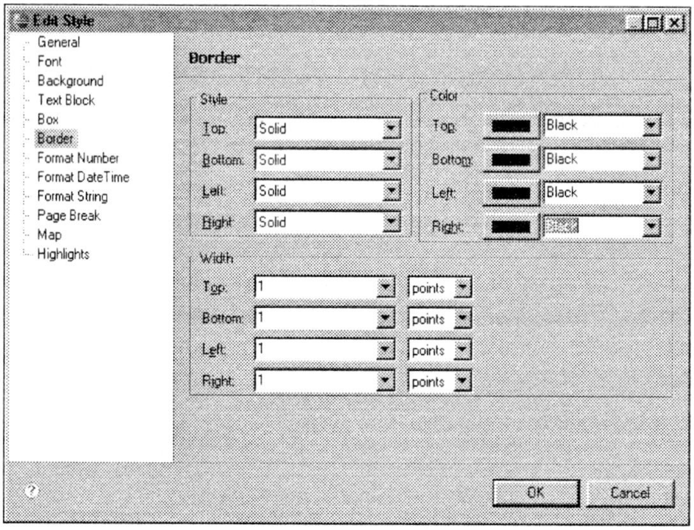

Figure 20-26 Border colors set to Black

7 Choose OK to save your change to the crosstab style.

8 In Outline, right-click the crosstab-cell style, then choose Edit Style.

9 Use the same steps to set all the cell border colors to Black, then choose OK.

In the layout editor, the lines around the cells and around the cross tab appear in black, as shown in Figure 20-27.

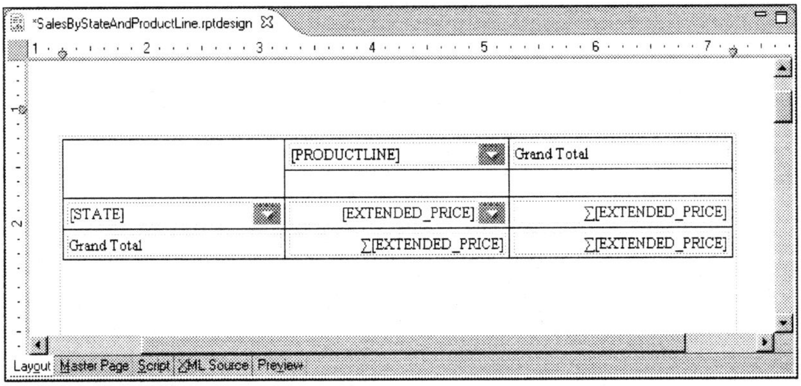
*SalesByStateAndProductLine.rptdesign
[PRODUCTLINE]
Grand Total
[STATE]
[EXTENDED_PRICE]
∑[EXTENDED_PRICE]
Grand Total
∑[EXTENDED_PRICE]
∑[EXTENDED_PRICE]
Layout
Master Page
Script
XML Source
Preview

Figure 20-27 Cross tab design showing black borders

10 Preview the report. Figure 20-28 shows a portion of the generated cross tab.

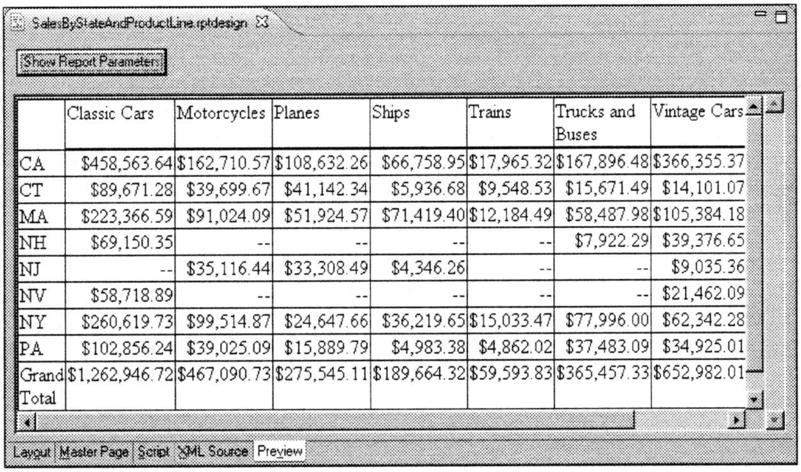
SalesByStateAndProductLine.rptdesign
Show Report Parameters
Classic Cars Motorcycles Planes Ships Trains Trucks and Buses Vintage Cars
CA $458,563.64 $162,710.57 $108,632.26 $66,758.95 $17,965.32 $167,896.48 $366,355.37
CT $89,671.28 $39,699.67 $41,142.34 $5,936.68 $9,548.53 $15,671.49 $14,101.07
MA $223,366.59 $91,024.09 $51,924.57 $71,419.40 $12,184.49 $58,487.98 $105,384.18
NH $69,150.35 -- -- -- -- $7,922.29 $39,376.65
NJ -- $35,116.44 $33,308.49 $4,346.26 -- -- $9,035.36
NV $58,718.89 -- -- -- -- -- $21,462.09
NY $260,619.73 $99,514.87 $24,647.66 $36,219.65 $15,033.47 $77,996.00 $62,342.28
PA $102,856.24 $39,025.09 $15,889.79 $4,983.38 $4,862.02 $37,483.09 $34,925.01
Grand Total $1,262,946.72 $467,090.73 $275,545.11 $189,664.32 $59,593.83 $365,457.33 $652,982.01
Layout
Master Page
Script
XML Source
Preview

Figure 20-28 Preview of the finished cross tab

You just learned how to build a basic cross tab that displays data from three fields, the minimum number. The rest of this chapter describes how to build more complex cross tabs.

Understanding cube terms

A data cube is a powerful object that structures multi-dimensional data so that applications can perform complex analyses without performing additional queries on the underlying data source. When you use BIRT Report Designer to design a cube, you see the following terms in the user interface. These terms are interchangeable.

- Dimension and group

- Measure and summary field

Dimension and measure are technical terms related to cubes, and will be familiar to report developers who are well-versed with cube concepts. Group and summary field, on the other hand, are descriptive terms, which are more relevant to report developers who are not familiar with cubes. Conceptually, groups and summary fields in a cube are equivalent to groups and summary fields in a listing report.

Figure 20-29 shows Cross Tab Cube Builder, and highlights the way that tool displays the synonymous terms.

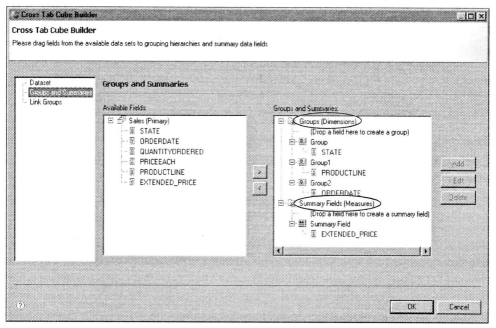

Figure 20-29   Terms used in Cross Tab Cube Builder

When you bind data from a cube to a cross tab, BIRT Report Designer generates an appropriate expression, based on the structure of the cube. Figure 20-30 shows the cross tab's Binding page, and highlights the cube-specific syntax that the column binding expressions use.

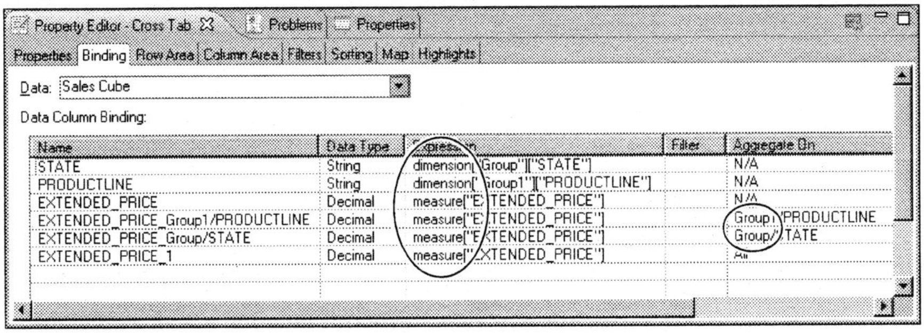

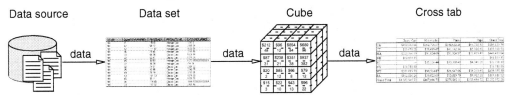

Figure 20-30   Terms used in the cross tab's Binding page

When discussing cubes, the rest of this chapter uses the terms dimension and measure, rather than the terms group and summary, which are used for structuring report layout items.

Setting up data for a cross tab

As the tutorial demonstrated, there is one additional step to perform when you set up data for a cross tab, compared to setting up data for other report elements, such as a table, list, or chart. Just as you do to prepare data for use by other report elements, you create at least one data source and data set. Unlike a table or a chart, however, you cannot directly insert a data set field in a cross tab.

For a cross tab, the extra step is to create a cube, whose data you insert in a cross tab. As the tutorial also demonstrated, you build a cube, using data from a data set. Figure 20-31 illustrates how the cross tab gets its data.

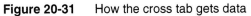

Figure 20-31   How the cross tab gets data

If you are wondering why there is an additional data entity, the answer is that the cube offers a far more powerful way to store numeric data for fast analysis.

About cubes

Commonly associated with online analytical processing (OLAP) technology, a cube is a multidimensional data structure that is optimized for analysis and reporting. A cube organizes data into dimensions and measures. Measures represent values that are counted or aggregated, such as costs or units of products. Dimensions are categories, such as products, customers, or sales periods, by which measures are aggregated. For example, a retail cube might contain data that supports viewing sales volume and cost of goods, both of which are measures, by store location, time period, and product lines, all of which are dimensions.

Dimensions can be hierarchical and contain multiple levels. For example, a region dimension can contain a region-country-state hierarchy. Similarly, a time dimension can contain a year-quarter-month-week hierarchy. Most cubes include a time dimension because, for most reports, showing measures by day, week, month, quarter, or year is essential to analyzing data. The time dimension is a special dimension. The cube groups dates stored in a field into any time period of your choice.

Planning the data

Before you build a data set or a cube, think about the aggregate data you want to display in the cross tab, and how you want to categorize the aggregate data. For example:

- Average score and high score by year by school district

- Sales volume by month by product by store

- Call volume and average call time by support person by day and by call type

After you identify the information to display in the cross tab, you know which data fields to define as dimensions and measures in the cube. In our first example, the measures are average score and high score, and the dimensions are year and school district. After you identify the contents of the cube, you know which data to retrieve from the data source. Figure 20-32 shows the data planning flow.

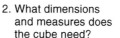

1. What information does the cross tab need to display?

2. What dimensions and measures does the cube need?

3. What data needs to be retrieved from the data source?

Figure 20-32   How to plan the data to display in a cross tab

Notice that the planning steps are in the reverse order of the implementation steps, that you start with the end result and work backward to determine the best way to get the results you want. If you have control of the data source as well—the database, for example—you can go a step further and create a database schema that supports the queries to return data for a cube.

Most report developers, however, neither create nor maintain corporate databases or other information systems. The rest of this section provides some guidelines for designing data sets and cubes, given the typical ways databases are structured.

Designing the cube

In BIRT, you can create a cube with any number of dimensions and measures. You might be tempted to store all measures against every combination of dimensions. This technique, however, is not practical in real-world applications. The number of aggregations increases exponentially with the number of measures and dimensions. The higher the number of aggregations to calculate, the greater the amount of time and computer resources required.

Observe the following rules:

- Cube data can be used in cross tabs only. In release 2.2.1, you cannot use cube data in a table, chart, or list.

- A cross tab can use data from one cube only. This requirement is similar to tables, lists, and charts using data from one data set only.

Therefore, for each cross tab you want to create, design a cube that provides just the data you want to display in that cross tab.

The cube's data structure maps nicely with the cross tab's structure. The cube organizes measures by dimensions, and the cross tab displays aggregate data (measures) by any number of data groups (dimensions). This natural symmetry makes designing a cube intuitive and straightforward. Determine what your users want to see and how they want to see it, and define the measures and dimensions for the cube accordingly.

Designing data sets for a cube

This design phase requires more thought and planning. The data set must accomplish two key things. It must retrieve data from the source in a resource-efficient manner and also in a way that makes sense for the cube. How you write the SQL query to get the data depends on how the database is structured. When planning how to get data for a cube, you also have to decide whether to build one data set or multiple data sets.

BIRT supports the creation of cubes using data from a single data set or multiple data sets to support the different ways data sources can be structured, and the different expertise levels of report developers. In other words, the decision to build one or multiple data sets to get data for a cube depends on how the data source is structured, and also on your grasp of OLAP design principles.

The cube builder in BIRT is designed for report developers with varying OLAP expertise. You do not have to know much about OLAP to build a data set or a cube for a cross tab, but if you have the expertise, you can design data sets that apply OLAP design principles for optimal performance.

It is beyond the scope of this book to teach OLAP principles, but a high-level discussion on the subject might help you decide if you want to explore the world of OLAP.

Comparing OLTP and OLAP

Online Transaction Processing (OLTP) systems and Online Analytical Processing (OLAP) systems are two common database structures. Each serves a different purpose.

OLTP is the standard, normalized database structure designed for transactions, where data inserts, updates, and deletes must be fast. One of the ways OLTP systems optimize the entry or updates of records is by minimizing repeated data. For example, complete information about an order includes an order number, a customer name, a bill-to address, a ship-to address, and a payment method. The order details include a product number, a product description, the quantity ordered, and the unit price. In a flat structure, each order detail record would need and include all that information. That is a lot of repeated information, which is why OLTP systems use relational technology to link the information. The Classic Models sample database is an example of an OLTP database. Figure 20-33 shows a partial view of the Classic Models schema. Tables are linked to one another by keys.

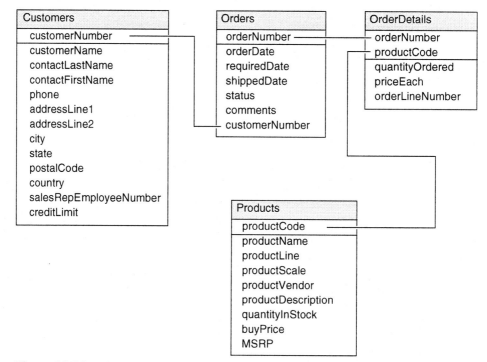

Figure 20-33   A partial view of the Classic Models schema

By contrast, OLAP is a database structure designed for performing analysis to reveal trends and patterns among data. This structure more closely represents the way people ask questions or want to view data. For example:

- What are the sales amounts for each product this month?

- Are product sales up or down compared to previous months?

- What products saw the greatest increase this quarter?

- In what regions did product sales increase this quarter?

Figure 20-34 shows an example of an OLAP structure.

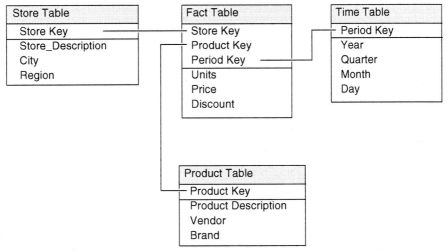

Figure 20-34   An OLAP schema

This particular OLAP structure is commonly referred to as a star schema because the schema diagram is shaped like a star, that is, one in which points radiate from a central table. The central table is called a fact table, and the supporting tables linked to it are dimension tables. As Figure 20-34 shows, the fact table contains the measures and keys to link to each dimension table. The dimension tables do not link to one another.

Many-to-one relationships exist between the keys in the fact table and the keys they reference in the dimension tables. For example, the Product table defines the products. Each row in the Product table represents a distinct product and has a unique product identifier. Each product identifier can occur multiple times in the Sales fact table, representing sales of that product during each period and in each store.

Designing a single data set

Design a single data set if:

- The database from which you are retrieving data uses an OLTP structure.

- You are well-versed in writing SQL joins. Because an OLTP structure minimizes repeated data, you typically have to join many tables to get all the data you need. The query you created in the tutorial joined four tables to get data for a cube that contained only two dimensions and one measure.

- You find it too complicated to create data sets from a OLTP structure to resemble a star schema. This exercise can feel like fitting a square peg into a round hole.

The disadvantage of creating a single data set is that, typically, it must use multiple joins. These joins are complex to create and increasing the number of joins can slow queries.

Designing multiple data sets in a star schema

Create multiple data sets to retrieve data for a cube if:

- The database from which you are retrieving data uses an OLAP star schema.

- You are familiar with star schemas.

- The number of joins required to get the data from multiple tables is too complex and degrades performance.

If the database uses a star schema, you can create data sets that mimic the structure, one data set for each fact table and dimension table in the star schema.

If the database uses an OLTP structure, you can also create one data set to retrieve the data to calculate the measures, and one data set for each dimension. Because you are trying to map data from an OLTP structure to data in a OLAP star schema, the mapping process is less intuitive, and you might also find that you still need to create multiple joins in each data set.

Building a multi-dataset cube

The tutorial earlier in this chapter walked through the steps for building a cube that used data from a single data set. In this section, you learn how to create a multi-dataset cube. Because the concepts and procedures are easier to understand with an example, this section walks through the steps for performing the following tasks:

- Creating the data sets to retrieve data from the Orders, OrderDetails, and Products tables in the Classic Models sample database

- Using data from the data sets to build a cube that contains a sales amount measure, a product line dimension, and a year dimension

How to create data sets for a multi-dataset cube

In this procedure, you create two data sets:

- A fact data set, SalesTotal, to retrieve the data for calculating the sales totals

- A dimension data set, Productlines, to retrieve data about the product lines

Note that we are not creating a separate data set for the year dimension, as is typical in a star schema. It is sometimes too complicated to create a pure star schema design when working with data stored in an OLTP system.

1 Create a new data set named SalesTotal. Create the following query:

```
select CLASSICMODELS.ORDERDETAILS.PRODUCTCODE,
CLASSICMODELS.ORDERS.SHIPPEDDATE,
CLASSICMODELS.ORDERDETAILS.QUANTITYORDERED *
    CLASSICMODELS.ORDERDETAILS.PRICEEACH as "EXTENDED_PRICE"

from CLASSICMODELS.ORDERDETAILS, CLASSICMODELS.ORDERS
where CLASSICMODELS.ORDERS.ORDERNUMBER =
    CLASSICMODELS.ORDERDETAILS.ORDERNUMBER
and CLASSICMODELS.ORDERS.STATUS = 'Shipped'
```

- The query retrieves PRODUCTCODE data because it is the key to later link to the PRODUCTLINE dimension.

- The query retrieves SHIPPEDDATE data to use for the year dimension.

- The query creates a calculated column, EXTENDED_PRICE, whose values will be aggregated to calculate the sales totals.

- The query creates a join between the Orders and OrderDetails tables to get all the necessary data about the orders. Because the data set is retrieving data from an OLTP database, joins are unavoidable.

- The query contains a filter condition to retrieve order data for orders that have been shipped, and therefore, that have been paid.

2 Create a new data set named Productlines. Create the following query:

```
select CLASSICMODELS.PRODUCTS.PRODUCTLINE,
CLASSICMODELS.PRODUCTS.PRODUCTCODE
from CLASSICMODELS.PRODUCTS
```

- The query retrieves PRODUCTLINE data to use for the PRODUCTLINE dimension.

- The query retrieves PRODUCTCODE data because it is the key that the SalesTotals data set will need to reference.

How to create a multi-dataset cube

1 In Data Explorer, right-click Data Cubes, then choose New Data Cube.

2 On the Dataset page of Cross Tab Cube Builder, supply the following information, as shown in Figure 20-35:

    1 In Name, specify a descriptive name, such as Sales Cube, for the cube.

    2 In Primary dataset, select SalesTotal. In a multi-dataset cube, the fact data set that retrieves the data to calculate measures is the primary data set.

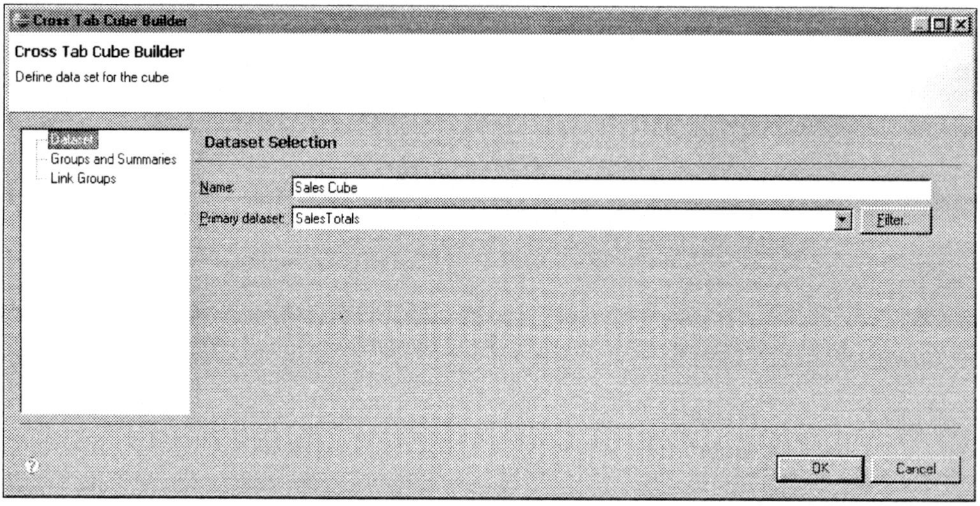

Figure 20-35   Name and primary data set specified for a cube

3 Choose Groups and Summaries to define the dimensions and measures for the cube. The Groups and Summaries page, shown in Figure 20-36, displays the available data sets and fields.

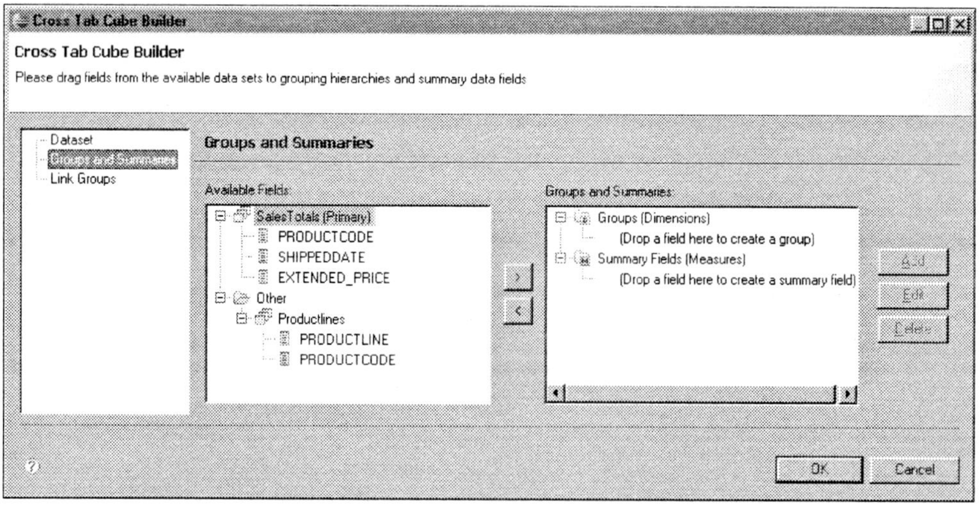

Figure 20-36   Groups and Summaries page shows the available data sets and fields

4 Define the year dimension of the cube.

1 Under the Sales Totals (Primary) data set, drag SHIPPEDDATE and drop it under Groups (Dimensions) in the drop location that displays (Drop a field here to create a group).

Group Level displays the different ways to group the dates. To display the dates as they appear in the data source, select Regular Group. To group the dates by any of the time periods, select Date Group.

2 Select Date Group, then select year, as shown in Figure 20-37.

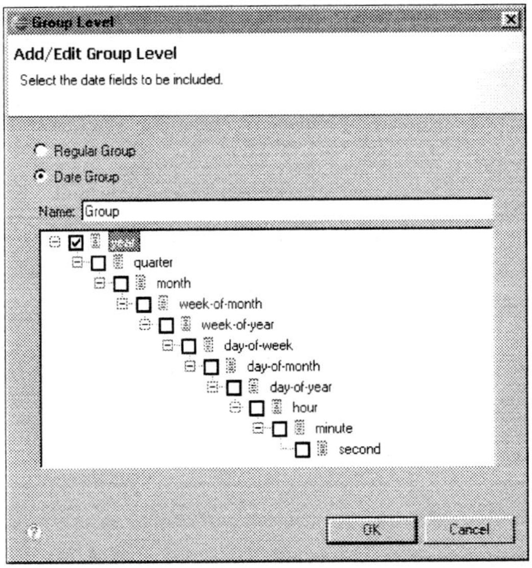

Figure 20-37   Group Level showing the year group selected

3 Choose OK to save the year dimension.

5 Define the product line dimension.

1 Under the Productlines data set, drag PRODUCTLINE and drop it under Groups (Dimensions) in the drop location that displays (Drop a field here to create a group).

2 Under the Productlines data set, drag PRODUCTCODE and drop it on the PRODUCTLINE dimension. This action creates a hierarchical relationship between PRODUCTLINE and PRODUCTCODE.

6 Define the cube's measure. Under the Sales Totals (Primary) data set, drag EXTENDED_PRICE and drop it under Summary Fields (Measures) in the drop location that displays (Drop a field here to create a summary field).

The Groups and Summaries page, shown in Figure 20-38, displays the dimensions and measure that you define.

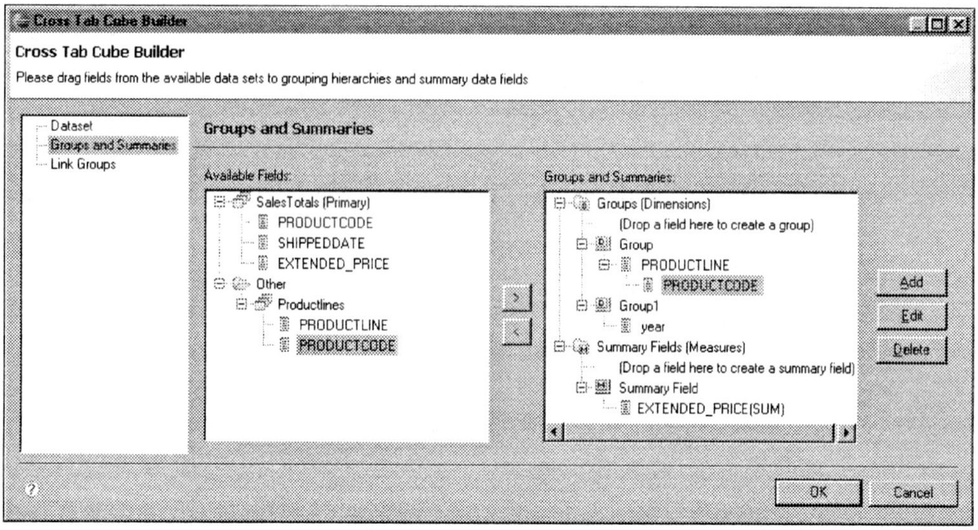

Figure 20-38 Groups and Summaries page shows the dimensions and measure

7 Link the data in the dimensions with the fact data set.

    1 Choose Link Groups. The Link Groups page displays the Productline dimension you created and the primary (fact) data set.

    2 Link the PRODUCTCODE field in both items, as shown in Figure 20-39.

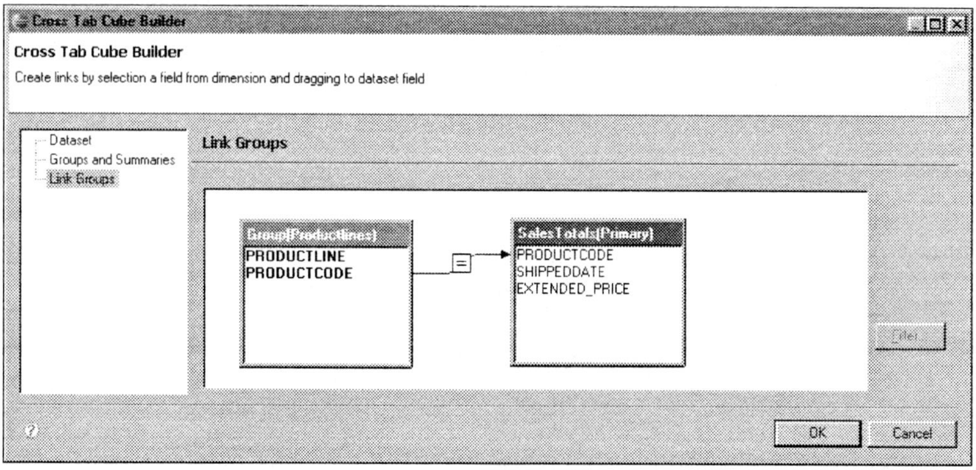

Figure 20-39 Link Groups page shows how the dimension and fact data sets are linked

    8 Choose OK to save the cube. You can now build a cross tab that uses data from this cube.

Figure 20-40 shows a cross tab that uses the year and PRODUCTLINE dimensions and the EXTENDED_PRICE measure from the cube.

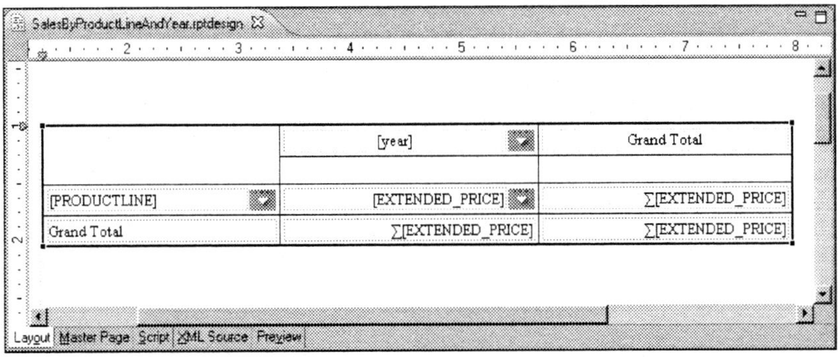

Figure 20-40   Cross tab design

Figure 20-41 shows the generated cross tab.

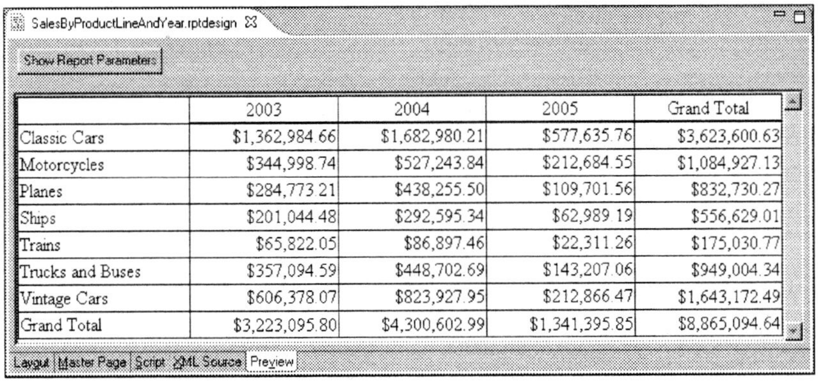

	2003	2004	2005	Grand Total
Classic Cars	$1,362,984.66	$1,682,980.21	$577,635.76	$3,623,600.63
Motorcycles	$344,998.74	$527,243.84	$212,684.55	$1,084,927.13
Planes	$284,773.21	$438,255.50	$109,701.56	$832,730.27
Ships	$201,044.48	$292,595.34	$62,989.19	$556,629.01
Trains	$65,822.05	$86,897.46	$22,311.26	$175,030.77
Trucks and Buses	$357,094.59	$448,702.69	$143,207.06	$949,004.34
Vintage Cars	$606,378.07	$823,927.95	$212,866.47	$1,643,172.49
Grand Total	$3,223,095.80	$4,300,602.99	$1,341,395.85	$8,865,094.64

Figure 20-41   Cross tab output

Building a cross tab

The tutorial earlier in this chapter walked you through the procedures for building a basic cross tab. In this section, you learn how to create more complex cross tabs, including how to display multiple dimensions and measures, and how to customize row and column headings.

Areas of a cross tab

A cross tab consists of the following three areas, as shown in Figure 20-42:

- The row area

- The column area

- The detail area

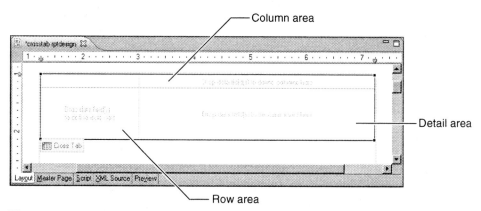

Figure 20-42 Cross tab row, column, and detail areas

The row and column areas are where you insert dimensions from a cube. The dimension values form the row and column headings of the cross tab. The detail area is where you insert a measure or measures from a cube to display aggregate data.

Displaying multiple dimensions in row and column areas

When you build a cross tab, you group the aggregate data by at least two dimensions, for example, sales totals by year and product line, or sales totals by year and state. Often, report users want to view aggregate data by more than two dimensions.

The cross tab in Figure 20-43 shows the sales total by region, state, product line, and product. To create the cross tab, two dimensions (State and Year) are inserted in the row area, and one dimension (Productlines) is inserted in the column area. The Productlines dimension has two levels, Productline and Productname.

SalesByProductLineAndProductAndStateAndTime.rptdesign

Show Report Parameters

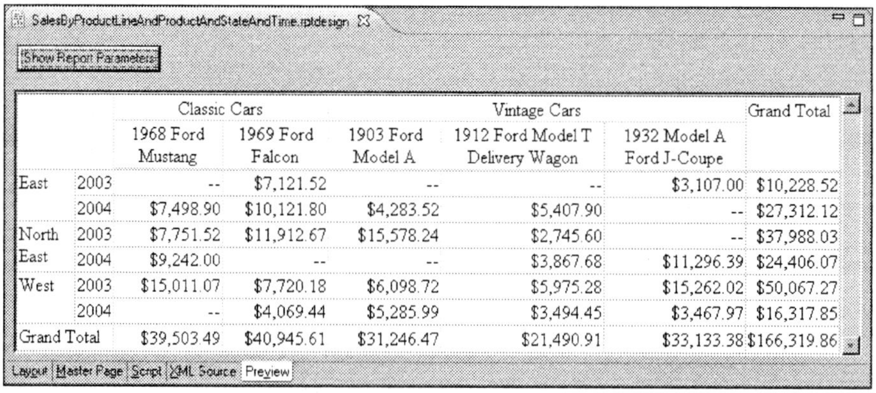

		Classic Cars		Vintage Cars			Grand Total
		1968 Ford Mustang	1969 Ford Falcon	1903 Ford Model A	1912 Ford Model T Delivery Wagon	1932 Model A Ford J-Coupe	
East	2003	--	$7,121.52	--	--	$3,107.00	$10,228.52
	2004	$7,498.90	$10,121.80	$4,283.52	$5,407.90	--	$27,312.12
North East	2003	$7,751.52	$11,912.67	$15,578.24	$2,745.60	--	$37,988.03
	2004	$9,242.00	--	--	$3,867.68	$11,296.39	$24,406.07
West	2003	$15,011.07	$7,720.18	$6,098.72	$5,975.28	$15,262.02	$50,067.27
	2004	--	$4,069.44	$5,285.99	$3,494.45	$3,467.97	$16,317.85
Grand Total		$39,503.49	$40,945.61	$31,246.47	$21,490.91	$33,133.38	$166,319.86

Layout Master Page Script XML Source Preview

Figure 20-43 Cross tab using multiple dimensions in the row and column areas

As the example shows, each additional dimension by which you group data appears as a column or row, and each additional dimension provides a more comprehensive and detailed view of the data. Just as you can define an unlimited number of dimensions for a cube, you can build a cross tab that displays aggregate data by as many dimensions as you want.

Calculating aggregate data by too many dimensions, however, can result in many empty cells, a problem commonly referred to as data sparsity. When designing a cube that contains more than two dimensions, make sure that processing time is not spent calculating zeros.

In addition, a cross tab that contains more than two or three dimensions in either the row or column area is difficult to read. Rather than display data by too many dimensions in a single cross tab, consider dividing the data into multiple cross tabs.

How to insert multiple dimensions in the row or column area

1 Drag a dimension from the cube and drop it in the row or column area of the cross tab.

2 Drop the second dimension next to the first dimension, as shown in Figure 20-44.

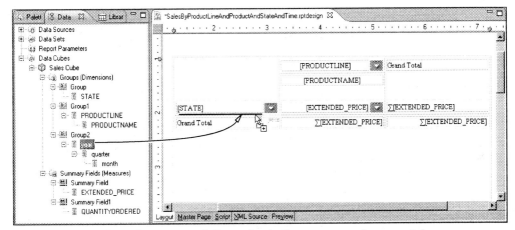

Figure 20-44   Dropping a second dimension in the row area of a cross tab

Figure 20-44 shows the straight cursor directly below the first dimension. The straight cursor can also be directly to the left of the first dimension. In either case, each successive dimension you place in the row area always appears to the right of the previously inserted dimension. Likewise, each successive dimension you place in the column area always appears below the previously inserted dimension. After you place the dimensions in the cross tab, you can move them to the desired location.

Displaying or hiding dimension levels

When you insert into the cross tab a dimension that contains multiple levels (for example, year, quarter, month), by default, the cross tab displays only the top level. You can, at any time, select additional levels to display. You can even skip levels. In a year-quarter-month hierarchy, you can, for example, display the year and the month.

How to display or hide levels

1 Click the down arrow button next to the data element, as shown in Figure 20-45.

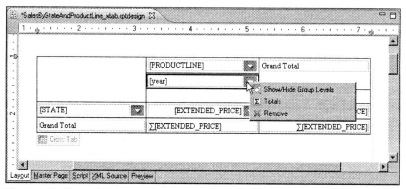

Figure 20-45 Displaying a menu for a selected element in the cross tab

2 Choose Show or Hide Group Levels.

3 On Show or Hide Group Levels, select the levels to display. Figure 20-46 shows an example of selecting all levels.

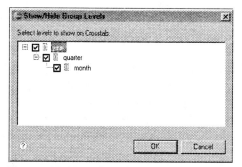

Figure 20-46 Show or Hide Group Levels

In the example, the time dimension has only three levels. If you want to display additional levels, such as week-of-month or day-of month, edit the definition of the time dimension in the cube builder.

4 Choose OK. BIRT creates a data element for each selected level, as shown in Figure 20-47.

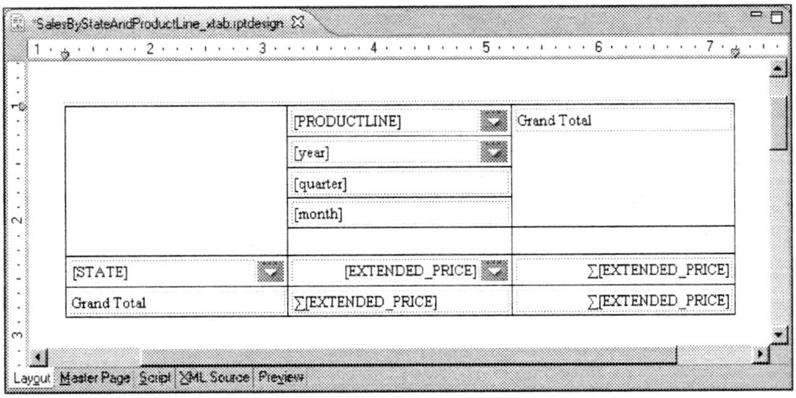

Figure 20-47 Cross tab displays a data element each for the year, quarter, and month levels

Displaying multiple measures

You can display any number of measures in a cross tab. A cross tab that displays aggregate data by product line and state can, for example, show the sales total in dollars, the number of units sold, the number of customers, and so on. Figure 20-48 shows a cross tab that displays two measures, sales total amounts and total units sold.

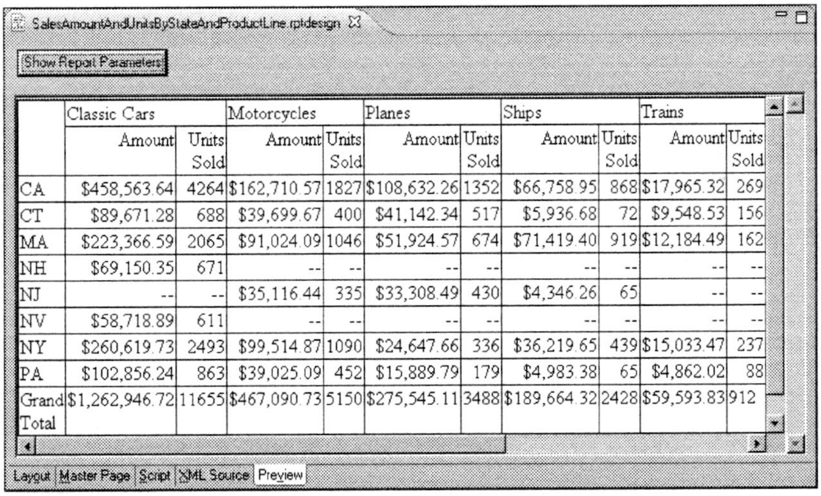

	Classic Cars		Motorcycles		Planes		Ships		Trains	
	Amount	Units Sold	Amount	Units Sold	Amount	Units Sold	Amount	Units Sold	Amount	Units Sold
CA	$458,563.64	4264	$162,710.57	1827	$108,632.26	1352	$66,758.95	868	$17,965.32	269
CT	$89,671.28	688	$39,699.67	400	$41,142.34	517	$5,936.68	72	$9,548.53	156
MA	$223,366.59	2065	$91,024.09	1046	$51,924.57	674	$71,419.40	919	$12,184.49	162
NH	$69,150.35	671	--	--	--	--	--	--	--	--
NJ	--	--	$35,116.44	335	$33,308.49	430	$4,346.26	65	--	--
NV	$58,718.89	611	--	--	--	--	--	--	--	--
NY	$260,619.73	2493	$99,514.87	1090	$24,647.66	336	$36,219.65	439	$15,033.47	237
PA	$102,856.24	863	$39,025.09	452	$15,889.79	179	$4,983.38	65	$4,862.02	88
Grand Total	$1,262,946.72	11655	$467,090.73	5150	$275,545.11	3488	$189,664.32	2428	$59,593.83	912

Figure 20-48 Cross tab displays two measures side by side

When you insert multiple measures, by default, the cross tab displays the measures horizontally as shown in Figure 20-48. You can specify that the cross tab display them vertically instead, as shown in Figure 20-49.

If you compare the cross tabs in Figure 20-48 and Figure 20-49, you see that displaying measures vertically reduces the width of the cross tab and increases its height. So, besides your preference for reading the values horizontally or vertically, you can use this layout option to adjust the height and width of a cross tab.

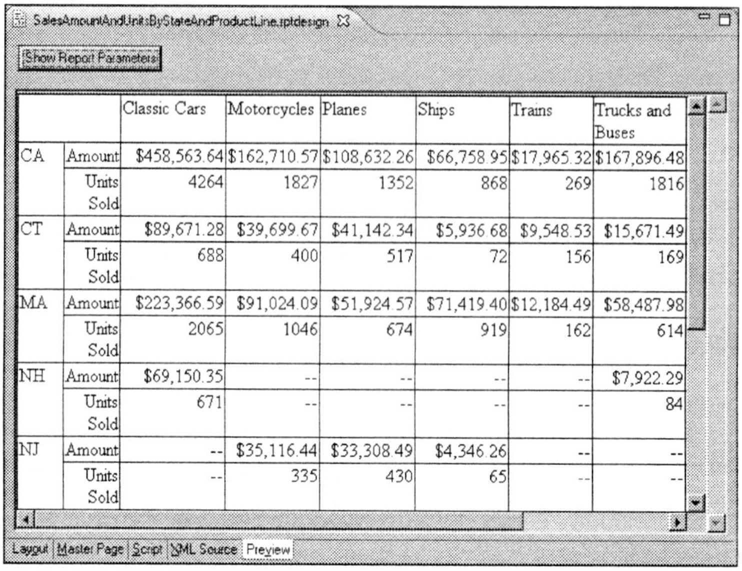

		Classic Cars	Motorcycles	Planes	Ships	Trains	Trucks and Buses
CA	Amount	$458,563.64	$162,710.57	$108,632.26	$66,758.95	$17,965.32	$167,896.48
	Units Sold	4264	1827	1352	868	269	1816
CT	Amount	$89,671.28	$39,699.67	$41,142.34	$5,936.68	$9,548.53	$15,671.49
	Units Sold	688	400	517	72	156	169
MA	Amount	$223,366.59	$91,024.09	$51,924.57	$71,419.40	$12,184.49	$58,487.98
	Units Sold	2065	1046	674	919	162	614
NH	Amount	$69,150.35	--	--	--	--	$7,922.29
	Units Sold	671	--	--	--	--	84
NJ	Amount	--	$35,116.44	$33,308.49	$4,346.26	--	--
	Units Sold	--	335	430	65	--	--

Figure 20-49   Cross tab displaying two measures, one above the other

How to insert multiple measures in a cross tab

1 Drag a measure from the cube and drop it in the detail area of the cross tab.

2 Similarly, insert the second measure next to the first measure.

- To display the second measure on the right of the first measure, drop the measure when the line cursor appears below the data element for the first measure, as shown in Figure 20-50.

- To display the second measure on the left of the first measure, drop the measure when the line cursor appears on the left of the data element for the first measure.

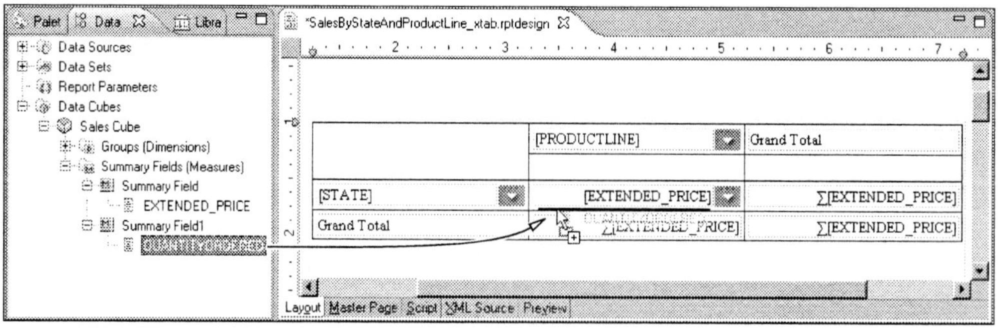

Figure 20-50   Inserting a measure on the right of another measure

How to display measures vertically

1 Select the cross tab.

2 In Property Editor, select General properties, then select Layout data fields in detail area vertically. Figure 20-51 shows this option selected.

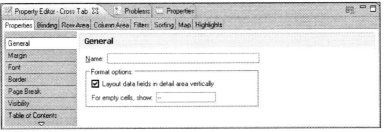

Figure 20-51 Select the option to display measures vertically

Adding subtotals and grand totals

You can display totals for each dimension that you add to a cross tab, and for each level within a multilevel dimension. The cross tab in Figure 20-52 displays sales data by product line, state, year, and quarter. The rows and columns that display the subtotals and grand totals are highlighted. BIRT does not create the subtotal and grand total rows and columns by default. You choose whether or not to display grand totals, and which subtotals to display.

SalesByStateAndProductLineAndTime.rptdesign

Show Report Parameters

			Classic Cars	Motorcycles	Planes	Ships	Trains	Trucks and Buses	Vintage Cars	Grand Total
CA	2003	1	--	--	--	--	--	$8,880.80	$18,701.35	$27,582.
		3	$78,643.82	$51,730.71	$10,300.99	$16,593.81	$7,027.48	$23,549.46	$42,823.09	$230,669.
		4	$61,577.32	$80,909.26	$32,308.36	$2,133.72	--	--	$64,858.98	$241,787.
		2003 Total	$140,221.14	$132,639.97	$42,609.35	$18,727.53	$7,027.48	$32,430.26	$126,383.42	$500,039.
	2004	1	$64,783.07	--	$23,797.47	$23,059.52	--	$36,390.78	$45,411.14	$193,441.
		2	--	$5,119.63	$33,228.69	--	--	--	$21,203.06	$59,551.
		3	$44,355.39	--	--	$3,351.85	$7,132.40	$25,285.24	$5,285.99	$85,410.
		4	$28,496.68	--	$2,434.25	--	--	$32,997.66	$67,536.80	$131,465.
		2004 Total	$137,635.14	$5,119.63	$59,460.41	$26,411.37	$7,132.40	$94,673.68	$139,436.99	$469,869.
	2005	1	$133,572.15	$24,950.97	--	$15,585.83	$3,805.44	$40,792.54	$68,642.90	$287,349.
		2	$47,135.21	--	$6,562.50	$6,034.22	--	--	$31,892.06	$91,623.
		2005 Total	$180,707.36	$24,950.97	$6,562.50	$21,620.05	$3,805.44	$40,792.54	$100,534.96	$378,973.
CT	2003	2	--	--	$13,814.21	$1,692.68	--	--	$1,525.40	$17,032.
		3	$3,797.26	$2,834.10	--	--	--	--	--	$6,631.
		4	$47,077.27	--	--	$4,244.00	$5,472.52	--	$6,224.47	$63,018.
		2003 Total	$50,874.53	$2,834.10	$13,814.21	$5,936.68	$5,472.52	--	$7,749.87	$86,681.

Layout | Master Page | Script | XML Source | Preview

Figure 20-52 Cross tab displays sales subtotals and grand totals

How to display subtotals and grand totals

This procedure assumes that you have already inserted dimensions and measures in the cross tab.

1 Select the cross tab.

2 In Property Editor, choose the Row Area tab or the Column Area tab to add a subtotal or grand total in the row area and column area, respectively. Figure 20-53 shows the Row Area tab selected.

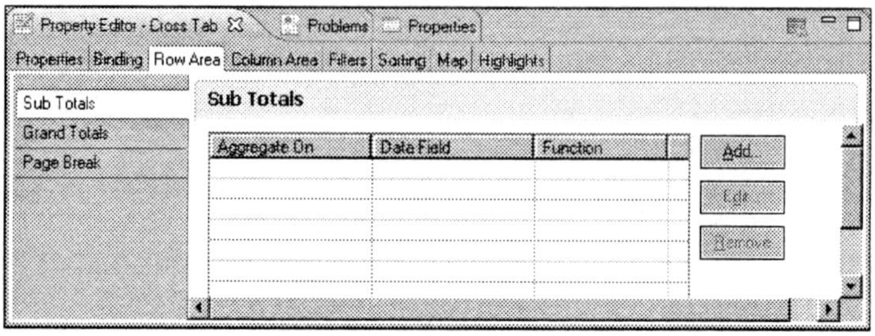

Figure 20-53   Adding a subtotal to a cross tab's row area

3 To create a subtotal, select Sub Totals, then choose Add. To create a grand total, select Grand Totals, then choose Add. A cross tab can always include grand totals. If, however, a row or column area consists of only one dimension, there can be no subtotals. The Add button is disabled if you cannot create a subtotal.

4 On Sub Total or Grand Total:

   1 In Aggregate On, select the dimension or dimension level whose total to display.

   2 In Data Field, select the field whose values to aggregate.

   3 In Function, select an aggregate function.

     Figure 20-54 shows an example of displaying subtotals for the year dimension.

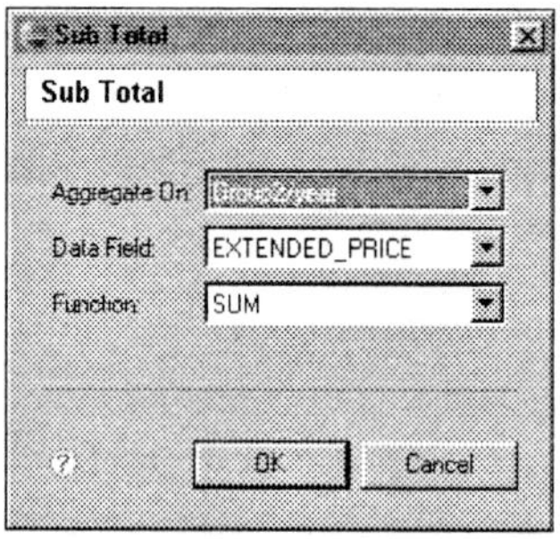

Figure 20-54   Specifying a subtotal in a cross tab

   4 Choose OK.

A new row or column is added to the cross tab, and it contains a label and a data element. For the subtotal example shown in Figure 20-54, a label in the new row displays [year]Total, and a data element displays Σ [EXTENDED_PRICE], as shown in Figure 20-55.

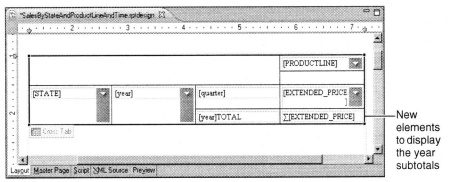

Figure 20-55   Elements that display year subtotals in a cross tab

Displaying user-defined values in row and column headings

So far, all the cross tab examples show row and column headings displaying values exactly as they appear in the data set fields. These values can sometimes by cryptic or ambiguous. You can replace such values with more descriptive terms. Sometimes, certain values appear infrequently in a set of rows. Assume, for example, that certain products sell very poorly. In a cross tab that displays sales data by product and month, rather than display a row for every product and show lots of empty cells, you can group all the unpopular products into one user-defined value named Others.

Compare the reports in Figure 20-56, Figure 20-57, and Figure 20-58. The report in Figure 20-56 shows sales by state and product line. The state values display exactly as they appear in the state field.

SalesByStateAndProductLine.rptdesign

Show Report Parameters

	Classic Cars	Motorcycles	Planes	Ships	Trains	Trucks and Buses	Vintage Cars	Grand Total
CA	$458,563.64	$162,710.57	$108,632.26	$66,758.95	$17,965.32	$167,896.48	$366,355.37	$1,348,882.59
CT	$89,671.28	$39,699.67	$41,142.34	$5,936.68	$9,548.53	$15,671.49	$14,101.07	$215,771.06
MA	$223,366.59	$91,024.09	$51,924.57	$71,419.40	$12,184.49	$58,487.98	$105,384.18	$613,791.30
NH	$69,150.35	--	--	--	--	$7,922.29	$39,376.65	$116,449.29
NJ	--	$35,116.44	$33,308.49	$4,346.26	--	--	$9,035.36	$81,806.55
NV	$58,718.89	--	--	--	--	--	$21,462.09	$80,180.98
NY	$260,619.73	$99,514.87	$24,647.66	$36,219.65	$15,033.47	$77,996.00	$62,342.28	$576,373.66
PA	$102,856.24	$39,025.09	$15,889.79	$4,983.38	$4,862.02	$37,483.09	$34,925.01	$240,024.62
Grand Total	$1,262,946.72	$467,090.73	$275,545.11	$189,664.32	$59,593.83	$365,457.33	$652,982.01	$3,273,280.05

Layout Master Page Script XML Source Preview

Figure 20-56   Cross tab displays sales totals by state and product line

The report in Figure 20-57 shows the same data, except that the abbreviated state names are replaced with full state names.

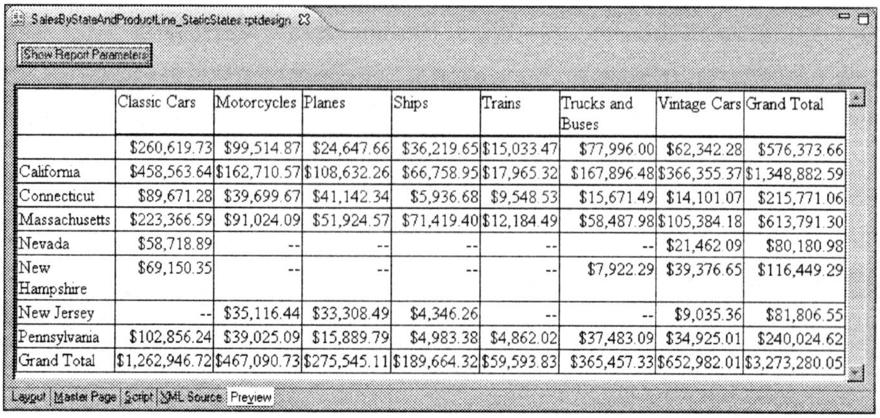

SalesByStateAndProductLine_StaticStates.rptdesign
Show Report Parameters
Layout Master Page Script XML Source Preview

	Classic Cars	Motorcycles	Planes	Ships	Trains	Trucks and Buses	Vintage Cars	Grand Total
	$260,619.73	$99,514.87	$24,647.66	$36,219.65	$15,033.47	$77,996.00	$62,342.28	$576,373.66
California	$458,563.64	$162,710.57	$108,632.26	$66,758.95	$17,965.32	$167,896.48	$366,355.37	$1,348,882.59
Connecticut	$89,671.28	$39,699.67	$41,142.34	$5,936.68	$9,548.53	$15,671.49	$14,101.07	$215,771.06
Massachusetts	$223,366.59	$91,024.09	$51,924.57	$71,419.40	$12,184.49	$58,487.98	$105,384.18	$613,791.30
Nevada	$58,718.89	--	--	--	--	--	$21,462.09	$80,180.98
New Hampshire	$69,150.35	--	--	--	--	$7,922.29	$39,376.65	$116,449.29
New Jersey	--	$35,116.44	$33,308.49	$4,346.26	--	--	$9,035.36	$81,806.55
Pennsylvania	$102,856.24	$39,025.09	$15,889.79	$4,983.38	$4,862.02	$37,483.09	$34,925.01	$240,024.62
Grand Total	$1,262,946.72	$467,090.73	$275,545.11	$189,664.32	$59,593.83	$365,457.33	$652,982.01	$3,273,280.05

Figure 20-57 Cross tab displays full state names

The report in Figure 20-58 shows sales data by regions instead of by state. The region values are not stored in a field. Rather, the region values were created using expressions that grouped states into user-defined regions. Grouping the data provides a different view of the data, and in this example, eliminates empty values from the cross tab. BIRT automatically calculates the new sales totals according to the user-defined groups.

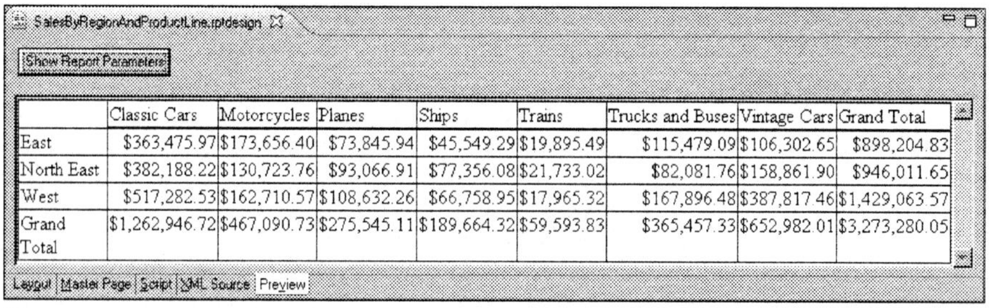

SalesByRegionAndProductLine.rptdesign
Show Report Parameters
Layout Master Page Script XML Source Preview

	Classic Cars	Motorcycles	Planes	Ships	Trains	Trucks and Buses	Vintage Cars	Grand Total
East	$363,475.97	$173,656.40	$73,845.94	$45,549.29	$19,895.49	$115,479.09	$106,302.65	$898,204.83
North East	$382,188.22	$130,723.76	$93,066.91	$77,356.08	$21,733.02	$82,081.76	$158,861.90	$946,011.65
West	$517,282.53	$162,710.57	$108,632.26	$66,758.95	$17,965.32	$167,896.48	$387,817.46	$1,429,063.57
Grand Total	$1,262,946.72	$467,090.73	$275,545.11	$189,664.32	$59,593.83	$365,457.33	$652,982.01	$3,273,280.05

Figure 20-58 Cross tab displays sales totals grouped into regions

How to specify user-defined values for row and column headings

This procedure assumes that you have already created a cube and defined the dimensions whose values populate the row and column headings.

1 In Data Explorer, double-click the cube. The Cross Tab Cube Builder appears.

2 Choose Groups and Summaries.

3 Select the dimension to edit, then choose Edit.

4 On Group Level, select Static. This option indicates that this dimension displays static values that you define.

5 Create a member-expression entry for each value to display.

- In Member, type the value to display in the cross tab.

- In Condition Expression, type the expression that indicates the value to replace.

Figure 20-59 shows examples of member-expression entries to display the following values:

- North East in place of CT, MA, and NH

- East in place of NJ, NY, and PA

- West in place of CA and NV

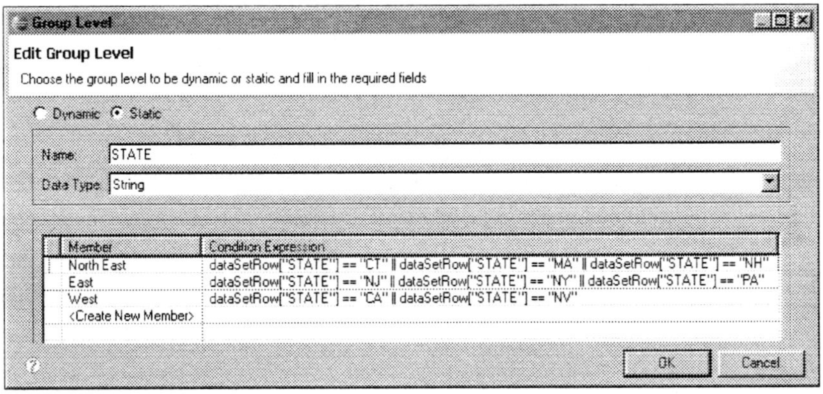

Figure 20-59   Group Level showing user-defined dimension values

Sorting cross tab data

By default, a cross tab displays data sorted by dimension values. In other words, values displayed in the row and column headings are sorted in ascending order. If you wish, you can sort the dimension values in descending order. A more common reporting requirement is to sort data by totals. Compare the cross tabs in Figure 20-60 and Figure 20-61. The cross tab in Figure 20-60 displays row and column heading values in the default ascending order. In the rows, the values are East–West. In the columns, the values are Classic Cars–Vintage Cars.

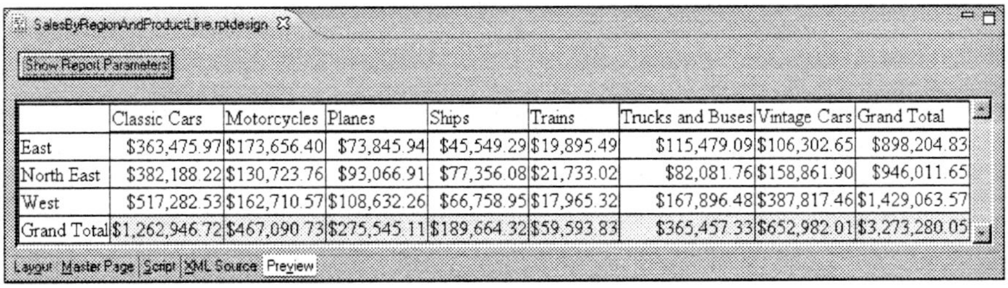

	Classic Cars	Motorcycles	Planes	Ships	Trains	Trucks and Buses	Vintage Cars	Grand Total
East	$363,475.97	$173,656.40	$73,845.94	$45,549.29	$19,895.49	$115,479.09	$106,302.65	$898,204.83
North East	$382,188.22	$130,723.76	$93,066.91	$77,356.08	$21,733.02	$82,081.76	$158,861.90	$946,011.65
West	$517,282.53	$162,710.57	$108,632.26	$66,758.95	$17,965.32	$167,896.48	$387,817.46	$1,429,063.57
Grand Total	$1,262,946.72	$467,090.73	$275,545.11	$189,664.32	$59,593.83	$365,457.33	$652,982.01	$3,273,280.05

Figure 20-60   Data sorted by default

The cross tab in Figure 20-61 displays data sorted by product grand totals, in ascending order. The product grand totals in both cross tabs are highlighted for easier comparison.

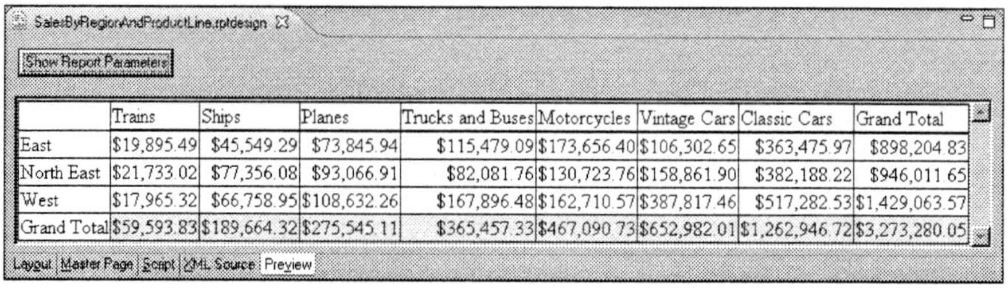

	Trains	Ships	Planes	Trucks and Buses	Motorcycles	Vintage Cars	Classic Cars	Grand Total
East	$19,895.49	$45,549.29	$73,845.94	$115,479.09	$173,656.40	$106,302.65	$363,475.97	$898,204.83
North East	$21,733.02	$77,356.08	$93,066.91	$82,081.76	$130,723.76	$158,861.90	$382,188.22	$946,011.65
West	$17,965.32	$66,758.95	$108,632.26	$167,896.48	$162,710.57	$387,817.46	$517,282.53	$1,429,063.57
Grand Total	$59,593.83	$189,664.32	$275,545.11	$365,457.33	$467,090.73	$652,982.01	$1,262,946.72	$3,273,280.05

Figure 20-61   Data sorted by product line grand totals in ascending order

Although the typical choice is to sort by dimension values or by totals as shown in the previous cross tab examples, you can also sort data for a specific dimension value. The cross tab in Figure 20-62 shows data sorted by product line totals for the West. As you can see, this type of sort can produce a confusing result because the sort is applied to a subset of the data, which makes the data in the rest of the cross tab appear random.

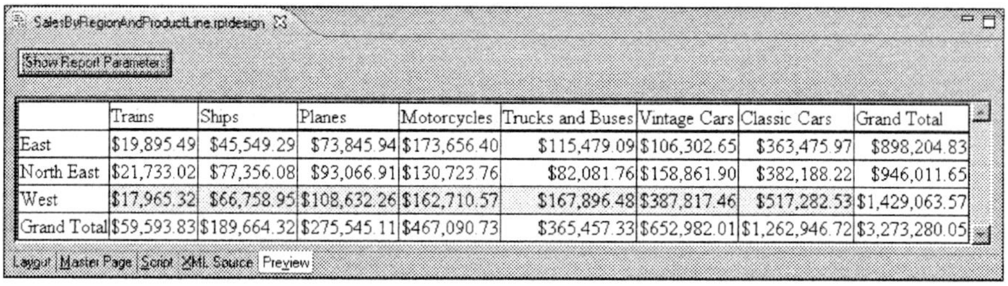

	Trains	Ships	Planes	Motorcycles	Trucks and Buses	Vintage Cars	Classic Cars	Grand Total
East	$19,895.49	$45,549.29	$73,845.94	$173,656.40	$115,479.09	$106,302.65	$363,475.97	$898,204.83
North East	$21,733.02	$77,356.08	$93,066.91	$130,723.76	$82,081.76	$158,861.90	$382,188.22	$946,011.65
West	$17,965.32	$66,758.95	$108,632.26	$162,710.57	$167,896.48	$387,817.46	$517,282.53	$1,429,063.57
Grand Total	$59,593.83	$189,664.32	$275,545.11	$467,090.73	$365,457.33	$652,982.01	$1,262,946.72	$3,273,280.05

Figure 20-62   Data sorted by product line totals in ascending order for the West

How to sort cross tab data

1   Select the cross tab, and on Property Editor, choose the Sorting tab.

2   On the Sorting page, choose Add.

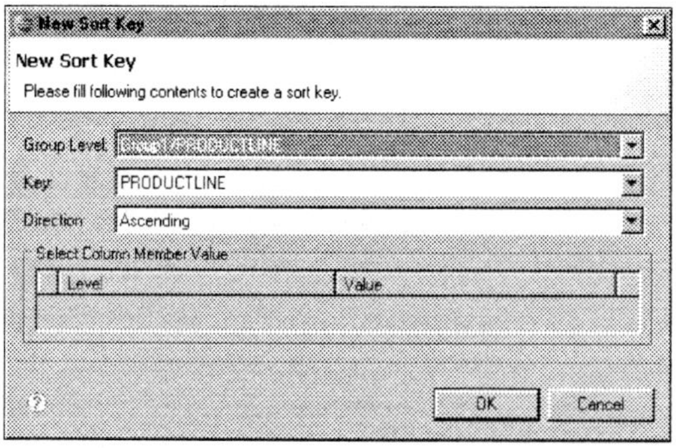

Figure 20-63   New Sort Key showing default sort values for the PRODUCTLINE dimension

By default, New Sort Key displays sort information for the first dimension in the column area, as shown in Figure 20-63. The default Key value, PRODUCTLINE, indicates that the values in the PRODUCTLINE dimension are sorted by product line name in ascending order.

3 On New Sort Key, supply the necessary sort information, as follows:

1 In Group Level, select the dimension on which to sort.

2 In Key, select the data on which to sort. Although the typical choice is to sort on totals, you can also sort data by a specific dimension value. Depending on your choice, you may be required to provide additional information about the dimension level and value on which to sort.

3 In Direction, select Ascending or Descending. Choose OK to save the sort definition.

Figure 20-64 shows an example of sorting on product line grand totals. This sort definition was created to generate the cross tab shown in Figure 20-61.

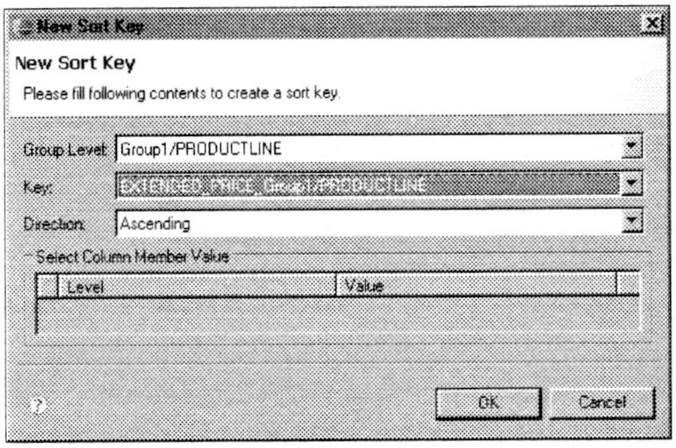

Figure 20-64   New Sort Key specifying sorting on product line grand totals

Figure 20-65 shows an example of sorting on a specific dimension value. This sort definition was created to generate the cross tab shown in Figure 20-62.

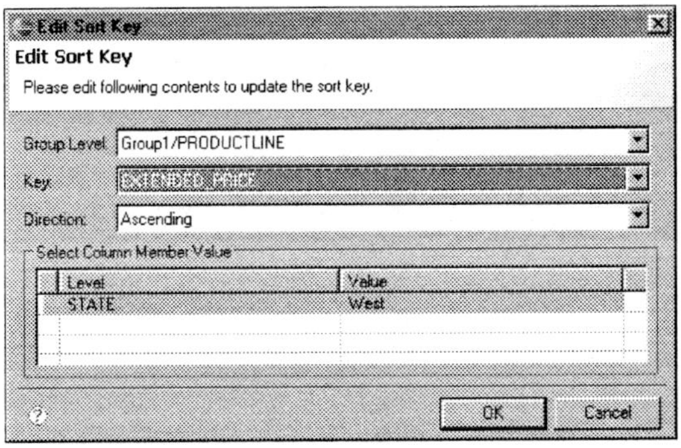

Figure 20-65   Edit Sort Key specifying sorting on a dimension value

Limiting the amount of data the cross tab displays

When you generate a report that contains a cross tab, BIRT creates one column or one row in the cross tab for each unique value in the dimensions that you insert in the cross tab. If you build a cross tab that displays sales totals by products in the column area and months of a particular year in the row area, and there are 100 products in the data set, the cross tab will consist of at least 100 columns, 12 rows and 1200 cells, not counting a row and column for the grand totals. This cross tab is obviously too wide to view on-screen or print. You can reverse the dimensions so that the product values appear as rows, and the month values as columns, but then the cross tab is much taller.

Although there is no limit to the amount of data that a cross tab can display, you improve the usability of the data if you limit the amount. After all, the main advantage of presenting data in a cross tab is the ability to compare and analyze information, preferably on a single page or screen.

As you do with any other type of report, you narrow the scope of data to include in a cross tab by creating filter conditions. If the data originates from a database, it is best, for performance reasons, to specify the filter condition in the SQL query. Alternatively, you can filter at the data set level, the cube level, and finally, at the cross tab level. The filtering option you select depends on whether other report elements or cross tabs are using the same data set or cube.

Enhancing Reports

Designing a Multipage Report

Most reports display and print on multiple pages. When you design a report, consider how a multipage report displays and prints. You can, for example, design a report so that page breaks occur at logical places. For a report that contains a series of subreports, you can specify page breaks to start each subreport on a new page.

You can also design a page layout that enhances the report's appearance and usability. A page layout specifies the style of the pages on which report data appears. You can specify, for example, that all pages display the report title in the top left corner, the company logo in the top right corner, a page number in the bottom right corner, and a report-generation date in the bottom left corner. You can also design special effects, such as a watermark that appears in the background. To design a page layout, you customize the report's master page.

Planning the page layout

Before you design a page layout, preview the report in the desired output format, and decide what changes, if any, to make to the default page layout. Consider the following design issues:

- Decide for which output format you are designing a page layout. A report design renders differently in the different output formats.

  - For an HTML report, an important decision is whether the report appears on a single scrollable page or on multiple pages in the report viewer. A single page is typical for online viewing, but, if the report is very long, displaying the report on multiple pages in the report viewer might be more suitable. If you choose to display an HTML report on a single page, decide if a master page is necessary. It does not make sense, for instance, to display a page number for a one-page report.

- ▪ For output formats that support pagination, such as PDF and DOC, decide the page dimensions, including paper size, margin sizes, header size, footer size, and page orientation. The default master page uses US letter size (8.5" x 11"). If you are developing a report for a locale that typically uses A4 paper, change the page size.

- ■ Decide the design of the master page. The default page layout displays the report-generation date in the bottom left corner of every page. Report designers typically customize the master page to reflect a corporate style or to provide additional information, such as page numbers or confidentiality statements. You can design a different master page for different output formats by displaying elements for one output and hiding them for another. You can also design and use different master pages in a single report.

Controlling pagination

Pagination is the division of a document into pages of a size you specify. It applies to the following output formats supported by BIRT: DOC, PDF, and PPT. In PPT, each report page is a PowerPoint slide. Reports in these formats display as much data as can fit on each page. This behavior can result in key sections appearing in the middle or at the bottom of a page. For most paginated reports, you will want to start certain sections at the top of a new page or avoid breaking a section across two pages.

By contrast, an XLS report appears on a single Excel worksheet; page breaks that you specify in the report design have no effect. Similarly, an HTML report, by default, displays on a single scrollable page. Page breaks that you specify, however, take effect, when an HTML report is viewed in the report viewer. When you preview a report in the layout editor or as HTML, the entire report always appears on one page.

Inserting page breaks

Reports that consist of a series of documents or distinct sections typically look more organized if each document or section appears on a separate page. For example, if a report consists of a cover letter, disclaimer information, and a summary report that is followed by a detailed report, you can insert page breaks to display each type of information on a separate page. Similarly, if a report groups sales data by state, then by customer, you can start the data for each state on a new page.

You can specify page breaks for the following elements:

- ■ Top-level elements

These are elements that are not placed in another element.

- Second-level elements

  These are elements that are placed in a top-level list, table, or grid. For example, if table A contains table B, and table B contains table C, you can specify a page break for table A and table B, but not for table C.

- Groups

  You can specify page breaks for data groups defined in top-level and second-level tables or lists.

You specify page breaks using the Page Break Before and Page Break After properties. Table 21-1 describes the values you can select for these properties.

Table 21-1   Values for Page Break Before and After properties

Page Break Before, Page Break After value	Description
Always	Always insert a page break before or after the selected element.
Auto	Insert a page break before or after the element as necessary. Auto is the default value.
Avoid	Avoid inserting a page break before or after the selected element.
Always Excluding First	Applies only to groups and Page Break Before. Always insert a page break before each instance of the selected group, but not before the first instance.
Always Excluding Last	Applies only to groups and Page Break After. Always insert a page break after each instance of the selected group, but not after the last instance.

The rest of this section provides examples of inserting page breaks for various elements. For simplicity, the examples of the generated reports shown in this section are in PDF format. You can assume that the other output formats that support pagination show similar results.

Inserting page breaks in a report with multiple sections and groups

Figure 21-1 shows a PDF report with default page breaks. In this report, the page break properties are set to Auto. Figure 21-2 shows the same report with page breaks after the Top Products and Top States reports and after each state group in the Sales By State and Product report. Notice in Figure 21-2 that the title, Sales By State and Product, repeats at the top of every page of that report. The Repeat Header option is set by default. If you want the report header to appear only once, at the beginning of the report, deselect the Repeat Header option.

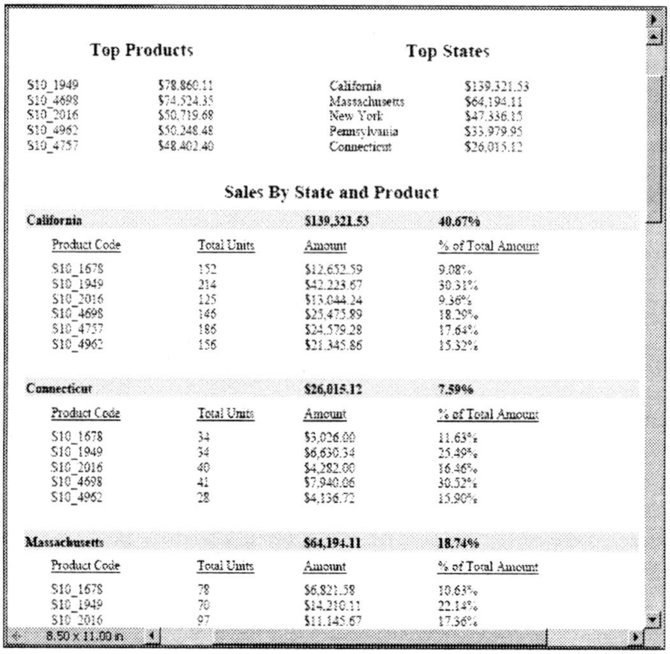

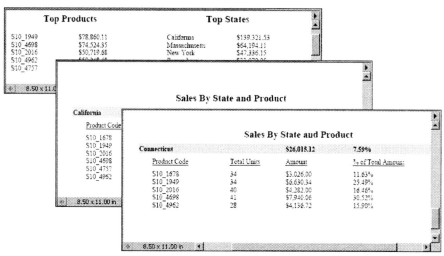

Figure 21-1 PDF report using default pagination

Figure 21-2 PDF report using custom pagination

Figure 21-3 shows the report design and indicates where and how page breaks are set. In this report design, page breaks are set as follows:

■ The Page Break After property of the grid at the top of the report is set to Always, which inserts a page break after the grid. Alternatively, selecting the top-level table element that appears after the grid and setting its Page Break Before property to Always achieves the same result.

- The Page Break After property of the state group is set to Always Excluding Last. This setting inserts a page break after each state group, except for the last group. If the Page Break After property is set to Always, the report displays a blank page after the last group. Alternatively, you can set the state group's Page Break Before property to Always Excluding First. This setting inserts a page break before each state group, except for the first group, and prevents a blank page from appearing before the first group.

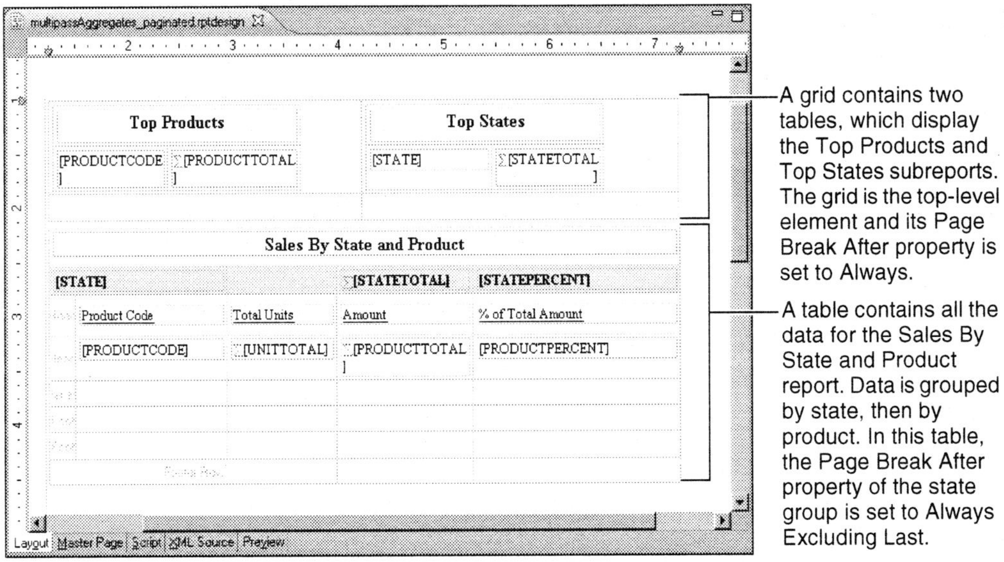

Figure 21-3   Page break property settings in a report design

Figure 21-4 shows a partial view of the group editor where you set the state group's Page Break After property.

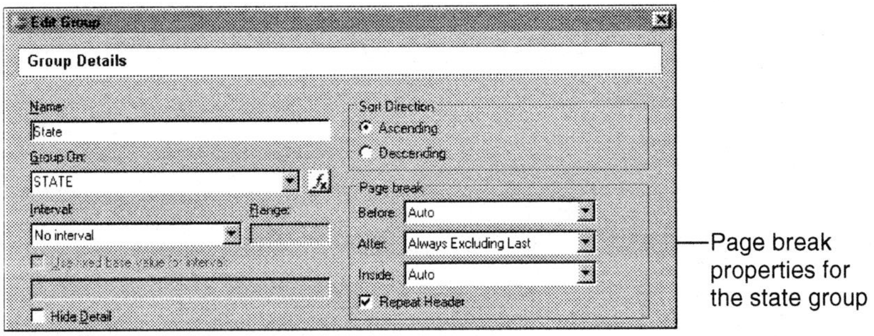

Figure 21-4   Page break properties for a group

Inserting page breaks in a master-detail report

In the next example, a report displays data with a master-detail relationship. An outer, top-level table contains two inner tables. The top-level table displays customer information. For each customer, the inner tables display order information and payment information, respectively. Figure 21-5 shows the PDF report that is paginated so that each customer's information starts on a new page.

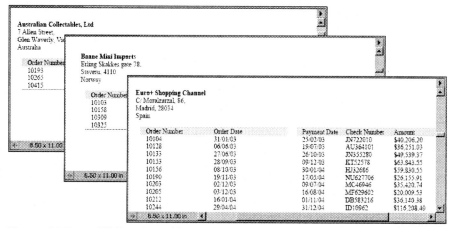

Figure 21-5 PDF output with each customer's data starting on a new page

Figure 21-6 shows the report design and indicates where and how the page break is set. The Page Break After property of the second-level table is set to Always.

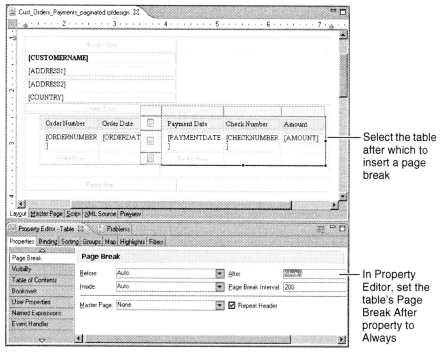

Figure 21-6 Report design that supports starting each customer's data on a new page

Specifying the number of rows per page

Specifying page breaks before or after selected sections or groups in a report is the typical way to control pagination. You can also insert a page break after a specified number of data rows. In a simple listing report that does not contain groups or multiple sections, you could, for example, display twenty rows on each page. Figure 21-7 shows two pages of a report that displays ten data rows per page.

Orders by Top Ten Customers

Euro+ Shopping Channel   **$820,689.54**

Order 10104

Product	Quantity	Price
1962 City of Detroit Streetcar	32	$1,705.92
Diamond T620 Semi-Skirted Tanker	33	$3,781.47
1950's Chicago Surface Lines Streetcar	49	$2,770.95
1954 Greyhound Scenicruiser	35	$1,818.25
1992 Porsche Cayenne Turbo Silver	26	$2,767.70
1958 Chevy Corvette Limited Edition	44	$1,338.04
1970 Dodge Coronet	35	$1,820.70
1970 Triumph Spitfire	38	$4,529.60
1992 Ferrari 360 Spider red	23	$3,816.85
1964 Mercedes Tour Bus	29	$3,559.17

Page: 1

Euro+ Shopping Channel   **$820,689.54**

Order 10104

Product	Quantity	Price
1998 Chrysler Plymouth Prowler	24	$3,261.60
1957 Chevy Pickup	41	$4,566.99
1969 Corvair Monza	34	$4,468.96

Order 10128

Product	Quantity	Price
The Mayflower	32	$2,328.00
1904 Buick Runabout	43	$3,321.32
Collectable Wooden Train	41	$3,307.47
1903 Ford Model A	41	$4,928.20

Order 10133

Product	Quantity	Price
ATA: B757-300	27	$3,107.43
American Airlines: B767-300	24	$1,841.52
1930 Buick Marquette Phaeton	27	$1,001.43

Page: 2

Figure 21-7   Report pages displaying ten data rows per page

To specify the number of rows per page, select the table element that contains the data and set the table's Page Break Interval property. The Page Break Interval property applies page breaks to all output formats, except HTML. Figure 21-8 shows the report design that generates the report shown in Figure 21-7. The selected table has its Page Break Interval property set to 10.

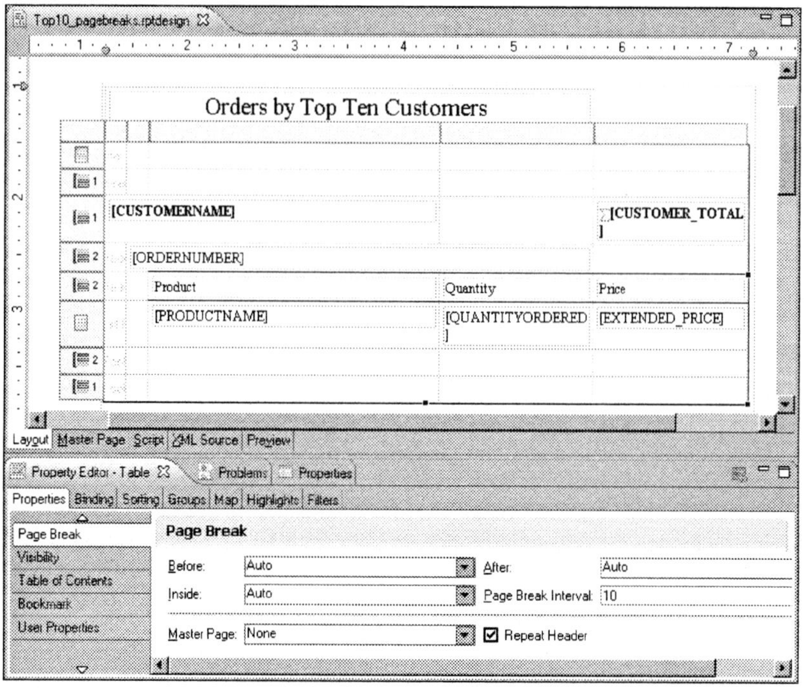

Figure 21-8   Table displaying its Page Break Interval property set to 10

Customizing the master page

The master page specifies the dimensions and style of the pages on which report data appears. You can specify, for example, that the page size is 7" x 9", the printable area is 6" x 8", the company logo always appears in the top right corner, and the page number appears in the bottom right corner.

The page size and margin settings apply only to reports in PDF, DOC, and PPT formats, where size dimensions matter, because these document types are page-oriented. For HTML reports, data appears directly in the BIRT report viewer or web browser and the layout of data adjusts to the size of the viewer or browser window.

Viewing the master page

When you create or open a report design, the layout editor always shows the report layout. To view the master page, use one of the following options:

- Choose Page→Master Page→Simple Master Page.
- Choose the Master Page tab at the bottom of the layout editor.

You can view either the report layout or the master page but not both at the same time. Figure 21-9 shows the default master page.

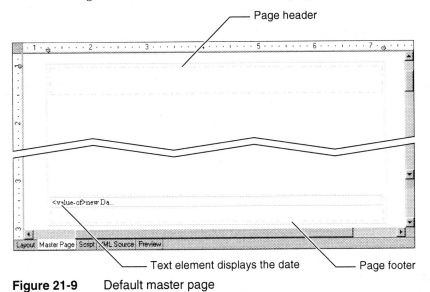

Figure 21-9   Default master page

Designing the page header and footer

The default master page includes a text element that displays the current date in the page footer. If you preview your report, you see that the current date appears on the bottom left of every report page. You can delete or edit this text element. You can add other elements to the master page by dragging them from the palette and dropping them in the page footer or header.

Observe the following rules:

- You can place elements in the header and footer only. You do not place elements in the report content area because the contents of those elements would overlap report data.

- You cannot place more than one element directly in the header or footer. To place multiple elements, insert a grid, then insert the elements in the grid.

Displaying page numbers, the current date, and other text

Common header and footer information includes the page number, report-generation date, company name, author name, copyright information, and confidentiality statements.

As Figure 21-10 shows, BIRT Report Designer provides predefined text elements for displaying some of these common items, including the current date, page number, author name, and file name. These items are available on the palette when the master page is displayed.

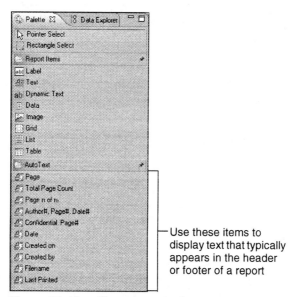

Use these items to
display text that typically
appears in the header
or footer of a report

Figure 21-10   Text elements for common header and footer items

For example, the date element is a text element that contains the following dynamic value:

```
<VALUE-OF>new Date()</VALUE-OF>
```

After you insert a predefined text element in the page header or footer, you can edit the text to display different information. For example, you can edit the date element to display the date in a different format. By default, the report displays the date according to the locale that is set on the machine on which the report is generated. You can use the format attribute to display the date in a custom format, as shown in the following expression:

```
<VALUE-OF format="MM-dd-yy">new Date()</VALUE-OF>
```

To display other text in the header or footer, you can use the other predefined text elements in the palette and edit the text content or insert a regular text or label element and type the text from scratch.

Remember, to display more than one element in the header or footer, you must first insert a grid, then insert the elements in the grid. The predefined Author#, Page#, Date# element creates a grid and three text elements, so you might find it convenient to insert this element, then edit the individual text elements.

As with any text element, you can also customize the appearance of the predefined elements, for example, to display text in a different style or color, or to align text in the center or right of the page.

How to display text in the header and footer

1 In the layout editor, choose the Master Page tab. The layout editor displays the master page. The palette displays additional elements under AutoText, specifically for use in the master page.

2 To display a single text element in the header or footer, drag the desired element from the palette, and drop it in the header or footer. For example, to display the page number, insert either the Page element or the Page n of m element.

3 To display multiple text elements in the header or footer:

　1 Insert the grid element in the header or footer. Delete the date element from the default footer first.

　2 On Insert Grid, specify the number of columns and rows for the grid. If, for example, you want to display two elements on the same line, specify 2 columns and 1 row.

　3 Insert each text element in a grid cell.

Displaying an image

You can insert static and dynamic images in a page header or footer. You insert an image in a master page the same way you insert an image in the report layout. The difference is that you cannot insert an image inside a table in the master page. Therefore, when you insert a dynamic image directly on the master page, the same image—the image in the first data row—appears on every page.

Specifying a header size

The size of the header in the generated report can be different when rendered in PDF and in HTML. For an HTML report, the header dynamically resizes to accommodate its contents, and the header always appears directly above the report content. In an HTML report, the header height property is ignored.

For a PDF report, the header also dynamically resizes to accommodate its contents. Unlike the HTML report, you can specify a fixed size for the header. If you specify a header size of one inch, and you insert an image that is half an inch in height, the report displays half an inch of space between the image and the report data. If the header size you specify, however, is not sufficient to display a large image, the report overrides the specified header size and resizes the header to display the image in its entirety.

Increasing the header size is one way to increase the space between the header content and the report content. However, because header size applies only to PDF output, this technique is not recommended if you want to create a master page that serves both PDF and HTML output equally well.

The preferred technique to add space between the header content and report content is to increase the padding at the bottom of the text or label element placed in the header. Alternatively, if you use a grid to organize multiple elements, you can add a row at the bottom of the grid and set the row size. Using either of these techniques, the extra space appears in both PDF and HTML output.

Specifying a footer size

Like the header, the size of the footer in the generated report can be different for PDF and HTML reports. In both types of reports, the footer dynamically resizes to fit its content. If you specify a footer size, the PDF report displays a footer section of the specified size, except when the contents exceed the specified size. The HTML report ignores the specified footer size.

How to specify a header or footer size

1   In the layout editor, choose the Master Page tab. The layout editor displays the master page.

2   In Property Editor, choose General properties. Property Editor displays the master page's general properties, as shown in Figure 21-11.

3   Specify a size for the header height, the footer height, or both.

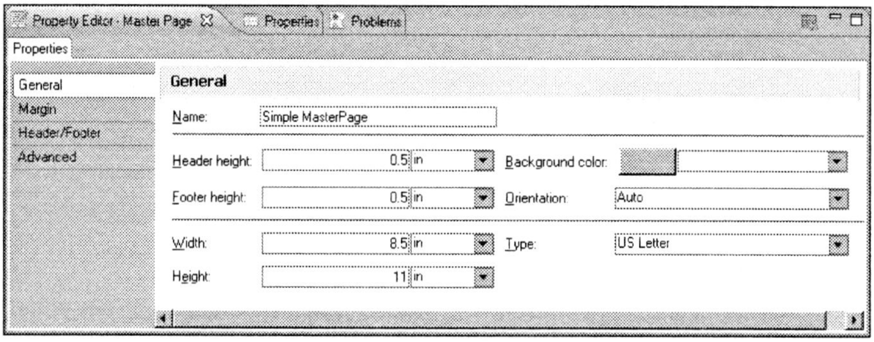

Figure 21-11   Master page properties in Property Editor

Excluding header content from the first page

It is common practice to display header content on every page except the first. For example, a report displays a title in bold and large font on the first page, but in a smaller font at the top of the other pages, as shown in Figure 21-12. To create this design:

■   Insert a text element in the report page to display the title on the first page.

■   Insert a text element in the master page header to display the title on subsequent pages. When you insert an element in the page header, it appears, by default, on every page in the report.

■   Turn off the Show header on first property. This property controls whether headers appear on all pages, or on all pages except the first.

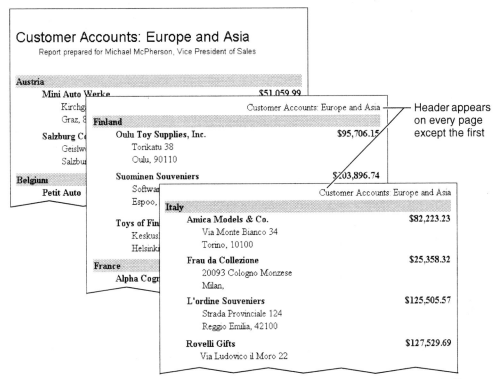

Figure 21-12 Report output when the Show header on first property is turned off

How to exclude header content from the first page

1 In the layout editor, choose Master Page. The layout editor displays the master page.

2 In Property Editor, choose Header/Footer. Property Editor displays the header and footer properties, as shown in Figure 21-13.

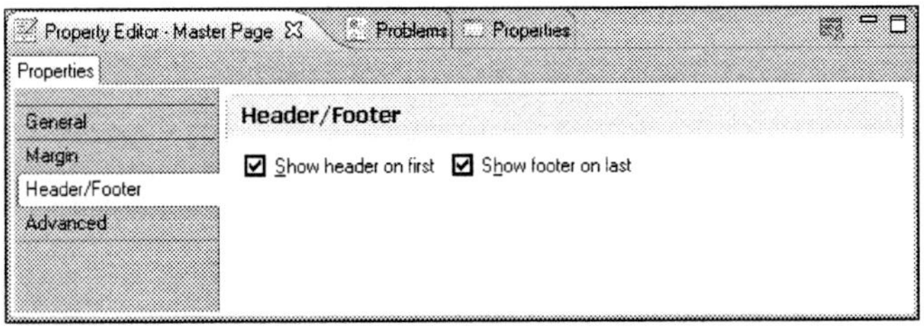

Figure 21-13 Header and footer properties

3 Deselect Show header on first.

4 Choose Preview to verify the report output. If the report contains more than one page, the header content appears on all pages except the first.

Displaying an image in the background

A page can contain an image that appears behind the report data. This effect is called a watermark. For example, a document in draft form can display the word Draft across the page. A government document can display a department seal in the background. Figure 21-14 shows examples of reports including watermarks.

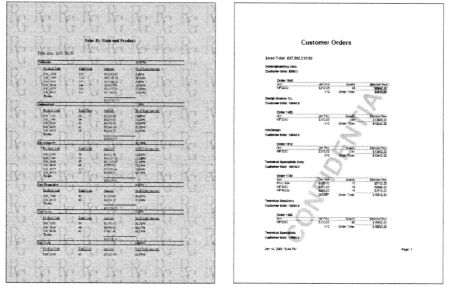

Figure 21-14   Reports including watermarks

When you design a watermark:

- Make sure the image recedes into the background and does not interfere with the readability of the report. For example, use very light-colored images.

- You can use a small image and repeat it so that it fills the entire page. In Figure 21-14, the report on the left shows this effect. Use this technique judiciously. As the example report shows, filling the page with colored images can reduce the readability of the report.

- You can use a large image that fills the page. In Figure 21-14, the report on the right shows this effect.

- Bear in mind that if any report elements in the report layout have background color, this color appears on top of the background image. Figure 21-15 shows this effect. If you want to display a watermark, limit the use of color in the report layout; otherwise the report readability is compromised.

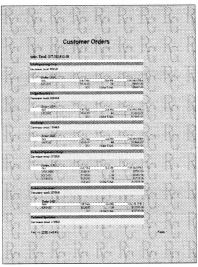

Figure 21-15   Report using colors and a watermark

To use an image as a watermark, select the master page. On Property Editor, select Advanced, expand Simple Master Page, then expand Background, as shown in Figure 21-16. Set the Background image property to the URL of the image file, such as:

```
http://mysite.com/images/logo.jpg
```

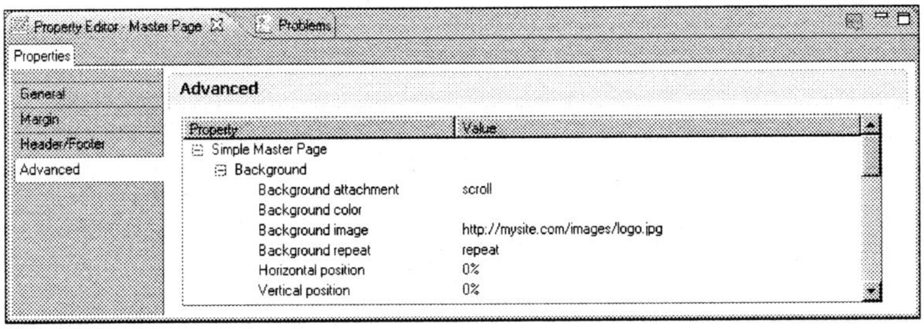

Figure 21-16   Property Editor showing advanced properties for the master page

You can specify a local file-system location, such as c:/images/logo.jpg. You should, however, use a local path for testing purposes only. When you deploy the report, the report will not be able to find the image on the local machine.

Designing the appearance of the background image

By default, a background image repeats to fill the page. You can change this behavior by setting the value of the Background repeat property as follows:

- Specify no-repeat to display the image once.

- Specify repeat-x to repeat the image across the page horizontally.

- Specify repeat-y to repeat the image across the page vertically.

Figure 21-17 shows the results of setting the Background repeat property to different values.

Background repeat = no-repeat   Background repeat = repeat-x   Background repeat = repeat-y

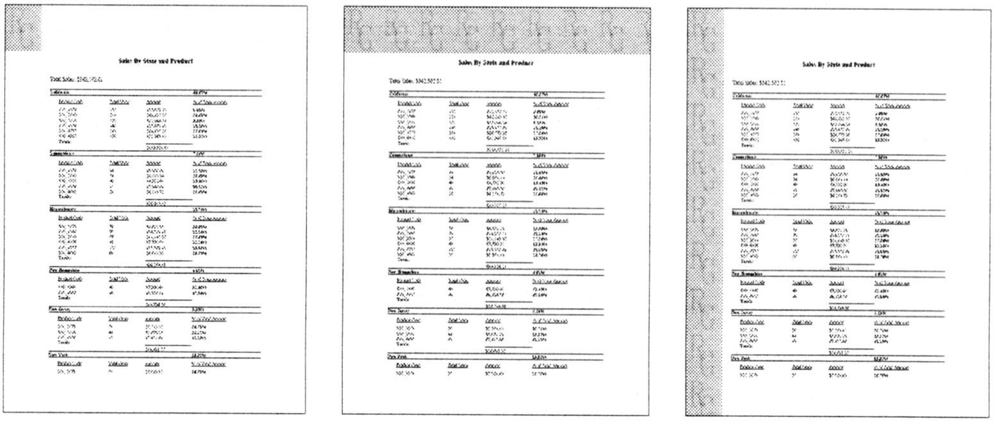

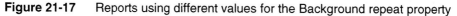

Figure 21-17 Reports using different values for the Background repeat property

Positioning the background image

If you set the Background repeat property to no-repeat, repeat-x, or repeat-y, you can reposition the image to display it on a different part of the page by using the Horizontal position and Vertical position properties. For Horizontal position, you can select the center, left, or right values. For Vertical position, you can select the bottom, center, or top values.

For both these properties, you can also specify a precise position or a percentage. For example, setting Horizontal position to 3 in displays the image 3 inches from the left of the page. Setting Vertical position to 25% displays the image at the top 25% of the page. You can use Dimension Builder, as shown in Figure 21-18, to specify a precise position by inches, millimeters, pixels, and so on.

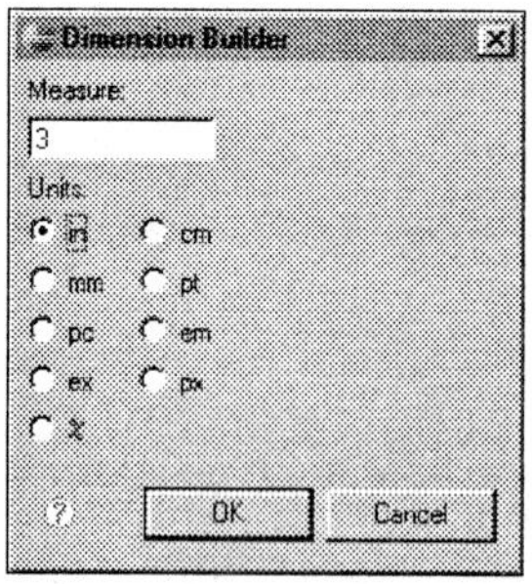

Figure 21-18 Dimension Builder

Figure 21-19 shows the results of setting the Background repeat, Horizontal position, and Vertical position properties to different values.

Background repeat = repeat-x
Vertical position = center

Background repeat = repeat-y
Horizontal position = 75%

Background repeat = no-repeat
Horizontal position = right
Vertical position = top

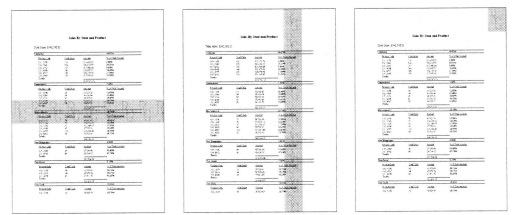

Figure 21-19 Reports using different background property values

Displaying different content in different output formats

You can design a master page that differs for different output formats. Simply select the element or elements on the master page that you want to display in a particular output format, then set the element's Visibility property accordingly. Figure 21-20 shows a picture element's Visibility property set to hide the picture in a PDF report.

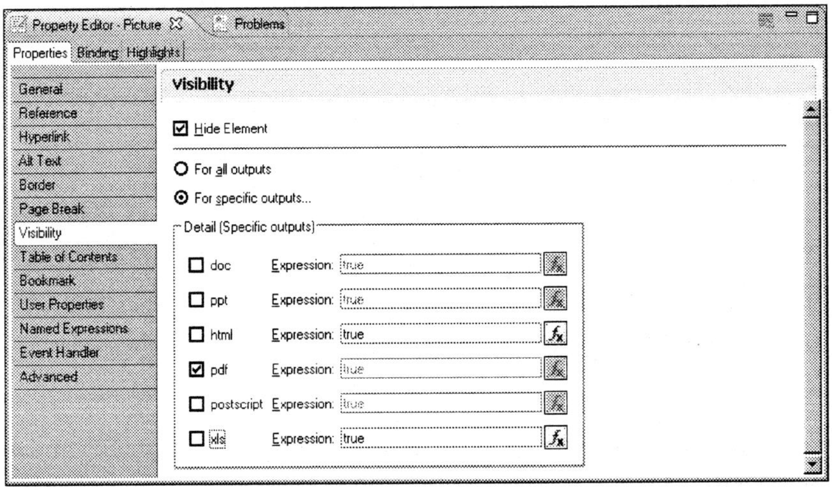

Figure 21-20 Hiding an element in PDF output only

You also have the option of disabling the master page for HTML reports. Sometimes, it makes sense to hide header and footer information for HTML reports, which display on a single page. For example, page numbers and report headers are not necessary for a one-page report. If the master page contains only these items, disabling the entire master page, rather than hiding individual elements on the master page, is more efficient.

To disable the master page for HTML reports, choose Window→Preferences, then choose Report Design—Preview, and deselect Enable master page content. Note that this option takes effect at the application level, not at the report level.

Specifying page size, orientation, and margins

As explained earlier, these page settings apply to page-oriented reports only. An HTML report displays directly in the report viewer and its size adjusts to the size of the viewer window. Report data in XLS format appears on a single worksheet.

The default master page uses the following settings:

- US letter size, 8.5" x 11"

- Portrait orientation

- Top and bottom margins of 1"

- Left and right margins of 1.25"

You can change these page settings in Property Editor. The General page of Property Editor for a master page is shown in Figure 21-21.

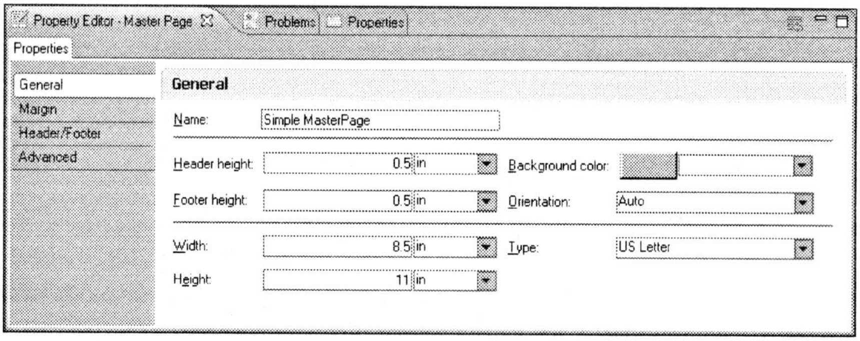

Figure 21-21   Master page properties

If you are designing a report for PDF, specify the page settings before you begin laying out report data. If, for example, you set the page width to a smaller size after you lay out the report data, you most probably have to adjust the report contents to fit in the new page size.

Using multiple master pages

You can use multiple master pages in a single report. A report can use different master pages to display, for example, one section of a report in portrait mode and another section in landscape mode. Using multiple master pages, you can also specify different background color, or different header and footer content for different sections of a report. Figure 21-22 shows a report that uses two master pages. The first page uses a master page that has portrait mode and a watermark. The second page uses a master page that has landscape mode and text in the footer.

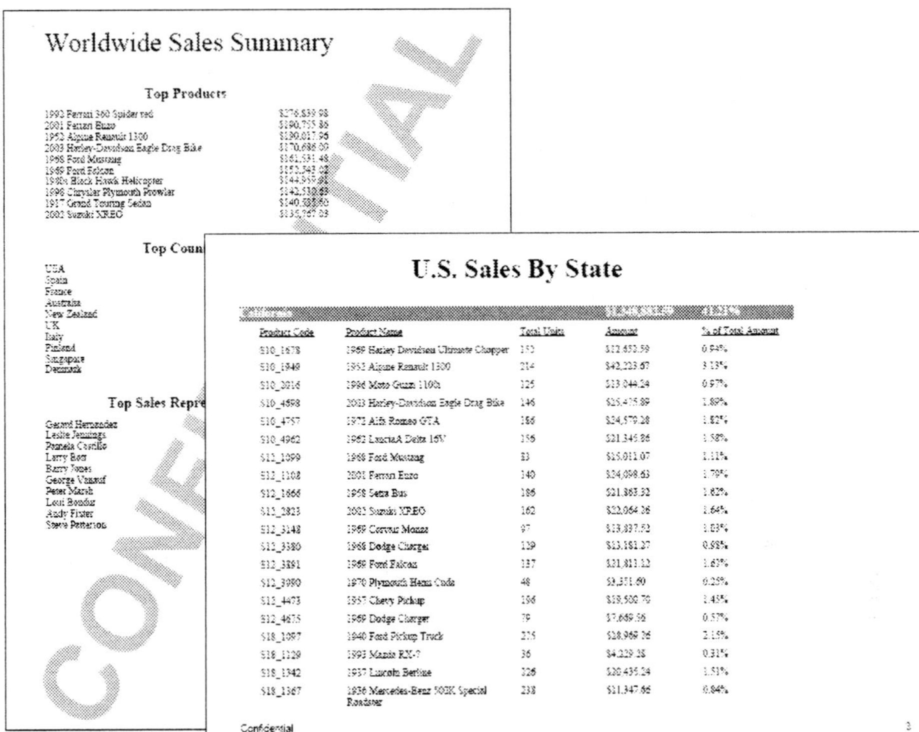

Figure 21-22   Report using two master pages to display different page styles

To use multiple master pages in a report:

- Create the master pages. You can create as many master pages as you want through the Outline view. Right-click MasterPages and choose Insert to add a new master page to the report design.

- Specify a page break for each report section that uses a different master page.

- Assign a master page to each report section.

For example, to design the report in Figure 21-22, two master pages, named Portrait and Landscape, were created. The Portrait master page was applied to the first report page, and the Landscape master page to the body of the report, using the following procedure:

- Select the report section that you want to appear on the title page, and on Property Editor, choose Page Break. On the Page Break page, set the Master Page property to Portrait. Then set the Page Break After property to Always. Figure 21-23 shows a grid selected, and its master page and page break properties set. The grid contains all the elements whose data appears on the first page.

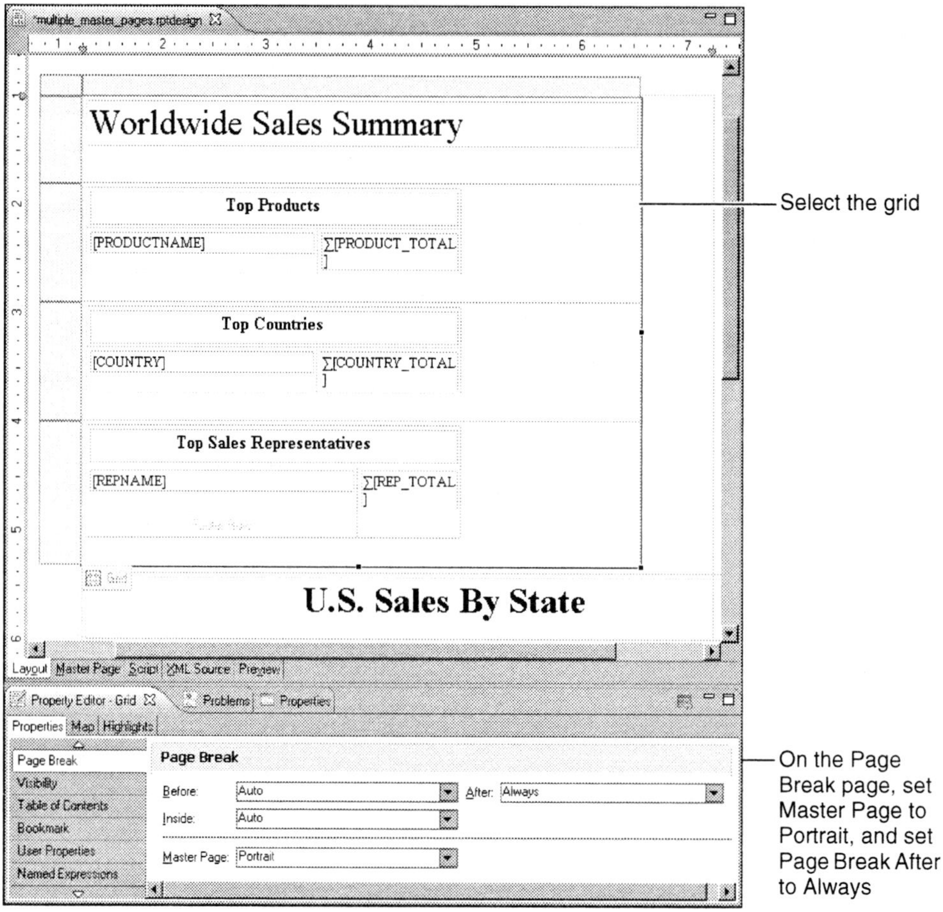

Figure 21-23   Page break and master page applied to selected grid

- Select the first element that appears on the body of the report, which starts on the next page. Set its master page to Landscape, as shown in Figure 21-24. The Landscape master page is used for the rest of the pages in the report.

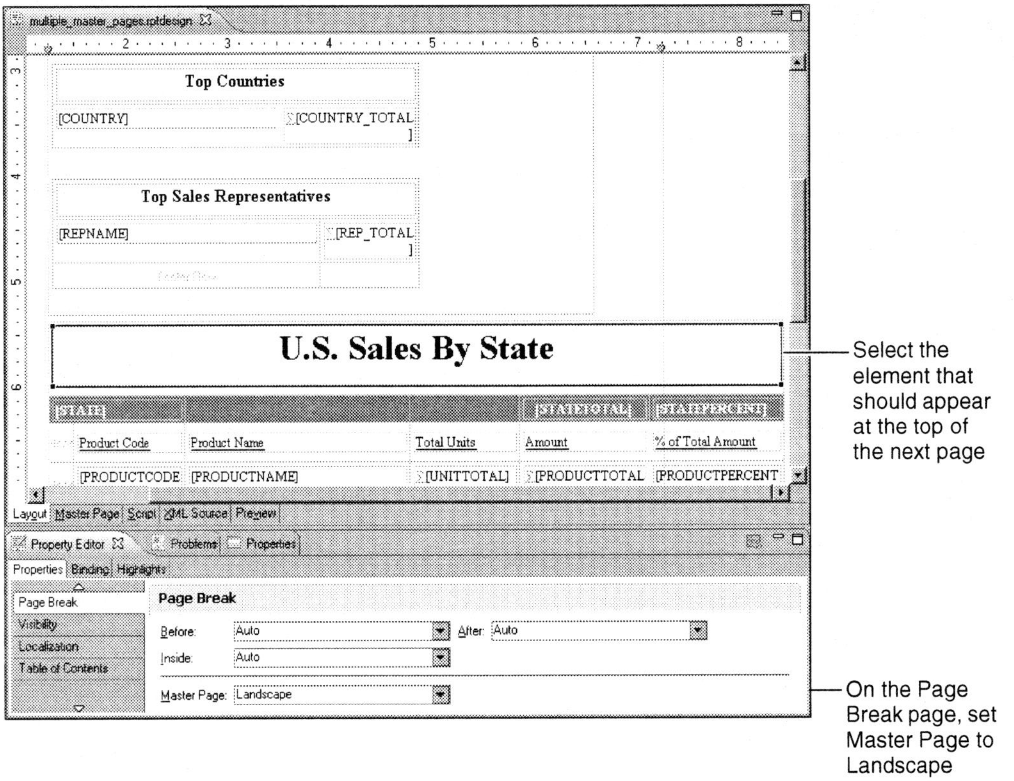

Figure 21-24 Master page applied to the first element in the body of the report

Adding Interactive Viewing Features

Some reports are long and complex, which can make it difficult for readers to locate and use the information that they need. If these reports will be viewed online, you can add interactive features that help users to navigate and explore reports.

Hyperlinks and tables of contents offer different ways for a user to find information or drill down to more detailed data. Interactive chart features enable you to customize the data that a chart displays and provide links to additional information. If designing an HTML report, you can add interactive elements common to web pages, such as buttons and check boxes, that do something when selected.

Not all report output formats support every interactive viewing feature. Output formats, such as PPT, XLS, and DOC, provide limited support. For example, interactive charts are available only in the BIRT report viewer; the table of contents appears only in the report viewer and in PDF; interactive web page elements apply to HTML reports only.

Creating hyperlinks

You can create a hyperlink that links one report element to another element, either in the same report or in a different report. A report, for example, can contain a summary listing with hyperlinks to detailed information. Similarly, a large report that consists of several subreports can contain a title page with hyperlinks to each subreport.

The report element that acts as the hyperlink is called the source report element. It must be a data, label, image, or chart element. The report element to which you link is called the target report element.

Figure 22-1 shows two pages of a report in the BIRT report viewer, and how clicking a hyperlink on the first page jumps to content on the sixth page. The first page of the report displays sales summary information in a table and a chart. The state names in the table and the slices of the pie chart are hyperlinks. When the user clicks a hyperlink, the report viewer displays the detailed sales information for the selected state, as shown in Figure 22-1.

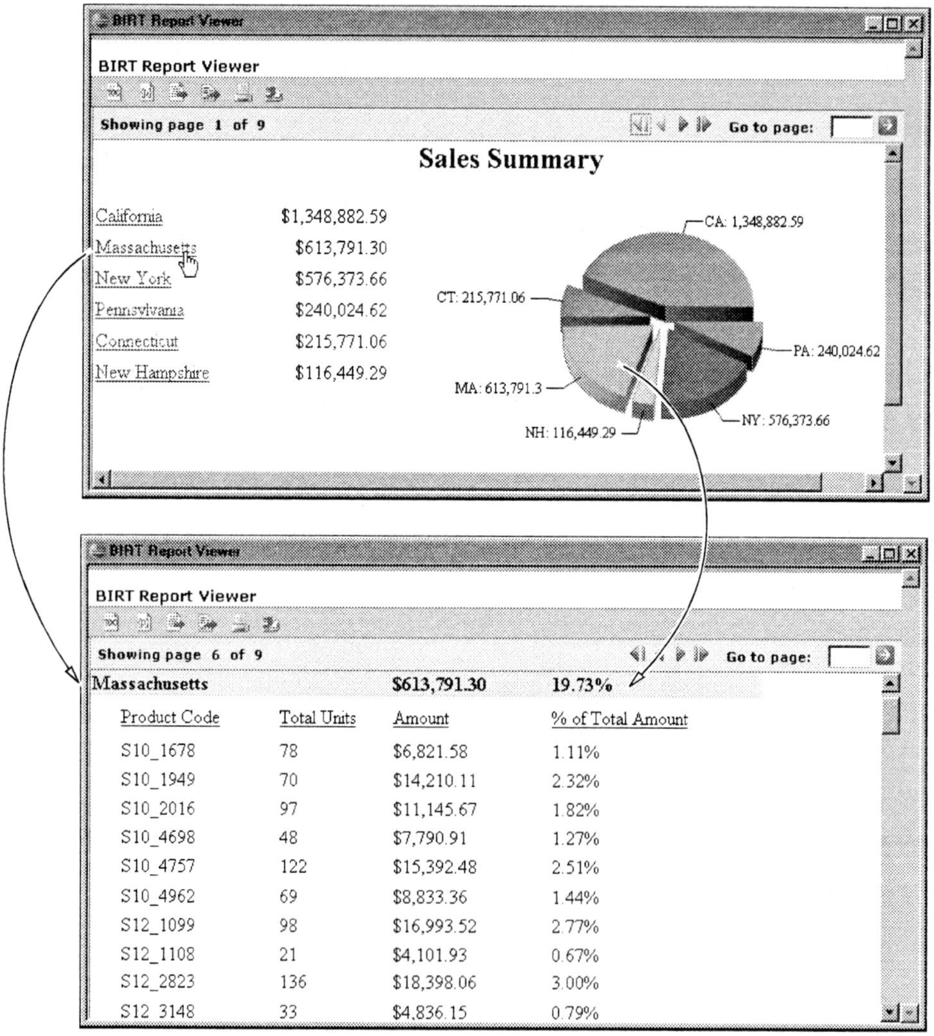

Figure 22-1   Clicking a hyperlink to go from one section in a report to another

Linking two sections in a report

To create a link from one report element to another element in the same report, you use a bookmark and a hyperlink. First, you define a bookmark for the target report element. Then, you define a hyperlink for the source report element. You perform these tasks in this sequence because the hyperlink requires the bookmark information.

Defining a bookmark

As its name suggests, a bookmark is a marker for finding a place in a report. When you define a bookmark, you specify information that determines how BIRT generates the bookmark. The information you supply for a bookmark can be one of the following:

- A name, such as "Bookmark 1" or "Bookmark for Sales Details Section". If you supply a name, you must enclose it within double quotation marks. Figure 22-2 shows an example.

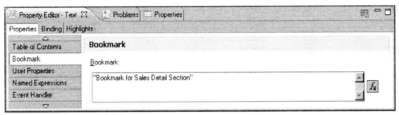

Figure 22-2   Using a name for the bookmark

Specify a name when you want to link to a specific static location in the report. For example, to link to the beginning of a particular subreport in a report, you can select the label element that displays the title of the subreport, then create a bookmark using a name.

- An expression, such as row["STATE"], as shown in Figure 22-3.

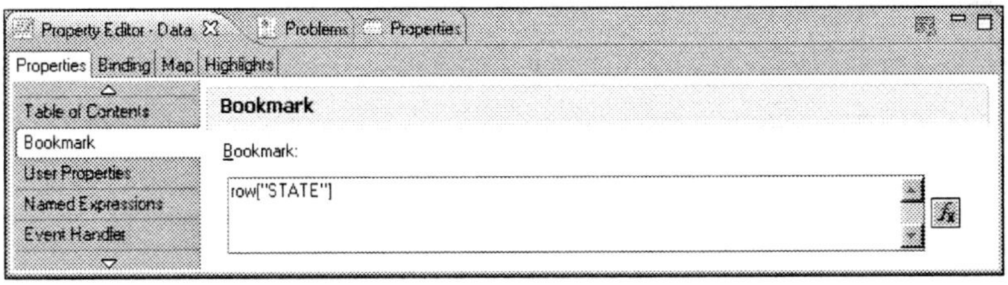

Figure 22-3   Using an expression for the bookmark

Specify an expression when you want to link to a location that is generated dynamically. The report shown in Figure 22-1 is such an example. In the Sales Detail section, the data element that displays the state name has a bookmark. The bookmark expression, row["STATE"], generates a dynamic bookmark for each state in the section.

How to define a bookmark

1 Select the target report element.

2 On Property Editor, under Properties, choose Bookmark.

3 In Bookmark, type the name of the bookmark or create an expression. You can use any bookmark name that does not start with "_TOC_." This string is reserved for internal use by BIRT.

Figure 22-4 shows the bookmark definition for the example report shown in Figure 22-1.

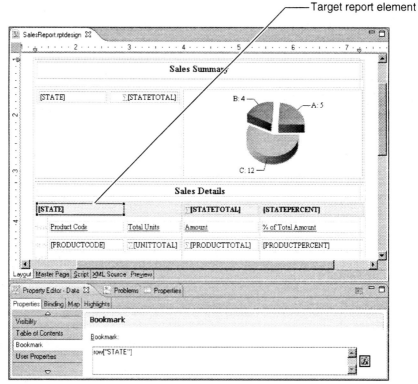

Figure 22-4   Bookmark definition for a selected data element

Defining a hyperlink

After you create the bookmark, you define a hyperlink that goes to the bookmark. When you define a hyperlink, you specify the following information:

- The type of hyperlink. To link two sections within a report, use Internal Bookmark.

- The bookmark to go to, or a link expression that changes the bookmark dynamically based on factors, such as report parameters, session values, or data values.

Use a link expression if you want to link to bookmarks conditionally. For example, the details to which you link for each customer in a customer listing report may be different depending on the role of the person viewing the report. Someone in the sales department may need to see purchase order details, while someone in the shipping department may need to see bill of lading information. Adding a script to change the bookmark based on user role accomplishes this result.

A hyperlink can only be defined for a data, label, image, or chart element. The hyperlink options are the same for all these elements. The way in which you access the hyperlink options, however, differs for a chart and the other elements. For a chart, you use the interactivity editor in the chart builder to access the hyperlink options. For the other elements, you use the Hyperlink page of Property Editor.

How to create a hyperlink that links two sections in a report

1 Select the source report element, then perform one of the following tasks:

- For a data, label, or image element, on Property Editor, choose Properties, then choose Hyperlink. On the Hyperlink page, choose the ellipsis button to open Hyperlink Options. Figure 22-5 shows the Hyperlink page and the selected data element for the example report shown in Figure 22-1.

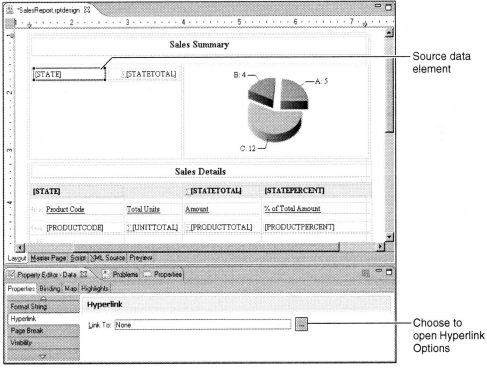

Figure 22-5   Selected data element and Hyperlink page

■ For a chart, perform the following steps to open Hyperlink Options:

1 Double-click the chart to open the chart builder.

2 Select Format Chart, then choose the chart element for which to define a hyperlink. The chart element can be a value series, the chart area, the legend, the x- and y-axis, or a title. Figure 22-6 shows an example of a pie chart's value series selected.

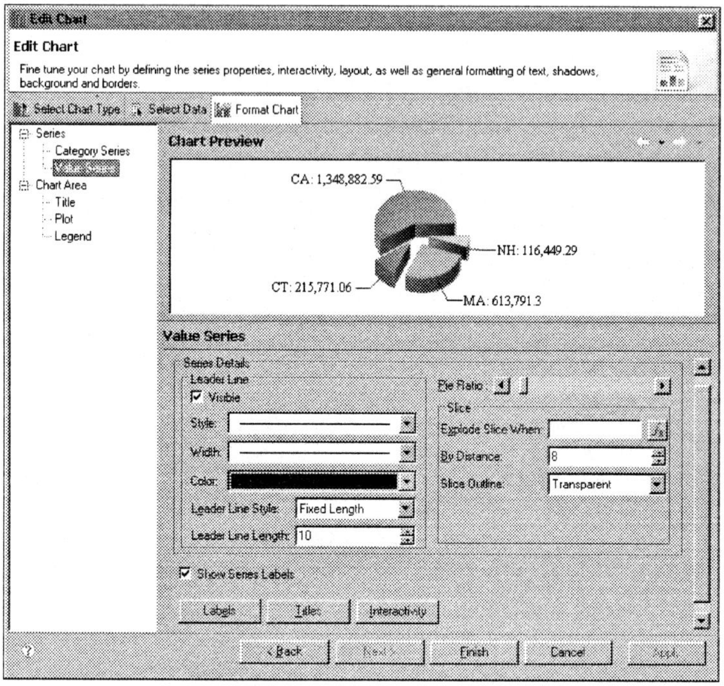

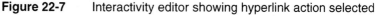

Figure 22-6   Edit chart displaying format options for value series

3 Choose Interactivity. On the interactivity editor, in Action, select Hyperlink.

4 Choose Edit Base URL to open Hyperlink Options. Figure 22-7 shows the hyperlink action selected in the interactivity editor.

Choose to open
Hyperlink Options

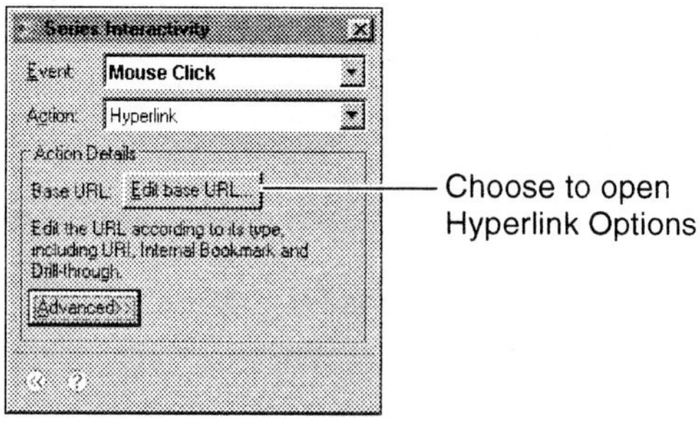

Figure 22-7   Interactivity editor showing hyperlink action selected

2 On Hyperlink Options, complete the following tasks:

   1 In Select Hyperlink Type, select Internal Bookmark.

   2 Do one of the following:

   ❏ In Bookmark, select a bookmark from the drop-down list. The list displays all the bookmarks that you defined for the report. The bookmark you select appears in both Bookmark and Linked Expression, as shown in Figure 22-8.

   ❏ In Linked Expression, choose the expression builder button, then build an expression.

   Figure 22-8 shows an example of a hyperlink definition that uses a bookmark value.

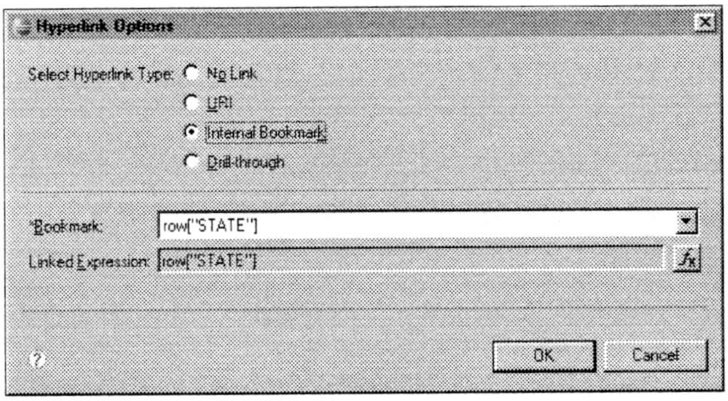

Figure 22-8   Hyperlink Options

   3 Choose OK.

3 Preview the report to test the hyperlink. In the previewer and the report viewer, a data or label element with a hyperlink appears as blue underlined text, and an image has a blue border. For a chart, a hyperlink does not have a different appearance, but a cursor shaped like a hand appears when you hover the mouse pointer over a hyperlink.

Linking to a section in a different report

Creating a link from one report to a different report is similar to creating a link between elements in the same report. You begin by creating a bookmark in the target report. Then, you create a hyperlink in the source report. This type of hyperlink is called a drill-through hyperlink, and requires you to supply additional information, including:

■ The name of the target report that contains the bookmark. The target report can be one of the following file types:

▪ Report design (.rptdesign). Specify a report design if you want to run a report to display current data when the user clicks the hyperlink, or if you want to generate a customized report based on a parameter value.

- Report document (.rptdocument). A report document is a previously executed report that contains cached data. Report document is the recommended target report type if the report is very large or if the report data changes infrequently.

- The bookmark in the target report to which to link. Alternatively, you can link to the target of a table of contents entry. The table of contents, described later in this chapter, is another mechanism for navigating from one report section to another.

- Using the same or a new window to open the target report.

- The output format in which to display the target report.

Figure 22-9 shows an example of hyperlink options specified to link to a bookmark, row["STATE"], in a target report named SalesDetails.rptdesign.

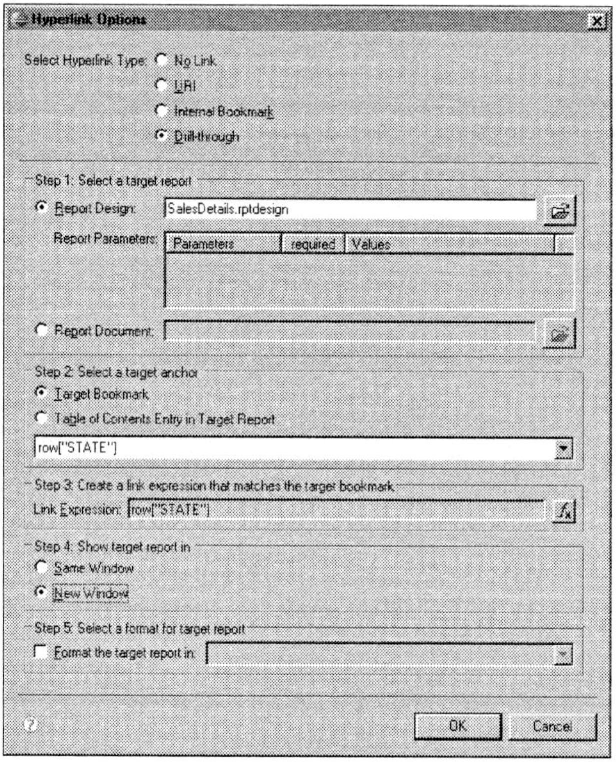

Figure 22-9   Hyperlink options for linking two reports

You can customize the data displayed by the target report and improve system response time by using report parameters. For example, instead of generating a target report that shows sales details for all states, you can use a target report design that has a report parameter that filters data by state. The report displays sales details only for the state whose hyperlink the user clicks. Typically, generating the filtered report is faster than generating a report with all the data.

To generate such a report, perform the following tasks:

- In the target report, create a report parameter to get the state value at run time.

- In the source report, define a hyperlink that runs the target report and passes the selected state value to the target report's parameter. Figure 22-10 shows a hyperlink definition where the row["STATE"] value is passed to the report parameter, RP_State, in the target report SalesDetail.rptdesign. When the target report you specify contains report parameters, you click under Parameters in Hyperlink Options to view a list of the parameters.

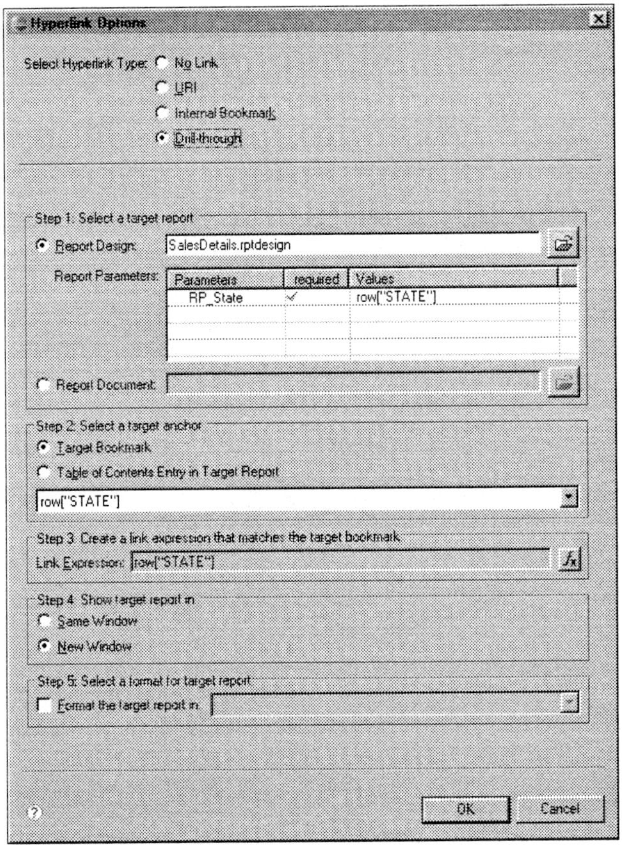

Figure 22-10   Hyperlink options for a link that passes a parameter

Linking to external content using a URI

You can use a hyperlink to open a document or a web page. These links provide users with easy access to additional sources of information, creating more interactive reports.

For example, you can use a hyperlink to:

- Open a company web page when a user chooses a label.

- Open a text file that contains detailed copyright information when a user chooses a label that displays a copyright statement.

- Open an image file or play a movie clip when a user chooses a thumbnail image in the report.

This type of hyperlink uses a Uniform Resource Identifier (URI) to locate a document, image, or web page. You provide the URI on Hyperlink Options, using the settings shown in Figure 22-11.

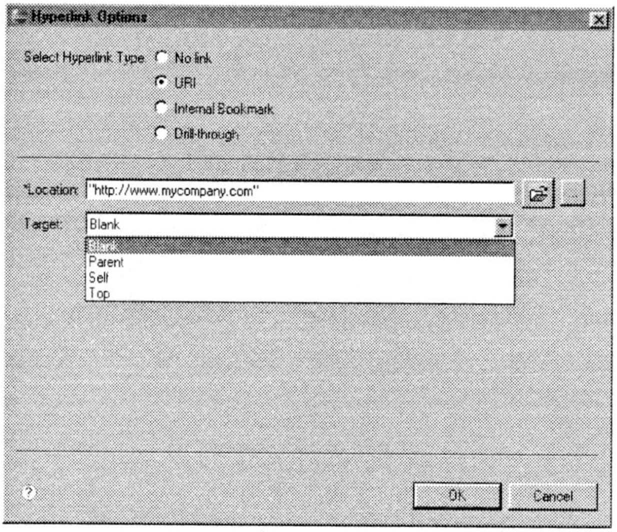

Figure 22-11   Hyperlink options for a URI

First, choose URI as the hyperlink type, then, in Location, supply the URI, as shown in the following examples:

```
"http://www.mycompany.com"
"http://mysite.com/legal_notices/copyright.html"
"http://mysite.com/images/executives.jpg"
"file:/C:/copyright/statement.txt"
```

The quotation marks are required. You can type a URI, navigate to and select a file, or use the expression builder to create an expression that evaluates to a URI. Use an expression to construct a URI dynamically when the full URI is not known at design time or if the URI changes depending on data retrieved from a data source.

In Target, specify where to open the target document. The choices correspond to the target attributes for an HTML anchor tag. Select Blank to open the target document in a new window. Select Parent, Self, or Top to open the target document in the same window.

Creating a table of contents

Like hyperlinks, a table of contents provides an effective way for a report user to navigate to specific locations in a large report. A table of contents displays a list of items that reflect the organization of the report. These items are known as table of contents entries. These entries are active links to locations within the report. The report developer can either use the default values for these entries or create custom values that are more meaningful to the report's users.

Figure 22-12 shows a report, in the report viewer, that displays products by product line. The table of contents, which appears to the left of the report when the TOC button is selected, lists all the product lines in the report. When the user selects a product line, the report viewer displays the corresponding section of the report. When viewing the report in PDF format, the table of contents entries appear as bookmarks to the left of the report.

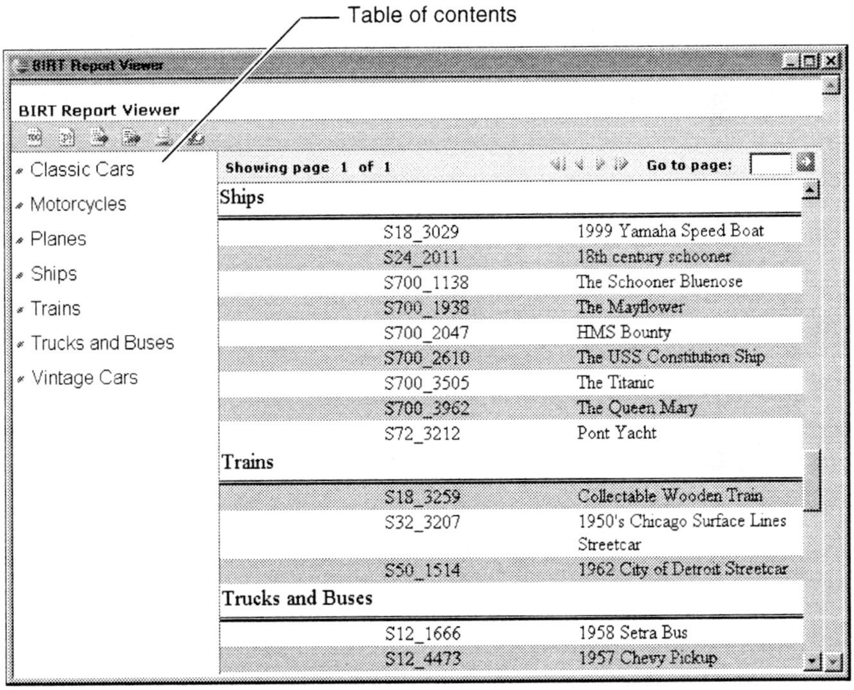

Figure 22-12   Report viewer displaying a table of contents next to a report

Using the default table of contents

By default, a grouped report includes a table of contents that displays the group values. For example, if the group key is a data set field named PRODUCTLINE, the table of contents displays all the values in the PRODUCTLINE field, as shown in the example report in Figure 22-12. To

generate this table of contents, BIRT defines the expression,
row["PRODUCTLINE"], in the Table of Contents Item Expression option in
the group editor, as shown in Figure 22-13.

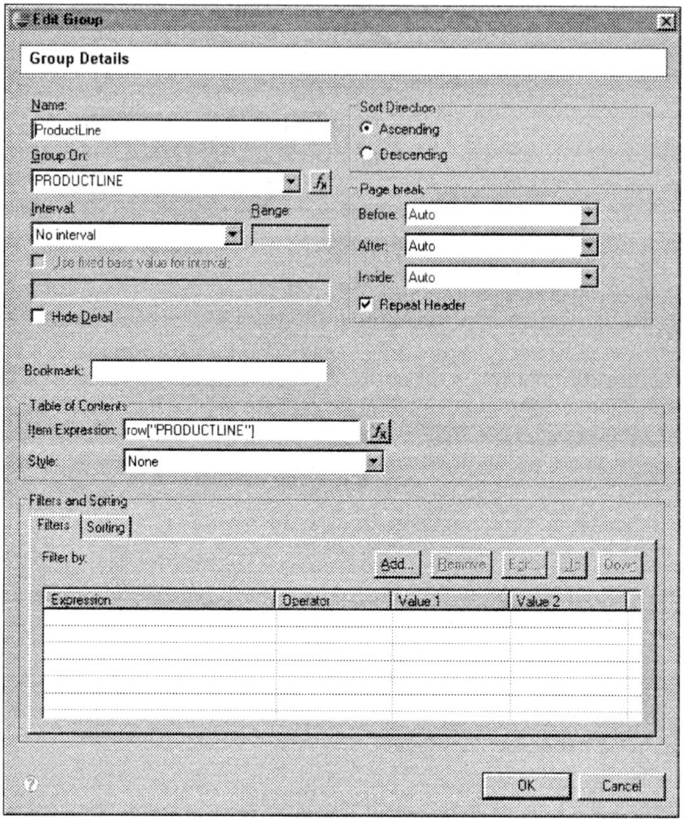

Figure 22-13   Edit Group displaying the default TOC item expression

BIRT creates a table of contents for every group in a report, not just for the
top-level group. For example, if you group order data by state, customers,
and order ID, the automatically generated table of contents displays a
hierarchy of group values that enable the user to navigate to a particular
state, customer, or order ID. If you do not want a group's values to appear in
the table of contents, simply delete the expression in the Table of Contents
Item Expression in the group editor.

Defining a custom table of contents

You can create a table of contents for other report elements, such as dynamic
images or data elements. Select the report element whose values to use in the
table of contents, choose Table of Contents in Property Editor, then specify an
expression that determines the values to display. For example, you can add a
nested table of contents to the report shown in Figure 22-12 to display
product codes under each product line. To create this table of contents, select

the [PRODUCTCODE] data element and specify row["PRODUCTCODE"] as
the expression for the Table of Contents property, as shown in Figure 22-14.

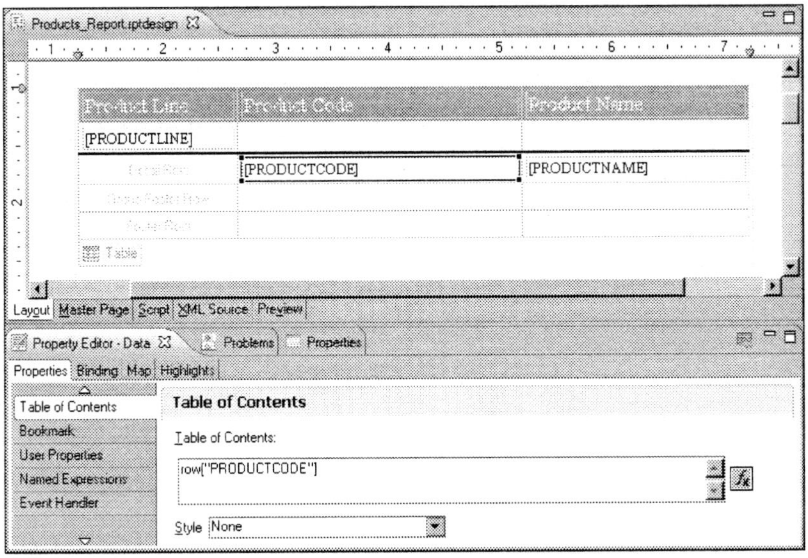

Figure 22-14 Table of Contents property for the selected data element

In the report viewer, the table of contents displays product codes within the
product line entries, as shown in Figure 22-15.

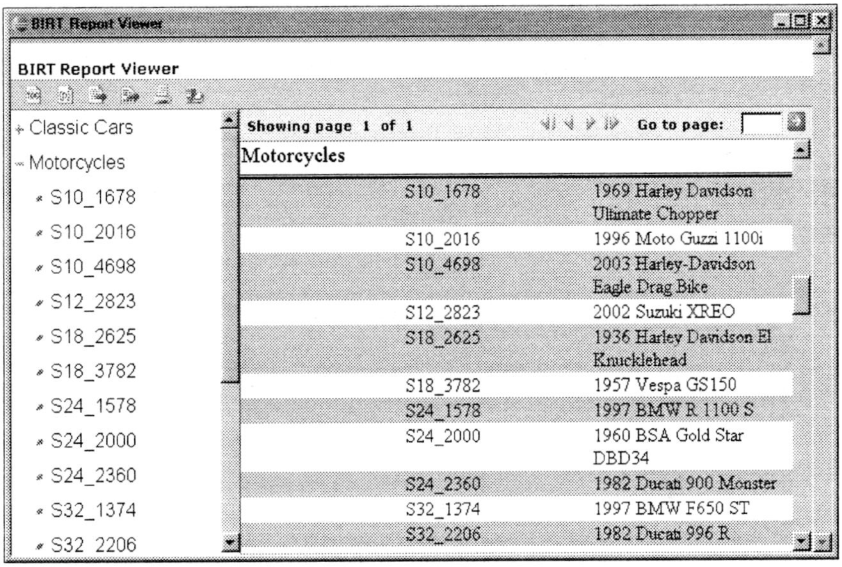

Figure 22-15 Report viewer displaying a nested table of contents

In some cases, you may not want the table of contents to display field values
exactly as they are saved in the data source. For example, the values might be

obscure. You can customize the table of contents expression to create a more informative table of contents entry. For example, to display a product name on a separate line after a product code, the table of contents expression would be as follows:

```
row["PRODUCTCODE"] + " \n" + row["PRODUCTNAME"]
```

You can provide any valid JavaScript expression as a table of contents expression. For example, to show that a product is obsolete, you can check the value of the OBSOLETE database field, as the following example shows:

```
if ( row["OBSOLETE"] == "yes" ) {
    row["PRODUCTCODE"] + " (Obsolete)"
} else {
    row["PRODUCTCODE"] + " \n" + row["PRODUCTNAME"]
}
```

Adding interactive chart features

You can bookmark or link to a chart or include a chart in the table of contents, as described earlier in this chapter. You can also use additional interactive features, available through the chart builder, to enhance the behavior of a chart in the report viewer.

An interactive chart feature supports a response to an event, such as the report user choosing an item or moving the mouse pointer over an item. The response can trigger an action, such as opening a web page, drilling to a detail report, or changing the appearance of the chart. For example, you can use a Tooltip to display the series total when a user places the mouse over a bar in a bar chart, as shown in Figure 22-16.

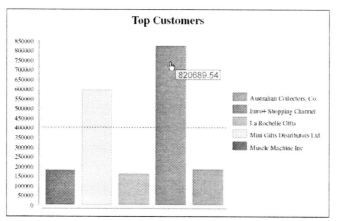

Figure 22-16   Chart showing a Tooltip

You can add an interactive feature to a value series, the chart area, a legend, marker lines, the x- and y-axis, or a title. Figure 22-17 identifies these elements.

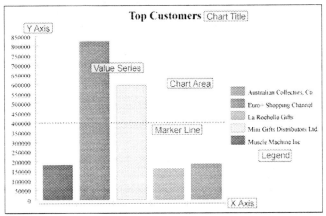

Figure 22-17   Elements selectable for chart interactivity

Start the process of adding interactivity to a chart by choosing Format Chart in the chart builder and selecting the chart element you wish to make interactive. Choose the Interactivity button, and the interactivity editor appears. Figure 22-18 shows the location of the Interactivity button for a chart legend.

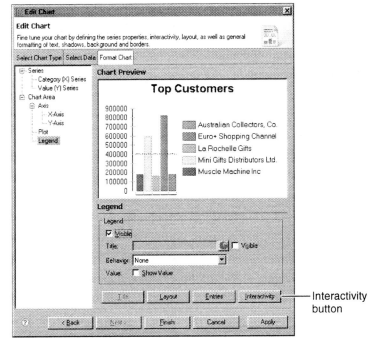

Figure 22-18   Accessing interactivity for a chart legend

The location of the button to invoke the interactivity editor varies by chart element. Table 22-1 lists the procedure used to invoke the interactivity editor for each element. Not all chart types have all elements listed in the table.

Table 22-1   Accessing chart interactivity options

Chart element	How to invoke the interactivity editor
Chart Area	Choose Interactivity on the Chart Area formatting page
Chart Title	Choose Interactivity on the Chart Area formatting page
Legend Area	Choose Interactivity on the Legend formatting page
X-Axis and Y-Axis	Choose Interactivity on the X-Axis or the Y-Axis formatting page
Marker	Choose Markers on the X-Axis or the Y-Axis formatting page. Axis Markers appears. Choose Interactivity.
Value Series	Choose Interactivity on the Value Series

Defining interactivity events and actions

You specify the type of event that triggers interactivity for the selected chart element and indicate the action you wish to perform in Interactivity. For example, in a chart legend, you can use a mouse click to toggle the visibility of the associated data point. Figure 22-19 shows the event type and action in Interactivity required to accomplish this event.

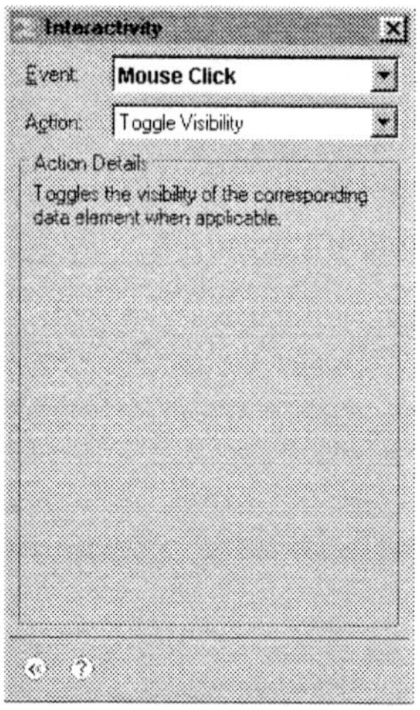

Figure 22-19   Toggle visibility on legend with mouse click

There are a variety of event types that can be used to trigger interactivity. Table 22-2 lists the type options available in the interactivity editor, and describes the UI gesture associated with each.

Table 22-2   Event types

Event type	Description
Mouse Click	Click the selected chart element.
Mouse Double-Click	Double-click on the selected element.
Mouse Down	Press and hold the mouse button down over the selected element.
Mouse Up	Release the mouse button above the selected chart element.
Mouse Over	Move the mouse pointer onto the selected element and leave it there.
Mouse Move	Pass the mouse pointer over the selected element.
Mouse Out	Move the mouse pointer off the selected element.
Focus	Put UI focus on the selected element with the mouse or tab navigation.
Blur	Remove UI focus from the selected element using either the mouse or tab navigation.
Key Press	Press a key while the mouse pointer is over the selected element.
Key Down	Press and hold a key down while the mouse pointer is over the selected element.
Key Up	Release a key while the mouse pointer is over the selected element.
Load	Load the chart in the viewer.

Table 22-3 lists the action options associated with each event type in the interactivity editor. You can add multiple interactive features to a chart element, but a particular event can produce only one action.

Table 22-3   Interactive features

Action name	Result
Hyperlink	Links to a web page, a document, or an image. Also used to link to another report.
Show Tooltip	Displays explanatory text over a chart element.
Toggle Visibility	Changes the visibility of a chart element, typically a series.
Invoke Script	Invokes a client-side script inside the viewer.
Highlight	Highlights a chart element, such as a data point.

(continues)

Table 22-3   Interactive features *(continued)*

Action name	Result
Toggle Data Point Visibility	Changes the visibility of a data point.

Chart formats and supported actions

Not all actions are available in all chart output formats. Highlighting and Tooltips, for example, are not available to charts in JPG and BMP format. Only SVG charts support all the interactive features. In addition, to use the interactive features, the report user must view the report in a browser that has an SVG plug-in and that supports JavaScript. To see how an interactive feature works in a chart, you must preview the report in the report viewer.

Adding interactive elements to an HTML report

Using JavaScript, you can add interactive HTML elements to a report. Some common elements, which you have probably seen on many web pages, include pop-up windows, alert messages, drop-down menus, and buttons. In an HTML report, you can add, for example, a button that, when clicked, expands or collapses a report section.

To add an interactive HTML element, perform the following tasks:

- Insert a text element and set its type to HTML.

- In the text editor, use the script tag to write JavaScript code that runs when an event, such as a mouse click, occurs.

Figure 22-20 shows a report design with a text element placed in the header row of a table that displays customer information.

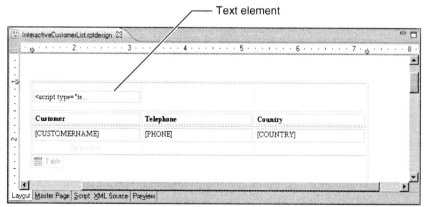

Figure 22-20   Report design that includes an HTML text element

Figure 22-21 shows an example of HTML text specified for the text element. Within the script tag is a user-defined function, showinfo( ), that displays the number of customer rows in a table. The last line of code creates a button that, when clicked, runs the showinfo( ) function.

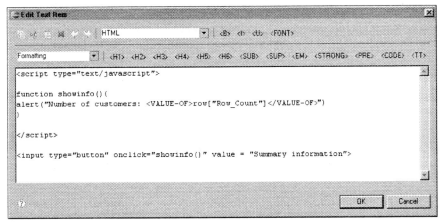

Figure 22-21   The text editor showing HTML text that includes a JavaScript function

Figure 22-22 shows the HTML output. A Summary information button appears at the top of the report. When the user clicks this button, a dialog appears and displays the information you specified.

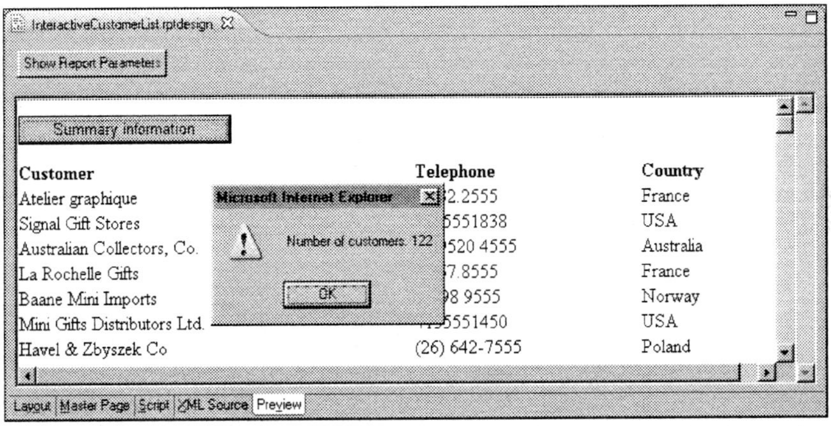

Figure 22-22   The previewer showing the report output and the dialog that appears when the Summary information button is clicked

Interactive HTML elements appear only in an HTML report. If your report is to be viewed in other formats, such as PDF, you need to hide the text element that contains the JavaScript code in all formats, except HTML. If you do not, the report displays the text element's code when it is viewed in a format other than HTML.

Identifying report elements for data export

Report users can export report data from the report viewer to a comma-separated values (.csv) file by choosing Export data. Users can use Export data to extract some or all of the data from a report, then use this data in another document or format. For example, a user could export customer sales data from a report for a previous quarter, then use the numbers in a spreadsheet to create a forecast for an upcoming one.

As a report developer, you can provide report elements with descriptive names so that the user can find the information easily.

How to export report data

1 In the report viewer, choose Export data, as shown in Figure 22-23.

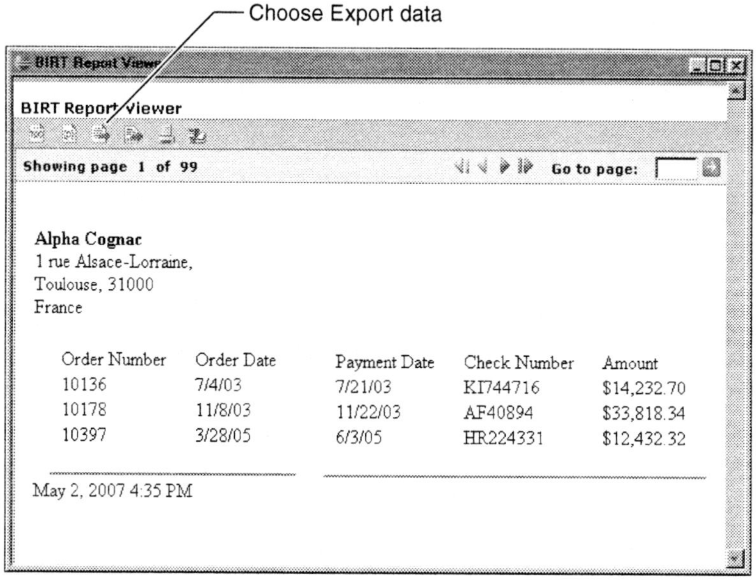

Figure 22-23 Export data button in the report viewer

2 When Export Data appears, as shown in Figure 22-24, select a result set from the drop-down list.

Available result sets lists the container elements, such as tables and charts, that contain data. By default, the names that are displayed in the list are internal names that begin with the prefix ELEMENT, for example, ELEMENT_50, ELEMENT_72, and so on.

3 Move the data that you want to export from Available Columns to Selected Columns.

4 Choose OK.

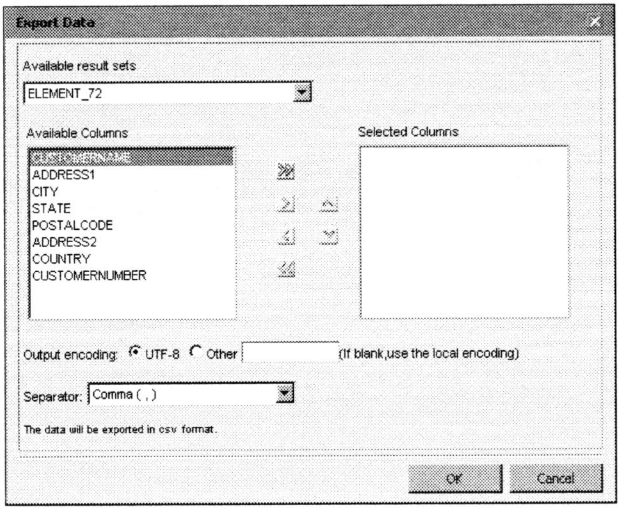

Figure 22-24   Export Data

5   On File Download, choose Save, then choose Save As and indicate where
to save the file.

How to identify a report element

To make it easier for report users to identify the section of the report they
wish to export data from, you can give each report element a more
meaningful name in Property Editor. For example, to give a more meaningful
name to the main table in a customer report, select the table in the layout
editor, and on General properties, in Name, type "Customer Data", as shown
in Figure 22-25.

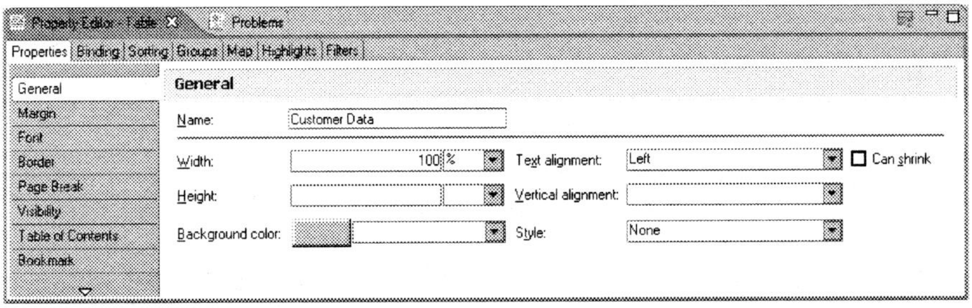

Figure 22-25   Giving an element a name in Property Editor

Building a Shared Report Development Framework

Previous chapters describe how to create and use data sources and data sets and lay out and format report items. A single report developer with a requirement for only a few reports can use these approaches effectively. For a larger project, either one with more developers or one that requires more reports, many designs need to use the same elements or layouts. In these cases, manual techniques are cumbersome. Developing the same components repeatedly wastes time and is prone to errors. Even if you use the copy-and-paste features of BIRT Report Designer, a report design does not provide convenient access to standard elements and layouts.

BIRT provides the following solutions for designing reports that must conform to standards, including using common design elements and data sources:

- A library

  This type of file stores customized report features, such as data sources, data sets, visual report items, styles, and master pages. Use a library in a report design to access the customized report elements. You can use multiple libraries in a single report design. By using multiple libraries, you can separate the styles and functionality that different projects or processes need.

  A library is a dynamic component of a report design. When a library developer makes changes to a library, the report design synchronizes itself with the changed library. In this way, changes propagate easily within a suite of report designs.

- A template

  This type of file provides a structure for a standard report layout. BIRT Report Designer provides a set of standard templates, such as Simple Listing and Grouped Listing report templates. A template can contain visual report items that appear in the report's layout, data sources and data sets, and master page layouts. A template can also use one or more libraries in the same way that a report design does.

  A template is a static framework on which to build a new report design. For this reason, a report design can derive from only one template. Additionally, when a template developer changes a template, report designs that are based on that template do not automatically reflect the changes to the template.

- A CSS file

  This type of file provides styles for formatting items in a report, similar to the formatting of items on a web page. Chapter 10, "Formatting Report Content," provides detailed information about using CSS files in BIRT.

Comparing report designs, libraries, and templates

By reading the earlier chapters in this book, you became familiar with the concepts of developing a report design. Developing a library or a template uses similar skills. All these file types use the same report elements from the palette, Data Explorer, and the Outline view in BIRT Report Designer, but you use each type for a different purpose. Figure 23-1, which illustrates the simplest outlines for each file type, shows the structural differences.

Report design　　　　　　　Library　　　　　　　　Template

Figure 23-1　　Basic structures of report designs, libraries, and templates

The following sections clarify the differences between these file types.

About the report design file type

The main purpose of a report design file is to generate reports by retrieving data from a data set and formatting that data into a layout. The file-name extension for a report design file is .rptdesign.

A report design can contain any number of report elements. Data sources, data sets, report parameters, and data cubes are non-visual elements that you access in Data Explorer. You place visual elements in the design by dragging them from the palette and dropping them in the layout. A report design can also include embedded images. You can access any element in a report design by using the Outline view. To display the Outline view, choose Window➤Show View➤Outline from the main menu.

To affect the appearance of the pages in a paginated report, you use the master page. To ensure a consistent appearance for multiple parts of a report design, you can create and apply styles.

About the library file type

The main purpose of a library is to provide developers of report designs with a shared repository of predesigned report elements. The file-name extension for a library file is .rptlibrary.

Like a report design, a library can include any number of report elements and any type of report element. You add elements to a library by using the palette and Data Explorer or by copying them from another BIRT file, such as a report design. If you have a report design that contains all the report elements that you need in a particular library, you can even create a library directly from that report design. Because a library is not a design, there is no Body node in the outline. Instead, a library has a Report Items node, which contains all the visual report items in the library.

When you have added the components to the library, you group related styles into a theme. This grouping provides quick access to all of the necessary styles for that theme. The Themes node in a library takes the place of the Styles node in the other file types. CSS files also support sharing styles across a team of report developers, but do not group the styles into themes.

To share a library across a team of report developers, set the resource folder for each developer to the same shared location, then publish the library to that folder. The developer uses Library Explorer to access report elements from the libraries.

About the template file type

The main purpose of a template is to provide a standard start position for a new report design. As such, the structure of a template file is identical to the structure of a report design file. The file-name extension for a template file is .rpttemplate.

A template includes the master pages that the report design uses and any number of report elements. In addition to standard report elements, a template file can include template report elements. These elements display instructions to the report developer about how to use the template. Designing a template is just the same as designing a report design. Indeed, you can create a report design, then save it as a template.

To share a template across a team of report developers, set the template folder for each developer to the same shared location, then publish the template to that folder. When a developer chooses File→New→Report, BIRT Report Designer lists all templates in that folder as well as the standard BIRT templates.

Sharing report elements in a library

A library provides a straightforward way to use custom styles and report elements. You can make any change to the properties of a report element and copy the element to a library. When you save a change to an element in a library, the customized element is available to any report design that uses the library directly.

When you use an element from a library in a report design, you can change any properties, but you cannot change the structure of the element. For example, if you use a table from a library, you can change the table's style or data binding, but you cannot add or remove cell contents, columns, or groups.

Figure 23-2 shows the structure of a report design that uses a library. The expanded Libraries item shows all the libraries that the report design uses. In this example, the report design uses three libraries. Because a report design can use multiple libraries, you can separate logical sets of report elements.

BIRT uses the concept of name space to identify the sets of report elements that each library contains. Using a separate name space for each library means that BIRT distinguishes between items that have the same name but appear in different libraries. For example, if you have a grid named Page Header in more than one library, BIRT uses the name space to determine which one to display in your report.

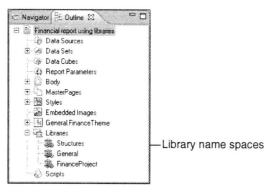

Figure 23-2   Outline view showing included libraries

Table 23-1 describes some of the many possible uses of elements from a library. This table gives only one example use for each type of report element.

When you start to design a suite of reports, you will find many more reasons to share report items.

Table 23-1   Examples of uses for shared report elements

Report element	Shared use
Data source	Typically, provides data sources for a whole reporting project. For example, an accounts department's project uses a database that holds customer invoices and sales orders. A marketing department's project uses a sales leads database as well as the one with customer invoice information. If you create a data source that is not a profile, change the data source in the library from a test data source to the live data source when the project is deployed.
Data set	Provides a data set for multiple reports that use the same data. For example, a suite of profit-and-loss reports can use the same tables. Take care when using a shared data set. You must ensure that a shared data set efficiently provides the correct rows for each report design that uses it. In some cases, using different data sets improves performance or accuracy.
Report parameter	Provides a standard parameter for a report design. For example, a shared report parameter can provide a standard appearance for a user to select from a list of customers or a standard set of cascading parameters for country, state, and city. You can provide the data sets for the shared parameters in the same library.
Data cube	Provides a standard data cube. Designing a data cube can be complex. After a data specialist designs the cube, report developers can use the shared cube to build cross tabs.
Label	Provides simply formatted, standard text for a report design. For example, a shared label can be a legal notice, such as "Company confidential" with the required font and size.
Text	Provides standard text that needs complex formatting. For example, a text element can display your company's standard terms and conditions of sale.
Dynamic text	Provides formatted text from a data field or expression. For example, a dynamic text element can display notes about a customer's order.
Data	Provides data or expressions. For example, a data element can display the result of a common calculation, such as the extended price of a line item in a purchase order.
Image	Provides a standard image, such as a company logo or a watermark for a company confidential document.

(continues)

Table 23-1 Examples of uses for shared report elements *(continued)*

Report element	Shared use
Grid	Provides a container for other report items. For example, a grid can display a number of static items, such as a company logo in an image element or an address in a label or text element.
List	Provides a container for data-driven report items. For example, a list can bind to a standard data set, such as customers or orders.
Table	Provides a container for data-driven report items in columns. For example, a table can bind to a data set for orders and contain data elements that display order number, order status, and order date.
Chart	Provides a graphical summary of data. For example, a bar chart can display its categories and series in a preferred arrangement. A report developer can use that chart from a library and bind the data fields without needing to know everything about how to design a chart.
Cross tab	Provides a standard cross tab. When used in conjunction with a shared data cube, report developers take advantage of the expertise of data modeling experts.
Style	Supports using standard style properties, such as company colors and fonts.

Dynamic library behavior

A key feature of a library is that it is dynamic. When you change a library, the same changes occur in report designs that use the library. For example, if the preferred font for your company changes from Times New Roman to Arial Unicode, you make the changes to styles in a library. When you generate a report from any design that uses styles from that library, or when you open or refresh the design in BIRT Report Designer, the changes take effect.

This dynamic behavior ensures that all report elements that derive from a library always use the current styles and properties. For this reason, when you implement a policy of using libraries, you must ensure that every custom element that more than one report design uses derives from a library element. If you use an element directly from the palette and customize it in the same way in multiple designs, the benefits of dynamic library updating are not available.

Sometimes, BIRT cannot apply changes from a modified library to a report design without additional action on the part of a report developer. The following list describes these situations:

- The name of the library changes or the library no longer exists.

- The library no longer contains an element that the report design uses.

- The name of the element in the library changes.

- The name of the element in the library refers to a different type of element.

If BIRT Report Designer opens a report design that has any of these problems, a warning message appears in the layout in place of the affected report element, as shown in Figure 23-3.

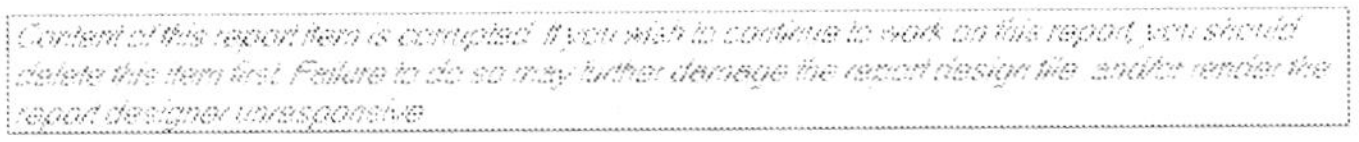

Figure 23-3   A report item that cannot access a library definition

To repair any of these conditions, you must delete the element that is causing the problem. Alternatively, if you are familiar with XML, you can edit the XML source of the report design. If you choose to edit the XML, you should back up the report design first.

Sharing styles

A library provides a flexible way to share sets of styles. A library groups styles into themes. For a library, the Outline view shows Themes instead of Styles. In a newly created library, Themes contains one theme, defaultTheme. By default, the library uses the styles in this theme to display report items in the layout.

Comparing themes and CSS files

As described in Chapter 10, "Formatting Report Content," you can also use CSS files to provide shared styles. Use a CSS file when your company already has a standard set of styles in an existing CSS file or if your report developers are familiar with using CSS. Remember that BIRT does not support the full range of properties that CSS provides. For this reason, you need to make sure that the appearance of your BIRT reports using CSS matches your needs. Use a theme from a library instead of a CSS file when you want to group related styles together.

Using a style from a theme

When you use a library in a report design, you can assign a single theme to the report design. Property Editor shows the theme that the report design is using, as shown in Figure 23-4. To assign a theme to a report design, you drag the theme from the library in Library Explorer and drop it onto the report design. This action makes all the styles in that theme available to items in the report design. Any predefined styles, such as grid, table, and so on, take effect immediately on items in the design.

You can use custom styles from the theme in the same way that you use custom styles that are defined in the report design itself. If you define a style with the same name in the report design as one in the library, BIRT uses the style that you define in the report design.

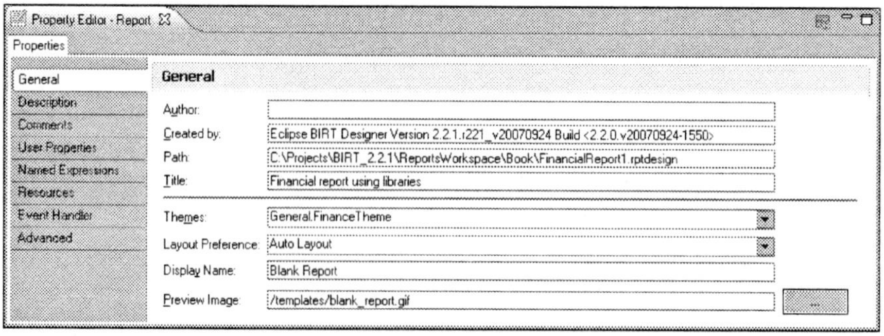

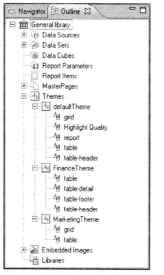

Figure 23-4   Properties for a report design that uses a theme

Because a library is dynamic, when you add styles to a theme, they become available to all report designs that use that theme. For example, consider a theme that does not have a style called table. Tables in a report design that uses this theme use the default style. Later, a library developer adds a style called table to the theme. Now the appearance of the tables in that design match the style that is defined in the theme.

Designing multiple themes

You can create multiple themes in a single library. For example, you can create styles in the default theme for use in most report designs, then make special themes for financial and marketing report designs, as shown in Figure 23-5. A report design can use styles from only one theme. For this reason, if you need some styles to be the same for all themes, you can copy the style from the theme in which you create the style to the other themes that need those styles.

Figure 23-5   Multiple themes in a library

Understanding library name space

When you use a library in a report design, BIRT assigns a name space to the library. This name space identifies every report element from the library that the report design uses. By default, BIRT Report Designer bases the name space on the file name of the library. For example, if the name of the library is FinanceProject.rptlibrary, the name space is FinanceProject. In Figure 23-2, earlier in this chapter, you see an example of how the Outline view displays the name space in a report design.

If you use more than one library with the same default name space, BIRT Report Designer prompts you for a name space for the second and subsequent libraries. In this case, provide a name space that distinguishes the library from the others but shows a relationship to the original library name.

Designing libraries for a shared environment

A library is a key tool for achieving consistent appearance in a suite of report designs. A library also reduces the amount of repetitive work that report developers must complete. To use libraries effectively, you should consider how to structure the libraries to make best use of their properties and functionality. Although you can use a single library that contains every custom component that your report designs need, this library could become very large and confusing for report developers.

One way to design a suite of libraries is first to make libraries that contain elements that are common to all reporting projects. After you create these general libraries, you can create a project-specific library for each reporting project. These project libraries can contain elements that are simple modifications of the standard report elements. They can also contain complex elements, such as tables nested within grids or lists. A library can refer to items in other libraries. For example, if your project library contains a grid for a report header that uses the company logo, you can include the logo from the general library in that grid. In this way, you build on the power of libraries by not having the same item in multiple locations.

For example, you can create the following libraries:

- A general library that contains standard items that all projects use, such as themes, an image element for the company logo, a text element that contains a confidentiality agreement, and master pages with grid elements with standard contents for page headers and footers

- A library that all projects use for complex items, for example, a table element with predefined behavior, such as highlighting

- For each project, one or more libraries that contain elements that are specific to the project, such as data sources

By building suites of libraries in this way, you provide the building blocks for a standard appearance for all reports, then you package the behavior and appearance of report elements that are appropriate to each reporting project.

You make the suite of libraries available to report developers by placing them in a repository that is known as the resource folder.

The final step in implementing libraries is to use a library in a report design. A report design can use any library in its project and in the resource folder. The design has access to all the customized elements in these libraries. Figure 23-6 shows a representation of an architecture for libraries and report designs.

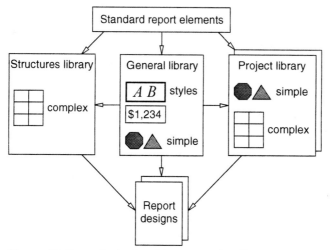

Figure 23-6   Project architecture using libraries

Defining a general library

The purpose of a general library is to provide a foundation for common elements that can appear in any report designs in any reporting project. A general library contains standard, simple items, such as a company logo image element. This library also contains a default theme that includes settings for predefined styles and any custom styles for all report designs. If multiple reporting projects need to use a different theme, place that theme in this library. You can also include common items such as master pages that use these basic components. Figure 23-5, earlier in this chapter, shows an example of such a library.

Defining a structures library

A structures library provides grids, lists, and tables to report designs. For example, imagine that most of your report designs use a table element. Initially, the table element in your library is identical in behavior to the table from the palette. Later, you discover a need to alternate the row colors for every table in every report design. You make the change to the tables in the library, and every report design that uses the table from the library now has the new feature. If your structures library did not contain table elements, you would have to make this change manually.

When you create grid, list, and table elements in a library, you need to consider the contents of the cells as well as the layout and behavior of the element itself. As discussed earlier in this chapter, when a report design uses an element from a library, the structure of the element is not modifiable. You can change only the properties of an element that is derived from an item in a library. For this reason, the recommended practice is to place a report item in every cell in a grid, list, or table that you define in a library. By changing the properties of the labels or data items after you place the element in a report design, you can use the same structure to achieve many different results.

Figure 23-7 shows an example of this approach. The table in the library has four columns. The cells in the header row contain labels, the cells in the detail row contain data elements, and the cells in the footer row contain a label and data elements. A report design uses two copies of the library table. One copy modifies the cell contents to show a list of customers in three columns with a fourth empty column. The other copy uses all four columns to display order information.

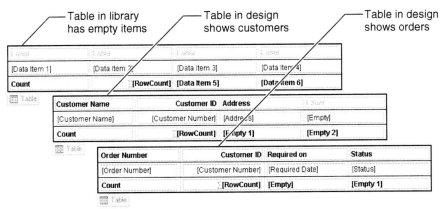

Figure 23-7   Customizing a table from a library

Defining a project library

The purpose of a project library is to provide customized report elements for report designs within a single reporting project.

The most common elements that are specific to a project are data sources. You can also include data sets in a project library, but, for best report generation speed, a report design should use a data set that is designed for its specific needs. A data set that a library provides is often too general for optimum efficiency because it retrieves more fields from that data source than most report designs require.

Other simple elements that a project library can contain are project-specific image elements and text elements with standard wording and formatting. A project library can also contain complex, structured elements, such as tables that have custom layout or behavior.

There are two ways to set up a project library.

- Customizing only the project-specific report elements

  Report developers use this library and the general libraries in every new report design for this project. They use the report items from the project library or from the palette. Use this technique if the project customizes only a few elements or provides only complex structures to complement the elements from the palette.

- Customizing every type of report element

  Report developers use this library in every new report design for the project. Instead of using report items directly from the palette or the general libraries, they use report items from the project library. Use this technique if the project customizes many elements or if the project's requirements are likely to change frequently.

Understanding the resource folder

BIRT Report Designer uses the resource folder as a repository for libraries. This folder should be one that all report developers can access, such as a directory on a shared network drive. The location of the resource folder is specified in the Preferences page, which you access by choosing Windows→Preferences from the main menu, then choosing the Report Design Resource item, as shown in Figure 23-8. You can browse to or type the name of your resource folder, then choose OK. BIRT Report Designer then uses this location to display libraries and other resources in Library Explorer.

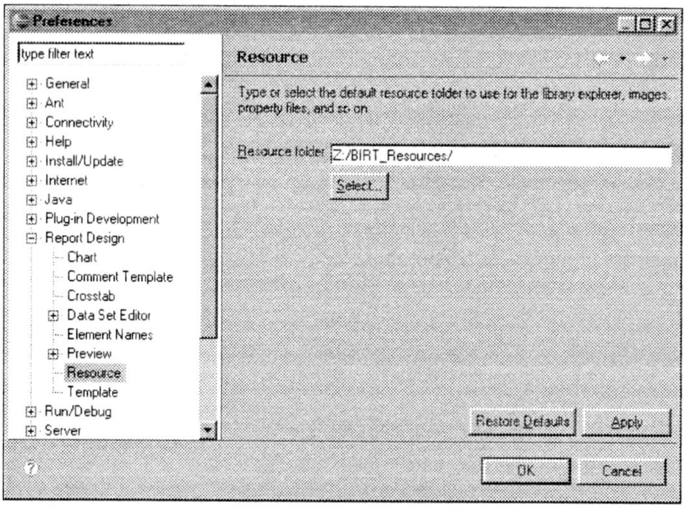

Figure 23-8   Setting up a resource folder

If you have a large number of libraries, you can use subfolders to organize the libraries in a logical way. For example, the \\SharedServer\Resource\General folder can contain the general libraries, and \\SharedServer\Resource\Finance can contain the Finance libraries.

To place a library into the resource folder, you can publish a library from your current workspace or you can add a library from an external location. You can also use standard file system commands to copy your library files to the resource folder. Make sure that your library has a meaningful file name because BIRT Report Designer displays this name to the report developers who use the resource folder.

How to publish a library from your workspace

1 Open the library in BIRT Report Designer.

2 Choose File→Place Library in Resource Folder.

3 On Publish Library, as shown in Figure 23-9, make changes to the file name and folder. For example, change the file name of the library if you need to make the name more meaningful. Use Browse if you want to place the library in a subfolder of the resource folder. Choose Finish.

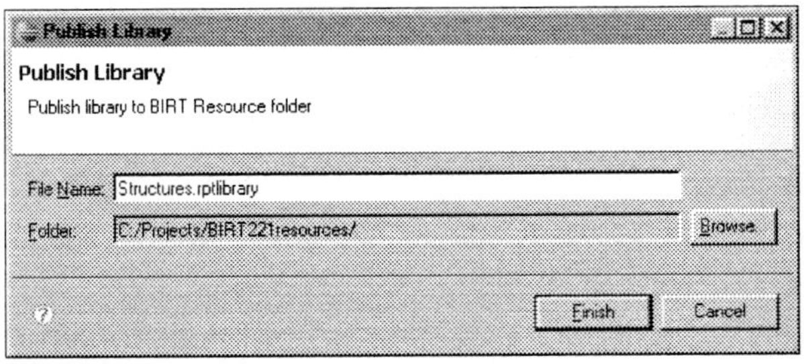

Figure 23-9   Publishing a library

4 On the context menu in Library Explorer, choose Refresh. The new library appears in the list of available libraries.

How to add an external library to the resource folder

1 On the context menu in Library Explorer, choose Add Library.

2 On Add Library, choose Browse to navigate to and select a library from the file system, as shown in Figure 23-10.

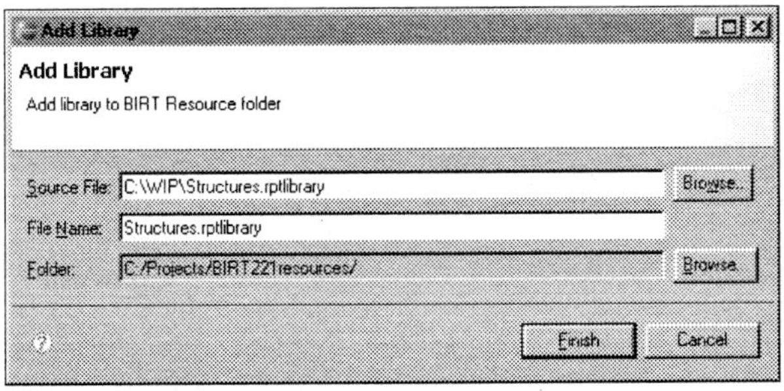

Figure 23-10   Adding an external library

3 You can also make changes to the file name and folder in the same way as for publishing a library from your workspace. Choose Finish.

4 On the context menu in Library Explorer, choose Refresh. The new library appears in the list of available libraries.

Using a library

BIRT Report Designer provides a tool, Library Explorer, which supports access to all libraries in the resource folder and its subfolders. Figure 23-11 shows the appearance of Library Explorer.

Figure 23-11　Library Explorer

Library Explorer shows all the elements in each library in a tree structure, the same as the structure of an open library in the Outline view. Because a library does not have a Body slot to order report sections in the report layout, visual report elements are in a Report Items slot. Figure 23-12 shows an example of how the elements in a library appear in Library Explorer.

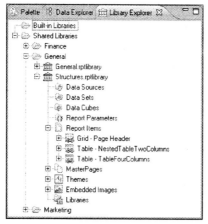

Figure 23-12　Library Explorer showing elements in a library

You use Library Explorer as a source for elements in your report design. You cannot change or create elements in a library in Library Explorer. You can only change elements in a library in your workspace that you open in the editor. You open a library in the editor in the same way that you open a report design, by using Navigator or, in BIRT RCP Report Designer, by choosing File➤Open. After making changes to a library in the editor, you place the new library into the resource folder, as described earlier in this chapter.

Library Explorer does not check actively for changes to libraries. For this reason, it does not immediately display changes to the list of available libraries or the items in an individual library. To update the view in Library Explorer, right-click inside it, and choose Refresh.

Accessing report elements from a library in a report design

Using report elements from a library is as straightforward as using items from the palette or data elements from Data Explorer. In Library Explorer, you expand the library that you need, and you expand the slot that you need to see the items available in the library. Next, you drag the component from the library to the place where you need it in your report design. For example, to select a visual report item, you expand Report Items inside the library. Then, you drag the report item to the layout of your report design. If this item is the first use that you make of a library, BIRT Report Designer displays a message to let you know that you added the library to the report design. The library item appears in the Outline view as an icon with a link, as shown in Figure 23-13.

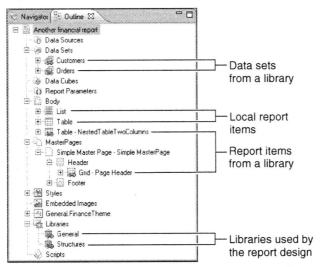

Figure 23-13   Outline view showing report items from a library

If a report item in the library is a structure such as a grid, you can only include the entire structure in your report design. You cannot select one piece of the structure, such as an image that is in a cell in the grid.

To add a data set from a library to a report design, drag the data set from Library Explorer onto the Data Sets slot in the Outline view. The data set appears in Data Explorer as well as in Outline. You do not need to drag the associated data source from the library unless you want to create a new data set specific to the report design.

When you select an element in your report design that comes from a library, Property Editor displays the extra field, Library, as shown in Figure 23-14.

This field shows the full path of the library that provides the definition of the element.

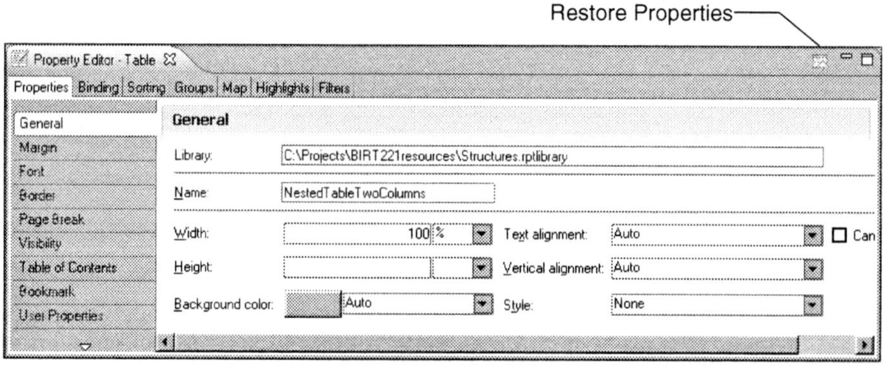

Restore Properties———

Figure 23-14   Property Editor for a table element from a library

Making local changes to a library element in a report design

Typically, when you use a library element in a report design, you need to modify the element's properties in some way. For example, you might want to increase the size of the text in a text element that contains a confidentiality agreement. As shown earlier in this chapter in Figure 23-7, you can also change the values and expressions in labels and other report items inside a library structure such as a table, but not the structure itself. You cannot add or remove columns or groups in a grid, list, or table element that comes from a library.

You make changes to the item's properties in the same way that you change any other item in the report design. The report design stores only the changes that you make to the report item. BIRT takes all other properties from the item in the library. In this way, BIRT retains the dynamic nature of the library item while supporting your local changes.

You can also make changes to the query in a data set from a library. To open the data set editor, you double-click the data set, in the same way as you do for any other data set.

If you need to revert to the original properties of the element, you select the Restore Properties button on Property Editor's tool bar. Figure 23-14 shows the location of this button. When you select this button, BIRT Report Designer prompts you to confirm that you want to discard your changes.

Using themes and styles from a library

To use a style from a library, you first set the Themes property of the report design to the library theme that contains the style that you need. The report design then has access to all the styles in that theme. As shown in Figure 23-15, the styles in the theme appear in the Outline view in a new slot, with the same name as the theme.

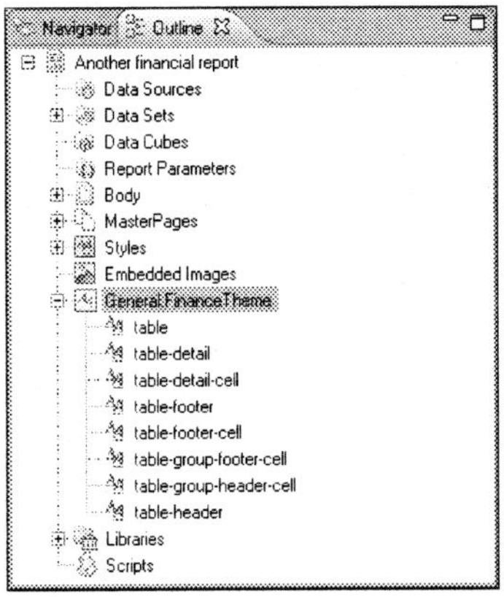

Figure 23-15   Theme styles in Outline

A report design has access to the themes in all the libraries that it uses, but it can use styles from only one theme. For this reason, the library developer must place all the necessary styles in each theme. Predefined styles in the theme, such as table or grid, take effect when you select the theme in Property Editor. Custom styles from the library are available in the list of styles in Property Editor for a report item.

A report design can use styles from a theme, from a CSS file, and from the report design itself. If any of these styles have the same names, BIRT uses the following rules to determine which style to use:

- If the report design defines a style, that style takes precedence over a style of the same name in a CSS file or a theme.

- A style from a CSS file takes precedence over a style of the same name in a theme.

- A style in a theme is used when there is no style of the same name defined in a CSS file or the report design itself.

To revert a report design to use no theme, set the Themes property of the report design to None. After you set this property, the Outline view no longer shows a Themes item. To remove the styles from a CSS file from a report design, right-click on the CSS file in the Styles slot in Outline and choose Delete.

How to set a theme for a report design

1   In Library Explorer, expand the library that contains the theme. Expand the Themes node in the library.

2   Drag the theme that you want to use from Library Explorer and drop it in the layout editor.

Any predefined styles in the theme take effect in the report design immediately. The appearance of any report items in the layout editor changes to match the styles in the theme. The library appears in the Libraries node of the Outline view.

How to drop a theme from a report design

You drop a theme from a report design by changing the Theme property of the report root item.

1 To access the report design's properties, in the Outline view, select the report root item.

Figure 23-16 shows this item selected. This item shows either the report design's file name or its title property value, if it has one.

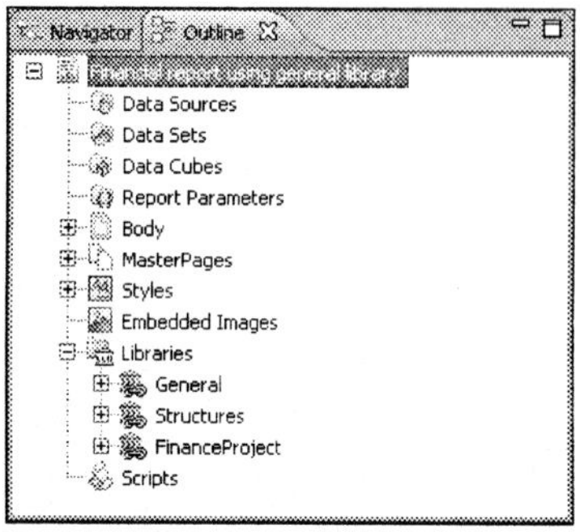

Figure 23-16 Report root item

2 In Property Editor, select None from the list in Themes, as shown in Figure 23-17.

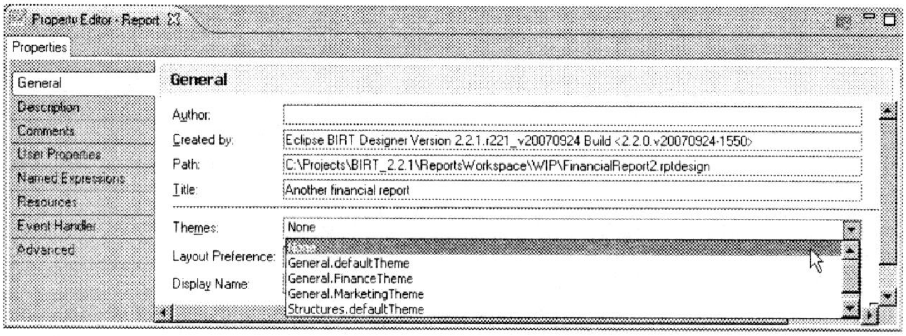

Figure 23-17 Selecting a theme in Property Editor

Now, the theme that the report design uses is None, which means that it uses only its own styles or styles from an included CSS file, not styles from a theme in a library.

Creating a library

BIRT Report Designer provides two ways to create a library. Use whichever technique best suits your requirements. The creation options are

■ Creating an empty library

From the Eclipse main menu, choose File➤New➤Library. Use this technique if you have no existing report designs or if you have many existing designs that use different styles or property settings. You can create a set of related report elements that do not depend on existing designs.

■ Creating a library from an existing report design

In the Outline view, right-click the report design root, and choose Export to Library. Use this technique if you have an existing report design that contains report elements that use the desired structure, properties, and styles. Report items that were in the Body slot in the report design appear in the Report Items slot in the new library. Custom styles in the report design appear in the defaultTheme theme in the library.

When you name a library file, BIRT uses this name to build the name space when you use the library in a report design. The name space appears in the Libraries node in the Outline view for the report design and in the names of themes, styles, and unmodified library report items that the report design uses.

After you create the library, you add report elements to the library. In many ways, this process is similar to adding elements to a report design. You add data sources and data sets to the library in exactly the same way as to a report design. You add styles to a theme in Outline, rather than directly to Styles. To add visual report items, you drag the item from the palette to the layout editor or to the Report Items node in Outline.

How to add an element to a library

Creating an element in a library uses the same wizards and dialogs as creating an element in a report design. After you add an element to a library, you make changes to it in the same way as you do in a report design.

1 Open or create a library.

2 In Data Explorer, create any required data sources and data sets.

3 To add a style, in the Outline view, expand the Themes node. Right-click a theme, then choose New Style.

4 To add a theme, in Outline, right-click the Themes node, and choose New Theme.

5 To add a report item, drag an item from the palette to Report Items in Outline. The new item appears both in Report Items and in the layout editor.

Editing a report item in a library

When you open a library in BIRT Report Designer, no layout appears in the layout editor because a library does not order sections in the layout. Instead, you design each report item separately by selecting an item from Report Items in the Outline view. Figure 23-18 shows an example of editing a table element in a library. After you change or add a report item in a library, you publish the changed library to the resources folder. Use the Refresh command on Library Explorer's context menu to see the changes.

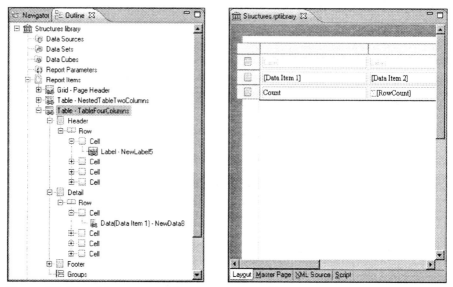

Figure 23-18 Library report item structure and layout

When you open a report design that uses the updated library, the changes take place immediately. To see the changes in an open report design that uses the library, expand the Libraries slot in the Outline view for the report design. Then, right-click the changed library and choose Refresh.

Sharing a report layout as a template

A template provides a straightforward way to use a custom layout and master pages for a suite of reports. You design a template in the same way that you design a report. A template can contain any report element, such as data sources, data sets, master pages, and any type of report item.

A template can use report elements and a theme from libraries in the same way as a report design does. In this way, templates extend the shared development effort that libraries provide. Libraries provide access to sets of individual report elements, and templates assemble them into a standard report layout. For example, a template for a bulk marketing letter can use a company logo from a general library and the marketing theme and a data source from the marketing project library. The report designs that build on the template get the addressees and the content for the letter from a report-specific data set.

You can develop a template directly or use an existing report design as the basis for a template. Figure 23-19 shows how the library architecture extends to building templates.

After you design a template, you publish the template to a shared location. You define this location on the Report Design Preferences—Template page.

You access this page by choosing Windows→Preferences. BIRT Report Designer checks this location when a report developer creates a new report design. The new template appears in the list of report templates in the New Report wizard. To provide visual assistance to the report developer, you can associate an image with the template. This image appears in the preview area of the wizard when the developer selects the template.

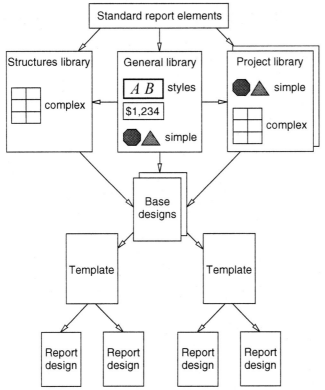

Figure 23-19   Project architecture using templates

Developing a custom template

BIRT Report Designer provides two ways to create a template. Use whichever technique best suits your requirements. The creation options are

- Creating an empty template

  From the main menu, choose File→New→Template. Use this technique if you have no existing report designs that have the required structure.

- Creating a template from an existing report design

  Open the report design. From the main menu, choose File→Register Template with New Report Wizard. Use this technique if you have an existing report design that has the structure that you need.

When you create a template, BIRT prompts you for template-specific properties. Figure 23-20 shows the properties and describes where they appear in the New Report wizard when you next create a new report. The only required property is Display Name.

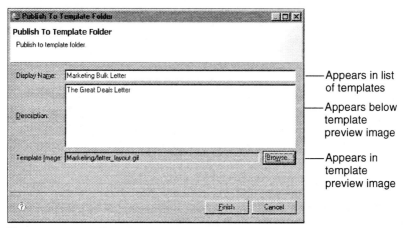

Figure 23-20   Template-specific properties

When the report developer selects a custom template in the New Report wizard, its preview image appears, if you supplied one. Figure 23-21 shows an example of a custom template that has a preview image.

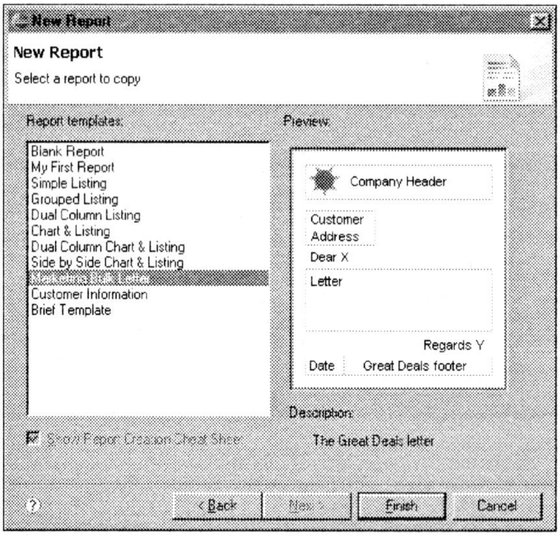

Figure 23-21   Using a custom template

If you do not supply some of the optional template properties, the New Report wizard displays default values. Figure 23-22 shows how such a template appears. No description appears for the template. Because you have not supplied a template image, BIRT Report Designer creates a thumbnail image of the layout of the template's layout in Preview.

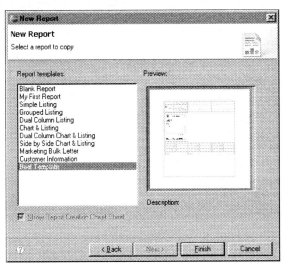

Figure 23-22 Template with no description or template image

When you create a template from a report design, the default image is the image from the template that you used to create the design. You can change the default image to a thumbnail by setting the template's Preview Image property in Property Editor.

Designing template report items

After you develop the structure of a template, you can choose to identify some or all of the items in the layout as template report items. When a report developer uses the template to create a report design, a template report item appears in the layout with an informational message. Double-clicking the template report item activates the item as a standard report item with the properties that you set when you designed the template.

A template can contain both template report items and normal report items. Use template report items for items that you want the report developer to modify for the new report design. Use normal report items for items that the report developer does not need to change.

Typically, you create template report items on simple report items, such as text or data elements inside a table or grid element. You can then make the container into a template element, with overall instructions for the items inside it. If you need to provide complex instructions for using a template, you can create a set of instructions for the template that is called a cheat sheet. BIRT RCP Report Designer does not support creating a cheat sheet. You need to use BIRT Report Designer, which includes the Eclipse Plug-in Development Environment. To create a cheat sheet, choose Help➤Help Contents. In the Eclipse online help, see the User Assistance Support topic inside the Platform Plug-in Developer Guide book's Programmer's Guide. Property Editor displays the Cheat sheet property in a template root's Advanced properties.

How to create a template report item

1 Create or open a template.

2 Add a report item to the layout, or select an existing item in the layout. For example, Figure 23-23 shows a text item inside a table item and its appearance in the Outline view.

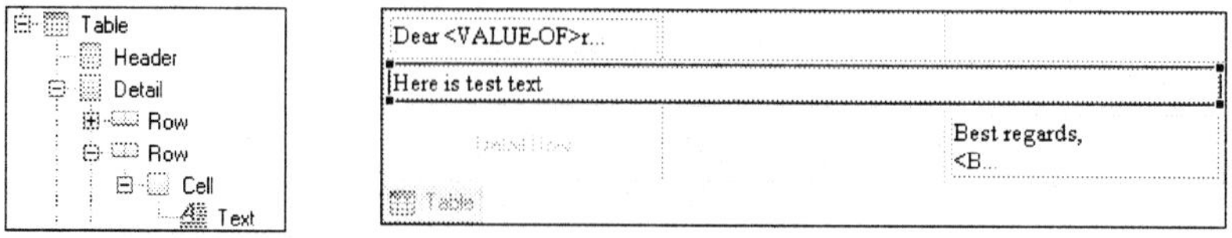

Figure 23-23 Standard appearance of text element and its icon

3 Right-click the report item, and choose Create Template Report Item.

4 On Create Template Report Item, type instructions to the report developer. These instructions explain how to use the report item. Figure 23-24 shows an example of some instructions.

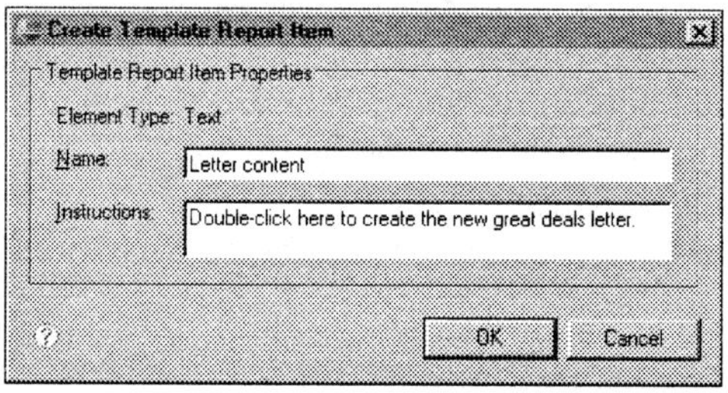

Figure 23-24 Providing instructions for a template report item

5 Choose OK.

The report item now appears in the layout as a template report item. The template report item displays an icon that is appropriate to the type of report item and the instructions that you provided. In Outline, the report item's icon changes to be a template item icon. Figure 23-25 shows how a text element appears after conversion to a template report item.

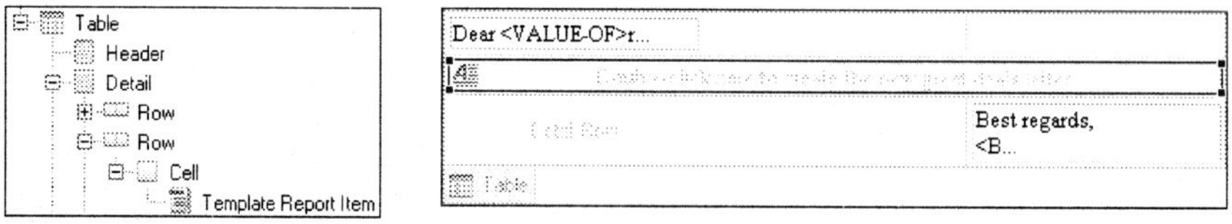

Figure 23-25 Text element as a template report item

Registering a template with the New Report wizard

To make a template available to report developers, you publish the template to a template folder. The default location of the template folder is the folder in the BIRT Report Designer user interface plug-in that contains the standard templates. Typically, this folder is not in a shared location, so you need to change it. You define the template folder within your Eclipse preferences. The standard BIRT templates remain available after you change the template folder to the new shared location.

Next, you publish the template. If the template has a preview image, copy the image to the resource folder, then select that shared image from the Publish to Template Folder wizard.

How to set up a template folder

1　From the Eclipse main menu, choose Window→Preferences.

2　In Preferences, expand Report Design, and choose Template.

3　To navigate to the template folder, choose Select, then choose OK.

How to publish a template

1　Open the report template.

2　Set the Preview Image property if you want the image that appears in the New Report wizard to be a thumbnail or an image file on the file system.

3　Choose File→Register Template with New Report Wizard.

4　In Publish to Template Folder, check the properties, as shown in Figure 23-26.

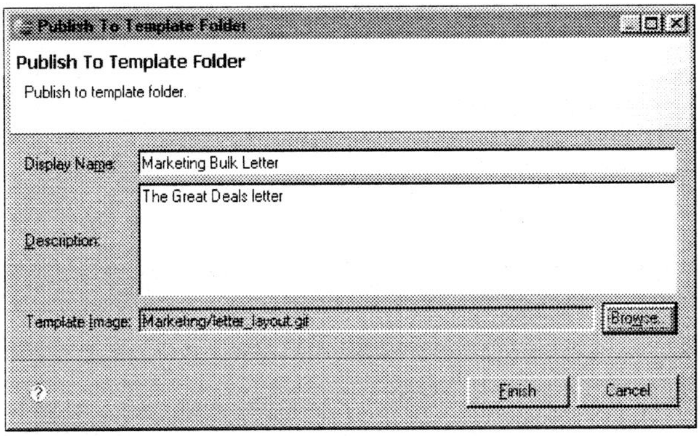

Figure 23-26　Publishing a template

5　Make any corrections to the display name and description.

6　To change the template image, first copy the required image to the shared resources folder. Choose Browse, then select the required image from those in the shared resources folder.

7　Choose Finish.

Using a custom template

To use a custom template as a starting point for a report design, you must define the template folder, following the instructions from earlier in this chapter. After you set up the template folder, the New Report wizard includes all custom templates in the list of available templates.

After you choose Finish in the New Report wizard, BIRT Report Designer displays the layout of the template in the layout editor. All the report elements in the template, such as data sources, data sets, and visual report items, are available for editing in the same way that you edit report elements in one of BIRT's predefined templates.

A template can include template report items as well as standard report items in the layout. You can see the appearance of a template report item in Figure 23-25, earlier in this chapter.

How to use a template report item

To use a template report item, you must create a report design from a template that contains a template report item. This example uses the predefined Chart and Listing template.

1 Create a report design. In the New Report wizard, choose the Chart and Listing predefined template.

2 In the layout editor, follow the instructions in the cheat sheet.

   The final instruction is to edit the chart. The chart item is a template report item. This item appears in the layout with an appropriate icon and instructional text, as shown in Figure 23-27. The text supplements the instructions in the cheat sheet. In this case, the instructions are similar.

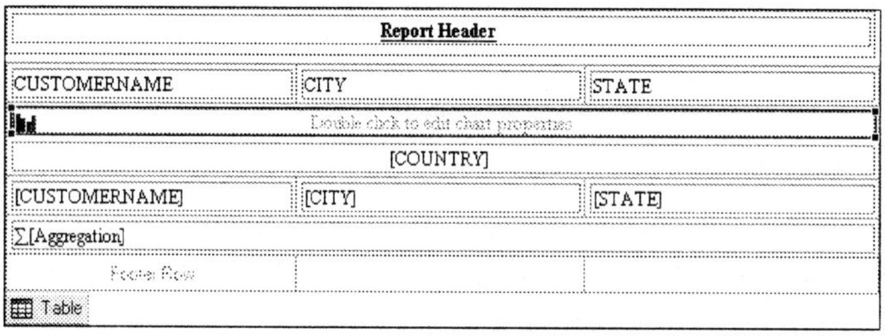

Figure 23-27   Using a template report item

When you double-click the template report item, the chart builder appears.

3 Set up the chart as described earlier in this book. The chart now appears as a standard chart element in the layout.

4 To discard the changes that you made to the chart, right-click the chart element, and choose Revert to Template Item. The chart now appears as the original template report item, as shown in Figure 23-27.

Localizing Text

When you insert label and text elements in a report, you typically type the text that you want to display. Use literal or static text if a report will always be viewed in one language or locale. If, however, a report will be translated into multiple languages, use resource keys rather than static text. The resource keys are translated, or localized, in resource files.

If you are not familiar with resource keys or resource files, think of resource keys as variables, and resource files as text files in which the variables are set to their values. If a report needs to appear in four languages, you create four resource files to define text values for each language. When a report runs, BIRT uses the machine's current locale, the resource keys, and the resource files to find the appropriate text value to display. Figure 24-1 shows the functions of resource files and resource keys in a localized report.

Resource files for English, Spanish, and French locales. Each file contains the resource key, greeting, and the localized version.

Report design uses the resource key, greeting, in a label element.

Report output when run in English, Spanish, and French locales, respectively.

```
greeting=Hello
    greeting=Hola
        greeting=Bonjour
```

```
greeting
```

```
Hello
    Hola
        Bonjour
```

Figure 24-1   Resource keys in resource files, the report design, and the report

You can specify resource keys for the following items:

- Static text in label, text, and chart elements. For example, you can localize report titles, column headings, chart titles, and other static labels.

- Text values that come from a data set field. Data values of date or number type do not need to be localized. BIRT automatically displays numbers and dates according to the locale to which the report user's machine is configured.

- Report parameters.

Overview of the localization process

The localization process for BIRT reports is similar to the localization process for Java applications. This section provides an overview of the entire process. Steps that you perform using BIRT Report Designer are described in more detail in later sections. The basic steps are as follows:

- Create the default resource file. The resource file is a text file with a .properties file-name extension. In this file, you define all the resource keys in key=value format, as shown in the following examples:

  ```
  hello=Hello
  thanks=Thank you
  ```

  If you know the text strings that you want to localize, you can create the resource file in an external text editor and define the keys before you build your report. Alternatively, you can create the resource file in BIRT Report Designer and define keys as you add label and text elements to the report.

- If you create the default resource file in an external text editor, place the file in the resource folder. If you create the resource file in BIRT Report Designer, the file is created in the resource folder. You specify the location of the resource folder on the Preferences page, which you access by choosing Window→Preferences from the main menu, then choosing Report Design→Resource.

- Assign the resource file to the report that you want to localize.

- For each report parameter, label, text, or chart element that you want to localize, choose the resource key to use.

- When you finish defining the keys in the default resource file, create a resource file for each language that the report will support. The file name must include the language code and, if necessary, the region code. The file name must be in the following format:

  ```
  <filename>_<ISO 639 language code>_
      <ISO 3166 region code>.properties
  ```

  For example, MyResources_en_US.properties is for U.S. English, and MyResources_en_UK.properties is for British English. For a list of supported language and region codes, see the Java reference documentation at the following URL:

```
http://java.sun.com
```

- In the localized resource files, use the same set of keys that are defined in the default resource file, and set their values to the translated strings. A quick way to create the keys is to make a copy of the default resource file, then edit the values. Unless you are multilingual, this task is typically done by a team of translators.

  The following examples show resource keys and values that could appear in two localized versions of the same information:

```
MyResources_fr.properties:

    hello=Bonjour
    thanks=Merci

MyResources_es.properties:

    hello=Hola
    thanks=Gracias
```

- Use the native2ascii command to convert the localized resource files to a format that the Java platform can use. The command requires an input file name and an output file name, so copy the resource file to a temporary file, then use the correct file name as the output file name.

  The following example converts a Japanese resource file:

```
copy MyResource_ja.properties temp.properties
native2ascii -encoding SJIS temp.properties
    MyResource_ja.properties
```

For more information about native2ascii and the list of supported encoding character sets, see the Java reference documentation at the following URL:

```
http://java.sun.com
```

- Place all the localized resource files in the resource folder. When a report runs, BIRT uses the appropriate resource file to find the localized text values to display. If BIRT cannot find a resource file for a specific locale, it uses the default resource file.

Assigning a resource file to a report

You can add as many resource files as you need to the resource folder. Different reports in a project can use different resource files. You can, however, assign only one resource file to a report. You assign a resource file to a report by completing one of the following tasks:

- Select a resource file that currently resides in the resource folder.

- Create a new resource file in BIRT Report Designer, then assign it to the report.

If you select an existing file, you can assign the keys that are defined in that file to report parameters, label, text, or chart elements. If you create a new resource file, it contains no keys. You define the keys as you add report parameters, label, or text elements to the report.

How to assign a resource file to a report

1 In the layout editor, select the report by clicking in an empty area on the report page.

2 In Property Editor, choose Resources. Property Editor displays the Resources page, as shown in Figure 24-2.

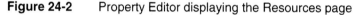

Figure 24-2   Property Editor displaying the Resources page

3 Choose Add, next to the Resource File field.

4 On Browse Resource Files, indicate which resource file to use by completing one of the following tasks:

- To use a resource file that currently exists in the resource folder, select the resource file displayed under Resource Folder.

- To create a new resource file using BIRT Report Designer, select Resource Folder. In New File Name, type a name for the new resource file, such as CustomerReportResources.properties, as shown in Figure 24-3. You must type the .properties file-name extension.

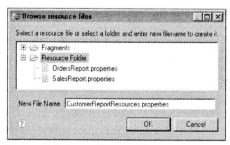

Figure 24-3   Browse Resource Files showing a new resource file

5 Choose OK.

The name of the resource file appears in Resource File on the Resources page of Property Editor. The report uses the selected resource file. You can, at any time, specify a different resource file to use. You can also specify no resource file by deleting the file name from the Resource File field on the Resources page.

Assigning a resource key to a label or text element

After you assign a resource file to a report, you can localize the text in label and text elements by assigning a resource key to each label or text element. You can assign a resource key that you defined earlier, or you can define a new resource key, then assign it to the label or text element.

How to assign an existing resource key to a label or text element

1 In the layout editor, select the label or text element that you want to localize.

2 In Property Editor, choose Localization, as shown in Figure 24-4.

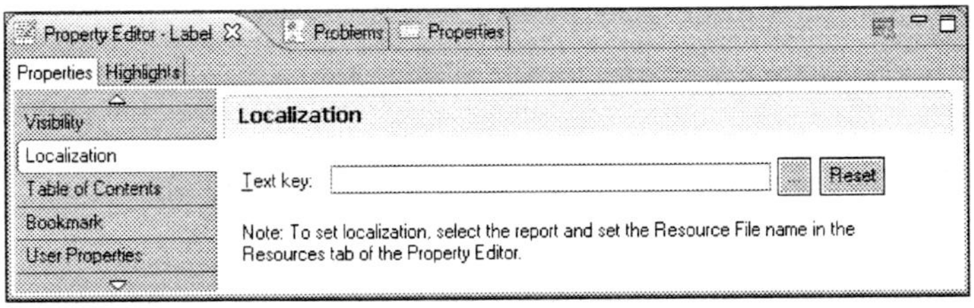

Figure 24-4 Property Editor displaying the Localization page

3 Choose the ellipsis (...) button that is next to the Text key field. This button is enabled only if you have already assigned a resource file to the report. Select Key displays the current list of keys and values that are defined in the resource file that the report uses, as shown in Figure 24-5.

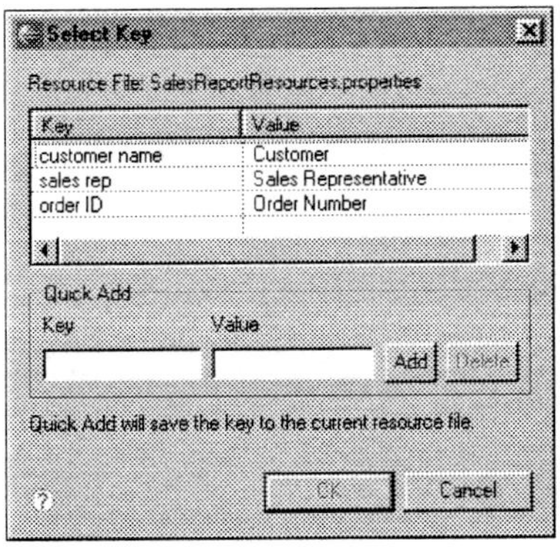

Figure 24-5 Select Key

4 Select the key to assign to the label or text element, then choose OK. In the layout editor, the label or text element displays the value that corresponds to the key.

How to define a new resource key

1 Select the label or text element that you want to localize.

2 In Property Editor, choose Localization.

3 Choose the ellipsis (...) button that is next to the Text key field. This button is enabled only if you have already assigned a resource file to the report. Select Key displays the list of keys and values that are defined in the resource file that the report uses.

4 If the key you want to assign is not in the list, add a new key as follows:

    1 In Quick Add, provide a key and value, then choose Add. The key is added to the resource file and appears in the list of keys.

    2 To assign the key to the label or text element, select the key from the list, then choose OK. In the layout editor, the label or text element displays the value that corresponds to the key.

Changing localized text in a label or text element to static text

If you change your mind about localizing a label or text element, you can remove the resource key and use static text instead.

How to remove a resource key from a label or text element

1 Select the label or text element.

2 In Property Editor, choose Localization. Property Editor displays localization information for the selected element, as shown in Figure 24-6.

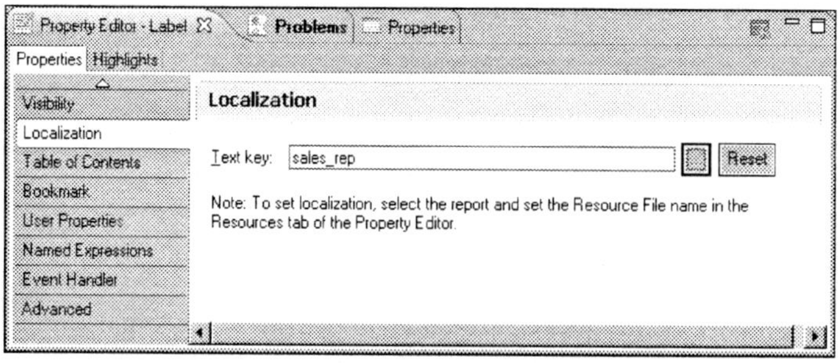

Figure 24-6   Localization properties for an element

3 Choose Reset. The label or text element displays either nothing or the default static text, if you specified any default text when you inserted the element.

Assigning a resource key to chart text

After you assign a resource file to your report, you can localize static text in a chart, such as the chart title and axis titles, by assigning a resource key to the chart text.

How to assign a resource key to chart text

1 In the layout editor, double-click the chart element to open the chart builder, then choose Format Chart.

2 Navigate to the section for the chart part that you want to localize. For example, to localize the chart title, navigate to the Chart Area section. To localize the y-axis title, navigate to the Y-Axis section. Figure 24-7 shows the portion of the chart builder that you use to work with the y-axis.

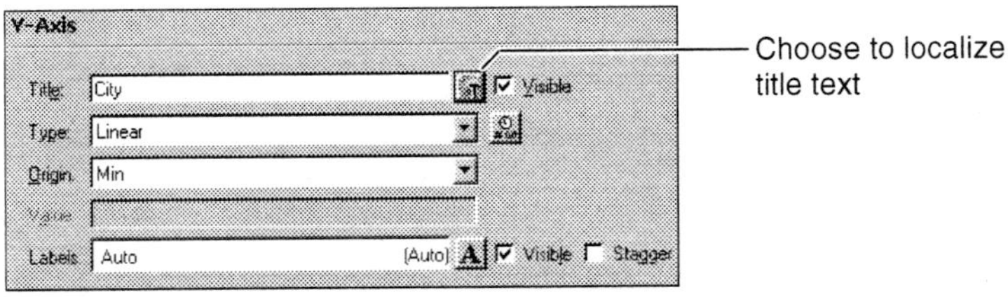

Figure 24-7   Localizing title text on the y-axis

3 Choose the button that is next to the field to localize. For the example in Figure 24-7, choose the button at the right of the Title field.

Externalize Text appears, as shown in Figure 24-8. Lookup Key displays, by default, the first key in the resource file. Default Value displays the current text label applied to the chart element.

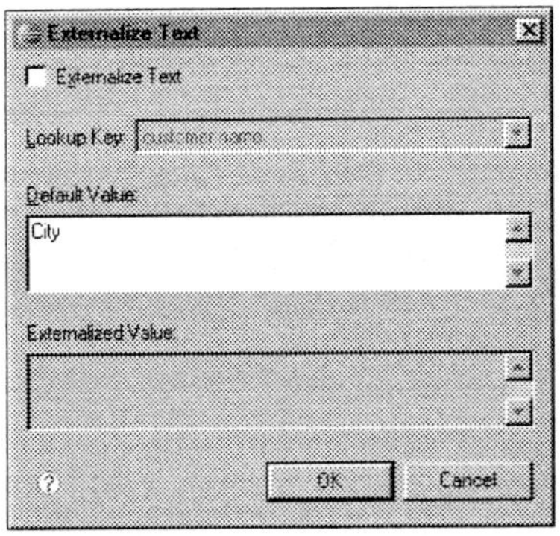

Figure 24-8   Externalize Text displaying default settings

4 Assign a resource key to the chart text as follows:

  1 Select Externalize Text. The list of resource keys is enabled in the drop-down list that is next to Lookup Key.

2 From the drop-down list, select a key to assign to the chart text. The value that corresponds to the key that you selected appears in Externalized Value, as shown in Figure 24-9.

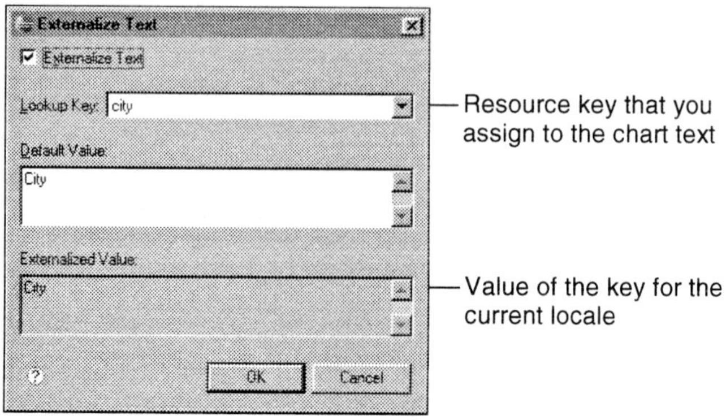

Figure 24-9   Resource key and its externalized value

If the key and value pair that you want to use for the chart text is not available, you can edit the resource file to add a new key. Information about this task appears later in this chapter.

3 Choose OK.

The Title field in Edit Chart shows the title's display value. To use a different resource key, choose the button to open the Externalize Text dialog, and select a different key from the Lookup Key list.

5 Choose Finish to close the chart builder and return to the layout editor. In the report design, the chart text displays the value that corresponds to the key that you selected.

Changing localized chart text to static text

If you change your mind about localizing text in a chart, you can remove the resource key and use static text instead.

How to remove a resource key from chart text

1 Navigate to the Format Chart section for the chart part that you want to change.

2 Choose the Externalize Text Editor button that is next to the field that you want to change.

Externalize Text displays the resource key that is assigned to the chart part, as shown in Figure 24-10.

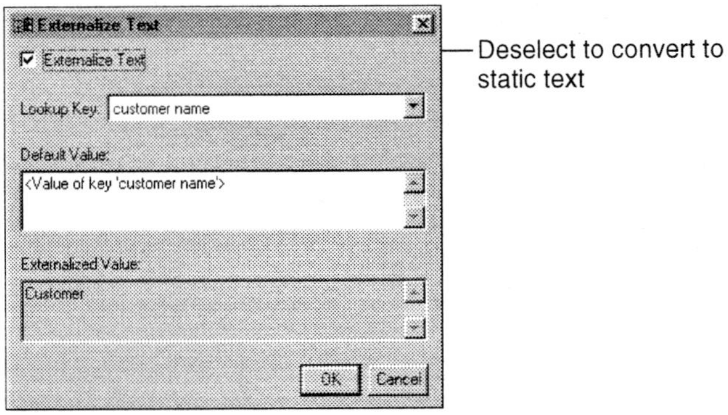

Figure 24-10 Externalize Text displaying the assigned resource key

3 Deselect Externalize Text.

4 In Default Value, type the static text to display for the chart part, then choose OK. The Title field in the chart builder shows the title's new display value.

5 Choose OK to return to the layout editor. In the report design, the chart displays the static text that you typed.

Assigning a resource key to a value in a data element

Localizing text data that originates from a data source requires that you know the data values at report design time because you map each data value to a resource key when you design the report. If you do not map a data value to a resource key, the report displays the original data value. Assuming the original values are in English, if you do not map every value in the data set field, your report will display data in two languages. For unmapped values, the report displays data in English. For mapped values, the report displays data in the language specified by the user's machine locale.

How to assign a resource key to a data value

1 In the layout editor, select the data element whose values you want to localize.

2 On Property Editor, choose the Map tab.

3 On Map List, choose Add to create a map rule.

4 On New Map Rule:

   1 In the first field, select from the drop-down list, Value of this data item. The field displays the expression that refers to the data set field, which contains the values you want to localize.

2 In the second field, select an operator from the list. For example:

   `Equal to`

3 In the third field, specify the value to replace. For example:

   `"Shipped"`

   You must enclose string values in quotation marks (" ").

   Skip the next field, "Then display following value". You enter a value for this field only if you want to map the data value to a literal text value.

4 Specify a resource key. Choose the ellipsis (...) button to select a resource key. You can access resource keys only if you have assigned a resource file to the report.

   Select Key displays the current list of keys and values that are defined in the resource file that the report uses.

   1 Perform one of the following steps:

      ❏ Select an existing key to assign to the data value.

      ❏ Under Quick Add, create a new key and value, choose Add, then select the key from the list.

   2 Choose OK to confirm your resource key selection. The resource key appears in the Resource Key field on New Map Rule. Figure 24-11 shows a completed map rule, which maps the value Cancelled to the localized value defined for the resource key cancelled.

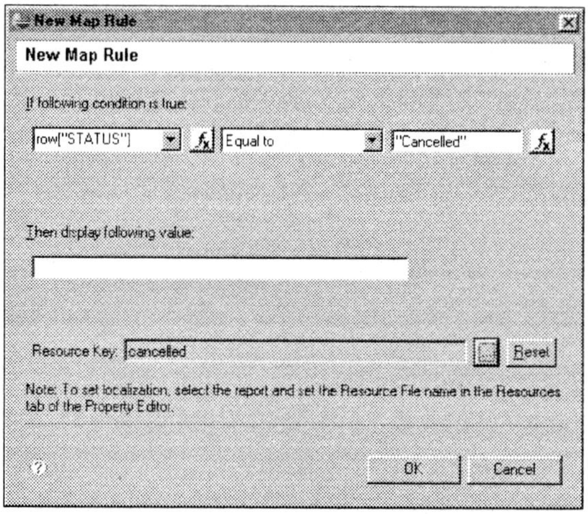

Figure 24-11   Map rule that maps a data value to a resource key

5 Choose OK to save the map rule. The rule that you created appears in Map List.

5 Repeat steps 3 through 4 to create additional rules, one for each data value that you want to replace. Figure 24-12 shows an example of six map rules that were created for a data element that displays order status.

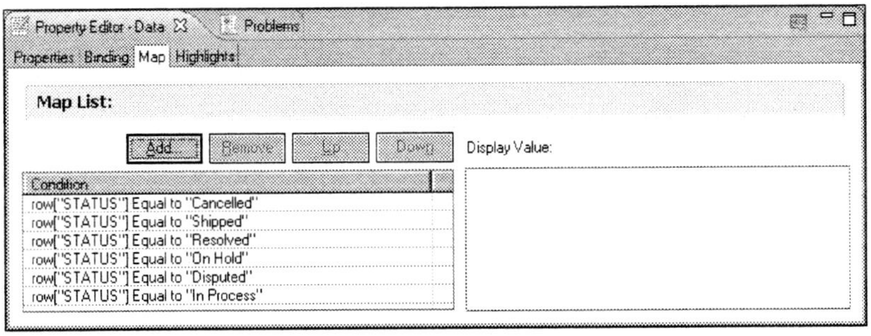

Figure 24-12   Six map rules for a data element

Assigning a resource key to a report parameter

You assign a resource key to a report parameter to localize the text that prompts report users to supply a value for the report parameter. If a report parameter displays a static list of values in radio buttons, a list box, or combo box, you can also localize each value. Figure 24-13 shows the dialog box, Enter Parameters, that displays report parameters to the report user. You can localize the name of a report parameter. In Enter Parameters, the report parameter name appears next to the curly braces symbol, **{ }**. You can also localize the values that appear next to radio buttons and in the list boxes.

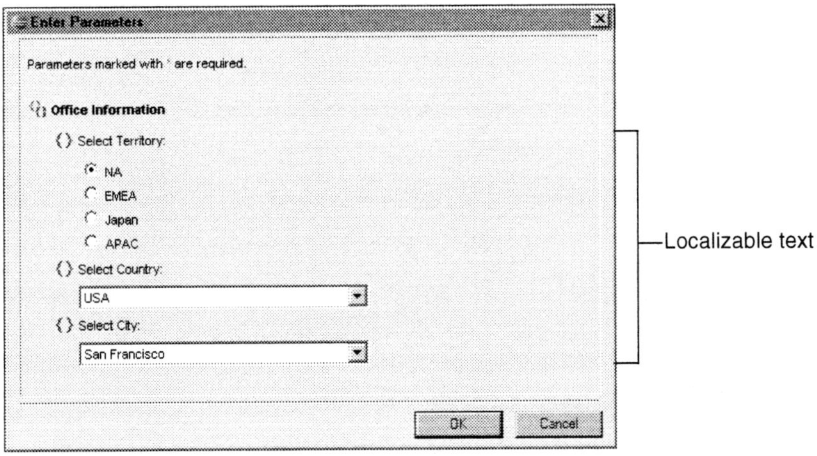

Figure 24-13   Text that can be localized in Enter Parameters

How to assign a resource key to a report parameter name

These instructions assume that you have already created the report parameters.

1 In Data Explorer, under Report Parameters, select the report parameter that you want to localize. Do not double-click the parameter, which opens the Edit Parameter dialog.

2 In Property Editor, choose Localization.

3 Choose the ellipsis (...) button that is next to the Text key field. Select Key displays the current list of keys and values that are defined in the resource file that the report uses.

4 Perform one of the following steps:

- Select an existing key to assign to the report parameter.

- Under Quick Add, create a new key, choose Add, then select the key from the list.

5 Choose OK.

How to assign a resource key to a report parameter value

These instructions assume that you have created the report parameter that displays a list of values in a list box, combo box, or radio buttons. The values must be static. Values that are derived dynamically at run time cannot be localized.

1 In Data Explorer, under Report Parameters, double-click the report parameter whose values you want to localize.

2 On Edit Parameter, in the Selection values table, select the value to localize, then choose Edit. Edit Selection Choice appears. Figure 24-14 shows an example of a radio button value (Shipped) selected for editing.

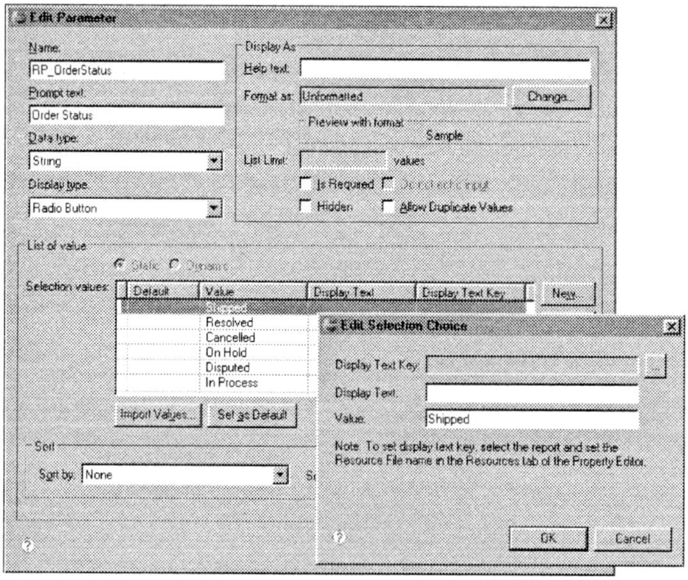

Figure 24-14   A parameter value selected for editing

3 On Edit Selection Choice, choose the ellipsis (...) button that is next to the Display Text Key field. This button is enabled only if you have already assigned a resource file to the report. Select Key displays the current list of keys and values that are defined in the resource file that the report uses.

4 On Select Key, perform one of the following steps, then choose OK:

- Select an existing key to assign to the report parameter value.

- Under Quick Add, create a new key, choose Add, then select the key from the list.

5 Choose OK to apply the key to the report parameter value.

On Edit Parameter, the Selection values table displays the actual value, the display value that the user sees, and the resource key mapped to the display value. Figure 24-15 shows an example of a localized parameter value.

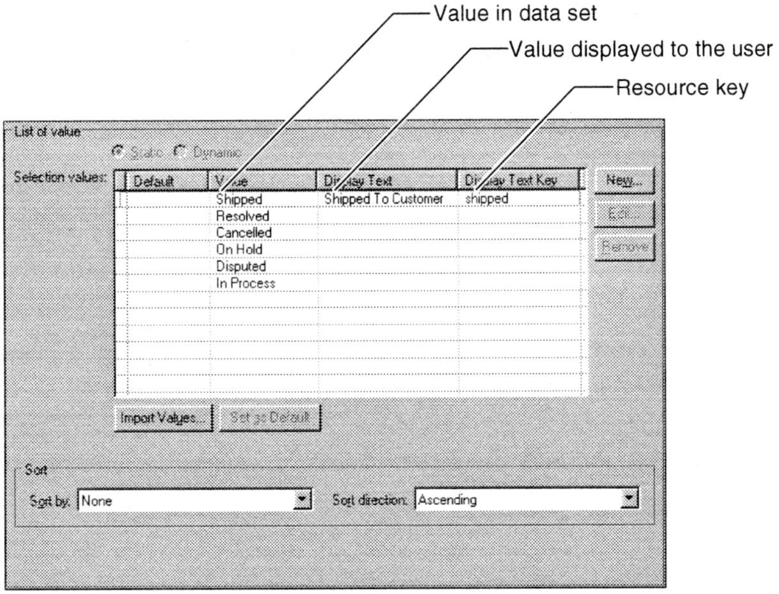

Figure 24-15   The Selection values table in the Edit Parameter dialog, used to display information about a localized parameter value

6 Repeat steps 2 to 5 to localize the remainder of the parameter values.

Editing a resource file

You often need to change the values of keys or add new keys as you design your report. You can accomplish these tasks through the localization properties page of Property Editor for a label or text element, but it is easier to edit the resource file directly.

When you edit the values of keys, the values in the report are updated automatically. If, however, you change a key name or delete a key, report text that uses that key does not display a value because BIRT cannot find the key. It is best to limit your edits to adding new keys or editing the values of the existing keys.

When editing a resource file, if you want to use spaces in the keys, you must precede the space with a backslash (\). For example:

```
order\ ID=Order Number
```

When you add a key through the Select Key dialog, and you type order ID as the key, BIRT adds the backslash automatically, which you see when you open the resource file.

Be aware that when you edit a resource file after it has been translated into locale-specific resource files, those locale-specific resource files must be updated also. Otherwise, the report will not display the text that you intended when it runs in other locales. For this reason, you should create localized resource files only after you have finalized the default resource file and finished creating and testing the report.

How to edit a resource file

Choose File➤Open File, navigate to the resource folder, then double-click the resource (.properties) file. The file that opens in the report editor displays the list of keys and their values, as shown in Figure 24-16.

Edit the file as needed, then save and close it.

Figure 24-16   Resource file opened in the report editor

Previewing a report in different locales

When you have completed all the localization tasks, preview the report in all the locales that it supports to verify that the localized text appears properly. BIRT Report Designer provides an easy way for you to preview a report in any locale without changing your machine's locale. You can test the report in a different locale by setting the locale option in BIRT's preview preferences.

How to preview a report in a different locale

1   Choose Window➤Preferences. Figure 24-17 shows Preferences as it appears in BIRT Report Designer. If you are using BIRT RCP Report

Designer, Preferences displays only report design options and not the Eclipse options.

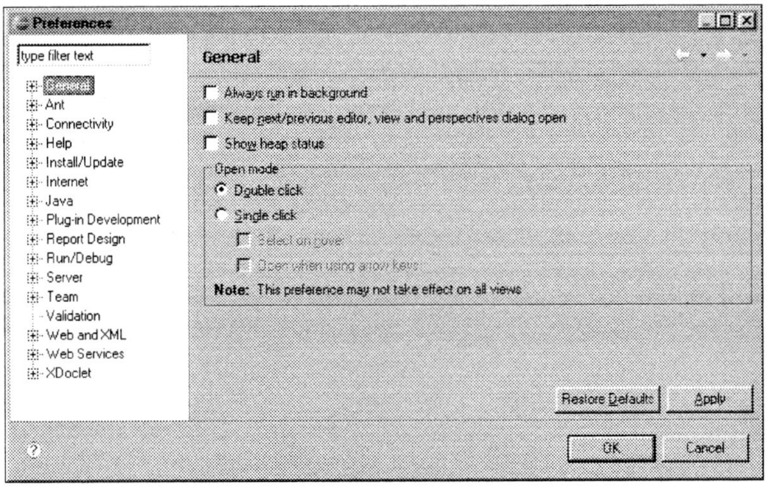

Figure 24-17   General preferences in BIRT Report Designer

2 On the left side of the dialog, expand Report Design, then choose Preview. The preview properties appear, as shown in Figure 24-18.

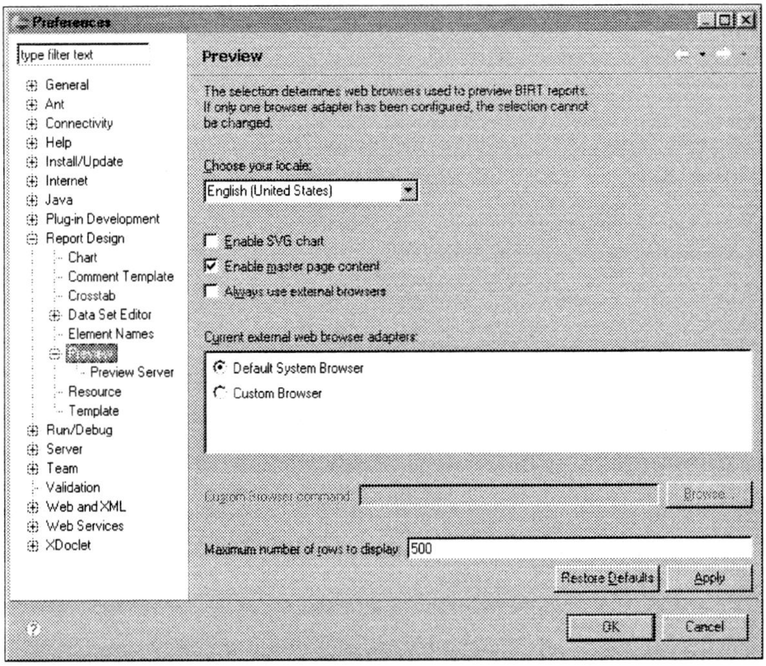

Figure 24-18   Preview preferences in BIRT Report Designer

3 Under Choose your locale, select a locale in which to preview your reports, then choose OK. The locale that you select applies only to previewed reports. It does not change the locale that your machine uses, nor does it change the localized text that appears in the report design.

4 Preview the report. The localized text appears in the language for the locale that you selected.

5 To preview your report in another language, repeat the previous steps to select a new locale.

abstract base class

A class that organizes a class hierarchy or defines methods and variables that apply to descendant classes. An abstract base class does not support the creation of instances.

Related terms
class, class hierarchy, descendant class, method, variable

aggregate function

A function that performs a calculation over a set of data rows. For example, SUM calculates the sum of values of a specified numeric field over a set of data rows. Examples of aggregate functions include AVERAGE, COUNT, MAX, MIN, and SUM.

Related terms
data row, field, function, value

Contrast with
aggregate row, aggregate value

aggregate row

A single row that summarizes data from a group of rows returned by a query. A SQL query that includes an aggregate expression and a Group By clause returns aggregate rows. For example, a row that totals all orders made by one customer is an aggregate row.

Related terms
data, query, row, SQL (Structured Query Language), value

Contrast with
aggregate value, data row, SQL SELECT statement

aggregate value

The result of applying an aggregate function to a set of data rows. For example, consider a set of data rows that have a field, SPEED, which has values: 20, 10, 30, 15, 40. Applying the aggregate function MAX to dataSetRow("SPEED"), produces the aggregate value, 40, which is the maximum value for the field.

Related terms
aggregate function, data row, field, value

alias
1 In a SQL SELECT statement, an alternative name given to a database table or column.

2 An alternative name that is given to a table column for use in an expression or in code in a script method. This name must be a valid variable name that begins with a letter and contains only alphanumeric characters.

Related terms
column, expression, method, SQL SELECT statement, table, variable
Contrast with
display name

ancestor class

A class in the inheritance hierarchy from which a particular class directly or indirectly derives.
Related terms
class, inheritance

Contrast with
class hierarchy, descendant class, subclass, superclass

applet
A small desktop application that usually performs a simple task, for example, a Java program that runs directly from the web browser.
Related terms
application, Java

application

A complete, self-contained program that performs a specific set of related tasks.
Contrast with
applet

application programming interface (API)

A set of routines, including functions, methods, and procedures, that exposes application functionality to support integration and extend applications.
Related terms
application, function, method, procedure

argument

A constant, expression, or variable that supplies data to a function or method.
Related terms
constant, data, expression, function, method, variable
Contrast with
parameter

array
A data variable that consists of sequentially indexed elements that have the same data type. Each element has a common name, a common data type, and a unique index number identifier. Changes to an element of an array do not affect other elements.

Related terms
data, data type, variable

assignment statement
A statement that assigns a value to a variable. For example:

```
StringToDisplay = "My Name"
```

Related terms
statement, value, variable

BIRT
See Business Intelligence and Reporting Tools (BIRT).

BIRT extension
See Business Intelligence and Reporting Tools (BIRT) extension.

BIRT Report Designer
See Business Intelligence and Reporting Tools (BIRT) Report Designer.

BIRT technology
See Business Intelligence and Reporting Tools (BIRT) technology.

bookmark
An expression that identifies a report element. A bookmark is used in a hyperlink expression.

Related terms
expression, hyperlink, report element

Boolean expression
An expression that evaluates to True or False. For example, Total > 3000 is a Boolean expression. If the condition is met, the condition evaluates to True. If the condition is not met, the condition evaluates to False.

Related term
expression

Contrast with
conditional expression, numeric expression

breakpoint
In BIRT Report Designer, a place marker in a program that is being debugged. At a breakpoint, execution pauses so that the report developer can examine and edit data values as necessary.

Related terms
Business Intelligence and Reporting Tools (BIRT) Report Designer, data, debug, value

bridge class

A class that maps the functionality of one class to the similar behavior of another class. For example, the JDBC-ODBC bridge class enables applications that use standard JDBC protocol to access a database that uses the ODBC protocol. BIRT Report Designer and BIRT RCP Report Designer use this type of class.

Related terms
application, Business Intelligence and Reporting Tools (BIRT) Report Designer, Business Intelligence and Reporting Tools (BIRT) Rich Client Platform (RCP) Report Designer, class, Java Database Connectivity (JDBC), open database connectivity (ODBC), protocol

Business Intelligence and Reporting Tools (BIRT)

A reporting platform that is built on the Eclipse platform, the industry standard for open source software development. BIRT provides a complete solution for extracting data, processing data to answer business questions, and presenting the results in a formatted document that is meaningful to end users.

Related terms
data, Eclipse, report

Contrast with
Business Intelligence and Reporting Tools (BIRT) extension

Business Intelligence and Reporting Tools (BIRT) Chart Engine

A tool that supports designing and deploying charts outside a report design. Using this engine, Java developers embed charting capabilities into an application. BIRT Chart Engine is a set of Eclipse plug-ins and Java archive (.jar) files. The chart engine is also known as the charting library.

Related terms
application, Business Intelligence and Reporting Tools (BIRT), chart, design, Eclipse platform, Java, Java archive (.jar) file, plug-in, report

Contrast with
Business Intelligence and Reporting Tools (BIRT) Report Engine

Business Intelligence and Reporting Tools (BIRT) Demo Database

A sample database that is used in tutorials in online help for BIRT Report Designer and BIRT RCP Report Designer. This package provides this demo database in Derby, Microsoft Access, and MySQL formats.

Related terms
Business Intelligence and Reporting Tools (BIRT), Business Intelligence and Reporting Tools (BIRT) Report Designer, Business Intelligence and Reporting Tools (BIRT) Rich Client Platform (RCP) Report Designer

Business Intelligence and Reporting Tools (BIRT) extension

A related set of extension points that adds custom functionality to the BIRT platform. BIRT extensions include

- Charting extension

- Open data access (ODA) extension

- Rendering extension

- Report item extension

Related terms
Business Intelligence and Reporting Tools (BIRT), charting extension, extension, extension point, rendering extension, report, report item extension

Business Intelligence and Reporting Tools (BIRT) Report Designer

A tool that builds BIRT report designs and previews reports that are generated from the designs. BIRT Report Designer is a set of plug-ins to the Eclipse platform and includes BIRT Chart Engine, BIRT Demo Database, and BIRT Report Engine. A report developer who uses this tool can access the full capabilities of the Eclipse platform.

Related terms
Business Intelligence and Reporting Tools (BIRT), Business Intelligence and Reporting Tools (BIRT) Chart Engine, Business Intelligence and Reporting Tools (BIRT) Demo Database, Business Intelligence and Reporting Tools (BIRT) Report Engine, design, Eclipse platform, plug-in, report

Contrast with
Business Intelligence and Reporting Tools (BIRT) Rich Client Platform (RCP) Report Designer

Business Intelligence and Reporting Tools (BIRT) Report Engine

A component that supports deploying BIRT charting, reporting, and viewing capabilities as a stand-alone application or on an application server. BIRT Report Engine consists of a set of Eclipse plug-ins, Java archive (.jar) files, web archive (.war) files, and web applications.

Related terms
application, Business Intelligence and Reporting Tools (BIRT), Java archive (.jar) file, plug-in, report, web archive (.war) file

Contrast with
Business Intelligence and Reporting Tools (BIRT) Chart Engine

Business Intelligence and Reporting Tools (BIRT) Rich Client Platform (RCP) Report Designer

A stand-alone tool that builds BIRT report designs and previews reports that are generated from the designs. BIRT RCP Report Designer uses the Eclipse Rich Client Platform. This tool includes BIRT Report Engine, BIRT Chart Engine, and BIRT Demo Database. BIRT RCP Report Designer supports report design and preview functionality without the additional overhead of the full Eclipse platform. BIRT RCP Report Designer does not support the Java-based scripting and the report debugger functionality the full Eclipse platform provides. BIRT RCP Report Designer can use, but not create, BIRT extensions.

Related terms

Business Intelligence and Reporting Tools (BIRT), Business Intelligence and Reporting Tools (BIRT) extension, Business Intelligence and Reporting Tools (BIRT) Chart Engine, Business Intelligence and Reporting Tools (BIRT) Demo Database, Business Intelligence and Reporting Tools (BIRT) Report Engine, debug, design, Eclipse platform, Eclipse Rich Client Platform (RCP), extension, JavaScript, library (.rptlibrary) file, plug-in, report

Contrast with

Business Intelligence and Reporting Tools (BIRT) Report Designer

Business Intelligence and Reporting Tools (BIRT) Samples

A sample of a BIRT report item extension and examples of BIRT charting applications. The report item extension sample is an Eclipse platform plug-in. The charting applications use BIRT Chart Engine. Java developers use these examples as models of how to design custom report items and embed charting capabilities in an application.

Related terms

application, Business Intelligence and Reporting Tools (BIRT), Business Intelligence and Reporting Tools (BIRT) Chart Engine, chart, design, Eclipse, Eclipse platform, Java, plug-in, report, report item, report item extension

Business Intelligence and Reporting Tools (BIRT) technology

A set of Java applications and APIs that support the design and deployment of a business report. BIRT applications include BIRT Report Designer, BIRT RCP Report Designer, and a report viewer web application servlet. The BIRT Java APIs provide programmatic access to BIRT functionality.

Related terms

application, application programming interface (API), Business Intelligence and Reporting Tools (BIRT), Business Intelligence and Reporting Tools (BIRT) Report Designer, Business Intelligence and Reporting Tools (BIRT) Rich Client Platform (RCP) Report Designer, Java, report viewer servlet

cascading parameters

Report parameters that have a hierarchical relationship. For example, the following parameters have a hierarchical relationship:

```
Country
    State
        City
```

In a group of cascading parameters, each report parameter displays a set of values. When a report user selects a value from the top-level parameter, the selected value determines the values that the next parameter displays, and so on. Cascading parameters display only relevant values to the user. Figure G-1 shows cascading parameters as they appear to a report user.

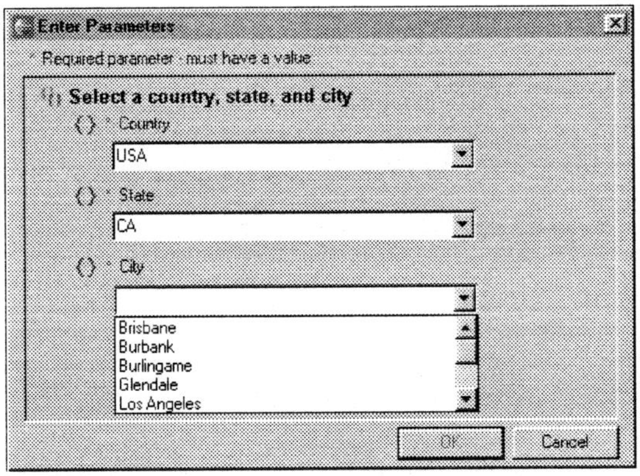

Figure G-1   Cascading parameters

Related terms
hierarchy, parameter, report, value

Contrast with
cascading style sheet (CSS)

cascading style sheet (CSS)

A file that contains a set of rules that attach formats and styles to specified HTML elements. For example, a cascading style sheet can specify the color, font, and size for an HTML heading.

Related terms
element, font, hypertext markup language (HTML), style

Contrast with
template

case sensitivity

A condition in which the letter case is significant for the purposes of comparison. For example, "McManus" does not match "MCMANUS" or "mcmanus" in a case-sensitive environment.

category

In an area, bar, line, step, or stock chart, one of the discrete values that organizes data on an axis that does not use a numerical scale. Typically, the x-axis of a chart displays category values. In a pie chart, category values are called orthogonal axis values and define which sectors appear in a pie.

Related terms
chart, data, value

Contrast with
series

cell

An intersection of a row and a column in a cross tab, grid element, or table element. Figure G-2 shows a cell.

Related terms
column, cross tab, grid element, row, table element

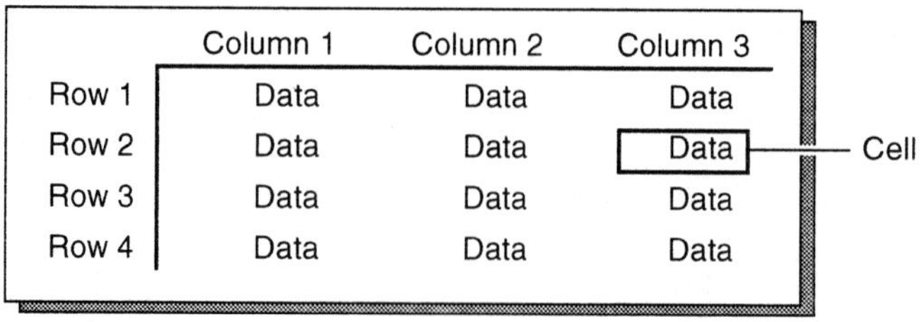

	Column 1	Column 2	Column 3
Row 1	Data	Data	Data
Row 2	Data	Data	Data
Row 3	Data	Data	Data
Row 4	Data	Data	Data

Figure G-2   Cell

character   An elementary mark that represents data, usually in the form of a graphic spatial arrangement of connected or adjacent strokes, such as a letter or a digit. A character is independent of font size and other display properties. For example, an uppercase C is a character.

Related term
data

Contrast with
character set, glyph

character set

A mapping of specific characters to code points. For example, in most character sets, the letter A maps to the hexadecimal value 0x21.

Related terms
character, code point

Contrast with
locale

chart   A graphic representation of data or the relationships among sets of data.

Related term
data

chart element

A report item that displays values from data rows in the form of a chart. The chart element can use data rows from the report design's data set or a different data set. A report item extension defines the chart element.

Related terms
chart, data, data row, data set, design, element, report, report item, report item extension, value

Contrast with
charting extension

chart engine

See Business Intelligence and Reporting Tools (BIRT) Chart Engine.

charting extension

A BIRT extension that adds a new type of chart, a new component to an existing chart type, or a new user interface component to the BIRT chart engine.

Related terms
Business Intelligence and Reporting Tools (BIRT), Business Intelligence and Reporting Tools (BIRT) extension, Business Intelligence and Reporting Tools (BIRT) Chart Engine, chart, extension

charting library

See Business Intelligence and Reporting Tools (BIRT) Chart Engine.

class
A set of methods and variables that defines the attributes and behavior of an object. All objects of a given class are identical in form and behavior but can contain different data in their variables.

Related terms
data, method, object, variable

Contrast with
subclass, superclass

class hierarchy

A tree structure that represents the inheritance relationships among a set of classes.

Related terms
class, inheritance

class name

A unique name for a class that permits unambiguous references to its public methods and variables.

Related terms
class, method, variable

class variable

A variable that all instances of a class share. The run-time system creates only one copy of a class variable. The value of the class variable is the same for all instances of the class, for example, the taxRate variable in an Order class.

Related terms
class, object, value, variable

Contrast with
dynamic variable, field variable, global variable, instance variable, local variable, member variable, static variable

code point
A hexadecimal value. Every character in a character set is represented by a code point. The computer uses the code point to process the character.

Related terms
character, character set

column   **1** A named field in a database table or query. For each data row, the column can have a different value, called the column value. The term column refers to the definition of the column, not to any particular value. Figure G-3 shows a column in a database table.

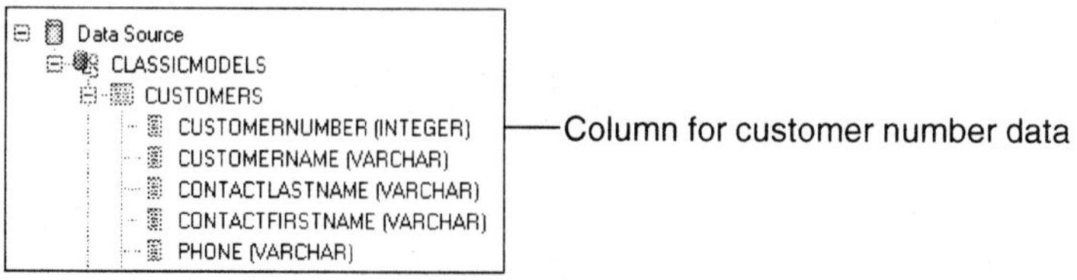

Figure G-3   Column in a database table

2 A vertical sequence of cells in a cross tab, grid element, or table element. Figure G-4 shows a column in a cross tab.

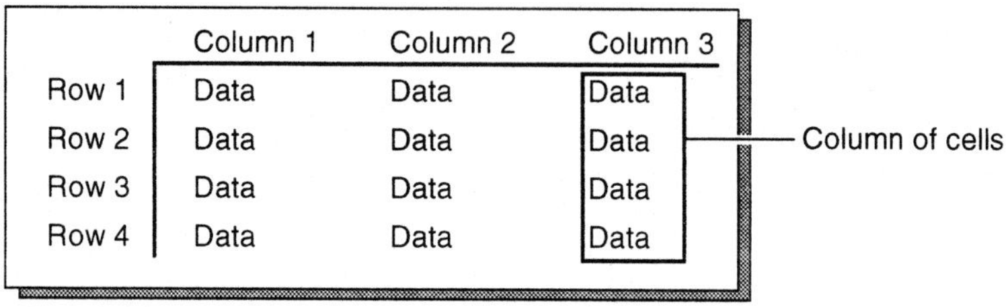

Figure G-4   Column in a cross tab

Related terms
cell, cross tab, data row, field, grid element, query, table, table element, value

column binding

A named column that defines an expression that specifies what data to return. For each piece of data to display in a report, there must be column binding. Column bindings form an intermediate layer between data-set data and report elements.

Related terms
column, data, data set, expression, report, report element

computed column

See computed field.

computed field

A field that displays the result of an expression rather than stored data.

Related terms
data, expression, field

Contrast with
computed value

computed value

> The result of a calculation that is defined by an expression. To display a computed value in a report, use a data element.
>
> **Related terms**
> data element, expression, report, value
>
> **Contrast with**
> computed field

conditional expression

> An expression that returns value A or value B depending on whether a Boolean expression evaluates to True or False.
>
> **Related term**
> Boolean expression, expression

configuration file

> In open data access (ODA), a file that specifies the ODA interface version of the driver and defines the structure, contents, and semantics of requests and responses between the open data source and the design tool.
>
> **Related terms**
> data source, interface, open data access (ODA), open data access (ODA) driver, request, response

Connection

> A Java object that provides access to a data source.
>
> **Related terms**
> data source, Java, object

constant

> An unchanging, predefined value. A constant does not change while a program is running, but the value of a field or variable can change.
>
> **Related terms**
> field, value, variable

constructor code

> Code that initializes an instance of a class.
>
> **Related terms**
> class, object

container

> 1   An application that acts as a master program to hold and execute a set of commands or to run other software routines. For example, application servers provide containers that support communication between applications and Enterprise JavaBeans.
>
> 2   A data structure that holds one or more different types of data. For example, a grid element can contain label elements and other report items.

Related terms
application, data, Enterprise JavaBean (EJB), grid element, label element, report item

containment

A relationship among instantiated objects in a report. One object, the container, incorporates other objects, the contents.

Related terms
container, instantiation, object, report

containment hierarchy

A hierarchy of objects in a report.

Related terms
hierarchy, object, report

converter   A tool that converts data from one format to another format.

Related terms
data, format

cross tab   A report that summarizes data from database table columns into a concise format for analysis. Data appears in a matrix with rows and columns. Every cell in a cross tab contains an aggregate value. A cross tab shows how one item relates to another, such as order totals by credit rating and order status. Figure G-5 shows a cross tab.

Order Totals by Credit Rating and Order Status

	A			B			C			Totals		
	Quantity	Ave Qty	Amount	Quantity	Ave Qty	Amount	Quantity	Ave Qty	Amount	Quantity	Ave Qty	Amount
Open	98,205	349	9,870,799	40,472	283	4,673,517	4,980	332	636,555	143,657	327	15,180,871
Closed	171,813	365	20,633,175	131,183	497	14,465,314	21,790	198	2,591,731	324,786	384	37,690,220
In Evaluation	90,969	469	12,136,326	22,168	411	2,596,936	0		0	113,137	456	14,732,262
Cancelled	23,944	855	3,029,520	0		0	0		0	23,944	855	3,029,520
Selected	10,540	527	1,375,204	0		0	0		0	10,540	527	1,375,204
Totals	395,471	398	47,044,024	193,823	420	21,735,767	26,770	214	3,228,286	616,064	390	72,008,077

Figure G-5   Cross tab

Related terms
aggregate value, cell, column, data, grid, report, row, table, value

Contrast with
aggregate function

cross-tab element

A report item that displays a cross tab. A cross tab displays aggregate values in a matrix with rows and columns.

Related terms
aggregate value, cross tab, report item

CSS   See cascading style sheet (CSS).

cube   A multidimensional data structure that provides multiple measures and dimensions to access and analyze large quantities of data. BIRT uses a cube to structure data for display in a cross-tab element.

Related terms
cross-tab element, data, dimension, measure, multidimensional data

custom data source

See open data access (ODA).

data   Information that is stored in databases, flat files, or other data sources that can appear in a report.

Related terms
data source, flat file, report

Contrast with
metadata

data element

A report item that displays a computed value or a value from a data set field.

Related terms
computed value, data set, element, field, report item, value

Contrast with
label element, Report Object Model (ROM) element, text element

Data Explorer

An Eclipse view that shows the data sources, data sets, report parameters, and data cubes that were created for use in a report. Use Data Explorer to create, edit, or delete these items. Figure G-6 shows Data Explorer.

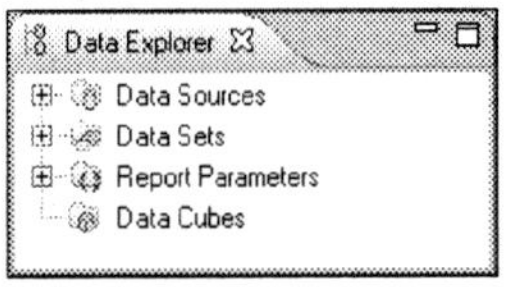

Figure G-6   Data Explorer

Related terms
cube, data set, data source, Eclipse view, parameter, report

data point   A point on a chart that corresponds to a particular pair of x- and y-axis values.

Related terms
chart, value

Contrast with
data row, data set

data row   One row of data that a data set returns. A data set, which specifies the data to retrieve from a data source, typically returns many data rows.

Related terms
data, data set, data source, row

Contrast with
data point, filter

data set   A description of the data to retrieve or compute from a data source.

Related terms
data, data source

Contrast with
data point, data row

data set field

See column.

data set parameter

A parameter that is associated with a data set column and passes an expression to extend dynamically the query's WHERE clause. A data set parameter restricts the number of data rows that the data set supplies to the report.

Related terms
column, data row, data set, expression, parameter, query, report

Contrast with
report parameter

data source

1   A SQL database or other repository of data also known as an input source. For example, a flat file can be a data source.

2   An object that contains the connection information for an external data source, such as a flat file, a SQL database, or another repository of data.

Related terms
data, flat file, SQL (Structured Query Language)

Contrast with
data row, data set

data type   1   A category for values that determines their characteristics, such as the information they can hold and the permitted operations.

2   The data type of a value determines the default appearance of the value in a report. This appearance depends on the locale in which a user generates the report. For example, the order in which year, month, and day appear in a date-and-time data value depends on the locale. BIRT uses three fundamental data types: date-and-time, numeric, and string. Data sources such as relational databases support more data types, which BIRT maps to the appropriate fundamental data type.

Related terms
Business Intelligence and Reporting Tools (BIRT), date-and-time data type, locale, numeric data type, report, String data type, value, variable

database connection

See data source.

database management system (DBMS)

Software that organizes simultaneous access to shared data. Database management systems store relationships among various data elements.

Related term
data

database schema

See schema.

date-and-time data type

A data type for date-and-time calculations. Report items can contain expressions or fields with a date-and-time data type. The appearance of date-and-time values in the report document is based on locale and format settings specified by your computer and the report design.

Related terms
data type, design, expression, field, format, locale, report, report item

debug   To detect, locate, and fix errors. Typically, debugging involves executing specific portions of a computer program and analyzing the operation of those portions.

declaration

The definition of a class, constant, method, or variable that specifies the name and, if appropriate, the data type.

Related terms
class, constant, data type, method, variable

derived class

See descendant class.

descendant class

A class that is based on another class.

Related term
class

Contrast with
subclass, superclass

design   1 To create a report specification. Designing a report includes selecting data, laying out the report visually, and saving the layout in a report design file.

2 A report specification. A report design (.rptdesign) file contains a report design.

Related terms
data, layout, report, report design (.rptdesign) file

DHTML (dynamic hypertext markup language)

See dynamic hypertext markup language (DHTML).

dimension   In a cube, fields such as products, customers, or orders, by which measures are aggregated.

Related terms
cube, field, measure

Contrast with
multidimensional data

display name

An alternative name for a table column, report parameter, chart series, or user-defined ROM property. BIRT Report Designer displays this alternative name in the user interface, for example, as a column heading in a report. This name can contain any character, including spaces and punctuation.

Related terms
Business Intelligence and Reporting Tools (BIRT) Report Designer, character, chart, column, Data Explorer, report, report parameter, Report Object Model (ROM), table, value

Contrast with
alias

document object model (DOM)

A model that defines the structure of a document such as an HTML or XML document. The document object model defines interfaces that dynamically create, access, and manipulate the internal structure of the document. The URL to the W3C document object model is

```
www.w3.org/DOM/
```

Related terms
extensible markup language (XML), hypertext markup language (HTML), interface, Uniform Resource Locator (URL), World Wide Web Consortium (W3C)

Contrast with
document type definition (DTD), structured content

document type definition (DTD)

A set of markup tags and the interpretation of those tags that together define the structure of an XML document.

Related terms
extensible markup language (XML), tag

Contrast with
document object model (DOM), schema, structured content

domain name

A name that defines a node on the internet. For example, the Eclipse Foundation's domain name is eclipse. The URL is

```
www.eclipse.org
```

Related terms
node, Uniform Resource Locator (URL)

driver   An interface that supports communication between an application and another application or a peripheral device such as a printer.

Related term
interface

dynamic hypertext markup language (DHTML)

An HTML extension that provides enhanced viewing capabilities and interactivity in a web page without the necessity for communication with a web server. The Document Object Model Group of the W3C develops DHTML standards.

Related terms
document object model (DOM), hypertext markup language (HTML), web page, web server, World Wide Web Consortium (W3C)

dynamic text element

A data element that displays text data that contains multiple style formats and a variable amount of text. A dynamic text element adjusts its size to accommodate varying amounts of data. Use a dynamic text element to display a data source field that contains formatted text. A dynamic text element supports plain or HTML text.

Related terms
data, data source, field, format, hypertext markup language (HTML)

Contrast with
text element

dynamic variable

A variable that changes during program execution. The program requests the memory allocation for a dynamic variable at run time.

Related term
variable

Contrast with
class variable, field variable, global variable, instance variable, local variable, member variable, static variable

Eclipse   An open platform for tool integration that is built by an open community of tool providers. The Eclipse platform is written in Java and includes extensive plug-in construction toolkits and examples.

Related terms
Eclipse platform, Java, plug-in

Contrast with
Business Intelligence and Reporting Tools (BIRT) extension

Eclipse Modeling Framework (EMF)

A Java framework and code generation facility for building tools and other applications that are based on a structured model. EMF uses XML schemas to generate the EMF model of a plug-in. For example, a BIRT chart type uses EMF to represent the chart structure and properties.

Related terms
application, Business Intelligence and Reporting Tools (BIRT) technology, chart, Eclipse, extensible markup language (XML), framework, Java, plug-in, property, schema

Eclipse perspective

A predefined layout of the Eclipse Workbench, including which Eclipse views are visible and where they appear. A perspective also controls what appears in certain menus and toolbars. A user can switch the perspective to work on a different task and can rearrange and customize a perspective to better suit a particular task. Figure G-7 shows the Eclipse Java perspective.

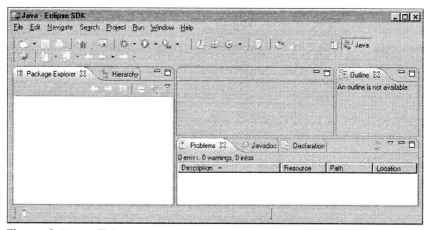

Figure G-7   Eclipse perspective

Related terms
Eclipse, Eclipse view, Eclipse Workbench

Eclipse platform

The core framework and services in which Eclipse plug-in extensions exist. The Eclipse platform provides the run-time environment in which plug-ins load and run. The Eclipse platform consists of a core component and a user interface component. The user interface component is known as the Eclipse Workbench. The core portion of the Eclipse platform is called the platform core or the core.

Eclipse Plug-in Development Environment (PDE)

An integrated design tool for creating, developing, testing, and deploying a plug-in. The Eclipse PDE provides wizards, editors, views, and launchers that support plug-in development. The Eclipse PDE supports host and run-time instances of a workbench project. The host instance provides the development environment. The run-time instance enables the launching of a plug-in for testing purposes.

Related terms
design, Eclipse, Eclipse project, Eclipse Workbench, object, plug-in

Eclipse project

A user-specified directory within an Eclipse workspace. An Eclipse project contains folders and files that are used for builds, version management, sharing, and resource organization.

Related terms
Eclipse, Eclipse workspace

Eclipse Rich Client Platform (RCP)

The Eclipse framework for building a client application that uses a minimal set of plug-ins. Eclipse Rich Client Platform (RCP) uses a subset of the components that are available in the Eclipse platform. An Eclipse rich client application is typically a specialized user interface that supports a specific function, such as the report development tools in the BIRT Rich Client Platform.

Related terms
application, Business Intelligence and Reporting Tools (BIRT), Eclipse, Eclipse platform, framework, plug-in, report

Eclipse view

A dockable window on the Eclipse Workbench, similar to a pane in Windows. An Eclipse view can be an editor, the Navigator, a palette of report items, a graphical report designer, or any other functional component that Eclipse or an Eclipse project provides. A view can have its own menus and toolbars. Multiple views can be visible at one time.

Related terms
design, Eclipse, Eclipse perspective, Eclipse project, Eclipse Workbench, Navigator, Palette, report, report item

Eclipse Workbench

The Eclipse desktop development environment, which supports the Eclipse perspectives.

Related terms
Eclipse, Eclipse perspective

Contrast with
Eclipse Plug-in Development Environment (PDE), Eclipse workspace

Eclipse workspace

A user-specified directory that contains one or more Eclipse projects. An Eclipse workspace is a general umbrella for managing resources in the Eclipse platform. The Eclipse platform can use one or more workspaces. A user can switch between workspaces.

Related terms
Eclipse platform, Eclipse project

Contrast with
Eclipse Workbench

EJB   See Enterprise JavaBean (EJB).

element   1   In Report Object Model (ROM), a component that describes a piece of a report. A ROM element typically has a name and a set of properties.

2   A tag-delimited structure in an XML or HTML document that contains a unit of data. For example, the root element of an HTML page starts with the beginning tag, <HTML>, and ends with the closing tag, </HTML>. This root element encloses all the other elements that define the contents of a page. An XML element must be well-formed, with both a beginning and a closing tag. In HTML, some tags, such as <br>, the forced line break tag, do not require a closing tag.

Related terms
data, extensible markup language (XML), hypertext markup language (HTML), property, report, Report Object Model (ROM), Report Object Model (ROM) element, tag, well-formed XML

Contrast with
report item

ellipsis button

 A button that opens tools that you use to perform tasks, such as navigating to a file, building an expression, or specifying localized text.

encapsulation

A technique of packaging-related functions and subroutines together. Encapsulation compartmentalizes the structure and behavior of a class, hiding the implementation details, so that parts of an object-oriented system need not depend upon or affect each other's internal details.

Related terms
class, function, object

Contrast with
object-oriented programming

enterprise   A large collection of networked computers that run on multiple platforms. Enterprise systems can include both mainframes and workstations that are integrated in a single, managed environment. Typical software products that are used in an enterprise environment include web browsers, applications, applets, web tools, and multiple databases that support a warehouse of information.

Related terms
applet, application

Contrast with
Enterprise JavaBean (EJB), enterprise reporting

Enterprise JavaBean (EJB)

A standards-based server-side component that encapsulates the business logic of an application. An EJB can provide access to data or model the data itself. Application servers provide the deployment environment for EJBs.

Related terms
application, data, JavaBean

Contrast with
Java

enterprise reporting

The production of a high volume of simple and complex structured documents that collect data from a variety of data sources. A large number of geographically distributed users who are working in both client/server and internet environments receive, work with, and modify these reports.

Related terms
data, data source, report

Contrast with
enterprise, structured content

event An action or occurrence recognized by an object. Each object responds to a predefined set of events that can be extended by the developer.

Related term
object

Contrast with
event handler, event listener

event handler

A Java or JavaScript method that is executed upon the firing of a BIRT event. BIRT fires events at various times in the report generation process. By writing custom code for the associated event handlers, the BIRT report developer can provide special handling at the time the events are fired. Report items, data sets, and data sources all have event handlers for which the report developer can provide custom code.

Related terms
Business Intelligence and Reporting Tools (BIRT), data set, data source, event, Java, JavaScript, method, report, report item

Contrast with
event listener

event listener

An interface that detects when a particular event occurs and runs a registered method in response to that event.

Related terms
event, method

Contrast with
event handler

exception   An abnormal situation that a program encounters. In some cases, the program handles the exception and returns a message to the user or application that is running the program. In other cases, the program cannot handle the exception, and the program terminates.

Related term
application

expression

A combination of constants, functions, literal values, names of fields, and operators that evaluates to a single value.

Related terms
constant, field, function, operator, value

Contrast with
regular expression

expression builder

A tool for selecting data fields, functions, and operators to write JavaScript expressions. Figure G-8 shows the expression builder.

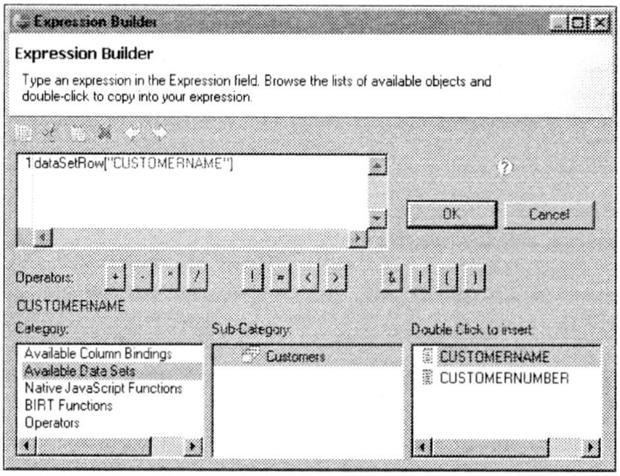

Figure G-8   Expression builder

Related terms
data, expression, field, function, JavaScript, operator

extensible markup language (XML)

A markup language that supports the interchange of data among data sources and applications. Using XML, a wide variety of applications, legacy systems, and databases can exchange information. XML is content-oriented rather than format-oriented. XML uses tags to structure data into nested elements. An XML schema that is structured according to the rules that were defined by the W3C describes the structure of the data. XML documents must be well-formed.

Related terms
application, data, data source, element, schema, tag, well-formed XML, World Wide Web Consortium (W3C)

Contrast with
hypertext markup language (HTML)

extension   A module that adds functionality to an application. BIRT consists of a set of extensions, called plug-ins, which add functionality to the Eclipse development environment.

Related terms
application, Business Intelligence and Reporting Tools (BIRT), Eclipse, plug-in

Contrast with
Business Intelligence and Reporting Tools (BIRT) extension, extension point

extension point

A defined place in an application where a developer adds custom functionality. The APIs in BIRT support adding custom functionality to the BIRT framework. In the Eclipse Plug-in Development Environment (PDE), a developer views the extension points in the PDE Manifest Editor to guide and control plug-in development tasks.

Related terms
application, application programming interface (API), Business Intelligence and Reporting Tools (BIRT), Eclipse Plug-in Development Environment (PDE), extension, framework, plug-in

Contrast with
Business Intelligence and Reporting Tools (BIRT) extension

field   The smallest identifiable part of a database table structure. In a relational database, a field is also called a column.

Related terms
column, table

field variable

In Java, a member variable with public visibility.

Related terms
Java, member, variable

Contrast with
class variable, dynamic variable, global variable, instance variable, local variable, member variable, static variable

file types   Table G-1 lists the report designer's file types.

Table G-1   File types

Display name	Glossary term	File type
BIRT Report Design	report design (.rptdesign) file	RPTDESIGN
BIRT Report Design Library	library (.rptlibrary) file	RPTLIBRARY
BIRT Report Design Template	report template (.rpttemplate) file	RPTTEMPLATE
BIRT Report Document	report document (.rptdocument) file	RPTDOCUMENT

filter   To exclude any data rows from the result set that do not meet a set of conditions. Some external data sources can filter data as specified by conditions that the query includes directly or through the use of report parameters. In addition, BIRT can filter data after retrieval from the external data source. Report developers can specify conditions for filtering in either the data set or a report item.

Related terms
Business Intelligence and Reporting Tools (BIRT), data, data row, data set, data source, query, report, report item, report parameter, result set

flat file   A file that contains data in the form of text.

Related term
data

Contrast with
data source

font   A family of characters of a given style. Fonts contain information that specifies typeface, weight, posture, and type size.

Related term
character

footer   1   A unit of information that appears at the bottom of a page.

2   A group footer is a unit of information that appears at the bottom of a group section.

Related terms
group, section

Contrast with
header

format   **1**   A set of standard options with which to display and print currency values, dates, numbers, and times.

2   A specification that describes layout and properties of report data or other information, for example, PDF or HTML.

Related terms
data, hypertext markup language (HTML), layout, property, report, value
Contrast with
style

forms-capable browser

A web browser that handles hypertext markup language (HTML) forms. HTML tags enable interactive forms, including check boxes, drop-down lists, fill-in text areas, and option buttons.
Related terms
hypertext markup language (HTML), tag

fragment   See plug-in fragment.

framework

A set of interrelated classes that provide an architecture for building an application.
Related terms
application, class

full outer join

See outer join.

function   A sequence of instructions that are defined as a separate unit within a program. To invoke the function, include its name as one of the instructions anywhere in the program. BIRT provides JavaScript functions to support building expressions.

Related terms
Business Intelligence and Reporting Tools (BIRT), expression, JavaScript
Contrast with
method

global variable

A variable that is available at all levels in an application. A global variable stays in memory in the scope of all executing procedures until the application terminates.
Related terms
application, procedure, scope, variable

Contrast with
class variable, dynamic variable, field variable, instance variable, local
variable, member variable, static variable

glyph
1 An image that is used for the visual representation of a character.

2 A specific letter form from a specific font. An uppercase C in Palatino
font is a glyph.

Related terms
character, font

grandchild class

See descendant class.

grandparent class

See ancestor class.

grid
See grid element.

grid element

A report item that contains and displays other report elements in a static
row and column format. A grid element aligns the cells horizontally and
vertically.

Figure G-9 shows a report title section that consists of an image element
and two text elements that are arranged in a grid element with one row
and two columns.

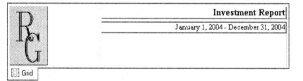

Figure G-9   Grid element

Related terms
cell, column, element, image element, report, report item, row, text
element

Contrast with
list element, table element

group
A set of data rows that have one or more column values in common. For
example, in a sales report, a group consists of all the orders that are placed
by a single customer.

Related terms
column, data row, report, value

Contrast with
group key, grouped report

grouped report

A report that organizes data in logical groups. Figure G-10 shows a grouped report.

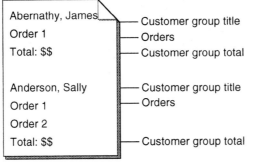

Figure G-10   Grouped report

Related terms
data, group, report

group key   A data set column that is used to group and sort data in a report. For example, a report developer can group and sort customers by credit rank.

Related terms
column, data, data set, group, report, sort

header   1   A unit of information that appears at the top of every page.

2   A group header is a unit of information that appears at the beginning of a group section.

Related terms
group, section
Contrast with
footer

hexadecimal number

A number in base 16. A hexadecimal number uses the digits 0 through 9 and the letters A through F. Each place represents a power of 16. By comparison, base 10 numbers use the digits 0 through 9. Each place represents a power of 10.
Contrast with
character set, octal number

hierarchy   Any tree structure that has a root and branches that do not converge.

HTML   See hypertext markup language (HTML).

HTML element

See element.

HTTP　　　　See hypertext transfer protocol (HTTP).

hyperlink

 A connection from one part of a report to another part of the same or different report. Typically, hyperlinks support access to related information within the same report, in another report, or in another application. A change from the standard cursor shape to a cursor shaped like a hand indicates a hyperlink.

Related terms
application, report

hypertext markup language (HTML)

A specification that determines the layout of a web page. HTML is the markup language that tells a parser that the text is a certain portion of a document on the web, for example, the title, heading, or body text. A web browser parses HTML to display a web page.

Related terms
layout, web page

Contrast with
dynamic hypertext markup language (DHTML), extensible markup language (XML)

hypertext markup language page

See web page.

hypertext transfer protocol (HTTP)

An internet standard that supports the exchange of information using the web.

Contrast with
protocol

identifier　　The name that is assigned to an item in a program such as a class, function, or variable.

Related terms
class, function, variable

image　　　A graphic that appears in a report. BIRT Report Designer supports .gif, .jpg, and .png file types.

Related terms
Business Intelligence and Reporting Tools (BIRT) Report Designer, report

Contrast with
image element

image element

 A report item that adds an image to a report design.

Related terms
design, element, image, report, report item

inheritance

A mechanism whereby one class of objects can be defined as a special case of a more general class and includes the method and variable definitions of the general class, known as a base or superclass. The superclass serves as the baseline for the appearance and behavior of the descendant class, which is also known as a subclass. In the subclass, the appearance and behavior can be further customized without affecting the superclass. Typically, a subclass augments or redefines the behavior and structure of its superclass or superclasses. Figure G-11 shows an example of inheritance.

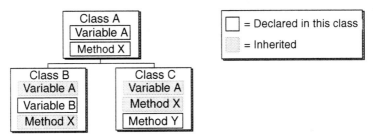

Figure G-11   Inheritance

Related terms
class, descendant class, file types, method, object, subclass, superclass, variable

Contrast with
abstract base class, hierarchy

inner join

1   A type of join that returns records from two tables that are based on their having specified values in the join fields. The most common type of inner join is one in which records are combined and returned when specified field values are equal. For example, if customer and order tables are joined on customer ID, the result set contains only combined customer and order records where the customer IDs are equal, excluding records for customers who have no orders.

2   When creating a joint data set in BIRT, a type of join that returns all rows from both data sets if the specified field values are equal. For example, if customer and order data sets are joined on customer ID, the joint data set returns only combined customer and order rows where the customer IDs are equal.

Related terms
Business Intelligence and Reporting Tools (BIRT) technology, data set, field, join, result set, row, table, value

Contrast with
outer join

input source

See data source.

instance   See object.

instance variable

A variable that other instances of a class do not share. The run-time system creates a new copy of an instance variable each time the system instantiates the class. An instance variable can contain a different value in each instance of a class, for example, the customerID variable in a Customer class.

Related terms
class, value, variable

Contrast with
class variable, dynamic variable, field variable, global variable, local variable, member variable, static variable

instantiation

The action of creating an object.

Related term
object

Contrast with
class

interface   **1**   The connection and interaction among hardware, software, and the user. Hardware interfaces include plugs, sockets, wires, and electrical pulses traveling through them in a particular pattern. Hardware interfaces include electrical timing considerations such as Ethernet and Token Ring, network topologies, RS-232 transmission, and the IDE, ESDI, SCSI, ISA, EISA, and Micro Channel. Software or programming interfaces are the languages, codes, and messages that programs use to communicate with each other and to the hardware and the user. Software interfaces include applications running on specific operating systems, SMTP e-mail, and LU 6.2 communications protocols.

2   In Java, an interface defines a set of methods to provide a required functionality. The interface provides a mechanism for classes to communicate in order to execute particular actions.

Related terms
application, class, Connection, Java, method, protocol

internationalization

The process of designing an application to work correctly in multiple locales.

Related terms
application, locale

Contrast with
localization

IP address   The unique 32-bit ID of a node on a TCP/IP network.

Related term
node

J2EE   See Java 2 Enterprise Edition (J2EE).

J2SE   See Java 2 Runtime Standard Edition (J2SE).

JAR   See Java archive (.jar) file.

Java   A programming language that is designed for writing client/server and networked applications, particularly for delivery on the web. Java can be used to write applets that animate a web page or create an interactive web site.

Related terms
applet, application, web page

Contrast with
JavaScript

Java 2 Enterprise Edition (J2EE)

A platform-independent environment that includes APIs, services, and transport protocols, and is used to develop and deploy web-based enterprise applications. Typically, this environment is used to develop highly scalable web-based applications. This environment builds on J2SE functionality and requires an accessible J2SE installation.

Related terms
application, application programming interface (API), enterprise, enterprise reporting, Java 2 Runtime Standard Edition (J2SE), protocol

Contrast with
Enterprise JavaBean (EJB), Java Development Kit (JDK)

Java 2 Runtime Standard Edition (J2SE)

A smaller-scale, platform-independent environment that provides supporting functionality to the capabilities of J2EE. The J2SE does not support Enterprise JavaBean or enterprise environment.

Related terms
enterprise, Enterprise JavaBean (EJB), Java 2 Enterprise Edition (J2EE)

Contrast with
Java Development Kit (JDK)

Java archive (.jar) file

A file format that is used to bundle Java applications.

Related terms
application, Java

Contrast with
web archive (.war) file

Java Database Connectivity (JDBC)

A standard protocol that Java uses to access database data sources in a platform-independent manner.

Related terms
data source, Java, protocol

Contrast with
data element, schema

Java Development Kit (JDK)

A Sun Microsystems software development kit that defines the Java API and is used to build Java programs. The kit contains software tools and other programs, examples, and documentation that enable software developers to create applications using the Java programming language.

Related terms
application, application programming interface (API), Java

Contrast with
Java 2 Enterprise Edition (J2EE), Java 2 Runtime Standard Edition (J2SE), JavaServer Page (JSP)

Java Naming and Directory Interface (JNDI)

A naming standard that provides clients with access to items such as EJBs.

Related term
Enterprise JavaBean (EJB)

Java Virtual Machine (JVM)

The Java SDK interpreter that converts Java bytecode into machine language for execution in a specified software and hardware configuration.

Related terms
Java, SDK (Software Development Kit)

JavaBean A reusable, standards-based component that is written in Java that encapsulates the business logic of an application. A JavaBean can provide access to data or model the data itself.

Related terms
application, data, encapsulation, Java

Contrast with
Enterprise JavaBean (EJB), enterprise reporting

JavaScript An interpreted, platform-independent language that is used to enhance web pages and provide additional functionality in web servers. For example, JavaScript can interact with the HTML of a web page to change an icon when the cursor moves across it.

Related terms
hypertext markup language (HTML), web page, web server

Contrast with
Java

JavaServer Page (JSP)

A standard Java extension that simplifies the creation and management of dynamic web pages. The code combines HTML and Java code in one document. The Java code uses tags that instruct the JSP container to generate a servlet.

Related terms
hypertext markup language (HTML), Java, servlet, tag, web page

JDBC   See Java Database Connectivity (JDBC).

JDK   See Java Development Kit (JDK).

JNDI   See Java Naming and Directory Interface (JNDI).

join   A SQL query operation that combines records from two tables and returns them in a result set that is based on the values in the join fields. Without additional qualification, join usually refers to one where field values are equal. For example, customer and order tables are joined on a common field such as customer ID. The result set contains combined customer and order records in which the customer IDs are equal.

Related terms
field, query, result set, SQL (Structured Query Language), table, value
Contrast with
inner join, join condition, outer join, SQL SELECT statement

join condition

A condition that specifies a match in the values of related fields in two tables. Typically, the values are equal. For example, if two tables have a field called customer ID, a join condition exists where the customer ID value in one table equals the customer ID value in the second table.

Related terms
field, join, table, value

joint data set

A data set that combines data from two data sets.
Related terms
data, data set

JSP   See JavaServer Page (JSP).

JVM   See Java Virtual Machine (JVM).

keyword   A reserved word that is recognized as part of a programming language.

label element

A report item that displays a short piece of static text in a report.
Related terms
report, report item

Contrast with
data element, text element

layout The designed appearance of a report. Designing the layout of a report entails placing report items on a page and arranging them in a way that helps the report user analyze the information easily. A report displays information in a tabular list, a series of paragraphs, a chart, or a series of subreports.

Related terms
chart, listing report, report, report item, subreport

layout editor

A window in a report designer in which a report developer arranges, formats, and sizes report elements.

Related terms
design, report

Contrast with
previewer, Property Editor, report editor, script editor

lazy load The capability in a run-time environment to load a code segment to memory only if it is needed. By lazily loading a code segment, the run-time environment minimizes start-up time and conserves memory resources. For example, BIRT Report Engine builds a registry at startup that contains the list of available plug-ins, then loads a plug-in only if the processing requires it.

Related terms
Business Intelligence and Reporting Tools (BIRT) Report Engine, plug-in

left outer join

See outer join.

library A collection of reusable and shareable report elements. A library can contain embedded images, styles, visual report items, JavaScript code, data sources, and data sets. A report developer uses a report designer to develop a library and to retrieve report elements from a library for use in a report design.

Related terms
Business Intelligence and Reporting Tools (BIRT) Report Designer, data set, data source, design, JavaScript, report element, report item, style

Contrast with
file types

library (.rptlibrary) file

In BIRT Report Designer, an XML file that contains reusable and shareable report elements. A report developer uses a report designer to create a library file directly or from a report design (.rptdesign) file.

Related terms

Business Intelligence and Reporting Tools (BIRT) Report Designer, design, extensible markup language (XML), report design (.rptdesign) file, report element

Contrast with

file types, report design (.rptdesign) file, report document (.rptdocument) file, report template (.rpttemplate) file

link   See hyperlink.

listener   See event listener.

list element

A report item that iterates through the data rows in a data set. The list element contains and displays other report items in a variety of layouts.

Related terms

data, data row, data set, element, layout, report item

Contrast with

grid element, table element

listing report

A report that provides a simple view of data. Figure G-12 shows a listing report.

Customer List		
Customer	**Phone**	**Contact**
ANG Resellers	(91) 745 6555	Alejandra Camino
AV Stores, Co.	(171) 555-1555	Rachel Ashworth
Alpha Cognac	61.77 6555	Annette Roulet

Figure G-12   Listing report

Related terms

data, report

local variable

A variable that is available only at the current level in an application. A local variable stays in memory in the scope of an executing procedure until the procedure terminates. When the procedure ends, the run-time system destroys the variable and returns the memory to the system.

Related terms

application, procedure, scope, variable

Contrast with

field variable, global variable

locale   A location and the language, date format, currency, sorting sequence, time format, and other such characteristics that are associated with that location. The location is not always identical to the country. There can be multiple languages and locales within one country. For example, China has two locales: Beijing and Hong Kong. Canada has two language-based locales: French and English.

Contrast with
localization

localization

The process of translating database content, printed documents, and software programs into another language. Report developers localize static text in a report so that the report displays text in another language that is appropriate to the locale configured on the user's machine.

Related terms
locale, report

Contrast with
internationalization

manifest   A text file in a Java archive (.jar) file that describes the contents of the archive.

Related term
Java archive (.jar) file

master page

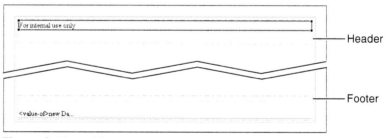

A predefined layout that specifies a consistent appearance for all pages of a report. A master page typically includes standard headers and footers that display information such as page numbers, a date, or a copyright statement.

The master page can contain report elements in the header and footer areas only, as shown in Figure G-13.

For internal use only ———————————————————— Header

<value-of>new Da... ———————————————————— Footer

Figure G-13   Master page layout

The master page's header and footer content appears on every page of the report in paginated formats, as shown in Figure G-14.

Related terms
Business Intelligence and Reporting Tools (BIRT), Business Intelligence and Reporting Tools (BIRT) Report Designer, footer, grid element, header, hypertext markup language (HTML), layout, previewer, report, template

measure   In a cube, values that are aggregated, such as average cost or total units of products.

Related terms
Business Intelligence and Reporting Tools (BIRT) technology, cube, value
Contrast with
dimension

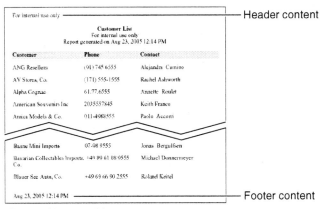

Figure G-14   Master page content

member   A method or variable that is defined in a class and provides or uses information about the state of a single object.

Related terms
class, method, object, variable
Contrast with
global variable, instance variable, static variable

member variable

A declared variable within a class. A set of member variables in a class contains the data or state for every object of that class.

Related terms
class, data, declaration, object, variable
Contrast with
class variable, dynamic variable, field variable, global variable, instance variable, local variable, static variable

metadata   Information about the structure of data that enables a program to process information. For example, a relational database stores metadata that describes the name, size, and data type of objects in a database, such as tables and columns.

Related terms
column, data, data type, table

method   A routine that provides functionality to an object or a class.
Related terms
class, object
Contrast with
data, function

modal window

A window that retains focus until explicitly closed by the user. Typically, dialog boxes and message windows are modal. For example, an error message dialog box remains on the screen until the user responds.

Contrast with
modeless window

mode

An operational state of a system. Mode implies that there are at least two possible states. Typically, there are many modes for both hardware and software.

modeless window

A window that solicits input but permits users to continue using the current application without closing the modeless window, for example, an Eclipse view.

Related terms
application, Eclipse view

Contrast with
modal window

multidimensional data

Any set of records that you can break down or filter according to the contents of individual fields or dimensions, such as product, location, or time. This data organization supports presenting and analyzing complex relationships.

Related terms
data, dimension, field, filter

multithreaded application

An application that handles multiple simultaneous users and sessions.

Related term
application

Navigator

In BIRT Report Designer, an Eclipse view that shows all projects and reports within each project. Each project is a directory in the file system. Use Navigator to manage report files, for example, deleting files, renaming files, or moving files from one project to another. Figure G-15 shows Navigator.

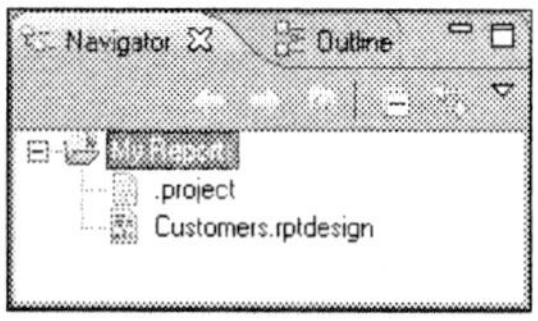

Figure G-15   Navigator

Related terms
Eclipse project, Eclipse view, report

node
A computer that is accessible on the internet.

Contrast with
domain name

null
A value that indicates that a variable or field contains no data.

Related terms
data, field, value, variable

numeric data type

A data type that is used for calculations that result in a value that is a number. Report items that contain expressions or fields with a numeric data type display numbers, based on the formats and locale settings that are specified by your computer and the report design.

Related terms
data type, design, expression, field, format, locale, report, report item, value

numeric expression

A numeric constant, a simple numeric variable, a scalar reference to a numeric array, a numeric-valued function reference, or a sequence of these items, that are separated by numeric operators. For example:

```
dataSetRow["PRICEEACH"] * dataSetRow["QUANTITYORDERED"]
```

Related terms
array, constant, function, operator, variable

Contrast with
Boolean expression

object
An instance of a particular class, including its characteristics, such as instance variables and methods.

Related terms
class, instance variable, method, variable

object-oriented programming

A technique for writing applications using classes, not algorithms, as the fundamental building blocks. The design methodology uses three main concepts: encapsulation, inheritance, and polymorphism.

Related terms
application, class, encapsulation, inheritance, polymorphism

Contrast with
object

octal number

A number in base 8. An octal number uses only the digits 0 through 7. Each place represents a power of 8. By comparison, base 10 numbers use the digits 0 through 9. Each place represents a power of 10.

Contrast with
hexadecimal number

ODA   See open data access (ODA).

online analytical processing (OLAP)

The process of analyzing, collecting, managing, and presenting multidimensional data.

Related terms
data, multidimensional data

online help

Information that appears on the computer screen to help the user understand an application.

Related term
application

open data access (ODA)

A technology that enables accessing data from standard and custom data sources. ODA uses XML data structures and Java interfaces to handle communication between the data source and the application that needs the data. Using ODA to access data from a data source requires an ODA driver and typically also includes an associated tool for designing queries on the data source. ODA provides interfaces for creating data drivers to establish connections, access metadata, and execute queries to retrieve data. ODA also provides interfaces to integrate query builder tools within an application designer tool. In BIRT, ODA is implemented using plug-ins to the Eclipse Data Tools Project.

Related terms
application, Business Intelligence and Reporting Tools (BIRT), Connection, data, data source, driver, extensible markup language (XML), interface, Java, metadata, open data access (ODA) driver, plug-in, query

open data access (ODA) driver

An ODA driver communicates between an arbitrary data source and an application during report execution. An ODA driver establishes a connection with a data source, accesses metadata about the data, and executes queries on the data source. Each ODA driver consists of a configuration file and classes that implement the ODA run-time Java interfaces that conform to ODA. In BIRT, ODA drivers are implemented as an Eclipse plug-in to the Data Tools Platform project.

Related terms
application, BIRT technology, class, Connection, data, data source, driver, Eclipse, interface, Java, metadata, open data access (ODA), plug-in, query

open database connectivity (ODBC)

A standard protocol that is used by software products as one of the database management system (DBMS) interfaces to connect applications and reports to databases that comply with this specification.

Related terms
application, database management system (DBMS), interface, protocol, report

Contrast with
Connection, data source, Java Database Connectivity (JDBC)

operator
A symbol or keyword that performs an operation on expressions.

Related terms
expression, keyword

outer join
A type of join that returns records from one table even when no matching values exist in the other table. The kinds of outer join are the left outer join, the right outer join, and the full outer join. The left outer join returns all records from the table on the left in the join operation, even when no matching values exist in the other table. The right outer join returns all records from the table on the right in the join operation. For example, if customers and orders tables are left outer joined on customer ID, the result set will contain all customer records, including records for customers who have no orders. The full outer join returns the results of both left and right outer joins. The result set contains all records from both tables.

A joint data set supports all outer join types between two data sets.

Related terms
Business Intelligence and Reporting Tools (BIRT) technology, data set, join, joint data set, query, result set, row, table, value

Contrast with
inner join

Outline
An Eclipse view that shows all report elements that comprise a report design, report library, or report template. Outline shows the report elements' containment hierarchy in a tree-structured diagram. Figure G-16 shows Outline.

Figure G-16   Outline

Related terms
design, Eclipse view, hierarchy, library, report, report element, template

package   A set of functionally related Java classes that are organized in one directory.

Related terms
class, Java

Palette   An Eclipse view that shows the visual report elements for organizing and displaying data in a report. Figure G-17 shows Palette.

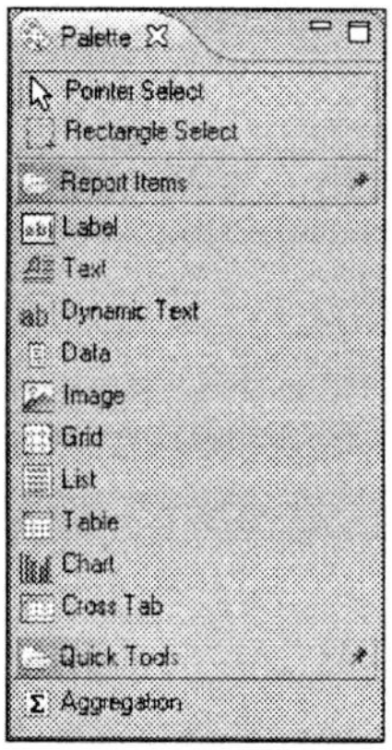

Figure G-17   Palette

Related terms
data, Eclipse view, report, report element

parameter   **1** A report element that provides input to the execution of the report. Parameters provide control over report data selection, processing, and formatting.

    2 The definition of an argument to a procedure.

Related terms
argument, data, format, procedure, report, report element

Contrast with
cascading parameters, data set parameter, report parameter

parent class

    See superclass.

password   An optional code that restricts user name access to a resource on a computer system.

pattern   A template or model for implementing a solution to a common problem in object-oriented programming or design. For example, the singleton design pattern restricts the instantiation of a class to only one object. The use of the singleton pattern prevents the proliferation of identical objects in a run-time environment and requires a programmer to manage access to the object in a multithreaded application.

Related terms
class, design, instantiation, multithreaded application, object, object-oriented programming

perspective

See Eclipse perspective.

platform

The software and hardware environment in which a program runs. Linux, MacOS, Microsoft Windows, Solaris OS, and UNIX are examples of software systems that run on hardware processors made by vendors such as AMD, Apple, Intel, IBM, Motorola, Sun, and Hewlett-Packard.

plug-in

1 An extension that is used by the Eclipse development environment. At run time, Eclipse scans its plug-in subdirectory to discover any extensions to the platform. Eclipse places the information about each extension in a registry, using lazy load to access the extension.

2 A software program that extends the capabilities of a web browser. For example, a plug-in gives you the ability to play audio samples or video movies.

Related terms
application, Eclipse, extension, lazy load
Contrast with
Eclipse Plug-in Development Environment (PDE)

plug-in fragment

A separately loaded plug-in that adds functionality to an existing plug-in, such as support for a new language in a localized application. The plug-in fragment manifest contains attributes that associate the fragment with the existing plug-in.

Related terms
application, localization, manifest, plug-in

polymorphism

The ability to provide different implementations with a common interface, simplifying the communication among objects. For example, defining a unique print method for each kind of document in a system supports printing any document by sending the instruction to print without concern for how that method is actually carried out for a given document.

Related terms
interface, method, object

portal

A web page that serves as a starting point for accessing information and applications on the internet or an intranet. The basic function of a portal is to aggregate information from different sources.

Related terms
application, web page
Contrast with
portlet

portlet   A window in a browser that provides a view of specific information that is available from a portal.
Related term
portal

previewer   A design tool that supports displaying a report or data.
Related terms
data, design, report
Contrast with
layout editor, script editor, Standard Viewer

procedure   A set of commands, input data, and statements that perform a specific set of operations. For example, methods are procedures.
Related terms
data, method, statement

process   A computer program that has no user interface. For example, the servlet that generates a BIRT report is a process.
Related terms
Business Intelligence and Reporting Tools (BIRT), interface, report, servlet

project   See Eclipse project.

Properties   A grouped alphabetical list of all properties of report elements in a report design. Experienced report developers use this Eclipse view to modify any property of a report element. Properties displays the same content as the Advanced page of Property Editor. Figure G-18 shows Properties.

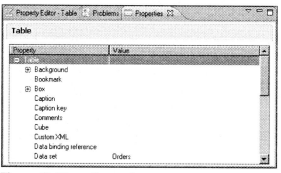

Figure G-18   Properties

Related terms
design, Eclipse view, property, Property Editor, report, report element

property

A characteristic of a report item that controls its appearance and behavior. For example, a report developer can specify a font size for a label element.

Related terms
font, label element, report item, value

Contrast with
method

Property Editor

An Eclipse view that displays sets of key properties of report elements in a report design. The report developer uses Property Editor to modify the properties of report elements. Figure G-19 shows Property Editor.

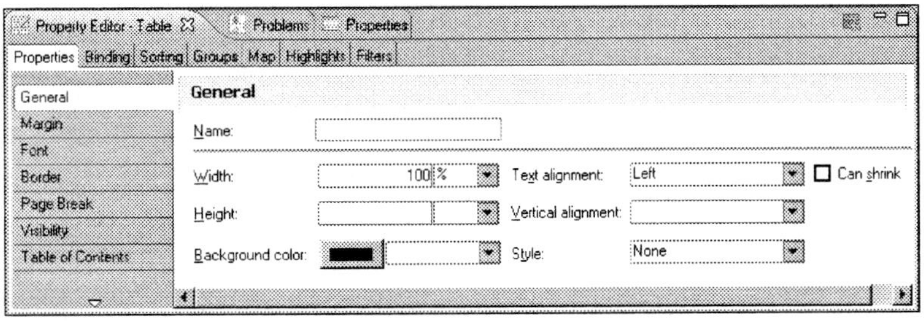

Figure G-19   Property Editor

Related terms
design, Eclipse view, property, report, report element

Contrast with
Properties

protocol

A communication standard for the exchange of information. For example, in TCP/IP, the internet protocol (IP) is the syntax and order in which messages are received and sent.

Related term
syntax

publish

To copy files to a shared folder to make them available to report users and developers. Libraries and resource files are published to the resources folder. Templates are published to the templates folder.

Related terms
library, report executable file, resource file, template

query

A statement that specifies which data rows to retrieve from a data source. For example, a query that retrieves data from a database typically is a SQL SELECT statement.

Related terms
data row, data source, SQL SELECT statement

range

A continuous set of values of any data type. For example, 1–31 is a numeric range.

Related terms
data type, value

regular expression

A JavaScript mechanism that matches patterns in text. The regular expression syntax can validate text data, find simple and complex strings of text within larger blocks of text, and substitute new text for old text.

Related terms
data, expression, JavaScript, syntax

rendering extension

A BIRT extension that produces a report in a specific format. For example, BIRT provides rendering extensions for HTML and PDF.

Related terms
Business Intelligence and Reporting Tools (BIRT), Business Intelligence and Reporting Tools (BIRT) extension, extension, hypertext markup language (HTML), report

report A category of documents that presents formatted and structured content from a data source, such as a database or text file.

Related terms
data source, format, structured content

report design (.rptdesign) file

An XML file that contains the complete description of a report. The report design file describes the structure and organization of the report, its constituent report items and their style attributes, its data sets, its data sources, and its Java and JavaScript event handler code. BIRT Report Designer creates the report design file and the BIRT Report Engine processes it to create a formatted report.

Related terms
Business Intelligence and Reporting Tools (BIRT), Business Intelligence and Reporting Tools (BIRT) Report Designer, Business Intelligence and Reporting Tools (BIRT) Report Engine, data set, data source, design, event handler, extensible markup language (XML), format, Java, JavaScript, report, report item, style

Contrast with
file types, library (.rptlibrary) file, report document (.rptdocument) file, report template (.rpttemplate) file

report document (.rptdocument) file

A binary file that encapsulates the report item identifier and additional information, such as data rows, pagination information, and table of contents information.

Related terms
Business Intelligence and Reporting Tools (BIRT) Report Engine, data row, report item

Contrast with
file types, library (.rptlibrary) file, report design (.rptdesign) file, report
template (.rpttemplate) file

report editor

In BIRT Report Designer, the main window where a report developer
designs and previews a report. The report editor supports opening
multiple report designs. For each report design, the report editor displays
these five pages: layout editor, master page editor, previewer, script
editor, and XML source editor.

Related terms
Business Intelligence and Reporting Tools (BIRT) Report Designer, design,
extensible markup language (XML), master page, layout editor,
previewer, report, script editor

Contrast with
report design (.rptdesign) file

report element

A visual or non-visual component of a report design. A visual report
element, such as a table or a label, is a report item. A non-visual report
element, such as a report parameter or a data source is a logical
component.

Related terms
data source, design, element, label element, report, report item, report
parameter, table element

report executable file

A file that contains instructions for generating a report document.

Related terms
file types, report

report item

A report element that you add to a report design to display content in the
report output. For example, a data element displays data from a data set
when you run a report.

Related terms
data, data element, data set, design, report, report element, run

report item extension

A BIRT extension that implements a custom report item.

Related terms
Business Intelligence and Reporting Tools (BIRT), Business Intelligence
and Reporting Tools (BIRT) extension, extension, report, report item

report library file

See library (.rptlibrary) file.

Report Object Model (ROM)

The set of XML report elements that BIRT technology uses to build a report design file. ROM defines report elements for both the visual and non-visual components of a report. The complete ROM specification is at:

```
http://www.eclipse.org/birt/ref
```

Related terms
Business Intelligence and Reporting Tools (BIRT) technology, design, element, extensible markup language (XML), report, report element

Contrast with
Report Object Model (ROM) element

Report Object Model definition file (rom.def)

The file that BIRT technology uses to generate and validate a report design. rom.def contains property definitions for the ROM elements. rom.def does not include definitions for report items that are defined by report item extensions, such as the chart element.

Related terms
Business Intelligence and Reporting Tools (BIRT) technology, chart element, design, property, report, report item, report item extension

Contrast with
Report Object Model (ROM), Report Object Model (ROM) element, Report Object Model (ROM) schema

Report Object Model (ROM) element

An XML element in rom.def that defines a report element.

Related terms
element, extensible markup language (XML), report element, Report Object Model definition file (rom.def)

Contrast with
report item, Report Object Model (ROM) schema

Report Object Model (ROM) schema

The XML schema that defines the rules for the structure of report design files. All BIRT report design files must conform to this schema. To validate a report design, open the file in a schema-aware XML viewer such as XML Spy. The ROM schema is at:

```
http://www.eclipse.org/birt/2005/design
```

Related terms
Business Intelligence and Reporting Tools (BIRT), design, extensible markup language (XML), report, Report Object Model (ROM), schema

Contrast with
Report Object Model definition file (rom.def)

report parameter

1 See parameter.

2 A report element that contains a value. Report parameters provide an opportunity for the user to type a value as input to the execution of the report.

Related terms
parameter, report, report element, value

Contrast with
cascading parameters, data set parameter

report template

See template.

report template (.rpttemplate) file

An XML file that contains a reusable design that a report developer can employ when developing a new report.

Related terms
design, extensible markup language (XML), file types, report, style, template

Contrast with
file types, library (.rptlibrary) file, report design (.rptdesign) file, report document (.rptdocument) file

report viewer servlet

A J2EE web application servlet that produces a report from a report design (.rptdesign) file or a report document (.rptdocument) file. When deployed to a J2EE application server, the report viewer servlet makes reports available for viewing over the web. The report viewer servlet is also the active component of the report previewer of BIRT Report Designer.

Related terms
application, Business Intelligence and Reporting Tools (BIRT) Report Designer, Java 2 Enterprise Edition (J2EE), previewer, report, report design (.rptdesign) file, report document (.rptdocument) file, servlet, web server

request A message that an application sends to a server to specify an operation for the server to perform.

Related term
application

Contrast with
response

reserved word

See keyword.

response A message that a server sends to an application. The response message contains the results of a requested operation.

Related term
application
Contrast with
request

resource file

A text file that contains the mapping from resource keys to string values for a particular locale. Resource files support producing a report with localized values for label and text elements.

Related terms
label element, locale, localization, resource key, text element, value

resource key

A unique value that maps to a string in a resource file. For example, the resource key, greeting, can map to Hello, Bonjour, and Hola in the resource files for English, French, and Spanish, respectively.

Related terms
label element, locale, localization, resource file, text element, value

result set   Data rows from an external data source. For example, the data rows that are returned by a SQL SELECT statement performed on a relational database are a result set.

Related terms
data, data row, data source, SQL SELECT statement

Rich Client Platform (RCP)

See Eclipse Rich Client Platform (RCP).

right outer join

See outer join.

ROM   See Report Object Model (ROM).

row   **1** A record in a table.

2 A horizontal sequence of cells in a grid element or table element.

Related terms
cell, grid element, table, table element
Contrast with
data row

RPTDESIGN

See report design (.rptdesign) file.

RPTDOCUMENT

See report document (.rptdocument) file.

RPTLIBRARY

See library (.rptlibrary) file.

RPTTEMPLATE

See report template (.rpttemplate) file.

run   To execute a program, utility, or other machine function.

schema **1** A database schema specifies the structure of database objects and the relationships between the data. The database objects are items such as tables.

2 An XML schema defines the structure of an XML document. An XML schema consists of element declarations and type definitions that describe a model for the information that a well-formed XML document must contain. The XML schema provides a common vocabulary and grammar for XML documents that support exchanging data among applications.

Related terms
application, data, element, extensible markup language (XML), object, report, table, well-formed XML

scope   The parts of a program in which a symbol or object exists or is visible. Where the element is declared determines the scope of a program element. Scopes can be nested. A method introduces a new scope for its parameters and local variables. A class introduces a scope for its member variables, member functions, and nested classes. Code in a method in one scope has visibility to other symbols in that same scope and, with certain exceptions, to symbols in outer scopes.

Related terms
class, function, member, method, object, parameter, variable

script editor

In the report editor in BIRT Report Designer, the page where a report developer adds or modifies JavaScript for a report element.

Related terms
Business Intelligence and Reporting Tools (BIRT) Report Designer, JavaScript, report, report editor, report element

Contrast with
layout editor, previewer

scripting language

See JavaScript.

SDK (Software Development Kit)

A collection of programming tools, utilities, compilers, debuggers, interpreters, and APIs that a developer uses to build an application to run on a specified technology platform. For example, the Java SDK supports developers in building an application that users can download across a network to run on any operating system. The Java Virtual Machine (JVM), the Java SDK interpreter, executes the application in the specified software and hardware configuration.

Related terms
application, application programming interface (API), Java, Java Virtual Machine (JVM), platform

section
A horizontal band in a report design. A section structures and formats related report items. A section uses a grid element, list element, or table element to contain data values, text, and images.

Related terms
data, design, grid element, image, list element, report, report item, table element, value

select
1 To highlight one or more items, for example, in a report design. A user-driven operation then affects the selected items. Figure G-20 shows selected items.

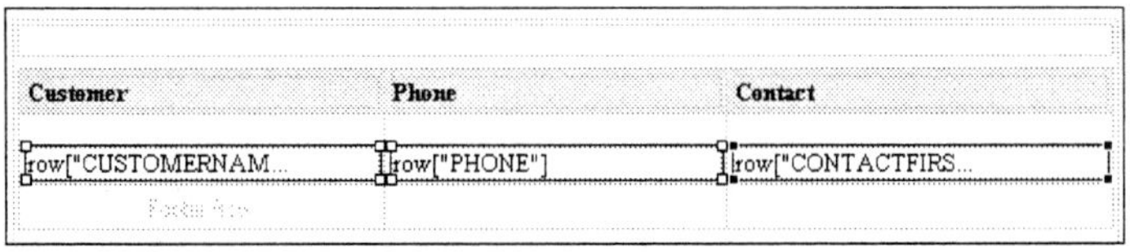

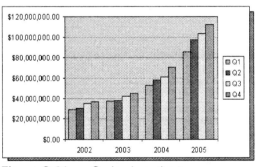

Customer	Phone	Contact
row["CUSTOMERNAM...	row["PHONE"]	row["CONTACTFIRS...

Figure G-20   Selected items

2 To highlight a check box or a list item in a dialog box.

Related terms
design, report

SELECT
See SQL SELECT statement.

series
A sequence of related values. In a chart, for example, a series is a set of related points. Figure G-21 shows a bar chart that displays a series of quarterly sales revenue figures over four years.

Figure G-21   Series in a chart

Related terms
chart, value

Contrast with
category

servlet A small Java application that runs on a web server to extend the server's functionality.

Related terms
application, Java, web server

simple object access protocol (SOAP)

A message-based protocol based on extensible markup language (XML). Use SOAP to access applications and their services on the web. SOAP employs XML syntax to send text commands across the internet using HTTP. SOAP supports implementing a messaging system.

Related terms
application, extensible markup language (XML), hypertext transfer protocol (HTTP), protocol, syntax

slot A construct that represents a set of ROM elements that are contained within another ROM element. For example, the body slot of the report design element can contain one or more of any type of report item. Figure G-22 shows a body slot.

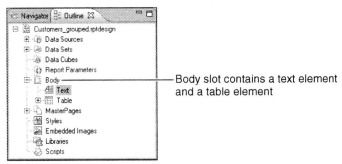

Body slot contains a text element and a table element

Figure G-22   Body slot

Related terms
design, element, report, report element, report item, Report Object Model (ROM) element

sort To specify the order in which data is processed or displayed. For example, customer names can be sorted in alphabetical order.

Related term
data

Contrast with
sort key

sort key A field that is used to sort data. For example, if you sort data by customer name, then the customer name field is a sort key. You can sort data using one or more sort keys.

Related terms
data, field, sort

SQL (Structured Query Language)

A language that is used to access and process data in a relational database.
For example, the following SQL query accesses a database's customers
table and retrieves the customer name and credit limit values where the
credit limit is less than or equal to 100000. The SQL query then sorts the
values by customer name:

```
SELECT customers.customerName,
customers.creditLimit
FROM customers
WHERE customers.creditLimit >= 100000
ORDER BY customers.customerName
```

Related terms
data, query, sort, table, value

Contrast with
SQL SELECT statement

SQL SELECT statement

A statement in SQL (Structured Query Language) that provides
instructions about which data to retrieve for a report.

Related terms
data, report, SQL (Structured Query Language), statement

Standard Viewer

A viewer that appears after the user runs a report. In the Standard Viewer,
the user can perform basic viewing tasks, such as navigating the report,
viewing parameter information, exporting data, and using a table of
contents.

Related terms
data, parameter, report

Contrast with
previewer, report viewer servlet

state   See instance variable.

statement   A syntactically complete unit in a programming language that expresses
one action, declaration, or definition.

static variable

A variable that is shared by all instances of a class and its descendant
classes. In Java, a static variable is known as a class variable. The compiler
specifies the memory allocation for a static variable. The program receives
the memory allocation for a static variable as the program loads.

Related terms
class, class variable, descendant class, Java, variable

Contrast with
dynamic variable, field variable, global variable, instance variable, local variable, member variable

String data type

A data type that consists of a sequence of contiguous characters including letters, numerals, spaces, and punctuation marks.

Related terms
character, data type

Contrast with
string expression

string expression

An expression that evaluates to a series of contiguous characters. Elements of the expression can include a function that returns a string, a string constant, a string literal, a string operator, or a string variable.

Related terms
character, constant, expression, function, operator, variable

Contrast with
String data type

structured content

A formatted document that displays information from one or more data sources.

Related terms
data source, format

Contrast with
report

Structured Query Language (SQL)

See SQL (Structured Query Language).

style

A named set of formatting characteristics, such as font, color, alignment, and borders, that report developers apply to a report item to control its appearance.

Related terms
design, font, format, report, report item

Contrast with
cascading style sheet (CSS)

style sheet

See cascading style sheet (CSS).

subclass

The immediate descendant class.

Related terms
class, descendant class

Contrast with
superclass

subreport   A report that appears inside another report. Typically, the subreport uses data values from the outer report.

Related terms
data, report, value

superclass

The immediate ancestor class.

Related terms
ancestor class, class

Contrast with
descendant class, subclass

syntax   The rules that govern the structure of a language.

tab   The label above a page in a dialog box that contains multiple pages.

Contrast with
label element

table   A named set of columns in a relational database.

Related term
column

Contrast with
table element

table element

A report item that contains and displays data in a row and column format. The table element iterates through the data rows in a data set. Figure G-23 shows a table element.

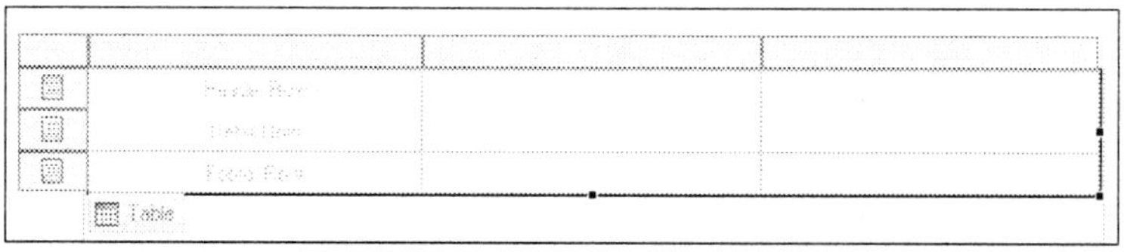

Figure G-23   Table element

Related terms
column, data, data row, data set, element, report item, row

Contrast with
grid element, list element, table

tag   An element in a markup language that identifies how to process a part of a document.

Related term
element

template   In BIRT Report Designer, a predefined structure for a report design. A report developer uses a report template to maintain a consistent style across a set of report designs and for streamlining the report design process. A report template can describe a complete report or a component of a report. BIRT Report Designer also supports custom templates.

In Figure G-24, New Report displays the available templates and Preview displays a representation of the report layout for the selected My First Report, a customer-listing-report template.

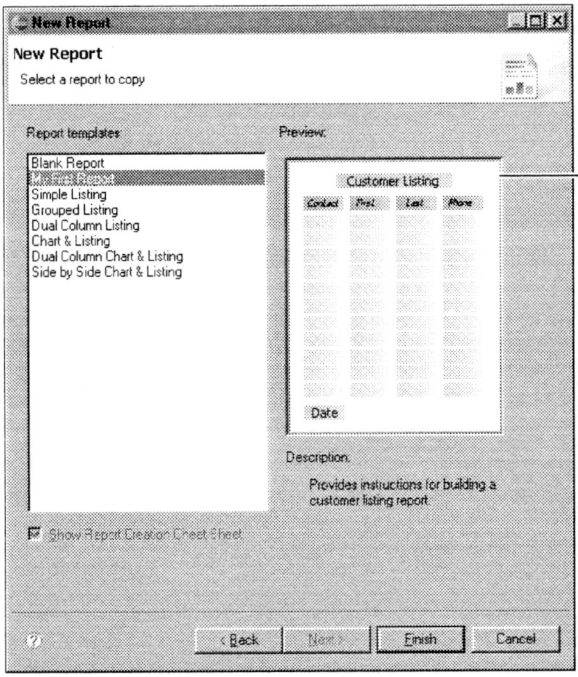

Customer listing report layout

Figure G-24   Template

Related terms
Business Intelligence and Reporting Tools (BIRT), Business Intelligence and Reporting Tools (BIRT) Report Designer, design, layout, listing report, report, report design (.rptdesign) file

Contrast with
report template (.rpttemplate) file

text element

A report item that displays user-specified text. The text can span multiple lines and can contain HTML formatting and dynamic values that are derived from data set fields or expressions.

Related terms
data set, expression, field, format, hypertext markup language (HTML), report item, value

Contrast with
data element, dynamic text element, label element

text file   See flat file.

theme   A set of related styles that are stored in a library (.rptlibrary) file. A theme provides a preferred appearance for the report items in a report design. A library file can store multiple themes. A report design can use styles from a single theme as well as styles defined in the report design itself.

Related terms
design, library (.rptlibrary) file, report, report item, style

Contrast with
cascading style sheet (CSS)

tick   A marker that occurs at regular intervals along the x- or y-axis of a chart. Typically, the value of each tick appears on the axis.

Related term
chart

Contrast with
tick interval

tick interval

The distance between ticks on an axis. Figure G-25 shows a tick interval in a chart.

Related terms
chart, tick

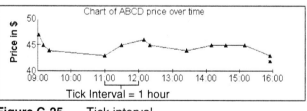

Figure G-25   Tick interval

toolbar   A bar that contains various buttons that provide access to common tasks. Different toolbars are available for different kinds of tasks.

translator   See converter.

type   See data type.

Unicode   A living language standard that is managed by the Technical Committee of the Unicode Consortium. The current Unicode standard provides code points for more than 65,000 characters. Unicode encoding has no dependency on a platform or software program and therefore provides a basis for software internationalization.

Related terms
code point, character, internationalization

Uniform Resource Locator (URL)

A character string that identifies the location and type of a piece of information that is accessible over the web. http:// is the familiar indicator that an item is accessible over the web. The URL typically includes the domain name, type of organization, and a precise location within the directory structure where the item is located.

Related terms
character, domain name, hypertext transfer protocol (HTTP)

Contrast with
Universal Resource Identifier (URI)

universal hyperlink

See hyperlink.

Universal Resource Identifier (URI)

A set of names and addresses in the form of short strings that identify resources on the web. Resources are documents, images, downloadable files, and so on.

Contrast with
Uniform Resource Locator (URL)

URL   See Uniform Resource Locator (URL).

value   1 A quantity that is assigned to a constant, variable, parameter, or symbol.

2 A specific occurrence of an attribute. For example, blue is a possible value for the attribute color.

Related terms
constant, parameter, variable

variable A named storage location for data that can be modified while a program runs. Each variable has a unique name that identifies it within its scope. Each variable is capable of containing a certain type of data.

Related terms
data, data type, scope

Contrast with
class variable, dynamic variable, field variable, global variable, instance variable, local variable, member variable, static variable

view   A predefined query that retrieves data from one or more tables in a relational database. Unlike a table, a view does not store data. Users can use views to select, delete, insert, and update data. The database uses the definition of the view to determine the appropriate action on the underlying tables. For example, a database handles a query on a view by combining the requested data from the underlying tables.

Related terms
data, query, table

Contrast with
Eclipse view

viewer   See previewer and Standard Viewer.

web archive (.war) file

A file format that is used to bundle web applications.

Related terms
application, format

Contrast with
Java archive (.jar) file

web page   A page that contains tags that a web browser interprets and displays.

Related term
tag

web server

A computer or a program that provides web services on the internet. A web server accepts requests that are based on the hypertext transfer protocol (HTTP). A web server also executes server-side scripts, such as ASPs and JSPs.

Related terms
hypertext transfer protocol (HTTP), JavaServer Page (JSP), request, web page

web services

A software system designed to support interoperable machine-to-machine interaction over a network. Web services refers to clients and servers that communicate using XML messages that adhere to the SOAP standard. Web services are invoked remotely using SOAP or HTTP-GET and HTTP-POST protocols. Web services are based on XML and return a response to the client in XML format. Web services are language-independent. They can be built and consumed on any operating system as long as that operating system supports the SOAP protocol and XML.

Related terms
extensible markup language (XML), hypertext markup language (HTML), protocol, simple object access protocol (SOAP)

well-formed XML

An XML document that follows syntax rules that were established in the XML 1.0 recommendation. Well-formed means that a document must contain one or more elements and that the root element must contain all the other elements. Each element must nest inside any enclosing elements, following the syntax rules.

Related terms
element, extensible markup language (XML), syntax

workbench

See Eclipse Workbench.

workspace

See Eclipse workspace.

World Wide Web Consortium (W3C)

An international, but unofficial, standards body that provides recommendations regarding web standards. The World Wide Web Consortium publishes several levels of documents, including notes, working drafts, proposed recommendations, and recommendations about web applications that are related to topics such as HTML and XML.

Related terms
application, extensible markup language (XML), hypertext markup language (HTML)

XML (extensible markup language)

See extensible markup language (XML).

XML element

See element.

XML PATH language (XPath)

XPath supports addressing an element or elements within an XML document based on a path through the document hierarchy.

Related terms
element, extensible markup language (XML)

XML schema

See schema.

XPath   See XML PATH language (XPath).

averages 254, 256, 257, 266
Avoid value (page breaks) 561
axes values
    See also charts
    adding gridlines to 499, 501
    adding markers to 497–501
    adding titles to 496
    changing line styles for 499, 500
    changing tick marks for 501
    changing type 503
    defining 438–441, 503
    defining multiple y 450, 455
    flipping 410, 411, 450
    formatting 496
    hiding labels for 497, 499
    highlighting 497, 499
    intersecting 504–505
    labeling 499, 501–503
    positioning tick marks for 499, 500
    rotating 474, 475
    scaling 450, 505–506
    selecting chart types and 430–432, 439
    setting interactive options for 596
    specifying range of 498
axis labels 459, 497, 499, 501–503
    See also data point labels
axis lines 499–501
axis markers 497, 498, 596
axis titles 459, 496
axis types 503

B

Background Color property 188, 189
background colors
    alternating 188, 189
    axis labels 503
    axis titles 497
    chart areas 478, 487, 489
    chart legends 493, 494, 496
    chart titles 491, 492
    curve-fitting labels 513
    customizing 480
    data point labels 511
    group headers 229, 244
    marker labels 499
    master pages 577
    styles 45, 175
    watermarks 572
Background image property 573

background images
    adding to charts 432, 479, 507
    adding to master pages 572
    repeating 572, 573
    repositioning 574
    selecting 479
Background repeat property 573, 574
backslash (\) character 642
bar charts
    See also charts
    changing bar position for 486
    coloring data series for 508
    creating 410
    formatting 462
    plotting data values for 431
    plotting multiple sets of bars 446
    stacking data series in 432
bar colors 508
bar orientation (charts) 410
bars (charts) 462, 464, 486
base values (groups) 218, 219
Between operator 309
BIGDECIMAL type indicator 71
binding
    aggregate values 259, 260, 261
    charts to report items 452
    columns to cross tabs 532
    columns to master reports 380
    data elements to computed fields 146
    data elements to images 151
    data set parameters to detail
        reports 385
    data set parameters to master
        reports 372
    data set parameters to report
        parameters 321–324, 347
    data sets to columns 122, 124
    data sets to lists 142, 162
    data sets to tables 138–140, 162
    data to reports 119
    parameters to data sources 85
    textual elements to data sets 158, 162
binding information. *See* column binding
    information
binding properties 85
Binding tab 119
BIRT 648
BIRT applications. *See* applications
BIRT Chart Engine 648

BIRT Demo Database 648
See also Classic Models sample
database
BIRT documentation xxiii, xxiv
BIRT extensions 648
BIRT Functions category 281
BIRT open source projects. *See* projects
BIRT RCP Report Designer
See also BIRT Report Designer; Rich
Client Platforms
creating cheat sheets and 625
defined 649
documentation conventions for 22
installing 10–11
removing cached pages for 12
requirements for 3
running projects and 20, 26
setting preview preferences and 642
specifying JVM for 12
starting 11, 23
testing installations for 11
updating 14, 15, 16
BIRT Report Designer
See also designs
building reports and 19, 21, 131, 532
configuring 5
data sources supported for 63
defined 649
documentation conventions for 22
drivers installed with 66
filtering data and 302, 303, 305
formatting data and 165, 166, 183, 186
grouping data and 212, 216, 224
installing 9–10
overview 21
requirements for 3, 5
sorting data and 209, 211
specifying JVM for 12
starting 10, 22
testing installations for 10
troubleshooting connections for 87
updating 14, 15
BIRT Report Designer Full Eclipse Install
software 9–10
BIRT Report Engine 649
BIRT report object model. *See* ROM
BIRT reports. *See* reports
BIRT Samples package 650
BIRT technology 650

BIRT web site xxi
BIRT.exe 11, 23
blank cells 526, 545
blank lines (delimited text files) 71
blank pages 563
blank report designs 34
blank rows and columns
deleting 136
generating output and 136
spacing elements with 193, 398, 402
blank space characters 48
block-level elements 47
Blur event type 597
BMP format 432
bold text style 167
Bookmark property 584
bookmarks 583, 584, 587, 588, 647
Boolean expressions 203, 294–295, 647
Boolean values 255, 294
Border property 248, 404, 530
border styles 404
borders
adding to cross tabs 530
adding to tables 404
adjusting spacing for 195, 405
cascading styles and 175
formatting properties and 165
grouping data and 229, 248
Borders property 195
bottom *n* logic filters 307
bottom *n* summary reports 274
break reports. *See* grouped reports
breakpoints 647
bridge class 648
bridge driver 66
Browse Resource Files dialog 632
browsers. *See* web browsers
bubble charts
See also charts
creating 414
formatting 462–463
bug reports 7
builds 7
bulleted lists 154
Business Intelligence and Reporting
Tools 648
See also BIRT
buttons
assigning values to 331, 332

charts

See also chart elements; specific chart type or part

accessing sample 31

adding background images to 432, 479, 507

adding to reports 133, 418, 422, 433

adjusting spacing in 478, 480

applying styles to 173

binding to report items 452

building combination 455

building queries for 445, 452

changing default titles for 424

comparing values with 411, 413, 415

creating 409, 430, 437

   tutorial for 416–429

customizing 459

defined 652

defining data types for 503, 505

defining interactive features for 432, 581, 594–598

defining series for 439

displaying changes over time in 411

displaying gauges or dashboards with 412, 456

displaying in layout editor 429

displaying multiple values with 414

displaying relationships to whole 410, 411, 413

displaying sample data for 420, 453, 454

displaying scheduling information in 415, 464

displaying trends with 411, 511, 512

filtering data for 451, 452

filtering data rows for 303

formatting values in 424, 477, 482, 496

grouping data and 434, 438, 442, 443, 444, 446

hiding data series in 507

hiding empty values in 461

highlighting values in 497

identifying data characteristics with 411

linking data sets to 437, 438

linking to 585, 586

localizing 635–637

missing labels in 501

overview 409, 437

predicting future values with 511

previewing 420, 422, 453, 454

removing resource keys for 636

rendering as images 432

resizing 422

selecting data for 420, 433, 437

setting background colors for 478–480

setting plot size for 488

sorting data for 438, 445

specifying output formats for 430, 432, 433

specifying type 409, 419, 430

standardizing 608, 628

tracking stock values with 415, 447

cheat sheet property 625

cheat sheets 625

class hierarchy 653

class names 653

class variables 653

See also instance variables; variables

classes

defined 653

formatting data and 168, 169

selecting driver 65

Classic Models sample database

See also demo database

building charts and 409, 417, 434

building cross tabs from 516

building listing reports and 32

building subreports and 372

connecting to 36

retrieving data from 37

–clean option 12, 87

client areas (charts) 485, 486

client-facing reports 19

CLOB fields 156, 158

CLOB values 154

closing values, plotting 415, 447, 473

code

adding to reports 25

changing libraries and 609

creating expressions and 279, 295

designing reports and 27

displaying 27, 28

loading 678

referencing columns and 110

setting interactive features and 598

testing and debugging 21, 27, 659

writing 25

data *(continued)*
   linking to 585, 588, 589
   localizing 637–639
   mapping to alternate values 201–203
   organizing 56, 208
   placing images behind 572, 573, 574
   plotting 420, 433, 437, 503, 505
   presenting 21, 54, 56, 131
   previewing 115
   reorganizing 42, 207, 208
   retrieving 54, 63, 89, 95
   selecting 90
   sorting. *See* sorting data
   specifying at run time 116
   standardizing 606, 607
   summarizing 57, 271
   viewing changes over time 411
   viewing deviation between 415
   viewing distinctions among 411
   viewing relationships among 409
   viewing relationships to whole 410, 411, 413
   viewing sample 453, 454
   viewing trends in 411, 511, 512
data binding. *See* column binding
data components. *See* data elements
data cube elements 607
data cubes 520, 532, 533–543, 607, 657
   See also multidimensional data
data elements
   See also data
   adding expressions to 157
   adding to designs 39, 133, 154
   aggregating values and 259, 263, 264
   aligning text in 190
   applying styles to 173
   assigning resource keys to 637–639
   binding to computed fields 146
   binding to data sets 123, 124
   binding to images 151
   copying 125
   defined 657
   displaying alternate values for 201–203
   displaying date values and 169, 394
   displaying report titles and 155
   displaying string values and 170
   formatting numeric values in 156, 167, 397

   formatting static text in 155
   placing in libraries 607
   placing in lists 141
   placing in tables 138
   reordering groups and 226, 227
Data Explorer
   accessing 36
   adding data sets to 37, 144, 617
   adding data sources to 36
   charting data and 437
   creating cascading parameters and 344, 345
   creating column bindings and 119
   creating column headings for 110
   creating data set parameters and 322
   creating data sources and 63
   creating report parameters and 318, 330, 336
   creating run-time connections and 84
   defined 657
   displaying data and 26, 167
   displaying field types and 278
   editing queries and 320
   editing report parameters and 332
   grouping parameters and 340, 341
   inserting data set fields from 142, 144
   localizing parameters and 640
   reordering parameters in 348–349
data filters
   See also filtering
   adding to designs 308, 310, 311
   applying 297
   charting data and 451, 452
   creating 303, 317
   defined 668
   defining XPath expressions for 301, 302
   matching string patterns and 289, 291
   setting at run time 317–325
   setting conditions for. *See* filter conditions
   specifying parameters as 317, 325, 327
data point labels 510, 511
data point markers 461
data point settings 510, 511
data points
   See also charts
   adding gridlines for 499
   arranging 439

data sets *(continued)*
  localizing 637
  naming 90, 93, 100
  overview 89
  placing in libraries 607, 613
  previewing 115, 310
  returning first value in 255
  returning from
    JDBC data sources 93
    stored procedures 95
    text files 97
    XML data sources 98, 100
  returning images 147
  returning last value in 255
  returning median value in 255
  selecting for charts 420, 433, 438
  setting up output columns for 110
  showing variation between 415
  testing 21
  troubleshooting 87
  verifying 21, 110, 115, 310
  viewing 26, 281
Data Sets folder 144
Data Sets slot 617
data source drivers. *See* drivers
data source elements 607
  See also data sources
Data Source Explorer 77
Data Source Name property 65, 72, 73
data source objects 63, 658
  See also data sources
Data Source property 96, 97, 100
data sources
  See also specific data source type
  accessing data in 20, 63, 64, 70, 73
  accessing multiple 367
  adding to designs 63
  associating with data sets 96, 100
  binding parameters to 85
  changing default names for 64
  charting data and 437, 438, 445
  combining data from multiple 113
  connecting to. *See* connections
  creating 36, 64, 73, 76, 79, 81
  defined 658
  defining connection profiles for 77, 79
  displaying 26
  displaying data from 144, 207
  filtering data in 297, 298, 305, 317, 325

overview 63
placing in libraries 607, 613
retrieving data from 89, 116, 297
reusing 76
sorting and unsupported 209
troubleshooting 87
data sparsity 545
data style (predefined) 173
Data Tools Platform 6
data type indicators 71
Data Type property 112
data types
  accessing text files and 70, 71, 73
  aggregating data and 260
  assigning to parameters 319, 322
  charting data and 445, 503, 505
  creating column bindings and 123, 124
  creating expressions and 278
  defined 658
  selecting for computed fields 112
database drivers 66, 67
  See also JDBC drivers
database management systems 659
database schemas 94, 534, 538, 539, 695
database structures 536
Database URL property 66, 69
database URLs 66, 69
databases
  See also Classic Models sample
    database; data sources
  accessing data in 81, 367
  connecting to 64
  creating data cubes and 536, 537, 538
  creating queries for 93–95
  displaying tables in 93
  displaying views in 94
  filtering data in 297, 298, 318, 325
  joining tables in 91, 113
  sorting and 209, 211
Dataset page (Cube Builder) 540
Dataset Parameter Binding dialog 385
DATE data type 71
date elements 568
  See also date values
date expressions 292–294
date formats
  changing 394
  charting data and 482, 484
  customizing 169, 170, 484, 568

getDay function 293
getHours function 293
getMinutes function 293
getMonth function 293
getSeconds function 293
getting started 19, 22, 23, 58
  See also tutorials
getYear function 293
global variables 669
  See also variables
Glossary 645
glyph 670
  See also character sets; fonts
gradient colors (charts) 479, 485
Gradient Editor 479
gradient patterns (charts) 479
Grand Total dialog 524, 550
grand totals
  See also totals
  aggregating data and 258, 261
  displaying in cross tabs 523, 549–551
grandchild classes. *See* descendant classes
grandparent classes. *See* ancestor classes
graphical applications 432
Graphical Editing Framework 6
graphical user interface
  See also user interface elements
  BIRT RCP Report Designer 24
  BIRT Report Designer 23
graphics 432
  See also images
graphs. *See* charts
grid cells 200
  See also cells
grid elements
  See also grids
  adding to designs 133, 134–136
  adding to libraries 608, 613, 617
  applying styles to 173
  defined 670
  inserting blank space with 398, 402, 570
  placing in page header and footers 568, 569
grid items. *See* grids
grid layouts 135
grid marks. *See* tick marks
grid style (predefined) 173
Grid tab 135

gridlines (charts) 460, 499, 501
Gridlines dialog 505
grids
  See also grid elements
  adding columns or rows to 135, 391
  adjusting spacing for 193
  aligning content in 190–191
  arranging multiple pies and 473
  building subreports and 368, 370
  changing 135
  creating 133, 134–136, 199
  defined 670
  displaying side-by-side tables in 391
  merging cells in 200
  organizing multiple elements and 568, 569
  placing data set fields in 144
  placing images in 147
  placing report elements in 134, 135
  removing columns or rows from 136
  resizing columns and rows in 194, 195
  specifying page breaks for 561, 562
  standardizing 608, 618
group editor. *See* Edit Group dialog
group fields. *See* group keys
group footer cells 247
group footer rows 215, 247, 258
group footers 174, 263, 434, 668
group header cells 229, 230
group header rows
  adding 228
  applying styles to 174
  placing aggregate values in 243, 258, 263
  placing summary values in 215
group headers 434, 671
  See also group headings
group headings
  creating 227–231, 246
  formatting 237
group keys 671
Group Level dialog 541
group names 227
Group On pick list (New Group) 214
group properties 214
group sections 444
grouped reports
  See also groups
  counting number of rows in 267

interactive chart features 432, 581, 594–598

interactive HTML elements 598–599
interactive images 432
interactive report viewer 29
interactive reports 581, 589
interactive textual content 154
Interactivity button 586
interactivity editor (charts) 586, 595, 596, 597
interfaces 95, 674
    See also application programming
        interfaces; user interface
internal bookmarks 584, 587
internationalization 56, 674
    See also locales
intersection options (charts) 504, 505
Interval pick list (New Group) 214, 218, 219, 220
Interval value 219
introductory information 141
Inventory.rptdesign 351
invoice numbers 292
Invoke Script action 597
IP addresses 674
Is False operator 309
Is Not Null operator 309
Is Null operator 309
Is True operator 309, 310, 313
IS-BOTTOM-N function 255
IS-BOTTOM-N-PERCENT function 255
IS-TOP-N function 255
IS-TOP-N-PERCENT function 255
italic text style 167

J

J2EE environments 675
J2SE environments 675
.jar files 12, 67, 69, 675
Java. *See* Java programming language
Java 2 Enterprise Edition. *See* J2EE
    environments
Java 2 Runtime Standard Edition. *See*
    J2SE environments
Java applets 646
Java archives. *See* .jar files
Java code 675
Java Database Connectivity. *See* JDBC
Java Development Kit 7

Java Development Kit. *See* JDK software
Java interfaces 674
Java Naming and Directory Interface 676
Java programming language 675
Java programs 676
Java Virtual Machines. *See* JVMs
JavaBeans 676
JavaScript
    See also source code
    case sensitivity for 279
    defined 676
    familiarity with 278
    multiline expressions and 279
    null values and 286
    regular expressions and 289, 291
JavaScript expressions. *See* expressions
JavaScript functions
    See also functions
    case sensitivity for 279
    concatenating values and 111
    converting case for 292
    creating group headings and 231
    entering in expressions 145
    filtering with 307
    getting specific characters with 231
    manipulating date or time values
        and 292, 293
    manipulating numbers and 282, 284
    manipulating string values and 284, 285, 287, 288, 290, 292
    viewing 281
JavaScript operators 281
JavaServer Pages. *See* JSPs
JDBC (defined) 676
JDBC data sets 90, 93, 298
JDBC data sources
    building queries for 93–95
    connecting to 64, 84
    creating 64
    displaying tables or views in 94
    filtering data in 298, 299, 317, 318, 325
    naming 65
    retrieving data from 90
    setting connection properties for 65
    troubleshooting 87
JDBC directory 68
JDBC driver manager 66, 67, 69
JDBC Driver Manager. *See* Manage JDBC
    Drivers dialog

math functions 281, 282
matrix reports. *See* cross-tab reports
MAX function 255
maximum values (charts) 505
measures
   See also cross tabs; data cubes
   adding 535, 540, 548
   defined 533, 680
   displaying 547, 549
   relationship to summary fields 532
MEDIAN function 255
median values 255
member variables 681
   See also field variables; variables
members 681
membership filters 324
membership test conditions 300
memo fields 292
memos 133, 154
Merge command 201
merging table or grid cells 200
message files 59
messages 203, 204, 206
metadata 681
meter charts
   See also charts
   changing dial scale for 467
   changing needle appearance for 467
   coloring series for 508, 509
   creating 412, 456–458, 466
   displaying multiple dials in 457
   displaying multiple meters in 456, 468
   displaying multiple needles in 456
   formatting 465–470
   highlighting values in 469
   labeling dials for 469
   setting dial size for 466
meter size 466
methods 681
   See also functions
Microsoft Windows systems. *See* Windows platforms
milestone build 7
milestone releases 15
MIN function 255
minimum values (charts) 505
minor gridlines 500, 501
minor tick marks 499, 501, 505
mock-ups 58

modal windows 682
mode 682
MODE function 255
modeless windows 682
modulus (%) operator 189, 190
month function 294
monthly reports 219
Mouse Click event type 597
Mouse Double-Click event type 597
Mouse Down event type 597
Mouse Move event type 597
Mouse Out event type 597
Mouse Over event type 597
Mouse Up event type 597
movie clips 590
moving
   image files 147
   parameter groups 348
   report parameters 348
   tables 391
moving averages 256
MOVINGAVE function 256
multicolumn page layouts 199–201
multi-dataset cubes 538, 539
multidimensional data 682
   See also data cubes
multidimensional data structures 533
multiline expressions 157, 279
multiline text 154, 494
multilingual reports. *See* locales;
   localization
multipage reports 559
multiple columns, selecting 97
multiple report elements 45, 47, 143
multiplication 282, 483
Multiplier property 483
multithreaded applications 682

N

name fields 286
name spaces 606, 611, 621
named perspectives 24
named styles 172
names
   See also aliases; display names
   accessing data and 119
   applying styles and 176, 177, 609, 619
   cascading parameters and 344, 345
   case sensitivity for 38, 279

Property Editor *(continued)*
  localizing data values and 637
  localizing report parameters and 640
  localizing text elements and 633, 634
  mapping data values and 201
  opening 42
  overview 26
  restoring property values and 618
  selecting elements and 45, 406
  sorting data and 42, 209, 554
  viewing binding information and 119
Property Editor command 42
property sheets. *See* Properties view
protocol 689
prototypes 66
prototyping reports 20, 53, 54, 58
publish 689
Publish Library dialog 615
Publish to Template Folder dialog 627
publishing libraries 59, 615
publishing report templates 622, 626, 627
purpose statements 54
pyramid charts 411
  See also charts

Q

quarterly reports 216, 219
QUARTILE function 256
queries
  See also SQL statements
  accessing multiple tables and 91
  building automatically 38
  building data cubes and 535, 538
  building linked subreports and 371
  building user-selection elements
    and 332, 336
  changing 618
  charting data and 445, 452
  creating 90, 93
  defined 689
  filtering data with 298, 302, 308, 317,
    320, 324, 556
    examples for 299
  limiting data returned by 91
  matching text patterns and 307
  previewing result sets for 115
  retrieving data with 90, 298
  sorting data with 209
  validating 38, 115

Query Text property 116, 117
Query wizard 96
quotation mark characters. *See* double
  quotation mark character; single
  quotation mark character

R

radio buttons
  assigning values to 331, 332
  formatting values for 329, 330, 338
  localizing text for 639, 640
  selecting values and 317
  setting default values for 330, 335
  sorting values for 336
  specifying as display type 329
  testing values for 349
randomly generated data 420, 454
range 689
  See also range of values
range fill colors 499
range filter conditions 300, 306
range markers (charts) 497, 498, 499
range of values
  defined 689
  highlighting in charts 497, 498
  searching 300, 306
  setting grouping intervals for 214, 218
Range setting (New Group) 218, 219, 220
RANK function 256
RCP (defined) 663
  See also Rich Client Platforms
read-only styles 178
record-level elements (XML) 100
records 71, 297
  See also rows
referencing column names 44
referencing data set fields 146, 279
RegExp objects 289, 290
  See also regular expressions
region codes 630, 631
region properties (charts) 470
Register Template with New Report
  Wizard command 623, 627
regular expressions 289, 290, 291, 690
relational databases 64
  See also databases
relational models 90
relational structures 90
relative paths 98

release build 7

removing. *See* deleting

renaming

   cascading style sheets 179

   column bindings 124

   columns 110, 418

   data sources 64

   resource keys 642

rendering environments 55

rendering extensions 690

   See also output formats

Repeat Header property 137, 561

replace function 285, 287

replacing

   multiple strings 285

   null values 287

   specific characters 289, 291

   text 44, 285, 292, 568

report components. *See* report elements; report items

report descriptions 141

Report Design command 23

report design environments 21–22

   See also BIRT; Eclipse

report design files

   building libraries and 604

   defined 690

   generating 27

   opening 27

Report Design perspective 10, 23

report design tools 25

report design views 24–27

report design window 25

   See also report editor

report designer packages 3

report designers 3, 22

   See also BIRT Report Designer; BIRT RCP Report Designer

report designs

   See also page layouts

   accessing 27

   adding data sources to 63

   adding libraries to 606, 611

   adding report elements to 26, 605, 616, 617

   adding to libraries 604

   adding to projects 32

   assigning themes to 609, 619

   copying and pasting data in 125

creating 19, 131, 603

defined 659

deriving from templates 604, 605, 627, 628

displaying 25, 27

embedding images in 147, 149

formatting data and 165, 172, 177, 182

grouping data in 212, 213, 216, 224, 226

hiding elements in 203, 205, 599

linking images to 147, 148, 585

localizing reports and 56, 630, 642

prototyping 54, 55, 58

registering as templates 623

removing styles from 619

removing themes from 620

returning values at run time for 315, 317, 336

saving 27, 233

selecting data for 90

setting filters in 308, 310, 311

sharing 121

standardizing 603, 604, 605, 611

updating libraries in 603, 608

report document files 690

report document model (BIRT). *See* ROM

report documents. *See* documents; reports

report editor 25, 422, 691

report elements

   See also specific type

   accessing data and 119, 120

   adding multiple 47, 143

   adding to designs 26, 605, 616, 617

   adding to libraries 605, 606, 611, 621

   adding to master pages 567, 575

   adding to report pages 26, 39, 142–152

   restrictions for 143

   adding to report sections 131, 134

   adding to templates 622, 625

   aligning 135, 190–191

   applying styles to 173, 174, 175, 182

   arranging in grids 134–136

   arranging in lists 140–142

   arranging in tables 136–140

   changing 608, 616, 618, 628

   creating column bindings for 123, 124, 139

   creating textual information and 153

   customizing 165, 172, 608, 614

resource keys *(continued)*
  localizing parameters and 639–641
  localizing text elements and 629, 630, 633–634
  removing 634, 636, 642
  renaming 642
  specifying 202, 630
  updating 642
resources 15, 26, 59
Resources page 632
response 693
response messages 693
restarting Eclipse 87
Restore Properties button 618
restoring JDBC drivers 69
result sets
  See also data sets; queries
  changing number of rows in 116
  defined 694
  limiting data in 91
  previewing data in 115
  retrieving multiple 95
  returning from multiple tables 91
  returning from stored procedures 95
  sorting data in 91
Revert to Template Item command 628
Rich Client Platforms 20, 22, 663
RIGHT JOIN clause 92
right outer joins. *See* outer joins
risers (charts) 411
roles 81
ROM (defined) 692
ROM definition file 692
ROM elements 692
ROM schemas 692
ROM specification 27
rom.def 692
rotating axes values 474, 475
rotating chart labels 502
rotating chart titles 491
row areas (cross tabs) 544, 545, 550
row boundaries 194
row headings 516, 544, 551
row heights 194
row numbers 256
row properties 194
rows
  See also records
  adding to grids 134, 135, 391

adding to tables 39, 137, 140
adjusting spacing between 49
aggregating values and 257, 258, 261, 265
aligning text in 190
alternating colors for 187–190
applying background colors to 45
applying styles to 174
building cross tabs and 516, 544, 545
changing number returned 116
charting data and 434, 444, 453
counting 255, 267
creating group headings and 229
defined 694
deleting 136
filtering 303, 310, 313, 320
generating computed values and 111
grouping data and 229, 230, 246, 444
hiding detail 215, 272
iterating through 158, 370, 382, 387
resizing 194
restricting retrieval of 298, 305
retrieving from databases 92
setting number per page 565
spacing report elements and 136, 193, 398
.rptdesign files. *See* report design files
.rptdocument files. *See* report document files
.rptlibrary files. *See* report library files
.rpttemplate files. *See* report template files
rules
  changing formatting 185
  creating formatting 183–185, 186, 188
  default precedence for 186
  deleting 187
  mapping data values and 201, 203
  reordering 187
  testing formatting 185, 187
run 695
running stored procedures 96
running totals 189, 256, 258, 264
RUNNINGCOUNT function 256
RUNNINGSUM function 256
run-time connections 81–86
run-time filters 317, 325
run-time parameters 320
run-time queries 324

S

stock charts *(continued)*
    creating 414
    formatting 473–474
    grouping values for 447–449
stocks, tracking value of 256, 415, 447
stored procedures 95
straight cursor 142
strike through text style 167
strikethrough text options 491
String data type 699
string expressions 284, 699
string fields 284, 300, 307
string formats 170, 171
    See also text formats
string functions 281, 284
string substitution 285
STRING type indicator 72
string types 167
strings
    computing values of 278, 284–292
    concatenating 47, 145, 286
    containing zero values 526
    converting case for 171, 211, 292
    converting numbers to 284
    converting to numbers 292
    defining URIs and 590
    displaying portions of 287–289
    displaying textual information
        and 153, 154
    entering at run time 331
    finding specific characters in 287
    formatting values 51, 155, 160, 170
    grouping by interval 217
    localizing reports and 56, 630, 638
    mapping alternate values to 202
    matching patterns in 289–292, 300, 307
    removing infinity symbol and 283, 284
    removing null values and 287
    replacing values in 285
    returning length of 288
    sorting 43, 211
structured content 131, 699
Structured Query Language. *See* SQL
structures libraries 612
style elements 608
style properties
    displaying 175
    embedding 51
    formatting reports and 165

inheriting 175
setting 176, 182
unsupported 177
style sheets
    defined 651
    grouping styles and 605, 609
    linking to reports 178–181
    removing styles from 619
    renaming 179
    reusing 57, 177
styles
    adding to libraries 608, 618, 621
    adding to themes 605, 610
    applying 173, 176, 182, 619
    changing 182, 530
    copying 610
    creating 45, 172, 174, 175
    customizing 46, 176
    defined 699
    deleting 182
    designing reports and 605, 609
    grouping 605, 609
    importing 172, 177, 178
    inheriting 175
    placing in libraries 608
    removing 619
    reusing 177
    saving 176
    setting for multiple elements 45
Sub Total dialog 550
subclasses 699
    See also descendant classes
subDate function 294
subreports
    adjusting spacing in 398–403
    aligning data in 370
    building data sets for 374, 376, 378
    creating 141, 368, 372–406
    customizing 393–407
    defined 700
    linking to 369–372, 581, 588
        tutorial for 385, 388
    overview 367
    placing side-by-side 391
    structuring 368, 370
    testing 367
    viewing nested elements in 392
subroutines. *See* procedures
substr function 288

Word formats 28
word processing 19
Workbench (Eclipse) 22, 663
worksheets. *See* Excel spreadsheets
workspace directory 15
Workspace Launcher 22
workspaces 22, 664
World Wide Web Consortium (W3C) 705
Wrapping width setting 494
WSDL documents 75
WTP plug-ins 7

X

x-axis
    See also axes values
    adding markers to 498
    building 438, 439, 440
    changing line styles for 500
    defining data series for 439
    overlapping labels and 501, 502
    rotating 474, 475
    scaling 505
    summarizing data for 443, 444
    transposing 450
x-axis labels 501, 502
x-axis titles 496
XLS formats 560
    See also Excel spreadsheets
XML (defined) 667
XML code 27
    See also source code
XML data 73
XML data mappings 98, 100, 300
XML data sets 100, 101, 300, 302
XML data sources
    accessing data in 73, 98, 100
    associating with data sets 100
    connecting to 73
    creating 73
    filtering data in 300–302
    generating charts and 432
    naming 73
    previewing data sets for 101
    retrieving data from 90, 298
XML DataSet page 100
XML documents 300, 704
XML editor 25, 27

XML elements 300, 664
XML files
    deleting column mappings for 101
    filtering 325
    mapping to data in 98, 100, 300
    selecting 73, 100
XML PATH language 705
XML reports 25
XML schema files 74
XML schemas 695
XML Source page 25
XML Source tab 28
XML specification 73
XPath expressions
    accessing XML data sources and 98, 300
    creating 98–100
    defined 705
    filtering with 301, 302
    mapping to XML data and 100
XPath functions 99
XPath property 101

Y

y-axis
    See also axes values
    adding a second 450, 455
    adding acceleration lines to 462
    adding gridlines to 499
    arranging tick marks on 499
    building 438, 439, 440
    defining data series for 439
    grouping values on 446, 447
    highlighting points on 498
    overlapping labels and 501, 502
    rotating 475
    scaling 450, 505, 506
    transposing 450
y-axis labels 501, 502
y-axis titles 496

Z

z-axis 431
z-axis rotation settings 475
zero values 266, 283, 526
zip codes 292
ZIP files. *See* archive files